One Team …
A Commitment to Quality

There's just one reason our team is dedicated to producing quality travel publications—you, our reader.

Throughout our guides we offer **practical information**, **touring tips** and **suggestions** for finding the best places for a break.

Michelin driving tours help you hit the highlights and quickly absorb the best of the region. Our descriptive **walking tours** make you your own guide, armed with directions, maps and expert information.

We scout out the attractions, classify them with **star ratings**, and describe in detail what you will find when you visit them.

Michelin maps featured throughout the guide offer vibrant, detailed and easy-to-follow outlines of everything from close-up museum plans to international maps.

Places to stay and eat are always a big part of travel, so we research **hotels and restaurants** that we think convey the essence of the destination, and arrange them by geographic area and price. We walk you through the best shopping districts and point you towards the host of entertainment and recreation possibilities on offer.

We **test, retest, check and recheck** to make sure that our guidebooks are truly just that: a personalized guide to help you make the most of your visit. And if you still want a speaking guide, we list local tour guides who will lead you on all the boat, bus, guided, historical, culinary, and other tours you shouldn't miss.

In short, we remove the guesswork involved with travel. After all, we want you to enjoy traveling with Michelin as much as we do.

The Michelin Green Guide Team

PLANNING YOUR TRIP

WELCOME TO ROME

SYMBOLS

🛈   **Tourist Information**
🕑   **Hours of Operation**
🕒   **Periods of Closure**
🙂   **A Bit of Advice**
🙂   **Details to Consider**
👓   **Entry Fees**
Kids   **Especially for Children**
👣   **Tours**
♿   **Wheelchair Accessible**

CONTENTS

DISCOVERING ROME

DISCOVERING ROME'S ENVIRONS 322

YOUR STAY IN ROME

HOW TO USE THIS GUIDE

Orientation

To help you grasp the "lay of the land" quickly and easily, so you'll feel confident and comfortable finding your way around the region, we offer the following tools in this guide:

- Detailed table of contents for an overview of what you'll find in the guide, and how the guide is organized.
- Map of Rome at the front to the guide, with the Principal Sights highlighted for easy reference.
- Detailed maps for major cities and villages, including driving tour maps and larger-scale maps for walking tours.
- Map of Rome Regional Driving Tours, each one numbered and color coded.
- Principal Sights organized alphabetically for quick reference.

Practicalities

At the front of the guide, you'll see a section called "Planning Your Trip" that contains information about planning your trip, the best time to go, different ways of getting to the region and getting around, and basic facts and tips for making the most of your visit. You'll find driving and themed tours, and suggestions for outdoor fun. There's also a calendar of popular annual events. Information on shopping, sightseeing, kids' activities and sports and recreational opportunities is included as well.

LODGINGS

We've made a selection of hotels and arranged them within the cities by price category to fit all budgets (*see the Legend on the cover flap for an explanation of the price categories*). For the most part, we've selected accommodations based on their unique regional quality, their Roman feel, as it were. So, unless the individual hotel embodies local ambience, it's rare that we include chain properties, which typically have their own imprint. If you want a more comprehensive selection of accommodations, see the red-cover **Michelin Guide Italia**.

RESTAURANTS

We thought you'd like to know the popular eating spots in Rome. So we selected restaurants that capture the Rome experience—those that have a unique regional flavor and local atmosphere. We're not rating the quality of the food per se. As we did with the hotels, we selected restaurants for many towns and villages, categorized by price to appeal to all wallets (*see the Legend on the cover flap for an explanation of the price categories*). If you want a more comprehensive selection of dining recommendations, see the red-cover **Michelin Guide Italia**.

Attractions

Principal Sights are arranged alphabetically. Within each Principal Sight, attractions for each town, village, or geographical area are divided into local Sights or Walking Tours, nearby Excursions to sights outside the town, or detailed Driving Tours—suggested itineraries for seeing several attractions around a major town. Contact information, admission charges and hours of operation are given for the majority of attractions. Unless otherwise noted, admission prices shown are for a single adult only. Discounts for children, seniors, students, teachers, etc. may be available; be sure to ask. If no admission charge is shown, entrance to the attraction is free.

If you're pressed for time, we recommend you visit the three- and two-star sights first: the stars are your guide.

STAR RATINGS

Michelin has used stars as a rating tool for more than 100 years:

★★★	Highly recommended
★★	Recommended
★	Interesting

SYMBOLS IN THE TEXT

Besides the stars, other symbols in the text indicate sights that are closed to the public ⚊ ; on-site eating facilities ✕; also see 👁 ; breakfast included in the nightly rate 🛏 ; on-site parking 🅿 ; spa facilities 🆂🅿🅰 ; camping facilities △ ; swimming pool 🛏 ; and beaches ⚊.

See the box appearing on the Contents page and the Legend on the cover flap for other symbols used in the text.

See the Maps explanation below for symbols appearing on the maps.

Throughout the guide you will find peach-coloured text boxes or sidebars containing anecdotal or background information. Green-coloured boxes contain information to help you save time or money.

Maps

All maps in this guide are oriented north, unless otherwise indicated by a directional arrow. The term "Local Map" refers to a map within the chapter or Tourism Region. See the map Legend at the back of the guide for an explanation of other map symbols. A complete list of the maps found in the guide appears at the back of this book.

Addresses, phone numbers, opening hours and prices published in this guide are accurate at press time. We welcome corrections and suggestions that may assist us in preparing the next edition. Please send your comments to:

Michelin Maps and Guides
Hannay House
39 Clarendon Road
Watford, Herts WD17 1JA
UK
travelpubsales@uk.michelin.com
www.michelin.co.uk

Michelin Maps and Guides
Editorial Department
P.O. Box 19001
Greenville, SC 29602-9001
USA
michelin.guides@us.michelin.com
www.michelintravel.com

Principal sights in Central Rome

Entrance stairwell, Vatican Museum
B. Kaufmann/MICHELIN

WHEN AND WHERE TO GO

When to Go

CLIMATE

Located 28km/17mi from the coast, Rome enjoys a mild Mediterranean climate: bright and crisp in winter, hot in summer. The most temperate months are May, September and October, and sometimes June, if the summer heat arrives late. During July and August, the temperature rarely dips below 30°C/86°F and the high humidity makes the heat hard to bear. September and October are splendid, with sunny skies and mild temperatures (although squalls sometimes dampen October). November is the wettest month of the year – often the result of heavy downpours – and the temperature falls, signalling winter. It can be cold in December, January and February, but only snows every 20 years or so. The mild weather returns again in March and April, occasionally accompanied by more rainfall.

BEST TIME TO VISIT

April, May, September or October provide the best weather. Unsurprisingly, these months attract the most visitors (especially over Easter). Some hard-core travellers – especially those without children or elderly companions – praise July and August, despite the heat. The city empties, as many Romans head to their second homes on the coast or in the mountains. However, many shops and services close down, and the shell of the city doesn't convey its dynamic character. In winter, the air is fresh, the light sharp and the sky often a clear blue. You may not even need a coat in December, as you wander among the street fairs and elaborate nativity scenes in unheated churches. The epicentre is the Piazza Navona, where stalls sell sweets and toys. Many feature Befana, the witch that brings Italian children toys on Epiphany.

Weekend Itineraries

A SNAPSHOT OF ROME

Day 1
One of the highlights of Rome is, of course, the **Colosseum**. Start your sightseeing at this famous monument and then continue to the **Roman Forum**, with the imposing white frills of the **Victor Emmanuel II monument** in the background. Exit via the **Piazza del Campidoglio**, then walk northwest to the **Pantheon** and the attractive Piazza della Rotonda, strolling from here to Piazza Navona. Rest at the **Café della Pace** (Via della Pace 3/7) and watch a colourful cast of characters funnel through the narrow medieval streets. Queue for authentic pizza at **Da Baffetto** (Via del Governo Vecchio 11). Savour a gelato from the humble **Da Quinto** (Via di Tor Millina 1) or more famous **I Tre Scalini** (Piazza Navona 28–3). Linger until nightfall, when buskers croon beside the piazza's illuminated fountains.

Day 2
Visitors interested in art and religion should spend the morning at **St Peter's** and **the Vatican** (even the briefest taste requires at least half a day); those keen on antiquity may prefer to explore the **Imperial Fora** and **the Capitoline Museums**. In the late afternoon, admire the Spanish Steps at **Piazza di Spagna**, then stroll along the elegant **Via dei Condotti** and Rome's main shopping street, the **Via del Corso.** The district of Trastevere is the perfect evening choice. Stray through the medieval streets, thick with bars, clubs and restaurants, patronized by tourists and locals alike. Standouts include the wine bar **Enoteca Ferrara** (Via del Moro 1a, Piazza Trilussa 41) and the pizzerias **Panattoni** (Viale Trastevere 53/5) and **Dar Poeta** (Vicolo del Bologna 45). Finish, as every trip must, at the **Trevi Fountain.** Tradition

claims one coin (cast backward over the left shoulder) ensures a return to Rome, two bring love, and three a wedding in the Eternal City.

ANCIENT ROME

Much of the ancient city remains visible, despite medieval stoneworkers quarrying the monuments. As you daydream the ruins back to life, remember that bright paint adorned the marble and tufa.

Day 1

The **Colosseum** is the best starting point. This grandiose amphitheatre once hosted shows and games, and its imposing size still recalls its former glory. Admire the nearby **Arch of Constantine**, still almost completely intact. A stroll through the **Roman Forum** takes you past remains of temples, basilicas and the august Senate House. On hot days, rest among the shady gardens and excavations on the **Palatine Hill**. Finish at the attractive Piazza della Rotonda, home of the **Pantheon**. Revitalize with a well-earned espresso at one of the nearby cafes that vie for the title of "city's best": **Tazzo d'Oro** (Via degli Orfani 8) or **Sant' Eustachio** (Piazza Sant' Eustachio 8).

Day 2

Visit the **Imperial Fora**, the **Capitoline Museums** and **Trajan's Market**, followed by **Caracalla's Baths**. Conclude with a ramble along the **Appian Way** and a peek at one of the many catacombs.

BAROQUE ROME

Few cities rival Rome in terms of Baroque splendour. Many of the greatest 17C artists lived and worked here, including famous names such as Bernini, Borromini, Caravaggio and Pietro da Cortona.

Day 1

Piazza Navona is the obvious starting point, with its magnificent Baroque masterpieces by Bernini (the Fountain of the Four Rivers) and Borromini (the Church of Sant'Agnese in Agone). Also worth seeing to the east of the piazza is the small church of Sant'Ivo alla Sapienza. Visit the **Galleria Doria Pamphili**, whose masterpieces include the famous *Rest after the Flight into Egypt* by Caravaggio. A short walk takes you to **Sant'Andrea della Valle**, one of the most elegant of the Baroque churches. Detour through the **Campo dei Fiori**, the famous open-air market, then continue west across the Tiber via the dramatic **Ponte Vittorio Emanuelle** to **St Peter's Basilica** and **the Vatican Museums**. Afternoon lines may be lengthy, but most guides shepherd groups past the queue.

Day 2

Begin at the lively **Piazza di Spagna**, and the nearby Baroque churches of **Sant'Andrea al Quirinale** and **San Carlo alle Quattro Fontane**. Nearby is the beautiful palazzo that once housed Cardinal Barberini, and now shelters a rich collection of 17C paintings. Walk north through the **Villa Borghese**, where you can admire sculptures by Bernini and rest in the park's attractive gardens. End the day at the famous **Trevi Fountain**, best seen illuminated at night. Legend promises that a coin tossed in the fountain ensures a return to Rome.

Longer Itineraries

The one-day itineraries listed below are designed for visitors who wish to see as much as possible in a short stay. Those interested in a particular historical and artistic period should consult the list to the right of the Principal Sights' map, as well as the suggestions given above. Maps of the various sights are at the guide's beginning and within the chapters in the *Discovering Rome* section (&see Map index at the end of the guide).

OPTION 1

Start in the **Imperial Fora**, then continue to the **Roman Forum** and the **Palatine Hill**, concentrating on the most important monuments (marked with stars in the main text) in all sites. Book ahead to visit the **Domus Aurea** (Nero's Golden House), not far from the Colosseum.

Stop at the **Colosseum**, pausing to admire the **Arch of Constantine**, then make your way to the **Basilica of St John Lateran**. En route to the basilica, make a brief stop at **San Clemente** to admire its magnificent mosaics.

OPTION 2

Start at the busy **Piazza Venezia**, dominated by the imposing bulk of the **monument to Vittorio Emanuele II** and continue towards the **Santa Maria d'Aracoeli** steps. After pausing to admire the Renaissance elegance of **Piazza del Campidoglio**, spend some time in the **Capitoline Museums** with a panoramic coffee break on the cafe terrace (Palazzo dei Conservatori). The **Chiesa del Gesù**, with its magnificent interior, is just a short walk away. From here, continue to the **Pantheon**, an exceptional domed structure dating from the 1C BC, and then on to **Piazza Navona**. The nearby church of **San Luigi dei Francesi** houses masterpieces by Caravaggio. Others well worth a visit include **Santa Maria della Pace**, the hidden gem of **Sant'Ivo alla Sapienza**, and **Sant'Andrea della Valle**.

OPTION 3

Begin at the colourful market in **Piazza Campo dei Fiori**. Barter for fresh produce or flowers, which gave this vibrant square its name. Next door is the quieter **Piazza Farnese** with grand fountains of Egyptian granite (adapted from the ancient Baths of Caracalla). The French Embassy and Academy occupy the palazzo there; Michaelangelo designed the upper storeys and the superb entablature. A stroll along Via di Monserrato and the elegant **Via Giulia** brings you to **Castel Sant'Angelo**. This papal fortress lies close to the centre of religious Rome: Via della Conciliazione leads directly to **St Peter's**. After admiring the famous square and enjoying a short tour inside the basilica, make your way to the magnificent **Vatican Museums** to visit the Sistine Chapel. Expect long lines, unless you've booked a guide (otherwise return another day and queue an hour or two before opening).

OPTION 4

After visiting **Santa Maria Maggiore**, a long ramble takes you towards **Piazza di Spagna**. En route, stop at **San Carlo alle Quattro Fontane** and **Sant'Andrea al Quirinale**, as well as making a short detour via **Piazza del Quirinale** to the **Trevi Fountain**. Explore the district between **Piazza di Spagna** and **Piazza del Popolo**, wandering along some of the most elegant streets in Rome (**Via del Corso** and **Via dei Condotti** for the latest fashions and gold, **Via Margutta** for arts and crafts and **Via del Babuino** for antiques). At sunset, climb the Pincian Hill for a breathtaking city view from the gardens.

Themed Visits

FRESCOES IN ROME

Frescoes that should not be missed include those in the **Sistine Chapel** and **Raphael Rooms** in the **Vatican Museums**. Also noteworthy here is the chapel of Nicholas V, a 15C work by Fra' Angelico and Benozzo Gozzoli, and the Chiaroscuri Rooms, adorned with unusual monochrome frescoes by pupils of Raphael. Staying west of the Tiber, visit the magnificent **Villa Farnesina**, decorated with 16C frescoes by Raphael, Giulio Romano, Giovanni da Udine, Baldassarre Peruzzi and Sodoma. From here, a walk up the Janiculum Hill takes you to the church of **San Pietro in Montorio**, which houses the fresco of the **Flagellation** by Sebastiano del Piombo. Below in Trastevere, discover a masterpiece of medieval painting: the **Last Judge-**

ment by Pietro Cavallini in the church of **Santa Cecilia**. Crossing the Tiber by the Ponte Garibaldi, continue to the **Chiesa del Gesù** to admire the ceiling by Baciccia, and then climb the steps of **Santa Maria d'Aracoeli** to see the **frescoes** by **Pinturicchio** in the chapel of San Bernardino da Siena. A diversion through the historic centre takes you to the Caelian Hill and the basilica of **San Clemente**, which houses 15C **frescoes** by Masolino da Panicale in the chapel of Santa Caterina. Return to Piazza Venezia and then head towards the Pantheon, pausing in the splendid Baroque church of **Sant'Ignazio** for the **fresco on the ceiling** with its unusual trompe l'oeil effect. The Carafa chapel in the church of **Santa Maria sopra Minerva** boasts delicate 15C **frescoes** by Filippino Lippi. The church of **San Luigi dei Francesi** – towards the Piazza Navona district – has **17C frescoes** by Il Domenichino, illustrating the legend of St Cecilia in the chapel of the same name. Cross Corso Vittorio Emanuele to reach the 16C **Palazzo della Cancelleria**, where Vasari spent 100 days adorning the Sala dei Cento Giorni. On the other side of the city, the church of **Santa Maria del Popolo** houses the Adoration of the Child by Pinturicchio in the Della Rovere chapel; the **salon** of **Palazzo Barberini**, overlooking the square of the same name, contains a Baroque fresco by Pietro da Cortona, celebrating the glory of the Barberini family.

St Peter's Basilica at night

G. Bludzin/MICHELIN

MUSEUMS IN ROME

The **Museo Nazionale Romano** collections feature in a number of different locations, the most important of which are the **Palazzo Massimo alle Terme**, the **Aula Ottagona** and **Palazzo Altemps**. Other notable exhibits are in the Sezione Epigrafica e Protostorica (at Diocletian's Baths) and at the Crypta Balbi. The **Capitoline Museums**, dedicated mainly to Roman art, are also of major importance. Unusual for its layout and location is the **Centrale Montemartini**, an old power station slightly outside the historic centre. The **Museo della Civiltà Romana** contains a large model of Rome during Constantine's reign, as well as scaled replicas of the low reliefs adorning Trajan's Column. Etruscan art has pride of place in the **Museo Nazionale di Villa Giulia**; the gold- and iron-work –along with the vivid tomb paintings – represent the best of this pre-Roman civilization. The **Galleria Borghese** exhibits both Renaissance masterpieces (Raphael) and works by Baroque masters such as Bernini and Caravaggio. The **Galleria Doria Pamphili** showcases works by Carracci, Caravaggio, Velázquez and Titian; while the **Galleria d'Arte Antica in Palazzo Barberini** displays paintings by Sodoma and Raphael. Explore non-European art in the **Museo Preistorico Etnografico L Pigorini** situated in the EUR district, near the **Museo delle Arti e Tradizioni Popolari Italiane**. Lastly, Rome's headliner is the **Vatican Collection**: a group of museums housing a vast collection of paintings, sculptures and other exhibits.

ART AND GARDENS

The following suggestions combine visits to art galleries and museums with leisurely strolls through quiet parks and gardens (known as *ville* in Italian), which provide welcome respite from the incessant traffic roar.

The most famous is, without a doubt, the **Villa Borghese**. Begun in the 17C by the cardinal of the same name, it bustles on Sundays with locals walking, jogging and enjoying the fresh air. Stroll past its lakes and statues, then linger in the magnificent **Galleria Borghese**, home to works by Raphael, Bernini and Caravaggio. Exhausted after the **Vatican Museums**? Relax in its beautiful **gardens** (reservation necessary). The itinerary suggested in the *GIANICOLO* chapter combines gardens, museums, shaded avenues and Renaissance residences: walk from **Villa Farnesina** to the **Orto Botanico**, visit **San Pietro in Montorio**, and finish with the panoramic **Janiculum walk**. Stroll in the delightful **Villa Celimontana park** after admiring the magnificent **mosaics in the church of San Clemente** or following a tiring walk among the ruins of the **Forum** and the **Colosseum**. Another green oasis – dotted with old churches – is the Aventine Hill. Enjoy the panoramic **Giardino degli Aranci** (Parco Savello) next to **Santa Sabina**, an impressive palaeo-Christian church founded in the 5C, or combine a visit to Santa Prisca with a walk through the rose gardens, the **Roseto Comunale**. Nor should you miss the **Casina delle Civette**, nestling in the elegant Villa Torlonia gardens on Via Nomentana, with its interesting collection of **Bel Époque stained-glass windows**.

UNUSUAL SIGHTS

Rome's most famous quirk is perhaps the view of St Peter's through the **Knights of Malta keyhole** of no 3, Piazza dei Cavalieri di Malta, on the Aventine Hill. Farther south in the city stands the **Cestius Pyramid**, the unusual mausoleum of a Roman magistrate, in the gorgeous oasis of the Protestant Cemetery, which also houses remains of English poets John Keats (1795–1821) and Percy Bysshe Shelley (1792–1822). The **Centrale Montemartini**, where a collection of ancient sculptures from the Capitoline Museums contrast with the turbines and engines of the old power station, is also of modern architectural interest. Spend the evening in the nearby **Testaccio district** –blue-collar home of the Roma football team – with its bars, restaurants, and the **Testaccio Village** (*see Entertainment in Your Stay in the City*), the setting for summer concerts and shows.

Back in the historic centre, the crypt of **Santa Maria della Concezione**, along the *dolce vita* Via Veneto, contains the bones of around 4,000 Capuchin monks, some of which are incorporated into its macabre decoration. According to legend, Salome requested the beheading of St John the Baptist – and the results are on display in the church of **San Silvestro in Capite**. In Via Giulia, the **oratory of Santa Maria della Morte** is known for its highly unusual decor: the skulls inserted into the walls recall the fact that the order that once lived here was responsible for the organisation of Christian funerals for the poor *(the oratory is open only for mass on Sunday evening at 6pm and is closed during August)*.

The eclectic architectural style of the small *palazzi* around **Piazza Mincio** in the **Coppedè district** dates from the beginning of the 20C. To the north of the city, not far from Porta Pia, the nearby **Villini district** is of the same period; the unusual **Villino Ximenes** is especially noteworthy here.

Although Rome contains the core of the Roman Catholic Church, it is also home to a modern **mosque** built in bold architectural style on the slopes of Monte Antenne, as well as a **synagogue** and the **Museum of Jewish Art**.

Lastly, architectural buffs adore the sporting complex of the **Foro Italico**, Fascist-built and renovated for the 1960 Olympic Games. The complex includes a swimming pool, the Marble Stadium, the Olympic Stadium and, on the opposite bank of the Tiber, the Palazzetto dello Sport.

FOUNTAINS

Rome's many fountains include grandiose Baroque creations, as well

Fontana del Nettuno

as more modest, traditional sculptures. Only the most famous or most unusual are mentioned below. For more history, refer to the index, or log onto www.romaturismo.it. Without a doubt, the most famous water feature is the **Trevi Fountain**, which dominates the small piazza of the same name. Of almost equal renown are the three installations in **Piazza Navona**, in particular the Fountain of the Four Rivers, a magnificent sculpture by Bernini. After window shopping along the elegant Via Condotti, rest at the Spanish Steps, where you can admire the unusual **Fontana della Barcaccia (boat fountain).** Legend states that the Via del Babuino (Baboon Street) took its name from the silenus on the **fountain close to the church of Sant'Atanasio**, given the statue's resemblance to a monkey. The **Fontana della Botticella**, close to Augustus's Mausoleum, is also of interest. The area between Via Veneto and Via XX Settembre is dotted with fountains: the **Fontana del Tritone** (Triton fountain) and the **Fontana delle Api (bee fountain)**, the symbol of the Barberini family, both by Bernini; the **four 16C fountains** adorning the crossroads of Via delle Quattro Fontane and Via XX Settembre, constructed by private citizens during the urban renovation promised by Sixtus V; and the **Fontana**

dell'Acqua Felice, crowned with a monumental statue of Moses. When exploring the Pantheon area, cool down at the 16C **fountain in Piazza della Rotonda** which, like so many others in Rome, was sculpted by Giacomo della Porta. Nearby is the typical **Fontana del Facchino**, the subject of a local legend (*see PANTHEON)*. The Campo dei Fiori district is full of fountains: the **fountain in Piazza Sant'Andrea della Valle**, the **fountains in Piazza Farnese**, the **Fontana del Mascherone** on Via Giulia (which spouted wine on ancient festival days), and the **Fontana della Terrina**.
Other fountains worthy of note include the delightful **Fontana delle Tartarughe (turtle fountain)** near Largo Argentina, which, according to legend, was built in a single night; the 16C **fountain in Piazza d'Aracoeli** at the foot of Capitol Hill; the unusual **Fontana della Navicella**, opposite the church of Santa Maria in Domnica; and the monumental **Fontana Paola** on the Janiculum.
Finally, sample the city's sweet aqueduct waters via the *nasone* (noses): the free-flowing street spigots. Seal the faucet's mouth with a thumb, forcing an arc of liquid through the small hole. *Cin cin!*

BRIDGES AND BANKS OF THE TIBER RIVER

The Tiber, which cuts the city in two, provides some fascinating views of the city (👁️see Themed Tours – On the Water). Follow the river either on foot or by bike (short sections of the bank have proper cycle tracks). Although major roads parallel the river, often carrying heavy traffic, the footpaths – shaded by lovely plane trees – still provide a pleasant walk. The most attractive section for walkers is without a doubt the stretch from the Ara Pacis Augustae to Piazza Bocca della Verità, near the site of the Ancient Romans' trading and military ports. The peaceful **Isola Tiberina**, still home to the Hospital of the Brothers of St John of God, stands besides the ruins of the **Ponte Rotto** (broken bridge). The ancients played upon its ship shape, constructing a travertine prow and other details. Its bridges are particularly evocative: **Ponte Cestio** leads to Trastevere and the Janiculum, and **Ponte Fabricio**, the city's oldest functional span that dates back to IC BC, leads to the synagogue and the old Jewish quarter (known as the "ghetto" – a shortening of the word for "neighbourhood," not an insult) on the opposite bank. Nearby is **Ponte Sisto**, built in the 15C by Pope Sixtus IV, which crosses the Tiber near Piazza Trilussa, a delightful corner of Trastevere; from the bridge there is a good view of the tiled rooftops of the Janiculum district. Another unforgettable view unfolds from **Ponte Sant'Angelo**. Its arches remain from the time of the Emperor Hadrian, but Bernini embellished them with beautiful angels in the 17C.

BIRD'S-EYE VIEWS

The best time to enjoy a view of the tiled rooftops and marble domes of the capital is undoubtedly at sunset, when the sky is streaked with pale red in winter and blazing scarlet in summer. Don't miss the magnificent **view from the Janiculum**. Wander along the pedestrian **Passegiata Gianicolo**, perhaps pausing under the formal equestrian statue at Piazza Garibaldi, also home to snack and balloon vendors, miniature pony rides and a puppet theatre. Equally impressive is the wide panorama from Piazzale Napoleone I in the **gardens on the Pincian Hill**, the **dome of St Peter's** and the **Piazza del Campidoglio**. For the best views, however, take a seat at the **Caffè Capitolino**, in Palazzo Caffarelli, or pause in the **Galleria del Palazzo Senatorio** during your visit to the Capitoline Museums. For an excellent view of the Roman Forum, walk along Via del Campidoglio to behind the Palazzo Senatorio, or climb the Palatine Hill, where the views from

Ponte Cestio

Courtesy of APT of Rome

The Palatine Hill, aerial view

Courtesy of APT of Rome

the **Orti Farnesiani** extend from the temples in the forum to the Basilica of Maxentius, the bell-tower of San Francesca Romana, and the Colosseum. Locals often joke that the best view of Rome is from the **Vittorio Emanuele II Monument**, mainly because you can't see the marble monstrosity underfoot. From the **terrace of Castel Sant'Angelo**, a panorma unfolds from the Borghese Gardens to the unmistakable dome of the Pantheon, the monument to Victor Emmanuel II, and the impressive dome of St Peter's. For a more peaceful scenic outlook, try the **Giardino degli Aranci** (Parco Savello) near Santa Sabina on the Aventine Hill; just be wary on the steep footpaths nearby, sometimes the haunt of flashers.

Gardens

Escape the city's hustle and bustle of the city, spread a picnic blanket alongside locals or stroll in the shade of the stately umbrella pines. Known as *ville* (villas), these gardens once belonged to noble families. Open from dawn to dusk, many contain museums, cafes and other recreational options (few public toilets, however).

Villa Borghese
In this large, popular park, decorated with statues and fountains, it is still possible to find quiet areas, such as the Giardino del Lago, an English-style garden with magnolias, aloe and yucca, or the Italianate Parco dei Daini. Home to the Villa Giulia – a national museum of exquisite Etruscan art – the vast green oasis also include a static-line balloon, a train trolley, bike rentals, an equestrian centre and the Bioparco, a zoo that boasts bears.

Roseto di Roma – This rose garden on the Aventine Hill is open exclusively during bloom (end of April to end of June). The prize-giving ceremony

G. Bludzin/MICHELIN

A fountain in the Pincio gardens

draws great crowds.

Villa Sciarra – In the Monteverde Vecchio district, this park is full of statues, fountains and antiquities, as well as playgrounds. It rediscovered its Baroque charm at the beginning of the century and is renowned for its collection of plants.

Villa Celimontana
see COLOSSEO-CELIO.
This is one of the few parks in Rome with a skating rink. It provides a popular backdrop for wedding photos and in summer hosts jazz concerts.

Villa Torlonia
see CATACOMBE DI PRISCILLA.
A rare species, known as the Californian palm, grows in the former residence of the Mussolini family. The Casina delle Civette contains a fine collection of Liberty-style stained glass, designs and other articles.

Villa Glori
see PARIOLI district.
Shaded by olive trees, this spacious garden has kids pony and donkey rides.

Villa Doria Pamphili
see GIANICOLO district.
The "lungs" of the western district, this park is very popular late in the evening with athletes and kite flyers. It houses a number of buildings, greenhouses, an 18C lake and many rare plants.

Parco dell'Appia Antica
One of Rome's original roads – the Via Appia Antica – closes to cars on Sundays. Pedestrians and cyclists rule the ancient *basoli*, the polygonal basalt paving stones. A two-hour guided bike tour departs the *Sede il Parco* (Park Seat) each Sunday at 10.30am (www.parcoappiaantica.org). Highlights include ancient catacombs (www.catacombe.roma.it), the *Quo Vadis?* church and the *Fosse Ardeatine*, the cave where Nazis massacred 335 Roman men and boys – now a pilgrimage site. Reach the park via the Archeobus or city buses 110, 218, 660 and 664 (www.atac.roma.it).

Orto Botanico di Villa Corsini
Not far from Trastevere, these gardens have a wonderful variety of cacti, orchids and tropicals. A small garden of flowers and plants with particularly strong scents has been planted for the benefit of the visually impaired.

Riserva Naturale di Monte Mario
This nature reserve has Prehistoric, Roman and Renaissance ruins.

Riserva Naturale del Litorale Romano
Typical Mediterranean vegetation sprouts here, alongside spacious open areas of dunes and holm oak woods. The oasis also contains Roman ruins from sites such as Ostia Antica, Trajan's Ports, ruins from the ancient Via Severiana and Pliny's villa.

Other Ways to Tour

BY BICYCLE

Rome is not an ideal city to explore by bike or moped because of its dense, chaotic traffic, heavy pollution and the uneven road surfaces. However, keen cyclists follow the bike path along the Tiber and explore the city's public parks. The only sections of dedicated cycle track run from Ponte Risorgimento to Villa Borghese and then from Villa Borghese to Villa Ada, and from Ponte Sublicio, in the south of the city, to Ponte della Magliana and on to Ponte di Mezzocammino.

Bicycle hire
Bicycles can be hired in the city centre: Piazza di Spagna, near the entrance to the metro; Piazza del Popolo, on the corner of the street containing Café Rosati *(open in summer, 6am-1am, in winter Sun mornings only)*; Via dei Fori Imperiali, near the Colosseo Metro stop *(open Mar-Oct, 10am-6pm [2am in summer])*; Villa Borghese underground car park, sector III.
On Sundays and public holidays bikes can be taken on Metro line B and the train to Lido di Ostia, for those interested in cycling outside the city or along the coast. A bike ticket costs €3.50 for 24 hours, second class.

BY SCOOTER

Mopeds (*motorini*) are the essential Roman mode of transport and fashion accessory. A credit card and photo identification – or cash deposit – may be required for a rental, costing about €30 per day, €170 per week.

Helmets are the law – one of the few heeded by the free-spirited Romans (and stringently enforced by the police). The smaller vehicles, like the standard 50cc put-puts, aren't approved to transport passengers, but often do. Mopeds can enter the historic centre (the limited traffic area "ZTL") and park free in blue-line area … or just about anywhere else they can wedge out of traffic. Drivers must be 14+ for models up to 50cc.

Brave souls can rent from **Scooter Hire** (Via Cavour 80a, Monti; ☎06 481 5669; www.scooterhire.it). **Romarent** also offers guided bike and scooter tours in English (Vicolo dei Bovari 7a, Centro Storico near the Piazza Navona; ☎06 689 6555; http://web. tiscali.it/romarent). Finally **EcoMoveRent** supplies scooters, along with bicycles, boats and airplanes (Via Varese 48/50, Esquilino; ☎06 44 704 518; www.ecomoverent.it).

The **Parco Gianicolense** offers atmospheric views of the cityscape, but its switchbacks and one-way streets promote panic and funnel drivers into the Vatican traffic jams. Instead, bump along the back streets of Trastevere or the Aventine Hill, away from the horns and hustle. Coasting past the Circus Maximus – the ancient Roman horse track – is especially evocative.

BY HORSE-DRAWN CARRIAGE

Carriages (*carozzella* or *botticella* in Roman dialect) can be hailed from St Peter's Square, the Colosseum, Piazza Venezia, Piazza di Spagna, Piazza Navona , near the Trevi Fountain, Via Veneto and Villa Borghese. ☎06 57 901. Rides normally have a fixed route and the cost ranges between €80 and €150 .

BY METRO AND BUS

In a rare display of cooperation, the metro, buses and trams work together under the company ATAC (Via Voluturno 65, Esquilino; ☎06 46 951, 800 431 784; www.metrebus.it). The city's rich history stunted the subway (*la metropolitana*). The overlapping ruins run deep, making tunnel excavation difficult. The city managed a simple two-line system, aimed mainly at suburban commuters. The metro is efficient and safe, but stay on-guard for pickpockets and groping in crowds.

New routes allow visitors to discover the historical centre from the comfort of a bus:

- ◆ **110** departs from Termini (Piazza dei Cinquecento) from 9am-8pm (summer) and from 10am-6pm (winter), with departures every 30min. A **non-stop** ticket costs €15.
- ◆ a €20 **stop and go** ticket allows passengers to hop on and off, as well as take the Archeobus.
- ◆ The ATAC ticket office is situated in zone C of Piazza dei Cinquecento.
- ◆ The Basilica line leaves Termini (Piazza dei Cinquecento) at 10.30am and 3pm and costs €7.75.

For further information or to make a booking, call ☎06 46 95 22 52 or 06 46 95 22 56 (open 9am-7pm). The ATAC website is www.atac.roma.it.

ON THE WATER

For an unusual view of the city, why not take a **boat trip** on the River Tiber? **EcoMoveRent** 100-minute tours depart every Wednesday, Friday and Saturday from 8pm-12am (April–December; Via Varese 48/50, Esquilino; ☎06 44 704 518; www. ecomoverent.it). The motorboat departs from the Ponte Umberto I, pivots under the Ponte Duca d'Aosta, then returns (€49-55 per person, maximum of four).

Tourvisa also runs dinner cruises between these bridges from May-Oct, at 10.30am and 12.45pm. The trip lasts approximately 1hr 30min and costs €53 per person. ☎06 44 63 481, www.tourvisa.it.

BY PLANE

For a bird's-eye view of the city in a Cessna 182 or Highlander, contact the dell'Urbe Airport at Via Salaria 825.

20min flights available. Advanced reservation necessary. Cost €70 per person; minimum of two people required. For information contact City Fly, ☎06 88 333, www.cityfly.com.

KNOW BEFORE YOU GO

Useful Websites

The Internet enables visitors to contact tourist offices, consult programmes and brochures and make bookings on line. The following sites provide information on Roman history and art, as well as giving practical suggestions.

Art and culture in Rome

Consult the official site of the Comune di Roma, which lists details of events and exhibitions taking place in the city: www.comune.roma.it

Practical information

The Comune di Roma's central database lists regularly updated addresses, plus details on transport, events, shows, sport and a range of other topics: www.romaturismo.it

The Imperial Fora

This site contains reconstructions of ancient Rome and virtual visits around the Fora via two web-cams. It also provides information on daily life in antiquity and on the excavation work in the fora: www.capitolium.org

For tourists and locals

Www.romainweb.com (in Italian only) and www.wantedinrome.com detail cultural events, museums, monuments, guided tours, cinemas and theatres, children's activities, shops, bars and nightclubs etc.

Cinecittà

This site provides information on the history of the Cinecittà film studios, as well as virtual reconstructions of famous sets, details of cinema events and festivals taking place around the world, and an introduction to digital technology and other facilities available at the studios: www.cinecitta.it

Touring Club Italia

Natives have a soft spot for TCI, purveyors of maps, guides and member discounts. The Milan-based association began in 1894 as the Touring Club Ciclistico Italiano (Cycling Touring Club of Italy). Today it caters to a wide range of travellers. A €25 annual membership includes discounts on car rentals, accomodations, ferries, spas, museums and historic sites (www.touringclub.it).

Tourist Offices

INTERNATIONAL

The **Ente Nazionale Italiano per il Turismo** (ENIT) has offices abroad and in Italy. *For local tourist information see below.*

UK

1 Princes Street, London W1B 2AY; ☎(020) 7408 1254; 00800 0048 2542 (free phone); Fax (020) 7493 6695; italy@italiantouristboard.co.uk; www.enit.it (Mon-Fri, 9am-5pm).

USA

Suite 1565, 630 Fifth Avenue, New York NY 10111; ☎(212) 245 5618; (212) 245 4822 (brochure line); enitny@ italiantourism.com; www.italiantourism.com (Mon-Fri, 9am-5pm). For Los Angeles, ☎(310) 820 1898; (310) 820 0098 (brochure line); enitla@italiantourism.com.

Canada

Italian Government Tourist Board, 175 Bloor St E, Suite 907 – South

Tower, Toronto, Ontario M4W 3R8;
☎(416) 925 4882; Fax (416) 925 4799;
enit.canada@on.aibn.com;
www.italiantourism.com.

Australia
Italian Government Tourist Office,
Level 4, 46 Market Street, Sidney, NSW
2000; ☎00612 92 621666; italia@
italiantourism.com.a

LOCAL

Azienda di Promozione Turistica (APT)
Via Parigi 11 (☎06 48 89 91 or
☎06 48 89 92 38), and at Fiumicino
Airport (☎06 65 95 60 74). Free
brochures and maps of the city.

Comune di Roma
information kiosks *(open 9am-6pm;
☎06 36 00 43 99; www.romaturismo.com)*
at:
- Termini Railway Station, Platform 2 ☎06 48 90 63 00
- Termini Railway Station, Piazza dei Cinquecento ☎06 47 82 51 94
- Castel Sant'Angelo, Piazza Pia ☎06 68 80 97 07
- Fori Imperiali, Piazza Tempio della Pace ☎06 69 92 43 07
- Piazza di Spagna, Largo Goldoni ☎06 68 13 60 61
- Piazza Navona, Piazza Cinque Lune ☎06 68 80 92 40
- Via Nazionale, opposite the Palazzo delle Esposizioni ☎06 47 82 45 25
- Trastevere, Piazza Sonnino ☎06 58 33 34 57
- San Giovanni, Piazza San Giovanni in Laterano ☎06 77 20 35 35.

International Visitors

ITALIAN EMBASSIES AND CONSULTATES

UK   Embassy
14 Three Kings' Yard,
London W1Y 2EH
☎(020) 7312 2200
Fax (020) 7312 2230
emblondon@embitaly.org.uk
www.embitaly.org.uk

USA   Embassy
3000 Whitehaven St, NW
Washington, DC 20008
☎(202) 616 4400
Fax (202) 518 2154
www.ambwashingtondc.esteri.it/

Canada   Embassy
275 Slater Street, 21st floor
Ottawa, Ontario K1P 5H9
☎(613) 232 2401/2/3
Fax (613) 233 1484
ambasciata.ottawa@esteri.it
www.ambottawa.esteri.it

UK   Consulates
38 Eaton Place
London SW1X 8AN
☎(020) 7235 9371
Fax (020) 7823 1609.

Rodwell Tower, 111 Piccadilly
Manchester M1 2HY
☎(0161) 236 9024
Fax (0161) 236 5574
passaporti@italconsulman.demon.co.uk

32 Melville Street,
Edinburgh EH3 7HA;
☎(0131) 226 3631;
Fax (0131) 226 6260;
consedimb@consedimb.demon.co.uk

USA   Consulate
690 Park Avenue
New York NY 10021
☎(212) 439 8600
Fax (212) 249 4945
info.newyork@esteri.it
www.consnewyork.esteri.it

Canada   Consulates
3489 Drummond Street
Montreal, Quebec H3G 1X6
☎(514) 849 8351
Fax (514) 499 9471
consolato.montreal@esteri.it
www.consmontreal.esteri.it

496 Huron Street
Toronto, Ontario M5T 1Y5;
☎(416) 921 3802
consolato.it@toronto.italconsulate.org
www.iictoronto.esteri.it

FOREIGN EMBASSIES IN ROME

Australia – Via Alessandria 215
00198 Rome; ☎06 85 27 21
Fax 06 8527 2300
www.italy.embassy.gov.au
Canada – Via GB de Rossi 27
00161 Rome; ☎06 44 59 81
rome@dfait-maeci.gc.ca
www.canada.it
Ireland – Piazza di Campitelli 3
00186 Rome; ☎06 69 79 121
Fax 06 67 92 354
irish.embassy@libero.it
New Zealand – Via Zara 28
00198 Rome; ☎06 441 7171
www.nzembassy.com
South Africa –Via Tanaro 14
00198 Rome; ☎06 852 541
www.sudafrica.it
UK – Via XX Settembre 80a, Rome
☎06 42 20 00 01; Fax 06 48 73 324
www.britain.it
USA – Via Veneto 119a, 00187 Rome
☎06 46 741; Fax 06 48 82 672
www.usembassy.it

DOCUMENTS

Passports – Brits must carry a valid
national passport. Citizens of other
European Union countries only need a
national identity card. In case of loss
or theft, report to the embassy or
consulate and the local police.

Visas – Entry visas are required by
Australian, New Zealand, Canadian
and US citizens (if stay exceeds three
months). Apply to the Italian
Consulate (visa issued same day; delay
if submitted by mail). US citizens may
find the booklet *Your Trip Abroad*
useful for visa requirements, customs
regulations, medical care etc. –
available from the Superintendent of
Documents, PO Box 371954,
Pittsburgh, PA 15250-7954,
☎(202) 512 1800; Fax (202) 512 2250;
www.access.gpo.gov

HEALTH

As the UK is a member of the European
Union, British subjects should obtain
medical form E111 from the Ministry
of Social Security, Newcastle-upon-Tyne,
or from main post offices, before
leaving home. Separate travel and
medical insurance is recommended.

CUSTOMS

EU member states have no limits,
provided the merchandise is for
personal use. Keep receipts for all
goods acquired abroad. Request the
leaflet *Duty Paid* from HM Customs
and Excise, Finchley Excise Advice
Centre, Berkeley House, 304 Regents
Park Road, London N3 2JY, ☎0845 010
9000; www.hmce.gov.uk
For non-Eu citizens, "duty-free" only
alleviates taxes at the shopping
source: you still must declare articles
in excess of your home country's
allowance. For example, the United
States permits $800 of goodies before
the taxman cometh (charging a flat
10% on the next $1,000), as long as
the traveller was abroad at least 48
hours and hasn't made another
international trip in the last 30 days
(more duty-free tips on www.customs.
treas.gov).
Edible souvenirs can fall foul of
officials (who mete out fines of $250
for forbidden foods). The US Customs
Service offers a free publication **Know
Before You Go** for US citizens, www.
customs.gov

DRIVING IN ROME

Also see the Getting Around chapter.

Nationals of the European Union
require a valid **national driving
licence**. Non-EU citizens may wish to
carry an **international driving licence**,
obtainable in the US from the
American Automobile Association,
US$18 for members and US$20 for non-
members. The AAA can be contacted
at 1000 AAA Drive, Heathrow FL 32746-
5080, ☎(407) 444 7000; www.aaa.
com/vacation/idpf.html
Other documents required include the
vehicle's current **log book** and a
green card for insurance.

Accessibility ♿

Accessible attractions include the Vatican Museums, Castel Sant' Angelo, Galleria Doria Pamphili, Palazzo delle Esposizioni, Museo della Civiltà Romana, Museo delle Navi Romane, St Peter's, San Giovanni in Laterano, Palazzo Venezia, the Galleria Nazionale d'Arte Moderna, Galleria Borghese and the Bioparc-Zoo. Rome's exceptional effort is the walkway between the Piazza Navona and the Trevi Fountain. Not only does smooth brick designate a pedestrian-friendly path, but Braille plaques explain the landmarks en route. Many Roman historic monuments do not have modern lifts or wheelchair facilities. For detailed information prior to departure contact **RADAR** (Royal Association for Disability and Rehabilitation), 12 City Forum, 250 City Road, London EC1V 8AF ☎(020) 7250 3222; Fax (020) 7250 0212; www.radar.org.uk. Request a free multilingual pamphlet, **Rome Accessibile**, from the tourism office (Azienda per il Turismo di Roma, Via Parigi 5, Esquiline; ☎06 3600 4399; www.romaturismo.com; open 9am–7pm Mon–Sat). Stock often run low, so try the publisher **CO.IN** as well (Via E. Giglioli 54A; ☎06 712 9011; www.coinsociale.it; open 9am–6pm Mon–Fri). The group also organizes an eight-seat shuttle bus, which should be booked several days in advance (airport runs are possible). English-speakers staff its **Roma per Tutti** advice line (☎06 7162 3919; www.romapertutti.it; open 9am–5pm Mon–Fri). The toll free number is only good within Italy (☎800 271 027; open 9am–5pm Mon–Fri, 9am–1pm Sat). A free guidebook with a CD-ROM, **Cammina Cammina**, offers information and itineraries in English and Italian (Sol.Co. Roma Piazza Vittorio Emanuele 31, Esquiline; ☎06 490 821; www.solcorona.net; open 9am–7pm Mon–Fri).
Explore Rome with **Accessible Journeys** (www.disabilitytravel.com), Flying Wheels Travel (www.flying-wheelstravel.com) and **Hands on Italia** (signed tours; www.handsonita-lia.com). **Access Able** offers excellent information (www.access-able.com), as do the **Society for Accessible Travel and Hospitality** (www.sath.org) and the **American Foundation for the Blind** (www.afb.org).
Sights in this guide marked with the symbols ♿ or (♿) have full or partial access for wheelchairs.

TRANSPORT

Two bus services have facilities for wheelchair access. Line 590 runs from Metro line A (inaccessible) on Viale Giulio Cesare to Piazza Cinecittà and line 157 links Via A. Mitelli (Tor Bella Monaca) to Termini Railway Station. All the stations on Metro line B, with the exception of Circo Massimo, Colosseo and Cavour have lifts. Many of the city buses now have lower platforms and so are suitable for wheelchair users. Large train stations have an office for the disabled (ufficio disabili); Termini's is beside platform one (☎06 488 1726). Request assistance 24 hours before travel.

GETTING THERE

By Plane

AIRLINES

Many airline companies fly direct to Rome. The following is a brief selection:

Alitalia

- 4 Portman Square, Marble Arch London W1H 9PS
  ☎(020) 7486 8432
  Fax (020) 7486 8431
  Reservations can also be made on ☎08705 448 259
  www.alitalia.co.uk
- 4-5 Dawson Street, Dublin 2
  ☎(01) 677 5171; Fax (01) 677 3373
  www.alitalia.ie
- 666 Fifth Avenue, New York NY 10103; ☎(212) 903 3300
  Fax (212) 903 3350.
  www.alitaliausa.com
- Viale Marchetti 111, 00148 Rome
  ☎06 65 621; alitalia.it

British Airways

- 156 Regent Street, London W1B 5LB;
  ☎0845 77 999 77 (enquiries); 0845 77 333 77 (reservations); Fax (020) 7434 4640 (reservations);
  www.britishairways.com
- USA – ☎(1-800) AIRWAYS.
- Via Bissolati 54, 00187 Rome;
  ☎199 712 266 (from Italy only).

For information on low-cost flights to Italy, *see Basic Information – Discounts.*

Major **US airlines** that fly to Rome include:

- **American Airlines** – www.aa.com
- **Continental Airlines** – www.continental.com
- **Delta Airlines** – www.delta.com
- **Northwest Airlines** – www.nwa.com (no direct flights to Rome)
- **United Airlines** – www.ual.com (no direct flights to Rome)
- **USAirways** – www.usairways.com

Tour operators offering flight-only or package holidays include:

- **Citalia** – ☎(020) 8686 0677 www.citalia.com
- **Italy Sky Shuttle** – ☎(020) 8241 5145

AIRPORTS

Rome is served by two airports: **Leonardo da Vinci Airport** at **Fiumicino** (26km/16mi SW of Rome) and **Ciampino Airport** (15km/10mi SE of Rome). For information about both airports: *www.adr.it.* Fiumicino handles domestic and international traffic. Ciampino concentrates on low-cost flights.

Ground Transportation

Fiumicino is linked to the centre by **train**: services to Roma-Termini (€11) depart every 30min, between 7.40am-10.30pm from the airport; between 7am-10pm from Roma-Termini; journey time 32min.

FM1 Fiumicino-Fara Sabina services run trains every 15min to Trastevere, Ostiense, Tuscolana and Tiburtina (€5.50). Going directly to these neighborhoods can save considerable time and hassle, but be careful: taxis are rare during rainstorms and late at night without booking.

Four COTRAL night buses loop between the airport, Termini and Tiburtina stations from 1.15am to 5am. Tickets are €3.60. Fiumicino's stop is outside the arrivals hall (☎06 575 31, 800 150 008; www.cotralspa.it).

A **taxi** to city centre takes 45 minutes and costs a flat rate of €60 for up to four passengers and luggage (only use the authorized white and yellow cabs at the stand).

Buses embark outside **Ciampino** arrivals hall every half-hour 6.50am–11.40pm and cost €1 (☎06 575 31, 800 150 008).

Purchase tickets at the bar inside the Departures Hall or from a vending machine. Drivers sell at a higher price, but are reluctant to make change – or even bother in the first place. Validate your ticket on the bus. Relax onboard, as Anagnina is the last stop. Once in the station, follow the underground passage to the Metro. Purchase an €1 subway ticket from the bar, newsstand or vending machines, which need correct change.

A private **bus service** also connects Termini to both airports. All information and schedule on www.terravision. it. Cost of ticket: €7-8 (one way), €12-14 (return).

Parking

In addition to a multi-storey car park, Fiumicino Airport also has a long-stay car park with a capacity for 3 000 vehicles. The car park sits east of the airport, and is directly linked to the Rome-Fiumicino motorway. A free bus shuttles to the domestic and international terminals every 10min during the day (from 7am-midnight) and every 20min at night. The cost of parking ranges from €8.78 per day for the first four days,€5.16 for the next four days and €3.10 from the ninth day onwards.

By Train

Italy has an extensive train network. Service is generally reliable and inexpensive – making rail the most pleasant way to explore the country (Ferrovie dello Stato; ☏8488-888-088; www.trenitalia.com).

Whenever possible, purchase tickets from an automated machine at the rail station, which has menus in English. The computer allows you to browse destinations, scrutinize schedules and pay by credit. Best of all, you avoid the long, panicked queues. Travel agents – with the FS sticker – may charge a slight commission.

Tickets are good for two months, but must be stamped before boarding. Orange validation machines stand at the end of each platform.

The mainline national and international trains arrive at **Stazione Termini** or **Tiburtina**. Termini is on both Metro

lines (**A** – Ottaviano-Anagnina and **B** – Laurentina-Rebibbia) and the bus station in the forecourt serves almost all the routes in Rome. Several nearby towns – such as Viterbo, Pantano and Ostia – are accessible on routes from the city: the Rome-Viterbo line leaves from Piazzale Flaminio Station; Rome-Pantano from Roma Laziali Station; the Rome-Lido line leaves from Porta San Paolo Station and makes three stops before Ostia Lido, one of which is the ruins at Ostia Antica.

Timetables are available at the Italian Tourist Office in London and from news-stands in Italy.

Useful numbers

Italian State Railways (Ferrovie dello Stato), ☏892021(information in Italy), information office at Termini Station ☏892021; information for disabled travellers ☏06 48 81 726; www.trenitalia.com
Ultima Travel, 424 Chester Road, Little Sutton, South Wirral CH66 3RB ☏0151 339 6171; fax 0151 339 9199.

By Coach/Bus

Coach services from Victoria Coach Station in London are operated by Eurolines, 4 Cardiff Road, Luton, Bedfordshire L41 1PP; ☏08705 143 219 (calls charged at standard rate); Fax 01582 400 694; welcome@ eurolinesuk.com; www.eurolines.co.uk Alternatively, contact National Express, 75 Davies Street, London W1K 5HT, ☏0870 901 3190; 08705 80 80 80; www.gobycoach.com.

By Car

The Michelin companion maps and plans for this guide are listed at the back of the guide.
On the outer edge of the city is the **Grande Raccordo Anulare** (GRA), a multi-lane ring road from which all the motorways (A1 to Florence and Bologna to the north, to Naples in the south; A12 to Fiumicino, Civitavecchia and the west coast; A24 east to Aquila

and the Adriatic) and main roads (*strada statale*) radiate.

The **Tangenziale Est** links the Stadio Olimpico to the Piazza San Giovanni in Laterano via such eastern quarters as Nomentano, Tiburtino, Prenestino.

If you are approaching Rome from the north along the A1, and heading north (Cassia, Flaminia or Salaria districts)

or west (Aurelia) of the city, leave the motorway at Roma Nord and follow the Grande Raccordo Anulare (GRA). For the eastern and southern districts of Rome, stay on the motorway, follow signs to Roma Est-Napoli and take the GRA at the Roma Est exit.

From the A16 and A24 motorways, the GRA is clearly signposted.

GETTING AROUND

Visitors are best advised to explore Rome by foot and on public transport because traffic in the city is heavy and parking places are difficult to find.

For information on hiring a bicycle or moped, ℰ *see When and Where to Go.*

By Public Transportation

Public transport services are organised by **ATAC** (Azienda Tramvie e Autobus del Comune di Roma, ☎ 800 43 17 84, open Mon-Fri, 8am-6pm or ☎ 06 46 951; www.atac.roma.it). City route plans are on sale in bookshops and kiosks; the plan *Rete dei Trasporti Urbani di Roma*, published by ATAC, is sold at the information kiosk in Piazza dei Cinquecento.

A typical Roman façade (detail)

B. Morandi/MICHELIN

Tickets should be purchased before the beginning of the journey and punched in the machine in the bus and on the underground.

Different types of ticket (*biglietto*) are sold at newspaper kiosks or in tobacconists' shops: those bearing the name **Metrebus** may be used on all means of transport – bus, tram, metro and overground FS (*Ferrovie Statali*) trains in second class except on services Roma Termini – Fiumicino Aeroporto and Ponte Galliera – Fiumicino Aeroporto. Individual tickets may also be acquired from machines at metro stations and end-of-line bus stops.

Tickets available include:

♦ a **BIT** ticket costing €1, is valid for a journey up to 1hr 15min on various lines from the time it is stamped;

♦ a **BIG** ticket, costing €4, is valid until midnight of the day of purchase;

♦ a **BTI** pass, costing €11, is valid for three days.

♦ a **CIS** pass, costing €16, is valid for one week.

A monthly pass is also available for €30. Bus and trams stops are indicated by a sign *fermata*; request stop = *fermata richiesta*. The entrance door (*salita*) is at the back of the bus and the exit (*uscita*) in the middle.

Buses operate from 5.30am-midnight. The following established routes are amongst the most useful:

♦ **64** and **40** from Termini Station to the Vatican, stopping at Via Nazionale, Piazza Venezia, near the Gesù Church, Largo di Torre Argentina and Corso Vittorio

Emanuele II. However, beware of pickpockets, notably at rush hour;

- **218** Piazza San Giovanni in Laterano south to Via Ardeatina (passing the north end of the Old Appian Way);
- **310** from Termini Station to Piazza Vescovio;
- **116** and **117** (weekdays only) run through the historic centre using electric minibuses. The former runs from Via Veneto and from Via Giulia, and the latter from Piazza San Giovanni in Laterano and from Piazza del Popolo;
- **85** Colosseum, Imperial Fora, Piazza Venezia, Via del Corso.

Trams operate from 5am-9pm. There are six lines; the following routes are amongst the most useful to tourists:

- **3** Trastevere, Colosseum, San Giovanni in Laterano, Piazza Thorwaldsen (Villa Giulia and the Galleria Nazionale d'Arte Moderna);
- **14** and **516** from the east side of the city (Via Prenestina) to Termini Station, Via Piazzale di Porta Maggiore and Piazza Vittorio Emanuele II;
- **19** from Piazza dei Gerani to the Olympic Village, stopping at Piazza dei Gerani, Piazzale del Verano, Viale Regina Margherita, Piazza Thorwaldsen, Via Flaminia and Viale Tiziano;
- **30b** from Piazzale Ostiense (Piramide de G Cestius) to Piazza Thorwaldsen, passing near the Galleria Nazionale d'Arte Moderna and Villa Borghese and through the city centre past the Colosseum, San Giovanni in Laterano and Piazza Porta Maggiore.
- **8** from Trastevere Station stopping at Viale Trastevere, Via Arenula and Via di Torre Argentina.

For more info: www.trambusopen.com

Metro (underground) trains operate from 5.30am-11.30pm; the section Termini-Rebibbia runs until 9pm weekdays and 11pm weekends and holidays. There are two lines:

- **Line A** runs from Battistini to Via Anagnina. The most useful stops include Flaminio (Piazza del Popolo, Spagna (Piazza di Spagna), Barberini (Piazza Barberini), Termini (Termini Station), San Giovanni (St John Lateran) and Cinecittà.
- **Line B** runs from Rebibbia to Laurentina via EUR. The most useful stops include Termini (Termini Station), Cavour (Piazza Cavour), Colosseo (Colosseum), Circo Massimo (near the Circus Maximus and the Baths of Caracalla), Piramide (Mausoleum of Caius Cestius), San Paolo (basilica of St Paul Without the Walls) and EUR Fermi (EUR district).

By Taxi

To call a taxi dial ☎06 35 70, ☎06 49 94, ☎06 88 177, ☎06 41 57, ☎06 55 51, or ☎06 66 45. Fixed starting charge: €2.33 rising €0.10 every 50 seconds. Extra charges apply for luggage (€1.03), night service (between 10pm–7am; €3.50) and Sundays and holidays (€3.50). Flat rates exist for each airport – Fiumicino €60 and Ciampino €30 for four passengers –but expect fare melodrama nonetheless.

By Car

Driving in Rome is not advised as access to the city centre is very difficult and parking severely restricted; many streets are reserved for pedestrians, taxis, buses and local residents. The historic centre is delineated as blue zone (fascia blu) from which private cars are excluded between 6.30am-7.30pm Mon-Fri and 2-6pm Sat.

ROAD REGULATIONS

Traffic drives on the right. The minimum driving age in Italy is 18 years of age. **Seat belts** must be worn in the front and back of the vehicle. Drivers must wear shoes, carry spare lights and a **red triangle** and a **yellow vest** to be displayed in case of a breakdown or accident.

A valid **driving licence** must be carried at all times.

Motorways (*autostrade* – subject to tolls) and dual carriageways *(superstrade)* are indicated by green signs; ordinary roads by blue signs; tourist sights by yellow signs.

Italian **motorway tolls** can be paid with money or with the **Viacard**, a magnetic card sold at the entrances and exits of the motorways, in Autogrill restaurants and in the offices of ACI (Automobile Club Italiano), Via Marsala 8, 00185 Rome, ☎06 99 81.

The following **speed restrictions** apply:
- 50kph in built-up areas;
- 90-110kph on open country roads;
- 90 (600cc)-130kph (excess of 1 000cc) on motorways depending on engine capacity.
- Low beams must be on at all times when driving on a Motorway.

PARKING

Consider purchasing a €26 parking card at the newsstands for longer visits. Otherwise, meters charge €1.03 per hour, except on weekends and evenings Avoid streets marked "*Sosta Vietata*" – no matter how many cars cluster there. Illegally parked vehicles may be toward (☎06 676 91). Hotel lots are the best option, but large garages include the Villa Borghese (Piazza Brasile), Parcheggio Ludovisi (60 Via Ludovisi); Parking Termini (near the train station) and Terminal Gianicolo (Via Gregorio VII). Other ACI car parks are scattered at random around town. The largest car parks are marked on the map on the inside back cover of the guide.

PETROL/GASOLINE

Fuel is sold as super, *senza piombo* (unleaded 95 octane), super plus or *Euro plus* (unleaded 98 octane) or *gasolio* (diesel).

Petrol (gas) stations are usually open between 7am-7pm. Many close at lunchtime (12.30pm-3pm), Sundays and public holidays and some refuse payment by credit card. As well as the service stations on the ring road (Raccordo Anulare), petrol can be bought 24hr a day from automatic petrol pumps or petrol stations throughout the city, including those at Corso Francia on the corner of Via di V. Stelluti, Via Salaria on the corner of Viale Somalia, Lungotevere Ripa, Piazzale della Radio, Via Prenestina 187 and Via Tuscolana 1530.

MAPS AND PLANS

A list of Michelin maps that would be useful for getting to Rome and finding your way around the city is given at the back of the guide (see Maps and Plans).

RESCUE SERVICE

The American Automotive Association and Royal Automobile Club both have reciprocal agreements with the Automobile Club d'Italia for breakdown assistance and general information (☎803 116).

RENTAL CARS

All the main car hire agencies have offices at Fiumicino Airport and Ciampino Airport and at Termini Railway Station. Weekly rentals cost between €300 and €400 for a medium-sized car. Agencies require a credit card, passport, license and a driver over 21 or 23. Outlets include:

AutoEuropa: ☎06 65 017450; www.autoeuropa.it
Avis: ☎199 100 133; www.avis.co.uk
Hertz: ☎199 112 211 – if calling from a mobile, dial ☎0248 233 662; www.hertz.co.uk
Italy by Car: ☎06 65 29 133; www.italybycar.com
Europcar: ☎800 014 410; www.europcar.co.uk
Maggiore: ☎848 867 067; www.maggiore.it
SIXT: ☎06 65 953547; www.maggiore.it
Targa Rent: ☎06 652 9336; www.targarent.it

WHAT TO SEE AND DO

Calendar of Events

Obtain calendar details from the Vatican Information Office (*Ufficio Informazioni Pellegrini e Turisti*) and from local tourist offices (APT).

JANUARY

6 JANUARY
Festival of the Befana: the last of the Twelve Days of Christmas; market stalls in Piazza Navona overflow with presents and sweets (*cenone* or candy coal). Befana, the good witch, brings presents to children.

21 JANUARY
In the Church of Sant'Agnese Fuori le Mura, the **saint's feast day** is celebrated with the benediction of two lambs. They're given to the Benedictines of Santa Ceciliam, who spin the wool into *paliums,* which each new archbishop receives from the Pope.

FEBRUARY

17 FEBRUARY
The Inquisition burned Giordano Bruno alive for heresy in 1600. Honor this freethinker at his poignant statue in Rome's Campo dei Fiori, where maskers caper through the famous piazza.

MARCH

EARLY MARCH
EuroChocolate Festival: Nine days of lectures, tastings, films and gorging on chocolate.
www.eurochocolate.roma.it

8 MARCH
Women's Festival (*Festa della Donne*) The day honors women, who are given yellow puffball blossoms (mimosa).

9 MARCH
The **blessing of automobiles** near the Church of Santa Francesca Romana, patron saint of drivers.

19 MARCH
In the Trionfale district on the **Feast of St Joseph** stalls sell typical *bignè*, a sort of doughnut, and *frittelle,* a sort of choux pastry.

OPEN MONUMENTS WEEKEND
Explore Italy's private gardens, monasteries, villas and castles for free. Rome opens St. Anthony's Abbey. The date falls on the weekend closest to the 21st, the first day of Spring.

ROMAN MARATHON
Thousands of runners dash past the ruins on the third Saturday of the month (www.maratoneta.it).

APRIL

The steps of Trinità dei Monti are decked with blooming azaleas, a dazzling sight.

GOOD FRIDAY
Stations of the Cross by night between the Colosseum and the Palatine Hill.

EASTER
At noon in St Peter's Square the Pope gives his *Urbi et Orbi* blessing.

21 APRIL
Solemn ceremony on the Capitoline Hill commemorates the anniversary of the 753 BC birth of the Eternal City.

25 APRIL
Liberation Day marks the end of German occupation in 1945.

MAY

Antique Fair in Via dei Coronari.
Roses in bloom in the municipal rose gardens of the Roseto di Roma (Via di Valle Murcia).

1 MAY
Parades and fiery speeches honor the nation's laborers. Businesses are closed on this popular holiday.

FIRST TWO WEEKS IN MAY
International Tennis Championship

JUNE

Industrial and Commercial Fair,
Via Cristoforo Colombo.

23-24 JUNE
On the **Feast of St John**, in the district bearing his name, there is great rejoicing: popular games and spectacles; snails in broth and roast pork.

29 JUNE
Service in St Peter's Basilica on the Feast of St Peter and St Paul, the most solemn of the religious festivals in Rome.

JUNE-JULY

Tevere-Expo: exhibition of Italian and international crafts on the Tiber banks.

15-30 JULY
Fiesta de Noantri: A week of singing, dancing and feasting in Trastevere to celebrate the eccentric neighborhood and – to a lesser degree – the Virgin of Carmine. *Noiantri* roughly means "our very own", a fitting motto for this area, famous for outsiders and foreigners.

JULY-AUGUST

Estate Romana (Roman Summer):
Concerts and spectacles held (especially in Caracalla's Baths).

5 AUGUST
Commemoration in the basilica of Santa Maria Maggiore of the miraculous fall of snow which led to the construction of the church: a shower of white flower petals is released in the Pauline Chapel.

15 AUGUST
Assumption Day (*Ferragosto*)
Celebrates the Virgin Mary's ascent to heaven. The entire nation goes on holiday – often for weeks.

SEPTEMBER

Throughout the month, Romans visit the peaceful Alban Hills, especially Ariccia, to savor *porchetta*, sandwiches of crispy roast pig, and wine (☎06 963 0896).

LATE SEPTEMBER
European Heritage Day: Private gardens and palaces open their doors – such as Doganella di Ninfa near Rome – on the fourth Sunday.

OCTOBER

ART FAIR
Wander Margutta Street and the nearby Via Orso, lined with paintings, handicrafts and exhibitions.

NOVEMBER

1 NOVEMBER
On All Saint's Day (*Tutti i Santi*), Catholics visit graveyards, as business grinds to a halt. Costumed children race in the squares, flinging confetti and shaving cream. Snack of the "bones of the dead" (*osso di morto*) from a pastry shop.

DECEMBER

The famous Piazza Navona hosts a month-long fair selling sweets, ornaments and toys. A handmade creche (*presepio*) or Epiphany witch (Befana) make the best souvenirs. Wander the brightly lit streets – Frattina, Condotti, Sistina and Del Babuino in particular – or the twisting alleys of Trastevere.

8 DECEMBER
Celebration of the doctrine of the Immaculate Conception in Piazza di Spagna in the presence of the Pope.

CHRISTMAS
In Via Giulia every year there is an exhibition of over 50 nativity scenes, with beautiful cribs in the following churches: Santi Cosma e Damiano, Santa Maria in Via, Sant'Alessio, Basilica dei Santi Apostoli, San Marcello, the Gesù Church, Santa Maria d'Aracoeli, Santa Maria del Popolo and Santa Maria Maggiore (13C crib).

Midnight mass is celebrated with particular solemnity in Santa Maria Maggiore and in Santa Maria d'Aracoeli. In St Peter's Square the Pope's blessing, *Urbi et Orbi*, is bestowed.

Activities for Children

Kids Unless they have studied some Roman history, young children are unlikely to enjoy trailing around ruins, museums and churches. However, Rome does have a number of sights that interest youngsters, especially in its large parks. The most popular of these is **Villa Borghese**, with its carousels, pony rides, and a zoo, now known as the **Bioparco**, with over 1 000 animals. A walk around the **Janiculum** delights with puppet shows every afternoon, miniature-horse rides, and the noon cannon blast. Other attractive public gardens include the vast **Villa Doria Pamphili**, whose small lake is now home to the gentle coypu, a type of aquatic rodent similar to a small beaver; the **Villa Sciarra** in old Monteverde; and **Villa Celimontana**, not far from the Colosseum. The **Orto Botanico**, behind Palazzo Corsini, is one of Italy's most important botanical gardens and contains a many rare plants.

The **Museo delle Paste Alimentari** (the National Pasta Museum), near the Trevi Fountain, is both informative and entertaining. The EUR district is also worth exploring as a family: visit the *Museo delle Arti e Tradizioni Popolari* (Folk Museum), enjoy the rides at the funfair (Luna Park), or walk around the small lake, stopping for an ice cream at the popular Giolitti gelateria.

Sightseeing

GENERAL INFORMATION

For information, free publications and maps, contact the APT or stop at one of the city information kiosks (*see Know Before You Go*).

PRICES AND HOURS

See Basic Information.
Information on admission times and charges for museums and monuments is given in the *Discovering Rome section of the guide*. Because of fluctuations in the cost of living and the constant change in opening times, the details should merely serve as a guideline. Phone ahead to confirm.

The prices indicated are for single adults benefiting from no special concession; reductions for children, students, the over-60s and parties should be requested on site and be backed by ID. Special conditions often exist for groups, but arrangements should be made in advance. For EU nationals, state-run or city-run museums provide free admission to

San Paolo Fuori Le Mura (St Paul Without the Walls), Interior

Courtesy of APT of Rome

visitors under 18 and over 65 with proof of identification, and a 50% reduction for visitors under 25. When visits to museums, churches or other sites are accompanied by a custodian, it is customary to leave a donation.

CHURCHES

The major basilicas (St Peter's, St John Lateran, St Paul Without the Walls, St Mary Major) are open from 7am-6pm, but most churches close at noon and reopen in the afternoon from 4-8pm; exceptions are marked in the *Selected Sights* section.

Visitors should be appropriately dressed: long trousers for men; no bare shoulders or very short skirts for women.

Churches are closed during services; tourists already inside should avoid disrupting the worshippers. As many of the works of art are positioned high up, it is a good idea to take binoculars. Small change is needed for the lights.

GUIDED TOURS

Travel agents and the ATAC offices in Piazza del Cinquecento provide details of organised guided tours in foreign languages. For independent group visits, contact the Sindacato Nazionale CISL, Centro Guide Turistiche, Via S. Maria alle Fornaci, 8 ☏ 06 63 90 409

BASIC INFORMATION

Business Hours

MUSEUMS, ARCHAEOLOGICAL SITES AND GARDENS

Museums are closed Mondays; on other days ticket offices usually shut 30min or 1hr before closing time. Ancient monuments, archaeological sites and public parks (Roman Forum, Colosseum, etc.) close about one hour before dusk, according to the following timetable:

9am-3pm,	1 **Nov**-mid **Jan**
9am-3.30pm,	mid **Jan**-mid **Feb**
9am-4pm,	mid **Feb**-mid **Mar**
9am-4.30pm,	mid **Mar**-last day of winter time
9am-5.30pm,	first day of summer-mid **Apr**
9am-6pm,	mid **Apr**-1 **Sep**
9am-5.30pm,	2 **Sep**- last day of summer time
9am-4.30pm,	first day of winter time-30 **Sep**
9am-4pm,	1–31 **Oct**

Many museums require visitors to leave bags and backpacks in a luggage deposit area. Flash photography is usually forbidden.

Discounts

The **Where to Stay** section details budget options, including B&Bs, *pensioni*, youth hostels, camp sites, and convents and monasteries.

TRAIN

The **Carta Club Eurostar** (€80, valid one year) gives a 10% discount on first-class travel throughout Italy. The **Carta Amicotreno** (€50, for travellers under 26) gives a 10% discount on some local trains and 20% off many medium- and long-distance routes.

AIRLINES

Several airlines offer budget fares to Rome and other destinations in Italy, although prices vary according to how far in advance the reservation is made.

- **Ryan Air**:
  www.ryanair.com
- **EasyJet**:
  www.easyjet.com
- **BMI**:
  www.flybmi.com
- **Evolavia**:
  www.evolavia.com

- **Hapag-Lloyd Express**:
  www.hlx.com
- **German Wings**:
  www.germanwings.com
- **Sky Europe:**
  www.skyeurope.com
- **Virgin Express**:
  www.virgin-express.com
- **Wizz**
  http://wizzair.com

Alitalia has various special offers for passengers buying their ticket one, two or three weeks before departure. The airline also offers special weekend rates for travellers departing on a Saturday and returning on a Sunday of the same weekend *(tipo corto)* and for the same type of ticket, but valid for a month *(tipo lungo)*.

FOR YOUNG PEOPLE

TRAIN
The **Carta Verde** (€40, valid for a year) gives young people a 10% discount in both first and second class, on all trains within Italy, and a 25% including fast Eurocity trains and Eurostar.

AIRLINES
Discounted rates are available for young people aged between 12 and 26 (under 26 on the day of departure).

FOR SENIOR CITIZENS

TRAIN
For travellers over 60 years of age, the **Carta d'Argento** (€30, valid for a year) offers a 15% discount in first and second class on the Italian section of all routes, including fast Euro-trains.

AIRLINES
Senior citizens are also eligible for discounts on some airlines.

FOR FAMILIES AND SMALL GROUPS

TRAIN
Families and groups of at least three people and no more than five are entitled to a 20% discount in both first and second class if they are travelling together. Children aged between four and 12 travel at half-price of the discounted fare and children under four travel free.

AIRLINES
Families qualify for discounted tickets on certain airlines, if they fulfil the following conditions: at least four people together, with a maximum of two adults and a minimum of two children (between the ages of two and 11). At least one of the adults must be a parent of the children.

Electricity

The voltage is 220V, 50 cycles per second, with a two-pin plug. Pack an adaptor for hairdryers, shavers, computers, etc. North American visitors may need a transformer for appliances beyond a laptop. Seek out an electrical (*elettricità*) or hardware (*ferramenta*) store.

Public Holidays

In addition to the usual Italian public and religious holidays listed below, Rome celebrates 21 April (the birth of Rome) and 29 June, the feast day of St Peter and St Paul, the patron saints of the city.

A working day is *un giorno feriale; giorni festivi* include Saturdays, Sundays and the following public holidays:

January	1 (*New Year*) and 6(*Epiphany*)
Easter	Sunday and Monday (*lunedì dell'Angelo*)
April	25 (*St Mark's Day* and *liberation in 1945*)
May	1 (*Festa dei Lavoratori*)
June	29 (*The Feast of St Peter and St Paul, patron saints of Rome*)
August	15 (*The Assumption – Ferragosto*)
November	1 (*All Saints – Tutti i Santi*)
December	8 (*Immaculate Conception*), 25 and 26 (*Christmas* and *St Stephen's Day*).

Mail/Post

In Italy post offices are open from 8.30am-1.50pm (Sat 11.50am). Some central branches open weekday afternoons until 6pm and Sat until 2pm. The main post office is at Piazza San Silvestro, and is open day and night; letters sent **poste restante** *(fermo posta)* arrive here.

Money

The unit of currency is the **euro** which is issued in notes (€5, €10, €20, €50, €100, €200 and €500) and in coins (1 cent, 2 cents, 5 cents, 10 cents, 20 cents, 50 cents, €1 and €2).

BANKS

Banks are usually open Monday to Friday, 8.30am–1.30pm and 2.30pm–4pm. Some branches open in the city centre and shopping centres on Saturday mornings, almost most are closed on Saturdays, Sundays and public holidays. Most hotels will change travellers' cheques. Money can be changed in post offices (except travellers' cheques), money-changing bureaux and at railway stations and airports. Commission is always charged.

CREDIT CARDS

Payment by credit card is widespread in shops, hotels and restaurants and in petrol stations. Money may also be withdrawn from a bank, but may incur interest pending repayment.

Newspapers

The main Roman newspapers (available throughout Italy) are *La Repubblica*, *Il Messaggero* and *Il Corriere della Sera*. The *Osservatore Romano* is the official newspaper of the Vatican City. Foreign newspapers are widely available throughout the city.

Pharmacies

These are identified by a red-and-white or emerald-neon cross. When closed, each advertises the names of the pharmacy on duty and a list of doctors on call. Some of the most central 24hr pharmacies include those at: Piazza dei Cinquecento 49/50/51 (Termini Station), Via Cola di Rienzo 213/215, Corso Vittorio Emanuele 343/343A, Corso Rinascimento 44/50, Piazza Barberini 49, Via Arenula 73,

EMERGENCY NUMBERS		
General Emergency Services	☎113	
Central Police Headquarters	☎06 46 86	Via S. Vitale 15
Foreign Residents' Bureau	☎06 86 21 02	Via S. Vitale
ACI Emergency Breakdown Service	☎803 116	
Police (emergencies)	☎06 67 691	
Fire Brigade	☎115	
Carabinieri (emergencies)	☎112	
Lost Property	☎06 58 16 040	Via N. Bettoni 1
Emergency Health Services	☎118	
Ambulance – Red Cross	☎06 55 10	
Permanent Medical Service	☎06 58 20 10 30	
San Camillo Hospital	☎06 58 701	Circonvallazione Gianicolense 87
Policlinico A Gemelli (hospital)	☎06 30 151	Largo Gemelli 8
Umberto I Hospital	☎06 49 971	Viale del Policlinico 155

Piazza della Repubblica 67 and Via Nazionale 228.

Taxes and Tipping

Italy lards on a variable tax – averaging 19% – to most goods and services. The *Imposta sul Valore Aggiunto* (IVA) mostly lurks unseen, part and parcel of the bill. Visitors from non-EU countries can claim back the IVA on merchandise over €155. Italians tip about five percent in a pizzeria or humble trattoria, or just round up to the nearest euro. The rate should rise in posher places, but never top ten percent.

€0.25 tips are appropriate for bar service. Taxi drivers expect around €0.50. as do cloakroom attendants, porters €0.50–1.00 per bag.

Telephones

The telephone service is organised by TELECOM ITALIA (formerly SIP). Each office has public booths where the customer pays for units used *(scatti)*. Reduced rates operate after 6.30pm and even less between 10pm-8am.

AREA CODES

It is now mandatory to dial the area code (06 for Rome), even when making a local call. For international calls dial 00 plus the following country codes:
- ☎ **61** for Australia
- ☎ **1** for Canada
- ☎ **64** for New Zealand
- ☎ **44** for the UK
- ☎ **1** for the USA

If calling from outside the country, the international code for Italy is 39 and the code for Rome is 06. Dial the full area code always.

PHONE CARDS

Telephone cards *(schede telefoniche)* are sold in denominations of €1, €5 and €10 and are supplied by CIT offices and post offices as well as tobacconists (sign bearing a white T on a black background).

PUBLIC PHONES

Telephone cards (sold in post offices and tobacconists) and telephone credit cards are accepted in call boxes. To make a call: lift the receiver, insert payment, await dial signal, punch in the number and wait for a response.

USEFUL NUMBERS

Directory Enquiries: ☎1240;
International Enquiries: ☎892412;
Urgent Calls: ☎4197;
TIM Customer Service: ☎119;
Vodaphone Customer Care: ☎190;
Traffic Information: ☎840042121.

Leonardo da Vinci-Fiumicino Airport
☎06 65 951; Ciampino Airport, ☎06 79 49 41.
Domestic Flight Reservations:
☎06 65 641;
International Flight Reservations:
☎06 65 642;
Flight Information: ☎06 65 95 36 40/ 40 01;
Passenger Information:
☎06 65 95 36 40, or 06 65 95 44 55.

Time

The time in Italy is usually the same as the rest of mainland Europe (one hour ahead of the United Kingdom) and changes during the last weekend in March and October between summer time *(ora legale)* and winter time *(ora solare)*.

Tobacconists

Tabacchi sell postcards, stamps, confectionery, phone cards, public transport tickets and lottery tickets in addition to cigarettes and tobacco. Those at Via del Corso 11 and Viale Trastevere 275 stay open all night.

St. Peter's Basilica, Vatican
©Charis Tsevis/SXC

CITY OF SEVEN HILLS

The Emperor Augustus 'found a city of clay and left it marble'. His legacy was over a millenia of beautification that leaves Rome today with centuries of elegant architecture piled high — ancient frescos flaking in basements, and amphitheatres topped with minimalist penthouses. Bathed in the gold of sunset, the mélange numbers among the world's most striking cities. The Italian capital is home to many of Europe's greatest wonders, such as the Pantheon and Forum, the Colosseum, St. Peter's, Piazza Navona, Spanish Steps, Trevi Fountain and the Villa Borghese. Like any beauty, she can be mercurial; cars and people jostle through narrow alleyways — the froth of sound and style often leaves visitors exhausted. Schedule long siestas to counterbalance the Eternal City's intensity.

Location

Rome lies about halfway down the shin of "the boot", some 24km/15mi inland from the Tyrrhenian Sea. The Tiber River, known to the ancients as the *flavus Tiber* (the fair or yellow Tiber), bisects the city. Its waters supposedly bore the legendary Romulus and Remus (🕮 *see History*) to the foot of the Palatine.

The Seven Hills

Historians emphasise the strategic location of Rome's seven hills, especially the **Palatine**, which was a staging post on the salt road (*Via Salaria*) and was first settled in the 8C BC. Its twin peaks gave a clear view of the Tiber River. Today the Palatine and the **Capitoline** hills rise west of the Colosseum, the **Caelian** to the south, the **Aventine** to the southwest. The **Esquiline** rises east of the Colosseum, the **Quirnal** and **Viminal** hills sit farther to the northeast.

The **Janiculum**, south of the Vatican across the river, didn't make the original cut, though it remains a key landmark, as does **Monte Testaccio**. Made from discarded ancient *amphorae* (terracotta shipping jars), the man-made hill rears 54m / 177 feet near the Pyramide Metro and Ostia Railway Station.

The Streetscape

No other city has managed to combine so successfully such a diverse heritage of Classical antiquities, medieval buildings, Renaissance palaces and Baroque churches. Far from being discordant, they constitute a logical continuity where revivals, influences and contrasts display the ingenuity of Roman architects and builders. Today, Rome still impresses as a lively urban core.

The main thoroughfares bustle with traffic, both vehicular and pedestrian. Yet, quiet alleyways wind between ochre-coloured facades to small market squares, or to stairs descending to charming fountains. Rome rewards a wanderer endlessly.

Climb high for **views** of the city's splendour. From the belvedere on the Janiculum Hill unfolds a rooftop panorama. Above the sea of terracotta tiles rise countless domes, such as the elegant Sant'Ivo alla Sapienza, the Pantheon, and the majestic orb of St Peter's, designed by Michelangelo. The **Pincio**, above the Piazza di Popolo, is another favourite sunset perch.

Rome is the **city of churches**: some 300 in all, a fitting number for the home of the Roman Catholicism. Since the 7C, pilgrims have visited the tombs of St Peter and St Paul and the catacombs, and, more recently, the Vatican State.

Rome is also famed for its **obelisks and water features**. Liquid dances throughout the city, from street nozzles to the Baroque splendour of the Trevi Fountain, the delicate Renaissance tracery of the Turtle Fountain, and a number of elaborate sculptures by Bernini. As for obelisks – Egyptian, Imperial and Papal – they seem to grow like trees: curiously perched on an elephant's back, contrasting starkly with the façade of the Pantheon, boldly mounted on the Fountain of the Four

Rivers, or even acting as the pointer for a gigantic sundial in Piazza Montecitorio.

A Visible Past

Rome's many famous monuments continue to delight tourists: the Pantheon and Forum, the majestic Colosseum, St Peter's, the Spanish Steps, the Trevi Fountain and the Villa Borghese, to name a few. The **ancient ruins** form the backbone of this stunning landscape; scattered around the city, these are often hemmed in by modern buildings. Their survival is amazing; armies repeatedly sacked Rome during the Middle Ages and in the past, the citizens themselves have torn down structures and even pastured cows in the Forum.

Others colonized the old temples and amphitheatres, building onto their tiers. Churches and monuments often have multiple layers, each dating to a different historical period. The best example is the basilica of San Clemente sul Celio, built in the 4C on Republican-era foundations, then reconstructed in the 12C, and modified in the 18C.

Another important characteristic of Rome is its old villas, where noble families once lived far from the madding crowds. Now public parks, the gardens of the Villa Borghese, Villa Doria and Villa Ada provide an attractive and essential splash of greenery.

Although Rome still operates under the emblem of the wolf and the old Republican formula SPQR (*Senatus Populusque Romanus*), not much remains of the marble glory of Augustus and the emperors. The Renaissance and Baroque have both left their marks, mainly as a consequence of the architectural ambition of many of the popes. And the modern citizens overlay it all with Vespas, fashion billboards, football flags and minimalist chic constructions.

Still, the Eternal City remains poetic and potent – dangerously so. As the poet Henry Wadsworth Longfellow warned: "Tis the centre to which all gravitates. One finds no rest elsewhere than here. There may be other cities that please us for a while, but Rome alone completely satisfies. It becomes to all a second native land by predilection, and not by accident of birth alone."

THE CITY TODAY

Rome has seen widespread and, especially after the Second World War, uncontrolled urban expansion. The modernisation of this busy capital city has meant increased traffic, which, in turn, has damaged Rome's ancient monuments.

The Eternal City

Rome had to double in size to fulfil its modern role as capital of a united Italy (since 1870). Architects used concrete, metal and glass to house its population, construct administrative buildings, and improve its traffic flow.

Italy's capital is not a quick study. The metropolis struts and shouts like Napoleon, languidly simmers like Sophia Loren and, then – just as the kaleidoscope shifts towards a coherent pattern – slips into business mode, shrewd-tongued and silk-suited. Rome is ephemeral, enigmatic. Small wonder early residents revered Janus, the two-faced ancient God of new beginnings, who looks forward, while peering back. The Eternal City, solid on the bedrock of history, reinvents itself daily.

Eleanor Clark best captured the chaos, contradictions and coquetry of this city in her 1950s classic, *Rome and a Villa*. "The ordinary traveller," she observed, "runs off in relief to Florence, to the single statement, the single moment of time, the charming unity of somewhat prison-like architecture, and is aware later of having retained from his tour of Rome some stirring around the heart, those images, huge, often grotesque, were what he had been looking for, only it would have take so long..."

HISTORY

According to legend, Aeneas, the heroic founder of Rome, was the son of Venus. Such divine origins helped to give credence to the city's grandiose destiny and its position as the "capital of the world." The decadence of the Empire led to the rise and fall of Rome, and despite becoming the cornerstone of the Christian world, the city was repeatedly sacked by barbarian tribes during the early Middle Ages. Restored to its former splendour during the era of the Papal States, Rome was finally declared the capital of a united Italy in 1870.

Origin and Growth

Before the Empire, before even the Etruscans, the peninsula was home to elephants, hippopotamuses, rhinoceroses – and the first Italians. *Homo Erectus* roamed this landscape from around 200,000 BC.

By 10,000 BC, more advanced humans displaced Neanderthals; most likely Cro-Magnons, who had fire, but no herds or agriculture. They dabbed crude art onto their cavern-homes, including the Grotto Polesini near Tivoli.

In Neolithic times, farmers and herders built clusters of huts, wove fabrics and cast pots. They were recognizably Mediterranean: short and narrow-headed. After 2,000 BC, this stock mixed with round-headed alpine people from central Europe.

Regional cultures emerged between 1,000-800 BC. The southern Villanovans occupied the site of Rome. They hammered bronze armour, fought with iron weapons and lived in round homes. Other tribes – mostly speaking Indo-European dialects – dwelt nearby, including the Oscans, Sabines, Latins and Umbrians.

The Tiber's left bank – eroded lava-flows from the Alban Hills (**Monti Albani**) – provided excellent defensive positions: particularly the Palatine. It rose steeply from the surrounding marsh with a clear view of the Tiber. This site was, moreover, an ideal staging post on the salt road (**Via Salaria**).

ROME'S LEGENDARY ORIGINS

According to Livy in his *Roman History* and the Greek historian Dionysius of Halicarnassus in his *Early Roman History*,

Aeneas, son of the goddess Venus and the mortal Anchises, fled from Troy as it fell. He landed at the Tiber's mouth and married Lavinia, the king of Latium's daughter. After his death, his son Ascanius (or Iulus) left to found Alba Longa (see Index). The last king of this Alban dynasty was Amulius, who deposed his brother Numitor and forced the latter's daughter, Rhea Silvia, to become a Vestal Virgin. Raped by the god Mars, she birthed the twins **Romulus** and **Remus,** whom Amulius set adrift on the Tiber. The basket carrying the infants washed up at the foot of the Palatine where they were nursed by a wolf and brought up by shepherds.

As ambitious adults, they decided to found a city. A dispute about sites and bird omens led to fratricide. Romulus alone founded the city on April 21, 753 BC, and populated it with outlaws who settled on the Capitoline (👉 *see CAMPI-DOGLIO – CAPITOLINO)*. Females were in short supply. So the first king threw a party, invited the local tribes and stole their daughters; this "Rape of the Sabine Women" later became an overly popular theme in classical art.

A succession of kings, alternately Sabine and Latin, until the Etruscans arrived.

THE ETRUSCANS

A band of 12 city states flourished from the eighth- to third-centuries BC. Brilliant urban planners, they transformed villages into city grids with temples, roads and drained fields. Their rock-cut theatres, tunnels and tombs honeycomb central Italy.

The Etruscans' origin is much-disputed; some even suggest this high civilization was Atlantis. Skillful jewellers, they cast metal sculptures (including the **Capitoline Wolf, Rome's symbol**), as well as painting frescoes and black clay pots.

The last three rulers were Etruscan and steadied the upstart city, at least initially. **Lucius Tarquinius Priscus** introduced drainpipes and games. **Servius Tullius** reorganized the army, bolstered the middle classes and encouraged a basic political assembly. This peace exploded in 510, when Romans expelled the tyrant **Tarquin Superbus**. The trigger was unclear: power struggles or grain shortage, perhaps. Legend points the finger at his son's rape of a pious wife, who then committed suicide (The Rape of Lucretia).

Try as they might, the Etruscans couldn't retake Rome. Unable to reach their southern settlements, the city-states dwindled. A 474 defeat at Cumae crushed their naval supremacy. Bullied by Celtic tribes to the north, the Etruscans were conquered by the Romans; Volsinii fell last in 265 BC.

Greek and Latin accounts claim moral superiority over the "debauched" people. Yet politics probably undermined the Etruscan League: internecine strife, cruelty towards peasants, elite snobbery, and perhaps just a little ruling-class corruption towards the end.

Many mourn the passing of this quicksilver artistic empire, which once nearly united the Italian peninsula. DH Lawrence, author of the classic 1932 travelogue *Etruscan Places*, rhapsodized about "the long-nosed, sensitive-footed, subtly smiling Etruscans, who made so little noise outside the cypress groves. "Italy to-day is far more Etruscan in its pulse than Roman: and will always be so. The Etruscan element is like the grass of the field and the sprouting of the corn, in Italy: it will always be so. Why try to revert to the Latin-Roman mechanism and suppression?"

THE MONARCHY (753-509 BC)

753 – Legendary foundation of Rome by **Romulus** on the Palatine Hill.

715-616 Reigns of three Sabine kings Numa Pompilius, Tullus Hostilius, Ancus Martius.

616-509 Etruscan hegemony: Tarquin the Elder, who laid out the Forum, Servius Tullius and Tarquin the Proud.

THE REPUBLIC (510-27 BC)

Tradition dates the Republic to 510 BC. Citizens expelled the ruling Tarquins, and granted executive and military power to two consuls, elected annually. The **Senate**, formed by the old patrician families, had a purely advisory role. **Praetors** bore judicial power, while **aediles** and **quaestors carried out** administrative and financial tasks; all these officials served for one year.

The city divided into two ordines: the **patricians** (aristocrats "able to trace their ancestors") and the **plebeians**, who were forbidden to assume political or priestly office, or to marry "up".

Inevitably, these groups clashed. The patricians saw their privileges gradually reduced over the years and a new mixed ruling class, known as the *nobilitas*, formed at the end of the 4C. The last prohibitions to fall were those relating to censorship and religious offices.

The patricians controlled many slaves, who formed the most wretched section of society, but who could be freed and become *liberti*. A boss-supplicant system – known as *clientela* – emerged during this period. A patron gave his clients financial or political assistance, and they

Museo Nazionale Romano

The Lupercalia (Altar to Mars and Venus), Palazzo Massimo alle Terme

returned this support during elections and tribunals.

This period saw Roman expansion within the Italian peninsula and across the Mediterranean. As the army grew in importance, so did the power of the men behind it. Its generals struggled for dominance throughout the late Republican period.

Proconsuls administered – and often plundered – the conquered provinces. During the Empire, the consuls' powers were united in one person, an emperor. Many later claimed divinity to re-enforce their right to rule.

494 Rome leaves the Latin League. First plebeians secession. They obtain a magistrature to defend their rights (tribunate of the plebeians).

451-449 The city codifies civil and penal laws in the **Twelve Tables**, described by Cicero as "the very height and pinnacle of the law".

396 Romans capture Etruscan Veia, which controlled the River Tiber, after a 10-year siege.

390 Invasions by the Gauls and Roman defeat on the River Allia. Sacking and burning of Rome (see CAMPIDOGLIO-CAPITOLINO).

367 Plebeians granted access to consulship, reform of magistrature of censorship, and proposal for the distribution of territorial areas to citizens (ager publicus).

343-341 Rome forms alliances with Greek cities of the Campania region. This leads to the **First Samnite War**.

326-304 **Second Samnite War**. Rome suffers the famous defeat of the **Claudine Forks**. Tactical reform of the legions (into groups of 60 men) guarantees Rome a partial victory.

312 Appius Claudius Caecus, writer and orator, becomes censor. Construction of the first section of the Appian Way.

298-290 **Third Samnite War**; Rome defeats the combined armies of the Samnites, Etruscans, Gauls and Umbrians at the battle of Sentinum, in the present-day Marche region. The victory brings central Italy under Roman control.

282-272 The capture of Tarentum – the last powerful Greek *polis* on

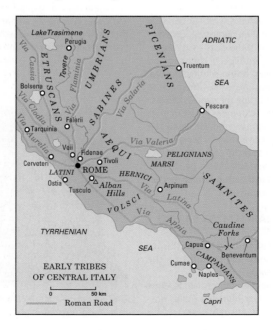

EARLY TRIBES OF CENTRAL ITALY

0   50 km

Roman Road

the peninsula – brings the Romans into contact with the Hellenic culture.

264-241 **First Punic War** between Rome and **Carthage**. After fierce fighting on land and at sea, Rome captures Sicily, with its prosperous cities, and the island becomes the first province governed by a propraetor. A few years later, Rome conquers Sardinia.

218-201 **Second Punic War** and march by Hannibal from Spain to Italy (elephants over the Alps!). **Hannibal** defeats the Romans in Ticinus, Trebia, Lake Trasimene, and Cannae, not far from Venosa. The Roman counter-offensive chases the Carthaginians out of Spain and prevents supplies from reaching Hannibal's army. **Scipio Africanus** (a young general from the noble Cornelii Scipiones family) settles in Sicily; from here he extends the fighting to Africa. Hannibal, summoned home, is defeated by the army of Scipio Africanus at Naraggara-Zama. The peace treaty gives the Romans control over the western section of the Mediterranean basin. The destructive war has far-reaching consequences in Italy, such as an influx of slaves, the destruction of small peasant farms, and an increase in the urban population, as food funnelled into Rome.

201 The first comedies of Plautus.

197-168 War in the east against the Hellenistic states of Macedonia, the Seleucids in Asia Minor and the Syrian-Mesopotamian region.

179 Construction of a wooden theatre. (Pompey finds a loophole and builds the first stone version – hitherto banned –in 55).

148-146 **Third Punic War**: capture and destruction of Carthage.

133-121 The brothers **Tiberius** and **Caius Gracchus**, both plebeian tribunes, inspire social and economic reforms. Angered, the Senate orders their assassinations.

111-105 War against Jugurtha of Numidia. The continuous strife and probable corruption of senators weakened the Roman republic. Two famous generals are victorious: **Caius Marius**, consul for the first time in 107, and Lucius **Sulla**.

91-88 War between Rome and its Italian allies, who demanded Roman citizenship. After much violent fighting, the toughest rebels are defeated, although citizenship is awarded to all Italian peoples.

88 **First Civil War** between the Senate (nobility) and people (*populares*). Lucius Sulla, supporter of the Senate and the *nobilitas*, is deprived of supreme command of the war against Mithridates in favour of **Marius**, a supporter of the *populares*. After marching on Rome to silence the *populares*, Sulla earns the war command.

87 Sulla departs. Caius Marius and Cornelius Cinna establish the rule of the *populares*.

84 Sulla returns and defeats Cinna (Marius was killed in 86). The following year, Sulla assumes dictatorial powers: exiles have no recourse to law, and their killers can claim their property. Fear, loathing and bloodshed ensue.

82-79 Sulla reforms the Republic. The Senate is strengthened and the powers of the plebeian tribunes reduced. Sulla retires from public life and dies the following year. He was described by one of his biographers as a frustrated monarch: unlike Augustus, he did not actually abolish the Republican political system.

73-70 **Licinius Crassus**, a rich businessman, is elected consul in

Caesar

Museo Nazionale, Napoli/GIRAUDON

quest of Britain and fighting against Germanic tribes. Troubles in Asia Minor, where in 54 Crassus is defeated and killed by the Parthians near Carrhae in Upper Mesopotamia.

49-45 Civil war between Caesar and Pompey.

49 Caesar becomes dictator.

48 Assassination of Pompey, who had taken refuge at the court of the Ptolemy in Egypt.

44 Assassination of Caesar on the **Ides of March** (15 March).

VENI, VIDI, VICI

Gaius Julius Caesar (101-44 BC)
Soldier and statesman, orator and writer (*The Gallic Wars* and *The Civil War*) – was instrumental in the establishment of the Roman Empire. A supporter of the *populares*, he proved his outstanding political abilities while he was still very young. In 58 Caesar became Governor of Cisalpine Gaul and of Provincia (now Provence); by 51 he had conquered the whole of Gaul, at the cost of perhaps a million lives. In January 49, he crossed the Rubicon (the boundary across which armies were not supposed to tread) and marched on Rome and its officials; Pompey, who had been sole consul since 52, and the Senate fled. Civil war followed. Pompey's army was defeated at Pharsalus in Thessaly, Pompey himself was murdered in Alexandria and his supporters fell in Africa and Spain.

70 with **Pompey**, after putting down the slave revolt led by Spartacus (6 000 prisoners crucified). Pompey is away fighting Mithridates and pirates until 62.

63 **Catiline Conspiracy**, secretly supported by Caesar. The conspiracy is put down by the consul, Cicero, the champion of the agreement drawn up between senators and *equites* (which included businessmen and speculators). Catiline is killed in battle near Pistoia.

60 **First Triumvirate**, a private agreement between Crassus, Pompey and Caesar is signed at Lucca. The following year Caesar was elected consul.

58-52 Caesar's campaign against the **Gauls**, followed by his con-

Augustus and His Achievements

Gaius Julius Caesar Octavianus was the first Roman Emperor, and remains among the most important. Shipwrecked in Hispania, the teen crossed hostile territory to rejoin Julius Caesar. Impressed, the ruler adopted his great-nephew. After the Ides of March – that fateful assassination – Octavius, though just 18, pushed for his inheritance. Seven years later, he had eliminated the competition, right down to the lovers Cleopatra and Mark Anthony.

In 27 BC, he offered to return power to the Roman Senate. They named him *princeps* (first leader) and Augustus ("grower"). He grew into a model leader, who inspired reform in politics, religion and the arts. As Historian Paul Zanker says: "Following the long, dark years of civil war, the Romans enjoyed 45 years of peace and security. Monarchy had at last brought orderly government to the vast empire, bread and circuses to the Roman plebs, and a tremendous boost to the economy. The Romans looked out at their empire filled with a powerful sense of mission," he wrote in *The Power of Images in the Age of Augustus*.

Early in 44, Caesar appointed himself consul and dictator for life; he gave his name to the month of his birth (July), pardoned his enemies and weakened the power of the senators by reducing their number to 900. On 15 March 44 BC (the Ides of March), while planning a campaign against the Parthians, he was stabbed to death by a group of senators in the Curia Pompeia.

43 — **Second Triumvirate** established: the young **Octavian** (Caesar's great-nephew and adopted heir, who took the name Gaius Julius Caesar Octavian – later "Augustus"), **Mark Antony** (Caesar's fellow consul) and **Lepidus**. Antony is assigned the east, Octavian the west and Lepidus Africa. Assassination of Cicero, who had attacked Antony in public debates.

31 — **Battle of Actium** (not far from Patras) between the troops of Octavian and those of Mark Antony (aligned politically – and romantically – with Cleopatra, Queen of Egypt). The lovers commit suicide; Octavian annexes Egypt to Rome and proclaims himself successor to the Ptolemy dynasty.

The Roman Empire

JULIO-CLAUDIAN DYNASTY (27 BC-AD 69)

27 — The Senate grants Octavian the title **Augustus** (from the Latin *"augere"* – "to grow").

14 BC — Augustus dies at Nola having witnessed the premature death of many family members. He is succeeded by **Tiberius**, the son of his wife Livia, distinguished for his military achievements in Germany and Pannonia. Proud of his family tradition (he belonged to the noble Claudian family), this introvert retired to Capri towards the end of his life (27 AD). The historian Tacitus was one of his most fierce detractors.

AD 30 — **Jesus of Nazareth**, known as Christ, is condemned to death.

37-41 — **Caligula** as *princeps* (head of State). He suffers from bouts of madness, but is determined to wield absolute power as Emperor, moving away from the compromise with Republican ideals achieved by Augustus. He is assassinated.

41-54 — **Claudius**, Caligula's uncle and a scholar of the Etruscan civilisation, assumes power. Britain annexed to the Empire. Some of Claudius's freed slaves, very loyal to him, are appointed in official posts. The reaction of the Senate is violent. **Seneca** is one of the victims of repression and is exiled to the island of Corsica.

54-68 — **Nero** as Emperor. Declared emperor after Caligula, Claudius wed Agrippina, then adopted her son **Nero**. Rumour claims she assassinated her husband, making her dotty offspring *princeps*. Nero's tutor Seneca succeeded in controlling the young Emperor's behaviour for the first five years, tempering his more absolute tendencies. The repression of a senatorial conspiracy led to the suicide of Seneca and to violent and authoritarian

Nero

Vatican
Naumachia

MAUSOLEUM OF AUGUSTUS

MAUSOLEUM OF HADRIAN
(Castel Sant' Angelo)

Nero's Circus
(Basilica di S. Pietro)

Pons Aelius

Pt͟a Cornelia

Nero's
Bridge

Pt͟a
Triomphalis

P⁺͟a Flaminia
(P⁺͟a del Popolo)

Via
Flaminia

Via

AURELIAN

Pt͟a Pinciana

Salarie

Via

Gardens
of Lucullus

PINCIAN

MARTIUS

30

VII

Ara Pacis

Antonine
Crematorium

IX

7

Hadrian's
Temple

Pt͟a Quirinalis

Pt͟a
Salutaris

Via

Temple
of Serapis

Alta

CAMPUS

Baths
of Nero

STADIUM
OF DOMITIAN
(P⁺͟a Navona)

PANTHEON

Saepta
Iulia

Pt͟a
Sanqualis

28

Corso

JANICULUM

TEVERE

6

Odeon
of Domitian

Baths
of Agrippa

24

13

8

Pompey's
Curia
and Theatre

3

Pons Agrippa

14

Portico
of Octavia

25

16

IMPERIAL
FORA

Pt͟a Septimiana

Pons
Aurelius

Circus
Flaminius

18

ROMAN
FORUM

5

CAPITOLINE

THEATRE OF MARCELLUS

12

VIII

2

Tiber Island

Pons Cestius

21

Forum
Olitorium

11

X

23

Aurelia

Pons Aemilius

22

2

19

10

PALATINE

Pt͟a Aurelia

Via

XIV

Pons Sublicius

Forum
Boarium

17

9

A. Traiana

AURELIAN

Msicina

Pt͟a Trigemina

XI

CIRCUS

15

Augustan
Naumachia

Probus
Bridge

26

MAXIMUS

Baths
of Sura

20

AVENTINE

Baths of Decius

XIII

XII

Depot

Portico
of Aemilius

Pt͟a
Lavernalis

Pt͟a Rausuculana

Pt͟a Portuensis

Pt͟a Naevia

WALL

OF

SERVIUS

TULLIUS

Warehouses

Mausoleum
of Caius Cestius

Warehouses

Pt͟a Ostiensis
(P⁺͟a S. Paolo)

Via

Portuensis

Via

Ostiensis

← PORTS OF CLAUDIUS AND TRAJAN

ROME DURING THE EMPIRE		Arch of Constantine	XI	1
		Arch of Janus	XI	2
Amphitheatrum Castrense	V	Arx	VIII	4
Antonine Crematorium	IX	Augustan Crematorium	IX	30
Ara Pacis	IX	Augustan Naumachia	XIV	

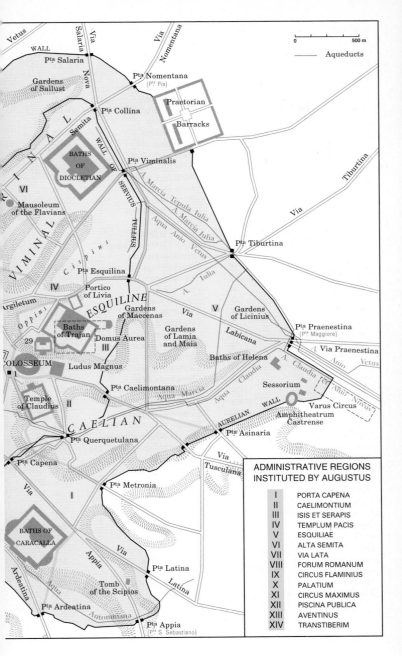

ADMINISTRATIVE REGIONS
INSTITUTED BY AUGUSTUS

I	PORTA CAPENA
II	CAELIMONTIUM
III	ISIS ET SERAPIS
IV	TEMPLUM PACIS
V	ESQUILIAE
VI	ALTA SEMITA
VII	VIA LATA
VIII	FORUM ROMANUM
IX	CIRCUS FLAMINIUS
X	PALATIUM
XI	CIRCUS MAXIMUS
XII	PISCINA PUBLICA
XIII	AVENTINUS
XIV	TRANSTIBERIM

Basilica of Constantine	IV	5	Baths of Decius		XIII
Basilica of Neptune	IX	6	Baths of Diocletian		VI
Baths of Agrippa	IX		Baths of Helena		V
Baths of Caracalla	XII		Baths of Nero		IX
Baths of Constantine	VI	28	Baths of Sura		XIII

Baths of Titus	III	29	Porta Nomentana	VI	
Baths of Trajan	III		Porta Ostiensis	XII-XIII	
Circus Flaminius	IX		Porta Pinciana	VI-VII	
Circus Maximus	XI		Porta Portuensis	XIV	
Colosseum	III		Porta Praenestina	V	
Column of Marcus Aurelius	IX	7	Porta Querquetulana	II	
Depot	XIII		Porta Quirinalis	VI	
Domus Augustana	X	9	Porta Raudusculana	XII-XIII	
Domus Aurea	III		Porta Salaria	VI	
Domus Flavia	X	10	Porta Salutaris	VI-VII	
Forum Boarium	XI		Porta Sanqualis	VI-VII	
Forum Olitorium	VIII-IX-XI		Porta Septimiana	XIV	
Gardens of Lamia and Maia	V		Porta Tiburtina	V	
Gardens of Licinius	V		Porta Trigemina	XI-XIII	
Gardens of Licullus	VII		Porta Triomphalis	IX	
Gardens of Maecenas	III		Porta Viminalis	IV-VI	
Gardens of Sallust	VI		Portico of Aemilius	XIII	
Hadrian's Temple	IX		Portico of Livia	III	
Imperial Fora	IV-VI-VII-VIII		Portico of Octavia	IX	
Largo Argentina Sacred Precinct	IX	3	Portico of the Argonautes	IX	13
Ludus Magnus	II		Pratorian Barracks	VI	
Mausoleum of Augustus	IX		Probus Bridge	XIII-XIV	
Mausoleum of Caius Cestius	XIII		Roman Forum	IV-VIII-X	
Mausoleum of Flavians	VI		Saepta Iulia	IX	
Mausoleum of Hadrian	IX		Septizonium	X	15
Nero's Bridge	IX-XIV		Sessorium	V	
Nero's Circus	IX		Stadium of Domitian	IX	
Odeon of Domitian	IX		Tabularium	VIII	16
Pantheon	IX		Temple of Aesculapius	XIV	21
Pompey's Curia	IX		Temple of Apollo (Palatine)	X	17
Pons Aelius	IX		Temple of Apollo Sosianus	IX	18
Pons Aemilius	IX-XIV		Temple of Cibele	X	19
Pons Agrippa	XI-XIV		Temple of Claudius	I-II	
Pons Aurelius	IX-XIV		Temple of Diana	XIII	20
Pons Cestius	XIV		Temple of Elagabalus	X	23
Pons Fabricius	IX-XIV	12	Temple of Fortuna Virilis	XI	22
Pons Sublicius	XI-XIV		Temple of Isis and Serapis	IX	24
Porta Appia	I		Temple of Jupiter Capitolinus	VIII	25
Porta Ardeatina	I-XII		Temple of Minerva	XIII	26
Porta Asinaria	II-V		Temple of Serapis	VI-VII	
Porta Aurelia	XIV		Temple of Venus and Rome	IV	27
Porta Caelimontana	II-III		Theatre of Balbus	IX	14
Porta Capena	I-XII		Theatre of Marcellus	IX	
Porta Collina	VI		Theatre of Pompey	IX	
Porta Cornelia	IX		Tiber Island	XIV	
Porta Esquilina	III-IV		Tiberius' Palace	X	11
Porta Flaminia	VII-IX		Tomb of the Scipios	I	
Porta Latina	I		Trajan's Column	XIII	8
Porta Lavernalis	XIII		Varus Circus	V	
Porta Metronia	I-II		Vatican Naumachia	IX	
Porta Naevia	XII		Warehouses	XIII	

behaviour by the Emperor. His diplomatic successes (the annexing of Armenia to the Roman Empire) did nothing to dispel the general level of discontent. Violent persecution of the Christians took place in 64, followed by the famous fire. The German legions rebelled and imposed Sulpicius Galba as the new Emperor. Nero committed suicide.

69 Succession disputed. Galba is followed by the prefect of Lusitania, Otho, who is in turn defeated and forced to commit suicide by Vitellius. Vitellius is challenged by Flavius Vespasian and **civil war** breaks out in the city of Rome. The Campidoglio fire damaged the Temple of Jupiter: a highly sacrilegious act.

FLAVIAN EMPERORS (AD 70-96)

Vespasian

Museo Capitolino, Roma/S. Chirol

69-79   After much destruction and a year of civil war, **Flavius Vespasian** – head of a troop responsible for putting down the Jewish revolt – is proclaimed Emperor. This skilful administrator restores the finances of the state and promulgates the *Lex de imperio,* which sets out the powers of the *princeps* (head of State) for the first time. He promotes the construction of public works, such as the huge Flavian Amphitheatre, now known as the **Colosseum**.

79-81   **Titus**, Vespasian's eldest son, becomes Emperor. In 79, Vesuvius erupts, destroying Herculaneum, Stabia and Pompeii. **Pliny the Elder** dies while valiantly attempting to rescue the victims.

81-96   Titus's brother, **Domitian**, becomes Emperor. He advocates anti-Senate policies, carries out military offensives in the Germanic regions and in Dacia with little success, and instigates the persecution of the Christians in 93. A conspiracy leads to his assassination.

ANTONINE EMPERORS AND ADOPTED HEIRS

96-98   **Nerva**, a former senator, becomes Emperor. He inaugurates the procedure of Emperors nominating their successor.

98-117   **Marcus Ulpius Trajan** is elected Emperor.

117-38   **Hadrian** becomes Emperor. He promotes peace, abandoning Mesopotamia and fortifying the boundaries (*limes*) of the empire. A cultured and passionate Hellenist, he travelled widely, spending time in Africa and Asia Minor. His reign was blighted by a serious Jewish revolt in Palestine, Egypt and Cyrene (131-35).

Trajan – The Best of Emperors

Marcus Ulpius Trajan was a Spaniard of Italian descent, and was the first Emperor to come from the provinces. Intelligent and energetic, he was described as the best of Emperors (*optimus princeps*). He carried out great public works such as building a forum with markets and two libraries (one Greek and one Latin), enlarging the ports of Ostia and Ancona, and constructing a bridge in Alcantara and an aqueduct in Segovia, both in Spain. In Italy, he instituted the *alimenta* for children, the first major example of social spending. His conquests in Dacia brought gold and slaves to Rome and helped to improve the economy of the Empire. He also led campaigns against the Parthians and penetrated as far as the Persian Gulf to enable the Empire to profit from the trade between the Far East and the Mediterranean. Other campaigns included those against the Nabataean kingdom and the capture of the capital Petra, an important commercial centre on the caravan route. In 117 he died of exhaustion while returning to Rome

Museo Capitolino, Roma/S. Chirol

Marcus Aurelius

138-61 A long period of peace under the reign of **Antoninus Pius**. During this period Rome had a population of around one million, a figure exceeded only by imperial Peking.

161-80 Reign of **Marcus Aurelius**, a Stoic philosopher and statesman who wrote a philosophical work in Greek, entitled *Meditations*. After a campaign against the Parthians, he faced the German tribes (Quadi and Marcomanni) in the Upper Danube region.

180-92 Reign of **Commodus**, son of Marcus Aurelius. Commodus was immature and not very capable; he was killed by a conspiracy of the Senate.

SEVERAN EMPERORS AND MILITARY ANARCHY (3C)

193-211 The African general **Septimius-Severus** becomes Emperor after the civil war between Albino and Nigro. He starts the offensive against the Parthians and the Scots. Government assumes the form of a military autocracy.

211-17 Rule of Aurelius Antoninus, known as **Caracalla**, a fierce and unstable character. In 212 he publishes the *Constitutio Antoniniana de civitate,* which granted citizenship to all free men in the Empire, probably for tax purposes. High inflation begins and continues until the early 4C.

218-22 Reign of **Elagabalus**, high priest of the sun god, El-Gabal, from the city of Emesa in Syria. His outrageous behaviour leads to his assassination.

222-35 **Severus Alexander** attempts to work with the Senate to prevent German tribes invading. He is killed by Maximinus from Thracia, an uncouth professional soldier. Military **anarchy** follows, along with German and Persian threats.

256-60 Persecution of Christians under **Valerian**. The Emperor and his army are defeated by the Persians and Valerian is held prisoner. He is succeeded by his son Gallienus, protector of the famous philosopher **Plotinus**, who opened a school in Rome.

270-75 **Aurelian**, a skilful general, takes Palmyra, a Syrian capital. Preoccupied by the invasion of Germanic tribes on Italian soil, Aurelian has a new wall built around Rome, later reinforced by Honorius. The wall had 16 gates and 383 towers.

IMPERIAL AUTOCRACY (4C-5C)

The Empire was reorganised under Diocletian and Constantine. Italy and Rome lost some of their importance, imperial power became autocratic, and administrative and fiscal reforms replaced the old Augustinian laws. Christianity became the religion of the Emperor and his family, and the seat of power shifted east, with the founding of Constantinople in 331.

284-305 **Diocletian**, a high-ranking official, becomes Emperor. He attempts to harness inflation with fixed prices and devises a system that splits the Empire administratively, at the same time guaranteeing a peaceful succession. The **tetrarchy**, or rule by four, creates two leaders under the title of Augustus, assisted by two Caesars (who were also heirs). In 286 **Maximian** becomes Augustus in Milan; Galerius is given the title of Caesar and control of the east in Mitrovizza, assisting Diocletian, and **Constantius-Chlorus** assists Maximian as his Caesar and settles in Trier, governing Gaul and Britain. Rome is no longer the capital, but assumes a symbolic value as the original home of the Empire.

303 Systematic persecution of Christians by Diocletian.

311 Galerius grants permits eastern Christians to worship.

306-37 Chlorus's son, **Constantine**, takes advantage of the dissolution of the tetrarchy and proclaims himself Augustus. He routs enemies, including the pagan, Maxentius, supported by the Senate.

337-60 The Empire is divided among Constantine's three sons who soon begin fighting. **Constantinus II**, supporter of the

ROMAN EMPIRE
As at the end of 2C AD

Roman territory at the end of the 2nd Punic War (201 BC)

The Empire at the end of the reign of Augustus (AD 14)

The Empire at the end of the Antonines' reign (AD 192)

Trajan's conquests abandoned at his death in AD 117

Fortified wall *(Limes)*   Spread of Christianity in 4C

Heruli
Scythians
CASPIAN SEA
EUXINE (BLACK SEA)
ARMENIA
BITHYNIA PONTUS
GALATIA CAPPADOCIA
CILICIA ○ Caesarea
Tarsus Carrhae ○ ASSYRIA
LYCIA- Tigris Parthians
PAMPHILIA SYRIA MESOPOTAMIA
CYPRUS ○ Palmyra Euphrates
○ Damascus
SEA ○ JUDEA PERSIAN GULF
○ Jerusalem
○ Alexandria ARABIA
EGYPT
RED SEA

0   500 km

Arian faith, emerges victorious. He visits to Rome.

360-63 **Julian** as Emperor. Cousin of Constantius II, he was a very cultured man. He embraces paganism and attempts to reinstate this ancient religion. Christian teachers are refused work, although there are no real acts of hostility towards the Church. He leads a successful campaign against the Persians, but dies near Ctesiphon, in Mesopotamia.

378 Disastrous Roman defeat at **Adrianopolis** (Thracia). The Em-peror Valentian is killed and the **Goths** establish themselves in the Balkans, often acting as mercenaries for the Roman army.

382 **Leo the Great** proclaims the Pope "Head of the Church" and the fount of episcopal authority, reinforcing the supremacy over Constantinople. During this period, Gratian, a pupil of Ambrose, renounces the traditional and pagan title of *Pontifex Maximus*, once the prerogative of all Emperors after Augustus.

379-95 **Theodosius I** resolves the problem of the Goths and reigns as sole Emperor (the last in Roman history). In 380 Nicean Christianity is proclaimed the state religion by the Emperor in Thessalonica. In 392, at the suggestion of **Ambrose** of Milan, paganism is outlawed. Following Theodosius's death, the Empire is divided between his sons: **Arcadius** in the east and **Honorius**, whose guardian was the Vandal general Stilicho, in the west.

Constantine and Christian Rome

Constantine ruled as sole Emperor. In 313 he issued an **edict** in Milan, along with Licinius, stating that henceforth all religions would be tolerated, except Manicheism. Christianity was therefore officially recognised for the first time and Constantine himself converted to the religion. In 325 the Emperor headed the **First Ecumenical Council** of Christianity, which was held in Nicaea (Asia Minor), during which the Arian heresy was outlawed. Constantine was responsible for the construction of basilicas in Jerusalem (Holy Sepulchre) and Rome (St Peter's and St John Lateran, which remained the Papal seat for centuries). The conversion of Constantine confirmed the birth of a Christian empire.

The Church of Rome assumed superiority over the other Bishoprics and the other four Patriarchates of Christianity because Peter and Paul were said to have preached and been martyred in Rome. Tertullian states that Paul was beheaded in 67 and in 2C AD the Gaulish writer Irenaeus recorded the *principalitas* of the Church of Rome. Other writers recounted Paul's martyrdom and Peter's crucifixion during the reign of Nero. Eusebius of Caesarea (4C AD) recalls the words of Gaius about the trophies of the Apostles: "I can point out the trophies of the apostles. For if you are willing to go to the Vatican or the Ostian Way, you will find the trophies of those who founded this Church". Gaius's trophy can be identified in the crypt of St Paul Without the Walls – and archaeological evidence would appear to agree with this interpretation; a more recent tradition suggests that the tomb of the first Pope is located in the catacombs of **St Peter's**. Christian preaching, according to Suetonius and Tacitus, would appear to have taken place near the Jewish community which was established in Trastevere as early as the end of the 1C BC (this community is therefore the oldest in Rome), and was soon to interest the Gentiles. The aristocrat Acilius Glabrio was martyred in 91 and **Flavius Clemens**, Domitian's cousin, was killed because he was Christian. It is believed that it was his wife Domitilla who donated the land for use as a Christian cemetery. A number of churches were built over the martyrs' tombs or near the homes of the rich protectors of the Christian community *(tituli)*.

403 After the invasion of the Po Plain by the Visigoth, **Alaric** (later defeated by Stilicho), Honorius leaves Milan and settles in Ravenna, defended by marshland. A conspiracy murders Stilicho in 407.

410 Alaric sacks Rome for three days. A huge outcry follows. Jerome and Augustine write pages on the desecration of the city. The previous year, various Germanic tribes had invaded Gaul. The west is on the verge of collapse.

430 **Aurelius Augustine**, a Christian writer and philosopher, dies at Ippona (in present-day Algeria), attacked by Vandals. He wrote the Confessions and a major work on the civilisation and decadence of Rome, *De Civitate Dei*.

455 **Genseric**, king of the Vandals, sacks Rome from his African territory with extreme ferocity. Just four years earlier, the Roman general Ezio had stopped the Huns in Gaul, and in 452 **Attila** had turned back at the Po Plain, either as a result of the intervention of the Pope, or from fear of an outbreak of plague in Italy.

476 The barbarian **Odoacer** deposes the last Emperor of the west, **Romulus Augustus**. The Emperor of the east is now universally recognised as the legitimate ruler.

Papal Power (6C-15C)

493 The Arian **Ostrogoths** settle in Italy. Their educated king, Theodoric, initiates a period of collaboration.

527-65 **Justinian** becomes Emperor of Byzantium. In 540, he orders his general Belisarius to invade Sicily. This leads to the disastrous Gothic War, which devastated parts of Italy and marks the ancient era's end. Belisarius captures, then loses Rome.

In 552, the eastern Empire annexes Italy.

568 Invasion by the **Lombards**, a Germanic people more unruly than the Visigoths. Rome, officially part of the Byzantine Empire, is, in fact, defended and sustained by the Pope. The Byzantine exarch has his residence in Ravenna. The disappearance of the Senate and the destruction of the city signals the beginning of Rome's decay.

590-604 Papacy of **Gregory the Great**, known as *Consul Dei* because of his political ability. A writer and theologian, he was responsible for the evangelisation of Britain. Under his Papacy, the Bishop of Rome becomes a moral and political force of European importance. In spite of this, records of the time (many of which are pilgrims') show Rome to be a small city, with a population of less than 20 000. The influx of monks from the east and the Greek language influences the city for two centuries.

752 Lombards threaten Rome. Pope Stephen II appeals for help from the king of the Franks, **Pepin the Short** (the Franks were Catholics, unlike the other Germanic tribes, who were Arian), marking the beginning of the alliance between the French and the Pope. The latter had little faith in Byzantium, involved in iconoclasm conflicts.

758 Donation of Querzy-sur-Oise. The Pope acquires Sutri and other territories, leading to the birth of the *Patrimonium Petri*, otherwise known as the **Papal States**.

800 **Charlemagne**, who had conquered the Lombards in 776, is crowned Emperor by Pope Leo III, despite the opposition of Byzantium, reviving the Roman Empire of the west.

Rome is the seat of this *Respublica Christiana*.

824 Ludovic the Pius, son and successor to Charlemagne, passes his *Constitutio* stating that no Pope could be elected without first swearing allegiance to the Emperor.

846 The Moors, landing at Ostia, sack the basilica of St Peter's. As a result, the Leonine Walls are built around the Vatican basilica in 852.

9C-10C Unsettled period for the Papacy. The aristocratic families of Rome (the Theophylacti, **Crescenzi** and later the Tuscolani) all push for the election of their family members, who are often weak and dissolute.

962 John XII calls **Otho I**, king of Germany, to Rome and crowns him Emperor. Otho imposes major reforms on the Papacy, establishing that a Pope could not be elected without the consent of the Emperor. In 963 Pope John XII is deposed and Leo VIII, a German prelate loyal to the Emperor, elected.

996 **Otho III** resides in Rome, on the Aventine, and dreams of restoring Rome to its ancient grandeur. The Pope is the scholar **Sylvester II**. In 998 the Emperor issues a *Privilegium* attesting the pre-eminence of Rome above all other cities in the Empire. Otho's death cuts short the city's renaissance in 1002.

1057 Stephen IX elected Pope without the Emperor's approval.

1075 **Gregory VII**, a strong advocate of absolute theocracy, confirms the superiority of the Papacy over the Empire and declares that laymen cannot make ecclesiastical appointments (the **Investiture Controversy**). He also denounces the sale and acquisition of Church goods and the marriage of priests. In his *Dictatus Papae* the Pope sets out the holy and political power of the Papacy, which exceeds that of all bishops and other Christians, including the Emperor. The Emperor Henry IV, angered by this statement, captures Rome. He is then expelled by the Norman army of Robert Guiscard, called upon by Gregory VII. Rome is violently sacked and its population massacred; many of those inhabitants not killed are sold as slaves.

1122 **Concordat of Worms**. The Pope and the Emperor reach a compromise to end the Investiture Controversy. At the suggestion of the canonist, Yves (Ivo) of Chartres, the Pope will from now on invest future bishops spiritually with a ring and pastoral staff; the Emperor will concede temporal power with a sceptre.

1130-55 Arnaldo da Brescia, a monk who was a pupil of the philosopher Abelard, attempts to reform the papacy and institute a republic in Rome, divided into *Comune*.

1153 Pope protected by **Frederick Barbarossa** under the Treaty of Constance. Arnaldo da Brescia captured and hanged. New conflict between the Pope and the Emperor. Rome fortified with towers (*Roma turrita*) built by powerful aristocratic families.

1198-1216 Papacy of **Innocent III**. Medieval papal theocracy culminates in this period.

1309-77 **Avignon captivity**. As a result of the influence of the French monarchy, the Popes (most of whom were French) move to Avignon. The Pope returns to Rome following the protests and prayers of Catherine of Siena, Bridget of Sweden and the poet Petrarch.

1347 Rome dominated by **Cola di Rienzo**, a notary of the city and ardent admirer of ancient history, who is eager to return the city to its former glory. His attempt fails miserably because of the hostility of the aristocratic families. After only three years, he exits the city. He returns with the Pope's support, but is soon forced to flee once more and is tragically slaughtered. The anonymous *The Life of Cola di Rienzo* captures his sad tale in the vulgar Roman dialect.

1357   Cardinal Egidio di Albornoz publishes his *Constitutiones Aegidianae*, laws with which the Papal States were ruled until the 19C.

1378-1417 Great Schism of the West. Two Popes reign simultaneously, one in Rome and one in Avignon. A third emerges in Pisa in 1409. Pope **Martin V** brings the seat of the Papacy back to Rome and rules.

1447-55 Nicholas V founds the **Vatican Library**, which today has around 500 000 books and 60 000 manuscripts. Rome becomes a centre of the European Humanist movement.

1453   Turks capture Constantinople, ending the eastern Empire. Humanist Pope Pius II (Enea Silvio Piccolomini) issues a protest over the apathy of western sovereigns.

The Modern Era

1494   The French king, **Charles VIII**, en route for Naples, enters Rome. This marks the beginning of foreign intervention in central and northern Italy.

1508-12 After a period of fighting to subjugate the aristocratic families to the power of the Church, **Julius II** goes to war to retain Romagna, to weaken the Venetian Republic and to expel the French king, Louis XII.

1517   **Luther**, who had visited Rome and been shocked by the immorality of the Curia, nails his 95 Theses on the church door at Wittenberg. The Medici Pope Leo X underestimates the danger of Luther's gesture.

6 May 1527 The **sack of Rome** by the Protestant Swiss and Spanish troops under Emperor Charles V, who holds the city for seven months. Only 32 000 of the 55 000 inhabitants remain. The later influx of central Italians distanced the Roman dialect from other southern strains. In November Clement VII surrenders to the imperial troops, promising a council to reorganise Catholicism.

1543-63 **Council of Trent** and birth of the Counter-Reformation.

1585-90 Pontificate of **Sixtus V**, during which crime and brigandry are rife. The Church and State are divided into 15 congregations at this time, a cardinal administers each. Sixtus V erected the obelisks of Piazza dell'Esquilino, Piazza del Popolo, Piazza San Pietro and Piazza San Giovanni in Laterano. He constructed the Via Sistina, partially linked the main churches and numerous districts of Rome with wide roads, rebuilt the Lateran and constructed the Scala Santa, replaced the statue of the Emperor on Trajan's Column with that of St Peter and had a chapel built to house his own tomb in the basilica of Santa Maria Maggiore.

1600   The philosopher **Giordano Bruno** is burnt at the stake in Campo dei Fiori.

1631   **Urban VIII** obtains the duchy of Urbino. The Papal States reach their greatest extent.

1791   Renunciation by the Papacy of Avignon and the Comtat-Venaissin, French annexes

1798   Rome occupied by the French troops of **Napoleon**; the Jacobin Roman Republic proclaimed. Pius VI dies in exile in Valence.

1800   The new Pope, Pius VII, is elected in Venice and returns to Rome, where the Republic is defeated. The following year the Pope signs a concordat with Napoleon.

1808 Rome occupied by the French. Following political disagreements (Pius VII refused to blockade Britain), the Papal States are invaded by Napoleonic troops and the Pope banished to Savona, then Fontainebleau. Pius VII returns to Rome in 1814.

1820-61 Struggle for the unification of the Italian States.

1848 **Pius IX** sends troops to fight the Austrians, during the First War of Independence. The Pope's conservative stance leads to the proclamation of the Roman Republic, defended by **Garibaldi** against the French troops, who ensure the return of the Pope.

CAPITAL OF ITALY

1870 Rome captured by the Italian army, ending the Pope's temporal authority Pope. Pius IX retires to the Vatican. The State proposes the Law of Guarantees, to safeguard the Pope's liberty, which is refused by the Pope. Rome becomes the Italian capital.

1915 Italy enters World War I on side of Allies.

28-29 October 1922 Fascist march on Rome. **Mussolini** named Prime Minister.

1929 Mussolini and Cardinal Gasparri sign the **Lateran Treaty** (renewed in 1984). Foundation of the Vatican City State.

1936 Mussolini forms axis with Nazi Germany.

1937 Creation of Cinecittà film studio and the Istituto Luce.

1940 Italy enters World War II on German side.

1943 San Lorenzo bombardment. King Victor Emmanuel III imprisons Mussolini. Armistice with Allies. Italy declares war on Germany.

1944 British and American forces liberate Rome.

1946 **Republic Proclaimed**. Rome becomes the administrative centre of the Lazio region.

1948 New constitution. Christian Democrats win elections.

1957 Treaty of Rome sets up the Common Market (now the European Union). Rome also becomes the headquarters of the Food and Agriculture Organisation (FAO), a United Nations organisation.

1960 Olympic Games held in Rome.

1963 Italian Socialist Party joins Christian Democrat-led coalition under Prime Minister Aldo Moro.

1963-65 **Second Vatican Council**, called by John XXIII (1958-63) and completed by Paul VI (1963-78). The Church tries to enter the modern world. Liturgical reform abolishes Latin in services.

1968 Clashes between students and police near Villa Giulia.

1960's-70's Right and left-wing terrorists jostle. Citizens cower inside during the "Years of Lead".

1972 Giulio Andreotti becomes prime minister, a post he will hold seven times.

1975 Holy Year celebrated.

1978 Former P.M. Aldo Moro kidnapped and killed by the Red Brigades. Paul VI dies and is succeeded by John Paul I, pope for only 33 days. The Archbishop of Cracow, Karol Wojtila, is elected and takes the name **John Paul II**. Abortion legalised.

1984 Renewal of the Lateran Pact between the Holy See and the Italian Government. Roman Catholicism loses status as state religion.

1990 Football World Cup held in the Eternal City.

1992 Mafia probes spark several years of arrests and investigations. Top anti-crime prosecutor, Giovanni Falcone, his wife and three bodyguards killed in car bomb attack.

2000 Celebration of the **Jubilee**.

2001 Silvio Berlusconi wins the general election, backed by a centre-right coalition. First constitutional referendum since 1946 creates greater autonomy to the country's 20 regions in tax, education and environment policies.

2002 Inauguration of the Rome Auditorium by Renzo Piano. Euro replaces the lira.

2003 PM Berlusconi appears in court on corruption charges.

2005 Death of **John Paul II**, election of the new pope **Benedict XIII**. Parliament ratifies EU constitution. Berlusconi resigns, then reforms government.

2006 Prodi becomes P.M. Giorgio Napolitano, a former communist, is elected as president.

2007 Romano Prodi resigns after a defeat on a foreign policy vote, but continues with a re-formed coalition government.

Influential Families

Many of Rome's powerful families funded monumental works, commissioned artistic treasures and occupied high levels of government.

BARBERINI

This Roman family, originally from Tuscany, produced Pope **Urban VIII** (1623-44). He funded the Barberini Palace on the Quirinal, upon which both the young **Bernini** and Borromini wor-

ked: it contains a magnificent picture gallery. He commissioned the Triton Fountain and the Fountain of the Bees in Piazza Barberini. A friend of Galileo, he was the first to employ Bernini – for a bust of himself and the baldaquin above the high altar in St Peter's Basilica.

BORGHESE

This noble family from Siena settled in Rome when one of its members was elected Pope **Paul V** (1605-21). The family has left its mark in the Palazzo Borghese, in the city centre, and in the Villa Borghese to the north of Rome. During his Papacy, the Villa became a museum and houses many important artworks collected over the years by generations of the family. Paul V also commissioned the Pauline Fountain (Fontana Paolina) on the Janiculum. He is buried in the Pauline Chapel in the church of Santa Maria Maggiore.

BORGIA

This Spanish family produced two Popes: **Calixtus III** (1455-58) and **Alexander VI** (1492-1503). During the latter's reign, America was discovered. He used Peruvian gold to decorate the ceiling of Santa Maria Maggiore; his coat of arms is shown there. Alexander VI also decorated the Vatican's Borgia Apartments. His son, **Cesare**, inspired Machiavelli to write *The Prince*; his daughter, **Lucrezia**, was the victim of family political intrigue.

CHIGI

MICHELIN

Originally came from Siena, these bankers became more important from the 15C through **Agostino Chigi**, who commissioned the young Raphael to decorate the Villa Farnesina. The Chigi Palace, official residence of the president of the Council of Ministers, owes its name to **Alexander VII** (1655-67), a member of the illustrious family who acquired it in the 17C. The Pope commissioned Bernini to build the colonnades of St Peter's. The Chigi coat of arms also appears on the fountain in Piazza d'Aracoeli.

COLONNA

MICHELIN

This ancient noble family was very powerful from the 13C to the 17C. The election of one of its members, **Martin V** (1417-31), as Pope during the Council

of Constance ended the Great Schism of the West. When the papacy returned to Rome, Martin concentrated totally, right up to his death, on reinstating the primacy of the Vatican.

DELLA ROVERE

MICHELIN

Two great Popes were born into this family from Savona: **Sixtus IV** and Julius II. **Sixtus IV** (1471-84), whose secular name was Francesco della Rovere, was a scholarly and industrious man. He wrote a thesis on the blood of Christ and a study on the Immaculate Conception. He was also rebuilt Sante Maria del Popolo and the constructed Santa Maria della Pace and the Sistine Chapel. Sixtus IV called upon some of the greatest artists of the day – including Botticelli, Ghirlandaio and Perugino – to decorate the chapel. Having appointed his nephews Gerolamo and Pietro Riario as Bishop and Archbishop of Imola, he came into conflict with Lorenzo de' Medici and was involved in the Pazzi conspiracy, which led to the assassination of Giuliano de' Medici (Lorenzo's brother) in Florence Cathedral, and to the massacre of the conspirators by the mob. Like his nephew Giuliano della Rovere (the future Pope Julius II), Sixtus IV was a warrior Pope; he fought against other Italian states and was victorious against Muhammad II, who had landed at Otranto and massacred many of the local inhabitants. **Julius II** (1503-13) was blessed with great gifts both as a politician and as a generous patron: the implementation of Bramante's design for St Peter's, the painting of the Vatican Rooms by Raphael, the designing of his mausoleum, which remained unfinished, by Michelangelo (in the church of San Pietro in Vincoli), and the collection of antique sculptures in the Vatican. He was also responsible for the building of Via Giulia, a long, straight thoroughfare between the bend in the Tiber and the island downstream.

FARNESE

MICHELIN

This aristocratic family from Umbria, already famous by the 12C, came to Rome through **Paul III** (1534-49), the Pope who convened the **Council of Trent** (1545-63). He was the driving force behind major projects. While still a cardinal, he commissioned Sangallo to build the Farnese Palace, finished by Michelangelo. When he became Pope, he turned again to the Florentine master for the *Last Judgement* in the Sistine Chapel and put him in charge of work on St Peter's Basilica.

MEDICI

MICHELIN

This Florentine merchant and banking family ruled Florence and the whole of

Tuscany from the 15C to the 18C. It produced several Popes: **Leo X** (1513-21), son of Lorenzo the Magnificent, a man of letters and patron of the arts, who put Raphael and Giulio Romano in charge of the Loggias in the Vatican: **Clement VII** (1523-34), an ally of François I, who was not able to prevent the sack of Rome or the Lutheran reforms which erupted during his Papacy; **Pius IV** (1559-65) who presided over the closure of the Council of Trent (1545-63); and **Leo XI**, who died a few days after he was elected in 1605, but who, while still a cardinal, had acquired the Villa Medici, which later became the French Academy in Rome.

PAMPHILI

MICHELIN

Originally from Umbria, the family settled in Rome during the 15C. In 1461 its members were honoured with the title of Counts of the Holy Roman Empire. In the 16C Giovanni Battista became Pope **Innocent X** (1644-55). He was responsible for many changes in Piazza Navona: the rebuilding of the Pamphili Palace, the transformation into a family chapel of the church of Sant'Agnese in Agone, for which the façade and dome were built by Borromini; and the building of the Fountain of the Four Rivers (Fontana dei Quattro Fiumi) which he commissioned from Bernini. He turned, however, to Borromini, a rival of Bernini, for the Palace for the Propagation of the Faith and the rebuilding of St John Lateran. The Villa Doria Pamphili was built for the Pope's nephew, whose wife inherited the palace that was known as Palazzo Doria Pamphili.

ART AND CULTURE

During the Republican period, art was valued for its practical and social significance, rather than for its aesthetic value. The priorities changed under the Roman Empire, when art celebrated power and demonstrated the prestige of the capital. The decadence of the Empire and the recognition of Christianity as the state religion saw the development of large basilicas; since then, these have often been restored or rebuilt. Many still welcome pilgrims today.

Art of Ancient Rome

ARCHITECTURE

The remains of only a few public works have survived from the period of the kings and the early Republic, such as the channel of the **Cloaca Maxima** (the Forum's vast drainage, dug in the 6C BC), the **town wall** built by **Servius Tullius** (578-534 BC), the **Appian Way** and the **Aqua Appia**, both the work of **Appius Claudius Caecus**, censor in 312 BC.

The major artistic influences came from the Etruscans, whose works they pillaged, and from the East. Victorious generals returned from there, dazzled by the splendours and accompanied by artists engaged in cities such as Athens or Alexandria.

Materials and techniques – Early Rome was built of very simple materials: **tufa**, a soft brownish stone, volcanic or calcareous in origin; and **peperine**, also of volcanic origin, which owes its name to its greyish hue and its granular texture, suggestive of grains of pepper (pepe in Italian). **Travertine**, a whitish limestone, mostly quarried near Tivoli, is a superior material to the earlier ones employed sparingly in the early centuries. **Marble** made rare appearances as a decorative material from the 2C BC, but became very popular under the Empire. **Brick** was first used in the 1C BC; it is usually seen today stripped of its marble facing.

The principles of classical Roman architecture were undoubtedly modelled upon those of ancient Greece. The mastery of three distinctive feats of civil engineering, however, heralded new building practices here. Firstly, the Romans discovered concrete, allowing them to build more quickly and therefore more prolifically. Secondly they learnt how to apply marble (and any other finely finished stone like granite, porphyry and alabaster) as surface decoration, rather than using large (and expensive) quantities as blocks. Today, many ruins are reduced to reddish or greying husks, long stripped of their marble facing and friezes.

Thirdly, the Romans learnt from their campaigns in the eastern Mediterranean (modern-day Turkey and Syria) the use of the arch, vaulting, squinches and, consequently, the art of constructing domes. At last they were able to break the linearity of the Hellenistic style with round arcs. They poured concrete between simple brick parapets to make solid walls or over brick layers to anchor the voussoirs of an archway, vault or dome. Indeed, the Romans seemingly avoided wooden coffering because of its expense. One particular feature of their concrete is its ability to harden through the centuries: the honeycomb appearance of ruins is largely due to brick erosion.

In their constructions the Romans used the **semicircular arch**. The one built over the Cloaca Maxima in about the 2C BC is a true masterpiece. There are some impressive examples of vaulting in the Domus Augustana, in the Pantheon, in Hadrian's Villa at Tivoli, in the Baths of Caracalla and in the Colosseum.

The Romans were masters of building theatres on level ground, rather than set into a hillside, as was the Greek practice. This involved the construction of vaults to support the terraces, as in the Theatre of Marcellus.

Classical orders – Greek architectural orders were employed, but with modifications: in the Tuscan or Roman Doric order, the column rests on a base rather than directly on the ground. The Ionic order was seldom used here; the Corinthian, however, was very popular – the Romans sometimes replaced the curling acanthus leaves on the capital with smooth overhanging leaves and substituted animals, gods, human figures for the central flower.

To the three Classical orders, they added a fourth, called Composite: a capital in which the four scrolls of the Ionic order surmounted the acanthus leaves. The entablature (comprising the architrave, frieze and cornice) was very ornate, richly decorated with pearls, ovoli and foliage.

The names of two architects have survived: Rabirius, active under Domitian (AD81-95), and Apollodorus of **Damascus** who worked for Trajan (AD98-117) and Hadrian (AD117-138).

Buildings and Monuments

Theatres – Pompey built the first permanent theatre (*Teatro di Pompeo*), which he passed off as a temple with semicircular steps, to avoid a ban. Unlike the Greeks, the Romans built on flat sites, using vaults to support the rows of seats which often ended in a colonnade. The space in front of the stage (orchestra) was reserved for actors and later people of rank, who came to watch the play. Thespians came on the stage, which was raised above the orchestra, through three doors in the wall at the back of the stage. Animals and chariots entered from the sides.

The rear wall, the most beautiful part of the theatre, was decorated with many columns, statues set in recesses, and facings of marble and mosaic. Behind the rear wall of the stage were the dressing rooms, storerooms and a portico overlooking a garden.

The stage hands were responsible for special effects: smoke, lights, thunder, apparitions and grand finales, gods and heroes who descended from heaven or disappeared into the clouds. The male actors wore masks to differentiate characters. The acoustics were influenced by the canvas awning slanting down over the stage, which concentrated the sound so it penetrated to the top row of the terraces and also, perhaps, by resonant vessels strategically placed to act as loud speakers. It has been suggested that when the actors sang, they stood in front of the rear wall of the stage so the doors acted as sounding boards.

Amphitheatres – Romans invented venues, such as the Colosseum, for displays of gymnastics and horse-drawn chariot races. Their main use, however, was for combats between gladiators, who were mostly slaves or prisoners. Wild beasts also battled. Romans considered these bloody events so important that candidates for public office incorporated them in their campaigns.

During the spectacle, slaves burned or sprayed perfume to neutralise the smell of the animals, covered the sand in the arena with red dust to hide the bloodstains and used lead-weighted whips to coerce human contestants or animals into the fray. Loud music played throughout the spectacle.

Amphitheatres were more or less oval in shape. The outer wall consisted of three storeys of arcades, surmounted by a wall with poles that supported the huge awnings. The most important spectators sat on a podium, protected by a balustrade; it was raised above the arena and positioned in the centre of one of the longer sides at the foot of the terraced area (*cavea*) which surrounded the arena on all sides.

Baths – Bathing occupied an important place in the Roman day, particularly during the Empire. Free public clubs

Baths of Caracalla

provided thermal pools, gymnasia and places to stroll, read or converse. Built on a large scale, the pleasure palaces contained columns, capitals, mosaics, coloured marbles, statues and frescoes.

Basilicas – Originally, basilicas accommodated law courts and stallholders, where people might congregate out of the sun or rain. The term, which means "royal portico", referred to it being a covered area. Rows of free-standing columns upheld the roof and divided the internal rectangular space into a "nave" flanked by two side aisles. Rome's first was the Basilica Porcia at the foot of the Capitolino in 185 BC. Unfortunately nothing remains. The use of basilicas for religious functions was assumed with the rise of the early Christian Church.

Triumphal arches – These monuments commemorated the triumph of a victorious general or raised a statue into prominent view. Some had only one opening (Arch of Titus); others had three (Arch of Septimus Severus, Arch of Constantine). Perhaps the original designs linked to the belief that a defeated army lost its powers of destruction on passing under the arch.

Circuses – The huge oblong arenas hosted popular chariot races; these include the Circus Maximus and Maxentius's Circus off the Old Appian Way.

Stadiums – These, too, were oblong in shape, but showcased athletic competitions. The site of Domitian's Stadium (Stadio di Domiziano) is now occupied by Piazza Navona.

Aqueducts – The impressive engineering of these great constructions has probably contributed more than anything else to the Roman reputation for building. The Aqua Appia, the oldest aqueduct, originally stretched more than 16km/10mi in length and was built in 312 BC by Appius Claudius the Blind. Approximately 100m/328ft of the aqueduct is still standing.

Roads – In some places, considerable stretches of the old paving are intact. The word *civus* alludes to a street going up or down hill; a *vicus* is a side street.

Temples and Worship

Temples celebrated the gods or an Emperor, who, since the time of Caesar, rose to divine status. Inspired by Etruscan and Greek models, their design varied from the elemental simplicity of the Temple of Fortuna Virilis to the more complex design of the Temple of Venus and Rome. Each temple had a place

The Roman Gods

Jupiter (*Zeus* in Greek), senior god and ruler of the heavens, the elements and light, is often shown with an eagle, holding a thunderbolt and wearing a crown.

Juno (*Hera*), his wife, protectress of womanhood and marriage, is shown with a peacock and a pomegranate.

Minerva (*Athena*), goddess of wisdom, is represented by an owl. She is the third member of the Capitoline Triad together with Juno and Jupiter, her father, from whose head she sprang fully armed, and is often shown with a shield and a helmet.

Apollo, god of beauty, the sun and the arts, sings to a lyre accompaniment and carries a bow like his sister **Diana** (*Artemis*), goddess of hunting, chastity and the moon (she wears a crescent moon on her head). The animal representing Diana is the doe.

Mercury (*Hermes*), protector of commerce and travel, wears winged sandals and carries a staff (caduceus) in his hand.

Vulcan (*Hephaistos*), god of fire, works in a forge with an anvil and hammer.

Vesta, goddess of the hearth, carries a simple flame as a symbol of fire in the home.

Mars (*Aries*), god of war, is identified by his weapons and his helmet.

Venus (*Aphrodite*), goddess of love and goodness, is represented by a dove. Born out of the foam of the sea, she is often represented standing in a shell or surrounded by sea deities such as Neptune (Poseidon), god of the sea who is armed with a trident.

Ceres (*Demeter*), protectress of the earth, tillage, corn and fecundity, is represented with a sheaf of corn and a scythe.

(cella) reserved for the statue of its divinity. Before this was a **pronaos,** set behind a colonnade. The whole structure stood on a podium.

As far as religion was concerned, Rome drew on all mythological sources for her deities; the 12 main gods and goddesses were the same in number, if not always in name, as their Greek counterparts on Mount Olympus. Public worship was held in the temples, but people also worshipped various household gods (*lares et penates*). Many houses had a sort of shrine **(lararium),** where offerings were made to the souls of ancestors.

Cult of the Dead

Tombs often lined the roads outside the city. Romans practised both burial and cremation. During the Republic, tombs with several chambers enclosed sarcophagi. The most common and elementary marker was a **tablet** (*cippus*), a simple block of stone bearing an inscription. More elaborately worked memorials, made of stone or marble, were called **steles** (*steli*).

Much later, large underground communal chambers **(colombarium)** became the popular form of burial for the poor and for slaves. Much like a dovecote, walls pocked small niches housed urns. The dead person was often "accompanied" on his journey to the other world with clothing, weapons, tools, jewellery (for a woman) and playthings (for a child).

Housing

Depending on their social and financial status, the ancient Romans lived in a multi-storey building **(insula)** containing several dwellings (see OSTIA ANTICA in the Excursions from Rome section), a small middle-class house, or a large-scale patrician house **(domus)**. Though luxurious, the latter seem modest by modern standards: simple walls and no windows.

These early houses contained a large rectangular room (*atrium*) with an open roof in the centre, which allowed rainwater (*pluvial*) to collect in a basin (*impluvium*). This atrium contained the room where the head of the family worked and received visitors, as well as other smaller rooms. Top-ranking officials, wealthy farmers and prosperous merchants had a second house, built in a more elegant Greek style, which was reserved for the family. Used only at certain times of the year, it consisted of rooms built round various atria and a colonnaded courtyard (*peristylium*), with a garden or sometimes a fishpond in the centre. In the dining room (*triclinium*), guests semi-reclined on couches.

SCULPTURE

In this discipline, the Romans most imitated Greek art. They erected mass produced sculptures all over town: pre-fab bodies in togas took custom heads. The Romans liked white and coloured marble, dark red spotted porphyry and alabaster. They also worked in bronze (Marcus Aurelius's statue).

Their originality sparked with **portraits**, fostered by aristocratic practice of wax death masks. Caesar's portraits always show a calm, reflective and energetic character, whereas Augustus, with his prominent ears, displays serenity and coldness. Malice unfurls in Vespasian's face and thick neck. Trajan must have had a very broad face and his hairstyle curiously accentuates this peculiarity. The equestrian statue of Marcus Aurelius is the sole survivor of a tradition established by Julius Caesar: the Emperor as an all-powerful conqueror.

The Romans also excelled in **historical low-relief sculptures**. The scenes on a sarcophagus or on Trajan's column are models of composition and precision.

Decorative sculpture, exceptionally rare in the Republican era as the sarcophagus of Scipio Barbatus shows, reached its apogee in the Augustan era with the **Ara Pacis**. One type of sculpture gave expression to **popular taste**, depicting various crafts and scenes from everyday life on the tombstones of working people.

Decadence in sculpture became apparent in the 3C AD: the folds of garments were scored too deep, making the figures rigid, the expressions became fixed because of excessive hollowing out of the pupil of the eye and the hair was carelessly treated.

PAINTING

A study of the frescoes in Pompeii has identified **four periods** in Roman painting. The "first style" consists of simple panels imitating marble facing. The "second style" is marked by architectural features in *trompe-l'œil,* to which small illustrated panels were added in the "third style". With the "fourth style" the *trompe-l'œil* became excessive and the decoration overloaded. Examples of Roman painting can be seen in Livia's House and the Griffin House on the Palatine and in the National Roman Museum (housed in the Palazzo Massimo alle Terme).

MOSAIC

This technique developed from an attempt to strengthen the floor surface, which was made of a mixture of broken tiles and chalk, by inserting pebbles and then small pieces of marble, which could be cut to a uniform size and arranged to form a design.

Roman workshops also copied the **opus sectile** technique, which originated in the East. A stencil of a decorative motif was applied to a marble base. The outline was traced on to the marble, then hollowed out and filled with small pieces of coloured marble. Examples are on display at the Picture Gallery in the Conservators' Palace and in the Ostia Museum (&see OSTIA ANTICA in the Excursions from Rome section).

Christian Art

The pagan cult of idols and the commandment in the Bible against "graven images" inhibited the spontaneous development of a new style of art among the early communities.

At first Christian art borrowed from the pagan repertoire those subjects which could be used as symbols: the vine, the dove, the anchor, etc. **Paintings** appeared on catacomb walls, following the earlier tradition; the oldest date from the 2C AD. The chief Christian building was the **basilica** (not to be confused with the secular pagan basilicas). Constantine erected the first over the tombs of Peter and Paul the Apostles (St Peter's in the Vatican; St Paul Without the Walls) and next to the Imperial Palace (St John Lateran).

Architectural Glossary

Some of the terms given below are further explained by the illustrations on the previous pages.

Words in italics are Italian

Altarpiece (or **ancona**): a large painting or sculpture adorning an altar.
Ambulatory: extension of aisles around the chancel for processionals.
Antependium: a covering over the front of an altar.

Low relief on the Arch of Constantine (detail)

G. Bludzin/MICHELIN

Apse: semicircular or polygonal end of a church behind the altar; the outer section is known as the chevet.

Apsidal chapel: small chapel off the ambulatory of a Romanesque or Gothic church.

Archivolt: arch moulding over an arcade or upper section of a doorway.

Atlantes (or **Telamones**): male figures used as supporting columns.

Atrium (or **four-sided portico**): a court enclosed by colonnades in front of the entrance to a palaeo-Christian or Romanesque church.

Avant-corps: part of a building which projects out from the main façade.

Bastion: in military architecture, a polygonal defensive structure projecting from the ramparts.

Bay: the area between two supporting columns or pillars.

Buttress: external support of a wall, which counterbalances the thrust of the vaults and arches.

Caisson (or **lacunar**): decorative square panel sunk into a flat roof or vaulted stonework.

Caryatid: female figure used as a supporting column.

Cathedra: high-backed throne in Gothic style.

Chancel: the part of the church behind the altar, with carved wooden stalls for the choir.

Ciborium: a canopy (baldaquin) over an altar.

Coffer (or **panel**): small square ornamental panel, painted or sculpted in various materials.

Console: projecting stone or wooden bracket which supports cornices or beams.

Corbel (or **truss**): triangular bracket, usually made of wood, supporting a roof.

Counter-façade: internal wall of church façade.

Cross (**church plan**): churches are usually built either in the plan of a Greek cross, with four arms of equal length, or a Latin cross, with one arm longer than the other three.

Exedra: section in the back of Roman basilicas containing seats; by extension, curved niche or semicircular recess outside.

Ghimberga: a triangular Gothic pediment adorning a portal.

Grotesque: a decorative style popular during the Renaissance in which parts of human, animal and plant forms are distorted and mixed. The term comes from the old Italian word *grotte*, the name given in the Renaissance period to the Roman ruins of the Domus Aurea.

High relief: sculpture or carved work projecting more than one half of its true proportions from the background (halfway between low relief and in-the-round figures).

Intrados: inner surface of an arch or vault.

Jamb (or **pier**): pillar flanking a doorway or window and supporting the arch above.

Keystone: topmost stone in an arch or vault.

Lantern: turret with windows on top of a dome.

Lesene (or **Lombard strips**): decorative band of pilasters joined at the top by an arched frieze.

Matroneo: the gallery reserved for women in palaeo-Christian and Romanesque churches.

Modillion: small bracket supporting a cornice.

Moulding: an ornamental shaped band which projects from the wall.

Narthex: interior vestibule of a church.

Overhang: overhanging or corbelled upper storey.

Ovolo: egg-shaped decoration.

Pala d'altare: Italian term for altarpiece.

Pediment: ornament in Classical architecture (usually triangular or semicircular) above a door or window.

Pendentive: connecting piece positioned at a corner of a square space to support an octagonal or circular dome.

Pilaster strip: structural column partially set into a wall.

Pluteus: decorated balustrade made from various materials, separating the chancel from the church.

Polyptych: a painting or relief consisting of several folding leaves or panels.

Portico: an open gallery facing the nave in palaeo-Christian churches; it later became a decorative feature of the external part of the church.

Ancient Art

Peripteral temple

Opisthodomos

Statue of the divinity to whom the temple was dedicated

Peristyle

Pronaos

Naos (cella)

Elevation of a Corinthian order temple

Pediment

Cornice

The section comprising the architrave, frieze and cornice is known as the **entablature**

Frieze

Architrave

Abacus

Capital with acanthus leaves

Fluted shaft

Torus

Stylobate

Doric

Tuscan

Ionic

Corinthian

Composite

R. Corbel/MICHELIN

Baths of Caracalla (3C AD)

Stadium

Cisterns

Library

Library

Palaestra:
the baths often
had gymnasium
areas for both
mental and physical
recreation

Palaestra

Calidarium:
hot water baths

Vestibule

Second tepidarium

Laconicum:
steam baths

Tepidarium:
tepid baths

Palaestra

Apodyterium:
changing room

Main entrance

Frigidarium:
cold baths

Colosseum (1C AD)

Corridors for the
spectators to move
around (originally
hidden by the steps)
which led into the
vomitoria, sloping
corridors which gave
access to the cavea

Elliptic cavea:
formed by terraces
for the spectators

Wall coping above
which the *velarium*,
a huge adjustable
awning which
sheltered spectators
from the sun, was
extended

Northern entrance to
the amphitheatre,
reserved for
the Emperor and
his suite. A further
three main entrances
corresponded to
the two axes of
the ellipsis

Ambulacrum

Entrance arches:
numbered from I to
LXXX (except the four
main entrances) to
correspond with the
entrance number on
the spectator's ticket;
seating was arranged
according to social
status

Arena: originally
covered by a wooden
floor

R. Corbel/MICHELIN

Arch of Constantine (4C AD)

Frieze depicting the campaign against Maxentius, Emperor in the East

Dedication

Attic: horizontal coping above the entablature

Entablature

Corinthian columns

Pedestal

Medallion

Side arch

Central arch

Castel Sant'Angelo: from mausoleum to fortress

Papal arms in marble (of Alexander VI) flanked by two statues personifying Winged Fame

Keep: central structure; here it is circular in form

Loggia

Casemate

Corbel: projecting structure with a bracket used to attack enemies from above

Towered wall

Curtain wall in brickwork

15C merlons on small arches supported by brackets

Bastion

R. Corbel/MICHELIN

Religious architecture

Sant'Andrea della Valle (1591-1623)

Intercommunicating chapels

Apsidal chapel

Nave

Transept crossing

Transept arm

Gesù Church, façade (1575)

Pediment

Double pediment
(semicircular and triangular)

Lantern

Dome

Four-cornered
section lesene

Connecting volute

Tambour

Corinthian
capital

Niche with
statue

String course
moulding

Half-column

R. Corbel/MICHELIN

San Giovanni in Laterano, interior (4C-17C)

Papal coat of arms

Coffered ceiling

Pendentive

Triumphal arch

Apsidal oven vault

Baldaquin with pinnacles

Tympanum

Aedicule

Column with Corinthian capital

Apsidal chapel

Papal altar

R. Corbel/MICHELIN

Civil architecture

Palazzo Senatorio (16C)

- Bell tower
- Balustrade
- Semicircular tympanum
- Belfry
- String course cornice
- Cartouche
- Lesene
- Triangular tympanum

Villa Borghese (17C)

- Corps de logis, recessed
- Cornice
- Oval niche
- Semicircular tympanum with a broken arch
- Niche
- Avant-corps
- String course
- Lesene
- Double staircase
- Terrace-covered portico
- Balustrade

R. Corbel/MICHELIN

Predella: base of an altarpiece, divided into small panels.

Presbiterio: the chancel or sanctuary of a church, reserved for the clergy.

Pronaos: the space in front of the *cella* or *naos* in Greek temples; later the columned portico in front of the entrance to a church or palace.

Protiro: small porch on columns in front of the portal in Romanesque churches.

Pulpit: an elevated dais from which sermons were preached.

Pyx: cylindrical box made of ivory or glazed copper for jewels or the Eucharistic host.

Retable: large and ornate altarpiece divided into several painted or carved panels, especially common in Spain after the 14C.

Rib: a projecting moulding or band on the underside of a dome or vault, which may be structural or ornamental.

Rustication: deliberately rough texture of dressed and uniformly cut stone which projects from the outer wall of a building and has deeply chiselled markings. In fashion during the Renaissance.

Splay: a surface of a wall that forms an oblique angle to the main surface of a doorway or window opening.

String course: projecting ornamental band or continuous moulding that separates one floor from another.

Tambour: a circular or polygonal structure supporting a dome.

Triforium: an open gallery above the arcade of the nave, comprised mainly of three-light windows.

Vault: arched structure forming a roof or ceiling; **barrel vault**: produced by a continuous rounded arch; **cross vault**: formed by the intersection of two barrel vaults; **oven vault**: semicircular in shape, usually over apsidal chapels, the termination of a barrel-vaulted nave.

Vaulting cell: one of the four segments of a cross vault.

Volute: architectural ornament in the form of a spiral scroll.

Window cross: a stone or wooden post which divides the opening of a window or door. The vertical posts are known as **mullions**.

Medieval Period

Only a few rare, but splendid, examples survive from the Middle Ages in Rome. Supplanted by Constantinople as the capital of the Empire and invaded by barbarians, by the 6C Rome was a ruined city with barely 20 000 inhabitants. In the 10C it became the battleground in the struggle between the Pope and the German Emperor. Until the 15C only simple constructions appeared.

ARCHITECTURE

Civil architecture consisted mainly of fortresses for noble families on strategic sites (Crescenzi House, Militia Tower).

Builders quarried ancient sites for **church decoration**: capitals, friezes and columns like those in Santa Maria Maggiore, Santa Sabina, etc. As such material grew scarcer, items from different sources blended into one church (columns in San Giorgio in Velabro, Santa Maria in Cosmedin, etc).

The **basilical plan** of the early churches was retained during the medieval era. It consisted of a rectangular building divided down its length into a nave flanked by two or four aisles separated by rows of columns; one of the shorter sides contained the entrance, the other the apse (with quarter-sphere vault). Between the apse and the nave and at right angles to them ran the transept. The nave extended above the side aisles and was lit by clerestories. It was covered by a pitched roof, left open or masked by a flat ceiling in the interior. The façade was often flanked by a bell tower (*campanile*). In Rome these towers are decorated with horizontal cornices dividing them into several storeys, with white miniature columns standing out against the brickwork and ceramic insets in brilliant colours.

By the 6C a rail had been introduced separating the congregation from the clergy and creating the chancel **(presbyterium)** on either side of the bishop's throne **(cathedra),** which stood in the apse. In front were the choristers in the **schola cantorum**. Churches also often housed a **martyrium** with the relics of

Mosaic in the apse of Santa Maria in Trastevere

B. Kaufmann/MICHELIN

the saint. The high altar was covered by a baldaquin or canopy **(ciborium)**.

SCULPTURE, PAINTING AND MOSAIC

The architect and sculptor **Arnolfo di Cambio** (c 1235-c 1302) moved to Rome from Florence around 1276. He created the baldaquins in St Paul Without the Walls and in Santa Cecilia, and the statue of Charles of Anjou in the Museo del Palazzo dei Conservatori.

Frescoes and mosaics were the chief forms of medieval decoration. The Romans had a taste for anecdotes and bright colours. The period from the 12C to the 14C is dominated by the **Cosmati**, all descended from one Cosma, who formed a guild of marble workers. Their workshops used fragments of ancient materials to create beautiful floors with decorative motifs of multicoloured marble and the furniture of a medieval church: episcopal throne, *ambones* (lecterns), paschal candlesticks. The early works, composed entirely of white marble, are very simple. Later they added porphyry and serpentine marble (green) cut in geometric shapes (roundels, lozenges etc). They produced lively effects with incrustations of enamels – blue, red and gold – on the friezes and wreathed columns of cloisters.

In the latter half of the 5C, Byzantine mosaics influenced Rome's style: figures with enigmatic expressions, often richly dressed, in conventional poses, which express the mysticism of the Eastern Church through symbolism.

Carolingian art brought a less rigid fashion, for example, works dating from the reign of Paschal I (817-24) (Santa Prassede; Santa Maria in Domnica). From the 11C to 13C the Roman workshops produced sumptuous masterpieces (the apse in San Clemente). **Pietro Cavallini**, the greatest artist in this period, must have worked in Rome at the end of the 13C and early in the 14C. He was both painter and mosaicist – a master of the different influences. His pure art is best expressed through the mosaic of the life of the Virgin in Santa Maria in Trastevere and by the fresco of the Last Judgement in Santa Cecilia. **Jacopo Torriti** and **Rusuti** were disciples of his.

Renaissance Art

After almost 10 centuries of invasions and plundering, the Popes brought new life and renewed prosperity to the capital of the Roman Catholic Church, thanks to the contribution of talented artists such as Michelangelo, Bramante and Raphael. This new explosion of art

The Annunciation by Filippino Lippi – Capella Carafa

attracted wealthy patrons to the city, and the period saw the construction of a number of fine Renaissance palazzi. After the Council of Trent, the canons of religious architecture were influenced mainly by the religious orders, who created an austere, yet grandiose style. In painting, the first hints of the bold new style could be seen. The Renaissance made less impact on Rome than on Florence. At the beginning of the 15C Rome was exhausted by the struggles of the Middle Ages and had nothing to show of artistic merit. By the end of the century, the city was an important archaeological centre and was famous for its abundant artistic activity commissioned by Popes and prelates. It was **Martin V** (1417-31), the first Pope after the Great Schism, who inaugurated this brilliant period. It all ended in 1527 when troops of Charles V sacked Rome.

ARCHITECTURE

The inspiration for Roman Renaissance buildings springs from classical monuments. The Colosseum's superimposed orders and engaged columns are imitated in the court of the Farnese Palace. The vaulting of Maxentius's Basilica led to the dome of St Peter's in the Vatican. And the Pantheon's curved and triangular interior pediments have been reproduced many times.

The **churches** are austere in appearance. The nave is covered by rib vaulting and flanked by apsidal side chapels; the arms of the transept end in rounded chapels. The first domes began to appear (Santa Maria del Popolo, Sant'Agostino). The screen-like façade has two stages: one above the other linked by scrolls. Broad flat surfaces predominate; shallow pilasters are preferred to columns. The first hints of the Counter-Reformation and the Baroque can be seen through broken lines, recesses and columns progressively more accentuated.

Sixtus IV (1471-84) was responsible for the majority of the Renaissance churches: Sant'Agostino, Santa Maria del Popolo and San Pietro in Montorio were built in his reign. He founded Santa Maria della Pace and made great alterations to the Church of the Holy Apostles.

The *palazzi* were large private houses between Via del Corso and the Tiber. Pilgrims crowded these streets, alongside the feast-day papal processions from the Vatican to the Lateran: Via del Governo Vecchio, Via dei Banchi Nuovi, Via dei Banchi Vecchi, Via di Monserrato, Via Giulia, etc. They supplanted the medieval fortresses; the Palazzo Venezia, begun in 1452, has retained its crenellations. From the outside the *palazzi* are gaunt and austere (barred windows on the ground floor). The inside was designed for a cultivated life-style, associated with sculptures and paintings.

SCULPTURE AND PAINTING

After working in Rome from 1496-1501 **Michelangelo** returned in 1505 to design a tomb for Julius II. Despite the magnificent monument, the Pope, preoccupied with the construction of St Peter's, suddenly lost interest. In 1508 the Pope summoned Michelangelo back and commissioned the Sistine Chapel. The painter revolutionised the concept of religious decor and produced a huge architectural structure, dominated by powerful figures (the Prophets, Sybils and *Ignudi* or naked figures) and panels illustrating episodes from Genesis. In both his painting and sculptures, Michelangelo emphasises the human body and radically changed the way man was represented. He portrays people as grandiose and dramatically aware of their own existence: physically powerful, muscular and tormented figures.

The other artist of major importance in the Renaissance period was **Raphael**. He, too, attempted to portray pure beauty, firstly in his gentle and balanced portraits, then by using the *sfumato* technique perfected by **Leonardo da Vinci**, and finally by acquiring the anatomical mastery of Michelangelo.

In **decorative sculpture,** delicate ornamental foliage and floral motifs often appear in gold (door frames, balustrades, etc). Funeral art flourished under **Andrea Bregno** and **Andrea Sansovino**, who combined a taste for decoration with ancient architecture.

AN ARTISTIC MELTING-POT

The Renaissance style reached Rome after being developed elsewhere and all the artists came from outside the city: the Umbrians were known for their gentle touch, the Tuscans for their elegant and intellectual art and the Lombards for their rich decoration.

- **Gentile da Fabriano** and **Pisanello** were summoned to Rome in 1427 by Martin V and Eugenius IV to decorate the nave of St John Lateran (destroyed 17C-18C).

- **Masolino da Panicale**, who came from Florence, painted St Catherine's Chapel in St Clement's Basilica between 1428 and 1430.
- From 1447-1451 **Fra Angelico**, also from Florence, decorated Nicholas V's Chapel in the Vatican.
- For the painting of the Sistine Chapel walls Sixtus IV called on **Pinturicchio**, **Perugino** and **Signorelli** from Umbria and on **Botticelli**, **Ghirlandaio**, **Cosimo Rosselli** and his son **Piero di Cosimo** from Florence. He also commissioned **Melozzo da Forli** to paint the Ascension in the apse of the Church of the Holy Apostles (fine fragments in the Vatican Picture Gallery and in the Quirinal Palace).
- In about 1485 **Pinturicchio** painted the life of St Bernard in Santa d'Aracoeli and a Nativity in Santa Maria del Popolo. Between 1492 and 1494 he decorated the Borgia Apartment in the Vatican for Alexander VI.
- From 1489-1493 **Filippino Lippi** was at work on the Carafa Chapel in Santa Maria Sopra Minerva.
- **Bramante**, who arrived in 1499, designed the tempietto beside San Pietro in Montorio (1502), built the cloisters at Santa Maria della Pace (1504) and extended the choir of Santa Maria del Popolo (1505-09).
- From 1508-12 **Michelangelo** was at work painting the ceiling of the Sistine Chapel for Julius II. In 1513 he began the Pope's tomb. The *Last Judgement* was painted between 1535 and 1541 and he worked on the dome of St Peter's from 1547 until his death in 1564. His last work was the Porta Pia (1561-64).
- From 1508-11 **Baldassarre Peruzzi** built the Villa Farnesina for Agostino Chigi.
- In 1508 **Raphael** began to paint the *Stanze* in the Vatican. In 1510 he designed the plan for the Chigi Chapel in Santa Maria del Popolo. From 1511 he worked on the decoration of the Villa Farnesina for Agostino Chigi. In 1512 he painted Isaiah in Sant'Agostino and the Sibyls in Santa Maria della Pace in 1514.
- **Sodoma** arrived in Rome from Milan in 1508 to paint the ceiling of the

Signature Room in the Vatican for Julius II. He worked on the Farnesina in about 1509.

– Early in the 16C **Jacopo Sansovino** built San Giovanni dei Fiorentini for Leo X.

– In 1515 **Antonio da Sangallo the Younger** began to build the Farnese Palace; Michelangelo took over in 1546.

Counter-Reformation

The Counter-Reformation, which covered the period from the reign of Paul III (1534-49) to the reign of Urban VIII (1623-44), was marked by the sack of Rome in 1527 and by the rise of Protestantism. The movement sought to put down the heretics, restore the primacy of Rome and to rally the faithful to the Church. The Society of Jesus, formed in 1540, proved to be a most efficacious instrument in the struggle. Henceforward the influential power of art was put at the service of the Faith.

Several successes ensued – the battle of Lepanto (1571), the conversion of Henri IV of France (1593) and the Jubilee (1600) – all expressed in an artistic style which presaged the Baroque.

ARCHITECTURE

The **church style** is sometimes called **"Jesuit"** because of the comprehensive contribution made by the Society of Jesus. The architecture combines an austere solemnity with a rich marble decor: churches appeared majestic and powerful. Designed to assemble the faithful together, these structures are vast. The Gesù Church is a typical example. The nave is broad and uncluttered, so that every member of the congregation could see the altar and hear the preaching. On the façade, the plain surfaces of the Renaissance are replaced with recesses and projections and engaged columns are gradually substituted for the flat pilasters.

The most flourishing period for **civil architecture** was the early years of the Counter-Reformation, during the reigns of Paul III, Julius III, Paul IV and Pius IV, who lived like Renaissance princes. The

family illustrates the Church triumphant: Paul V acquired the Borghese Palace and built the Pauline Fountain; his nephew, Cardinal Scipione Borghese, led a cultivated life, evident from the splendours of the Palazzo Pallavicini and the "Palazzina" Borghese, which now houses the Borghese Gallery.

SCULPTURE AND PAINTING

In the spirit of the Counter-Reformation, painting had to exalt the themes rejected by the Protestants: the Virgin, the primacy of St Peter, the doctrine of the Eucharist, the cult of the saints and their intercession for the souls in purgatory.

Mannerist

Wild emotion and wit burst onto the European art scene between 1520 and 1600. This movement – perhaps best personified by Michelangelo Buonarroti – rejected the serene balance of the High Renaissance.

Figures bend, bounce and bulge muscles in paintings. Colors fly off canvases. Reference and dirty jokes lace through virtuoso compositions. Fountains play music or wheeze animal cries. Branches weave into bowers. Hydraulics mischievously squirt visitors. Mannerism (from the Italian *maniera*, "style") is all about self-conscious grandstanding.

The pranks and preening reflected the new status of artists: no longer craftsmen, they were admired as intellectuals beside scholars, poets and humanists. Some experts connect the trippy hues, illogical compression of space and convoluted poses to the upheaval of the plague, Reformation and sack of Rome in 1527.

Lazio –the area around the capital – is the epicenter of Mannerist gardens with Vignola's V**illa Lante** in Bagnaia and **Palazzo Farnese** in Caprarola and Ligorio's **Villa d'Este** in Tivoli and **Monster Park** in Bomarzo. Examples in Rome include Raphael's **Villa Madama** and the tatty remains of the Farnese garden on the Palatine hill.

In sculpture there is the work of two of Michelangelo's close followers: **Ammanati** (1511-92) and **Guglielmo della Porta** (?1500-77). The end of the period is marked by the presence in Rome of **Pietro Bernini** (1562-1629), the father of Gian Lorenzo Bernini.

Among the painters are **Daniele da Volterra,** who worked with Michelangelo, **Giovanni da Udine**, **Sermoneta**, **Francesco Penni** and **Giulio Romano**, who formed part of the "Roman School" around Raphael. The style of the next generation – **Federico** and **Taddeo Zuccari**, **Pomarancio**, **Cesare Nebbia**, **Cavaliere d'Arpino** etc – is a direct development of Raphael's art. **Barocci**, whose soft and emotional style never lapsed into affectation, deserves a special place.

In their attempts to imitate, the Mannerist painters were often guilty of excess. Their colours are pallid, as if faded by the light; fresco paintings are framed with stucco or gilding or elaborate combinations of marble; large areas are often divided into smaller panels which are easier to paint.

Reaction

Reaction to Mannerism began with the earthy and often offensive **Caravaggio**, who heralded the first signs of the Baroque, and the **Bologna group**, led by the **Carracci** who ran an academy in Bologna from 1585-95: Ludovico (1555-1619), founder of the academy, and his cousins Agostino (1557-1602) and **Annibale** (1560-1609), who were brothers. **Guido Reni** (1575-1642), **Domenichino** (1581-1641) and **Guercino** (1591-1666) tried to achieve more verity of expression without abandoning idealism.

Michelangelo Merisi (1573-1610), known as **Caravaggio** after the name of his home village near Bergamo, began to work in Rome with Cavaliere d'Arpino in 1588. But he was quarrelsome and had to flee from the city in 1606 after murdering a man over a tennis match.

Never a dull moment then, as Caravaggio swashbuckles through history beating acquaintances, murdering and fleeing the authorities. Biographer Peter Robb explains: "He is portrayed as a violent, psychotic man, but he was much more wronged than wronging. His actions were entirely defensive.

"Caravaggio was hounded from the moment he became famous. He lived in an ugly, repressive society." Robb explains that the emotion-choked paintings exploded on the "decadent, stilted world of Roman art. His vigorous, clean realism was absolutely stunning."

He claims the bad boy was harassed – and ultimately killed – for love. The traditional view holds that Caravaggio set off for Rome and a papal pardon. Arrested by mistake, he missed the boat – which contained paintings he hoped would influence his case. Enraged, he followed on foot up the coast, where he caught fever and died in the wilds.

"He was murdered. It was revenge," Robb insists. "Many mysterious and sinister things happened in the last years of his life. He slept with a sword under his bed – that is the behaviour of a hunted man... He suffered some overnight reversal of fortune in Malta, where he was celebrated. I think it was a sexual crime and that's why it has been dropped from the records."

Roman Baroque

THE STYLE

The Baroque style is characterised by its theatrical architecture, comprising a riot of concave and convex curves and twisted columns, sculptures that capture a moment of action, and are embellished by *putti* statues and golden rays, and *trompe l'oeil* ceilings suggesting non-existent domes. The dominant feature is movement, pulling the eye from façade to fountain to piazza, each sight as superb as the last. This rich, dramatic style found the perfect home in the Italian capital, evolving over the years to create its own specific quirks, now known as "Roman Baroque".

The Baroque style evolved in the 17C and 18C. Several theories expound the origin of the term: in Portuguese "*baroco*" alludes to an uneven or irregular pearl (from which the French derived the term *baroque* meaning "bizarre, eccentric, profusely decorative"). In both cases, however, the attributed meaning tends to be pejorative, deriding the conscious deviation from established rules, and canons of harmony and beauty. It was a long time before the style was re-evaluated and appreciated.

Baroque, meanwhile, enjoyed a great vogue in the papal city during the reign of Urban VIII (1623-44), becoming synonymous with the triumph of Catholicism over heresy. The Church, with its newly acquired strength and spiritual power, and the Popes, with their desire to glorify God through new works of art, attracted illustrious talent to the city.

LEADING ARTISTS

The two most important artists in the world of Roman Baroque art were **Gian Lorenzo Bernini** and **Francesco Borromini**.

Gian Lorenzo Bernini (1598-1680) was born in Naples.

Early on, Cardinal Scipione Borghese recognised Bernini's genius and commissioned sculptures for his villa (now in the Borghese Gallery). At the age of 17, he produced his first work, *Jupiter and the Goat Amalthea,* followed by the magnificent sculptural groups of the *Rape of Proserpina, Apollo and Daphne,* and *David*. On the election of Urban VIII, he was appointed official artist to the papal court and to the Barberini family. After Maderno's death in 1629, the Pope put him in charge of the rebuilding of St Peter's Basilica.

During the reign of Innocent X (1644-55), Bernini sculpted his extraordinary *Ecstasy of St Theresa* and the *Fountain of the Four Rivers* (see PIAZZA NAVONA). Under Alexander VII (1655-67), he built the church of St Andrew on the Quirinal, the colonnade enclosing St Peter's Square, redesigned St Peter's Chair and built the Royal Stair (Scala Regia) in the Vatican Palace. Eventually he was summoned to Paris by Louis XIV and his minister, Colbert, to mastermind the façade of the Cour Carrée in the Louvre, but as the King turned his attention to Versailles, Bernini's design was never carried out.

Not only an architect and sculptor, Bernini probably painted hundred pictures, of which only a few have survived. He produced a great deal of work, rose rapidly and was very successful.

His genius was recognised in his lifetime and he received many decorations; his contemporaries saw in him another Michelangelo. He was welcome in the most brilliant circles; he put on plays for his friends, designing the stage sets, writing the words and playing a role. He was fleetingly eclipsed by Borromini when Innocent X succeeded Urban VIII, but soon returned to favour with his *Fountain of the Four Rivers*.

Francesco Borromini (1599-1667) was the son of Giovanni Domenico Castelli, an architect to the Visconti family in Milan. He trained as a stonemason and acquired great technical experience. The artist worked as Carlo Maderno's assistant on St Peter's, Sant'Andrea della Valle and the Barberini Palace. In 1625, he received the title of *maestro* and in 1628 took his mother's name: Borromini. He based his art on rigour and sobriety, excluding marble decorations and paintings. In Borromini's art, the Baroque style is expressed by architectural lines that he cut and curved with a sure hand. As an architect, he was critical of Bernini's over-dramatic and excessive style. Unsurprisingly, the two artists were supported by different patrons: the papal court favoured Bernini; Borromini's style agreed mainly with the religious orders, such as the Trinitarians and the followers of St Philip Neri.

San Carlo alle Quattro Fontane, Borromini's first full-scale work, probably shows his genius at its best (1638, although he envisioned the façade much later, in the year when he died). At the same period, he designed the Oratory of St Philip Neri, typical of his original and balanced style. Around 1643 he built the small church of Sant'Ivo alla Sapienza, with its convex and concave curves culminating in a multi-lobed cupola. These projects earned him the protection of Fra Spada, who became Innocent X's adviser. The Pope raised him to the first rank and appointed him to renovate St John Lateran for the Jubilee of 1650.

Borromini, an introvert who shunned the world, lived in constant anxiety and never knew the fame enjoyed by his rival. One night, in a fit of anguish and anger against his servant, he took his own life. Other architects worked in Rome at that period. **Carlo Maderno**, responsible for the façades of St Peter's and Santa

Susanna, and **Giacomo della Porta**, probably the most active architect around 1580, were both great admirers of Michelangelo and are often included among the Mannerists. **Flaminio Ponzio** worked for the Borghese (front of their palace, Pauline Fountain). **Giovanni Battista Soria** designed the façades of Santa Maria della Vittoria and St Gregory the Great. The well-proportioned architecture of **Pietro da Cortona** is most attractive (St Luke and St Martina, the façade of Santa Maria in Via Lata, the dome of San Carlo al Corso). In contrast with the dramatic architecture of Bernini and Borromini, this artist took his inspiration from the 16C models of Bramante and Palladio. He paid particular attention to the position of his work in an urban context (the façade of Santa Maria della Pace). The name of **Carlo Rainaldi** deserves to be remembered for his work in Santa Maria in Campitelli (1655-65) and for his arrangement of the "twin" churches in the Piazza del Popolo, which frame the entrance to Via del Corso.

Baroque Art

An inherent quality of Baroque art is restlessness – movement and contrast. Water, with its undulations and reflection, was an essential element. Effects dazzled from expensive materials, such as marble and precious stones. Cesare Ripa's dictionary, which appeared in 1594, explained how to express an abstract idea – even in stone.

In **architecture**, building plans hoped to express movement (San Carlo alle Quattro Fontane, Sant'Andrea al Quirinale). Façades were embellished with disengaged columns, bold projections, curved contours and recesses.

Flowing garments and figures expressing abstract qualities dominated **sculpture**. The altarpieces are decorated with pictures of marble and wreathed columns; the latter, a feature of ancient Roman art, were very popular with Bernini (baldaquin in St Peter's). Church interiors are full of cherubs perched on pediments and cornices.

In addition to the sculptors associated with Bernini (Antonio Raggi, Ercole Ferrata, Francesco Mochi, etc), mention must be made of **Alessandro Algardi** (1592-1654), inspired by classical art; he produced remarkable portraits and marble pictures, including the funerary monument of Leo XI in St Peter's.

Baroque **painters** sought to achieve effects of perspective and *trompe-l'œil* with spiralling or diagonal compositions. They included **Pietro da Cortona**, an architect, as well as an interior designer, whose masterpiece is the fresco depicting the triumph of the Barberini family in the palace of the same name. Also worthy of note is Giovanni Battista Gaulli. Known as **Baciccia**, he was a Bernini protégé who frescoed the Chiesa del Gesù ceiling. The artist **Giovanni**

Ceiling by Andrea Pozzo in Sant'Ignazio

B. Kaufmann/ MICHELIN

Sant'Ivo alla Sapienza

Lanfranco (1582-1647), from Parma, painted the dome of Sant'Andrea della Valle with great technical skill. **Andrea Pozzo**, a Jesuit, who was a painter, studied the theory of architecture and had a passion for *trompe-l'œil*. The best expression of which is without a doubt his fresco on the ceiling of the church of Sant'Ignazio: it is hard to believe that the cupola figured here is only an illusion. His book *Prospettiva de' pittori e architetti* appeared in 1693 and circulated throughout Europe.

Rome attracted artists of all nationalities. Rubens made several visits; he admired Michelangelo, the Carracci and Caravaggio and completed the apse paintings of the New Church. During his long stay, Velazquez painted a fine portrait of Innocent X (*now in the Galleria Doria Pamphili*).

Classicism

The 18C etchings of Piranesi don't always resonate now. After 1870, in an attempt to fulfil its role as the new-minted capital, the city spewed forth vast new residential districts. During the Fascist period, the layout transformed further. Buildings such as the Law Courts ("*palazzaccio*"), the monument to Victor Emmanuel II (the "wedding-cake" or "typewriter"), and the Palazzo delle Cività del Lavoro

("square colosseum") may initially have been un-popular, but they now form a familiar backdrop.

NEO-CLASSICISM

This trend developed from the middle of the 18C until the early 19C and was marked by a return to Greek and Roman architecture, recently re-discovered during the excavations of Herculaneum, Pompeii and Paestum. Following Baroque exuberance, neo-classicism was characterised by simplicity and symmetry, even a touch of frigidity. This was the period when Winckelmann, who was Librarian at the Vatican and in charge of Roman antiquities, published his works on art. Francesco Milizia launched his criticism of the Baroque and superfluous decoration, while praising the simplicity and nobility of ancient monuments.

Piranesi (1720-78), engraver and architect, took up permanent residence in Rome in 1754. He produced some 2 000 engravings, including the series "Views of Rome", published in 1750: an incomparable collection full of charm and melancholy. He also designed the attractive Piazza dei Cavalieri di Malta.

Antonio Canova (1757-1821) was the showy talent at this time and Napoleon's favourite sculptor. His works' calm regularity enchanted his contemporaries.

In architecture, mention should be made of **Giuseppe Valadier**, who laid out Piazza del Popolo (1816-20). While non-Italians, such as the German Mengs and the French at the Villa Medici, stand out in painting (*see PIAZZA DI SPAGNA*).

The end of the 19C saw artists – such as Cesare Maccari (frescoes in the Palazzo Madama) and Guilio Aristide Sartorio (frieze in the chamber of the Parliament building) – working in Rome.

MODERN ART

An exponent of Roman Futurism, **Giacomo Balla** (1861-1958) moved to Rome in 1895. With Fortunato Depero, he signed the 1915 manifesto of the "Futurist Reconstruction of the Universe"; after 1930 his painting reverted to pre-Futurist themes. Other important artists were **Mario Mafai** (1902-65) and **Gino Bon-**

Gigantic statues of athletes in the Stadio dei Marmi, Foro Italico

ichi (also known as Scipione) (1904-33), members of the Roman School, which Renato Guttuso joined in 1931. The major developments in both painting and sculpture can be seen in the National Gallery of Modern Art.

ARCHITECTURE AND TOWN PLANNING

For its first 20 years as the capital of Italy, Rome was a building site. The town plans of 1871 and 1883 provided for the construction of housing for the new civil servants around Piazza Vittorio Emanuele, Piazza dell'Independenza, at Castro Pretorio and in the Prati; for the demolition of the slum districts of the inner city; for the construction of administrative buildings; for the establishment of banks and newspapers; and for the provision of arterial roads. Via del Corso and Via Nazionale, which were opened soon after the inclusion of Rome in the kingdom of Italy, were followed by Corso Vittorio Emanuele II and Via XX Settembre.

First Quarter of the 20C

The government undertook more public works. In 1902, the Humbert I tunnel linked the Quirinal and the business centre. Extensive parks, formerly the private property of the great families, opened or, like the Villa Ludovisi, sold as building lots for residential development. Romans constructed the Tiber embankment and cut away the Campidoglio to make room for the monument to Victor Emmanuel II. The International Exhibition in 1911 developed the district around Piazza Mazzini , while a benefactor contributed a huge museum of modern art in a leafy setting. The year 1920 brought the beginning of the garden suburbs: near to Monte Sacro in the north and at Garbatella in the south.

Mussolini's Rome

The arrival of Mussolini in 1922 ushered in a policy of grandiose town planning linked to the Fascist ideology which favoured a return to Ancient grandeur. Three new streets – Corso del Rinascimento, Via della Botteghe Oscure and Via del Teatro di Marcello – were opened up to allow traffic to penetrate the Campus Martius. Via dei Fori Imperiali was opened in 1932 to give a clear view of the Colosseum from Piazza Venezia. The reconciliation of the Church and State, sealed in the Lateran Treaty in 1929, was marked by the opening of Via della Conciliazione (1936) to the detriment of the medieval district of the Borgo. As it had been decided that Rome should expand towards the sea, construction began on the new district known as EUR.

From the Second World War to the Present Day

The Holy Year in 1950, when masses of pilgrims were expected, saw the completion of both Via Cristoforo Colombo and the railway station (Stazione Termini). The Flaminia Stadium, the small Sports Palace in Via Flaminia and the Sports Palace in EUR were built for the 1960 Olympic Games. The Olympic Village in Via Flaminia was built on a site cleared of old run-down housing. Corso di Francia, a wide elevated highway, is also a daring piece of architectural design. In the west, Via Olimpica connects the Foro Italico to EUR. In 1961 the international airport at Fiumicino (Leonardo da Vinci) was built to complement the existing one at Ciampino. In 1970 the main orbital road round the city (Grande Raccordo Anulare – 70km/44mi) was finished.

Among Rome's modern buildings, mention should be made of the RAI block (▶ *see MONTE MARIO*), the British Embassy (▶ *see PORTA PIA*), buildings in EUR, the Chamber for Papal Audiences built by Pier Luigi Nervi in 1971 and the Gregorian

The Grand Tour

A continental tour of one or two years, culminating in a visit to Rome, was a pecu-liarly British custom which lasted 300 years, reaching its height in the 18C when the Grand Tour formed part of a gentleman's education. A young man would set out with a tutor, known as a "bear leader", who would superintend his studies, protect him from bad company and show him the sights. On arriving in Rome, preferably at Easter time, these early tourists would set out "equipped with all things needful to measure the dimensions of the antiquities they would be shown". It was impor-tant to engage a good guide such as Winckelmann, a German archaeologist, who was superintendent of antiquities in Rome, or Gavin Hamilton, who became well known as a dealer and antiquary. The tour had great influence at home on man-ners, architectural style and the formation of art collections. Lord Burlington, the arbiter of good taste in the early 18C, made two tours, which led to his patronage of William Kent and the introduction of the Palladian style into England.

Many English artists studied in Rome: Richard Wilson (1752-56); Sir Joshua Reynolds (1750-52); and Sir George Romney (1773-75), whose portraits show the influence of the Classical style in their backgrounds and draperies; John Flaxman, the sculptor (1787-94), nicknamed the "English Michelangelo", who encouraged John Gibson to become a pupil of Canova. Benjamin West (1760-63) and John Copley (1774) from America visited Rome before settling in London.

In the 19C, instead of the established tour of the most famous cities, works of art and monuments, with its accent on antiquities, visitors preferred to settle in less well-known towns, taking an interest in Italian life and customs and even in the nationalist movement. Charles Dickens visited Rome in 1845 while writing a travel book, Pictures of Italy.

Rome provided poetic inspiration: in May 1817 **Byron** toured the ruins gathering material for the Fourth Canto of Childe Harold; **Shelley** composed Prometheus Unbound and The Cenci while lodging in the Corso in 1819; in 1860 Robert and Elizabeth Barrett Browning made a visit to Rome which inspired his greatest work, The Ring and the Book, a poem based on a 17C Roman murder trial.

Rome still attracted many artists: Eastlake made invaluable purchases of early Italian art for the National Gallery in London; Turner visited Rome twice (1819, 1828) and used quotations from Childe Harold as titles for his paintings. From America came William Page (1849-60), who painted portraits of Robert and Elizabeth Browning; he had trained under Samuel Morse, an artist who studied in Europe in 1832 and invented the electric telegraph.

Many American writers visited Rome: Washington Irving (1804-06), Fenimore Cooper (1820-27), Longfellow (1828), Hermann Melville (1856-57), Nathaniel Hawthorne (1858-59) and Mark Twain (1867), while collecting material for Innocents Abroad. Most famous of all was Henry James, who first visited Italy in 1869; his first impor-tant novel was set in Rome.

Profane and Christian Museums (both in the Vatican), and the more recent structures by American architect Richard Maier (the *Ara Pacis* museum and the Church of Tor tre Teste) and Italian Renzo Piano (Rome Auditorium).

Literature

Rome has long been a popular subject for foreign writers , detailed by travellers such as Mark Twain, Stendhal and Goethe. However, perhaps the best portraits of this fascinating and contrasting city appear in the satire of the Roman author Bellini, or more recently in the complex novels of Alberto Moravia.

Rome's contribution to Italian literature is an important one. Over a period spanning at least seven centuries (from the 3C BC to the famous sack of Rome in AD 410), Latin literature flourished. The different literary genres included epics, by writers such as **Ennius** (239-169 BC), **Virgil** (70-19 BC), **Lucan** (39-65) and **Statius** (40-96); comic dramas by **Plautus** (?250-184 BC) and **Terence** (?184-?159 BC; satirical works by **Lucilius** (?168-102 BC), **Horace** (65-8 BC) and **Juvenal** (2C AD); didactic poetry by **Lucretius** (?98-?55 BC); love poetry by **Catullus** (87-?55 BC), **Propertius** (97-16 BC), **Tibullus** (55-19 BC) and **Ovid** (43 BC-AD 17); rhetorical and philosophical prose by **Cicero** (106-43 BC) and **Seneca** (?4 BC-AD 65); and romances by **Petronius** (2C AD) and **Apuleius** (AD 125-180).

Historians have left fascinating accounts. **Caesar** (100-44 BC) wrote about his own military campaigns in *The Gallic Wars* and *The Civil War*. Two monographs by **Sallust** (86-35 BC) have survived, the *Bellum Lugurthinum* (an account of the war in Numidia from 105-11 BC) and the *Bellum Catilinae*, on the Catiline conspiracy of 63 BC, which was also the subject of four famous orations by **Cicero** (known as the *Catilinarie*). These works, along with others by the same author (such as the *Pro Murena* and *Pro Milone*), paint an illuminating picture of the political climate during this period of the Republic.

Other annalistic works include the *Libri Ab Urbe Condita* by **Livy** (59 BC-AD 17), containing vivid descriptions of events that took place between the founding of the city and the 9C BC (of which about 30 books have survived intact), and the *Annales* (a history of the period from the death of Augustus to that of Nero) and *Historiae* (the period from Galba to Domitian) by **Tacitus** (55-117).

These official histories are complemented by the *Lives of the Caesars* (from Julius Caesar to Domitian) by **Suetonius** (?70-?125) – a kind of biography – and the 10 books of the *Epistulae* by **Pliny the Younger** (61-113), letters on a range of themes written to characters of the time, including the Emperor Trajan, which are fascinating for their portrait of high society during the Imperial era. In contrast, **Petronius** paints a grotesque and parodistic portrait of this society in his *Satiricon* (brilliantly adapted for cinema by the director Fellini).

From the Middle Ages Rome gradually lost her supremacy in the literary arts to other cities in Italy (especially Florence). Not until the founding of the Roman Academy by **Pomponio Leto** (1428-97) did the city regain literary eminence. This role was consolidated by the **Arcadia Society**, founded in 1690 by **Giambattista Felice Zappi** (1667-1719) and his wife Faustina Maratti (1680-1745). This society, situated at the time on the Janiculum Hill, championed a style reminiscent of the *Canzoniere* by Petrarch, as opposed to the Baroque "bad taste" of the 17C. Among the main exponents of this style were **Paolo Rolli** (1687-1785) and **Pietro Metastasio** (1698-1782). The latter was appointed official poet at the Imperial court in Vienna and his melodramas, such as *Catone in Utica* and *Dido Abandoned*, met with notable success both in Italy and abroad.

The city played a marginal role in cultural debate during the Enlightenment, a movement that greatly influenced Milan and Naples. Writers who visited Rome seemed to appreciate its unique nature, which gave rise to extremes of high praise or fierce condemnation. Although **Goethe** hurled abuse at the noise in Via del Corso during the Carnival, he confessed that he felt reborn the day he arrived in Rome (*Italianische Reise – Italian Journey*). **Mark Twain** did not look

BOOKS

Rome has long been a favourite subject with writers of all nationalities. The selection below includes recommendations of guide books, fiction and historical works on the city.

Art and Architecture

Roman Building Jean Pierre Adam (Routledge 1999)
Roman Art and Architecture Sir Mortimer Wheeler (Thames & Hudson 1964)
A Handbook of Roman Art: A Survey of the Visual Arts of the Roman World Martin Henig (Phaidon 1995)
Roman Imperial Architecture JB Ward Perkings (Penguin 1981)
Lives of the Artists G Vasari (Penguin Classics 1965, 1987 [2 vols])
The Italian Painters of the Renaissance B Berenson (Ursus Press 1999)

Commentaries and Fiction

Pictures from Italy Charles Dickens (1846, Penguin Books 1998)
Italian Journey Wolfgang Goethe (1788, Penguin Books 1970)
Italian Hours Henry James (1909, Penguin Books 1995)
Daisy Miller Henry James (1878, Penguin Books 1986)
The Child of Pleasure Gabriele d'Annunzio (1889, Dedalus Ltd 1990)

History

A History of Italy Stuart Woolf (Routledge 1979, 1991)
A Traveller's History of Italy Valerio Lintner (The Windrush Press 1989, 1993)
Roman Society D Dudley (Penguin 1991)
The Romans: An Introduction to their History and Civilization K Christ (University of Chicago Press 1985 [translated from German])
Rome: Its People, Life and Customs UE Paoli (Bristol Classical Press 1990 [translated from Italian])
Renaissance Rome: 1500-59 P Partner (University of Chicago Press 1980)
The Counter Reformation AG Dickens (Thames & Hudson 1969)
The Risorgimento and the Unification of Italy D Beales (Addison Wesley Longman Higher Education 1982)
Italy in the Age of the Risorgimento H Hearder (Addison Wesley Longman Higher Education 1983)
The Pope and the Duce PC Kent (Macmillan Press Ltd 1981)

Jubilee

The Holy Year in Rome: Past and Present EM Jung-Inglessis (International Scholars Publications 1998)
Pilgrims at Prayer (Cassell 1999)
Pilgrims in Rome (Cassell 1999)
Pilgrims at Prayer: The Official Vatican Prayerbook for the Jubilee Year 2000 (Continuum Publishing Company 1999)

People

Stories of Rome Livy, translated by R Nicholls (1982)
The Caesars Allan Massie (Sceptre 1994)
The Italians Luigi Barzini (Penguin 1964, 1991)
Romans, their Lives and Times Michael Sheridan (Phoenix Paperbacks 1995)
Rome, the Biography of a City Christopher Hibbert (Penguin 1995)
The New Italians Charles Richards (Penguin 1995)

Useful Guides

Guide to the Vatican Museums; Guide to the Vatican City (Monumenti, Musei e Gallerie Pontificie)
The Companion Guide to Rome Georgina Masson (Companion Guides 1998)

favourably on the papacy or its superstitious trappings. He claimed that walking through the streets of Rome it was difficult to believe in the city's magnificent past (*The Innocents Abroad*). **Leopardi** had a deeply disturbing impression of the city at the beginning of the 19C; he saw it as somehow shut in, lacking in imagination, and full of "quite repulsive" women. **Giuseppe Gioacchino Belli** (1791-1863) wrote in dialect, using popular themes similar to those of the Romantic movement. Belli wrote over 2 000 sonnets (*sonetti*), which portray the life of the common people, using the language and vocabulary of the lower social classes. He succeeds in painting a clear picture of Roman society, divided between the aristocracy and clerics on the one hand, and the "plebs" on the other, interspersed with occasional references to folklore. Another author who wrote in the Roman dialect was Carlo Alberto Salustri, better known as **Trilussa** (1873-1950), whose colourful and witty works describe popular dissatisfaction with the Fascist regime of the time.

A superb evocation of Rome is found in *Il Piacere* (1889) by **Gabriele D'Annunzio**. The author describes 16C courts and sumptuously decorated Baroque palaces in great detail, providing the backdrop for the elegant receptions and grand banquets held by high society. Places appear as symbols of the various characters, so that the city almost becomes a protagonist in the novel.

Two other leading lights of the city were **Vincenzo Cardarelli** (1887-1959) and **Antonio Baldini** (1889-1962) who produced the magazine *La Ronda* between 1919 and 1923.

Among contemporary writers, **Alberto Moravia** (1907-90) described the apathy and inadequacy of Rome's bourgeoisie in *Gli Indifferenti* and *La Noia*, and put forward a clear portrayal of the lower echelons of Italian society in *La Romana*, *Raconti romani* and *La Ciociara* (successfully adapted for the cinema by De Sica). During WWII, author **Elsa Morante** hid in villages south of Rome with Moravia. Thirty years later, in 1974, she based a sweeping novel on this fugitive existence. The story revolves around Ida Mancuso: widowed, raped and abandoned, yet resilient. As *Esquire* reviewer Alfred Kazan observed, *History* is "one of the few novels in any language that renders the full horror of Hitler's war, the war that never gets into the books".

Born and educated in Milan, **Carlo Emilio Gadda** (1893-1973) owed some of his fame to a novel based in Rome, entitled *Quer pasticciaccio brutto de via Merulana* (1946). The title translates literally as "That Awful Mess on Via Merulana". The novel effectively portrays Rome during the Fascist period, set around events taking place in 1927 and depicting all strata of society, from the bourgeoisie to the working class. Much of the novel's success lies in its use of the Roman dialect, for which Gadda consulted with friends who were experts on the subject, resulting in a new, bold and original mix of language.

An important figure in the cultural world of the 1960s and 1970s was **Pier Paolo Pasolini** (1922-75), also not orginally from Rome. This widely debated figure was a poet, novelist, critic, film director and dramatist. He portrayed a sadly realistic picture of the Roman underclass in *Ragazzi di vita* and *Una vita violenta*.

For a wide array of writing about the city, turn to *Smiles of Rome*. Editor Susan Cahill compiled this Literary Companion. Sample Freud on Michelangelo, Edith Wharton on the Villa Borghese and **Eleanor Clark**, author of the classic travelogue *Rome and a Villa*, on the Pyramid of Cestius in the Protestant Cemetery (where the remains of both Keats and Shelley lie).

Cinema

Rome has always provided the perfect backdrop for the big screen and for a few decades it was also home to the most important film studios in Europe, **Cinecittà**. (The name, pronounced cheenay chee-TAH, means "cinema city"). The Fascist dictator Benito Mussolini founded the lot in 1937, aping Hitler's and Stalin's propaganda machines. Set on the Via Tuscolano (see *CASTELLI ROMANI*), the studios covered an area of 600 000m²/6 456 000sq ft and housed 16 film sets, offices, restaurants, a huge pool for shooting water scenes and all the latest technology and gadgetry. These state-of-the-art facilities contributed to an increase in domestic film production, which was now completely autonomous. In the first six years, some 300 films were produced here –and not all were Fascist boosterism. "Black" films championed the cause, while middle-class melodramas – called "white telephone" after that ubiquitous prop – peddled escapism.

Cinecittà is also the cradle of neo-realism (the Italian School of *cinéma vérité*). Although films of this type are usually shot outside, giants like **Vittorio de Sica** and **Roberto Rossellini** did make some of their earliest works in the studios. The main theme of the neo-realists was the war and all its tragic consequences. In *Roma città aperta* (1945), *Paisà* (1946) and *Germania anno zero* (1948), Rossellini portrayed Nazi-Fascist oppression. De Sica, in *Sciuscià* (1946) and *Ladri di Biciclette* (1948), drew a portrait of post-war unemployment and misery. In *Riso amaro* (1949) and *Pasqua di Sangue* (1950), **De Santis** described a working class divided between submission to the dominant ideology and revolutionary aspirations.

The government began discouraging left-leaning productions in the 1950s. Gritty truths gave way to gloss, earning Cinecittà the nickname "Hollywood on the Tiber". Cheap and cheerful, the studio fostered American feature films like *Roman Holiday, The Quiet American, Ben Hur, Quo Vadis?* and *The Pink Panther*. Elizabeth Taylor first met her great love, Richard Burton, while filming *Cleopatra* here. And the world learned what to call the photographers pursuing the pair – *paparazzi* – thanks to **Federico Fellini**'s *La Dolce Vita*. The director captured many of the Eternal City's most enduring cinematic images, including Anita Ekberg and Marcello Mastroianni in the Trevi Fountain, and the bubble-headed fabulousness of the Via Veneto. He shunned locations and constructed lavish foam copies of monuments, including St Peter's cupola, on the lot (Soundstage Five, Europe's largest, was his preferred workspace for four decades). He considered the studio a temple of dreams: "For me, every journey starts and ends at the studios of Cinecittà... It's my ideal world, the cosmic space before the Big Bang".

For Italian cinema, the 1960s were a golden age. Supported by a powerful industrial infrastructure, the studios produced more than 200 films a year – and of the best quality. **Luchino Visconti** was a key player during this era. His early work focused mainly on themes relating to social injustice. Later films examined the decadence and disenchantment of the middle classes. Among his masterpieces were *Ossessione* (1943), *Notti bianche* (1957) and *Ludwig* (1972).

Sound of the cinema

"Mussolini didn't want to hear any foreign languages, so we started dubbing," Francesco Vairano – one of the nation's top dubbing directors – told *The Walrus Magazine*. Indeed, today *versioni originali* are scarce: Italians, quite rightly, fell in love with the sound of their own voices. The mouthpieces of the stars often become celebrities in their own right, like Giuseppe Rinaldi, the rugged voice of Marlon Brando, Robert Redford and Paul Newman. Emilio Cigoli gritted out lines for both John Wayne and Clark Gable. Oreste Lionello capered as Woody Allen. Greta Garbo even wrote a fan letter to her Italian songbird, actress Tina Latenzi.

Laurel and Hardy rode dubbing to new heights of success in this country. Originally mouthed by Italian-American actors, the soundtrack produced much hilarity in the olde worlde. So the pair remained in dialect, while the supporting cast purred fluently. A nation-wide contest appointed Alberto Sordi the bumpkin-emigrant voice of Ollie. By the time this comic actor died in 2003, he'd starred in almost 200 films, including Fellini's *I Vitelloni*. Soldi was so popular, Rome appointed him mayor for a day on his 80th birthday – and 250,000 locals mourned at his funeral.

The 1960s also brought a new generation of directors keen to record their political and social commitment, such as **Pasolini**, **Rosi** and **Bertolucci**. During the same period, the work of **Sergio Leone**, who produced a vast quantity of "spaghetti westerns", also kept the studios at Cinecittà in the limelight.

From the 1970s into the 90s, Italian cinema suffered a crisis, both in terms of production and creativity, which only a few *films d'auteur* managed to resist. Among the most recent are *La Famiglia* (1987) by **Ettore Scola**, *Caro Diario* (1994) and *La Stanza del Figlio* (2001) by **Nanni Moretti**, none of which were produced at Cinecittà. In 1997, the government sold the ailing studio to private companies, captained by Diego Della Valle, who runs JP Tod's, the Italian shoe company. A $25m infusion attracted Martin Scorsese's *Gangs of New York* (2002) and Mel Gibson's *The Passion of Christ* (2004), among other high-profile projects, but the studio still struggles. And computers threaten its strong suits: superb artisans and space for replica worlds. As Cinecittà celebrates its 70th birthday in 2007, big hopes lie with special-effects technology, pay-per-view television and a proposed theme park.

ITALIAN FILMS

Rome was a favourite venue for directors of Italian neo-realist films during the late 1940s and the city continues to be a popular backdrop for Italian cinema today. Below is a list of well-known movies that were shot in the capital.

Roma, città aperta by R Rossellini, 1945. A portrayal of the Italian Resistance in Nazi-occupied Rome. This film represents a landmark in the history of Italian cinema, with a memorable performance by Anna Magnani.

Ladri di biciclette by V de Sica, 1948. This film depicts the working-class districts of Rome in the post-war period, when a bicycle represented survival. Another masterpiece of neo-realism.

Domenica d'agosto by L Emmer, 1949. Episodes from daily life taking place at the same time on a Sunday in August on the road leading from Rome to the beach in Ostia.

Roman Holiday by W Wyler, 1953. This brilliant comedy tells the story of a princess discovering Rome on the back of a Vespa, in the company of a journalist. A delightful performance by Audrey Hepburn.

Le notti di Cabiria by F Fellini, 1957. Giulietta Masina stars in this extraordinary tale of a prostitute who dreams of true love, surrounded by exploiters and cynics.

Poveri ma belli by D Risi, 1958. This entertaining film features cars, beautiful women, parties and music from the 1950s, as well as Marisa Allasio, a famous actress of the time.

I soliti ignoti by M Monicelli, 1958. A group of unemployed, penniless youths organise the robbery of a security firm in this realistic portrayal of poverty in the 1950s.

Fantasmi a Roma by A Pietrangeli, 1960. This clever surrealist comedy recounts the story of four ghosts who succeed in saving an old palazzo from demolition.

La dolce vita by F Fellini, 1960. Delightful shots of Rome serve as a backdrop to the portrayal of an empty-headed generation with little interest in anything other than forgetting the past and enjoying themselves.

Satyricon by F Fellini, 1969. A satirical portrayal of the decadence of the Roman Empire, based on Petronius.

Roma by F Fellini, 1971. An autobiographical journey of the great Fellini shot in the city that served as a backdrop to his earliest films.

C'eravamo tanto amati by E Scola, 1974. Three friends who were in the Resistance together meet up again in Rome years later and bitterly compare their loss of hope and illusions.

In nome del papa re by L Magni, 1977. This splendid film portrays corruption and violence in the Papal Court during the final years of the Papal States, with a magnificent performance by Nino Manfredi.

Un borghese piccolo piccolo by M Monicelli, 1977. Alberto Sordi in one

Rooftops of the Eternal City

B. Morandi/MICHELIN

of his few dramatic performances in this film about a father who takes justice into his own hands after his son is killed in an armed robbery.

Una giornata particolare by E Scola, 1977. This film tells the story of an intense relationship between a resigned housewife (Sophia Loren) and a homosexual anti-fascist (Marcello Mastroianni) on the day in May 1938 when Hitler visited Rome and was welcomed by Mussolini.

Un sacco bello by C Verdone, 1979. One of the first comedies in Roman cinema. The three episodes of this film portray an average man from Rome, with all his faults and qualities.

Bianca by N Moretti, 1983. Nanni Moretti brings a hint of subtle irony to his portrayal of a high school teacher in search of himself, as he attempts to reconcile his ideals with reality.

Caro Diario by N Moretti, 1994. One of the three episodes that make up this film is a wonderful autobiographical trip through Rome by scooter. Entertaining and full of irony.

La parola amore esiste by M Calopresti, 1998. A story of loneliness, love and psychological hardship, made by one of the up-and-coming directors in Italian cinema.

The Talented Mr. Ripley by A Minghella, 1999. Remake of the classic novel, starting Matt Damon as Tom Ripley, a loner who takes over the life of playboy Dickie Greenleaf (Jude Law). The gripping thriller also stars Gwyneth Paltrow as Dickie's girlfriend.

Gangs of New York by M Scorcese, 2002. The great director's exploration of the development of Irish gangs in 19th century New York. Largely filmed in Cinecittà, the film stars Daniel Day-Lewis and Leonardo DiCaprio.

Ocean's 12 by S Soderbergh, 2004. This sequel to the 2001 caper finds the gang (including George Clooney, Brad Pitt, and Matt Damon) atempting three European heists in Rome, Amsterdam, and Paris. Things won't be that easy this time, however, with a rival thief (Vincent Cassel) and a beautiful Europol agent (Catherine Zeta-Jones) out to foil their plans.

The Passion of the Christ by M Gibson, 2004. A depiction of the last twelve hours in the life of Jesus Christ, filmed in the ancient language of Aramaic.

Rome 2005. This HBO miniseries chronicles the families of two Roman soldiers living during the reign of Julius Caesar. Filmed entirely in Rome and Cinecittà.

The Third Mother by D Argento, 2007 In the final trilogy installment, an American art student unwittingly opens an ancient urn that unleashes the world's most powerful witch.

- a. *Charming guesthouse*
- b. *Room for 50€ or less per night*
- c. *That little extra, not to be missed*

Can't decide ?

Then simply open a copy of Michelin Guide Charming Places in France !

- Hotels and guesthouses offering value for money
- Regionally based selection
- Establishments offering wining and dining breaks
- Establishments offering activity breaks
- Regional maps with establishments pinpointed for easy reference

The pleasure of travel with Michelin Maps and Guides.

*Piazza del Popolo from
the Pincian Hill*
G. Bludzin/MICHELIN

APPIA ANTICA★★

MICHELIN MAP 38 U 15 TO W 15-16

METRO LINE A: SAN GIOVANNI

The Old Appian Way is a narrow road, flanked by rows of graceful pine trees, ruins and ancient tombs. It runs through a semi-rural oasis, spared the prolific construction seen elsewhere around Rome. With its catacombs and the Quo Vadis Church, the "Queen of Roads" is an important part of Christian history.

Information: *www.parcoappiaantica.org.*

▶ **Orient Yourself:** Mon-Sat the Old Appian Way is accessible by car only as far as the tomb of Cecilia Metella; beyond that, visitors must walk or cycle. City buses service the Via Appia Antica. The **110** loops from the Viale Aventino out to the Porta Domine Quo Vadis and Catacombe di San Calisto, among other stops. The **218** runs a similar route from Piazza San Giovanni, stopping at the Fosse Ardeatine. The **660** circuits between metro at Colli Albani and the Tomba di Cecilia Metella. The petite **Archeobus** makes hourly stops at 14 sites, running from Termini Station to the Baths of Caracalla, along the Via Appia Antica to the Villa dei Quintili and the Parco degli Aquedotti (reserve ahead, as the shuttle fills quickly. ⏱Open June–Sept 9.45am–4.45pm; Oct–May 9.45am–3.45pm. ✆€10. ☎06 469 54695. www.trambusopen.com

Parking: Various lots dot the green pastureland. Try the Largo Martiri Fosse Ardeatine for the catacombs; the Via Arco di Travertino for the Via Latina tombs and Via Lemonia for the Parco degli Acquedotti. Sundays are car-free. However, police allow access to *Le Catacombe di San Callisto,* a museum.

Don't Miss: The most interesting part of the Old Appian Way (*Via Appia Antica*) passes the catacombs and the nearby ancient monuments (Romulus's Tomb, Maxentius's Circus and the tomb of Cecilia Metella). The catacombs of St Callistus, St Sebastian and Domitilla are particularly worthy of note.

Organizing Your Time: Allow half a day (3hr for the catacombs of St Callistus, St Sebastian and Domitilla). Best days to visit are Thu, Fri and Sat, when all the monuments and catacombs are open. Guides lead speedy tours; follow closely or risk getting lost in the gloom.

Kids: Bike rides along the ancient highway. Rentals cluster around the *Sede il Parco* (Park Seat), which itself charges €10 a day or €3 per hour for the first three hours (Sun and holidays, open from 10am–6pm; ☎06 512 6314).

Also See: The itinerary can be combined with an excursion to the *CASTELLI ROMANI* by turning left into Via Casal Rotondo and taking Appia Nuova (no 7) towards the *Grande Raccordo Anulare* (GRA) – Albano.

A Bit of History

The first-century poet Publius Papinius Statius dubbed this the *regina viarum* (Queen of Roads). The route once stretched from the city's core to Brindisi on the Adriatic coast, where ships sailed east, forming the umbilicus of the Empire. All its citizens – living and dead – mingled here. Tombs and monuments to notable citizens line the ramrod-straight "highway of antiquity".

The Via Appia is familiar from the saga of Spartacus. The charismatic ex-gladi-ator led a slave revolt, known as the Third Servile War, and defeated many Roman legions. After his defeat, some 6,000 crucified slaves lined the Via Appia all the way to Capua.

In the Middle Ages the Appian Way became unsafe; members of the Caetani family converted the tomb of Cecilia Metella into a fortress and plundered passing travellers. This led to the opening of the New Appian Way. Late in the 17C the Old and New Appian Ways were linked by the Via Appia Pignatelli.

The Catacombs

In medieval Rome the Latin expression *"ad catacumbas"* referred to St Sebastian's Cemetery, which lay in a hollow beside the Appian Way. When other similar cemeteries emerged in the 16C, they borrowed the name. "**Catacomb**" now means an underground Christian cemetery composed of several storeys that generally extend downwards.

HV Morton observed in his 1957 classic *A Traveler in Rome*: "About fifty catacombs are grouped in circle around Rome and new ones continue to be discovered … Father Marchi estimated that six million Christians must have been buried in the catacombs and that is all the galleries were placed end to end, they would stretch for 600 miles."

Christians in the catacombs

Until the middle of the 2C, Christians had no formal cemeteries. Often a sympathetic family would volunteer a private burial ground. The situation changed early in the 3C, when Pope Zephyrinus put Callistus in charge of the cemetery on the Appian Way.

For a long time the catacombs were simply graveyards where Christians came to pray at the tomb of loved ones.

Domine, Quo Vadis?

While fleeing persecution in Rome, **Peter** supposedly met Christ on the Via Appia and asked "**Domine, quo vadis?** (Lord, whither goest thou?)."

"To Rome, to be crucified a second time," he replied and disappeared, leaving his footprints in the road. Ashamed of his weakness, Peter returned to Rome and met his death. A church marks the spot of the legendary encounter.

Visits became more frequent in the 3C when the persecutions (by Septimius Severus in 202, Decius in 250, Valerian in 257 and Diocletian in 295) created many martyrs; the Popes strongly urged the faithful to pray at their tombs. The catacombs, however, were never a place of refuge. The imperial authorities closed them at the height of the persecution. Only rarely, when they had broken the closure rule, were Christians killed in the catacombs.

After a period of great popularity in the 4C, the catacombs were abandoned (except for St Sebastian's: always a place of pilgrimage). In the 5C and 6C, barbarians ravaged the Roman countryside. Gradually the martyrs' relics were trans-

Decorative Motifs

Originally, Christians decorated their tombs with motifs found on pagan tombs (garlands of flowers, birds and cherubs). Then other motifs began to appear, illustrating the metaphors of the Holy Scriptures, depicting scenes from the Bible and symbolising manifestations of spiritual life. The meaning of the paintings and symbols found in the catacombs is still a subject of much controversy.

The **dove** holding a twig in its beak is a symbol of reconciliation between God and man. The **anchor** signifies hope; sometimes the horizontal bar is stressed to form a cross. The **fish** is a symbol for Christ: the Greek word for fish is composed of the initial letter of each word in the Greek phrase meaning "Jesus Christ, God's son, Saviour."

The **dolphin** which comes to the rescue of shipwrecked sailors indicates Jesus the Saviour. The **fisherman** means a preacher because of Jesus's words to his disciples "I will make you to become fishers of men."

Jonah and the whale foretells the Resurrection.

The **Good Shepherd** or Jesus searching for the lost sheep was one of the most popular ways of representing Christ among early Christians.

Other favourite scenes were the miracle of the feeding of the 5 000, the healing of the man suffering with the palsy and the baptism of Jesus, or the institution of baptism.

ferred to the city and churches built to house them.

In the 16C, Archaeologist Antonio Bosio re-discovered an ancient cemetery in Via Salaria. Their systematic investigation is primarily due to archaeologist Giovanni Battista de Rossi (1822-94).

Modern Memorial

During WWII, a partisan bomb killed 32 Wehrmacht soldiers on the Via Rassella. The next evening, the SS took 335 Roman men and boys – the standard ten-to-one reprisal, plus three – outside Rome to the **Fosse Ardeatine**, a quarry connected to early Christian catacombs. Eleanor Clark evoked the site's horror in *Rome and Villa*: [They were] taken out to this bleak country place ... shot in the nape of the neck, and dumped into a pit." She concluded: "It is considered by many people the most moving war memorial in Europe."

Seventy-seven were Jews, the rest political prisoners. German troops exploded the tunnel to hide the death chamber. Later, a Roman court condemned former SS officers Erich Priebke and Karl Hass to life imprisonment for the massacre in March 1998.

Sights

Catacombe di San Callisto★★★
(St Calixtus Catacombs)

Via Appia Antica 78 🕭Guided tours *only, various languages (45min).* 🕐Daily *(except Wed), 9am-12pm and 2–5pm (5pm in winter).* 🕐Closed 1 Jan, Feb, Easter and *Christmas.* €7; no charge the last Sun *in Sep. Lucina's precinct open to specialists only.* ☎06 51 30 15 80 or 06 51 30 151; Fax *06 51 30 15 67; www.catacombe.roma.it.*
Over 20km / 12mi of tunnels connect half a million tombs in Rome's first official Christian cemetery. The catacombs sprawl between the Appian Way, Via Ardeatina and Via delle Sette Chiese. This cemetery, resting place of almost all the 3C Popes, is also famous for its paintings. The Christian cemetery could have grown from the tomb of the patrician Caecilii.

By the 2C, the Church owned the site and developed a huge burial ground, probably thanks to **Calixtus**. A Trastevere native, this slave oversaw money for his Christian master. Financial failure prompted him to flee. He was caught, denounced as a Christian and sentenced to hard labour in the Sardinian quarries. Released under an amnesty, he was excluded from Rome by the Pope, Victor I, who regarded him as an adventurer. Calixtus returned to favour under Zephyrinus, Victor's successor. He was made a deacon and appointed administrator of the cemetery that bears his name. In 217, he succeeded as pope: five years later he died. He was buried in Calepodius's Cemetery on the Aurelian Way, near the Janiculum, where his tomb is.

Cripta dei papi (Papal Crypt)

Calixtus decided this should be the popes' official burial place and interred his 3C colleagues in this chamber's walls. Among them was Sixtus II, killed on 6 August 258, together with four of his deacons, while holding a forbidden meeting in the cemetery.

The marble plaques sealing the *loculi* bear the names and titles of the dead Popes. The Greek letters "M T P" – an allusion to "martyr," meaning witness – underscore the names of Pontianus and Fabian; the former was deported to Sardinia where he died in 235; the latter was a victim of the Emperor Decius, who organised one of the worst persecutions ever suffered by the Christians.

Cripta di Santa Cecilia (St Cecilia's Crypt)

Pilgrims already venerated this chamber as St Cecilia's tomb in the 7C. Two centuries later, Paschal I found her sarcophagus in the *loculus*, which now contains a copy of Maderno's statue of the saint (👁 *see TRASTEVERE: Santa Cecilia*).

Sala dei Sacramenti (Sacraments' Crypt)

This group of chambers boasts paintings from the late 2C or early 3C. All the familiar catacomb themes appear here, but no purely decorative motifs. Calixtus's cemetery also contains the crypt of Pope Eusebius (309-10; he was deported to Sicily, but his successor recovered the body); the crypt where Pope Caius (283-96) is buried; and the crypt where, Pope Melchiades (also Miltiades) (311-14) may lie.

Lucina's Precinct, named after a noble Roman lady, and the Papal Crypt form the oldest part of the cemetery. One chamber shows two faint illustrations of the Eucharist.

Catacombe di Domitilla★★★
(Domitilla Catacombs)

Entrance at Via delle Sette Chiese 282. Guided tours only, various languages (45min), daily (except Tue), 9am-12pm and 2-5pm. Closed Tue; 1 Jan, Easter and Christmas. €7; no charge the last Sun in Sep. 06 785 0350. /Fax 06 51 10 342; www.catacombe.roma.it

This extensive network of galleries began in the private cemetery of Domitilla, whose uncle, the Emperor Domitian (81-96), belonged to the rich Flavian family. In 95 Domitilla's husband, **Flavius Clemens**, was denounced as a Christian and executed on Domitian's orders. Domitilla was exiled to the Isle of Pandataria.

Basilica dei Santi Nereo e Achilleo

Domitilla's Catacombs became famous in the 4C, when a basilica marked the graves of St Nereus and St Achilleus. According to legend, they were her servants, who also converted to Christianity. In fact they were two soldiers martyred under Diocletian (284-305). The **basilica** consisted of a nave and two side aisles preceded by a narthex, was built between 390 and 395 to the detriment of the upper galleries. The saints' sarcophagi probably lay in the apse near

St Petronilla's (transferred to the Vatican in the 8C). Pieces of the original structure – in particular of the *schola cantorum* – have been re-instated.

Here, in the late 6C, Gregory the Great preached one of his homilies deploring the misery suffered under the barbarian menace. Two centuries later, the basilica was deserted; in future the saints were venerated within the city walls in the new church dedicated to Nereus and Achilleus (see *TERME DI CARACALLA: Santi Nereo e Achilleo*), built by Leo III.

Cubicolo di Veneranda

This chamber behind the apse testifies to the popular enthusiasm for the cemetery in the 4C. The faithful were keen to be buried near the tomb of a saint, hence Veneranda next to St Petronilla. A fresco on the *arcosolium* (boxed tomb) shows them both entering paradise.

Vestibolo dei Flavi

One of the oldest parts of the cemetery, the Flavian Vestibule, is 2C: a long wide gallery decorated with vine tendrils, birds and cupids. Late in the 3C, Christians created a room for the funeral meal on the entrance's right. Linked is a *cubiculum* named after Love and Psyche.

Ipogeo dei Flavi Aureli

To the left of the basilica is another 2C *hypogeum* (underground noble tomb) with the names of the freed men employed by the Flavians and the Aurelians. Here are simple Christian symbols, such as the anchor or a monogram. Domitilla's Catacombs contain a multitude of galleries and sarcophagus rooms, like the *cubiculum* of Diogenes and the *cubiculum* of Ampliatus.

Catacombe di San Sebastiano★★★
(St Sebastian Catacombs)

Guided tours only, various languages (45min), daily (except Sun), 8.30am-12pm and 2.30-5.30pm (5pm in winter). Closed mid-Nov to mid-Dec, 1 Jan, Easter and Christmas. €5. 06 78 50 350. www.catacombe.roma.it
Near the catacombs, the Appian Way passes through a valley. On its slopes

stood houses and *columbarii* (dovecotelike chambers for ashes). Below three mausoleums were erected, which probably marked the cemetery's beginning. In the 4C, a basilica with a nave and two aisles was built above the earlier structures and surrounded by mausoleums (those round the apse and on the south side remain). Here, close to places sacred to the apostles Peter and Paul, St Sebastian was buried. He was a soldier martyred during the persecution in Diocletian's reign (284-305). His cult became so popular that in the 5C a crypt was excavated around his tomb. The basilica was altered in the 13C and then rebuilt in the 17C for Cardinal Scipio Borghese; the new church rose above the nave of the previous building.

The tour of St Sebastian's Catacombs includes a *colombarium*. Other graves, similar to the one on display, also exist.

Mausoleums

These three structures – with their brick façades, pediments and travertine door frames – probably date from the early 1C. Two mausoleums contain beautiful stucco decorations. Pagan and Christian dead intermingled here, it seems; the central mausoleum contains the Greek symbol for "the Son of God". The right-hand one is decorated with paintings and bears the name of its owner, Clodius Hermes.

Triclia

This section of the catacombs has proved the most controversial. The graffiti on the walls –invoking the Apostles Peter and Paul –suggest that from 258 onwards Christians met here to celebrate their memory. Possibly the saints' relics had been lodged here temporarily while the basilicas of St Peter in the Vatican and St Paul Without the Walls were being built. The participants sat on the stone benches for the meal.

Catacombe e cripta di San Sebastiano

In the Middle Ages, a ceaseless procession of pilgrims came to invoke the martyr's name against the plague. The searing pain of bubonic boils was thought to equal the agony of his multiple arrow wounds. Sadly, they damaged the network of galleries, which had developed from the 4C round St Sebastian's tomb.

Mausoleo di Quirino e Domus Petri

One chamber contains the graffito *Domus Petri* (Peter's House). The other, built in the 5C, was the **mausoleum of St Quirinus,** who was martyred in Pannonia (western Hungary).

Present basilica

The atmosphere in the single nave – with its white walls and beautiful 17C painted, wooden ceiling –is fairly solemn and chill. In the relics chapel (*right*) is exhibited the stone that supposedly bears Christs' footprints. It may, in fact, be an old votive offering. St Sebastian's Chapel (*left*), built in the 17C over his tomb, contains a statue of the saint by one of Bernini's pupils (17C). In the sacristy is a beautiful 14C wooden crucifix.

Additional Sights

Circo di Massenzio e Tomba di Romolo (Maxentius's Circus and Romulus's Tomb)

Via Appia Antica 153 Open (except Mon) Apr-Sept 9am-7pm, Oct-Mar 9am–5pm. Closed Mon €2.60. 06 78 01 324 and 06 71 03 819; Fax 06 68 92 115.
Emperor Maxentius (306-312) built his Imperial residence beside the Appian Way. He erected a handsome tomb nearby when his young son died in 309 and also a hippodrome for chariot races. The oblong shape of the circus is well preserved, as are the stables. Note also the remains of the two towers, which stood at the western end flanking the stalls, and the magistrates' box.

Tomba di Romolo

The **tomb of Romulus**, surrounded by a wall punctuated by a quadriporticus, is a domed rotunda preceded by a pronaos in a style reminiscent of the Pantheon. It is partly hidden by a barnacle-like house encrusting the front.

Fosse Ardeatine

Open daily, 8.15am-5pm. Closed 1 Jan, Easter, 1 May, 15 Aug and Christmas. *No charge.* 06 51 36 742. These tombs commemorate a particularly painful episode during the Second World War. Here on 24 March 1944 the Nazis killed 335 Italians as a reprisal for an attack by the Resistance in Rome in Via Rasella, in which 32 German soldiers were killed. The tombs (*fosse*) of the victims are sheltered by a sanctuary; a museum gives information on the period.

Tomba di Cecilia Metella★

Via Appia Antica 161 ( ) Open daily (except Mon), 9am-1hr before dusk (last admission 1hr before closing time). Closed Mon; 1 Jan, 1 May, 25 Dec €6, €20 "Roma archeologica" card valid for 7 days. 06 39 96 77 00. www.pierreci.it
The iconic grave honors the wife of Crassus, one of Caesar's generals. The family of Pope Boniface VIII transformed her flashy sepulcher into a defensive tower in 1303. They incorporated it into the adjacent 11C fortress, which extended across the road. Its bulky silhouette is one of the best known in the Roman countryside. On the entrance's left is the way into the tomb's conical funeral chamber.

Excursion

From Tomba di Cecilia Metella to Casal Rotondo

5km/3mi. 800m/875yd beyond Cecilia Metella's tomb the Old Appian Way becomes a one-way road.

Although the road surface is poor, this stretch of the Old Appian Way provides pleasant countryside views. The reddish tones of the tombs and the ruined aqueducts blend with the dark green of the cypresses and umbrella pines. These memorials – shaped like pyramids or *tumuli* – were some of the finest in Rome. Now topped by mounded dirt and undergrowth, only inscriptions or a few carvings may remain. The tomb on the right after the junction with Via Erode Attico was long thought to honour **one of the Curiatii**, the Alba Longa triplets who battled their local counterparts, the

Horatii, to end a war. Only one Roman survived – and then killed his sister, who grieved her Curiatius fiancee.

Quintilian Villa

Via Appia Nuova 1089. ♿️🕐Open daily (except Mon), in summer, 9am-1hr before dusk; rest of the year, 9am-5.30pm (last admission 1hr before closing time). 🕐Closed Mon; 1 Jan and Christmas. Tours with archaeologist available by prior appointment. ✎€6; €20 for a "Roma archeologica" card, valid for 7 days. ☎06 39 96 08 071. www.pierreci.it

This villa (Villa dei Quintili) was once a huge property dating to the time of Hadrian (117-38); part of it was turned into a fortress in the 15C.

Casal Rotondo

This cylindrical mausoleum dates from the Republican era; it is now topped by a farmhouse. From this point, there is a fine view (*left*) of aqueduct ruins.

AVENTINO ★

MICHELIN MAP 38 P 11-12
METRO LINE B: CIRCO MASSIMO

From ancient Roman times through to the Fascist era, the Aventine has played an important role in the history of Italy and its capital city. Today, the pleasant residential district is dotted with magnificent villas, embassies and opulent religious houses. The area is also home to a number of palaeo-Christian churches; well worth a visit. A superb view of Rome can be enjoyed from the attractive *Giardino degli Aranci* **(the Parco Savello).**

▸ **Orient Yourself:** The Aventine is the southernmost of the seven hills of Rome (about 40m/131ft high); it has two peaks separated by a gully down that runs Viale Aventino. The tour described below winds its way over the westernmost side of the hill, overlooking the Tiber, which is separated from the Palatine Hill by the wide oblong Circus Maximus.

🏛 **Don't miss:** Santa Sabina, the view from the *Giardino degli Aranci*

Kids **Especially for kids:** The keyhole in the piazza Cavalieri di Malta.

👣 **Also See:** Neighbouring sights are described in the following chapters: *BOCCA DELLA VERITÀ; PIRAMIDE CESTIA-TESTACCIO.*

A Bit of History

Throughout the Roman Republic, this popular district was mainly populated by merchants who traded on the Tiber banks. They built many religious shrines; among the oldest are the Temples to Diana, Ceres and Minerva, between Via di S. Melania and Via di S. Domenico. During the Empire, the Aventine became a residential area. Trajan lived there before becoming emperor and his friend Licinius Sura constructed private baths nearby (*northwest of the church of Santa Prisca*); Decius also built a bathhouse there in 242. Such luxury aroused the envy of the Visigoths. In 410, under their leader Alaric, they sacked Rome for three days, leaving the Aventine devastated.

Plebeian Stronghold

After the expulsion of the last king (509 BC), the Republic was marked by a struggle between the patricians and the plebeians. In the 5C BC, the weary plebeians withdrew to the Aventine as a protest. Menenius Agrippa, who was sent to reason with them. As a result of the crisis, two tribunes were elected from among the plebeians to protect them against the consuls.

Death of a tribune

The plebeian tribune Caius Gracchus and his brother Tiberius (**the Gracchi**) greatly influenced the Republic. Continuing the work begun by Tiberius (assassinated in 133 BC), Caius proposed reforms in the ownership of land. He took refuge from the consul's mercenaries on the Aventine, until forced to flee over the Sublician Bridge to the foot of the Janiculum, where he was murdered in 121 BC.

Visit

From the Piazzale Ugo la Malfa unfolds a fine **view**★ of the ruins of the semicircular façade of the Domus Augustana on the Palatine Hill.

In the square stands a **Monument to Giuseppe Mazzini** (1805-72), a writer and politician. In 1849, he proclaimed the Republic of Rome, but papal power was restored by the French under General Oudinot.

Circus Maximus

The great circus – in the Murcia Valley between the Palatine and the Aventine, now transformed into a long esplanade – was the largest in Rome. It was used exclusively for two-, three- and four-horse chariot races, which drew larger crowds than any other spectacle.

The track (over 500m/550yd long) was bordered by banks of seats; the stand at the northwest end was reserved for the magistrates in charge of the spectacle. Beneath it were the stalls; at the southeast end stood an archway.

From the 4C BC, the arena was divided by a central reservation, called the *spina*, which linked the two conical turning-posts (*metae*).

In the Augustan era, the Circus Maximus became truly grandiose. An obelisk (now in the Piazza del Popolo) more than 23m/75ft high was erected on the *spina* and a splendid stand was built below Flavian's Palace for the emperor and his family. The Circus Maximus could accommodate 150 000 spectators.

The emperors continued to make improvements. Claudius (41-54) replaced the wooden turning-posts with new ones in gilded bronze and marbled the stables. After the fire in 64, his successor Nero extended the circus to 600m/656yd long and 200m/219yd wide. Domitian (81-96) and Trajan (98-117) increased the number of stands and the capacity of the circus grew to 300 000 places.

BOCCA DELLA VERITÀ

Monumento a Giuseppe Mazzini	A	Torretta Frangipane	B

The major events took place during the September games, which originated in the 6C BC. They became pure entertainment, an imperial gift to the people. A passion for racing often led the emperors to foul excesses: Vitellius (68-69) had his favourite charioteer's rivals put to death; Caracalla (211-17) dealt out the same fate to another team.

The few remains near the Porta Capena belong to Trajan's period. The little tower at this end dates from the Middle Ages; it was part of a fortress built by the noble Frangipani family.

▶ *Take Via di Valle Murcia on the right of the Mazzini monument.*

The road is bordered by the **Rome Rose Garden** (*Roseto di Roma*), which usually blooms in May.

▶ *Turn left into Clivo dei Publicii.*

Santa Prisca

Open 8am-12pm and 4pm-7pm. €4. *For information and reservations, contact the Centro Servizi per l'Archeologia, Mon to Fri, 9am-6pm,* 06 39 96 74 00. *www.archeorm.arti.beniculturali.it*
The church is one of the first places of Christian worship in Rome. Though reconstructed in the 17C and 18C, its origin stretches back to the 2C.

WHERE TO EAT

See "Where to Eat" in the Your Stay in Rome section at the end of the guide.

SHOPPING

Archivio Fonografico – *Viale Aventino 59 –* 06 57 42 93 – *Open Mon-Fri noon-7pm; Sat 10.30am-1pm and 3.30-7pm; Sun 10.30am-1pm.* The only outward signs of this shop are a small sign and a bell. Appearances can be deceptive, however, as the Archivio Fonografico sells a wide selection of records and CDs, ranging from old songs to classical music. As an added bonus, visitors can listen to their prospective purchases from the comfort of one of the armchairs in the "living room."

Various legends connect to the name of the holy woman venerated here. Prisca may have be the first woman martyred in the city. Another tale claims Prisca was the wife of Aquila, mentioned by St Paul in his Epistle to the Romans: "Greet Prisca and Aquila, my helpers in Christ Jesus, who have for my life laid down their own necks..."

Excavations uncovered a late 2C **mithraeum**, a cave-like shrine of the mystery cult (*access from the south aisle of the church*). Contemporary with it is a twin-nave building, which may have been an earlier Christian structure. *Open 2nd and 4th Sun of the month, 4pm.* €5.
Traces of even older buildings, dating from the late 1C and early 2C have been found nearby; they may belong to Trajan's residence (98-117) or to the house of his friend, Licinius Sura, next to the baths he built (*Terme di Sura*).

▶ *Take Via del Tempio di Diana, Via Eufemiano and then Via SA Magno.*

Parco Savello

Better known as the **Giardino degli Aranci**, this park hugs the apse of Santa Sabina. In the 10C, fortifications were built to defend the hill; in the 13C they became the stronghold of the Savelli family. The northwest side, high above the river, offers a pleasant **view**★.

Santa Sabina★★

Open 6.30am-12.45pm and 3pm-7pm (6pm in winter). Cloisters and gardens open by appointment only 06 57 94 01.
Bishop Peter of Illyria built this church in the 5C. In the 16C, Sixtus V (1585-90) and his architect Domenico Fontana transformed the interior into typical Counter-Reformation style. Together with subsequent Baroque additions, this effaced the medieval character. Extensive restoration has revived its glory.

Exterior – Opening into the nave is a very beautiful **door**★★ made of cypress wood; it belonged to the original church and dates from the 5C. The two leaves are divided into panels, 18 bear the original low-relief carvings: scenes from the Old and New Testaments. High on the left is a Crucifixion, the oldest

The light, spacious interior of Santa Sabina

B. Kaufmann / MICHELIN

representation of this scene in a public place.

Interior★★ – The well-proportioned interior with light streaming through the clerestory windows reflects the vigorous expansion of the early Christian Church.

The basilical plan consists of a nave and two aisles separated by two rows of columns with Corinthian capitals directly supporting a very light arcade. The mosaic above the entrance shows female figures – allegories of the church of the Jews ("*Ecclesia ex circumcisione*") converted by St Peter and the church of the Gentiles ("*Ecclesia ex gentibus*") converted by St Paul.

Nave: the frieze of tessellated marble above and between the arches dates from the 5C.

Chancel: the rich marble decor (*schola cantorum, presbyterium, ambones*) dating from the 9C and destroyed by Sixtus V has been reconstructed from fragments of the original; the *ambones* (Early Christian pulpits) and the Paschal candlestick are also replicas. The Mannerist mosaic in the apse by Taddeo Zuccari (retouched in the 19C and 20C) replaced the original 16C mosaic.

At the east end of the aisle is a chapel dedicated to the Virgin in the 15C by Cardinal Poggio del Monte di Auxia; his tomb recalls the funeral art of Lombardy at the time of the Renaissance, introduced to Rome by Andrea Bregno.

North aisle: the 17C Baroque chapel dedicated to St Catherine of Siena has been preserved; its multicoloured marbles, frescoes and painted dome clash with the serenity of the rest of the church.

In the monks' garden, perfumed by roses and geraniums and shaded by clementine and lemon trees, is a sculpture of the Last Supper (1974) by Gismondi. (*For access, apply to the sacristan.*)

Sant'Alessio (St Alexis)

🕐 *Open 8:30am-12:30pm and 3:30 pm-6:30pm.* Legends abound here. On the left, immediately inside the door, is St Alexis's staircase: the son of a patrician family, he set out for the Holy Land as a mendicant, returning to Rome to die. His family did not recognise him and he spent his last days beneath the staircase of his father's house. The legend of the "beggar beneath the stairs" was one of the subjects of 15C mystery plays.

▶ *Continue along the road to Piazza dei Cavalieri di Malta.*

This charming **square** was designed by Piranesi in the 18C.

An Unexpected View

The door into the Priory of the **Knights of Malta** (Villa del Priorato di Malta, no 3 Piazza dei Cavalieri di Malta) is famous for the view through the keyhole, which reveals the dome of St Peter's at the end of a well-clipped avenue of trees.

BOCCA DELLA VERITÀ★★

MICHELIN MAP 38 N 11-12
METRO LINE B: CIRCO MASSIMIO
800M/880 YD FROM PIAZZA DELLA BOCCA DELLA VERITÀ

The Piazza della Bocca della Verità takes its name from the carved face in the portico of the church of Santa Maria in Cosmedin. Legend claims the "mouth of truth" consumes the hands of liars. In the classic 1953 film *Roman Holiday*, Gregory Peck's improv – and his co-star's ensuing screech – sealed the modern celebrity of this sculpture, which is probably an ancient drain cover. The piazza lies in a pleasant district not far from the river, close to ancient temples and palaeo-Christian and Renaissance churches.

▶ **Orient Yourself:** The small piazza lies on an area of flat land alongside the Tiber, wedged between the Capitoline and Palatine Hills, with the Aventine Hill to the south. The marshy Velabro Valley occupied this area in ancient times.

Especially for Kids: Doing a "Gregory Peck" at the Mouth of Truth.

🕐 **Organising Your Time:** Allow 1hr 30min.

✍ **Also See:** Neighbouring sights are described in the following chapters: *AVENTINO; CAMPIDOGLIO-CAPITOLINO; ISOLA TIBERINA-TORRE ARGENTINA; TRASTEVERE.*

A Bit of History

As early as 6C BC, crowds thronged the vegetable and cattle markets here. This area was also a religious centre, containing several temples. Caesar began construction of the magnificent Theatre of Marcellus. Nearby was the Circus Flaminius, a vast oblong arena, where chariot races, hunting events and processions took place.

In the Middle Ages, the area was heavily populated, particularly by artisans. Small businesses abounded, owned in particular by Jews. The removal of the Ghetto in 1888, the clearances undertaken in 1926 to reveal the ancient monuments and the opening of new roads all destroyed a good portion of the narrow lanes and old houses.

Forum Holitorium and Forum Boarium

Not far from the Roman Forum, the administrative and political centre, lay other trade *fora*. One of them, the veg-

The slender bell-tower of Santa Maria in Cosmedin

B. Kaufmann/MICHELIN

etable market (**Forum Holitorium**), extended from the Porticus of Octavia along the riverbank to Vicus Jugarius. Another, the cattle market (**Forum Boarium**), extended further south to the foot of the Aventine and reached as far east as the Arch of Janus (*Arco di Giano*) and the Arch of the Moneychangers (*Arco degli Argentari*). These two markets were next to the Port of Rome. Boats sailed up the Tiber, then navigable, and moored by the left bank level with the Pons Aemilius (*Ponte Rotto*). This district also contained altars. Hercules, thought to have driven Geryon's cattle through the Forum Boarium, was honoured for his victory over Cacus (◐*see Scala di Caco*), the blind cow thief. Parallel to the Temple of Apollo, traces have been found of another, attributed to the Roman goddess of war, Bellona. Three temples stood side by side on the site of the church of San Nicola in Carcere. Not far from the church of St Omobono, beside the Vicus Jugarius, a group of sanctuaries has been uncovered; further south stands the Temple of Fortune which Servius Tullius, the slave who became king, dedicated to the god who changes man's destiny. Naturally Portumnus, the protector of harbours, had a place of worship too; this has sometimes been identified as the very old sanctuary known as the Temple of Fortuna Virilis. Upstream from the Forum Boarium and its quays must have been the military port, known as *Navalia inferiora*. In 338 BC, when Rome embarked on the conquest of the Mediterranean, her citizens came to admire the ships captured at Antium. They displayed the prows on the Rostra in the Forum. It was here, too, that Cato of Utica disembarked in 58 BC laden with treasures from King Ptolemy Auletes, after an expedition to Cyprus.

Walking Tour

Piazza della Bocca della Verità★
This open space more or less covers the site of the Forum Boarium. The combination of ancient, medieval and Baroque buildings, framed by umbrella pines and pink and white oleanders, makes a typical Roman scene. Opposite the medieval

Bocca Della Verità
In the porch is the marble disc known as the **Bocca della Verità** (Mouth of Truth). According to popular legend, the mouth would snap shut on the hand of anyone with a guilty conscience. The name was also attributed to the fact that the mouth had never spoken. The face is that of a marine divinity, perhaps the Ocean, with two bulls' horns symbolising the surging power of the sea. The plaque is, in fact, a drain cover, possibly from the nearby Temple of Hercules.

façade of Santa Maria in Cosmedin stands an 18C fountain supported by two tritons.

Santa Maria in Cosmedin★★
◐*Closed for restoration.* ☎*06 67 81 419.* The church's soaring **bell-tower**★ with its bold arcading was built early in the 12C and is one of the most elegant in Rome.

Foundation
In the 6C, the district between the Aventine and the Tiber was inhabited by Greeks, who like other foreign enclaves, formed themselves into a fighting force (*schola*) to protect Rome from the Lombards. In order to feed these soldiers, the Church formed **deaconries** (*diaconiae*), composed of religious and lay people. Their duty was to fix the price of wheat and to distribute the grain, sometimes free

Piazza della Bocca della Verità
● Columns of the "Statio Annonae"

of charge. Here lay one of its deaconries, with an oratory in a storerooms. It was enlarged in the 8C by Pope Hadrian I and became the Greek church, called Santa Maria in Schola Greca. It later became Santa Maria in Cosmedin, named for a district of Constantinople.

Early in the 12C, the church was restored; the porch and campanile were added by Pope Gelasius II and Pope Callistus II. The church was restored to its medieval appearance in the 19C.

Interior

In the north aisle, on either side of the entrance door and in the sacristy, are huge Corinthian columns, once part of the deaconry. The beautiful floor and marble furnishings (ambones, Paschal candlesticks, canopy above the high altar and the episcopal throne) are all Cosmati work. The *schola cantorum* (1) for the choristers and the presbytery (2) for the priests are 19C reconstructions. The presbytery has been screened off by a *pergula*, a colonnade hung with curtains, which are drawn at certain moments in the Eastern liturgy. The 8C crypt is original for this period.

The beautiful 8C mosaic (3) in the sacristy comes from St Peter's Basilica.

▸ *From Piazza Bocca della Verità go east into Via del Velabro.*

The valley of the **Velabro** (*Velabrum*), between the Palatine and Capitoline Hills, was once marshy and malarial.

Arco di Giano (Arch of Janus)

This massive 4C construction with four faces, each pierced by an arch, spanned a busy crossroads. It marked the northern edge of the Forum Boarium. The name reflects the power of the god Janus to protect junctions.

Arco degli Argentari (Arch of the Moneychangers)

This construction is more like a monumental gate against the west wall of San Giorgio in Velabro. The Guild of Moneychangers built it to honour the Emperor Septimius Severus and his wife, Giulia Domna, who both appear on the arch (*inside right panel*). The sharp relief and the abundance of decoration are characteristic of 3C art.

San Giorgio in Velabro★

Founded originally as a deaconry in the 7C, the church was rebuilt and enlarged by Pope Gregory IV (827-44). Since its 1926 restoration, San Giorgio in Velabro has recaptured the charm of the Roman churches of the Middle Ages. The façade, the porch and the bell tower date from the 12C. The interior has a monumental simplicity. In the Middle Ages, Rome was poor: builders used existing foundations resulting in asymmetrical designs; columns and capitals were also recycled. The apsidal fresco of Christ flanked by the Virgin and St George, St Peter and St Sebastian is by **Pietro Cavallini** (1295).

▶ *At the west end of Via del Velabro turn right into Via di S Giovanni Decollato.*

Oratorio di San Giovanni Decollato★

Visit by guided tour by arrangement only (apply to Governatore della Circonfraternità della Misericordia, Via San Giovanni Decollato 22, 00186 Roma). ☎06 67 91 890 *(mornings only).*

The Oratory of the Confraternity of St John the Beheaded was built at the end of the 15C to assist people who had been condemned to death. Those who died in a state of grace were buried beneath the cloisters.

The decoration is by a group of Mannerist artists drawing inspiration from Michelangelo and Raphael. Starting from the right-hand wall, near the altar, are: *The Angel Gabriel appears to Zacharias* (Jacopino del Conte); on the left of the painting is a portrait of Michelangelo, who was himself a member of the brotherhood; *The Visitation* (Salviati); *Birth of St John the Baptist* (Salviati); above the entrance: *St John the Baptist preaching* (Jacopino del Conte); *Baptism of Christ* (Jacopino del Conte). On the left-hand wall, near the entrance: *Arrest of St John the Baptist* (Battista Franco); *Dance of Salome* (Pirro Ligorio); *Beheading of St John the Baptist*. On either side of the altar: *St Andrew and St Bartholomew* (Salviati); Above the altar: *Deposition* (Jacopino del Conte).

▶ *Continue north and east into Via della Consolazione.*

Santa Maria della Consolazione

🕐*Open 6am-12pm and 3.30pm-6pm.* Pause before the broad white façade of the church, at the top of the steps. A 14C chronicler recounts how a prisoner condemned to death asked for an image of the Virgin near the place of execution on the Capitol. As she brought comfort to poor wretches about to die, she was called the **Virgin of Consolation**.

The first church was built in 1470. In the 16C, a hospital was added; it was constructed between 1583 and 1600, according to plans by Martino Longhi the Elder. He also began the façade of the church, which was eventually completed in the 19C in a style inspired by the Counter-Reformation.

▶ *Take Vico Jugario and Via Petroselli to return to Piazza Bocca della Verità.*

Casa dei Crescenzi

This curious building is one of the rare remains of *"Roma Turrita"* when the city bristled with fortresses. This 12C structure defended a toll bridge (*Ponte Rotto*), controlled by the Crescenzi family. The random antique elements demonstrate how insensitively the Roman monuments were despoiled.

Tempio della Fortuna Virilis★

The attribution of this 2C BC temple to human fortune is without foundation. Some archaeologists think it is a sanctuary to Portumnus, the god of rivers and harbours. One of the best preserved temples in Rome, it has an austere air typical of the Republican era.

Tempio di Vesta★

Another case of false identification, since only one temple honoured Vesta (Roman Forum). More likely, this site was sacred to Hercules, shown by the base of the statue of the god found nearby.

With its well-proportioned fluted columns and Corinthian capitals, it is an elegant building, which dates from the reign of Augustus. A church was established in the *cella* in the Middle Ages. In the 16C, it was dedicated to St Mary of the Sun, after an image of the Virgin found in the Tiber, which shone.

CAMPIDOGLIO-CAPITOLINO★★★

MICHELIN MAP 38 M 11-12

Once known as the "head of the world," Rome's smallest hill is also her most famous; the Capitoline ("Campidoglio" in Italian). Today it remains the seat of the local authority that administers the capital. A stepped ramp – the Cordonata –leads to the magnificent square designed by Michelangelo and to the oldest public museums in the world, the Musei Capitolini. From the recently restored Tabularium unfurls a breathtaking view of the Roman Forum.

▶ **Orient Yourself:** The hill has two summits: the **Capitolino** and the **Arx** (the Citadel), upon which the church of Santa Maria d'Aracoeli is situated. The dip between them is now occupied by the Piazza del Campidoglio. The tour starts at the monumental Aracoeli staircase.

🕒 **Organising Your Time:** Allow 1hr 30min.

🧒 **Especially for Kids:** The Capitoline Museums often run children's programmes. The cafe terrace is perfect for a gelato break.

👣 **Also See:** Neighbouring sights are described in the following chapters: *BOCCA DELLA VERITÀ; FORO ROMANO-PALATINO; ISOLA TIBERINA-TORRE ARGENTINA; PIAZZA VENEZIA.*

A Bit of History

In 1764, Edward Gibbon observed, "in the gloom of the evening, as I sat musing on the Capitol, while the barefoot fryars were chanting their litanies in the temple of Jupiter, that I conceived the first thought of my history... the decline and fall of the Roman Empire."

In antiquity, this area was both the city's religious and political centre, providing access to the Forum and dominated by the Temple of **Jupiter Capitolinus** on the Capitoline and that of **Juno Moneta** (Counsellor) perched on the citadel. The impressive Tabularium, the depositary of the Roman state archives, was built in the late-Republican period; the Palazzo Senatorio subsequently layered atop this structure. On the southwest edge of the Capitoline Hill, above Via della Consolazione, is the bluff where the legendary **Tarpeian Rock** stood. From here traitors were hurled to their death during the republic.

Jupiter Capitolinus

By 6C BC, the Etruscan king, Tarquin the Proud, had already built a temple on the Capitol to Jupiter, the Best and Greatest. This was considered second only to the heavens as the god's abode. During triumphs, the generals, dressed in gold and purple, rode here bearing an ivory sceptre surmounted by an eagle, the symbol of Jupiter.

The temple was built on the Etruscan plan and divided into three sanctuaries, the central one to Jupiter and those on either side to Juno and Minerva: the Capitoline Triad. The city treasure was kept beneath Jupiter's statue. In the sanctuary dedicated to Juno, the Romans placed a silver statue in memory of the **"geese of the Capitol,"** (their cries alerted the Romans, when the Gauls attacked). Destroyed by fire, the temple was rebuilt twice, by Augustus and Domitian.

Walking Tour

Scalinata d'Aracoeli (Aracoeli Steps)

In 1348, the plague ravaged Italy; Rome miraculously was spared and built the steps as an offering of thanks. The first person to climb them was **Cola di Rienzo**. At this time, the pope was in Avignon; Rome was in a state of anarchy at the hands of the noble families. Cola decided to revive the city's grandeur. He stood atop the steps dressed like an emperor and roused the people with his speeches. **Petrarch** had begged the pope to restore the capital. In 1354, he set out to lend support to Cola di Rienzo, but learned that the "tribune of Rome" had been killed in a riot by a servant of the Colonna family. Atop the steps, there is a fine **view**★ of the dome of St Peter's, the Synagogue *(left)* and Sant'Andrea della Valle and the Gesù Church.

Santa Maria d'Aracoeli★★

◷ *Open 9am-12.30pm and 2.30pm-5.30pm.* The **citadel** *(arx)* long defended the northern flank of the Palatine, which was naturally protected to the west by the Tiber. During the republic, a temple was built here to *Juno Moneta* (Counsellor). Legend claims the Virgin and Child appeared to the Emperor **Augustus** here after he had asked the Tiburtine Sibyl whether there would one day be a greater man than himself.

Following the arrival in 552 of General Narses from Greece, several Greek monasteries were established in Rome. One occupied an oratory, later turned into the church of Santa Maria d'Aracoeli in 1250 by Franciscan monks. The name comes from an altar *(ara)* dedicated to the goddess of the sky or from the Citadel *(arx)*.

Interior

The interior is built on the basilical plan and contains several works of art. The side chapels and the aisle ceilings were added in the 16C and 17C. The **wood-coffered ceiling** was an ex-voto offering by **Marcantonio Colonna**, who fought with the troops of the Holy League at Lepanto in Greece on 7 October 1571, when the Christians won against the Turks. The **floor** is one of the best preserved examples of the work of the Cosmati, Romans who worked in marble between the 12C and the 14C. **Cardinal d'Albret's tomb** (1) is one of **Andrea Bregno**'s best works. The fine working of motifs, particularly on the sarcophagus, and the use of architectural elements (pilasters, arcades) are characteristic of his style. Next to it, **Giovanni Crivelli's tombstone** (2) is attributed to **Donatello**, whose signature used to be legible, it is said, but was worn away when the stone lay on the ground. The decorative **frescoes**★ in the **Cappella di San Bernardino da Siena** (3) were

TAKING A BREAK

Caffè Capitolino – *Piazzale Caffarelli 4 – ☎06 69 19 05 64 –* ◷*Open Tues-Sun, 9am-8pm – closed Mon – www. museicapitolini.org.* On the terrace of Palazzo Caffarelli, the Capitoline Museum bar provides a stunning panorama. Sandwiches and hot and cold drinks, including a range of cocktails, are served here. The view is particularly impressive at sunset.

La Dolce Roma – *Via Portico d'Ottavia 20/b – ☎06 68 92 196 –* ◷*Open Tue-Sat, 8.30am-1.30pm and 3.30-8pm; closed Sun, 10am-1pm.* Although situated in the Jewish quarter, this pasticceria offers a range of cakes and pastries that have a decidedly Austrian (apple strudel or sachertorte) and American (apple pie, carrot cake and peanut butter cookies) influence.

painted by **Pinturicchio** in about 1485 and illustrate the life and death of Bernardino. The funeral scene *(left wall)* shows some portraits against a landscape. The huge statue of Gregory XIII (**4**) complements that of Paul III (**5**); both are Counter-Reformation works. In the passage leading to the side door there is a tomb (**6**) designed by Michelangelo of a young man, Cecchino Bracci.

🕭 *Step outside to admire the doorway.*

A **mosaic of the Virgin and Child** (**7**) stands over the side door on the exterior. It comes from the Cosmati workshop and reveals the influence of **Pietro Cavallini**, the greatest Roman artist in the Middle Ages. His style blends balanced composition, Byzantine influence and knowledge of classical art.

🕭 *Although Piazza del Campidoglio can be reached from the side door of the church (down the steps), it is best approached up the "Cordonata" from the bottom of the hill. Sometimes in spring a side passage is open.*

▸ *Go back into the church.*

The **tomb of Luca Cavelli** (**8**) contains an ancient sarcophagus reused for the burial of Luca Savelli. The mosaic decoration and the tiny *Virgin and Child* are the work of Arnolfo di Cambio (14C). Like the floor, the **ambones** (9) are Cosmati work. They belong to the elaborate compositions typical of the late 12C.

The **Cappella di Sant'Elena** (10) is an elegant 17C domed construction. Beneath the porphyry urn is a 12C altar decorated with Romanesque sculptures and mosaic insets commemorating the appearance of the Virgin to Augustus.

Cardinal Matteo d'Acquasparta's Monument (11) is a typical Italian Gothic tomb (vertical composition with angels drawing curtains round the deathbed). The painting of the Virgin and Child is related to the art of Pietro Cavallini. Cardinal d'Acquasparta, Vicar General of the Franciscans, who died in 1302, is mentioned by Dante in his *Divine Comedy* as a man who relaxed his rule's severity. In the left transept is a statue (12) of Leo X (16C).

The **Cappella del Santo Bambino** (the chapel of the Holy Child) (13) took its name from a statuette, which, according to legend, had miraculous curative powers;

> ## The Root of 'Money'
>
> The word "money" comes from the Italian *"moneta,"* the name of the goddess Juno, whose temple once stood here. This derivation is explained by the fact that the building was also used as the Roman mint.

many letters were addressed to it from all over the world. It was stolen on 1 'February 1994.

The **third side chapel in the north aisle** (14) was decorated in the 15C with frescoes by Benozzo Gozzoli, Fra Angelico's assistant; only St Antony of Padua remains above the altar. In the pre-Christmas period young children gather in the adjoining **chapel** (15) to recite verses before Santo Bambino.

▷ *Down Aracoeli Steps; then left.*

La "Cordonata"

Michelangelo's design for this ramp was not faithfully executed. The two lions guarding the entrance are Egyptian (restored in 1955). Found on the Campus Martius, they were placed here in 1582. In 1588 **Giacomo della Porta** converted them into fountains, which once flowed with red and white wine on feast days. A **statue** of Cola di Rienzo was erected in the 19C on the spot where he was killed.

Piazza del Campidoglio★★★

Every visitor should pause a moment in **Capitol Square**, a haven where charm and majesty mingle in harmony. In the Middle Ages the piazza was known as *"Monte Caprino"* (Goat Hill); animals grazed among the ruins. Change came in the 16C. On the occasion of Charles V's visit in 1536, Pope Paul III decided that Rome, which had been sacked nine years earlier by the same Charles V, should be restored to its former elegance. He commissioned **Michelangelo** to draw plans for the Capitoline. The design was executed over the next 100 years or so and altered in certain respects. The square is lined by three buildings (Palazzo Senatorio, Palazzo dei Conservatori and Palazzo Nuovo) and is shaped like a trapezium to accommodate the position of the Palazzo dei Conservatori (Conservators' Palace), which had already been built. Michelangelo turned the square round to face the modern city, rather than the Forum. The balustrade with its overlarge statues was not his idea.

At the centre of his beautiful geometric design, executed only recently, is a copy of the equestrian statue of Marcus Aurelius. The original –which graced the square for many years and has undergone extensive restoration – is on display in the Palazzo Nuovo.

On Saturdays, the square is particularly busy; after the wedding ceremonies in the register office of the Palazzo dei Conservatori, newlyweds pose for photos by the statue of the Tiber and the wolf's head or on the Cordonata Steps.

Statue dei Dioscuri★

The two knights are shown standing beside their horses (👉 *see Tempio di Castore e Polluce*). The statues are Roman and date from the late Empire; they were found in the 16C on the Campus Martius and restored (one head is modern).

Trofei di Mario

Marius's Trophies is the name given to the sculptures (1C BC) that commemorate Domitian's conquest of the German people. Until the 16C, they adorned a fountain in Piazza Vittorio Emanuele II.

Milestones

Next to the statues of Constantine and Constantine II. Here stand the first and seventh markers from the Appian Way.

Palazzo Senatorio★★★ (Senate House)

👉 *Closed to the public; occupied by the offices of the local authority. The Tabularium is described as part of the Musei Capitolini (👉 see below).*

In 1143, under the influence of **Arnold of Brescia**, the Roman people deprived the pope of his temporal power and set up the Roman Commune. Senators were created to lead the government; their meeting palace was constructed like a castle on the ruins of the *Tabularium* (the 1C BC storage building for the bronze *tabulae* that recorded legal business). Michelangelo kept the walls of this old building, but designed a new façade. His plans were carried out from 1582-1605 by Giacomo della Porta and then by Girolamo Rainaldi.

The Rape of the Sabines and Tarpeia

With his brother dead and the new city established, Romulus was anxious to increase the population. Since the Campidoglio was declared a safe haven, the area soon became crowded with outlaws: a pack of men. To counter this imbalance, Romulus decided to lure the young Sabine women from a neighbouring tribe with a series of games. The rapacious Romans carried off the ladies. Outraged, Titus Tatius, king of the Sabines, set out to rescue his womenfolk. A bloody confrontation could have ensued. Except the Sabine women threw themselves between their fathers and husbands. Thus a new alliance was formed between Romulus and Titus Tatius.

Martino Longhi the Elder built the municipal tower from 1578-82.

The double staircase is the only part completed during Michelangelo's life. The fountain –added in 1588 on Sixtus V's initiative – was not part of the original design. The goddess of Rome, in porphyry and marble, seems lost in her recess, perched on a disproportionately high pedestal. The flanking statues come from Constantine's baths on the Quirinal and represent the Nile and the Tiber. The right-hand one was originally the Tigris: a replacement wolf's head revised the theme.

Some blocks of stone from the old **Arx Capitolina** (Citadel) can be seen in a little garden on the left of the Senate House.

Palazzo dei Conservatori and Palazzo Nuovo★★★

The **Conservators' Palace** was built in the 15C to house the meetings of the Conservators, magistrats who governed the town with the Senators. It was altered in 1568 by Giacomo della Porta according to Michelangelo's designs.

Although not built until 1654, the New Palace, the work of Girolamo and Carlo Rainaldi, was identical to the Conservators' Palace. At this time, the Via delle Tre Pile was opened and the development of the Capitol was complete. The two palaces house the collections of the Musei Capitolini (&see below); with their porticos at ground level and façades decorated with a single order of flat pilasters, they form an elegant ensemble.

▸ *From Piazza del Campidoglio take Via del Campidoglio on the right of Palazzo Senatorio.*

From the corner of the palace, catch a beautiful **view**★★ of the Roman Forum and in particular the Tabularium, the Portico of the Dei Consentes, the Temple of Vespasian and the Temple of Concord.

▸ *Return to Piazza del Campidoglio and take the steps on the left of the Palazzo dei Conservatori and then Via del Tempio di Giove.*

Below Via del Tempio di Giove are several stone blocks: a corner of the Temple of Jupiter. Beyond is a pleasant garden overlooking the so-called Tarpeian Rock (& see below), which gives a good **view** of the Roman Forum, the Palatine and other hills.

▸ *Take Via di Monte Caprino and go down to the left to Piazza della Consolazione.*

Rupe Tarpea

Via della Consolazione, an extension of Vico Jugario, is dominated on the left by the southern slope of the Capitol, where, after considerable hesitation, scholars have sited the **Tarpeian Rock**.

In ancient times, the *Vicus Jugarius* (now called *Vico Jugario*) was lined with the shops of craftsmen making yokes. It wound aunder the Capitol and connected the *Forum Holitorium* to the Roman Forum.

⊘The ruins here have a somewhat unsavoury reputation. Families and solo travellers should take caution.

▸ *Cross Via del Teatro di Marcello.*

San Nicola in Carcere

⏱*Open Mon-Fri, 7am-12pm and 4pm-5pm, Sat-Sun 9:30am-1pm and 4pm-7pm.*

Crypt open Thur 10:30am-12pm. ◷*Closed Aug and Christmas.* ☎*06 68 69 972.*

The 11C little church stands on the ruins of three Republican temples that over-looked the **Forum Holitorium** (◔ *see BOCCA DELLA VERITÀ).*

The church has been restored several times: Giacomo della Porta designed the façade in 1599. The nave stands on the site of the cella and pronaos of the middle temple. The tower, originally defensive, dates from the 12C when the district belonged to the Perleoni family. The words *"in carcere"* refer to a Byzantine prison that occupied the left-hand temple in the 7C and 8C.

The crypt contains the foundations of ancient temples; fragments of a frieze are visible from the roof of the church.

Teatro di Marcello★★

The **Theatre of Marcellus** was begun by Caesar and completed between 13-11 BC by Augustus, who dedicated it to Marcellus, his sister Octavia's son.

The two tiers of arches that remain were probably topped by a third row of Corinthian pilasters. They form the semicircular part of the building, which contained the tiers of seats; the stage backed onto the river. Holding 15 000 spectators, it was the second largest theatre in Rome after Pompey's in the Campus Martius. Its severe and sober style, with the three architectural orders – Doric, Ionic and Corinthian – served as a model for the Colosseum, which was built of the same stone: travertine from the Tivoli quarry. On the day of the inauguration, Augustus suffered a slight mishap that Suetonius recorded: "the official chair *(sella curulis)* gave way beneath him and he fell backwards."

The theatre was damaged in the fire in AD 64 and was finally abandoned early in the 4C. Workmen soon quarried it; some stone repaired the Ponte Cestio in the 4C. Houses were built against the walls and in 1150 it was transformed into a fortress and saved from further depredations.

In the 16C, the noble family of Savelli turned it into a palace. The remains of this house, which was built by Baldassarre Peruzzi, which are visible today above the old arches. The palace later passed to the Orsini. The ancient theatre was excavated from 1926-29.

Tempio di Apollo Sosiano★★

Romans venerated the Greek god Apollo chiefly for his power to ward off disease. The first temple dedicated to him was raised on this site in the 5C BC. In 34 BC, Caius Sosius, governor of Cilicia and Syria, rebuilt the sanctuary in marble and it became known as the **Temple of Apollo Sosianus**. The three elegant fluted **columns★★** with Corinthian capitals belonged to the temple's porch *(pronaos)* and were re-erected in 1940.

▸ *Turn left into Piazza di Campitelli.*

Santa Maria in Campitelli

◷*Open 7am-12pm and 4pm-7.30pm.* When the plague struck in 1656, the citizens prayed ceaselessly before the Virgin in the church of Santa Maria in Portico. Now demolished, this church stood on the riverside site of the present Anagrafe. After the epidemic, they built a new sanctuary to house the holy image. The first stone of Santa Maria in Campitelli was laid in September 1661. The building was entrusted to **Carlo Rainaldi** (1611-91), who drew up his own design and oversaw the construction.

The exterior, like the interior, is a forest of columns. Variety and movement are provided by the broken and curved pediments, the jutting cornices and multiple recessing.

The **interior★** space is defined by the columns. The variation on the Greek cross plan (extended and constricted towards the apse), the grandiose elevation of the vault and the dome and the alternating projections and recesses create a bold effect of perspective.

The church contains a few fine 17C paintings including a canvas of *St Anne, St Joachim and Mary (second chapel on the right)* by Luca Giordano (1632-1705), whose picture frame is supported by two kneeling angels. Another Baroque painting *(left of the choir)* is by Giovanni Battista Gaulli (**Baciccia**, 1639-1709).

▸ *Turn right into Via dei Delfini which leads to Piazza Margana.*

Piazza Margana is a charming and peaceful small square among narrow medieval streets and seemingly far removed from the noise and chaos of modern Rome. The **Margana Tower** *(part of Via Margana 40)* rises from the remains of a Roman portico; a column with an Ionic capital is still extant.

Fountain in Piazza d'Aracoeli

This fountain is by Giacomo della Porta (1589), the great aquatic designer. In the 17C, the Chigi family added its arms and 100 years later the base was replaced by the present circular basin.

Musei Capitolini★★★

Allow at least 3hr. Open daily (except Mon), 9am-8pm (ticket office closes 7pm). ⏰*Closed Mon ; 1 Jan, 1 May and Christmas.* ✆*€6.20, €8,30 joint ticket with Centrale Montemartini.* ☎*06 39 96 78 00. www.museicapitolini.org*

The collections of classical art in the Capitoline Museums were started by Sixtus IV in 1471, enlarged by Pius V in 1566 and opened to the public in 1734 by Clement XII. This excellent 18C assembly has changed little since and ranks as one of the most important in Rome.

Palazzo Nuovo

The fountain in the courtyard is dominated by the recumbent statue of a god christened **"Marforio."** The huge peaceful figure seems a little bored watching the water in the basin. Life once was more exciting, granted. In the Middle Ages, he was one of "talking statues" papered in satirical notes directed against the people in power.

Marforio originally lived next to the church of St Luke and St Martina. The cost of moving him (1595) was so great

that the government raised the price of wine. Thus he "wrote" to Pasquino, another talking statue, that the Romans were having to do without wine, so that he could preside over a fountain.

On the right is the famous **equestrian statue of Marcus Aurelius,**★★ which was transferred from the square outside St John Lateran to Piazza del Campidoglio by Michelangelo in 1538. Full of admiration, he restored it himself. Cast in bronze and once gilded, it is a fine example of late 2C Roman realism.

▶ *Take the stairs to the first floor.*

Gallery

The rooms in the museum are connected by a gallery. The collection is not arranged according to any particular historical or artistic criteria.

Sala delle Colombe (I)

The Dove Room takes its name from the finely crafted **mosaic**★★ that decorated Hadrian's villa at Tivoli. It is probably a 2C AD copy of a 2C BC Greek mosaic from Pergamum. The interesting **mosaic of the masks** (2C AD) is also on display.

The statue of a young girl holding a dove in her arms and warding off a serpent is a Roman copy of a 2C BC Hellenistic sculpture. During restoration, the serpent was substituted for the original animal (a dog or a cat).

Gabinetto della Venere (II)

This charming room was built at the beginning of the 19C to house the famous *Capitoline Venus*★★★. The Greek original, which inspired this statue (1C BC), depicted the goddess leaving her bath, with a double gesture of modesty.

Sala degli Imperatori (III)

This room houses some 70 portraits of famous people. In the male depictions, note the evolution from short to long beards, favoured by philosophers; in women's fashion, hairstyles morphed from tall layers of curls to the later penchant for ringlets. Every emperor is represented here. Noteworthy are two portraits of **Octavian Augustus**: one at the time of the Battle of Actium (*upper*

FIRST FLOOR

0   10 m

I

II

Gallery

III   IV   Salon   V   VI

Piazza   del   Campidoglio

row), the other (*facing the window*) as an older man, crowned with myrtle.

Sala dei Filosofi (IV)
The Philosopher's Room contains over 80 busts of poets, philosophers and rhetoricians. Homer's blindness makes him easily identifiable.

Salone
This room is the most typical of the museum. Note the two contrasting statues of **centaurs**★★: the young buck happy and laughing; the older one sad and tired. Other works exhibited in the room include the elegant *Apollo with Cthara* – a 2C BC copy of an original by Praxiteles – and the **Wounded Amazon**★, a fine Roman copy of a statue sculpted by Polyclitus.

Sala del Fauno (V)
Here stands the famous *Drunken Faun*,★★ made from precious red marble and dating from Hadrian's reign. Also worthy of note is the statue of a child wringing a goose's neck, a 2C Roman sculpture, inspired by a bronze by the Greek Boethos.

Sala del Gladiatore (VI)
The magnificent sculpture in the middle was long thought to be a gladiator. It is, in fact, the *Dying Gaul*★★★, a Roman imitation of a work in bronze or perhaps even an original work from the Pergamum School (late 3C, early 2C BC). All the nobility and suffering of agony are sensitively expressed in this work, which ranks among antiquity's finest.

▶ *Return to the ground floor and continue to the Tabularium (basement).*

Palazzo Senatorio-Tabularium
Excavated in 1930, an underground passage links the Palazzo Nuovo to the Palazzo dei Conservatori. It leads to the rooms of the Tabularium, which housed the Roman archives in the 1C BC, and later became a storehouse and prison (⚫ *see FORO ROMANO-PALATINO*). The gallery overlooks the Roman Forum and offers a magnificent view ★★.

▶ *Return to the connecting gallery and take the stairs back to the ground floor of the Palazzo dei Conservatori.*

Palazzo dei Conservatori
In the internal courtyard are the Gothic arches of the 15C palace *(right)* and a few pieces of a colossal statue of **Constantine** (4C).

▶ *Take the stairs to the upper floor.*

On the first landing are some **high-relief sculptures**: these depict a sacrifice, the triumph and clemency of Marcus Aurelius and Hadrian's entry into the city. The rooms of the *Appartamento dei Conservatori*, decorated from the 16C onwards, recall the grandeur and magnificence of ancient Rome. The frescoes in these rooms depict episodes from the Republican era.

Sala degli Orazi e dei Curiazi (Horatii and Curatii Room) (I)
The marble statue of **Urban VIII** was sculpted by **Bernini** and his pupils; that of **Innocent X**, in bronze, is a masterly piece by Algardi dating from the mid-17C. Other works on temporary display in the room include parts of the bronze statue of Constantine and a statue of Hercules in gilded bronze.
Cavaliere d'Arpino painted the frescoes at the end of the 16C. Treated like tapestries and framed by fake drapes

The Colossus of Constantine in the courtyard of the Palazzo dei Conservatori

and marble friezes, they depict episodes from the foundation of Rome.

Sala dei Capitani (II)

The Captains' Room is named after the 16C-17C statues of papal generals Marcantonio Colonna and Alessandro Farnese, which are displayed there. The **coffered ceiling**★ with historical scenes painted in the panels comes from a 16C palace, now demolished.

Sala dei Trionfi (Triumph Room) (III)

The painted frieze on the walls dates from the 16C and illustrates the triumph of Emilius Paulus over Perseus, king of Macedon in 168 BC.

This room houses the famous *"Spinario"*★★, an original Greek work or a very good 1C BC copy. The charming pose of this boy – removing a thorn from his foot – and the studied treatment of his hair and face make this an admirable work.

The bust of *Junius Brutus*★★ is a magnificent bronze portrait (3C BC) of the first consul, whose legendary severity and integrity found expression in this head.

Sala della Lupa (IV)

Here is the famous bronze of the *She-Wolf*★★★, the "mother of Rome" and city icon. In antiquity, the wolf stood on the Capitol and was struck by lightening in 65 BC, as the marks on the rear paws seem to testify. The statue dates from the 6C or 5C BC and could be the work of a Greek or Etruscan artist. The twins were added during the Renaissance.

Sala delle Oche (V)

Two small bronze geese give this room its name. Mounted in a beautiful stucco frame, they recall a famous incident in Roman history, when a gaggle saved the city from Gauls. Also on display here are the head of Medusa by Bernini and a bust of Michelangelo.

▶ *Room VI leads into Room X.*

Sala degli Arazzi (Tapestry Room) (X)

The huge tapestries were woven in a Roman workshop in the 18C; they depict works exhibited in the museum.

Sala di Annibale (Hannibal's Room) (XI)

The museum's only original 16C frescoes depict episodes from the Punic Wars. The 16C **chapel** (XII) to the right is dedicated to the Virgin, St Peter and St Paul.

▶ *Exit through the Sala degli Orazi e Curiazi.*

At the end of the corridor are the three **Sale dei Fasti Moderni** (XIII-XV), which house the Marsia – an important Roman reproduction (2-1C BC) of a Greek original – and a few Egyptian works.

▶ *Take the stairs to the second floor.*

Pinacoteca

On the entrance landing are two fine panels of *marble intarsia* work depicting tigresses attacking cattle. These 4C Roman works use the *opus sectile* technique, developed mainly in Egypt.

Central Italy from the Middle Ages to the 16C (I)

Most of the paintings on display in this room are religious in nature.

The 16C in Ferrara (II)

These paintings combine the bold colouring so typical of the Venetian School with the spatial solidity that is characteristic of the Central Italian School.

The 16C in Venice (III)

Venice, with Florence and Rome, was one of the most important centres of Italian painting during the Renaissance period. A characteristic feature was the attention paid to colour, rather than form. Here, note the Baptism of Christ, an early work by Titian, which balances colour and composition exquisitely, and Veronese's *Rape of Europa*.

▶ *Return to Room II and turn right.*

The 16C in Emilia (V)

In addition to paintings from the Emilian School, this room contains two works by Cavalier d'Arpino.

Painting in Bologna from the Carracci to Guido Reni (VI)

These 16C and 17C works demonstrate the new religious sensitivity characterised by the Carracci, and the elegant Classicism of Guido Reni *(St Sebastian)*.

Sala di Santa Petronilla (VII)

Dominant is the large **painting**★ by Guercino in honour of St Petronella. It's particularly noteworthy for the harmony of blue and brown hues, and the tortuous vertical lines, presaging the Baroque style. Also on display are a number of masterpieces from the early 17C Roman School. The *Gypsy Fortune-teller*★★ is an early work by Caravaggio. In *St John the Baptist*★★, the same artist pays tribute to Michelangelo's Sistine nudes and portrays the saint as a young boy, contrasting sharply with traditional religious iconography. Finally, spare a moment for *Romulus and Remus* by Rubens.

The 17C in Rome (IV)

This room houses paintings by both Italian and foreign artists.

Sala di Pietro da Cortona (VIII)

Pietro da Cortona was the first major Baroque painter; his work is characterised by the fluid, asymmetrical lines of his *Rape of the Sabine Women*★★.

Galleria Cini (Cini Gallery)

This rooms contains 18C porcelain from Meissen, Capodimonte and Cin; several tapestries; a series of views of Rome by Vanvitelli; portraits from the 15C-17C (including a self-portrait by Velázquez and two double portraits by Van Dyck); and examples of 18C painting.

CAMPO DEI FIORI★★

MICHELIN MAP 38 L 10-11, M 10-11

The area around Campo dei Fiori is one of the liveliest districts in Rome, with narrow streets full of boutiques, cafés, restaurants and artisans' workshops. The early morning bustle of the market gives way to diners, strollers and kids playing football on the cobblestones. In small squares, graceful **palazzos** stand alongside older, shabbier properties. Set between the Piazza Navona and Trastevere, this neighbourhood is a marvellous one to wander – just remain alert for motorini (mopeds), cars and pickpockets in the alleys.

▸ **Orient Yourself:** The walk follows the narrow streets of the district lying between the Tiber, Corso Vittorio Emanuele II and the Capitol.

🕓 **Organising Your Time:** Allow 2hrs.

⊙ **Don't Miss:** morning and night in the Campo dei Fiori, S. Andrea della Valle, Piazza Farnese at night, when the fountains and palazzi glow.

☝ **Also See:** *CASTEL SANT'ANGELO; GIANICOLO; ISOLA TIBERINA-TORRE ARGENTINA; PANTHEON; PIAZZA NAVONA.*

A Bit of History

In antiquity, the district was just to the south of the Campus Martius. **Pompey** set several important buildings here: a huge theatre, the first in Rome to be built of stone; a temple to Venus and a *curia* to house occasional meetings of the Senate. A decisive event in Roman history occurred in the latter: on the Ides of March, 44 BC, Brutus and other conspirators assassinated **Julius Caesar** at the foot of Pompey's statue. Almost nothing remains of this building.

The first Christian sanctuary here was San Lorenzo in Damaso, founded in 380. In the Middle Ages, palaces and houses of worship grew in number. The churches were quite simple buildings, serving tradesmen. The various guilds gave a certain character to the district: many leather curriers *(vaccinari)*, boiler-makers *(calderari)*, and rope-makers *(funari)* prospered along the streets, crowded by pilgrims heading to St Peter's.

After Charles V's troops sacked Rome in 1527, civil architecture revived. Cardinal Riario spent his gambling profits on the Palazzo della Cancelleria, thus countering the scruples of his relative, Sixtus IV. Cardinal Farnese, later Pope Paul III, built the prestigious palace that bears his family name.

Walking Tour

Piazza Campo dei Fiori★

The square's name ("Field of Flowers") probably goes back to the Middle Ages, when the area was one vast meadow, dominated by the fortress of the power-

---

Campo dei Fiori Market

This morning bazaar is one of the busiest and most lively in Rome. A regular visitor is the knife-sharpener with his pedal-powered grindstone. Cheese and cream, cured meats, fruit and vegetables, meat and poultry, colourful arrays of flowers, accented voices trading local gossip and exchanging ills for miraculous cures: the market is active from about 6.30am–2pm Mon-Sat. On Sunday afternoons, artists display paintings in the square. Later in the day, patrons lounge outside the bars and restaurants, as the bongo-drummers gather around the statue of the scientific martyr Giordano Bruno. The Campo dei Fiori remains lively until about 2am.

Address Book

WHERE TO EAT

See "Where to Eat" in the Your Stay in Rome section at the end of the guide.

TAKING A BREAK

Forno di Campo de' Fiori di Bartocci e Roscioli – *Piazza Campo dei Fiori 22 (vicolo del Gallo). ☎06 68 80 66 62. Closed Sun*. This bakery, visible from the street, is besieged by locals for its excellent pizza and bread.

Pica – *Via della Seggiola 12 ☎06 68 68 405 – Open 8.30am-midnight – Closed Sun morning*. This *gelateria* is renowned for its rice and ricotta ice creams. No surcharge for the tables outside.

BARS

Bookowsky – *Via Pomponio Leto 1. ☎06 68 33 844. Open Tue-Sun, noon-3pm and 8.30pm-2am. Closed Mon*. Browse among the books in this literary café, while enjoying a glass of wine, accompanied by canapés, bruschetta and other snacks.

The Library – *Vicolo della Cancelleria 7. ☎333 351 7581. www.thelibrary.it Open Tues–Sun 12pm–2am. Closed Mon*. A new addition to this gentrifying neighborhood, this *feng-shui* designed bar targets an international crowd. Lounge on a couch beside the indoor fountain or tickle the ivories. Owner Dana serves a light menu and provides wi-fi. Live music and DJ Fri & Sat.

Vineria Reggio – *Piazza Campo dei Fiori 15 – ☎06 68 80 32 68 – Open Mon-Sat 8.30am–2am; Sun 4pm–2am*. Opposite the statue of Giordano Bruno, this typical wine bar – with its wooden benches in front of the long bar and its outdoor terrace – is a favourite pre- and post-dinner meeting place for locals.

SHOPPING

Comics Bazar – *Via dei Banchi Vecchi 127/128 – ☎06 68 80 29 23. www.comicsbazar.com – Open Mon-Sat, 9.30am-7.30pm – Closed Sun*. Furniture – including items by Thonet – and bric-a-brac jumble together in this curio shop.

Fahrenheit 451 – *Piazza Campo dei Fiori 44 – ☎06 68 75 930 – libreriafahrenheit@tiscalinet.it – Open Tue-Sat, 10am-12.30pm and 4pm-midnight; Mon, 4pm-midnight; Sun, 9.30am-1.30pm and 6pm-midnight*. Although this bookshop on Campo dei Fiori looks tiny, inside it is a maze of small rooms and nooks and crannies that are perfect for browsing.

Libreria del Viaggiatore – *Via del Pellegrino 78 – ☎06 68 80 10 48 – Open Tue-Sat, 10am-2pm and 4-8pm*. As its name suggests, this small shop specialises in travel literature.

Franco Borini – *Via dei Pettinari 86/87*. Extreme footwear stars here: square-toed shoes, extremely high heels and bright colours abound.

---

ful Orsini family. By the 16C, the area was Rome's centre, a meeting place for people of all ranks, crowded with inns. The **"Hostaria della Vacca"** belonged to **Vanozza Caetani** (1442-1518), famous for her liaison with Rodrigo **Borgia**, who became Pope **Alexander VI**. She bore him several children, including the poisonous Cesare and Lucrezia. The façade of her hostelry still bears the Borgia arms, alongside those of Vanozza and one of her husbands'.

The Campo hosted all sorts of festivals, as well as executions. At the centre stands a statue of Giordano Bruno, a monk burned for heresy on 17 February 1600, during the Counter-Reformation. Every morning, the square bustles with an extensive food market.

Palazzo della Cancelleria★★

🕐 *Open Mon 4-7pm, Sat 9am-noon.* 🕐*Closed Sun & Vatican holidays.* ⊗€3 *(pay at the Vatican: Porta Sant'Anna). Apply to Signora Meli, ☎06 06 69 89 34 05.*

The **Chancery Palace** was built by an unidentified architect between 1483 and 1513 for Cardinal Raffaele Riario, upon whom "honours and riches were heaped" by his great-uncle Pope Sixtus IV. The palazzo housed the law courts,

CASTEL S. ANGELO   PIAZZA NAVONA   PANTHEON

Pal. del Governo Vecchio
Oratorio dei Filippini
Pal. Sforza Cesarini
★★S. AGNESE IN AGONE
Palazzo Madama
S. Eustachio
★★★ PIAZZA NAVONA
Pal. Tursi
Vecchio
Pal. Pamphili
Chiesa Nuova ★
Pal. d. Sapienza
Pal. Maccarani
Pal. Lancellotti
P.za di Pasquino
Pal. Lante
Corso
★ Pal. Braschi
San Pantaleo
Teatro Valle
S. Lorenzo in Damaso
P.za S. Andrea della Valle
Pal. d. Valle
Pal. Ricci
★★PAL. DELLA CANCELLERIA
Pellegrino
Vittorio
Pal. Massimo
★ Pal. d. Farnesina ai Baullari
Via del
S. Maria di Monserrato
★★S. ANDREA D.VALLE
Emanuele II
S. Eligio degli Orefici
Monserrato
Arco d. Acetari
Pal. Vidoni
V. dei Baullari
V. del Sudario
Giulia
Hostaria della Vacca
★PIAZZA CAMPO DEI FIORI
Via di Grotta Pinta
V. S. Caterina
P.za Farnese
V. dei Giubbonari
S. Carlo ai Catinari
Pal. Falconieri
PAL. FARNESE ★★
P.za Capo di Ferro
Cappella ★
S. Maria della Morte
V. del Mascherone
V. dell'Arco del Monte
P.za del M.te di Pietà
Fontana del Mascherone
B. Cairoli
★ Palazzo Spada
Pal. d. Monte di Pietà
P.za
★★ VILLA FARNESINA
Palazzo Cenci
Porta Settimiana
MIN. DI GRAZIA E GIUSTIZIA
Piazza Trilussa
Vallati
P.te Garibaldi
0   100 m
★★TRASTEVERE
TRASTEVERE

GIANICOLO   ISOLA TIBERINA-TORRE ARGENTINA

TEVERE   Lungotevere   della   Farnesina   Tebaldi   Giulia   Lungotevere   dei   Vallati

during the Napoleonic occupation (1809-14). Now it's occupied by the Papal Chancery, which drafts pontifical acts (⌖ see "VATICANO-S. PIETRO).

Michelangelo's "Fake" Cupid

Cardinal Riario's (architect of the Palazzo della Cancelleria) well-known taste for antiquities gave Michelangelo the idea of sculpting a magnificent Cupid, skilfully applying an artificial patina of age and selling it to the Cardinal for 200 ducats as a genuine antique. The collector got wind of the deceit and decided to recover his money and return the statue to the artist, but Michelangelo never saw his Cupid again. It was transferred to France and disappeared.

Façade and courtyard

This palazzo is the most elegant product of Rome's Renaissance. The broad smooth surfaces, the straight lines and the shallow pilasters of the façade give it a majestic quality. The granite columns of the courtyard arcade – a harmonious composition attributed to Bramante – come from San Lorenzo in Damaso.

Interior

On the main floor of the palace are the Aula Magna (the Great Hall) and the so-called *Sala dei "Cento Giorni"* (Room of the Hundred Days –perhaps how long its painting took). The latter contains a fresco by Giorgio Vasari, which depicts the meeting of Paul III, Charles V and François I in 1538 in Nice.

San Lorenzo in Damaso
Within Palazzo della Cancelleria.
The church, founded by Pope Damasus in the 4C, was later rebuilt as part of the palace. It was used as a stable under Napoleon and restored during the 19C. The ceiling, damaged by fire in 1939, has been entirely renewed.
The church consists of a nave and side aisles preceded by a vestibule. The first chapel on the right contains a 14C wooden crucifix; the last chapel on the left in the nave contains a 12C Virgin inspired by Byzantine icons.

▶ *Turn right into Corso Vittorio Emanuele II.*

Palazzo della Farnesina ai Baullari★
This little Renaissance building was begun in 1523 for Thomas le Roy, a French diplomat accredited to the Holy See. Raised to the peerage by François I of France, he added the lily of France to the ermine of Brittany, his country of origin. The lily was mistaken for the iris of the Farnese and the building was called the "Piccola Farnesina." As it overlooks **Via dei Baullari** (luggage-makers), it acquired the name of Farnesina ai Baullari. The Corso Vittorio Emanuele II façade was erected from 1898-1904; the original Renaissance style can be admired by walking around the building. The interior, which was radically restored in the 19C, houses ancient sculpture left by Baron Giovanni Barracco.

▶ *Continue along Corso Vittorio Emanuele II.*

Sant'Andrea della Valle★★
Piazza Sant'Andrea della Valle is graced with a fountain attributed to Carlo Maderno: it bears the eagle and dragon of the Borghese family and was probably put up for Pope Paul V.
Construction of the **church** began in 1591 under the direction of **Giacomo della Porta**: it was completed between 1608 and 1623 by **Carlo Maderno**. The **façade**★★ (1661-67), one of the most elegant of the Baroque style, was built by **Carlo Rainaldi**. The two-storey elevation ripples with columns and projections; the original scrolls intended to unite the two levels have been replaced by angels with a spread wing – although only the left-hand statue was executed.

Interior
The Latin-cross plan with a single nave flanked by intercommunicating side chapels, as in the Gesù Church, is typical of the Counter-Reformation. The severity of the art of this period is to be found in the extremely sober architecture of the second chapel on the right and the altar in the right transept. Conversely, the nave vaulting and left transept were decorated early in the 20C.
The dome★★, built by Carlo Maderno, is one of the loveliest in the city and second only to St Peter's in size. It was painted between 1624 and 1627 by **Lanfranco**, the first artist to handle a curved surface successfully. The *Glory of Paradise*, with its rich colouring, is an imitation of Correggio's effort on the dome of Parma Cathedral. The Evangelists on the pendentives were painted by Domenichino. The vigour and expressiveness are reminiscent of Michelangelo's art.
The upper section of the **apse**★, which was frescoed by **Domenichino** (1624-28), is in late Renaissance style: *St Andrew is led to his death (right); the Calling of St Andrew and St Peter (centre); the Flagellation of St Andrew (left); St Andrew being received into heaven (above); St Peter and St Andrew are shown the Saviour by St John the Baptist (arcade centre).*
The Piccolomini Popes' tombs lie above the last bay in the nave before the transept. The monuments to Pius II (*left*) and Pius III (*right*) are typical of late-15C funeral art.

▶ *Take Via dei Chiavari beside the church.*

Via dei Giubbonari runs very close to the site of Pompey's great theatre (*Teatro di Pompeo*), of which nothing remains except the semicircular line followed by the houses in Via di Grotta Pinta. By tra-

dition, it is the street where doublet-makers (*giubbone* = doublet), silk merchants and garment repairers worked. It remains very commercial. Behind the theatre, the great crowned portico of Pompey's Curia is where Julius Caesar was fatally stabbed in 44 BC. The remains of the Curia can be seen in the Largo Argentina Sacred Precinct (&see Area Sacra del Largo Argentina).
Turn right into Via dei Giubbonari and left into a side street leading into Piazza del Monte di Pietà, where the Cappella del Monte di Pietà can be seen.

▶ *Take Via dell'Arco del Monte; turn right into Piazza Capo di Ferro.*

Palazzo Spada★

The Piano Nobile is open just one Sun each month in the morning. ☎06 68 32 409.
During the 16th century, cardinals went to great lengths to "keep up with the neighbours". Gerolamo Capo di Ferro built this lavish white-stucco edifice, which was later acquired by Cardinal Bernardino Spada and finally by the Council of State. On the **façade** are statues of Roman patrons – such as Romulus, Numa and Augustus – and faithful dogs. One inscription reads: "The dictator Julius Caesar: He filled the whole world with his enemy's gore, and at the end he drenched the senate with his own blood."
The Caesar motif reoccurs within the **Galleria Spada**. (&see Additional Sights).The collection includes a statue of Pompey, which may have witnessed the famous assassination in 44BC. For some 20 years, until the last war, an elderly Frenchwoman appeared faithfully on the Ides of March and deposited a bouquet of scarlet carnations at the statue's feet.
The delicate execution of the friezes in the **courtyard**★★ is quite admirable.

Borromini "Perspective"

On the ground floor, behind the library and visible from the courtyard. Inquire about access.
The colonnade stretches into the distance – or at least appears to, thanks to clever a *trompe l'oeil* effect. In fact, the tunnel is a mere 9m/29ft feet with a petite two-foot statue. For a modest tip, the guard will sometimes escort sceptics behind the glass partition.

▶ *Continue to Piazza Farnese.*

Palazzo Farnese★★

⊶*Rarely open to the public.* ☎06 68 89 28 18. www.france-italia.it
At either end of this quiet and elegant piazza are two huge granite basins found in the Baths of Caracalla and converted into fountains in 1626. On the far side stands one of the most beautiful Roman palaces, which bears the name of the family for whom it was built. The fame of the Farnese began when Cardinal Alessandro was elected Pope in 1534, taking the name of **Paul III**. As the first Pope of the Counter-Reformation, he set up the Council of Trent, yet conducted his reign like a Renaissance monarch: he had four children whose mother has not been identified, made three of them legitimate and loaded them with riches. He was a patron of the arts, continuing the work on St Peter's and the Sistine Chapel and building the Farnese Palace. He and his descendants amassed a magnificent collection of works of art. One of his grandchildren, Ranuccio (1530-65), commissioned Salviati to celebrate the glory of the Farnese in a series of frescoes. Another, Odoardo (1573-1626), invited the Carracci to paint the gallery on the first floor. The last of the Farnese was Elizabeth (1692-1766), who married Philip V of Spain. Their son, Don Carlos of Bourbon, who became king of Naples in 1735, inherited the Farnese family riches; almost all the works of art from the Farnese Palace are now in the Naples Archaeological Museum or in the Royal Palace at Capodimonte.
The palace was purchased by the French Government in 1911 and bought back by the Italian Government in 1936. It was then leased to France for 99 years in exchange for the La Rochefoucauld-Doudeauville Palace, the building occupied by the Italian Embassy in Paris.

Façade

The absence of pilasters and the clear horizontal lines contribute to a masterpiece of balance and proportion. Construction began in 1515 on Cardinal Alessandro Farnese's orders, to the designs of his favourite architect, Antonio da Sangallo the Younger. When Sangallo died in 1546, Michelangelo took over. He retained the first-floor windows, framed by columns with alternate pediments, curved or triangular like the recesses in the Pantheon. He added the impressive upper cornice and over the central balcony he carved the irises of the Farnese coat of arms (not to be confused with the French lily). Recent restoration work has brought to light a delicate decorative design in pinkish tones.

The **courtyard** (⊶ not open to the public) is a model of Renaissance elegance, designed by three great architects: Sangallo, Vignola and Michelangelo. The rear **façade** – overlooking Via Giulia – is the best example of the building's elegance.

Its treasures include remarkable **frescoes** (1595-1603) by Annibale Carracci (in the Farnese Gallery) with the assistance of his brother Agostino and his pupils Domenichino and Lanfranco.

▸ *To admire the rear façade of the palace, take Via del Mascherone and turn right into Via Giulia (for a description of Via Giulia, ⟲see CASTEL S. ANGELO).*

At the intersection of Via del Mascherone and Via Giulia stands the 1626 **Fontana del Mascherone**. Carlo Rainaldi combined two ancient sculptures at the old ferry landing: a vast marble basin and a grotesque face with a vacuous expression. The mask dribbles water from the Acqua Paola, though for festivals, it would spout red wine. Sadly, this tradition has fallen by the wayside.

Via Giulia then runs past the Farnese Palace's **rear façade**. This was designed by Vignola who took over from Michelangelo as architect. In 1573 he was succeeded by Giacomo della Porta, who built the loggia. In 1603, the *"Passetto Farnese,"* the bridge over Via Giulia, linked the palace to the convent of Santa Maria della Morte and to several rooms where the Farnese kept their collection of Antiquities. Legend claims Alessandro Farnese,

one of the most blatantly rapacious rulers in papal Rome, disliked crossing the Tiber on public bridges with the riff-raff. He envisioned a private walkway connecting the Palazzo with the Villa Farnesina: a mighty status symbol, the 16th-century equivalent of, say, an executive heliopad. Michelangelo designed the graceful archway, now trailing with ivy, but span stopped well short of the river.

The Farnese vanity contrasts badly with the hospices and confraternities in the area, such as Santissima Trinità dei Pelligrini and **Santa Maria dell'Orazione e della Morte**. Dedicated to burial of the poor, it contained a spacious morgue-hall and easy river-access to net floating bodies each morning.

The 1737 facade by Fernando Fuga reflects this mission: gaping skulls flank the door. The two plaques, which invite alms, don't pull punches either. One image, black etched in ghostly white marble, shows a winged skeleton with a banner reading *"hodie mihi, cras tibi"* (essentially "your turn next"). The other begs on behalf of country plague victims, depicting a skeleton gloating over a human body.

▸ *Farther on turn right into Via di S Caterina and left into Via de Monserrato.*

Under the kindly eyes of its many beautiful madonnas, **Via di Monserrato** is lined by craft and antique shops, by palaces where the many Spanish prelates, who came to Rome in the suite of

Diplomatic Incident

The Farnese Palace has been occupied by the French Embassy since 1635. On 20 August 1662, a serious confrontation between the Papal States and the French king arose out of a street brawl near the Sistine Bridge. Two men died: a Corsican in the Papal Guard and a footman attending the carriage of the ambassador's wife. Following this incident, under the Treaty of Pisa Pope Alexander VII was forced to retract and to exclude any Corsican from his service.

the Borgia Popes (Calixtus III and Alexander VI), used to live. Many of the courtyards are worth a glance: the beauties of the Renaissance have not all disappeared. The church of **Santa Maria di Monserrato** is the Spanish national church.

▶ *Turn left into Via della Barchetta.*

Sant'Eligio degli Orefici

🕐*Open 10am-1pm.* 🕐*Closed 28 July-3 Sept and 22-31 Dec. To visit, press the intercom at Via S. Eligio 9 (custodian) or Via S. Eligio 7 (office). Donations welcome.* ☎/*Fax 06 68 68 260.*

Raphael began this church of the goldsmiths, often considered one of the purest expressions of the Renaissance (1516). A **cupola** crowns this small gem, laid out in an austere Greek cross plan. The *chiesa* is damp, somewhat gloomy, heavily restored and rarely open, but nonetheless outstanding.

▶ *Return to Via di Monserrato.*

The elegant **Palazzo Ricci**, tucked in at the back of its attractive little Renaissance square, has great charm; the façade bears traces of decorations by Polidoro da Caravaggio and Maturino da Firenze.
Via del Pellegrino, created by Sixtus IV in 1483 to provide pilgrims with easier access to St Peter's, was once home to a number of bookshops and printing houses. The façade of Palazzo della Cancelleria facing Via del Pellegrino is decorated with fine corner balconies and ground-floor arcades of shops.
The small and picturesque **Via Arco degli Acetari,** a popular photo spot, heads away from Via del Pellegrino directly in front of the *palazzo*.

Additional Sights

Museo Barracco
(Barracco Museum)

🕐*Open 9am–7pm.* 🕐*Closed Mon.* ⊛€3. ☎*06 68 80 68 48.*

The collections range over Egyptian, Assyrian, Greek and Roman sculpture to the end of antiquity. The museum also houses many original Greek statues.

The elegant internal courtyard stairs lead to the first floor, where the arch bears admirable 17C frescoes. The **Egyptian sculptures** date from the third millennium and include the head hewn in black granite of the young Pharaoh Ramses II, and two low-relief sculptures dating from the Old Kingdom, IV Dynasty *(Room I)*. Among the **Assyrian exhibits** *(Room II)*, note the low relief showing a group of women in a palm grove (late 8C BC); on display in the same room are a very beautiful woman's funeral mask in gilded pasteboard from the period of Ptolemy, an interesting head in painted stucco of a mummy from Ermopoli, and Egyptian art from the Roman period (2C). **Rooms III and IV** house a group of **Etruscan and Cypriot works**: Etruscan *antefixae* and memorial stones; a woman's head (2C BC) found near Bolsena; a little statute of the god Bes, a minor Egyptian deity also venerated by other races; interesting Cypriot statues such as the *quadriga* (6C BC). On the second floor are **Greek, Roman and medieval works of art**.

Galleria Spada★

In Palazzo Spada. 🕐*Open Tue-Sun, 8.30am-7.30pm.* 🕐*Closed Mon, 1 Jan, 1 May and at Christmas.* ⊛€5. ☎*06 68 74 896 ; Fax 06 68 61 158.*

The gallery presents Cardinal Spada's collection in its original setting: typical of a wealthy Roman in the 17C. The cardinal was the patron of Guercino and Guido Reni, whose noble manner pleased him. At the same time, he was interested in *bambocciate*, realistic paintings which appeared in Rome in about 1630 in the circle of the painter Pieter Van Laer, a Dutchman nicknamed *Il Bamboccio* (the puppet) because of a physical deformity.
The gallery is of interest both for its collection and for the building in which this is housed. In Room I, crowned by an 18C ceiling, note two canvases by **Guido Reni** (1575-1642): *Portrait of Cardinal Bernardino Spada*, a good example of the artist's use of pure delicate line, and the *Slave of Ripa Grande*.
The frieze along the top of the walls in **Room II** (tempera on canvas) is, in fact,

Houses in the picturesque Via dell'Arco degli Acetari

the same design repeated four times. The original frieze can be seen on the wall opposite the window and was produced by Perin del Vaga, possibly as a model for a tapestry to be placed under the Last Judgement in the Sistine Chapel, which was never completed. Room III, created in the 17C, was the cardinal's original gallery. On the ceiling, a series of panels dating from the end of the 17C portrays allegories of the four continents of the world (the first two panels), the four elements and the four seasons. The decoration of the fascia around the top of the walls is echoed by the trompe-l'oeil low reliefs in the two middle panels. The console tables in gilded wood are by late 17C Roman craftsmen. Paintings on display include a delightful and masterly *Landscape with Windmills* by Bruegel the Elder (1607) and the allegory of the *Massacre of the Innocents*, a masterpiece by Pietro Testa (first half of the 17C); note how the violent contrast between light and dark accentuates the dramatic aspect of this work. Jesus (escaping in the boat) is depicted embracing the cross, symbol of the Passion.

The two globes in the centre of the room (one of the earth, the second of the heavens) are by the Dutch cartographer and printer, Bleau (Caesius) and date from 1616 and 1622.

Room IV contains works influenced by Caravaggio. Particularly noteworthy is the portrait of an enraptured Saint Cecilia (149) by Artemisia Gentileschi.

Cappella del Monte di Pietà★

🕐*Open mornings only by prior appointment.* ☎*06 67 07 84 95.*

This small oval **chapel** within the Monte di Pietà Palace is a gem of Baroque art. Originally the work of Maderno, it was then redesigned by the architects Giovanni Antonio de' Rossi (who worked with Bernini) and Carlo Bizzaccheri (a pupil of Carlo Fontana). He took over after the maestro's death in 1695 and was responsible for the entrance hall and dome.

The chapel was consecrated in 1641, although decoration was not completed until 1725. The interior retains a number of works whose themes reinforce the aim of the institution: to put down usury.

CASTEL SANT'ANGELO★★

MICHELIN MAP 38 K 9-10, L 9-10.

This itinerary focuses on the River Tiber, the fortress-like building of Castel Sant'Angelo, and one of the most famous and romantic districts of Rome, dominated by the old fortress of the popes. The dome of St Peter's presides over this landscape. The other bank of the river is home to expensive antique shops in streets such as Via Giulia and Via dei Coronari, where the Madonna icons smile down on the alleys, recalling the old pilgrimage route.

▶ **Orient Yourself:** Castel Sant'Angelo is in the northwest section of Rome's historic centre, on a sharp loop of the Tiber. From here, Via della Conciliazione runs straight up to the Vatican City. The walk starts at the castle and then crosses the Tiber via the magnificent Ponte Sant'Angelo.

Don't Miss: the Castel S. Angelo terrace views, Via Giulia, Via dei Coronari

Organising Your Time: Allow 2hr 30min.

Also See: *CAMPO DEI FIORI; PIAZZA NAVONA; VATICANO-SAN PIETRO.*

A Bit of History

This district, densely populated in the Middle Ages, was gradually cleared and redeveloped as a centre for commerce. **Sixtus IV** (1471-84) initiated the transformation. On the route of religious processions between the Vatican and the basilica of St John Lateran, magnificent mansions were built, lining Via Banco di Santo Spirito, Via dei Banchi Nuovi and Via del Governo Vecchio.

Visit

Open daily (except Mon), 9am-7pm (last admission 6.30pm). Closed Mon, 1 Jan and Christmas. €5, €20 for a "Roma archeologica" card, valid for nine archaeological sites. 06 681 91 11. www.castelsantangelo.com.

WHERE TO EAT

See "Where to Eat" in the Your Stay in Rome section.

SHOPPING

Invito alla Lettura – Corso Vittorio Emanuele 283. 06 68 64 832. www.invitoallalettura.com. Open Mon 9am-midnight; Tue-Thu 9am-1am; Fri-Sat 9am-2am; Sun 10am-midnight. This lovely bookshop organises signings, readings and lectures.

The Castel Sant'Angelo squats upon ancient chunks of peperine and travertine stone. The angel statue dominates the whole complex. Entry is through the old mausoleum entrance, raised 3m/10ft higher than its original position.

Mausoleo di Adriano (Hadrian's Mausoleum)

This fortress-like building was intended as a sepulchre for **Hadrian** and his family. Begun by the emperor in AD 135, it was finished four years later by his adopted son and successor Antoninus Pius. The base (84m/276ft square) is surmounted by a drum (20m/66ft high), on which was heaped a small mound of earth (*tumulus*). It was crowned by a statue of the emperor and a bronze *quadriga* (four-horse chariot). The mausoleum contained the urns of all the rulers from Hadrian to Septimius Severus (AD 211). When Aurelian walled the city in 270, he turned it into a fortress.

Fortress

During the medieval struggle between the papacy and the noble families, the structure became a fortified stronghold. Nicholas V (1447-55) built a brick storey atop and added turrets at the corners. The octagonal bastions were the work of Alexander VI (1492-1503). In 1527 Clement VII took refuge there from the troops of Charles V and made several rooms habitable. These were later improved by Paul III, who already knew the castle, as he was imprisoned there by Innocent VIII when he was only Cardinal Alexander Farnese. In his autobiography, sculptor and metalworker **Benvenuto Cellini** admits that he, too, had been jailed there, as had Cagliostro, according to rumors. After the unification of Italy, the Castel Sant'Angelo became a barracks and military prison. Today, surrounded by a public garden, it knows only the assaults of tourists.

A high defensive wall – the **Passetto**, built by Leo IV (847-55) – links the castle to the Vatican Palace. Alexander VI created a passage along the top, so the Pope could retreat under siege.

Spiral Ramp

The entrance to the spiral ramp is below on the right, next to the entrance to the Tiber embankment. When the castle was a mausoleum, the ramp (125m/410ft) led up to the chamber where the funeral urns were kept. The walls were originally covered in marble, the floor was paved with mosaic, and the vault was decorated with stucco.

The Angel's Castle

In 590, Pope Gregory the Great led a procession against the plague decimating the city. Suddenly, atop the mausoleum, appeared an angel sheathing his sword. The gesture was interpreted as a sign that the plague would abate. In gratitude, the pope built a chapel on the mausoleum.

Main courtyard

This is also known as the Angel Courtyard from the 16C statue that graced the castle's crown until the 18C. On the right are medieval rooms, now the lower armoury. The end of the courtyard is closed by a shrine designed by Michelangelo. It forms the side wall of the chapel built for Leo X and probably stands on the site of Gregory the Great's cell (*see above*).

▸ *On the left are the Papal rooms.* Sala dell'Apollo

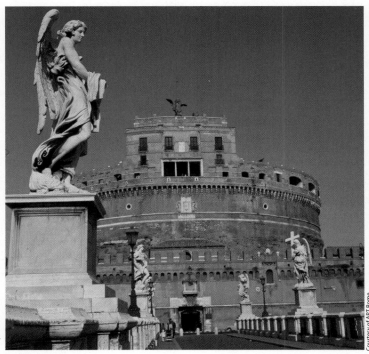

Castel Sant'Angelo

Courtesy of APT Rome

Access from Sala della Giustizia or from the main courtyard. Over the doorways and fireplace is the name of Pope Paul III and the date 1547. The room takes its name from its paintings, attributed to Perin del Vaga. The fine panels and ceiling illustrate mythological figures and grotesques. One of the two openings is the door to the lift (🕯 *see above).* The other leads to a 9m/29ft-deep shaft into a small room. Castel Sant'Angelo has many such trapdoors and secret passageways, which have given rise to a number of gruesome legends.

Sala di Clemente VII
The wooden ceilings bear the name of Pope Clement VII, and 15C and 16C paintings.

▶ *From Sala dell'Apollo take the tiny hall to the semicircular courtyard.*

Bagno di Clemente VII★
Access from the corridor separating Cortile di Alessandro VI from Cortile Leone X and the stairs up on the left. The beautiful decor by Giovanni da Udine, a pupil of Raphael, is evidence of the civilised lifestyle of the pope in the 16C.

Prigioni (Prisons)
Access by steps leading down from Alexander VI's Court. Beatrice Cenci (🕯 see Palazzo Cenci) Giordano Bruno, the heretic monk, and Benvenuto Cellini are supposed to have been imprisoned here.

Oil and grain store

The jars could hold 22 000 litres/4 839gal of oil and the capacity of the five large silos was about 100kg/3 700cwt of grain. It was Alexander VI who made these provisions in case of siege.

▶ *Return to Alexander VI's Court and take the steps up from the centre of the semicircle, which lead to the loggias of Pius IV, Paul III and Julius II (walking anticlockwise).*

Loggia di Pio IV (Pius IV's Loggia)

The rooms that open onto the loggia were living quarters for the staff. The loggia was rebuilt in the 19C to house political prisoners. Here, for many years, the gun was fired announcing noon.

▶ *Bear left.*

Loggia di Paolo III (Paul III's Loggia)

The Pope commissioned Antonio da Sangallo (the Younger) to design the loggia (*which faces north*) in 1543, and had it decorated with stucco work and grotesques.

▶ *Continue beyond the restaurant-bar.*

On the left is the upper armoury (*armeria superiore*), containing arms and uniforms of the Italian and papal armies.

Loggia di Giulio II (Julius II's Loggia)

It faces south with a fine view of St Angelo Bridge (*Ponte Sant'Angelo*) and the city of Rome. Giuliano da Sangallo probably built this loggia for Julius II.

▶ *Steps lead to the papal apartment.*

Appartamento papale★ (Papal apartment)

After the siege of 1527, when Clement VII sought refuge in Castel Sant'Angelo, Paul III had a suite of rooms constructed on top of the castle. These are protected by the succession of ramps and steps. **The Sala del Consiglio** (*Sala Paolina*) was a waiting room for visitors to the pope. Its floor is marble and the frescoes

are by a group of artists instructed by Perin del Vaga, a Florentine artist who followed Raphael. The name of the **Camera del Perseo** (Perseus's Room) is derived from the frieze by del Vaga himself. In the **Camera di Amore e Psiche** (Cupid and Psyche's Room), the frieze illustrates the story of the beautiful girl beloved by Venus's son.

▶ *Return to the Sala del Consiglio and, after the steps, turn into the corridor decorated with frescoes.*

Two sets of steps – linked by a passage – lead up to the **library** and two series of rooms (*one above the other*), named after their decorations: **Hadrian's Mausoleum Room** and the **Festoon Room**, which opens into a smaller apartment where Cagliostro was imprisoned, now comprising the **Dolphin Room** and the **Salamander Room**.

▶ *Return to the library.*

The **Sala del Tesoro** (Treasure Room), at the centre of the fortress, is a circular chamber. Its walnut presses contain the papal records, transferred here from the Vatican in 1870.

▶ *Beside the Sala del Tesoro.*

Scala Romana (Roman Staircase)

The staircase, part of Hadrian's Mausoleum, leads to the Hall of Flags and Columns (*Sala Rotonda*) and the terrace.

Terrace

The bronze statue of the angel (repaired in 18C) presides over a **panorama**★★★, one of Rome's most famous. From left to right: the Prati district and the green patch of the Villa Borghese; close to the castle, the great white mass of the Law Courts, then the Quirinal Palace, the Militia Tower and the shallow dome of the Pantheon; further right, the monument to Victor Emmanuel II and the domes and turrets of the city: the Gesù Church, St Ivo's corkscrew tower, the belfry of Santa Maria dell'Anima with its ceramic tiles, Sant'Andrea delle Valle, San Carlo ai Catinari and the Synagogue.

On the extreme right is the Janiculum Hill, San Giovanni dei Fiorentini, Via della Conciliazione, St Peter's and the Vatican Palace linked to Castel Sant'Angelo by the "Passetto," Monte Mario.

It is also possible to walk along the parapets to the four bastions: St John's, St Matthew's, St Mark's (which gives access to the "*Passetto*") and St Luke's.

Local Walking Tour

Ponte Sant'Angelo★
Supremely elegant, this bridge dates to Hadrian's era – the three central arches, at least. The 17C others were altered when the Tiber embankments were built in 1892-94. The statues of St Peter and St Paul (south bank) were erected by Clement VII in 1530; the ten Baroque angels are the work of **Bernini**, commissioned by Clement IX (1667-69).

▶ *Cross the Ponte Sant'Angelo and bear right into Via Paola.*

San Giovanni dei Fiorentini
Open 9am-12pm and 3pm-6pm. Pope Leo X, a Medici from Florence, decided to build a "national" church for his fellow countrymen in Rome. Famous Renaissance artists competed for the commission, including Peruzzi, Michelangelo and Raphael: Jacopo Sansovino won. Work began early in the 16C; it was continued by Antonio da Sangallo and Giacomo della Porta and completed in 1614 by Carlo Maderno. The 18C façade is late Counter-Reformation style. The chancel is Baroque.

Ironically, the aesthete **Borromini** rests in this patchwork construction. Near the main altar, his simple tomb reflects the shame of suicide (the architect had a long, messy death, allowing time to repent, pass away in the "grace of God" and receive a Christian burial).

The basilica's modern notoriety comes from its **pet masses**, where "domestic animals" are blessed.

Via Giulia★
The Via Giulia slices through the historic district. Part of the pilgrimage route, this wide, straight avenue once led the faithful to St. Peters. In fact, the road replaced a snarl of alleys, where brigands and pickpockets lurked. The 16C urban renewal produced one of the city's best addresses. For elegance and unity, Bramante was supposed to design all the buildings. The plan failed.

At Via Giulia's debut, prices were low enough even for artists. The irreverent goldsmith Benvenuto **Cellini** lived here, as did Sangallo the Younger (his home, number 79, was the Tuscan Embassy before unification). **Raphael** died before his rustic design at Via Giulia 85 was completed. Today a hodgepodge of palaces line the street, now flanked by antique shops and fancy restaurants.

Palazzo Sacchetti
No 66 Via Giulia. It may have been designed by Sangallo the Younger, architect of the Farnese Palace or by Annibale Lippi, the architect of the Villa Medici; both buildings were commissioned in the 16C by Cardinal Ricci di Montepulciano.

Between the next two side turnings on the right, Vicolo del Cefalo and Via del Gonfalone, are huge blocks of masonry. Bramante designed law courts for Julius II, which never progressed beyond these foundations. The Romans christened them "the Via Giulia sofas."

Pope Innocent X built the model prison at No52 "for a safer and more humane imprisonment of the guilty," as the inscription explains. Now Valadier's structure houses the **Museum of Criminology,** full of antique papal torture instruments (*entrance on Via del Gonfalone 29. Open Tues-Sat 9am-1pm; Tues & Thurs 2.30–6.30pm. Closed Sun, holidays and 13–25 Aug.* ☎ *06 68300234 www.museocriminologico.it*).

▶ *Turn left into Vicolo del Malpasso and left again into Via dei Banchi Vecchi.*

It was in **Via dei Banchi Vecchi**, the street of bankers in the 15C, that the **Palazzo Sforza Cesarini** was built by Pope Alexander VI, then only a cardinal.

▶ *Turn right into Via Sforza Cesarini and cross Corso Vittorio Emanuele II to reach Piazza della Chiesa Nuova.*

Chiesa Nuova★ (New Church)

The church was founded in the 12C as Santa Maria in Vallicella; the name probably alludes to a little valley nearby. The history of the church is linked to **St Philip Neri**, the Florentine founder of the Oratorians. In 1605, they rebuilt Santa Maria into the New Church.

The **façade** is decorated with the shallow pilasters and recessed columns typical of the Counter-Reformation. Neri wanted the **interior** to be plain, but during the Counter-Reformation, it was given a more elaborate Baroque format inspired by **Pietro da Cortona**. On the coffered stucco ceiling, he painted *St Philip's Vision* (1664-65). During construction, Neri had a vision of the Virgin supporting the ceiling, which threatened to collapse onto the altar.

Cortona enjoyed equal celebrity in Rome with Bernini. Between 1648 and 1651, he had already painted the dome, which depicts Christ abolishing punishment for mankind. In the pendentives, he placed the Prophets Isaiah, Jeremiah, Ezekiel and Daniel (1659-60). Meanwhile, he began an Assumption on the vault of the apse.

The chapel (*left of the chancel*) contains the remains of St Philip Neri and is decorated in grandiose style with gold, bronze and marble encrusted with mother-of-pearl.

A number of Mannerist and Baroque paintings star here, including three early works by **Rubens** (1608) in the chancel and the Presentation in the Temple by Cavalier d'Arpino (*first chapel on the left*). The chapel (*left transept*) contains a picture by Barocci, in a style typical of the late-16C. A beautiful Visitation (*fourth chapel on the left*) is by the same painter. On the altar in the sacristy (*entrance via the chapel in the left transept*) stands a beautiful marble sculpture of St Philip with an angel, executed in 1640 by Alessandro Algardi.

Oratorio dei Filippini

Closed for restoration at time of going to press. ☎06 67 10 81 17. www.comune.roma.it

Adjoining the New Church, the Oratorio was built between 1637 and 1662 to house the assemblies of the Congregation of the Oratory, where laity and clergy met under St Philip Neri.

Now know as **Borromini Hall**, it hosts conferences and various cultural activities. In addition to the Oratorian priests, the vast palace also houses the Vallicelliana Library, the Roman Library, the archives of the city of Rome, which include a collection of Roman newspapers dating back to the 18C, and various cultural institutes.

The **façade**★ overlooking Piazza della Chiesa Nuova is, in fact, the side elevation, designed by Borromini to form a unit with the church. Monumental, yet subtle, it is an interaction of calm and frenzied movement characteristic of this great Baroque architect..

Fontana della "Terrina"

Romans moved the **fountain** here in 1925; it had stood in the Campo dei Fiori until 1899. The basin was carved in 1590, but a few years later was covered with a travertine lid bearing the inscription: "Love God, do good and let others talk."

▷ *Take Via della Chiesa Nuova beside the church and turn right into Via del Governo Vecchio.*

Via del Governo Vecchio

One of the district's main streets, it continued the Papal Way as Via di Parione. Now it's lined with artisans' workshops, junk shops and antique dealers. Some of the Renaissance palaces still bear noble coats of arms. By Piazza di Pasquino sits the **Pasquino**, a fragment of a Hellenistic statuary group. This "talking statue" bears witness to the frustrations of citizens, who have posted rants –usually against war or the government – on it since the 16 C.

Palazzo del Governo Vecchio

The building at no 39 was completed in 1478. In 1624 it became the residence of the Governor of Rome. When the Government was transferred to the Palazzo Madama under Benedict XIV (1740-58), it became known as the Old Government Palace. The attractive doorway has friezes and diaper-work.

▷ *Return to Piazza dell'Orologio.*

Piazza dell'Orologio

The plain Oratory ends unexpectedly in a graceful clock tower. The wrought-iron scrollwork on the bell cage is Borromini's work (1647-49). Beneath the clock is a mosaic of the Virgin of Vallicella. On the corner is a beautiful **Madonna**, surrounded by a "glory" of cherubs.

▷ *Take Via dei Banchi Nuovi.*

Via dei Banchi Nuovi and Via Banco di Santo Spirito

By the 15C, bankers from Florence, Siena and Genoa had set up shop. Their fortunes were immense and intricately linked to the Holy See. The Papal State also granted them concessions on mining and customs dues. The bankers controlled the finances of the pope and the great noble families.

Together with money-changing, conducted in the streets, there was gambling. People bet on the election of the pope and the sex of unborn babies.

Until 1541, a working mint inhabited the **Palazzo del Banco di Santo Spirito**. From the end of Via Banco di Santo Spirito, stretches a pleasant view of Castel Sant'Angelo and its bridge.

Via dei Coronari★

One of the city's most attractive streets, this *via* boasts antique shops and palaces glowing in ochre and stone. During festivals, it rolls out a red carpet, studded with open-flame braziers. Overall it has retained the form acquired under Sixtus IV (1471-84). Dei Coronari is named for the vendors of rosaries (*corone*), who targeted pilgrims.

Arco dei Banchi

The Bankers' Arch leads to the Chigi bank. On the left is a Latin inscription, which comes from the nearby church of St Celsus and St Julian: it marks the Tiber's highwater mark in 1277.

▷ *Turn left under Arco dei Banchi.*

Ponte Vittorio Emanuele II (Victor Emmanuel II Bridge)

Nero built a bridge here in AD 60, which collapsed in the 4C. The present construction, decorated with allegorical groups and winged Victories, was begun soon after the unification and completed in 1911, linking Rome and the Vatican.

▷ *Cross the bridge to the right (north) bank and turn right.*

On the left is the imposing **Santo Spirito Hospital**, founded by Innocent III and rebuilt in the 15C by Sixtus IV. The **Church of the Santissima Annunciata** (Most Holy Annunciation), although small, is graced by an attractive façade full of movement (18C).

Santo Spirito in Sassia

🕐*Open 9am-7pm*. The church was built in the 8C for Anglo-Saxon pilgrims and rebuilt in the 16C, after being sacked. The architect was **Sangallo the Younger,** who died before its completion. The façade – which bears the arms of Sixtus V (1585-90), in whose reign the building was finished – is in the Renaissance style. The interior, beneath a beautiful coffered ceiling, is richly deco-

---

Madonnas

In Rome images of the Madonna smile from almost every street – at intersections, along alleyways, at the corner of a piazza. They may be painted, frescoed or in terracotta bas-relief, brightly coloured or monochrome. They seem to keep a watchful eye over passersby and many still retain the little lanterns, which for many years often provided the only illumination after sunset.

In January 1854, Rome introduced street lighting by gas – in Via del Corso. James Shepherd, an Englishman, was instrumental; he's now buried in the Testaccio Cemetery. In December, the street Madonnas were the object of a particular cult: peasants from the Abruzzi mountains, dressed in sheep skins, would perform on their bagpipes before their favourite shrine, accepting a small payment.

rated with paintings in the Mannerist style. There is a fine 16C organ.

Palazzo di Giustizia
The **Law Courts**, nicknamed the "*Palazzaccio*," were built from 1889-1911 by Guglielmo Calderini. They rank among the most conspicuous modern buildings in Rome. With a bronze *quadriga* by Ximenes (1855-1926) and colossal statuary, the Law Courts can claim both Classical and Baroque inspiration.

CATACOMBE DI PRISCILLA★

MICHELIN MAP 38 B 14-15, D 16-G 15-16, F 17.

The fascinating district around Via Nomentana stands outside the old walls northeast of the city. It is wedged between the River Aniene to the north, and the intersection of Via Nomentana and Viale Regina Margherita to the south. Sights include the palaeo-Christian churches of Sant'Agnese and Santa Costanza, the catacombs of Priscilla and the mosque, one of the most interesting recent buildings. Pleasant residential streets are lined with elegant palazzi and dotted with the attractive gardens of patrician villas.

Also See: *PORTA PIA-TERMINI; SAN LORENZO FUORI LE MURA.*

A Bit of History

Developed during the Fascist era, many streets bear names of countries that made up the Italian Empire. The large blocks of comfortable 1930s flats and elegant, ochre-coloured palazzi give way in the **Piazza Mincio** to extravagantly decorated buildings. Here reigns a mixture of Renaissance, Baroque and Egyptian styles, designed between 1922 and 1926 by the architect Gino Coppedè. The vast **Parco di Villa Ada** contains the *Monte Antenne*. Livy told of a city here that retaliated after the rape of the Sabine women; Romulus conquered it.

Chiesa di Sant'Agnese Fuori le Mura and Mausoleo di Santa Costanza★

The buildings' history begins with the death of Agnes, a 12-year-old martyred under Diocletian (284-305).
Legend of St Agnes – Both St Ambrose and Damasus, writing soon after the Diocletian persecution, mention this child-saint, grounding the 6C legend in truth. Agnes refused to marry the son of the Praetor, declaring that she had vowed her soul to God. She was condemned to stand naked in a place of ill repute – and was miraculously covered. She then escaped the stake unscathed, the flames turning on her executioners. Finally she was beheaded with a sword and buried in the Via Nomentana cemetery.
Legend of St Constantia – The saint's name is derived from that of Constantia, the Emperor Constantine's daughter or granddaughter. Suffering from leprosy, she spent a night by the saint's tomb. The

young martyr appeared in a dream, urging her to convert to Christianity; she woke cured.

Early church – After 337 **Constantia** erected a huge basilica near St Agnes's tomb. This fell into ruin, but a small chapel survived on the site of St Agnes' tomb. Rebuilt and enlarged by Pope Honorius (625-38), it is now known as St Agnes' Church and has been much restored.

Sant'Agnese Fuori le Mura★

Open 8am-noon and 4-7.30pm. ☎06 86 10 840; www.santagnese.net
The church of St Agnes Without the Walls can be reached from below (Via Sant'Agnese) or above (Via Nomentana through the convent courtyard and down a long flight of steps into the narthex). The walls are covered with fragments from the catacombs.

The ceiling and baldaquin are 17C. During the 1605-21 restoration, the bones of St Agnes were discovered next to another body, probably that of Emerentiana, who continued to pray by St Agnes's body when the other Christians fled from the stones thrown by pagans. Paul V enshrined her beneath the altar. The 7C **mosaic**★ is typical of Roman art with Byzantine influences.

S. AGNESE–S. COSTANZA

★★S. Costanza (Mausoleo)
BASILICA
S. Agnese fuori le Mura★
Via Nomentana

— Extant parts   — Non-extant parts

Catacombs

Open daily (except Sun and public holiday mornings and Mon afternoons), 9am-noon and 4-6pm. Guided tours only. €5. ☎06 86 10 840.
The oldest part dates back to the 2C. After St Agnes's burial, the graves spread behind the apse and down between the church and the mausoleum.

Mausoleo di Santa Costanza★★

Open 9am-noon and 3.30-6pm; Sun and public holidays 3.30-6pm only. Closed Mon afternoon. ☎06 86 10 840.
The Emperor Constantine's daughters, Helen and Constantia, were buried in this circular 4C mausoleum. It was probably converted into a church in the 13C. The outline of an oval vestibule can still be traced in front of the entrance. The rotunda is covered by a dome resting on a drum. The surrounding barrel-vaulted gallery is still adorned with its original 4C **mosaic**★. The vault has a variety of motifs: floral and geometric details, portraits in medallions, vine tendrils entwined with harvest scenes. The mosaics in the side recesses have Christian themes.

Sights

Catacombe di Priscilla★★

Guided tours only (45min; available in several languages), 8.30am–12.00pm and 2.30–5.30pm (5pm in winter). Closed Mon, Easter and Christmas. €5; no charge last Sun in Sept. ☎06 44 65 610 or 06 44 67 601.
The catacombs developed out of a private underground chamber (*hypogeum*) beneath the house of the Acilii, a noble family to which Priscilla belonged. Converts, they allowed the Christian community to bury its dead here. During the 3C, two storeys of galleries developed round the *hypogeum*. In the 4C, St Sylvester's Basilica, where several popes lie, was built by Pope Sylvester (314-35) over the Christian graves. The **Chapel of the Taking of the Veil** (*Cappella della Velata*) is named after the fresco, thought to represent three episodes in the dead woman's life: marriage, worship, motherhood. The **Chapel of the Virgin and**

Address Book

WHERE TO EAT

See "Where to Eat" in the Your Stay in Rome section at the end of the guide.

PASTRY SHOPS AND ICE-CREAM PARLOURS

Cavalletti – *Via Nemorense 179/181.* ☎06 86 32 48 14. Open Wed-Mon, 7.30am-1.30pm and 2.30-8pm. Known throughout the city for its light *mille-feuilles*, this small pasticceria also bakes excellent Neapolitan cakes and pastries, and lemon tarts.

Cds Artigiana Dolciumi – *Via S. Maria Goretti 24.* ☎06 86 21 86 22. Open 9am-2pm and 3-7pm. A small shop specialising in chestnut-based products: jams, cakes and marrons glacés.

Marinari – *Piazza S. Emerenziana 20/21.* ☎06 86 21 93 32. Open Tue-Sun, 7am-9pm. This pasticceria is renowned for its cream and berry tarts, and also offers a range of desserts and savoury snacks.

Romoli – *Viale Eritrea 140.* ☎06 86 21 62 08. Open until 2am. This popular bar-pasticceria sells a wide selection of filled *fagottini* (stuffed parcels). Try the dama, a house speciality, split in half and filled with a choice of cream, confectioner's cream, chocolate or nutella.

Di Lanzallotto Domenico – *Viale Somalia 96.* ☎06 86 21 22 57. Open Wed-Mon 7am-midnight. This gelateria attracts the crowds on summer evenings with its nutella-flavoured ice-cream, which is more like a mousse than an ice cream. Other excellent flavours are also available.

Duse (da Giovanni) – *Via Duse 1/e, zona Parioli.* ☎06 80 79 30 00. Open Mon-Sat, 8am-midnight. Known to one and all as "Da Giovanni," this small gelateria presides over one of the most elegant districts. Recommended for its excellent ice cream with unusual flavours such as date, passion fruit, papaya and mandarin.

CAFÉS

Excape Internet Café – *Viale Somalia 227.* ☎06 86 32 94 92. Open Mon-Sat, 9.30am-2am, Sun, 5pm-2am. As well as its 30 computers with Internet access, this high-tech café also has a range of original video games. In the summer, customers can surf the Net outdoors.

SHOPPING

Città 2000 – *Via Domenico Cassini 4.* ☎06 80 83 000. music@citta2000.it. Open Mon–Sat 9am–1.30pm and 3.30–8pm. This shop, near Viale Parioli, sells a variety of music, including trip-hop, fusion and jazz, as well as rare items.

Gatti e Antonelli – *Via Nemorense 211.* ☎06 86 21 80 44. Open Mon-Wed and Fri-Sat 7am-1.30pm and 4.30-7.30pm. This shop may make the best pasta in Rome.

Cooperativa Agricola Stella – *Via Garigliono 68.* ☎06 85 42 681. Open Mon-Sat until 8pm. Cheese-lovers can taste some excellent mozzarella and ricotta made from buffalo's milk.

Child★ (*Cappella della Vergine col Bambino*) contains the earliest representation of the Virgin (*on the ceiling*). The **Greek Chapel**★ (*Cappella Greca*) consists of two chambers. Over the arch in the inner room is a painting, possibly a 2C interpretation of the Eucharist.

Moschea★

Open Wed and Sat, 9-11.30am. For groups, by appointment only. Closed Aug and during Ramadan. ☎06 80 82 167.

The mosque, set in Mount Antenne, is part of the Islamic Centre: a library, an auditorium for 300 people, and several rooms for meetings and lectures. Typical Roman materials, such as brick and travertine stone, underline its connection to the city. The **interior**★ is the real masterpiece; the prayer hall is surmounted by a large stepped dome and 16 side domes, supported on 32 sunken pillars. This allows light to run around the base (170m/555ft). Utterly sublime.

Casina delle Civette

Open Apr-Sep, 9am-7pm; rest of the year, 9am-5pm. Closed Mon, 1 Jan, 1 May, 15 Aug and Christmas. Guided tours available (1hr). €2.50, no charge on 21 Apr. ☎06 44 25 00 72 or 06 44 25 00 88.

This original medieval-style building is hidden amid the green surroundings of **Villa Torlonia** and houses a small museum, which exhibits beautiful Liberty **stained-glass windows**★.

COLOSSEO-CELIO ★★★

MICHELIN MAP 38 M 13-14, N 13-14, P 13-14

METRO LINE B: COLOSSEO

This walk spans several centuries, focusing on the Colosseum and the Arch of Constantine, built in the time of the Emperors and now crowded with souvenir stalls, horse-drawn carriages and tourist groups; it then heads to the Caelian Hill, one of the greenest of the seven hills of Rome, to explore the many medieval treasures of this tranquil district.

▶ **Orient Yourself:** The Colosseum stands in the heart of Rome, southeast of the Forum.

Don't Miss: The Colosseum, of course, Michelangelo's Moses in S. Pietro in Vincoli, the mosaics of S. Clemente, the tranquil Villa Celimontana park.

Organizing Your Time: 2 hrs.

Especially for Kids: The Colosseum, with its tales of gladiators, naval battles and ferocious beasts, always fascinates.

Also See: FORO ROMANO-PALATINO, S. GIOVANNI IN LATERANO, S. MARIA MAGGIORE-ESQUILINO, TERME DI CARACALLA

Colosseo ★★★
(Colosseum)

(♿) ⏱Open summer, 8:30am-1hr before dusk; winter, 8:30am-5.30pm (last admission 1hr before closing time). ⏱Closed 1 Jan and Christmas. ✏ €8 (combined ticket with Palatine Hill and its museums); €20 for a "Roma archeologica" card, valid for nine archaeological sites. ☎06 39 96 77 00; www.pierreci.it

The Colosseum is the heart of ancient Rome, dominating the flat southeast end of the Forum. Though quarried and eroded, this amphitheatre remains one of the most enduring symbols of the city – if not all western civilization.

The stone blocks were brought from the quarries at Albulae, near Tivoli, along

specially built roads, 6m/20ft wide. Doric, Ionic and Corinthian columns support three tiers of arcades.

A Bit of History

Vespasian, the first of the Flavian emperors, devoted part of the huge area occupied by Nero's Domus Aurea (Golden House) to public entertainment. He transformed a lake-bed into the world's largest Roman amphitheatre. The Colosseum, begun in AD 72, took that name either because it stood near the huge **statue of Nero** or because of its own massive dimensions (527m/1 728ft in circumference and 57m/187ft high).

The circuses it hosted were originally rites to maintain good relations between the city and the gods. For many years, spectators attended bare-headed, as at a sacrifice.

The Colosseum, though still incomplete, was inaugurated in AD 80 by Titus, Vespasian's son. The spectacle lasted 100 days. The racing and the duels between gladiators were followed by bouts between men and wild animals: 5 000 beasts died. Even naval engagements were re-enacted in the flooded arena. In 249, to celebrate the millennium of the founding of Rome, 1 000 pairs of gladiators met in combat; 32 elephants, a dozen tigers and over 50 lions, brought from the provinces, were killed.

WHERE TO EAT

See "Where to Eat" in the Your Stay in Rome section at the end of the guide.

PIZZA BY THE SLICE
Pizzeria Leonina – Via Leonina 84 – ☎06 48 27 744 – ⏱Closed Sat and Sun. – 🍴. This tiny shop, situated just a few steps from the Colosseum, is always packed at lunchtime. It offers a wide range of pizzas to suit all tastes, including traditional and innovative combinations, such as squash pizza.

The spectacle usually lasted from dawn to dusk. Some were very cruel and spattered much blood. Others, like the presentation of wild animals, were like modern circus acts. Contrary to popular belief, Christians were never martyred here. Gladiatorial duels were banned in 404 by the Emperor Honorius. Wild animal fights disappeared in the 6C. In the 13C, the Frangipani family turned the Colosseum into a fortress, which then passed to the Annibaldi. In the 15C, it became a quarry: builders hauled away huge blocks of travertine for the Palazzo Venezia, Palazzo della Cancelleria and St Peter's Basilica. Benedict XIV stopped this in the 18C, by consecrating the building to the Christian martyrs thought to have perished there.

According to custom, one should stand before the Colosseum, and – in Byron's well-known words –quote the prophecy made early in the 8C by the Venerable Bede, an English monk and historian:

The Colosseum

> *"While stands the Colosseum,*
> *Rome shall stand;*
> *When falls the Colosseum,*
> *Rome shall fall;*
> *And when Rome falls,*
> *also the world."*

Visit

In Domitian's time, sailors would extend a linen awning to protect the spectators from sun and rain. Prime spots were reserved for the emperor and his suite, and for the Prefect of Rome and the magistrates. The *cavea*, the **terraces**, began 4m/13ft above the arena. First came the *podium*, protected by a balustrade and with marble seats for VIPs. Then came three tiers, separated by passages and divided by sloping corridors (*vomitoria*). Places were allotted according to social station. The women sat at the top under a colonnade; the slaves stood on the terrace above. The Colosseum probably had 45 000 seats and standing space for 5 000.

The gladiators, dressed in purple and gold, entered through doors at either end of the longer axis. Marching in ranks, they toured the arena and then halted before the emperor. Right arms raised, they pronounced the formula: *Ave, Imperator, morituri te salutant* ("Hail, Emperor, those who are about to die salute thee"). During excavations, the arena floor disappeared, revealing the underground warren where animals waited before being brought to the surface by ramps and lifts.

Not all Romans approved of these events. At the end of the 1C, the satirist Juvenal famously snarked: "This degraded people clamours with covetous anxiety for only two things in the world, bread and circuses."

Arco di Trionfo di Constantio★★★
(Arch of Constantine)

This magnificent construction, with its three arches, was built in 315 by the Senate and the Roman people three years after Constantine's victory over his rival Maxentius at the Milvian Bridge (ⓒ see MONTE MARIO). The abundant decoration was not all 4C work. Many sculptures were taken from 2C monuments (by Trajan, Hadrian and Marcus Aurelius). Like the Colosseum, the arch eventually merged into medieval fortifications.

North Face
The statues of four Dacian prisoners on the upper storey belonged to a monument erected in honour of Trajan (98-117). The four low reliefs between the statues date from the 2C (a further three are part of the collection of the Musei Capitolini); they belonged to monuments set up in honour of the Emperor Marcus Aurelius. The four medallions come from a monument to Hadrian (117-138). The subjects are hunting and sacrifices. The other 4C sculptures illustrate the reign of Constantine.

South Face
The design is identical to that on the north face. At the top are four low reliefs belonging to the same series as those in the Musei Capitolini and on the other side of the arch; on the left, two incidents in the wars of Marcus Aurelius; on the right, the Emperor addresses his army beside a sacrificial ceremony (below are the animals being led to the sacrifice).

Meta Sudans
Built by Titus and repaired by Constantine, this fountain was a cone of porous stone that oozed water. Named for the *meta* – the pivot pole in a chariot race – this unusual waterwork marked the turning point in a Roman triumphal procession, when a general entered the Via Sacra and the Forum. Mussolini demolished the remains to create a traffic circle. Now excavated, its foundations are displayed in the pedestrian area.

San Pietro in Vincoli to Santi Quattro Coronati

▸ *Go to Via di S. Giovanni on the east side of the Colosseum.*

The ruins on the street's north side may have belonged to the **Ludus Magnus**, a gymnasium for training gladiators.

▸ *Proceed north up Via N. Salvi and Via di Terme di Tito. Turn left into Via Eudossiana to reach Piazza San Pietro in Vincoli.*

San Pietro in Vincoli★
(St Peter in Chains)

ⓒ*Open 7am-12:30pm and 3:30pm-6pm.*
The church was consecrated in the 5C by Sixtus III (432-40), although it probably stands on a much older construction. One of the chief tourist attractions in Rome, it contains the famous *Moses* by **Michelangelo**. It also attracts pilgrims who venerate the chains that bound St Peter.
In 1475 Cardinal Giuliano **della Rovere** added the porch, which would be quite elegant if an upper storey had not been added in the 16C.
The broad interior is divided into a nave and two aisles by two rows of Doric marble columns. The medieval decor was altered in the 17C and 18C: the nave was vaulted and painted with frescoes.
On the left of the main door is the tomb of Antonio and Piero Pollaiuolo, famous Renaissance artists from Florence.

Mausoleo di Giulio II
(Julius II's Mausoleum)
This monument occasioned the meeting of two of the most powerful personalities of the Renaissance: **Julius II** and **Michelangelo**. The pope, with his unquenchable appetite for grandeur, wanted a tomb of such splendour that it would reflect his glory forever. In 1505, he summoned Michelangelo from Florence to assist. The tomb would dominate the centre of St Peter's Basilica, three storeys high, with 40 huge statues and bronze low reliefs: all surmounted by the sarcophagus. Michelangelo spent eight months

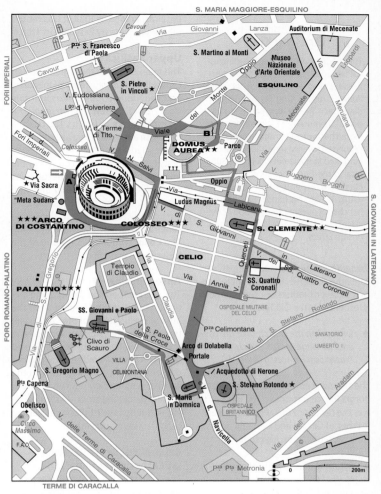

S. MARIA MAGGIORE-ESQUILINO

TERME DI CARACALLA

Antica ubicazione della statua di Nerone .... A   Pianta incisa delle Terme di Traiano .... B

---

in Carrara choosing marble. While there, he dreamed of sculpting a single gigantic figure out of the mountain of marble. He returned to Rome and a pope who had a new pet: **Bramante**. Hurt, Michelangelo retreated to Florence. After Julius II's death in 1513, the project declined steadily. Michelangelo sculpted only the *Slaves* (in Florence and Paris) and *Moses*; he began the statues of the daughters of Laban, Leah and Rachel, but left the mausoleum to his pupils.

Moses★★★

Pope Paul III grew tired of Michelangelo working on the tomb of Julius II. Anxious for him to start on the *Last Judgement* in the Sistine Chapel, the pope visited the

sculptor at work. There one of his cardinals remarked with great diplomacy that *Moses* was so beautiful that it alone would suffice to honour the grave.

The authoritative attitude of the huge seated figure is enhanced by the steady gaze of the eyes.

St Peter's Chains

The chains lie in the *confessio* beneath the chancel. Originally one bound the apostle in Jerusalem, the other in Rome. The legend of their miraculous joining began in the 13C.

Crypt

⊶ *Not open to the public.* The crypt is visible through the grill in the *confessio* (*beneath the high altar*). A fine 4C sarcophagus conserves the relics of the Maccabees, seven brothers whose martyrdom is recounted in the Old Testament.

▶ *On leaving the church take the covered passage (right), which leads to Piazza San Francesco di Paola.*

The steps are dominated by the former Borgia Palace (attractive 16C loggia); it was the residence of Vannozza Caetani, mother of Caesar and Lucrezia Borgia, the children of Pope Alexander VI.

▶ *Return via Piazza San Pietro in Vincoli to Via Eudossiana which leads into Viale del Monte Oppio.*

The **Parco del Colle Oppio** contains the relics of **Trajan's Baths** (*Terme di Traiano*). The immense palace built by Nero, known as the *Domus Aurea* (Golden House), once stood here.

▶ *Walk south along Via Labicana and then turn right towards San Clemente.*

Basilica di San Clemente★★

🕐 *Open 9am-12:30pm and 3:30pm-6:30pm*. The church was founded in the 4C in a private house belonging to a Christian (*titulus*) and was immediately dedicated to St Clement, the fourth Pope. It is, therefore, one of the oldest Roman basilicas. Ruined in 1084, it was rebuilt on the same site by Paschal II in 1108.

Upper Basilica

The main entrance through an atrium shows the simple austerity of medieval buildings (*usual entrance into south aisle from Via di S. Giovanni in Laterano*). The interior has preserved its 12C basilica plan with a nave and two aisles divided by recycled ancient columns. The unity of style, however, has been broken by the addition of Baroque stucco decorations and 18C alterations (ceiling and wall frescoes). The marble furnishings are particularly remarkable: in the *schola cantorum* (1) where the choristers sang. The **Cosmati** floor (12C) is one of the best preserved in Rome.

Apse Mosaic★★★

This 12C composition has dazzling colours, symbolism and beauty. Atop the apse is an illustration of the Crucifixion: on the cross are 12 doves, symbolising the Apostles, flanked by the Virgin and St John. Above is Paradise, shown in irridescent colours (*fan-shaped*) with the hand of god holding out the crown to his son. Below the cross are stags coming to quench their thirst (symbolising candidates for baptism).

Cappella di Santa Caterina (St Catherine's Chapel) (2)

The decorative **frescoes**★ by **Masolino da Panicale** (1383-1447) combine a taste for the attitudes, thin faces and subtle colours of the Primitives with the early Renaissance search for well-defined space: consider the architectural decor in the Annunciation scene above the entrance arcade.

The scene to the left of the arcade shows St Christopher carrying Jesus; in the chapel are scenes from the life of St Catherine of Alexandria (*left wall*), the Crucifixion (*end wall*) and scenes from the life of St Ambrose (*right wall – damaged*).

Lower Basilica

🕐 *Open 9am-12.30pm and 3:30-6:30pm, Sun and public holidays, 10am-12.30pm and 3-6pm*. 🕐 *Closed Christmas*. €3. ☎06 70 45 10 18.

▶ *From the north aisle steps lead down to the lower basilica (4C).*

This basilica consists of a narthex, a nave and two aisles and an apse. The upper basilica is built over the nave and south aisle of the lower one; a wall supporting the upper construction (**3**) divides the lower church into four.

Frescoes★

Some of these (**4**) date from the 11C and 12C; others are older (9C). Those in the nave (**5**) – notable for their good state of preservation and their lively scenes – illustrate the legend of Sisinius, Prefect of Rome. He went to arrest his wife, who was attending a clandestine Mass celebrated by Pope Clement, but was struck blind in the presence of the holy man. Above this scene, his servants, also blinded, carry off a column thinking it's his wife.

The figures are accompanied by sentences – ye olde cartoon captions. The language is often quite colourful and an extremely rare example of the transition from classical to vulgar Latin.

Mithraeum

Beneath the 4C basilica are the remains of two houses built in Republican times. The one beneath the apse was converted in the 3C into a *mithraeum*, a small temple for the cult of the god **Mithras**. Initiates sat on parallel stone benches. A statue of the god stood at the far end; central is the altar showing the god cutting the throat of the bull. Symbols of evil try to prevent the sacrifice that releases life-giving forces.

▶ *Take Via dei SS. Quattro Coronati.*

Santi Quattro Coronati

In the Middle Ages, the church of the **Four Crowned Saints** was part of a fortress that protected the Lateran Palace against attack. The Early Christian Church (4C) – erected by Leo IV (847-55) –lasted until 1084, when it was sacked and left in ruins by Robert Guiscard's troops. Paschal II (1099-1118) built a much smaller church, shorter and without side aisles. From the 12C to the 15C

S. CLEMENTE

Upper Basilica

0   10 m

Mithraeum

Lower Basilica   (▬▬ 4C construction)

Basilica di San Clemente

it belonged to Benedictine monks, but in the 16C the whole building passed to a community of Augustinian nuns.

Neither archaeologists nor historians can identify the saints honoured. The story of four martyred soldiers is mixed up with the story of five sculptors martyred in Pannonia (western Hungary). According to a list of martyrs, their remains all rest in this crypt.

Visit

The door beneath the tower, which served as a belfry in the 9C, leads into an outer courtyard. The wall opposite the entrance was the eastern façade of the early church.

The **interior** of the church is as Paschal II left it. The wooden ceiling and the women's galleries (*matronea*) date from the 16C. In the apse are 17C paintings and stuccoes depicting two groups of saints venerated in the church with a glory of saints in the vault. The crypt goes back to Leo IV's era. The sarcophagi of four martyrs were found in it, together with the silver reliquary containing St Sebastian's head.

Chiostro★

The Benedictines added these delightful **cloisters** in the 13C. The Augustinian nuns replaced the simple roof with vaulting. The ornamental basin dates from the time of Paschal II. The charming simplicity of the small columns is offset by the capitals, which are decorated with waterlily leaves. In the eastern walk is St Barbara's Chapel, with three small apses, added by Leo IV (9C).

Cappella di San Silvestro★

Entrance beneath the portico in the inner courtyard. Key available in the convent entrance on the north side of the inner court. The 13C **chapel of St Sylvester** contains curious frescoes, very naïve in execution. Beneath the figure of Christ, –flanked by Mary, John the Baptist and the Apostles – is an illustration of the legend of Pope Sylvester (314-35) curing the Emperor Constantine's leprosy.

Arco di Dolabella to San Gregorio Magno

▶ *From Via dei SS. Quattro Coronati, walk south to Piazza Celimontana.*

Arco di Dolabella

The 1C **Arch of Dolabella** – at the narrow entrance to Via S. Paolo della Croce – carries the remains of **Nero's Aqueduct**, which supplied water to the Palatine Hill from the Porta Maggiore. Nearby is an attractive **doorway**; it was decorated by Roman marble workers in the 13C with a mosaic showing Christ flanked by two figures, one black and one white, representing the Trinitarians, who ransomed captives. This sect had a hospice next to the church of San Tomaso in Formis.

Santo Stefano Rotondo★

Closed for restoration at the time of press. ☎06 42 11 99 .

The unusual round plan was inspired by the church of the Holy Sepulchre in Jerusalem. Built on the Caelian Hill in the late 4C to early 5C, it was dedicated to St Stephen (*Stefano*) by the pope at the end of the 5C. The church was originally one of the most opulent in Rome. By 1450, it lost its roof and for conservation purposes, the outer aisle was demolished and walls built along the line of columns of the second circle. The diameter of the basilica was thus reduced from 65m/213ft to 40m/131ft. In the 16C, Pomarancio (1530-92) painted the walls with 34 frescoes of martyrdom.

A charming 2C **mithraeum** is still visible beneath the church. The cult of the god Mithras, who was usually depicted in the act of killing a bull, was widespread among soldiers from the East and was particularly common during the reign of the Antonine emperors. ⏱*Only open the fourth Sat of the month at 11am, by appointment;* ☎06 39 96 77 00.

Santa Maria in Domnica

⏱*Open 9am-12:30pm and 4:30pm-7pm.*

The **Navicella Fountain**, in front of the church porch, was created in 1931 out of a 16C sculpture, in imitation of an ancient boat. This church, a favourite for weddings, has retained a rural charm. Founded in the 7C, it was greatly altered during the Renaissance. The façade and elegant, round-arched porch were restored at the request of Pope Leo X (1513-21) by Andrea **Sansovino**; the Pope's name is echoed by the lions on the keystones. The interior has retained certain 9C features: the basilica plan with a nave and two aisles, the columns with antique capitals and the beautiful apsidal **mosaic**★, an example of the artistic renewal that took place in the reign of Paschal I (817-24). The artist has abandoned the Byzantine rigidity for a more lifelike representation: a current of air seems to stir the raiment of the angels, grouped round the Virgin.

Kids At the end of the church is an entrance to the **Villa Celimontana** park. In its center is the intimate piazza dei S.S. Giovanni e Paolo.

▶ *Walk through the Villa Celimontana Park (entrance next to the church) to Piazza dei Santi Giovanni e Paolo.*

Basilica dei Santi Giovanni e Paolo

Domus antica (Ancient house) ⏱*Closed Tue and Wed.* ☎*06 70 05 745.*

The quiet square is dominated by the porch and the bold campanile, both dating from the 12C. The tower rests on the foundations of the **Temple of Claudius** (*Tempio di Claudio*), visible beneath the porch of the convent of the Passionist Fathers. Its history is similar to that of other buildings on the Caelian Hill: in the 4C, a certain Pammachius established a church in a private house; it was sacked by Robert Guiscard's Normans in 1084, but rebuilt in the 12C.

The five arches above the porch and the gallery, which comprise the upper stage of the façade, belong to the original building. Two handsome medieval marble lions guard the entrance. The **interior** dates almost entirely from the 18C. The main interest lies underground in the rooms of the **ancient house**★ where excavations have revealed traces of beautiful paintings (*access by steps at the west end of the north aisle. Open 10am–1pm and 3–6pm. Closed Tues & Wed.* ☎*06 70 45 45 44. www.caseromane.it.*)

At the foot of the stairs is a *nymphaeum* decorated with a marine fresco, (**1**) dating from the 2C; its fine state of preservation is due to a coat of whitewash applied to cover up the pagan decor when the house became a Christian place of worship. There follows a suite of parallel rooms beneath the nave and the south aisle; one (**2**) contains traces of sophisticated paintings of adolescents and spirits among garlands of flowers, vine tendrils and birds. The introduction of Christianity is evoked in a vaulted room; one wall (**3**) shows a woman at prayer, her arms extended as if on the cross.

▶ *Take Clivo di Scauro on the left.*

This tranquil, picturesque little street, built in the 2C BC by the Roman magistrate Scauro, passes under the medieval buttresses of the church. From here the apse of the basilica, the only one of its kind

Monte Celio (Caelian Hill)

The Caelian is the greenest and most pleasant of the seven hills of Rome. When Alba broke its peace treaty with Rome – following the combat between the Horatii and Curiatii – King Tullus Hostilius captured the rebellious city and transferred its population to the Caelian Hill. It was continuously inhabited until the 11C, when the Investiture Controversy brought war to Rome. In 1084, the army of Robert Guiscard "liberated" the papal capital from the German troops, but caused terrible devastation. Since then, there has been little rebuilding on the Caelian Hill. Both Basilica di Santi Giovanni e Paolo and Santo Stefano Rotondo are sited on the Caelian Hill.

in Rome, can be admired. With its small columns it is reminiscent of Romanesque churches in Lombardy.

▶ *At the end of Clivo di Scauro, the road turns to the left and the church of San Gregorio Magno comes into view.*

ROMAN HOUSES ON THE CAELIAN HILL

▬ Roman wall   ▢ Excavations

▦ Substructure of the basilica

San Gregorio Magno (St Gregory the Great)

Open 9am-5pm. Closed Mon. Chapels: €2.60 ☎06 488 10 94.

Its imposing 17C façade rises atop a steep flight of steps, framed by cypresses and umbrella pines. It was begun in 1633 by **GB Soria** for Cardinal Scipione Borghese (the eagle and dragon of his arms appear above the lower arches). Legend tells how in the 6C Gregory converted his house into a church and convent. From here, he sent a group of monks to evangelise England; among them were **St Augustine**, the first Archbishop of Canterbury, St Lawrence, St Melitas, St Justus and St Honorius. All succeeded him to the see of Canterbury. Beyond the façade is a four-sided portico.

In the chapel at the head of the south aisle stands Gregory's altar (15C), decorated with low reliefs of his legend. At the head of the north aisle is a chapel decorated with 17C paintings; it contains a curious Virgin on the wall (13C) and, opposite, a 15C tabernacle.

▶ *At the top of the steps, enter the small square to the left of the church.*

In the small square, there are three **chapels**, linked by a portico of antique columns. In St Sylvia's chapel (*right*), dedicated to St Gregory's mother, the apse is painted with a concert of angels (1608) by Guido **Reni**. St Andrew's Chapel (*centre*) has the *Flagellation of St Andrew* (1608) by **Domenichino** and the saint going to his martyrdom by Guido Reni.

The altarpiece is by Pomarancio and portrays the Virgin with St Andrew and St Gregory. St Barbara's Chapel (*left*) was first restored in the 17C. According to legend, St Gregory to offer meals to the poor; one day an angel came to sit with them, an event recorded in fresco.

Domus Aurea★★ (Golden House)

Entrance in Viale Domus Aurea, behind the Colle Oppio gardens. The west wing of the building is still undergoing restoration and refurbishment. Limited hours during repairs: open Tues–Fri 10am-4pm (last admission 1hr before closing time). Closed Sat-Mon, 1 Jan and Christmas. €5 + €1 compulsory booking fee. ☎06 39 96 77 00. www.pierreci.it

The **Golden House** is the palace built by **Nero** after the fire in AD 64. The vestibule was on the Velia (where the Arch of Titus stands) and contained the famous statue of Nero; the rooms were on the Oppian Hill. In the hollow between, now occupied by the Colosseum, was a vast lake, and all around were gardens and vineyards. Inside, Suetonius reported "the dining-room ceilings were composed of movable ivory tiles pierced with holes so that flowers or perfume could be sprinkled on the guests below; the main dining room was circular and turned continually on its axis, day and night, like the world."

Nero committed suicide in AD 68, after the Senate condemned him. The lake was

DOMUS AUREA
0   30 m

Constructed by Nero   Constructed by Trajan

drained and the Colosseum erected here. Then the upper part of the house was razed and the remainder lumped into foundations for the Baths of Titus and Trajan. The Golden House was not discovered until the Renaissance. Raphael and some of his fellow artists were very enthusiastic about the paintings: geometric designs, foliated scrolls, and decorations with faces and animals. These underground grottoes – gave these motifs the name "**grotesques**".

Tour

This residence, whose beautiful brick façade belonged to Trajan's Baths, was divided into two wings. The imperial apartments were in the left wing; the right housed the banqueting halls, galleries and libraries. The visit starts in one of the side galleries (1), built in front of Nero's house as a basement to Trajan's Baths, and continues through a series of rather dark rooms, one of which houses remains of the buildings destroyed by the fire of 64 (2). The visitor then arrives at the Nymphaeum of Ulysses and Polyphemus and the Room of the Golden Vault (3), both of which were decorated by Fabullus with brilliantly coloured landscapes and mythological scenes. The visit continues to the cryptoporticus that links the two wings; signatures of artists who snuck into the ruins are on the corridor ceiling. Just before the eastern wing, the Room of Achilles (4) is decorated with friezes and garlands. The eastern wing houses the Octagonal Room (5), where the skilful architectural design may be fully appreciated. The room is well lit by an opening and blossoms into a nymphaeum and four *triclinia*. The visit ends in the Room of Hector and Andromache (6), where the Laocoön statue perhaps emerged in 1506 (now on display in the Vatican).

EUR★

MICHELIN MAP 38 T2, T3, U2, U3, U4, V2 AND V 3
METRO LINE B: EUR PALASPORT OR EUR FERMI

Loved and loathed, this Fascist-built neighbourhood stands south of Rome. EUR stands for "Esposizione Universale di Roma," a boastful movement that inspired all this monumental, modern white marble and grand avenues. According to art historian Sylvia Pressouyre, in "a certain light, the district resembles the imaginary cities painted by Giorgio de Chirico". Leisure options here include pedal boats on the lake, a fair ground and, soon perhaps, a theme park at Cinecittà, Italy's epic film studios.

▶ **Orient Yourself:** EUR lies between the Via del Mare leading to Ostia to the west and Via Laurentina to the east. It's intersected by Via Cristoforo Colombo.

⊛ **Don't Miss:** Roman Civilisation Museum and the *Palazzo della Civiltà del Lavoro*.

⊙ **Organizing Your Time**: 4 hrs, if you wish to include a museum.

Kids **Especially for Kids:** the model of ancient Rome in the Museum of Roman Civilisation, the other museums, the *gelateria* Giolitti on the lakeside.

⌖ **Also See:** The itinerary can combine with *OSTIA ANTICA*. Catch a train from Magliana Station (Metro B: EUR-Magliana) or Ostiense Station (Metro B: Piramide).

A Bit of History

In 1937, the government conceived a grandiose project for a 1942 universal exhibition. The idea was to develop along the motorway linking Rome and Ostia. The contract was given to the architect Marcello Piacentini. Building began in 1939; on 10 June 1940, Italy entered the war allied to Germany and work stopped the next year. Following Rome's bombing and the fall of the Fascists, the scheme was abandoned. Two events – Holy Year in 1950 and the 1960 Olympic Games – brought EUR to the fore again. The new Via Cristoforo

Colombo and metro stimulated an administrative and cultural centre, a business forum and residences. The **Sports Palace**, by Piacentini and Pier Luigi Nervi, and the cycle racetrack were built for the Olympics. Today, EUR's colossal white buildings look much like the scheme proposed by the Fascists.

Sights

Museo della Civiltà Romana★★

(assisted visits). ⏱Open Tue-Sun 9am-2pm (last admission 30min before closing time). ⏱Closed Mon, 1 Jan, 1 May and Christmas. ↝€6.20; no charge on 21 Apr. ☎06 59 26 135 and 06 59 26 041. www2.comune.roma.it/ museociviltaromana.

The huge **Museum of Roman Civilisation** sprawls in two buildings linked by a portico. It illustrates the city's history from foundation through the empire. Exhibits really drive home the fact that a peasant people conquered their known world – and influenced the rest of it for more than 1 000 years.

Kids The highlight is a large **model of ancient Rome** (5C BC), called the *"plastico"*. Other replicas bring to life the well-

Model of Rome

The visit to the museum concludes with a superb 1:250 scale model★★ of Rome at the time of Constantine (306-37), made by the architect Italo Gismondi in 1937. The model shows the city in all its glory and allows the visitor to identify its many monuments, some of which survive today and others which no longer exist.

known monuments, such as the Colosseum, Domitian's Stadium (*Stadio di Domiziano*), and Hadrian's Villa. Of particular interest is the model depicting the spiral of low-relief panels on **Trajan's Column** (*Room LI*).

Museo delle Arti e Tradizioni Popolari★ (Folk Museum)

Piazza Marconi 8. ⏱Tues–Fri 9am–6pm, Sat–Sun 9am–8pm. ⏱Closed Mon, 1 Jan, 1 May, 25 December. ☎06 59 12 669; www.popolari.arti.beniculturali.it ↝€4.

This beautiful museum introduces visitors to Italian folklore and traditions. Exhibits start with a collection of old vehicles, including some fine Sicilian carriages and a grape-cart. To the left of the stairs, slightly out of view, is a beautiful Venetian **gondola**. Other displays explore peasant life, bread-making, farming, hunting, sailing and fishing. **Kids** Children enjoy the musical instruments, puppets and marionettes.

Museo Preistorico Etnografico L. Pigorini★

⏱Open Sun-Wed 9am-2pm. ⏱Closed Mon. ↝€4. ☎06 59 12 669. www.pigorini.arti.beniculturali.it.

Kids The **Museum of Ethnography and Prehistory** houses one of the largest ethnographic collections in the world. At the entrance is a wooden pirogue dating from 5 500 BC found on Lake Bracciano. The rich **African Section** assembles more than 60 000 objects, including weapons, utensils, costumes and religious articles. The **Oceanic Section** features masks, sculptures and paintings. A huge ceremonial canoe from the Trobriand Islands provides the focal point of the room.

The second floor is dedicated to Italian prehistory. The last room focuses on the increasing Eastern influence, during the early Etruscan era (late-8C to mid-6C BC). The **Praenestina fibul★** bears one of the oldest inscriptions in Latin.

Museo dell'Alto Medioevo

Viale Lincoln 3. ⏱Open Wed-Sun 9am-2pm (last admission 1.30pm). ⏱Closed Mon, 1 Jan, 1 May and Christmas. ↝€2. ☎06 54 22 819.

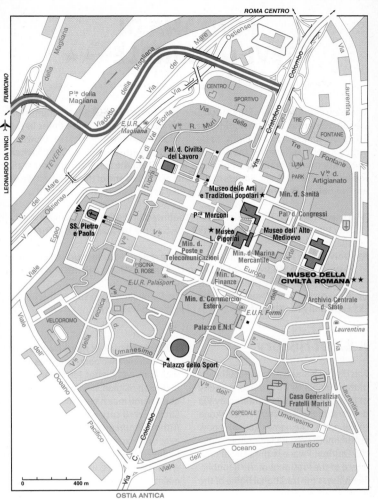

ROMA CENTRO

FIUMICINO

LEONARDO DA VINCI

TEVERE

OSTIA ANTICA

0   400 m

The **Medieval Museum** contains exhibits covering the 5C to the 11C, as well as plans of classical and Christian Rome.

Piazza Marconi
A marble obelisk (finished in 1950) has been raised to the glory of the Italian physicist Guglielmo Marconi (1874-1937), inventor of wireless telegraphy.

Palazzo della Civiltà del Lavoro
In 1938, three architects – Guerrini, La Padula and Romano – designed EUR's most iconic building. Its stark mass is accentuated by only by arches, a sort of Swiss-cheese effect. Fellini exploited this oddity in his 1962 film *Le Tentazioni*

del Dottor Antonio. Giantess Anita Ekberg chased a professor outside the "square Colosseum". The building houses working conditions organisations.

Santi Pietro e Paolo
This spectacular travertine church, dedicated to **St Peter and St Paul**, was built between 1937 and 1941 on the highest point in the EUR. Set among shrubs and flowers, its white mass dominates the whole district. Atop the steps stand two large statues of St Peter and St Paul. The Greek cross plan is stressed by the clean angles and sober lines. The dome, covered in little tiles overlapping like fish scales, rests on a drum pierced by *oculi*.

FONTANA DI TREVI-QUIRINALE★★★

MICHELIN MAP 38 K 12-13, L 12-13
METRO LINE A: BARBERINI (500M/550 YD FROM THE FONTANA DI TREVI)

The Trevi Fountain, one of the most famous sights in Rome, has been immortalised in numerous films, including the American-produced "Three Coins in the Fountain" and Federico Fellini's "La Dolce Vita." Nowadays the square is crowded with souvenir sellers and tourists, yet it's still breath-taking, especially when the white marble monument glows at night. From the fountain, a short walk leads to the Quirinal Hill, Rome's highest. Its piazza has one of the city's best views and is home to the President's palace, as well as fine palazzi and churches.

▶ **Orient Yourself:** This district is to the southwest of the Quirinal, the most northerly hill, and is bordered by Via del Corso to the west and Via del Tritone to the north.

⊚ **Don't Miss:** The Trevi fountain at night, the duelling architectures of Bernini e Borromini in S. Andrea al Quirinale and S. Carlo alle Quattro Fontane, Carracci's *Mangiafagioli* in the Galleria di Palazzo Colonna.

🕓 **Organizing Your Time:** 2 hrs 30 min. The Quirinale is open Sun.

Kids Especially for Kids: The museums of pasta and waxworks.

A Bit of History

This district is situated to the southwest of the Quirinal Hill, the most northerly of Rome's hills, and is bordered by Via del Corso to the west and Via del Tritone to the north. The name Quirinal is now synonymous with Italian politics, since the Quirinal Palace is the official residence of the President of the Republic. The hill was the traditional home of the Sabines and took its name from one of their lesser-known gods, **Quirinus**, who, with Mars and Jupiter, formed the basis of Roman religion. It is thought that the god's name may have derived from the Sabine word curi, which meant spear. Although uncertainty surrounds his exact role and attributes, Quirinus is believed to have been a warrior god who, unlike Mars, was responsible for maintaining peace and order in the city.

J. Malburet/MICHELIN

Piazza di Trevi, with the famous fountain in the foreground

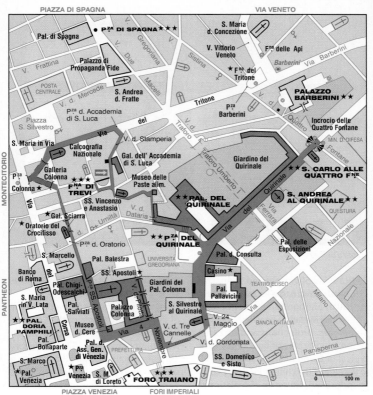

A legend identifies this god with the founder of Rome: during a solar eclipse, Romulus is said to have disappeared and been captured by the gods, who then transformed him into Quirinus. Until the end of the 19C only the fringes of the city reached the Quirinal; the Flavian Mausoleum (Mausoleo dei Flavi) was built there by Domitian (81-96); Caracalla built a temple to Serapis (the ruins survived until the Middle Ages); Constantine built a bathhouse that disappeared in the 17C.

Walking Tour

Fontana di Trevi★★★

This late Baroque fountain, one of Rome's most famous monuments, is an impressive sight, made all the more striking by its position in a tiny piazza. The key to the work is given in two high-relief carvings: in 19 BC Agrippa decided to build a long canal (20km/13mi) to

bring water to Rome (*left*). He named it "Acqua Vergine" after a young virgin who revealed the spring to the Roman soldiers (*right*).

Repairs were made under Pope Nicholas V and Urban VIII. Clement XII commissioned Nicolà Salvi (1732) to adorn the end of the canal with a fountain. It fills the whole width of the façade, which gives the impression of a commemorative arch. Salubrity and Abundance flank the central figure, the Ocean, which rides in a chariot drawn by two sea horses and two tritons, and provides a photogenic spectacle for the faithful tourists. Tradition claims one coin (cast backward over the left shoulder) ensures a return to Rome, two bring love and three a wedding in the Eternal City. Romantic notions aside, be wary of pickpockets here.

Church

In front of the fountain, set slightly back from the square, stands the church

Palazzo del Quirinale

dedicated to St Vincent and St Anastasius (**Santi Vincenzo e Anastasio**), built in 1650 by Martino Longhi the Younger for Cardinal Mazarin. Detached columns, pediments, projections and recesses create an interplay of light and shade typical of Baroque art. Vicolo Modelli, to the side of the church, leads to Piazza Scanderberg, home to the National Pasta Museum (☟ *See the section "Additional Sights"*).

▶ *South of the church turn left into Via della Dataria, which leads to Piazza del Quirinale.*

Piazza del Quirinale★★

Lined by handsome palaces, adorned with an obelisk and ancient statues and refreshed by a fountain, the square typifies Roman elegance. Sixtus V (1585-90) transferred statues of the **Dioscuri** from Contantine's Baths nearby; they are fine Roman copies of original Greek works. Some two centuries later, Pius VI moved them slightly apart to fit an obelisk, which formerly stood at the entrance to Augustus's mausoleum. Finally Pius VII (1800-23) completed the group with a handsome antique basin : a water trough when the Forum was the "Campo Vaccino" where cows grazed.

Palazzo del Quirinale★★

⟐ ☟*Open Sun, 8.30am–noon.* ☟*Closed 2 Jan, 27 Mar, 24 Apr, 1 May, 3 May, 3 Jul–11 Sept, and 18 and 25 Dec €5.* ☎*06 46 99 1. www.quirinale.it*

The **Quirinal Palace** is the work of some of the finest architects of the Counter-Reformation and the Baroque period. It was commissioned in 1573 by Gregory XIII from Martino Longhi the Elder as a summer residence for the popes. Sixtus V commissioned Ottaviano Mascherino, Domenico Fontana and Flaminio Ponzio. Under Paul V Carlo, **Maderno** added the monumental door with its two half-reclining statues of St Peter and St Paul. **Bernini** was brought in by Alexander VII. The palace was completed by Ferdinando Fuga for Clement XII.

The courtyard of the presidential palace –guarded by sentries who must be 1.82m/6ft 3in – leads to the grand staircase. The fresco of Christ (*above the arch*) by **Melozzo da Forlì** (1438-94) was originally part of the Ascension in the church of the Holy Apostles. The tour includes a succession of rooms, all sumptuously decorated, the chapel painted by **Guido Reni** (*Annunciation* on the altar piece), and the Pauline Chapel.

Palazzo della Consulta

The **façade**★ is by **Ferdinando Fuga** (18C), who favoured Baroque motifs. The three doorways – their pediments crowded with statues and sculptures, and the coat of arms of Clement XII, supported by a swarm of cherubs – make a lively contrast with the bare façade of the Quirinal

G. Bludain/MICHELIN

Palace. This is now the seat of the Constitutional Court.

▶ *Take Via del Quirinale.*

The east wing of the palace, overlooking Via del Quirinale, was built in the 17C and 18C.

Sant'Andrea al Quirinale★★

🕐Open Wed–Mon, 8am-noon and 4-7pm; 🕐Closed Tues, Aug. ☎06 85 30 17 58. *Donations welcome.*
St Andrew on the Quirinal by **Bernini** and St Charles by the Four Fountains (*San Carlo alle Quattro Fontane*) by **Borromini** express with unusual clarity the genius of two artists whose styles were diametrically opposed. The façade of the former, which opens into a semicircular atrium, bears a crown showing the arms of Cardinal Camillo Pamphili, Innocent X's nephew, who commissioned the church in 1658.

Interior★★

The interior, as in San Carlo, is elliptical, but oriented on the shorter axis and defined by the entrance and the magnificent choir stalls. The deep rectangular side chapels and the false portico in front of the high altar give a feeling of spaciousness, which helps to disguise the true proportions of the church. **Bernini**'s skilful use of coloured marble, gilding and stucco figures has created a rich and beautiful decor. The second chapel on the right contains three paintings by Baciccia (1639-1709); the *Crucifixion of St Andrew* by Jacques Courtois (1621-76), known as the Burgundian, can be admired in the apse. The gilt *Glory* by Raggi over the high altar, lit from above, is a reminder that Bernini had a great liking for theatricality. In a chapel to the left (1) note the painting by Carlo Maratta (1625-1713) showing the Virgin appearing to St Stanislas.
St Stanislas's Rooms (*Camere di San Stanislao*) (2) contain a recumbent statue of the saint in marble by Pierre Legros (*entered from the fourth chapel on the right; apply to the sacristan*).
In the **sacristy (3)** there is a beautiful vault in *trompe-l'œil*.

▶ *Continue along Via del Quirinale.*

Via del Quirinale
Sant'Andrea al Quirinale

San Carlo alle Quattro Fontane★★

🕐Open Mon–Fri 10am-1pm, 3-6pm; Sat 10am-1pm; Sun & hols noon–1, 3–6pm.
The **church of St Charles at the Four Fountains**, also known as San Carlino, is probably the best expression of **Borromini**'s creative genius. Commissioned in 1638, it was his first known work. The façade, added some 30 years later, was his last; it was unfinished when he committed suicide in 1667. It reveals the torment of a man whose art was full of contradictory statements: every curve is followed by a counter curve (in particular the façade and the cornices). A convex shrine (below the medallion) is set against the central concave section of the upper storey.

Interior★★

The form is that of an ellipse oriented on the longer axis. The movement is supplied by the alternating concave and convex surfaces of the walls themselves. The confined space – no larger, it is said, than one of the pillars supporting the dome of St Peter's – is perfectly suited to the architect's distinctive style. It is affected and austere, bizarre and elegant and quite out of sympathy with the Baroque taste for sheer size. The intricately designed coffering in the dome is surmounted by a lantern harbouring the Holy Ghost.

Cloisters★

Borromini's cloisters – two orders of Doric columns and slightly convex canted corners – are perfectly proportioned.

▶ *Continue to the crossroads with Via delle Quattro Fontane.*

Address Book

WHERE TO EAT

♿ See "Where to Eat" in the Your Stay in Rome section at the end of the guide.

ICE CREAM

Il Gelato di S. Crispino – *Via della Panetteria 42. ☎06 67 93 924. www. ilgelatodisancrispino.it. Open Mon, Wed–Thurs and Sun noon–12.30am, Fri–Sat noon–1.30am. Closed Tues.* The owners of this gelateria, considered one of Rome's best, only make flavours they like themselves and serve in cups, not cones. Flavours include honey, ginger and cinnamon, Armagnac, liquorice, meringue with hazelnut and chocolate and cream with Pantelleria raisin wine.

SHOPPING

Becker & Musicò – *Via di S. Vincenzo 29. ☎06 67 85 435. Open 10am-7.30pm.* Becker & Musicò specialises in articles for smokers, and also has a workshop, which makes wooden pipes from the white heath tree (*Erica arborea*).

Farmacia Pesci – *Piazza Fontana di Trevi 89. ☎06 67 92 210. Open Mon-Fri, 8am-8pm, Sat 8am–1pm. Closed Sun.* Rome's oldest pharmacy, dating back to the mid-16C, retains a number of its old features, including jars, documents and the huge structure that once separated the laboratory from the shop.

Fratelli Viganò – *Via Minghetti 7/8. ☎06 67 95 147. Open Mon–Sat 10am–1pm and 5–7.30pm. Closed Sun.* One of the oldest Roman stores, it sells a wide range of men's clothing, as well as hats, including the genuine Panama.

Mel Bookstore – *Via Nazionale 254/255. ☎06 48 85 405. Open Mon–Sat 9am–8pm; Sun 10am–1.30pm and 4.30–8pm.* This bookshop is tastefully decorated in early-20C style and offers a wide selection. A pleasant café occupies the top floor.

Incrocio delle Quattro Fontane

The **Four Fountains crossroads** was created by Sixtus V (1585-90), who introduced more alterations than the city had known since the empire's end. His aim was to link the main basilicas with broad straight roads. These four straight streets opened up **views**★ of the obelisks in front of the Trinità dei Monti (*west*), the Porta Pia (*north*), the west end of Santa Maria Maggiore in Piazza dell'Esquilino (*east*) and in Piazza del Quirinale (*south*). The crossroads corners' are canted to allow four 16C fountains.

▶ To get to the Palazzo delle Esposizioni, return to Via del Quirinale and turn left onto Via Ferrara.

Palazzo delle Esposizioni

⚒ *Closed for restoration at the time of going to press. Temporary exhibitions, cinema and theatre productions. Entrances at Via Nazionale 194 and Via Milano 9a. Café and restaurant.* The **Exhibition Hall**, opened in 1883, was designed by the architect Pio Piancentini. The main prospect is neo-Classical and its large central arch and two side entrances are reminiscent of a commemorative arch. Architect C Dardi shoe-horned in new technical and lighting systems, and fresh facilities: a conference room and cinema for 200 people, a 130-seat theatre, cafeteria, bookshop and a restaurant.

▶ Return to Piazza del Quirinale and take Via 24 Maggio.

Palazzo Pallavicini

🕙 *Open first of the month, 10am-noon and 3–5pm (appointment only). Closed 1 Jan. Contact Amministrazione Pallavicini, Viale Mazzarino 14, 00184 Roma, at least three weeks before. ☎06 48 14 344.*

The courtyard has palm trees, laurels, pines and holm oaks. On two sides loom the 1603 palace built by Cardinal Scipio Borghese, more or less atop Constantine's Baths. Just inside the main gates stands the **Casino,**★ opening onto a terrace. This charming 17C pavilion is famous for the **Aurora fresco** on the ceiling by Guido Reni, a pupil of the Carracci. The goddess is shown opening the gates of heaven to the sun's chariot.

On the right (*Via 24 Maggio*), the impressive doorway is the entrance to the **garden of the Palazzo Colonna**.

San Silvestro al Quirinale

Entrance to the left of the façade. ○━*Closed for restoration at press date.* ☎*06 67 90 240.*
The façade of the church of **St Sylvester on the Quirinal** is purely decorative; a 19C construction to disguise the difference in level between the church and the street. The latter had been widened and lowered; the church truncated.

The interior decor is surprisingly rich. The 16C coffered ceiling was restored in the 19C. Among the Mannerist decorations are some paintings in the **first chapel** on the left by Polidoro da Caravaggio and Maturino da Firenze (*see PIAZZA NAVONA: Via della Maschera d'Oro*). The floor has been paved with fragments of ceramic tiles, recycled from the Raphael Loggia in the Vatican.

In the left arm of the transept is a beautiful octagonal domed **chapel**★: Domenichino painted the medallions in the pendentives (1628); the stucco statues of Mary Magdalene (*left of the entrance*) and St John (*left of the chancel*) were sculpted at the same time by Alessandro Algardi.

The **chancel** vault is decorated with a late-16C fresco on a beautiful grey base. To the left of the chancel is a door opening onto a quiet terrace. Here Vittoria **Colonna**, who had composed poems to the glory of her dead husband, spent many hours in the company of scholars and holy men. Sometimes Michelangelo joined them. He developed a great affection for this noble and cultivated lady and was present at her death.

▶ *Turn right into Via della Cordonata and right again into Via 4 Novembre.*

Palazzo Colonna

The palace dates from the 15C, but was rebuilt in 1730. It is linked to its gardens by four arches spanning the Via Pilotta. **Pope Martin V** (1417-31), a member of the Colonna family, took up residence here when he returned to Rome after the Great Schism of the West. The **picture gallery**, a suite of richly furnished rooms, contains many 15C-18C paintings.

▶ *Take Via 4 Novembre west; turn left into Piazza Santi Apostoli.*

Kids In the square at No.67 is the **Museo delle Cere** (Waxworks Museum). ♿⊙*Open 9am-8pm.* €*6.* ☎*06 67 96 482.* *www.museodellecere.it*

Basilica dei Santi Dodici Apostoli★(Basilica of the Twelve Holy Apostles)

⊙*Open Mon–Sat 9.30am-noon and 4-8pm, Sun 4–5pm.* ☎*06 69 95 71.*
The church goes back to the 6C, when a basilica on the site was dedicated by Popes Pelagius I and John III to the Apostles Philip and James the Less.

Napoleonic Storm

In 1808, Napoleon was declared king of Italy and his brother Joseph king of Naples. Pius VII, as head of the Papal States, refused to apply an economic blockade or to recognise any king other than Ferdinand IV of Naples. On 2 February, General Miollis was ordered to enter Rome with 8 000 French soldiers to bring His Holiness to reason. Pius VII shut himself in the **Quirinal Palace (** *see entry in this section*).

In Vienna, on the evening of 17 May 1809, Napoleon wiped the Papal States off the map of Europe. Pius VII issued a Bull of Excommunication: "Let sovereigns learn once and for all that they are subject by the law of Christ to our throne and our commands." At dawn several French soldiers were found dead in the streets of Rome. On 7 July 1809, French troops broke down the door of the palace. The pope, in cape and stole, awaited them. Despite their great respect for Pius VII, the soldiers spirited him away to spend the rest of the Napoleonic era at Fontainebleau. Thus Napoleon rendered "unto Caesar the things that are Caesar's and unto God the things that are God's."

The greatest alterations were carried out by Sixtus IV (1471-84), of which only the lower part of the porch remains. The loggia above was closed with rectangular windows in the Baroque era and topped with a balustrade and statues. The upper section is 19C neo-Classical. In the porch, guarding the entrance, are three lions from the medieval building. The chancel contains the Renaissance tombs of the two Riario cardinals, Pietro and Raffaele, who helped their uncle, Sixtus IV, to reconstruct the church: **Cardinal Pietro Riario's tomb**★ (*left*) is the result of three masters of funerary art working in collaboration: Andrea Bregno, Mino da Fiesole and Giovanni Dalmata.

The **monument to Clement XIV** – at the top of the left aisle – is the first work executed in Rome by the neo-Classical sculptor Antonio Canova (1787).

Palazzo Chigi-Odescalchi

The palace, in front of the basilica of the Holy Apostles, was redesigned by **Bernini** when the Chigi family acquired it in 1664. The master's involvement in the project laid down rules that greatly influenced the architecture of central and northern Europe.

Palazzo Balestra

At the end of the square stands a Baroque palace (now occupied by the Banco di Roma). Here the **Stuarts**, the royal family of Scotland and England, lived in exile. Originally known as Palazzo Muti, it was given to James Stuart, the Old Pretender, in 1719, when he married Maria Clementina Sobieska of Poland. His two sons, Charles Edward, the Young Pretender, and Henry, Cardinal of York, were born in the palace. "Bonnie Prince Charlie" returned to die there in 1788.

Oratorio del Crocifisso★ (Oratory of the Crucifix)

The building's construction was entrusted to Tommaso dei Cavalieri, a young Roman noble, who inspired a warm affection in Michelangelo. Nonetheless he chose as his adviser one of the master's bitterest enemies, Nanni di Baccio Bigio. The façade was designed by Giacomo della Porta in 1561. It marked the beginning of a brilliant career, which led to work on the Capitol and at St Peter's (1573). The façade, which harmonises so well with the square it overlooks, bears traces of Michelangelo's teaching). The interior is decorated with frescoes by Mannerist artists.

▶ *Take the alley on the right of the oratory.*

The **Galleria Sciarra**★ – with its metal framework, glass canopy and fine paintings – is a highly original and lovely late-19C arcade.

▶ *Continue north along Via di Santa Maria in Via.*

Galleria Colonna

This arcade was built in 1923 linking Via di Santa Maria in Via with Via del Corso and Piazza Colonna.

Santa Maria in Via

St Mary's Church has miraculous origins: an image of the Virgin, painted on a tile, fell into a well. It overflowed and the icon reappeared. Many pilgrims still come to drink the water and to venerate the "Madonna of the Well" (*Madonna del Pozzo*). The late-17C Baroque façade is by Francesco da Volterra and Carlo Rainaldi.

▶ *Turn right into Via del Tritone.*

Via del Tritone

This street is full of shops and is one of the busiest in Rome; it links the city centre with the northeastern suburbs.

▶ *From Piazza dell'Accademia di S. Luca, take Via della Stamperia.*

Palazzo Carpegna houses the Galleria dell'Accademia di San Luca.

The **Calcographia** (*6 Via della Stamperia*) houses over 23 000 engravings, including some by Giovan Battista Piranesi (1720-78), who produced some remarkable views of Rome. The collection now belongs to the Istituto Nazionale per la Grafica (*also see GIANICOLO*).

Paintings of elegant women in the Galleria Sciarra

G. Bludzin/MICHELIN

Additional Sights

Galleria di Palazzo Colonna★
Entrance at no 17 Via della Pilotta. Time: 30min. ⊙Open Sat 9am-1pm; Mon–Fri and Sun by appointment only. ⊙Closed in Aug. ☜€7. ☎06 67 84 350. www.galleri acolonna.it

In the Sala della Colonna Bellica (Column Room), note Narcissus at the fountain by **Tintoretto** (1518-94) and a portrait, which may be of Vittoria Colonna. The name of the room is a reference to the red column: the family emblem. A cannon ball is lodged in the steps down to the salon. It was fired by the French troops who besieged Rome in 1849 in an attempt to re-establish Pius IX.

The Salone★★ (Salon) offers a very handsome perspective, resplendent with gilt, mirrors, crystal chandeliers, yellow marble and paintings. The **Sala degli Scrigni** (Casket Room) contains two **caskets**★, small 17C chests: one in ebony decorated with ivory low-relief carvings; the other in sandalwood. In the **Sala dell'apoteosi di Martino V,** note the fine portrait of a gentleman (197) by Paul Veronese (1528-88) and the famous

Peasant Eating Beans★ (43), attributed to Annibale Carracci (1560-1609).

Galleria dell'Accademia di San Luca (St Luke's Academy Gallery)
⊙ Open Mon–Sat 10am-12.30pm. ⊙Closed Sun, Jul and Aug. ☎06 67 98 850

This displays works by members of the academy, founded in 1577. Note the *Portrait of Clement IX* by Baciccia (1639-1709), a fresco fragment by Raphael, *Judith and Holophernes* by the Venetian Piazzetta (1682-1754) and a *Virgin and Angels* by Sir Anthony van Dyck.

Museo Nazionale delle Paste Alimentari
♿⊙Open 9.30am-5.30pm. ⊙Closed on public holidays. ☜€10. ☎06 69 91 119; www.pastainmuseum.com

Kids Housed in Palazzo Scanderberg, the **National Pasta Museum** charts the history of this staple, starting with the raw materials and their nutritious components, and finishing with amusing portrayals of famous people enjoying the end product. Displays are both imaginative and informative.

FORI IMPERIALI★★★

MICHELIN MAP 38 L 12-13 M 12-13

METRO LINE B: COLOSSEO OR CAVOUR

(BOTH METRO STATIONS ARE APPROXIMATELY 400M/440YDS FROM THE FORO DI AUGUSTO)

Now crowded with souvenir stalls and tourists, the imperial Fora once evoked the power and splendour of ancient Rome. Glimpses are still possible, amid the traffic and hustle of the modern city, in Trajan's Markets and the column celebrating his victory over the Dacians. Further from the vortex of Piazza Venezia, quiet corners unfold into medieval alleys. The once-disreputable Suburra district now gleams with craft shops and student hang-outs.

▶ **Orient Yourself:** The imperial *fora* extend roughly from the *Basilica di Massenzio e Costantino* (Maxentius and Constantine) to Piazza Venezia. They fill the valley between Capitoline Hill to the southwest and the Quirinal and Viminal Hills to the northeast.

◉ **Don't Miss:** The markets and column of Trajan.

◔ **Organizing Your Time:** Allow 2 hrs.

◔ **Also See:** *COLOSSEO-CELIO; FONTANA DI TREVI-QUIRINALE; FORO ROMANO-PALATINO; PIAZZA VENEZIA; SANTA MARIA MAGGIORE-ESQUILINO.*

A Bit of History

The Roman Forum grew too small to hold the Assemblies of the People, the judicial hearings, the conduct of public affairs and commercial matters. Caesar constructed a new meeting place to the north; the trend continued with Augustus, Vespasian, Nerva and Trajan. These complexes flexed the imperial muscle with porticoes, temples, libraries and basilicas. The old forum was not in any way abandoned. Octavius erected a temple there to the divinity of Caesar; as the Emperor Augustus, he was himself honoured with a commemorative arch in 19 BC, although work on his own forum had been underway over 10 years.

A temple to Vespasian stood at the foot of the Capitoline Hill.

Badly quarried and pillaged during the medieval era and Renaissance, the imperial *fora* disappeared under new buildings. The Fascists cleared the area for military parades. They demolished 16C structures, levelled the Velian Hill and sketchily excavated the imperial level, then paved the **Via dei Fori Imperiali** right through the area.

This wide road passes through the imperial *fora* in a straight line from Piazza Venezia, opening a clear view of the Colosseum, a solid reminder of Roman grandeur. Pedestrians can stroll here on Sundays, when the road is closed to traffic until 6pm, like much of the historic centre and the Appian Way.

Mercati Di Traiano★★
(Trajan's Market)

Via IV Novembre 94, but during restoration the entrance is on Piazza Madonna di Loreto, near Trajan's column) ⚷ *Site partially closed for restoration at the time of print.* ♿◔*Open Tues–Sun 9am–2pm.* ◔*Closed Mon, 1 Jan, 1 May, Christmas.* ✆*€6.* ☎*06 67 97 702. www.capitolium. org/eng/fori/mercatitraiano.htm*

Trajan's Market

The **Museo dei Fori Imperiali** should open in October 2007 in the old market buildings. The museum will display artefacts uncovered in recent digs.

About 150 shops occupied the terraces against the Quirinal Hill above the forum. The market was not simply a retail space – like the Forum Boarium and the Forum Holitorium – but a centre for the acquisition, division and redistribution of supplies, administered by the imperial authorities.

First is a magnificent vaulted room where the civil servants may have worked. The buttresses are of interest; no equivalent structure has been found among the monuments of ancient Rome. **Via Biberatica**★ serves the upper part of the semicircle, which forms the façade of the market and is lined with well-preserved shops and houses. The street's name may have derived from the Latin verb *bibere* (to drink), suggesting that it was once home to a number of taverns. The original paving remains, curving from the Torre del Grillo to the Via Quattro Novembre.

From Via Biberatica, walk down through the market. The long, vaulted shops on the first floor probably hawked wine and oil; they open on to a vaulted arcade.

Semicircular Façade

The façade and the tiers demonstrate the genius of architect **Apollodorus of Damascus**, who gave a monumental appearance to this utilitarian complex. The shallow shops on the ground floor opened directly onto the curving street; they may have sold fruit and flowers.

Foro Traiano★★★

Visitors enter the Fora at Largo Romolo e Remo. The Visitor Center dei Fori Imperiali (in front of the Basilica dei Santi Cosma e Damiano) organises tours and audio guides and provides brochures. ○*Open 9:30am-7:30pm;* ☎*06 67 97 702.*

Trajan's Forum consisted of a covered market with a concave façade and the forum itself: a square, the Basilica Ulpia, Trajan's Column, two libraries and the Temple of Trajan.

The forum was inaugurated by Trajan, the best of the Antonine Emperors, in 113. Its construction had involved work on a huge scale, including the cutting back and levelling of a spur of the Quirinal, which extended towards the Capitoline. Just as Caesar had financed his forum with booty from the Gauls, so Trajan spent the spoils of war with the Dacians, a redoubtable people who lived in what is now Romania. Even after the emperor's death, the prestige of his forum did not fade. It hosted official demonstrations: here Hadrian publicly burned the records of debts of certain citizens. And Marcus Aurelius (161-80) auctioned his treasures to finance wars against the Marcomanni (German tribe). Trajan's Forum – extending from Caesar's to beyond the two domed churches of St Mary of Loreto and the Holy Name of Mary – was the largest of the imperial *fora* and certainly the most beautiful. Historian **Ammianus Marcellinus** (c 330-400) recounts a visit made by **Constantinus II** (356). The eastern emperor was speechless at the Forum, "the sanctuary of the old power... but on arriving in Trajan's Forum... he was stupefied."

Forum

The entrance was set in a slightly curved wall facing southeast. The northeast and southwest walls were relieved by two apses, one of which is still visible, running parallel with the concave façade of the market and marked by two columns (one remains). The wall on the apse's far left is the forum's outer wall: huge blocks of peperine and travertine.

Colonna Traiana★★★
(Trajan's Column)

Originally there were rooftop terraces on the libraries, which made it easier to view this extraordinary work. Designed by **Apollodorus of Damascus**, the column stands about 38m/125ft high and consists of 17 marble drums. Battle tales –Trajan versus the Dacians – spiral upward. Laid in a straight line, the sculpture would be 200m/656ft long; no other imperial victories were celebrated with so much genius and effort. The column's also noteworthy technically (the precise seam between drums) and historically, as a record of the Dacian campaigns and of Roman military technique. Learn more about the carving and examine a replica close-up at the Museo della Civiltà Romana (see *EUR*).

The shaft's diameter is not uniform; two-thirds of the way up, it bulges slightly to prevent the illusion of concavity. The size of the panels and the figures also increases towards the top of the column, originally brilliantly coloured.

A bronze statue of Trajan stood atop the column (probably installed posthumously). In 1587, Pope Sixtus V replaced it with a statue of St Peter, one of Rome's patrons. Although a pagan monument, Trajan's Column was never maltreated by the Christians, who believed the prayers of St Gregory saved the emperor's soul.

158

A golden urn – containing Trajan's ashes – resided inside the column, until its theft in the Middle Ages.

Inside remains a spiral staircase *(not open)*, lit by windows in the decorative panels. The skillful design makes them scarcely visible outside.

Trajan's successor, Hadrian, erected a temple to the deified emperor, but the ruins have been erased.

Basilica Ulpia and Libraries

Named after Trajan's family, this basilica ends in two semicircles, one below at the corner of Via Magnanapoli. It was opulent with five aisles, a marble floor and two storeys of marble and granite columns (some standing, some marked by their bases). Beyond lay two public libraries (*biblioteca*): one contained Greek works, the other Latin manuscripts and Trajan's personal records. Between the two was a courtyard; at its centre stood Trajan's Column, a masterpiece of classical art.

Piazza del Foro

At the centre of the forum stood an equestrian statue in gilded bronze of the Emperor Trajan (*statua equestre di*

Colonna Traiana

Courtesy of APT Rome

Traiano), which Constantinus II dreamed of imitating. Historian Marcellinus recounts that a prince in the imperial suite made a subtle suggestion: "Begin, sir, by building a stable in this style … so that the horse you envisage will be as well housed as this one." Down the sides of the forum ran porticoes with statues of illustrious men.

> There is an overall view of the ruins from Via Alessandrina.

Foro Di Augusto★★

Augustus's Forum is separated from Trajan's Forum by a building (**1**) constructed by Domitian, which later housed the Knights of Rhodes (*see below*). The edifice is embellished with a fine 15C loggia. Octavian, who took the name **Augustus** as emperor, wanted to avenge the murder of his dear adopted dad Caesar. He finally defeated the murderers, Cassius and Brutus, at Philippi (a town in northern Greece) in 42 BC. He vowed to dedicate a temple to *Mars Ultor* (the Avenger), sited in a new forum. Building began in 31 BC, after a considerable amount of demolition work. The site extended from the old Forum to the edge of the unsavoury Suburra district. A high wall isolated it from the hovels and frequent fires; its irregular line reveals the difficulties the builders had to overcome.

The two sides facing southeast and northwest bowed into two semicircles, which are still visible. In the recesses stood bronze statues of the most famous citizens "who had brought Rome from insignificance to greatness" (Suetonius): Aeneas, the kings of Alba, the founding fathers of the Julian family, Romulus, Marius, Sulla and other great generals of the Republican era.

Against the centre of the back wall stood the **Temple of Mars Ultor,** which was approached by a majestic flight of steps. A few columns to the front and side remain. This temple played an important role in public life; it served as a reliquary for Caesar's sword. Here the members of the imperial family came for the ceremony of the *toga virilis,* a rite of manhood (at about 17). Here too the magistrates appointed to the provinces were invested with authority (*imperium*). And they also deposited the trophies of their victories here on their return.

The basilicas

These were formed by two porticoes, one on each side of the temple, in front of the semicircular recesses. Marble statues stood between the columns. Two have been re-erected in front of a room (**2**)**,** which housed a colossal statue of Mars or Augustus.

Two flights of steps flanked the temple and linked Augustus's Forum with Suburra. Atop the steps, near the three re-erected columns, is a fine arch, known as Arco dei Pantani. (👁 *There is a better view of it from Via Tor de' Conti.*)

Augustus's successors made further embellishments: **Tiberius** (14-37) erected two commemorative arches (**3**), one on each side of the temple, in honour of Drusus and Germanicus, who pacified Germany and Pannonia (western Hungary). The Emperor Claudius (41-54) continued to dispense justice there. According to Suetonius:

"One day, when he was hearing a case in Augustus's Forum, he was attracted by the cooking smells coming from the Temple of Mars next door: leaving his court, he went to join the Salian priests at their table."

Foro Di Nerva

Although begun by Domitian, this forum was completed and inaugurated by Nerva in 98. Very little remains of the long and narrow complex, traversed by the Argiletum, a street linking the old Roman Forum with the Suburra district. For this reason, it was also known as the *Forum Transitorium.* Here stood the Temple of Minerva; its lovely ruins were still visible early in the 17C, until Pope Paul V had them demolished. The columns and cornices were used in the construction of the Pauline Fountain on the Janiculum. Against the east wall stand two beautiful **columns**★ (**4**) and some fragments of a frieze, which adorned the wall enclosing the forum.

The junction of Via dei Fori Imperiali and Via Cavour stands more or less at the point where the Fora of Nerva *(west)* and Vespasian *(east)* met. Little remains.

Foro Di Vespasiano

This forum was built by Vespasian from 71-75. It formed a square adjoining the old Forum and extended approximately from the Basilica of Maxentius and Constantine in the south to the Conti Tower (*Torre dei Conti*) in the north. In the south corner was a library, now occupied by the church of St Cosmas and St Damian. It was also called the "Peace Forum". To commemorate his conquest of the Jews in 71, Vespasian erected a Temple of Peace. It housed treasures looted from the Jewish Temple in Jerusalem: the golden seven-branched candlestick, the tablets of the Law of Moses and the silver trumpets.

Foro Di Cesare★★

For his forum, Caesar chose a central position at the foot of the Capitoline, near the old Roman Forum. In order to clear the site, he had to relocate the

Curia Hostilia and the *Comitium*, and purchase and demolish the elegant houses already in situ. This exercise cost the exorbitant sum of 60 million *sesterci*, according to Cicero (then consul and a friend of Caesar's). However, Suetonius – the emperor's biographer – puts the figure at 100 million. Negotiations began in 54 BC, when Caesar was rich with the booty gained in the conquest of Gaul (58-51 BC); work started three years later. This forum was rectangular and extended from the *Curia* (east) to *Via di San Pietro in Carcere* (west), the long sides running more or less parallel with the Clivus Argentarius. Domitian undertook restoration work (81-96), following the fire that destroyed part of the Capitoline in 80. Trajan completed the work. About two-thirds of Caesar's forum has been uncovered; the rest is beneath Via dei Fori Imperiali.

The ruins

First to catch the eye are three beautiful standing columns, richly sculpted, which belonged to the **Temple of Venus Genitrix** and date from the time of Domitian and Trajan. Caesar claimed that his family (the *gens Iulia*) descended from Venus through her son, Aeneas, and the Trojan War hero's son, Iulus. He dedicated a temple to her after his victory at Pharsalus against Pompey, who was killed by Ptolemy, Cleopatra's brother. This temple, to the north of the forum, was a veritable museum: besides the statue of Venus in the cella, there was a golden statue of Cleopatra, some Greek paintings and, in front, a statue of Caesar's horse. This extraordinary animal had curiously split hooves, which resembled human feet. Soothsayers claimed this abnormality was a sign of divine intervention and meant that his master would be ruler of the world.

The edge of the forum was lined with shops, still visible beneath the *Clivus Argentarius*. During Trajan's reign (2C), a portico was added down the long side nearest the Clivus Argentarius. Its two long rows of granite columns still remain. It has been identified as the **Basilica Argentaria,** where the money-changers (*argentari*) plied their trade.

Additional Sights

Santi Luca e Martina (Church of St Luke and St Martina)

On the site of the Senate archive (*Secretarium Senatus*, an annex of the *Curia*), a church was built in about the 7C and dedicated to Martina, who had been martyred under Septimius Severus. From 1588, it also honoured St Luke, since in that year Pope Sixtus V gave the church to the members of St Luke's Academy, a guild of painters who recognised the evangelist as its patron saint. According to a 6C legend, he had painted a portrait of the Virgin Mary.

In 1634, a terracotta sarcophagus was found containing the remains of St Martina. Cardinal Francesco Barberini commissioned Pietro da Cortona to build a new shrine above the old one. Da Cortona designed a beautiful **façade**★. Its shallow convex curve is reminiscent of the style of Borromini. So, too, is the interior, designed on the Greek cross plan and decorated with pale stuccoes that reveal a search for complicated forms.

The **Carcere Mamertino**, the old Roman prison, stands opposite the church.

▶ *Follow the Clivus Argentarius and cross Via dei Fori Imperiali. Walk alongside Trajan's Forum as far as Trajan's Column.*

Note the symmetry of the domes of **SS. Nome di Maria and Santa Maria di Loreto**. In 1507, the latter was begun by Antonio da Sangallo the Younger to a square design and was completed in 1577 by Giacomo del Duca, from Sicily.

Torre delle Milizie★ (Militia Tower)

Entrance from Trajan's Market. ◷*Open Tues-Sun Mar-Oct 9am-7pm; Nov–Feb 9am–5.* ◷*Closed Mon, 6 Jan, Easter, 25 April, 1 May, 29 June, 15 Aug and Christmas.* €6.20. ☎06 67 90 048. www.roma-beniculturali.it/mercatitraianei/

This is one of the best-preserved buildings of medieval Rome. It was the keep of a castle built by Pope Gregory IX (1227-41), At this time, the papacy often used force to establish faith in the empire. The tower leans slightly because of an earthquake in the 14C; it has lost its top storey and crenellations. It has been known as "Nero's Tower": legends claim the mad emperor, dressed in theatrical costume, watched the great fire from here. Rumors insist he sparked the inferno: "charmed by the beauty of the flames," in Suetonius's account, while strumming his lyre and singing.

From Via Quattro Novembre, there is a view of the beautiful trees in the terraced public gardens of the **Villa Aldobrandini** and of the Baroque façade of the **church of San Domenico e San Sisto** (completed in 1655).

▷ *Turn right into Salita del Grillo.*

This quiet, picturesque street takes its name from the Marquess del Grillo, known for his jokes and jibes. Beside the arcade stands the **tower** of his mansion.

Casa dei Cavalieri di Rodi (House of the Knights of Rhodes)

🕐*Open Tue and Thu, 10am–1pm.* 🕐*Closed Aug and holidays* 👣*Guided tours only (45min).* ⊙*€2.10. Apply at least two weeks in advance to the Ufficio Monumenti medievali e moderni, Mon-Fri, 9am-1pm.* ☎*06 67 10 26 09, fax 06 67 10 42 91.*

Marco Bembo, Bishop of Vicenza and Cardinal of St Mark's Basilica, was appointed Grand Master of the Order of the Knight Hospitallers of St John by his uncle Pope Paul II (1464-71). He reconstructed this building, part of a medieval convent on the remains of the Temple of Mars Ultor. Some of the windows show that Venetian craftsmen were employed. The beautiful 15C loggia overlooking Trajan's Forum is supported on Roman columns. Their capitals are carved with leaves and rosettes; the walls are decorated with frescoes.

▷ *Continue along Via Tor de' Conti.*

The Via Tor de' Conti skirts the imposing wall built of large blocks of tufa and travertine, which separated Augustus's

FONTANA DI TREVI-QUIRINALE

FORO ROMANO-PALATINO · COLOSSEO-CELIO

Forum from the slummy Suburra district. Note the fine arch (*Arco dei Pentani*) that marked the entrance to the Forum. At the end of the street can be seen the imposing mass of the **Torre de' Conti**. Pope Innocent III had it built around 1238 with material taken from Nerva's Forum. The tower was inhabited until a 1348 earthquake reduced it to the shambles seen today.

▶ *Turn left into Via Madonna dei Monti and left again into Via del Boschetto to reach Via Panisperna.*

The peaceful Via Madonna dei Monti leads to what was the **Suburra** district, the most disreputable in ancient Rome. This zone, which harboured thieves and hired assassins, bequeathed its name to a nearby square. The narrow alleys, now lively with craft shops, were once frequented by the scandalous Empress Messalina, who frequented the local brothels in secret.

Via Panisperna crosses the **Viminale**, one of the seven hills of Rome, which probably takes its name from the very large number of willow trees or from the temple dedicated to Jupiter Vimineus that stood there. The tree-lined courtyard of the **church of San Lorenzo in Panisperna** (St Lawrence in Panisperna) is a tiny oasis from another era, separating this place of worship from the chaos of the city. On 10 August, the feast of St Lawrence, the nuns carry on an age-old tradition of offering blessed bread.

Carcere Mamertino (Mamertine Prison)

🕐 *Open daily 9am–noon and 2.30–5pm (6pm in summer). Donations welcome.* 🚶 *Guided tour available (10min).* ☎ *06 67 92 902.*

The Mamertine Prison was the Roman State jail; it consists of two rooms, one above the other, hollowed out of the Capitoline Hill beneath the church of San Giuseppe dei Falegnami (St Joseph of the Carpenters).

On the right of the entrance is a list of names of well-known people who perished here. In 104 BC, **Jugurtha** died of starvation, while his conqueror Marius led his victory parade through the forum. **Vercingetorix** was beheaded here in 46 BC, after Caesar's triumph. However, enemy chiefs often escaped death; Jugurtha and Vercingetorix had not been considered worthy of such clemency. It was here, on 5 December 65 BC, that Catiline's fellow conspirators were strangled after Cicero's fourth rabble-rousing speech.

In the Middle Ages, a legend arose that **St Peter** had been imprisoned here; hence the name *San Pietro in Carcere* (St Peter in Prison). On the left of the entrance is a list of Christian martyrs who died in the prison. At the head of the staircase linking the two rooms is a hollowed-out stone said to bear the imprint of the Apostle's head, as he was jostled by his jailers.

The lower chamber (*tullianum*) was built at the end of the 4C BC out of huge blocks of tufa arranged in a vault and was used as a cistern or a tomb. Legend tells how Peter and Paul made water miraculously spout from the earth, so they could baptise their gaolers. The spring and the pillar, to which the prisoners were chained, can still be seen.

FORO ROMANO-PALATINO★★★

MICHELIN MAP 38 M 12-13, N 12-13.
METRO LINE B: COLOSSEO.

The core of ancient Rome, the Forum has decayed into a sea of columns, crumbled walls and monumental arches. Now wildflowers and stray cats rule these ruins, the crucible of western civilisation for 12 centuries.

Historian Georgina Masson noted that: "though they revered it as the cradle of their institutions, the Romans continued to alter, add to and rebuild the temples in the Forum. This was partly due to damage by fire and earthquake, but also to their desire to make it worthy of the growing power of Rome." This rich mix is the obvious starting point for a visit to Italy's capital city.

Overlooking the Forum is the Palatine Hill, where umbrella pines shade the impressive husks of aristocratic houses. Quiet and gracious, this landscape invites travelers to stroll and daydream antiquity back to life.

▶ **Orient Yourself:** The Forum unfurls southeast of the Capitoline, flowing up towards the verdant Palatine hill. Enter from the Largo Romolo e Remo or by the Arch of Titus. One of the city's few public restrooms hides by the Temple of Castor and Pollux on the northwestern end of the Forum. The Palatine has ticket booths near the Arch of Titus and on the Via di San Gregorio. Metro stop Colosseo is closest.

🐾 **Don't Miss:** View the ruins from the Capitoline terrace and the Farnese Gardens on the Palatine Hill.

🕐 **Organizing Your Time:** Allow a half day to explore properly. Even the most cursory walk-through would absorb an hour.

Kids **Especially for Kids:** Gameboard carved on the steps of the Bascilica Julia.

👣 **See also:** *CAMPIDOGLIO-CAPITOLINO, COLOSSEO-CELIO, FORI IMPERIALI, PIAZZA VENEZIA*

Foro Romano

A Bit of History

In about 750 BC, the site was a marshy valley, subject to flooding by the Tiber and by streams from the seven surrounding hills (👣*see Map of Rome during the Empire*). Small villages of rough shacks grew up the hillsides. Their inhabitants, the Latins and the Sabines, were farmers who would fight each other, when pressed. The valley, which later became the Forum, was a burial ground and a meeting place. Here too people traded and worshipped.

Two centuries later, the marshy valley had become a real town square, thanks to the **Etruscans**. The origin of this high civilisation remains uncertain, but this north-central people spread down the boot to *Magna Graecia* (southern Italy).

In Rome, they built a citadel on the Capitoline, unified the villages and organised the social life of the community. Etruscan kings governed here from 616 to 509 BC. They fortified the city and drained the Forum into the Tiber, through the channel that became the Great Sewer (*Cloaca Maxima*).

Legend claims the **Lapis Niger** (black rock) marked the tomb of city father Romulus; most likely it was a sanctuary of Vulcan. Numa Pompilius, the second king, built the **Temple to Vesta**, the hearth goddess. Virgins tended the eternal flame here – and became powerful priestesses and document-keepers.

The Republican Era

Romans overthrew the last Etruscan king, Tarquin the Proud, in 509 BC and instituted the consulate. During this Republican era, Rome began to develop into the capital of an empire. The Forum, barely 2ha/5 acres in extent, hosted many pivotal events.

The city state warred with its neighbours, expanding its territory steadily. All victorious generals processed in triumph through the Forum. A slave rode behind them in the chariot, holding a crown above their heads and whispering "look behind" or "you are only mortal." The Roman conquests brought immense riches: the confiscated enemy treasuries, indemnities paid by the conquered nations and the tributes from the provinces. Money-changing, loans and credit were arranged in the Forum. The **Temple of Saturn** dates to 496 BC, the fabled "Golden Era" and served as the state treasury.

The men who decided the destiny of Rome met in the **Comitium**. Here stood the **Curia**, the seat of the highest level of Republican government. Two hundred senators, appointed for life, decided foreign policy, directed military operations, drew up peace treaties and enacted measures for public safety. Opposite the Curia was the *Rostra*, where orators held forth. In 185 BC, the **Basilica Porcia**, the first building of this sort in Rome, was erected so citizens to assemble under cover.

For 100 years, the Republican regime tore itself to pieces in civil war. In 52 BC, the tribune Clodius was killed by Milo; and creamated at the Comitium. The fire spread, destroying the Curia and the **Basilica Porcia**. In 44 BC, Caesar rebuilt the *Curia* and moved the *Rostra*.

Little remains, as early buildings were of tufa, peperine or wood. Augustus boasted that he inherited a town built of brick and left a city of marble. Later emperors followed suit, making the site more and more splendid.

The Forum during the Empire

In the Augustan era, the huge popular assemblies and the troop reviews shifted to the Campus Martius. The Forum became the chosen site for monuments: commemorative arches, basilicas and temples dedicated to emperors deified after their death.

The 2C BC satirist Plautus recorded that every sort frequented the crossroads of the empire: "vicious or virtuous, honest or dishonest. If you want to meet a perjurer, go to the Comitium; for a liar and a braggart, try the Temple of Venus Cloacina; for wealthy married wasters, near the Basilica. There, too, you will find well-perfumed prostitutes and men ready to do a deal, while the fish market is frequented by members of the eating clubs. Wealthy and reputable citizens stroll in the lower Forum; the middle Forum near the canal is favoured by the merely showy set ... "

In the 3C, building halted: not only for lack of space, but also because of the spread of Christianity. The emperors resisted, but in AD 391, Theodosius finally closed the pagan temples. The Forum's downfall began in 410, when Alaric the Goth descended from the Danube. His savage hordes torched the *Curia* and the Basilica Aemilia. Then followed an earthquake in 442, the depredations of Genseric's Vandals in 455, the armies of Theodoric in 500 and of Belisarius in 537, after which the Forum was dead. Rome's prestige no longer lay in grandiose monuments. Instead, the world celebrated the city as the resting place of St Peter the Apostle.

From the Middle Ages to the Renaissance

Once the Church became organised, the Bishop of Rome – the Pope – was recognised as the head of Christianity. Gradually the imperial buildings were converted into places of Christian worship. Some still survive, a curious juxtaposition of traditions; many have disap-

---

Via Panisperna 89

From 1926-37, this building was home to the group of young Italian physicists known as the "boys of Via Panisperna". Enrico Fermi, a 25-year-old wunderkind was their leader, nicknamed "the Pope". He fled to America in the 1930's to protect his Jewish wife Laura. Four years later, Fermi won the Nobel Prize, after designing the first man-made nuclear reactor and discovering beta decay. The *palazzo* now houses the offices of the *Polizia di Stato* (State Police).

peared. In the 9C, the buildings began to crumble and earth massed around them, burying the ruins.

The Pope and the Holy Roman Emperor sparked a civil war between the noble Roman families in the 12C. They fortified ancient structures; towers rose between the Temple of Antoninus and Faustina and Caesar's Forum. They also quarried old buildings. Decorations embellished churches and palaces; the statues and columns were baked in lime kilns to produce chalk.

The deserted Forum became a sewage farm. By the 15C the pillars of the Temple of Vespasian were half underground and the podium of the Temple of the Dioscuri was completely buried; both were surrounded by fields. The Forum had become a cows' field (campo vaccino). Near the Temple of the Dioscuri the marble basin of a fountain was being used as a drinking trough for animals; it is now in the Piazza del Quirinale. When Charles V visited Rome in 1536, Pope Paul III laid out a broad avenue from the Arch of Titus to the Arch of Septimius Severus.

Excavations

Many famous archaeologists, Italians and non-Italians, dug here; Carlo Fea, who began investigations in 1803, Antonio Nibby, Bunsen and Canina, Pietro Rosa, Giuseppe Fiorelli, Rodolfo Lanciani, H Jordan, C Hülsen and Giacomo Boni, who reached the oldest levels. Today Rome Reborn and the Pompey Project reconstruct the city via virtual reality.

Visit

Certain parts of the ruins may be closed owing to lack of staff or restoration work. From the Capitoline entrance, descend into the Forum; immediately on the right are the remains of the Basilica Emilia. &♿ *Open daily 8.30am–1hr before dusk (5.30pm in winter). Last admission 1hr before closing time.* *Closed 1 Jan, 1 May and Christmas.* ☎ *06 39 96 77 00. www. pierreci.it*

Basilica Emilia (Basilica Aemilia)

Rome's second basilica (179 BC) was frequently restored and reconstructed; a 1C effort remains visible. Like all the ancient basilicas, it served no religious purpose. The huge covered hall sheltered business transactions and judicial hearings, as well as citizens' meetings. Along the south side of the basilica there was a line of shops opening into a portico. Behind these jewellery and perfume boutiques lay the main hall, divided by two rows of coloured marble columns with a finely carved entablature of white marble. In the southeast corner is a Latin **inscription (1)** to Augustus's adopted grandsons, Caius and Lucius, who died before reaching manhood.

Via Sacra★ (Sacred Way)

This was the most famous street in ancient Rome. The Temple of Vesta and the Regia flanked the Sacred Way, along which victorious generals processed. Dressed like Jupiter and standing in a

J. Malburet/MICHELIN

four-horse chariot, they proceeded to the Capitoline Hill to thank the god Jupiter for his protection.

Santuario di Venere Cloacina (Sanctuary of Venus Cloacina) **(2)** – A travertine circle marks the site dedicated to the goddess who protected the main sewer (*cloaca*); traces of its steps are still visible. Here in the 5C BC, the centurion Verginius saved his daughter Virginia from a spurned suitor, Appius Claudius. The government official abused his power and claimed she was a slave. Verginius stabbed his child to preserve her freedom. The people rioted, overthrew the decemvirs and re-established the Roman Republic.

Argiletum – This street, one of the busiest in Rome, separated the Basilica Aemilia from the Curia and led to Suburra, a slum district. Sections of travertine paving remain.

Curia★★

🕐*May close at 1pm for administrative reasons.* The brick building visible today is not where the **Senate** met in the Republican period. The first Curia was more or less on the site of the chancel and left transept of St Luke's Church, but facing in a different direction. In the 1C BC, Caesar moved and enlarged it; Diocletian remodelled in the 3C.

The structure was less austere than it is today: the façade, faced with marble and stucco, was surmounted by a tympanum covered in travertine; the bronze door was removed to St John Lateran by Alexander VII in the 17C.

The Curia was a *templum*, a consecrated place, where an augur communicated the wishes of the gods. He would read omens: interpreting the flight of birds, the eating patterns of sacred chickens, and unusual events. Every sitting of the Senate began with this ritual.

The senators did not have fixed seats. Once the agenda had been read, each – according to the order fixed by a list – gave his opinion.

The Senate's power waned in imperial times. At the very most, after an emperor's death, they could condemn him and oppose his deification.

The mystery of the Statue of Victory - At the far end of the Curia, there are traces of a pedestal where Victory stood. Octavian contributed this golden statue in 29 BC, after he defeated the armies of Antony and Cleopatra, and became the ruler of the empire. For over three centuries, the emperors worshipped the statue, burning incense on the altar. At their funerals, it led the cortège, which culminated in the deification.

Such pagan capers couldn't last. The statue of Victory became an offence to Christianity. In 382, the Emperor Gratian removed it. The statue has been lost to history since.

Bassorilievi di Traiano★★ (Trajan's Plutei) – The *Curia* houses two sculpted panels found in the Forum and probably commissioned by Trajan or his successor Hadrian to decorate the Rostra. On the back are represented the three animals sacrificed during the purification ceremony: a pig, a sheep and a bull. The sculptor set these scenes against a local background, showing several of the Forum buildings.

Lapis Niger (Black Stone) (3)

In 1899, Giacomo Boni, the Forum's lead excavator, discovered black marble slabs (currently protected by a low fence). Beneath these, lay a *stele* with an obscure inscription. The ancients believed this area contained the tomb of Romulus, Faustulus (the shepherd who saw the wolf suckling the twins) or Hostus Hostilius, the father of the third king.

Comitium

🕐 *See The Republican Era, above.* It extended from the Curia to the *Lapis Niger* and contained a fountain with a circular base (remains are still visible).

Decennalia Caesarum (4)

In 286, Diocletian decentralised the government; he took charge of the eastern empire and Maximian of the western. Seven years later, they entrusted Gaul and Britain to Constantius, and the Balkan peninsula to Galerius. The first 10 years' reign (*decennalia*) of the two Caesars and the 20 years of the *Augusti* were celebrated with a column of which only the base remains. The carving shows sacrificial animals and religious ceremonies.

Rostra★

After 338 BC, the **orators' platform** was always called the *Rostra*. In that year, the Romans attacked Antium (modern Anzio), then notorious for its pirates, and captured the enemies' prows (*rostra*), which they fixed to the platform. In the Republican period, it stood between the *Lapis Niger* and the present *Curia*. The remains seen today are those of the *Rostra* moved in 44 BC by Julius Caesar. After his assassination, Octavian, **Antony** and Lepidus formed the second triumvirate (late October 43 BC). The period of proscriptions began; **Cicero** was one of the most famous victims. An enemy of Antony, whose illegal acts and imperial ambitions he denounced, the orator was murdered by agents of the triumvirate. His hands and head were exposed on the *Rostra*.

Arco di Trionfo di Settimio Severo★★ (Triumphal Arch of Septimius Severus)

The arch was built in 203 and is surmounted by statues of Septimius Severus, his two sons (Caracalla and Geta) and the figure of Victory. The emperor had just won a series of victories over the Parthians (197-202) and organised a new province, Mesopotamia In the 3C, architecture became more complicated: four detached Corinthian columns form a false portico. Decoration is abundant.

Umbilicus Urbis (5)

This 3C circular temple marked the symbolic centre of the city.

Altare di Vulcano (6)

The **Altar of Vulcan**, a venerable hollow in the tufa, goes back to the time of the

PIAZZA VENEZIA, FORI IMPERIALI

kings. Under the Republic, the day of 23 August was devoted to the *Volcanalia* Festival: little fishes – or other animals symbolising human lives that people wished to preserve – were offered to the god of fire.

Colonna miliare d'Oro (7)

The **Golden Milestone** marble column, covered with gilded bronze, was set up by Augustus to mark the point from which mileages were measured. It displayed the distances between the capital and the empire's major cities.

At the Capitoline's foot, splendid monuments flanked the **Clivus Capitolinus**, the road used for religious processions and military triumphs. It led from the Forum to the Temple of Jupiter.

▶ *Backtrack to the Temple of Caesar.*

Tempio del Divo Giulio (Temple of "Divine" Julius Caesar)

Almost nothing is left of this building, which started the cult of emperor worship. On the evening of the Ides of March 44 BC, the body of Caesar, who had been stabbed to death in the Curia of Pompey, was carried to the Forum and cremated before the *Rostra*. A column and altar were set up nearby, but were immediately pulled down by Caesar's enemies. They were replaced by a temple consecrated by Octavian in 29 BC to the "god" Julius Caesar.

In a semicircular recess at ground level stood a round altar (traces visible). In the *cella* was a statue of Caesar, a star on his head. Suetonius explains why he was often represented in this way: "after his apotheosis, during the first days of the games given in his honour by his successor Augustus, a comet appeared at about the eleventh hour and burned for seven days; it was thought to be Caesar's soul being admitted to heaven...."

When Octavian defeated the fleets of Antony and Cleopatra, he took the prows (*rostra*) of the enemy ships and fixed them to the terrace of Caesar's Temple; the terrace became known as Caesar's *Rostra* and later emperors often spoke from there.

Arco di Trionfo di Augusto (Triumphal Arch of Augustus)

Two commemorative arches were erected by Augustus between the Temples of Caesar and Castor. The first was built in 29 BC, after his victory at Actium in Greece. Ten years later, as the first became dilapidated, a second celebrated Augustus's recovery of the Roman standards, which had been captured by the Parthians. Only the foundations have been discovered (the bases of two pillars are visible).

Tempio di Castore e Polluce★★★ (Temple of Castor and Pollux)

This early 5C temple honoured Castor and Pollux, known as "the **Dioscuri**": offspring of Leda and the Swan (Jupiter), the twins were brothers to Clytemnestra and Helen of Troy. The chief remains are three columns supporting an architrave fragment: one of the most famous sights of the Roman Forum. The temple's history is surrounded by legends. Early in the 5C BC, Rome attacked its poor, envious neighbours: the conflict came to a head on the shores of Lake Regillus. During the battle, the Romans saw two divine knights fighting on their side: Castor and Pollux. They subsequently announced the victory to the people gathered in the Forum; their thirsty horses drank at Juturna's spring. The son of the dictator Postumius, who had directed the battle against the Latins, erected a temple here.

The three beautiful columns, which were pulled down in 1811, date from a reconstruction undertaken in the Augustan era and belong to the long left-hand side of the sanctuary. The very high podium, the magnitude of the Corinthian capitals and the use of very white marble combine with majestic effect.

The mad Emperor **Caligula** (AD 37-41) built a bridge from the Temple of Castor and Pollux (the antechamber to his palace) to the Temple of Jupiter on the Capitol, so that he could converse with the god, whom he considered his equal, or sometimes even take his place.

Basilica Giulia★★ (Basilica Julia)

In 170 BC, the Censor Sempronius Gracchus, father of the tribunes Tiberius and Caius, built a basilica on this site, which was called "Sempronia." In 55 BC, Julius Caesar, who was consul, replaced it with another basilica, larger and more elegant, which started the trend for gigantic buildings in the Forum. At 109m/358ft long, 40m/131ft wide, it was paved with precious marble in the centre and white marble in the side aisles. Kids Close observation reveals geometric designs marked out by idlers for their games. Julius Caesar was murdered before the basilica was finished; it still bears his name, though Augustus completed it.

Colonne votive (Votive columns)

There were seven, probably erected during Diocletian's reign (AD 284-305) to commemorate army generals. Two have been partly reconstructed.

Lago di Curzio (10)

The **Curtian Lake** refers to a circular paved area, protected by a roof and a railing. During the early Republic, it was a cleft full of water that could not be drained. The Oracle pronounced that the opening would close when Rome threw her dearest treasure into it. A valuable young soldier called **Curtius** rode into it fully armed and the abyss shrivelled to a small pool. The adjacent 1C BC low-relief sculpture illustrating the legend is now housed in the *Museo del Palazzo dei Conservatori*.

Colonna di Foca★ (Phocas's Column)

In AD 608, the eastern Emperor Phocas gave the Pantheon to Pope Boniface IV and it was turned into a church. In gratitude, the donor's statue was set in the Forum. The column had to be taken from an existing building, because no artists were capable of producing such fine sculpture. This monument was the last erected here.

The sacred **fig tree,** symbol of the one that shaded the cradle of Romulus and Remus, the **vine** and the **olive tree (8)**, icons of agricultural prosperity, have all been replanted. Here also stood the very popular statue of Marsyas, brought from Greece in the 2C BC. It represented a Silenus – looking, as they all did, like an old satyr, very ugly and often drunk – wearing a skin over his shoulders. He wore a Phrygian cap, symbol of liberty; newly-freed slaves would come and touch the statue.

The **inscription (9)**, reconstructed in bronze letters, bears the name of "Naevius" and commemorates the paving carried out by this magistrate in 15 BC.

Tempio di Saturno★★★ (Temple of Saturn)

From 497 onwards, a temple dedicated to Saturn stood on this site. This god supposedly taught the Romans to cultivate the earth; hence his prestige with this peasant people. Restored several times under the Republic, the temple was then rebuilt in the 4C after a fire. The eight columns of the *pronaos* that remain date from this period; the travertine podium goes back to the 1C BC.

The **Saturnalia** took place here, the wild December festival that overturned the social structure – helping the sun rise again. Distinctions between masters and slaves were suspended; the latter were even entitled to free speech.

The basement housed the **state treasury**. This place may have been chosen because the cult of Saturn was associated with that of Ops, the goddess of abundance. The Senate administered the treasure, assisted by the censors and the quaestors.

Portico degli Dei Consenti★ (Portico of the Di Consentes)

The best view is from the Capitoline Hill and Via del Foro Romano. These 12 Corinthian columns were reconstructed in 1858. The portico was built by Domitian in honour of the 12 great gods in the Roman pantheon, who met in council to assist Jupiter. Their statues stood in the portico, two by two: Jupiter and Juno, Neptune and Minerva, Mars and Venus, Apollo and Diana, Vulcan and Vesta, Mercury and Ceres.

It was restored in 367 by the Prefect of Rome, Vettius Agorius Praetextatus, who had been a friend of **Julian the Apostate** and shared his great sympathy for the pagan religions. Certainly, this was the last gesture to paganism in Rome, where 37 Popes had already acceded to the throne of St Peter.

Tabularium

See Musei Capitolini, CAMPIDOGLIO-CAPITOLINO. The podium and a few extant pillars form the base of the Senatorial Palace. The *Tabularium* filled the depression between the Citadel and the Capitol, the two peaks of the Capitoline Hill. Its façade formed the west side of the Forum. It was built in 78 BC to house the state records, including some bronze tablets of the old Roman laws, hence the name. The use of peperine, a very simple building material, and of the Doric order, a plain architectural style, typify the austerity of Republican architecture.

Tempio di Vespasiano★★ (Temple of Vespasian)

Three very elegant columns, excavated by Valadier in 1811, are still standing; they formed a corner of the earlier part of the temple. Above the architrave is a detailed decorative frieze: a cornice with dentil, ovolo and palm leaf moulding above a band decorated with bucranes and sacrificial instruments. The temple was approached by steps from the Clivus Capitolinus.

Vespasian became emperor in AD 69 following the struggles among the pretenders to Nero's seat. He therefore established a hereditary monarchy founded on primogeniture. He announced to the Senate that "his sons would succeed him or there would be no successor." His elder son Titus assumed the mantle of power and began a temple in honour of his father, who had been deified on his death. In practice, if an emperor ruled well, the Senate would issue a decree raising him to the rank of the gods. All that was needed was a witness who saw an eagle carry off the soul during the cremation.

Titus died before the temple was finished; Domitian, his brother, completed the building and dedicated his two predecessors. Their statues stood on a pedestal in the *cella*.

Tempio della Concordia (Temple of Concord)

The Romans always attributed a divine character to the mysterious forces that influenced events. Thus they worshipped as gods such abstract ideas as concord, justice, liberty and abundance. Most of these divinities were represented by the statue of a female figure: the attributes of Concord were two linked hands and a dove.

The Forum had a Temple of Concord since 367 BC; it commemorated the re-establishment of peace between the patricians and the plebeians, who had been at odds since the beginning of the 5C BC. Some two-and-a-half centuries later – when the assassination of the people's tribune, Caius Gracchus, had restored peace at home – Concord was again honoured and the temple rebuilt.

The plan of the building is quite unusual: the *cella* extends laterally beyond the width of the *pronaos*, which was reached by steps from the *Clivus Capitolinus*.

▶ *Retrace your steps and go around the Temple of Castor and Pollux.*

The Legend of the Shields

One day King Numa received a shield (*ancile*) from heaven which was thought to foretell victory for the Romans. He entrusted it for safekeeping to the priests of the cult of Mars, and to prevent it from being stolen he had 11 copies made; all were kept in the Regia. The workman who made the shields asked as his reward to be remembered in the chanting that accompanied the procession of the shields.

The Regia and the House of the Vestals mark the limit of the Forum at the time of the kings and the Republic. The section extending to the Arch of Titus was added later.

Cinta sacra di Giuturna (Sacred Precinct of Juturna) (12)

Juturna was a nymph who reigned over all the springs in Latium. Lovestruck Jupiter made her immortal. Her shrine contained a spring which played a part in the legend of the Dioscuri. In the basin stands an altar, probably 2C, with low-relief sculptures representing Castor and Pollux and a woman bearing a long torch (*on the front and back*), and Leda and the swan, and Jupiter (*on the sides*). The adjacent **aedicule** (13), partially reconstructed, the round well and the altar were also part of the sacred precinct. The well is inscribed with the name of Barbatius Pollio, who put up a dedication to Juturna, probably in the reign of Augustus; low-relief figures on the altar.

Santa Maria Antiqua

↝ *Closed for restoration at the time of going to press. Church open to groups of scholars and individuals by writing the Ufficio Permessi of the Soprintendenza Archeologica di Roma. ☏06 39 08 071; Fax 06 39 75 09 50; www.archeorm.arti.beni-culturali.it/sma/* Paintings dating from the Byzantine period can still be seen in this 6C church.

Oratorio dei Martiri (Oratory of the Forty Martyrs) (14)

The original purpose of the building is unknown; in the 7C it was decorated with paintings and dedicated to the 40 martyrs of Sebastea in Armenia, who were exposed in chains on a frozen pond.

Tempio e Atrio delle Vestali★★★ (Temple and Atrium of the Vestal Virgins)

In the days when fire was still a precious commodity, the village on the Palatine where Romulus lived must have included a round hut, similar to all the other huts, where the communal fire was kept alight. This process was organised around Vesta, the goddess of fire.

The institution of the cult in Rome goes back to Romulus or Numa Pompilius (715-672 BC). A group of priestesses, known as the Vestal Virgins, at first four in number but later increased to six, officiated in the cult of Vesta.

When the first temple was built, probably late in the 6C BC, it conserved the circular form of the earlier hut. It was destroyed by fire and rebuilt several times, always in circular form, until the time of Septimius Severus. Only the central foundation and a few marble fragments survived to be used in the 1930 reconstruction. It was an enclosed shrine, surrounded by a portico supported on 20 fluted Corinthian columns; the frieze showed the instruments of sacrifice in low relief. The cella housed an altar where the fire was kept burning constantly. There was also a secret place, where certain objects which were supposed to have made Rome's fortune were jealously guarded; they included the famous Palladium, a statuette in wood or bone of the goddess Pallas, which was able to protect the city which possessed it. It had fallen from the sky on the city of Troy, possibly thrown by Zeus on Olympus. The Romans thought it had come into their possession through Aeneas, who had stolen it from Troy and brought it to Italy.

Next to the temple was the house of the Vestal Virgins: the **Atrium Vestae**. It was a large two-storey building enclosing a courtyard with a portico, containing two pools of water and a garden.

The Vestal Virgins were chosen from the patrician families. They entered into service at the age of 10 and stayed for at least 30 years: 10 as pupils, 10 performing their duties and 10 teaching. Most of the Vestals spent their whole lives in the house. Discipline was strict: a virgin who let the fire go out, a portent of disaster for Rome, was severely punished and one who broke her vow of chastity was buried alive. From the 3C, statues were erected to the Vestals in recognition of their service. Some of these statues with an inscription on the base have been placed in the courtyard of the house.

Regia

Religious observance in Rome centred on the Regia and the Temple of Vesta. The Regia was held to have been the residence (16) of King Numa Pompilius, who succeeded Romulus and organised the state religion. Later it was the residence of the Pontifex Maximus, the head

Temple of Antonius and Faustina

Courtesy of APT Rome

of the college of priests. During the Regal period it was the Pontifex Maximus who kept the religious records. Under the Republic he took charge of the national religion and became so influential that the Emperors appointed themselves to the position.

Tempio di Antonino e Faustina★★ (Temple of Antoninus and Faustina)

The Emperor Antoninus Pius, who succeeded Hadrian in 138 AD, belonged to a rich family originally from Nîmes in France. He was well known for his kindness and reigned for 23 years in peace and moderation. On the death of his wife, Faustina, in AD 141, he raised her to the ranks of the goddesses, in spite of her scandalous behaviour. A huge temple to her was erected in the Forum.

When Antoninus himself died, in AD 161, the Senate decided to dedicate the temple to both husband and wife.

The beautiful monolithic columns of the pronaos still stand on their high podium. The frieze of griffins and candelabra on the entablature is a masterpiece of fine craftsmanship.

In the 11C the church of San Lorenzo in Miranda was established in the ruins. When Charles V visited Rome in 1536 the façade of the church was set back to reveal the colonnade. In 1602 the church was rebuilt.

Excavations beside the Temple of Antoninus and Faustina have uncovered a **cemetery (17)** dating from the time of Romulus (8C-7C BC).

Tempio di Romolo (Temple of Romulus)

The Romulus to whom the temple is thought to be dedicated was not the founder of Rome but the son of the Emperor Maxentius. Romulus died in 307.

Dating from the early 4C, the construction is circular and flanked by two rooms with apses: it may have been built in honour of Constantine, to celebrate his victory over Maxentius in 312, or in honour of the divine city of Rome. In the 6C, when the room behind the temple became the church of St Cosmas and St Damian, the temple itself became a vestibule to the church.

The doorway between two porphyry columns in the concave façade is closed by the original 4C **bronze doors**★; the lock still works.

On the left of the Temple of Romulus are traces of six small rooms on either side of a corridor; they may have belonged to a brothel in the Republican era.

The remains of a medieval arcaded building **(19)** high above the Sacred Way indicate how much the ground level in the Forum had risen by the Middle Ages.

Higher up the slope, quite in harmony with the Ancient monuments below, is the church of Santa Francesca Romana with its Romanesque belfry and three parapet statues.

Basilica di Massenzio e Costantino★★★ (Basilica of Maxentius and Constantine)

This building is well known for its summer symphony concerts. Maxentius was proclaimed Emperor by the people after the abdication of joint rulers, Maximian, his father, and Diocletian, in 305. Almost immediately he began to build a basilica, the last to be erected in Rome. Built of brick beneath a groined vault, it was different from the other two basilicas, Aemilia and Julia. It was rectangular and divided into three by huge pillars flanked by columns; one long side ran parallel to the Sacred Way and the other followed the line of the present Via dei Fori Imperiali; one of the short sides constituted the main façade (facing east towards the Colosseum) and the other projected in an apse.

The Imperial throne, however, was coveted by Constantine, son of the Emperor Constantius, who had reigned jointly with Maximian and Diocletian. He defeated Maxentius at the battle of the Milvian Bridge in 312 and completed the basilica with modifications. He moved the entrance to the façade overlooking the Sacred Way and graced it with a portico of four porphyry columns (*still visible*); an apse was added to the opposite façade. This grandiose building housed some colossal statues; fragments of the statue of Constantine, which stood in the west apse, can still be seen in the courtyard of the Palazzo dei Conservatori. The gilded bronze tiles were used in the 7C to roof St Peter's Basilica.

Antiquarium

The exhibits in this museum, which is housed in a former convent attached to the church of Santa Francesca Romana, are mostly connected with the Roman Forum: the earliest traces of Ancient Rome taken from tombs dating from 1 000-600 BC or found in the Forum or on the Palatine (hut-shaped urns and hollow tree trunks used as coffins).

Arco di Trionfo di Tito★★ (Triumphal Arch of Titus)

The arch stands on the **Velia**, a spur of the Palatine jutting out towards the Esquiline, and appears in all the views of the Forum.

Titus, the eldest son of Vespasian, succeeded his father as Emperor but his reign was brief: from AD 79-81. In 70 he had captured Jerusalem, thus bringing to a successful conclusion a campaign his father had been pursuing since 66. After his death an arch was erected to commemorate his success. The fall of Jerusalem was among the most tragic events in Jewish history. The city was destroyed and the temple, the spiritual bond between Jews of the diaspora, was burned down. In its place Hadrian built a sanctuary to Jupiter and the city was called Aelia Capitolina (Hadrian's family name was Aelius). The single archway of the Arch of Titus was restored by Luigi Valadier in 1821.

At the centre of the panelled vault is a sculpture depicting the apotheosis of

Titus: his soul is carried up to heaven by an eagle; this event made him eligible for deification.

The frieze (*above the arch on the side facing the Colosseum*) is indistinct: in a sacrificial procession a recumbent figure represents the Jordan, symbolising the defeat of Palestine.

The two low reliefs under the vault are among the masterpieces of Roman sculpture. On one side, Titus rides in his chariot in triumph, crowned with victory. On the other, the triumphal procession exhibits the booty pillaged from the temple in Jerusalem: the sevenbranch candlestick which Moses had made and placed in the Tabernacle as commanded by God on Mount Sinai, the table for the shewbread which was placed in the temple each week in the name of the 12 tribes of Israel, and the silver trumpets which announced the festivals.

It was on the Velia that Nero built the vestibule to his Golden House.

Tempio di Giove Statore (Temple of Jupiter Stator)

On 8 November 63 BC **Cicero** delivered his first Catiline oration here before the Senate. Feelings ran high among his audience, who were impressed by the security measures considered necessary to protect the State.

▶ *Bear right up the hill (Clivus Palatinus) to the Palatine.*

Palatino

Of the seven hills of Rome, it is the Palatine Hill that captures the visitor's imagination. As the cradle of the Eternal City it is a prime archaeological site. Since the Renaissance it has offered pleasant walks among flower beds and shady trees.

Byron wrote of the beauty of the Palatine and its overgrown ruins:

"Cypress and ivy,
weed and wallflower grown
Matted and mass'd together,
hillocks heap'd

On what were chambers,
arch crush'd, column strown
In fragments, choked up vaults,
and frescos steep'd
In subterranean damps...."

Origins

It was inconvenient for political reasons that **Romulus** and **Remus** (🛈 *see INTRODUCTION*), twin sons of the Vestal Rhea Silvia and the god Mars, should survive. They were therefore abandoned on the banks of the Tiber but the river was in spate and their cradle came to rest on the Palatine. They survived thanks to a shewolf which suckled them in the Lupercal cave. The shepherd Faustulus, who witnessed this unusual event, took charge of the twins and brought them up.

In the middle of the 8C BC Romulus ploughed a deep furrow around the Palatine lifting his ploughshare in three places. This was the beginning of Rome, a symbolic enclosure with three gateways: the Porta Mugonia, the Porta Romana and the Porta Scalae Caci.

This is obviously a legendary account ... but in 1949 traces of huts thought to date from the 8C and 7C BC were excavated on the legendary site of Romulus's house. During the Republic the Palatine was a quiet residential area. **Cicero** lived on the hill, as did Antony, the Triumvir, and Agrippa – Octavian's friend before becoming his son-in-law. Foreigners came to visit the shepherd's hut and the wolf's cave in the southwest face of the hill.

In 63 BC "on the ninth day before the Kalends of October, a little before daybreak" Octavian was born. When he became the Emperor Augustus, the Palatine began to alter. He enlarged his

The nymphaeum in the Domus Flavia, built during the time of Domitian

B. Kaufmann/MICHELIN

house and then rebuilt it after it was destroyed by fire in the 3 BC. Tiberius, who succeeded him, Caligula, Claudius and Nero all lived on the Palatine, but it was **Domitian**, the last Flavian Emperor (AD 81-96), who transformed the hill by turning it into the Imperial Palace and gave it the appearance that has now been revealed by archaeologists. The hollow which divided it into two peaks (Germalus and Palatium) was filled with new buildings, whose ruins now occupy the central section of the plateau: they are the **Domus Flavia** and the **Domus Augustana**; the **Stadium** also dates from this period. In 191 the buildings on the Palatine were seriously damaged by fire. The Emperor Septimius Severus was not content with simply undertaking repairs. He enlarged the Imperial Palace to the south and built a monumental façade, the Septizonium, parallel with the Old Appian Way, so that travellers arriving in Rome by this route would be immediately impressed by the grandeur of the capital. This section of the palace remained standing until Pope Sixtus V demolished it to provide building materials at the end of the 16C.

The Palatine began to go into decline in the 3C when Diocletian, Galerius, Maximian and Constantius deserted Rome and built new Imperial residences in Nicomedia, Sirmium, Milan and Trier respectively. In 330 **Constantine** moved the Imperial capital to Constantinople, formerly Byzantium, and the Palatine was abandoned.

The Christians generally ignored the Palatine plateau and built only on the slopes: in the 4C a sanctuary was dedicated to St Anastasia on the south side; on the north face the church of St Sebastian was established in what had been a temple to the sun; its builder Emperor Elagabalus dreamed of a religion combining the various Oriental cults and appointed himself high priest to the sun god.

In the 11C and 12C Rome became the prize in the struggles between the Pope and the Emperor and was studded with fortresses and towers; hence the descrip-

tion *Roma turrita*. The Frangipani family, who supported the Emperor, fortified the whole of the southeast face of the Palatine. By the time of the Renaissance the buildings on the Palatine (from which the word "palace" is derived) were in ruins. The wealthy Roman families built villas on the site, surrounding them with vineyards and gardens: the Barberini near to St Sebastian, the Farnese on the northwest part of the hill between Tiberius's and Caligula's palaces. In the 16C the Mattei built a villa on the site of the Domus Augustana; three centuries

★ T. di Venere e Roma ↑
■ Arco di Tito ★★
Via — Sacra ★
Meta Sudans
PIAZZA DEL COLOSSEO
COLOSSEO-CELIO
P⁰ Mugonia
★★★ ARCO DI CONSTANTINO
Clivus Palatinus
Via di S. Bonaventura
Vigna
S. Sebastiano
Tempio di Eliogabalo
Barberini
S. Bonaventura
Via di S. Gregorio
DOMUS ★
Lararium
Sala del Trono
FLAVIA
★★ DOMUS
Peristilium 4
Museo Palatino ★
AUGUSTANA
5
★ STADIO
Peristilium 6
8
Terme di Settimio Severo
Septizonium
N
Cerchi

later an Englishman, Charles Mills, converted it into a sort of Romantic Gothic castle. This extraordinary building was demolished at the end of the 19C at the instigation of P Rosa, the archaeologist in charge of the excavations.

Excavations

Investigative digging began in 1724 at the suggestion of Francis I of Parma, who had inherited the Farnese Villa. The Domus Flavia was the first building to see the light of day. About 50 years later a Frenchman, the Abbé Rancoureuil, exca-

vated the Domus Augustana and the buildings overlooking the Circus Maximus. In 1860, under Napoleon III, archaeologists discovered Tiberius's Palace, Livia's House and the Temple of Apollo, which was first attributed to Jupiter. The identification of the buildings on the Palatine has provoked passionate argument between archaeologists and historians. Many of the constructions have never been discovered but excavations on the Palatine continue, particularly in the area of the Temple of Apollo.

Very little of the ruined buildings remains standing and it requires a great effort of the imagination to evoke the splendour of the Ancient palaces on the Palatine.

Tour

&♿ ⏱ *Open daily 9am-1hr before dusk (5.30pm in winter). Last admission 1hr before closing time. ⏱Closed 1 Jan and Christmas. €8, combined ticket with the Colosseum; €20 for a "Roma archeologica" card, valid for nine archaeological sites. ☎06 39 96 77 00; www.pierreci.it ⚷ At the time of publication the Orti Farnese, the Cabins of Romulus, and the House of Augustus were closed for restoration.*

Clivus Palatinus

This road approximately follows the hollow between the two peaks: the Palatium to the left, the Germalus to the right.

▷ *Walk straight up the path (south) leaving on the right the steps which go up to the Farnese Gardens.*

The rectangular ditch marks the site of Domitian's Arch. The sections of high brick wall facing down the hill belonged to the portico of the Domus Flavia. The path emerges at the top of the hill in the centre of the artificial plateau which was created when Domitian filled in the hollow between the Palatium and the Germalus.

Domus Flavia★

This was the centre of official Imperial activity. Although the buildings have been razed to the ground, it is still possible to envisage them. There were three rooms behind the portico:

● the **Lararium** – the shrine of the household gods, the Lares – was the Emperor's private chapel;
● the **Throne Room** (Sala del Trono) was enormous (over 30m/98ft wide by 40m/131ft long) with huge statues standing in the recesses in the walls;
● the **Basilica**, where the Emperor dispensed justice, had an apse at one end and a row of columns down each of the long sides. Outside the

west wall are traces of the west portico of the Domus.

Behind these three rooms is a courtyard **(Peristilium)** originally surrounded by a portico (traces of the columns remain). Suetonius wrote that Domitian was so hated by everyone for his injustice and cruelty that he had the walls of the portico faced with phengite (a very shiny stone) so that he could "see by reflection what was going on behind his back." The octagonal basin at the centre of the court, which is now planted with flowers, was probably a fountain.

Beyond the peristyle is the **Triclinium**, the dining room, which was certainly the most beautiful room in the palace; part of the coloured marble floor has been preserved. It was supported on little brick pillars to allow the passage of warm air produced by an underground stove to heat the room.

The triclinium was flanked to right and left by two small leisure rooms, known in Latin as the nymphaea. The one on the right is well preserved.

The extant building in the far corner of the *nymphaeum* dates from the Farnese era (16C).

The traces of walls, columns and apses on the terrace behind the triclinium may mark the site of the libraries of the Imperial Palace.

Sale sotterranee★ (Underground rooms) – These rooms are all that remained of houses from the Republican era and of Nero's constructions when they were buried under Domitian's building projects.

● Beneath the basilica, a rectangular room: the paintings with which it was decorated are conserved in a room east of the Antiquarium; they probably date from the Augustan era and depict the cult of Isis.

● Beneath the lararium, the **Griffin House** (Casa dei Grifi), sometimes also erroneously called "Catilina's house": it was built in the 2C BC (walls composed of irregular-sized stones mixed with mortar), altered in the 1C BC (walls composed of regular stone blocks arranged in a diamond pattern) and then altered again by Nero; many of the paintings have been removed to the Antiquarium for safe keeping; one room contains a stucco relief of two griffins face to face.

- Beneath the peristyle: a circular chamber containing a well which communicates with another room by a passage. The discovery of this complex early this century caused quite a stir among archaeologists who thought they had found the Mundus. At the time of the founding of Rome the Mundus was a well into which a handful of earth was thrown by each new immigrant who, through this symbolic gesture, became a citizen of the new city. In fact, it is probably only a silo for water or grain.

Museo Palatino

The **Palatine Museum** is housed in a building which once belonged to the Convent of the Visitation, built over the ruins of Domitian's Imperial Palace (structural remains of which can be seen in Rooms 3 and 4), and contains articles and fragments found on the Palatine. The ground floor is dedicated to the period spanning the foundation of Rome (model of 8-7C BC huts built on the Germalus) and the Republican era; the upper floor contains exhibits relating to the Imperial period. Exhibits include remains of "second style" frescoes from Augustus's House, with architectural cornices and columns and suspended festoons of leaves and flowers between them; a collection of portraits of Emperors and famous characters; and two inlaid-marble panels which demonstrate the fine quality of wall decoration during the Nero period (AD 54-68). At the end of Room 9, the statue known as the Borghese Hera, a Roman copy of a Greek work from the end of the 5C BC, towers over the other exhibits.

Domus Augustana★★

This is not Augustus's own private house but the official Imperial residence. The rooms are arranged around two peristyles (*peristilium*); one is very much lower than the other. At the centre of the upper peristyle (**4**), marked by an umbrella pine, is the base of a construction which was reached by a bridge from the edge of the surrounding basin. Around the sides are various living rooms.

The rooms on the south side of the upper peristyle overlook the lower peristyle. The central basin (**6**), which is composed of a pattern of compartments, was designed to collect rain water. The palace itself faces the Circus Maximus from behind a concave façade.

Even in ruins the Domus Augustana gives an impression of grandeur and luxury because of its sophisticated design, its soaring walls and the daring of some of the vaulting.

Stadio★ (Stadium)

This was one of Domitian's projects. It looks like a gigantic trough (some 145m/159yd long) surrounded by a two-storey portico. Some say it was designed to stage private games and spectacles for the Emperor; others say it was a garden or an athletics ground. The small oval track (**7**) at the southern end dates from the 6C and is the work of Theodoric, the Ostrogoth, who occupied the Palatine at that period. The huge recess (**8**) in the centre of the long east side may have been reserved for the Emperor.

On the east side of the Stadium are the ruins of a bathhouse attributed to Septimius Severus but probably built by Maxentius.

▶ *Pass the museum and retrace your steps.*

Tempio di Apollo (Temple of Apollo)

For many years this temple was thought to be dedicated to Jupiter but it is probably the one mentioned by Suetonius: Augustus built a temple to Apollo "in a corner of his house on the Palatine which had been struck by lightning and which, according to the omens, Apollo was claiming for himself."

The temple is fenced off; the podium and a column of the *pronaos* are recognisable.

Casa di Livia★★ (Livia's House)

This house, which is named after Augustus's wife, was probably where the Emperor himself lived. The diamond pattern on the walls and the style of the decor date the building to the end of the Republic. The wall paintings which had already deteriorated somewhat were detached and erected just in front of the walls to which they belonged; this means they can be appreciated in their original setting. The names given to the various rooms do not necessarily correspond to their use. On either side of the centre room (*tablinum* – study) are two narrow rooms (wings) where wax images of the family ancestors were kept or which, in more modest houses, were used as storerooms.

Left wing – The lower part of the wall is decorated to look like marble; above are panels showing people and griffins face to face.

Tablinum – On the right-hand wall: a central panel, surrounded by architectural motifs, shows Io, Argos's daughter; Zeus fell in love with her and turned her into a heifer to protect her from the fury of his wife, Hera, who was nevertheless suspicious and set Argus, who had 100 eyes, to watch over the animal. The painting shows Hermes, who was sent by Zeus to rescue Io.

On the left-hand wall: lead pipes engraved with the name IVLIAE AV (Julia Augusta). The archaeologists who discovered this inscription in 1869 thought it referred to Augustus's wife, the Empress, and attributed the house to Livia.

The rear wall depicts Galatea fleeing from Polyphemus.

Right wing – The decorations on the left-hand wall, although damaged by the opening of the door, are still fresh: simulated columns flanking beautiful garlands of fruit and leaves from which hang baskets, sticks, horned animal heads, lyres and other representations of nature. Above, on a yellow ground, is a frieze showing people at work in the open air.

Cisterne (Cisterns) (2)

They date from the 6C BC; one is shaped like a beehive and the other is uncovered.

Scala di Caco (Cacus's Steps)

This was one of the three original approaches to the Palatine. The steps are named after a local villain, **Cacus**, who is linked in legend to Hercules. When Hercules was returning to the Argos with the cattle stolen from Geryon, he halted on the banks of the Tiber. Cacus, an evil three-headed monster who breathed fire from his three mouths, took the opportunity to steal three animals. He made them walk backwards to avoid detection but Hercules was not fooled and he killed Cacus.

Capanne del villagio di Romolo (Cabins from Romulus's village) (1)

Together with the Forum cemetery these huts form some of the earliest traces of the city (8C-7C BC). The modern roof which covers them creates a real reliquary. Three huts have been discovered, oval or rectangular and sunk in the ground. The ring of holes held the posts which supported the walls and the roof. The gap in the south side (facing the Tiber) marks the doorway and is flanked by smaller post holes which indicate the possibility of a porch. The ditch surrounding each emplacement was probably to drain off the rain water from the roof.

Tempio di Cibele (Temple of Cybele)

Cybele, the great goddess of Phrygia (also called the Mother of the Gods, the Great Mother or Magna Mater), was the personification of the powers of nature. Her cult was introduced into Rome late in the 3C or early in the 2C BC. In 204 BC, at the height of the Second Punic War, a hail of stones fell on Rome. The priests appealed to the gods and the Senate was obliged to send for the **"black stone,"** symbol of the goddess Cybele, from Pessinus in Asia Minor. The temple on the Palatine was inaugurated in 191 and then rebuilt by Augustus after several fires. Today only the base of the *cella* walls remains in the shade of a group of holm oaks.

Each year from 4-20 April a festival took place in front of the temple. Called the Megalesia, it consisted of theatrical presentations and circus acts and had been founded in 204 in honour of Cybele. Terence's comedy "Andria" was played for the first time during the festival in 168 BC, but on that occasion the audience preferred the tightrope walkers,

PALATII VILLAE BVRGHESIAE PROSPECTVS

J.W. Baur, View of Villa Borghese

"… that Gallery, which resembles the Theatre of the Universe, the Collection of Wonders, and the Longing of the Human Gaze." Thus Scipione Francucci, man of letters, in his short poem of 1613 described for the first time the collection of paintings and antique sculptures that belonged to Cardinal Scipione, nephew of Pope Paul V (1605-1621). A year later, the collection was to be transferred to the recently built Villa Borghese lying just outside the Porta Pinciana and future symbol of the "Golden Age" of the Borghese family. The Villa's uniqueness remains unchanged today thanks to its outstanding location, serenely blending architecture and nature, compared by L. Lepureo (1628) to the Garden of the Hesperides or Parnassus, and also thanks to the richness of its collections - the original core, still intact today, is the result of the choices made by its creator and owner. Built in accordance with the suburban architectural model of the Classical Age - with the pars urbana *and* pars rustica *- the villa was conceived, right from its 17th-century beginnings, as a kind of* ante litteram *museum, a microcosm of every form of art. Situated in the depths of the countryside beyond the Aurelian Walls, the Palazzina did not reflect the mores of the inhabited Urbe, unlike the other Borghese residences in Rome during the second decade of the 17th century (the Palazzi of Borgo, Campus Martius and Monte Cavallo).*
The villa was built in response to the family's need for a private residence and diplomatic seat, and to accomodate Scipione's passion for collecting. Rather than exalting the nobility of his family, it was to celebrate the seduction of antique art recreating it by means of various architectural, sculptural and figurative formal solutions, and above all, by means of its very appearance. Described by J. Evelyn (1644) as a "citadel surrounded by walls with

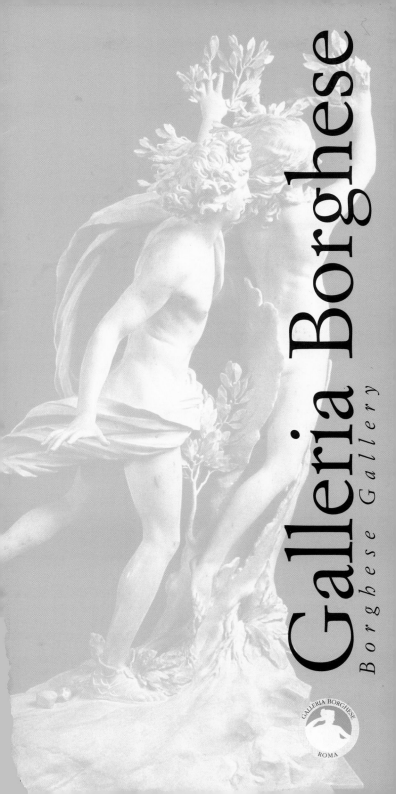

Galleria Borghese

Borghese Gallery

GALLERIA BORGHESE

ROMA

the "Garden of the Perpectives" or "Garden of Narcissus" named after the original bronze statue later replaced by a marble Venus on a basin made of African marble. Stretching out from the sides of the Palazzina like wings were two secret gardens that extended the spatiality of the interior to the outside. The park was divided into three areas enclosed by walls that were later knocked down, and its open spaces were regularly crossed by avenues.

Caravaggio, Boy with a Baskeet of Fruit

The collection's character was influenced by the capricious nature of its owner who had little love of affairs of state and was more inclined to indulge his personal whims and, above all, his passion for art. The original core is characterised by Scipione's interest in every form of antique and Classical art - to the exclusion of medieval works - and his openness to the most innovative artistic movements of his times. Its richness was the result of unscrupulous appropriation and tyrannical extortion by the "cardinal nepote" leading the inclusion of the collection of the Cavalier D'Arpino with paintings by Caravaggio, of Domenichino's Diana (1613), of the paintings from the Ferrara School including works by Garofalo and Dosso Dossi, and of Raphael's Deposition (1507). These were joined by gifts and acquisitions such as the antique sculptures of Tiberio Ceuli (1607), the collections of the sculptor Giovanni Battista della Porta (1608), of the Patriarch of Aquileia (1609), of Cesare d'Este with paintings by Dosso (acquired with the help of Cardinal E. Bentivoglio, and of Cardinal Sfondrato (1608), with Venetian works by Titian and G. Reni.
Thanks to the variety of the Cardinal's choices the most significant movements and the most brilliant Italian and foreign artists of the Cinquecento and Seicento - Titian, Caravaggio, Bernini and Rubens - are documented in the gallery. Towards the end of the 17th century the collection reached its height with the entry of numerous works from Olimpia Aldobrandini's inheritance (1682). A second significant artistic contribution took place towards the

A. Canova, Pauline Bonaparte

end of the 18th century (1770) when Marcantonio IV Borghese (1730-1800) launched the radical restructuring of the entire villa (1770-1800), causing the interior decoration and the landscaping of the gardens to reflect the more elegant style of Neoclassicism.

He entrusted the supervision of the work to the architect Antonio Asprucci who called upon a famous group of Italian and foreign artists and painters to renew the various rooms (G. Hamilton, T. M. Conca, B. Gagneraux, L. Pecheux, etc.).

The interior of the villa was decorated throughout: the walls were covered with polychrome marble Roman stucco and the 17th-century peperino *fireplaces were replaced by others embellished by precious materials. Canvas paintings echoing the original iconography of the sculpture in the the various rooms (The Rooms of Apollo and Daphne, of Silenus, of the Hermaphrodite) were applied to the ceilings which were divided into panels by elegant architectural mouldings. The floors were also renewed with precious Roman marble inlays. The inspiration for the splendid Egyptian Room (Room VII) on the ground floor (described and completed in 1782) lay in the culture of exoticism and contemporary travel books.*

The changes made to the exterior by A. Asprucci were over-invasive: the reliefs, no longer in harmony with the style of the period, were stripped from the façade, and the 17th-century staircase in the forecourt was eliminated for the same motive. The most serious loss was sustained in 1807 when Camillo Borghese, the husband of Pauline Bonaparte, sold a large part of the archaeological collection to Napoleon for thirteen million francs (these works now form the Louvre's Borghese Collection). Camillo Borghese would later try to compensate for this loss. It was, in fact, during this period (1805-08) that A. Canova was commissioned to portray Pauline as Venus Victrix, *while the acquisition of Correggio's* Danae *(1530-1531) dates to 1827.*

Dancing Satyr

In 1833 a new fideicommissum (a legal act that forbade the dispersal of any of the listed items) was drawn up in order to protect the collection which was purchased together with the Palazzina and the park, by the Italian state in 1902.

Paola Mangia

the Capitol and later eliminated by L. Canino, was reconstructed in accordance with the original plan. Descriptions made by Manilli and Montelatici during the second half of the 17th century say that the original interior decoration (no longer extant, with the exception of the wall paintings in the chapel) was rather simple and consisted of "dressed leather" applied to the walls and printed with blue and gold, the two colours of the Borghese family arms - the eagle and the dragon -, and "red velvet from Imola". Costly tapestries, some of which designed by Veronese, formed the main ornamentation while the furnishings consisted of numerous tables made of polished or painted wood or set with polychrome marble inlays, fine cabinet work, mirrors, and curios concealing surprises like the "seat of revenge" and the stool containing a "device of a horribly shrieking monster". Although the possibility of lodging in the palazzo with family members and servants existed, these stays never lasted more than one day and one night. The 17th-century structure of Ponzio and Vasanzio's villa recalled the classical-type models of the Cinquecento, represented by Baldassarre Peruzzi's Farnesina (1509) or by Annibale Lippi's Villa Medici (1544).

Recent restoration work, completed in 1997, renewed the original white marble-like colour of the façade. The U-shaped plan has two projecting side wings, a central portico surmounted by a terrace, a façade decorated with antique sculptures reflecting the Mannerist styles that had already been tried out in the casino created by Pirro Ligorio for Pius IV or in the above mentioned Villa Medici on the Pincian Hill. Lying between the two towers "for the family" set at the corners of the back wall was an open loggia (closed in the 18th century) containing a fresco by Lanfranco called the Council of the Gods (1624-25). It looked onto

Raffaello, Lady with a Unicorn

towers", it represented a perfect location rivalling Classical villas like the villa of Lucullus on the Pincian Hill, or Renaissance villas like the Villa Medici (1544), or the villa of Scipione's rival Cardinal Pietro Aldobrandini in Frascati (1598-1604), and the Cardinal would in fact dedicate the greater part of it to his archaeological collection. The exterior was intended to provide a foretaste of the antique climate within; numerous sculptures were placed in the gardens, while the façade was embellished with elegantly distributed statues, documented in the watercolour painting by Johann Wilhelm Baur (1636). Set into the south front was a Roman equestrian statue, restored by Pietro Bernini for the occasion and depicting Marcus Curtius Flinging himself into the Chasm. During the 18th century it was transferred into the entrance hall and set high up on the wall. The day after the election of Pope Paul V (May 1605), the "old vineyard by the Muro Torto" was bequeathed to Scipione together with the entire art collection. It was then that work on the building was begun under the supervision of the architect Flaminio Ponzio, succeeded at his death (1613) by the Dutch architect Jan van Santen known as Vasanzio.

As early as 1613, a number of statues were transferred into the Casino, and by August 1615, Gian Lorenzo Bernini's The Goat Amalthea had been installed. These were followed by four marble groups directly commissioned by Scipione, conceived as "antique statues" and intended to rival the masterpieces of classic antiquity. By this date (1615) the Palazzina was already functioning: the two hundred pieces forming the archaeological collection (installed on the ground floor) and part of the furnishings had already been transferred there, although the installation of the paintings, previously housed in the town villa of Borgo, would not take place until a later date. In 1997, the double travertine staircase set "in front of the palazzo" recalling Michelangelo's staircase at

GROUND FLOOR

P   portico
S   entrance Hall
C   chapel

ROOMS

1   of Pauline
2   of David
3   of Apollo and Daphne
4   of the Emperors
5   of the Hermaphrodite
6   of Aeneas and Anchises
7   Egyptian
8   of Silenus

FIRST FLOOR Picture Gallery

T   terrace
S   entrance Hall
9   16th-century Florentine School
10   16th-century Italian Mannerism
11   16th-century Ferrarese School
12   16th-century Sienese
     Lombard and Venetian Schools
13   16th-century Florentine School
14   Gallery of Lanfranco,
     17th-century painting
15   16th-century Ferrarese,
     Venetian and Brescian Schools
16   16th-century Florentine
     Mannerism
17   17th- and 18th-century painting
18   17th-century painting
19   17th-century painting in Rome
20   16th-century Venetian School

SERVICES AND AMENITIES

→   Entrance
❶   Tickets and information
❷   Bookshop
❸   Cloakroom
❹   Audio-guides and guided tours
❺   Lecture and Multimedia Hall
❻   Educational Area
❼   Bar and Restaurant
❽   Toilets
❾   Lifts and Stairs

The Borghese Museum and Gallery
P.le del Museo Borghese, 5
00197 Rome

Museum switchboard
• Tel. 06 8416542

Opening hours
• Monday closed
• Tuesday to Sunday: 9 a.m. - 7 p.m.
  Opening hours may vary.
  Visitors are requested to contact the
  booking ticket service previously.

Compulsory booking
• Bookings: Tel. 06 32810
• Group Bookings: Fax 06 32651329
  (Access and facilities for the handicapped
  are provided).

Didactic service
• Bookings: tel 06 8413979 fax 06 8840756

Guided tours
• Tel. 06 22582493 - fax 06 8555952
• info.tour@libero.it

Free entrance (compulsory booking € 2,00)
• Italian citezens under 18 and over 65;
  students from Architecture and Arts (only
  History of Art) Faculties, employees of the
  Ministry of Cultural Heritage and Activities;
  guided tours authorised by the Lazio
  Region; members of the Emergency Services
  whilst on dury; members of ICOM; foreign
  citizens (according to the agreements
  between states currently in force).

Transport
• Buses nos. 52, 53, 88, 116, 119, 910

Services
• Lavatories
• Cloakroom
• Bookshop
• Bar

• Entering the museum rooms with bags,
  backbags, pushchairs, umbrelias or cameras
• Switching on mobile phones in the
  museum rooms
• Filming and photographing
• Smoking in the museum
• Eating in the exhibition rooms
  Are forbidden.

Ministero per i Beni e le Attività Culturali
• freephone number 800991199

perhaps because Terence did not have Plautus's biting wit "nor his coarse jokes, his broad humour, his puns, his quips ...."

Domus Tiberiana

The arches facing the Temple of Cybele belonged to the rear façade of Tiberius' Palace. Only a few traces of this huge rectangular building are visible since Cardinal Farnese's gardens cover the greater part of it.

The main façade of the palace faced the Forum. Caligula extended the building as far as Via Nova; Trajan and Hadrian added the ranges overlooking Clivus Victoriae.

Cryptoporticus

This is a network of passages, partially underground, which probably linked the various Imperial buildings which occupied the hill. It dates from Nero's reign, although the arm linking up with Domitian's Domus Flavia must have been added later.

The stuccoes which decorated the vaulting in the section of the passage near Livia's House have been removed to the Antiquarium and replaced by copies.

The oval basin (3) on the left of the steps leading up to the Farnese Gardens was a fish tank in the southeast corner of Tiberius's Palace.

Orti Farnesiani (Farnese Gardens)

The gardens were laid out in the middle of the 16C by Cardinal Alexander Farnese, Paul III's nephew. The entrance, set in a semicircle at the level of the Forum (which was higher then than now), gave access to a series of terraces rising up the north face of the Palatine. On the flat top of the hill, over the ruins of Tiberius's Palace, stretched the Farnese's magnificent botanical garden, one of the richest in the world at that time. The northwest corner of the gardens gives an excellent **view**★★ of the Forum, the Tabularium, the Senatorial Palace, the monument to Victor Emmanuel II, the domes of the church of St Luke and St Martina and of the two churches next to Trajan's Column, the Militia Tower etc. In the northeast corner of the gardens are two buildings (reconstructed) which formed a complex comprising two aviaries above a nymphaeum. From the terrace there is a pleasant **view**★★, particularly at sunset, of the basilica of Maxentius, the belfry of Santa Francesca Romana and the upper storeys of the Colosseum.

Below the aviaries there used to be a monumental gate marking the entrance to the gardens. It was begun by Vignola and completed by Girolamo Rainaldi but taken down in 1882. It now stands on the east side of Via di S. Gregorio.

▶ *Leave the Palatine by Clivus Palatinus, turning right into Via Sacra at the Arch of Titus to visit the other monuments which belong to the Forum.*

Tempio di Venere e Roma★ (Temple of Venus and Rome)

The temple was built between AD 121-136 by Hadrian, completed by Antoninus Pius and restored by Maxentius, on the site of the vestibule to Nero's Golden House. It was the largest temple in Rome (110m/361ft by 53m/174ft) and designed in the Greek style with steps on all sides (the majority of Roman temples had only one flight of steps leading up to the *pronaos*). It was surrounded by a colonnade and uniquely comprised two cellae with apses back to back. One was dedicated to the goddess Rome and faced the Forum; the other was dedicated to Venus and faced the Colosseum.

The plans for the temple were drawn up by Hadrian, who was keen on architecture. He also designed two gigantic seated figures to be set in niches which were disproportionately small. Trajan's brilliant architect, Apollodorus of Damascus, commented that "if the figures tried to stand they would bump their heads on the vault." He had already poured scorn on the Emperor's rather peculiar taste for painting pumpkins. It was too much; Hadrian had the architect silenced once and for all.

The part of the temple which faces the Forum has been incorporated into the church of Santa Francesca Romana and the adjoining convent of Olivetan monks. An idea of the temple's appearance is given by a few columns which were re-erected in 1935; the position of the missing parts is marked by bushes of privet, box and oleander.

Santa Francesca Romana

🕐*Open 9:30am-12pm and 4pm-7pm.* In the 8C an oratory dedicated to St Peter and St Paul was built in the western half of the Temple of Venus and Rome by Pope Paul I. In the following century it replaced the church of Santa Maria Antiqua in the Forum and was called Santa Maria Nova. The church was placed under the patronage of Santa Francesca Romana (**St Frances of Rome**) when she was canonised in 1608.

The 12C Romanesque **bell-tower**★ is one of the most elegant in Rome.

The façade by Carlo Lombardi (1615) is characteristic of the Counter-Reformation. The use of a single order of flat pilasters resting on a high portico lends it a certain solemnity. Inside there is a beautiful 17C coffered ceiling.

Apsidal mosaic – The Virgin and Child are enthroned between St Peter and St Andrew, St James and St John. The mosaic dates from c 1160 at a period when mosaic art was marked by a certain eclecticism: the vivid colours of the Ancient art, together with the rigidity of the figures, is typical of Byzantine art.

Right transept – Two stones are preserved behind a grating; they are supposed to bear the print of St Peter's knees. He prayed at length to God to prevent Simon Magus from flying and Simon crashed to earth near the church. The A*cts of the Apostles* (VIII, 9-25) tell the story of the sorcerer who practised in Samaria and who wanted to acquire spiritual powers from the Apostles for money. He is the source of the word simony.

There is also a monument (16C) to Gregory XI, the last French Pope, who brought the Holy See back to Rome from Avignon in 1377. The central low relief shows St Peter entering Rome; the flanking statues are Faith and Prudence.

Crypt – Opposite the remains of St Frances of Rome is a marble low relief showing the saint and an angel (17C work by one of Bernini's pupils).

Sacristy – Beautiful painting of Santa Maria Nova showing a Virgin and Child which art historians date to the 5C or 8C.

▶ *Take Via dei Fori Imperiali.*

Santi Cosma e Damiano (Basilica of St Cosmas and St Damian)

🕐*Open 8am-1pm and 3pm-7pm.* The basilica was dedicated in 526 by Pope Felix IV to two saints of Arabian origin, Cosmas and Damian, twin brothers whose help was invoked to cure illness. The church was established in the Temple of Romulus and in an adjacent room which had been the library of Vespasian's Forum; it was the first Christian church to occupy a pagan building in the Roman Forum. When the relics of the two saints were discovered in the 16C the Popes began to alter the original church. In the 17C Clement VIII reduced the width of the nave by creating side chapels which cut off the outer edges of the mosaic on the chancel arch. The floor was raised, a doorway opened in the west wall and a plaster arcade added in front of the apse.

Ceiling★ – Beautiful 17C coffered ceiling showing the triumph of St Cosmas and St Damian (*centre*) and (*at each end*) the coat of arms with the bees of Cardinal Francesco Barberini, who promoted the greater part of the 17C alterations.

Mosaics★ – Those on the chancel arch date from the late 7C and show the Lamb of God surrounded by seven candelabra and four angels. The angels on the left and right, symbolising the Evangelists, St Luke and St John, have survived the 17C alterations. The lamb and the throne were restored in 1936.

The mosaics in the apse date from the 6C. In the centre is the figure of Christ against a sunset sky. At his sides are the Apostles Peter and Paul presenting St Cosmas and St Damian, dressed in brown. On the left is Pope Felix IV offering a model of his church and on the right St Theodore dressed in a handsome chlamys (short mantle), like a Byzantine courtier. Below, partially screened by the Baroque altar (1637), is the Paschal Lamb surrounded by 12 beautiful angels representing the apostles and the Church.

Southeast chapel – *Facing the entrance.* Above the altar is a curious fresco showing the living Christ on the cross, a work in the Byzantine style, repainted in the 17C.

GIANICOLO ★

MICHELIN MAP 38 L 9, N9

South of the Vatican rises this cool, leafy hill, where locals stroll and savour the magnificent views of their city. In summertime the Fontana Paola – the grand fountain at a belvedere – transforms into a sprawling open-air theatre complex, as do many nooks in this neighbourhood.

▶ **Orient Yourself:** The Janiculum Hill, or Gianicolo in Italian, stands on the west bank of the Tiber. The area's girded by 17C walls built by Urbano VIII, which include the grand Porta San Pancrazio. Beyond the hill to the west lies Villa Doria Pamphili, one of the city's largest areas of greenery.

⊚ **Don't Miss:** The noon cannon, il Tempietto at San Pietro in Montorio, views from the Fontana Paola and the Passegiata Gianicolo. Gardners enjoy the Villa Farnesina.

🕐 **Organizing Your Time:** Allow 2 hrs.

Kids **Especially for Kids:** The puppet show (Sat–Sun), carousel and pony rides near the Piazzale G. Garidbaldi. The playgrounds of the Villa Doria Pamphili.

A Bit of History

Legend claims that the two-faced god Janus founded a city on the **Janiculum** Hill (*Monte Gianicolo*). One of his children, Tiber, gave his name to the river. The *Gianicolo* was a country district until the 17C, when Urban VIII constructed a defensive wall with bastions along the present-day Viale delle Mura Aurelie and Viale delle Mura Gianicolensi.

From Mucius Scaevola to Garibaldi

Myth and truth entertwine in this area, so crucial to Rome's development.

The oldest tale goes back to the 6C BC, when the town had broken free of the Etruscan kings and was besieged by **Lars Porsenna**. **Mucius**. This young Roman noble infiltrated the enemy camp on the *Gianicolo* to assassinate their chief. He mistakenly killed one of the aides instead and was arrested. To prove to Lars Porsenna that life was of little account to a Roman defending his country, Mucius burned away his right hand on a brasier. Porsenna was so struck by this bravery that he let him go. Mucius was nicknamed "*Scaevola*", left-handed.

In his footsteps came Cloelia. According to Livy, she showed courage "without precedent among women." Held hostage in Porsenna's camp, she escaped with her companions and made them swim the Tiber to reach Rome.

While banqueting on the hill in 1611, the scientist **Galileo Galilei** tested a new

Council of the Gods (detail of vault fresco), Galleria della Villa Farnesina

telescope. In daylight, he managed to read the inscription on Saint John Lateran several miles away.

In 1849, one of the battles in the struggle for Italian unity raged here. **Garibaldi** defended the Gianicolo valiantly in the name of the Roman Republic against the French troops commanded by Marshal Oudinot. Tales claim he would take his morning coffee within view of the enemies, taunting them. On 4 July, the Papal Government was re-established after a month of bloody combat, particularly in the Villa Pamphili.

Later, in 1862, the great general uttered famous war cry – "*Roma o morte*" (Rome or death) – now memorialized on a Mussolini-built marble monument on the Via Garibaldi.

Villa Farnesina★★

&. ⏰*Open daily 9am–1pm; 9am–4pm 15 March–30 June, 15 Sept–31 Oct, 1-31 Dec. Mon–Sat 9am-1pm.* ✎€5. ☎06 68 02 72 68. *www.lincei.it/informazioni/villafar nesina/index*

The villa was set in this garden in 1508-11 for Agostino Chigi, the great banker. Known as "the Magnificent", he entertained his guests, including Pope Leo X, in sumptuous style. Designed as a suburban house, it has two projecting wings. For the construction and the decor, Chigi

commissioned the best Renaissance artists: **Baldassarre Peruzzi**, architect and painter, and Raphael with his usual following of Giulio Romano, Francesco Penni, Giovanni da Udine, Sebastiano del Piombo and Sodoma.

The friendship linking all these men is enshrined in Villa Farnesina: Agostino Chigi was Raphael's most ardent patron and Leo X had a sincere affection for him. None of them saw the sack of the city, which brought the Roman Renaissance to an end. Raphael died, aged 37, on Good Friday 1520; a few days later came Chigi's death; the following year Leo X succumbed to a "slight fever."

Later, in the 16C, the villa was sold to Cardinal Alessandro Farnese and assumed the name of its new owner.

The Interior

This painting collection is one of the gems of the Renaissance. On the ceiling of the **gallery,** along the garden front, is a fresco depicting the legend of Cupid and Psyche (in the centre *The Council of the Gods* and *The Marriage of Cupid and Psyche*), painted by Raphael, assisted by Giulio Romano, Francesco Penni and Giovanni da Udine. Finished in 1520, these paintings contain elements, which became characteristic of the Mannerist style (a series of scenes, as in a tapestry, framed by garlands).

At the eastern end of the gallery is the **Galatea** room (1511) where Nereus's sea maiden has been painted by **Raphael** riding in a shell drawn by dolphins (*right of the entrance*). The monstrous Polyphemus, as well as the scenes from Ovid's *Metamorphoses* (*in the lunettes*), are by **Sebastiano del Piombo**. The Constellations on the ceiling are the work of **Baldassarre Peruzzi**. The young man's head painted in grisaille (*left of the entrance*) is probably by Sebastiano del Piombo, but tradition attributes it to Michelangelo, who wanted to show Raphael that his figures were too small.

On the **first floor,** the **salon** is decorated with landscapes in *trompe-l'œil* by Peruzzi and his assistants; views of Rome are revealed between the painted columns.

In the next room, formerly a bedroom, the *Marriage of Roxana and Alexander* is by Sodoma (1477-1549). Dismissed by

French Interlude

On 31 August 1797, the Ambassador of the Directory, **Joseph Bonaparte**, accompanied by the young General Léonard Duphot, settled in the Palazzo Corsini (⏰ *See Walking Tour*). On 28 December, a a few revolutionaries led a riot in front of the palace. They called for the intervention of the French against the papal government. Shots were fired and General Duphot was killed.

On 10 February 1798, General Berthier besieged Rome and drove out Pius VI, who died in exile in Valence in France. Until 29 September 1799, Rome took its cue from the French Republic.

Julius II in favour of Raphael, Sodoma was commissioned by Agostino Chigi to decorate this room, probably in 1509. In a Renaissance setting, Alexander extends the crown to Roxana against a cloud of cherubs. The merit of this pleasant painting lies in the beauty of the figures, and the harmony and balance of the composition.

These qualities are lacking in the other scenes: Alexander and Darius's mother, Vulcan and three little angels (*on either side of the chimney piece*), the battle scene. To the left of the entrance are Alexander and Bucephalus (late 16C).

Gabinetto Nazionale delle Stampe

🚹 ○ *Open 8.30am-1.30pm (also 2.30-4.30pm Tue and Thu, by appointment); Sat (by appointment only).* ○ *Closed Sun and public holidays, 29 Jun, 10-19 Aug and 27-30 Dec. No charge.* ☎ *06 69 98 01.*

The National Printing Office has been accommodated in Villa Farnesina since 1950. In 1975, it merged with the *Calcografia Nazionale* to form the *Istituto Nazionale per la Grafica*, a body that houses an archive of prints and drawings from the 15C-19C. Highlights include Baroque works of the Roman and Florentine Schools. The reference section includes photographic material and computer databases, which can be consulted by appointment only.

Walking Tour

Palazzo Corsini

○ *Via della Lungara 10, the Galleria Corsini is open Tue-Sun 9am–3:30pm, Sun 9am–1:30pm.* ○ *Closed Mon, 25 Dec and 1 Jan.* ≈ *€4.* ☎ *06 68802323. www.galleriaborghese.it*

The palace was built in the 15C by the Riario, nephews of Sixtus IV, and passed in the 18C to Cardinal Corsini, nephew of Clement XII, who had it rebuilt by Ferdinando Fuga. It now houses the **Galleria Corsini,** with works by Caravaggio, Rubens, and Van Dyck, and the

/ Villa Doria Pamphili

Accademia dei Lincei, a learned society of scholars and men of letters.

▶ *South side of Palazzo Corsini; street of the same name leads to Orto Botanico.*

Orto Botanico (Botanic Garden)

Largo Cristina di Svezia. Enter via the Via della Lungara. 🚹 ○ *Open Tue-Sat, 9.30am–5.30pm (Apr-Oct, 6.30pm).* ○ *Closed Mon, Sun, in Aug and on public holidays. Audioguides available.* ≈ *€2.* ☎ *06 49 91 71 07. http://www.ips.it/musis/muort_f0.html*

Rome's University –"La Sapienza" – runs this garden, which contains over 3 500 species and eight glasshouses. Relax among the luxuriant vegetation and curiously wild upper slops, dotted with crumbling fountains and staircases.

Porta Settimiana

One of the gates in the Aurelian Wall (*Mura Aureliane*), it stands at the intersection of the Via Garibaldi. Alexander VI (1492-1503) reinforced it with merlons.

▶ *Turn right into Via Garibaldi; beyond the junction with Via G. Mameli, take the second steps on the right which lead to San Pietro in Montorio.*

San Pietro in Montorio★

🕐*Open 9am-12pm and 4pm-6pm.*
Legend claims St Peter was crucified here, though the church is best known for **Bramante**'s tempietto (🔍*See below*). It has a commanding view of Rome and was built in Sixtus IV's reign at the end of the 15C by Ferdinand II of Spain. The simple façade is typical of the Renaissance, as is the interior, which consists of a nave flanked by apsidal chapels. The chancel was damaged in the siege of 1849 and has been restored. Several Renaissance works have survived, particularly the *Flagellation★* (*first chapel on the right*), a fresco by Sebastiano del Piombo, clearly influenced by the monumental art of Michelangelo.

The ceiling in the next chapel was painted by **Baldassarre Peruzzi** (1481-1536). The pale fresco of the Virgin, by Pomarancio (1552-1626), and the two transept chapels were added at the Counter-Reformation. In the right-hand chapel the allegorical figures on the tombs and the cherubs on the balustrade are by Bartolomeo Ammanati, a pupil of Michelangelo. Beatrice Cenci is buried beneath the high altar.
Bernini designed the second chapel on the left in the Baroque period.

Il tempietto★★

▷ *Access through the gates on the right (outside) and through the fourth chapel on the right (inside).*

This charming miniature temple was one of Bramante's first works on his arrival in Rome in 1499. Despite its small scale, the construction has all the grandeur and rigorous conformity of a classical building. Perfectly proportioned, it is surrounded by a portico, supported on Doric columns and surmounted by a dome. Behind the building in a little chapel is a small cavity said to have held St Peter's cross.

View of Rome★★

▷ *From the open space in front of the church.*

The view extends from Monte Mario (*left*) and Castel Sant'Angelo to the gaudy "wedding cake" monument to Victor Emmanuel II. You can also see the arches of the Basilica of Maxentius in the Forum; further right again, beyond the green Palatine, is the façade of St John Lateran spiked with statues.

▷ *Return to Via Garibaldi.*

On the left is a **monument** set up in 1941 for soldiers who died fighting for Garibaldi – and Rome's inclusion in Italy.

Fontana Paola (Pauline Fountain)

This fountain was commissioned by Pope **Paul V**; its shape – a commemorative arch – shows the nascent taste for Baroque pomp. In summertime, outdoor stages colonize the area and an impromptu cafe sprawls in the road.

View of Rome

From the square in front of the *Ospedale del Bambino Gesù* (Hospital of the Infant Jesus 🔍*See local tour map in this section*), there is a spectacular **view★★★** of Rome. To the left is the drum of Castel Sant'Angelo surmounted by its angel and the white mass of the Law Courts; just below the Janiculum, across the river, is the dome of San Giovanni dei Fiorentini; in the background on the edge of the park is the Villa Medici with its two towers and the dome of San Carlo al Corso; slightly to the right are the two belfries of the Trinità dei Monti; then the Quirinal Palace behind the shallow dome of the Pantheon; next, nearer the river, is the high dome of Sant'Andrea delle Valle with the lower dome of the Gesù Church behind it; in the background is the Militia Tower; before it rise the monument to Victor Emmanuel II and the flat façade of Santa Maria d'Aracoeli.

▶ *Either make a detour uphill to Porta San Pancrazio and the road of the same name which leads to the Villa Doria Pamphili (1km/0.5mi – 45min on foot return) or turn right into Passeggiata del Gianicolo.*

Villa Doria Pamphili

▶ *The Via di San Pancrazio is a narrow road, packed with high-speed traffic. Nervous pedestrians – or those with small children – should enter through another park gate.*

A vast public park surrounds a 17C country house (*casino*), which is decorated with statues and low relief sculptures and set among terraces.

Kids A popular place for picnics, the park also has grotto-fountains and playgrounds that appeal to families. Restrictions about playing on the grass, however bizarre, are often enforced.

Passeggiata del Gianicolo (Janiculum Walk)

This road winds along the crest of the hill beneath the umbrella pines; it is lined by busts of Garibaldi's men and has some of the finest **views**★★★ of Rome.

Kids A carousel, pony rides and balloon vendors hold sway here. On weekends, 10am–3pm, a puppet show runs; the content is often smackdown Punch and Judy skits, which may alarm toddlers.

Monumento a Giuseppe Garibaldi (Giuseppe Garibaldi Monument)

Historian A.J.P. Taylor claims "Garibaldi is the only wholly admirable figure in modern history." The dashing and charismatic patriot led many of the battles that unified Italy (the *Risorgimento*).

In Emilio Gallori's grandiose work (1895), the hero is shown on horseback. Garibaldi strugged to reduce the temporal power of the papacy. In 1929, the Vatican requested the statue be turned, so it no longer gazed at Saint Peter's. Wags now point out that the horse's bottom faces the heart of Catholicism. From here unfurls a **view**★★★ of Rome from Villa Medici to St John Lateran; in the distance are the Alban Hills. The cannon is fired daily at noon from below the parapet.

Monumento ad Anita Garibaldi (Anita Garibaldi Monument)

The hero's Brazilian wife, who often fought beside him, scored a much better monument. Astride a rearing horse, she carries a baby and a pistol. Anita died – ill, pregnant and in Giuseppe's arms – after the 1849 retreat. Eleven years later, when Garibaldi rode to hail Victor Emanuel II as king of Italy, he wore Anita's striped scarf over his gray poncho. Further on, near the lighthouse, there is a fine **view**★★★ over the whole of the city of Rome.

▶ *Farther on, go down the steps on the right that cut off the hairpin bend of the Passeggiata.*

The old tree stump is all that remains of the oak tree beneath which Tasso sat and reflected on all his misfortunes (inscription).

Sant'Onofrio

🕐 *Open 8:30am–2:30pm; Sat 9:30am–3:30pm.* 🕐 *Closed in Aug.* ☏ *06 68 64 498.* This church has retained the appearance and atmosphere of a hermitage, which it received from its founder, a monk of the order of the Hermits of St Jerome, in 1434. Here **Tasso** (1544-95) came to die, pursued to the end, even to madness, by his religious doubts. His poem, *The Liberation of Jerusalem*, is a masterpiece of Italian Renaissance poetry. Chateaubriand, too, would have liked to finish his days here; on the outside wall of the church overlooking the river is a long quotation from his *Memories from Beyond the Grave*. On the right of the main door beneath the arcade are frescoes by **Domenichino,** illustrating the life of St Jerome (1605). The attractive frescoes in the **apse**★ were probably painted by Baldassarre Peruzzi assisted by Pinturicchio.

Art Gallery

Galleria Nazionale d'Arte Antica (National Art Gallery)

In Palazzo Corsini. &. ☉*Open Tues–Sat 8:30am–1:50pm and Sun 8:30am–7pm.* ☉*Closed 1 Jan, 1 May and Christmas.* ☛*Guided tours available.* ⌨ € 4. ☏*06 65 42 323.*

This gallery houses a collection of mainly 17C and 18C paintings with special emphasis on the Venetian, Emilian and Neapolitan schools. Particularly worthy of note are the *Portrait of Philip II* by Titian, in which the stiff posture and death-like complexion are striking; St John the Baptist by Caravaggio; and, in the room devoted to Tuscan primitives, an admirable *Triptych* by **Fra Angelico** showing the *Last Judgement*, the *Ascension and Pentecost*. This painter, who experienced the silence of the cloister, expressed his deep faith by painting serene and saintly faces (central panel of the *Last Judgement*) and a Christ who inspires adoration (right panel of the *Ascension*).

ISOLA TIBERINA-TORRE ARGENTINA★★

MICHELIN MAP 38 L11, M11, N11

The peace of *Isola Tiberina* **(Tiber Island) provides a striking contrast to the hustle and bustle of the "Ghetto" (old Jewish district), which extends along Via del Portico d'Ottavia. Though emptied in WWII, this district is still home to many traditional shops, such as haberdasheries, fabric shops and groceries specialising in kosher food, as well as to the impressive synagogue. Amid the ancient ruins and medieval alleys are a good choice of bars, restaurants and trattorias.**

▶ **Orient Yourself:** This walk runs from Isola Tiberina to the old Jewish district on the east bank of the Tiber. From the Jewish district, the walk continues to Largo di Torre Argentina, where the incessant noise of cars, buses and trams provides an anachronistic backdrop to one of the city's oldest archaeological sites.

🙂 **Don't Miss:** The Porticus of Octavia near the Theatre of Marcellus. The lively ghetto neighborhood. Fried Roman-Jewish artichokes (*carciofi alla giudia*) at Evangelista (*Via delle Zoccolette 11a;* ☏*06 687 5810*)or Da Giggetto (*Via del Portico d'Ottavia 21A;* ☏*06 6861105. www.giggettoalportico.com*).

☉ **Organising Your Time:** Allow 1hr 30mins.

Kids **Especially for Kids:** Romans designed the Tiber Island to resemble a ship. Outdoor cinema screens here in the summertime.

🚶 **Also See:** *BOCCA DELLA VERITÀ; CAMPIDOGLIO-CAPITOLINO; CAMPO DEI FIORI; PANTHEON; TRASTEVERE.*

1 Isola Tiberina★

Romans drove Tarquin the Proud, last king of his line, from the city in the 6C BC. They piled his crops into the Tiber; legend claims this seeded the island. The ancients also believed its shape echoes that of the boat which brought Aesculapius, the god of medicine, from Epidauros in Greece. To stress the resemblance, the southern point was paved with slabs of travertine round an obelisk, set up like a mast. Aesculapius is said to have arrived in Rome in 293 BC in the form of a serpent. The boat had scarcely come alongside, when the serpent disembarked and hid on the island; the Romans obligingly built at temple on the spot. The sanctuary site is now occupied by St Bartholomew's Church. The hospital of the Brothers of St John of God (*Fatebenefratelli* – literally "do-good-brothers") continues the island's medical tradition.

San Bartolomeo
(St Bartholomew's Church)

Its Baroque façade and the Romanesque bell-tower (12C) rise from the centre of the island. Inside the building, at the centre of the great staircase, is a cylindrical well-head (c 12m/39ft deep) surmounted by an ancient column carved with 12C saintly figures. One of the cannon balls fired during the French siege in 1849 is lodged in the wall *(left)* of the Lady Chapel at the back. **Kids** South of *Ponte Fabricio*, near the church, are the remains of the travertine, which faced the bow of the **"ship"** of Aesculapius. Tradition says that Rahere, courtier to Henry I of England, recovered from an attack of malaria, usually fatal then, in hospital attached to this church. In thanks, he founded a priory and a hospital in London's Smithfield, which still stand (*see the Green Guide London*).

▸ *Return to the square and take the steps opposite the church, which lead to the bank of the Tiber. Downstream of the island, in the middle of the river, are the remains of Ponte Rotto.*

Ponte Rotto

In origin "the Broken Bridge" goes back to the **Pons Aemilius**, built here mid-2C BC. It had already collapsed twice when Pope Gregory XII rebuilt it in about 1575. It collapsed again in 1598 and only one arch now remains. The channel of the **Cloaca Maxima** – the Forum's great sewer, dug in the 6C BC and still in use today – can be seen from the *Ponte Rotto* and *Ponte Palatino*.

Ponte Cestio (Pons Cestius)

This bridge links the Tiber Island to the popular, bustling Trastevere district. Its origins go back to the 1C BC; it was partially rebuilt in the 19C.

▸ *Cross to the north side of the island.*

Ponte Fabricio★ (Pons Fabricius)

The only intact classical span in Rome, it is sometimes also known as the "Bridge of Four Heads," because of the multi-faced Hermes set at the far end. Built in 62 BC by the consul Fabricius, it links the left bank with Tiber Island.

▸ *Cross the bridge.*

②From Isola Tiberina to Torre Argentina

Ghetto

Jews lived in Rome since ancient times, but their numbers increased after Pompey captured Jerusalem (1C BC) and again after the destruction of the Temple of Jerusalem, and the campaigns of Vespasian and Titus in Palestine (1C AD). Immigrants also arrived after the expulsion of Jews from Spain in 1492.

This ethnic group, which once lived in Trastevere, moved to the left bank of the Tiber in the 13C. In 1556, Pope Paul IV had the area enclosed within a wall, which ran from Ponte Fabricio, along Via del Portico di Ottavia and around Piazza delle Cinque Scole. This crowded, disease-ridden ghetto was home to some 4 000 people and its gates were opened at dawn and closed at dusk. Jews were prohibited from any commercial activities, with the exception of money-lending and selling fabrics, which explains the large number of haberdasheries and fabric shops here. In 1848, the walls were taken down, in 1870 the new Italian State abolished all restrictions, and in 1885 this insalubrious district was completely demolished, with the exception of the houses on Via della Reginella. In 1943, during the German occupation, more than 2 000 residents of the ghetto were deported; very few returned. Since WWII, the district gradually repopulated and today it has a lively atmosphere.

Sinagoga (Synagogue)

The synagogue, inaugurated in 1904, occupies part of the old ghetto. It was designed by Costa and Armanni and is dominated by its large dome, visible from all over Rome.

Museo della Comunità Ebraica (Hebrew Museum)

Open Jun-Aug, Mon–Thu 9am–7:30pm, Fri 9am–1:30pm, Sun 9am–noon; Sep–May, Mon–Thu 9am–4:30pm, Fri 9am–1:30pm, Sun 9am–noon. Closed Sat and Jewish holidays. Guided tours available (1hr). €6. 06 68 40 06 61.

Inside the synagogue is a display of souvenirs of the Jewish community in Rome, together with liturgical articles.

▸ *Take Via Portico di Ottavia.*

Portico di Ottavia
(Portico of Octavia)

One of the richest monuments in Rome, it vast dimensions stretched as the present *Piazza di Campitelli* and the church of *Santa Caterina dei Funari*. All that now remains is part of the entrance porch (*propylaea*), which faces the Tiber. Septimius Severus (193-211) funded the remaining Corinthian columns and entablature.

The original portico had been built in the 2C BC, as an enclosure for two temples dedicated to Juno and Jupiter respectively. Augustus rebuilt the portico, which he dedicated to his sister Octavia, and included two public libraries, one Latin and one Greek, as well as an assembly hall where the Senate sometimes met. The lower archaeological area in now accessible via a pedestrian passage open from 9am-sundown.

Sant'Angelo in Pescheria

Nowadays the *propylaea* of the Portico of Octavia serves only as a monumental entrance to the little church of *Sant'Angelo in Pescheria* (founded in the 8C).

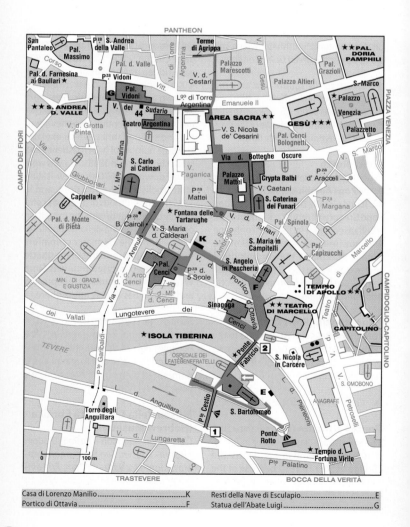

Casa di Lorenzo Manilio .... K	Resti della Nave di Esculapio .... E
Portico di Ottavia .... F	Statua dell'Abate Luigi .... G

Horatius Cocles and the Pons Sublicius

Downstream from *Ponte Rotto* and its modern neighbour, the Palatine Bridge, was the *Pons Sublicius*. This was the first to span the Tiber, built to foster relations between the Latins on the Palatine and the Etruscans on the right bank.

Each year on 14 May, the ancient offered human figures made of willow to appease the river. The bridge was made of wood and the law forbade any iron in its repair: it had to be easily dismantled if diplomacy failed. This happened when the last Etruscan king, Tarquin the Proud, was driven out of Rome in the 6C BC. While his men crow-barred the *Pons Sublicius* apart, the Roman Horatius Cocles alone held back the enemy: "withering the Etruscan leaders with his look, he challenged them one by one or taunted them." Finally the bridge was breached. Horatius jumped into the Tiber and rejoined his men. He was treated as a hero: he was granted land, his statue was put up in the Comitium and "every citizen set aside part of his own income to be given to Horatius."

The incident is also well known through Lord Macaulay's stirring ballad Horatius from his *Lays of Ancient Rome*.

The name, like those of the neighbouring streets, recalls the **fish market** that occupied the antique ruins in the 12C. The stalls and activity on the huge paving stones made this one of the most picturesque corners of Rome.

▶ *Turn left into Piazza delle Cinque Scole.*

The name of this piazza, Square of the Five Schools, refers to the fact that the synagogues serving the Ghetto once stood here. The arch and two columns on the left are the remains of a 1C building.

Palazzo Cenci

The narrow streets that surround the palace repeat like variations on a theme: the name of the great family involved in a scandal, which hit the headlines in the 16C. The palace itself stands on a slight rise (*Monte Cenci*) formed by the rubble from ancient buildings (perhaps the *Circus Flaminius*).

▶ *Follow Via S. Maria de' Calderari. Turn right into Via Arenula and then left into Via dei Giubbonari.*

San Carlo ai Catinari

🕐*Open 9am-12pm and 4pm-6pm.*
The grandiose, but rather heavy, Counter-Reformation façade of this church was erected between 1635 and 1638. The **interior**★, which is shaped like a Greek cross, is dominated by a hand-some coffered dome. The artists who painted *Sant'Andrea della Valle* are found here too: **Domenichino** painted the Cardinal Virtues on the pendentives of the dome; in the apse **Lanfranco** accomplished his last work (1647), the *Apotheosis of St Charles Borromeo*; above the high altar is St Charles Borromeo leading a procession in Milan to ward off the plague by **Pietro da Cortona** (1650); the 17C St Cecilia's Chapel (*right of the chan-*

An "Angelic Parricide"

The scandal broke on 9 September 1598. In those days a bold man could get away with almost anything – especially Francesco Cenci, whose father had been Pius V's treasurer. A cruel and perverted man, Francesco was eventually murdered at the instigation of his daughter **Beatrice**, with the support of her brother Giacomo and Francesco's wife Lucrezia. Pope Clement VIII sentenced them to death despite public opinion, which supported the plea of self-defence. The scandal – incest, opium and crime were all involved – inflamed Rome. The guilty parties were beheaded on 11 September 1599 in *Piazza di Ponte Sant'Angelo*. Each year on 11 September, a mass is celebrated in St Thomas' Church in *Piazzetta di Monte Cenci* for the soul of Beatrice Cenci.

AREA SACRA DEL LARGO ARGENTINA

Remains of St Nicholas' Church

Extant parts — Non-extant parts

▶ *Continue on Via del Sudario as far as Largo Torre Argentina.*

Teatro Argentina (Argentina Theatre)

The first performance of the *Barber of Seville* took place here in 1816 and was one of the most resounding failures in the annals of opera. Perhaps Pauline Borghese was behind it: she wanted to help the tenor avenge himself on Rossini, who had refused to alter the score.

cel) is verging on the rococo, with its strained perspective, its broken lines and animated stucco figures.

▶ *Take Via Monte della Farina, which runs alongside the west side of the church, as far as Piazza Vidoni.*

Statua dell'Abate Luigi

This statue of a Roman in a toga is one of the famous "talking" statues, which exchanged comments with Pasquino, Madam Lucrezia and Marforio.

▶ *Turn right into Via del Sudario.*

Casa del Burcardo (Johannes Burckard's House)

◷*Open Mon–Fri 9am–1.30pm.* ◷*Closed Sat–Sun, public holidays and during Aug.* ☎*06 68 80 67 55.*

A tower once stood where **Burckard**, the papal Master of Ceremonies, built his house in 1503. He called it **Torre Argentina** after the Latin name *"Argentoratum"* for Strasbourg, his home town. The house, now restored, is in the Gothic and Renaissance style. It contains a library and a collection of masks, theatrical costumes and playbills.

Palazzo Vidoni

Via del Sudario, 10-16. The Caffarelli, a rich Roman family, asked Raphael to design a palce here in 1500. Its robust elegance was altered in the 18C and 19C, when the façade was enlarged and re-sited to face the Corso Vittorio Emanuele II and the top storey added.

Area Sacra del Largo Argentina★★ (Largo Argentina Sacred Precincts)

This is the name given to a group of Roman Republican ruins in the *Largo Argentina*. This marshy ground –near the *Campus Martius* – often flooded. Traces of five levels from the 5C BC to the beginning of the empire have been revealed. In antiquity, this large precinct was at the heart of a busy district: to the southeast stood the theatre built by Balbus in Augustus's reign, to the west Pompey's Theatre and Curia (*Teatro e Curia di Pompeo*), to the north the rear façade of Agrippa's Baths (*Terme di Agrippa*) and the Saepta.Archaeologists remain unsure what deities were honoured here, so the temples are known as A, B, C and D. The tower and portico were part of a group of medieval houses.

Temple C

The oldest dates back to the 6C or 5C BC and follows the Etruscan model: a triple *cella* (containing three shrines) and a fairly high podium without columns.

Temple A

The first building on this site dates from the 4C or 3C BC. The present remains of are from the 2C or 1C BC. Temple A was converted into a church to St Nicholas.

Temple B

This 2C BC circular structure may have been dedicated to Juno. The tufa podium was covered by one of peperine, smothered in turn by stucco.

Temple D

The greater part of this temple lies beneath the road (*Via Florida*).

The north and east sides of the precinct were bounded by a portico (**1**). The high wall (**2**) on the west side behind Temple A belonged to a public lavatory. The drainage trough is still visible. Further south several large blocks (**3**) have been identified as the remains of Pompey's Curia, where, in 44 BC, Julius Caesar was assassinated during the Ides of March.

Largo Argentina Cat Sanctuary

Largo di Torre Argentina, corner of Via Florida & Via Arenula. *Open noon–6pm.* *Donations welcome.* *06 687 2133.* *www.romancats.de.*

Strays are an epidemic in Rome. Women –known as "*gattare*," cat ladies –informally cared for the abandoned animals here since the 1929 excavations began until 1993 (the star Anna Magnani numbered among them). A volunteer group now cares for 250–300 at a time. Still only 50% of the kittens survive.

▶ *Take Via de' Cestari and turn left into Via Arco della Ciambella.*

Wedged between no. 9 and no. 15 *Via Arco della Ciambella*, a small fragment of wall is all that remains of the **Terme di Agrippa**, the oldest baths in Rome. Built in 19 BC, these were supplied by a purpose-built aqueduct. Part of the channel still runs under *Via dei Condotti* and waters a number of fountains, including the *Fontana di Trevi*.

▶ *Return to Largo Argentina and continue to Via delle Botteghe Oscure.*

Via delle Botteghe Oscure was famous in the Middle Ages for its dimly lit basement shops ("*oscura*" means "dark" in Italian), which had been set up in the ruins of **Balbus' Theatre** (1C BC). The **Crypta Balbi** archaeological site, which houses part of the *Museo Nazionale Romano* (*see end of chapter*) sits here. The name of the street is also associated with the Italian Communist Party (now known as the *Democratici di Sinistra*), whose main office can be seen at no 4.

▶ *Turn right into Via Caetani.*

A commemorative bronze plaque marks the spot where the body of the statesman **Aldo Moro** was found on 9 May 1978, 54 days after he had been kidnapped by Red Brigade terrorists.

Santa Caterina ai Funari

This church has a very graceful façade, built between 1500 and 1564; the shallow pilasters are typical of the Renaissance, but garlands attempt the decorative effects typical of the Mannerist period. Note the unusual bell-tower.

Palazzo Mattei

Via dei Funari 31 or Via Caetani 32. Five palaces were built by the Mattei in the 16C and 17C. Carlo Maderno (1598-1611) was the architect.

▶ *Follow Via dei Funari as far as Piazza Mattei.*

Fontana delle Tartarughe★ (Turtle Fountain)

This charming late Renaissance work (1581-84) was by Taddeo Landini, probably from a design by **Giacomo della Porta**. Legend tells how Duke Mattei gambled away his fortune in one night. His fiancée's father gave him the bum's rush. To prove that a Mattei, even when ruined, could achieve wonders, he had the fountain built overnight.

Crypt

Crypta Balbi

Open 9am-7:45pm *Closed Mon, 1 Jan and Christmas.* *€4.* *06 39 96 77 00 071; ww.pierreci.it.*

Part of the *Museo Nazionale Romano,* it's housed in medieval buildings above a portico, added to the theatre by Lucius Cornelius Balbus in 13 BC.

The different levels, which include the basement crypt, house displays which explain the history of the site through archaeological finds, reconstructions, ceramics and excavations. Lively and lovely, the Crypto Balbi is a neglected gem among the city's museums.

MONTECITORIO★★

MICHELIN MAP 38 K 10-11.
METRO LINE A: SPAGNA
APPROXIMATELY 700M/770 YD FROM PIAZZA DI MONTECITORIO

This district lies between the Tiber and Via del Corso, which marks the boundary with the Fontana di Trevi and Quirinale quarter. Piazza Navona and the Pantheon lie a few hundred metres to the south. The best way to discover the district is on foot, heading out from bustling Piazza di Montecitorio, fronted by banks, newspaper offices, department stores, restaurants and cafés. Also home to the Italian Chamber of Deputies, the piazza is surrounded by narrow Renaissance-style streets lined with elegant, luxury shops. Go farther away from the square, and the atmosphere changes: the charming, quiet streets of the quarter beyond Via della Scrofa are dotted with 16C buildings and arts and crafts workshops.

▶ **Orient Yourself**: This district lies between the Tiber and Via del Corso, which marks the boundary with the Fontana di Trevi and Quirinale quarter.

Don't Miss: Caravaggio's *La Madonna dei Pellegrini* in S. Agostino, the Palazzo Altemps national museum

Also See: *FONTANA DI TREVI- QUIRINALE; PANTHEON; PIAZZA NAVONA & DI SPAGNA.*

A Bit of History

This district corresponds to the northern part of the **Campus Martius**, which was mostly reserved for the colossal tombs belonging to the Imperial families and the funeral pyres *(ustrina)*.

Like the other districts of the city through which the pilgrims passed on their way to the Vatican, this one was raised out of its medieval misery under Sixtus IV (1471-84). In his 13 years on the Papal throne he changed the face of Rome, using the money from the sale of indulgences to pay for his projects. Early in the 16C Leo X cleared the way for Via Leonina (now Via di Ripetta) to run from the Porta del Popolo, through which foreigners from the north entered the city, to the Mausoleum of Augustus.

In the second half of the 19C the old river port of the **Ripetta** was destroyed. It had been built in 1706, a set of curving riverside steps, of which Piranesi has left some attractive engravings. It was one of the most famous views in Rome.

Walking Tour

Piazza di Montecitorio

In the square stands a 6C BC **Egyptian obelisk**, re-erected in 1792 by Pius VI.

Brought back from Heliopolis by Augustus in the 10C BC, it served as the pointer for a gigantic sun dial, more or less on the site of *San Lorenzo in Lucina*.

Palazzo di Montecitorio

♿☞*Guided tour (30min) of the Chamber of Deputies first Sun of the month 10am–5.30pm. Times may change as a result of political events taking place. Consult the www.Camera.it, section "servizi ai cittadini."* ⏱*Closed during Aug and Sept.* ☎*06 67 601.*

The parliament meets where the Antonine family cremated its dead. **Bernini** began this *palazzo* in 1650, completed 47 years later by Carlo Fontana. Little remains of Bernini's Baroque fantasies: rough-hewn stones frame some windows and the effect is rustic, despite the clock tower. Since 1870, it's housed the Chamber of Deputies, thus demonstrations often add to the piazza's bustle.

Piazza Colonna★

This square is one of the most crowded places in Rome, being at the junction of the two main shopping streets (Via del Corso and Via del Tritone). The **column**★ at the centre of the square was probably erected between 176 and 193 in honour of **Marcus Aurelius** (161-80), who preferred philosophy to war but was forced to campaign on the banks of the Danube. He died at the front, of the plague. His victories were short-lived and did not contain the barbarian thrust. Just as Trajan's Column illustrated that Emperor's exploits against the Dacians, so Marcus Aurelius's Column depicts the significant episodes in his wars, with low-relief carvings arranged in a spiral. The carving was done by a group of sculptors and the designs were probably the work of several artists. To make the work more visible, the scenes are larger and in higher relief than those on Trajan's Column, but the quality of the craftsmanship has suffered. In 1589, Pope Sixtus V had the crowning statue of the emperor replaced with one of St Paul.

Palazzo Chigi

The building was begun in 1562 to designs by **Giacomo della Porta**. Carlo Maderno continued it, according to the severe concepts of the Counter-Reformation. The palace was completed in 1630 in the Baroque era. Two decades later, Pope Alexander VII purchased it for his family, after whom it is named. Since 1917, *Palazzo Chigi* has housed the Ministry of Foreign Affairs (post WWI), the Head of the Government (Fascist period) and now it belongs to the Presidency of the Council of Ministers.

▷ *Take the street between Palazzo di Montecitorio and Palazzo Chigi; turn left into Piazza del Parlamento and left again into Via di Campo Marzio.*

In the reign of Octavius Augustus, a vast area of the Campus Martius was occupied by an enormous **solar clock** (160m/ 525ft by 60m/197ft). Some pieces of travertine paving, marked with bronze insets representing the signs of the zodiac, are beneath Via di Campo Marzio.

▷ *Bear right into Via di Stelletta, right into Via della Scrofa and immediately left into Via dei Portoghesi.*

Torre della Scimmia (Monkey Tower)

The building on the corner of *Via dei Portoghesi* and *Via dei Pianellari* incorporates a 15C tower. It has been immortalised by the American novelist, Nathaniel Hawthorne (1804-64): The family living here owned a very naughty monkey. One day it climbed atop the tower carrying the new-born child. The father was terrified. After praying to the Virgin, he decided to whistle to the monkey and call it back. It slid down the drainpipe, holding the child, safe and sound. Since then, at the top, a light burns continuously before an image of the Virgin.

Sant'Antonio dei Portoghesi

🕐 Open Mon–Fri 8:30am–1pm and 3–6pm; Sat, Sun and holidays 8:30am–noon and 3–6pm. ☎ 06 68 80 24 96; www.ipsa-roma.com.

The 17 C Portuguese national church has an attractive Rococo façade; the interior is gorgeous with gold, stucco, marble and paintings. The first righthand chapel contains a monument by Canova.

▸ Take Via dei Panellari.

Sant'Agostino★

🕐 Open Mon–Sat 7am–1pm and 4:30–7:30pm, Sun 3:30–7:30pm.

The church, dedicated to St Augustine of Hippo, was built between 1479–1483. The broad travertine façade, with its rose windows, was one of the city's first Renaissance efforts. The two orders are linked by large loose scrolls; the powerful moulding adds character.

The interior, decorated by Luigi Vanvitelli in 1760, has been cluttered by 19C additions, which rob it of its soaring elegance, now only faintly perceptible in the nave. The church contains several fine works of art: near the main door is the Madonna del Parto★ (1521) by **Jacopo Sansovino**. The third pillar on the left in the nave bears a fresco by **Raphael** (1512) of the Prophet Isaiah★, which owes much to the Sistine Chapel.

The first chapel on the left contains the Madonna of the Pilgrims★★★ (1605) by Caravaggio. His contemporaries slammed this work for its rugged pilgrims, inspired by ordinary people, and for the ugliness of the man's feet. Even the Virgin nurses her bonny baby in a very realistic manner.

▸ Return to San Antonio dei Portoghesi and continue west along Via dell'Orso.

Locanda dell'Orso (Bear Inn)

From the Middle Ages to the Renaissance, this district consisted almost entirely of inns, which provided lodgings for pilgrims making their way to St Peter's.

The hostelry at the sign of the bear was set up in a fine 15C building. Montaigne stayed here for a few days during his visit to Rome in 1580.

Palazzo Altemps★★★
(Museo Nazionale Romano)

This palace, along with Palazzo Massimo alle Terme, the Terme di Diocleziano (🕐 see PORTA PIA-TERMINI) and the Crypta Balbi (🕐 see ISOLA TIBERINA-TORRE ARGENTINA), houses the **Museo Nazionale Romano**. ♿🕐 Open Tues–Sun 9am-7.45pm (last admission 6.45pm). 🕐 Closed Mon, 1 Jan, 1 May and Christmas. ☜€7. 🔊 Guided tours and audioguides (1hr 30min) in various languages. ☎ 06 39 96 77 00; www.archeorm.arti.beniculturali.it

The palace was begun in about 1480 by Girolamo Riario, Sixtus IV's nephew. In 1568 it was acquired by Cardinal Marco Sittico Altemps who had it rebuilt by Martino Longhi the Elder. In 1725 it became the residence of Cardinal de Polignac, the French Ambassador. Recently restored and reopened to the public, the museum now houses the Ludovisi-Boncompagni collection. In the first half of the 17C Cardinal Ludovico decided to decorate his villa with a substantial number of Ancient statues, some of which had been found during construction of the villa itself (in the area known in Antiquity as the Sallustian Gardens), and others which had been purchased by the Cardinal (some probably from the Altemps family). The statues were restored very much according to the ideas and criteria of the 17C. Some of the greatest artists of the time, including Algardi and Bernini, were called upon to work on the statues; they not only restored them but replaced any missing parts. One of the more unusual aspects of this collection is the strange (and nowadays unthinkable) combination of the Ancient original and the Baroque restoration.

Of equal interest is the recently restored palace itself, with its frescoed drawing rooms, old 15C and 16C structures and beautiful ceilings.

Visit

A harmonious 16C courtyard – designed by Antonio da Sangallo the Elder, Baldassarre Peruzzi and Martino Longhi the Elder – greets visitors. Four Roman statues can be seen under the northern portico (copies of Greek originals),

PALAZZO ALTEMPS

FIRST FLOOR

GROUND FLOOR

▣ Tourist information	⇕ Lift	▥▥ Toilets
⌒ Audio guide	Ⓐ Stairs	◿ Bookshop
⚇ Wheelchair access	△ Cloakroom	◎ Telephone

arranged in their original location. The loggia above bears a beautiful fresco (*see below*).

Cross the Atrium of Antoninus Pius (*Atrio di Antonino il Pio*), who is depicted wearing only a cloak, and enter the room dedicated to the Ludovico marble statues. Two heavily restored statues of Apollo with his lyre (*Apollo Citaredo*) can be seen in the *Sala delle Erme*. The Athena Algardi is a good example of 17C restoration work; perhaps it originally portrayed Hygeia. In the next room is the *Athena Parthenos*, a 1C Greek copy thought to have been inspired by the imposing statue (12m/39ft high) sculpted by Phidias for the Parthenon. On the first floor, the *Sala delle Prospettive Dipinte* contains late 16C frescoes with a false colonnade. The 15C **fresco★**

in the **Sala della Piattaia** is of outstanding beauty. This room takes its name from the kitchenware painted on the walls. *Orestes and Electra*★ (*Oreste ed Elettra*) is the work of the Greek sculptor Menelaos and dates from the 1C AD. The *Ares Ludovisi*★★, recently identified as Apollo, is a Roman copy of a statue from the Hellenistic period.

The **Sala delle Storie di Mosè** (Room of the Stories of Moses) contains the most famous exhibit of the collection, the **Ludovisi Throne**★★★ (*Trono Ludovisi*). This strange monument suggests a throne for a cult statue (probably part of a ritual ornament from a place of worship) and was found in the Villa Ludovisi in 1887. This Greek masterpiece dates from the early classical period (5C BC). The main panel shows a young woman being assisted by two attendants, who shield her body with a veil. Archaeologists have interpreted this scene as the birth of Aphrodite (Venus), goddess of love, who emerged from the sea foam, accompanied by the Seasons, whose feet brush the pebbles of the shore. The very light, delicate mantle gently envelops the lower half of the goddess's body, its rippling folds echoing the curves of the tunic about her neck. The artist has endowed the face of Aphrodite with joyful serenity. In the side panels, a naked woman plays the flute, while another, fully clothed, burns incense – these figures are often regarded as embodiments of sensuality (the courtesan) and modesty (the wife). In the same room is the monumental head known as the *Hera Ludovisi*, which is, in fact, a portrait of Antonia, wife of the Emperor Drusus and mother of Claudius.

Decoration of the **Loggia dipinta**★★ was commissioned at the end of the 16C by Marco Sittico Altemps. The fresco mimics an arboured garden, intertwining vegetal, animal and cupid motifs. The portraits of the Caesars from the Ludovisi collection are displayed here.

Three of the most interesting exhibits are in the *Salone del Camino*. The *Gaul taking his own life*★★★ (*Galata suicida*), a Roman copy of an original Greek bronze, dominates the centre of the room. Note the strength and movement of the barbarian, with the dramatic twist of the bust, and the forlorn stance of the wife, supported only by her husband's hand. This is a magnificent example of Hellenistic art, copied for Julius Caesar after his Gallic victory. The *Dying Gaul (Galata morente)* in the Capitoline Museum is part of the same group (*see CAMPIDOGLIO-CAPITOLINO*).

The 3C **Grande Ludovisi**★★ **sarcophagus** (*sarcofago Grande Ludovisi*) depicts battles between the Romans and the barbarians. The victorious Romans can be seen in the top level; in the middle, the soldiers attack the barbarians, depicted on the bottom. Note the different characteristics: the Romans appear proud and courageous; the barbarians wince in pain. The delicate face of the **Ludovisi Erinyes**★ (*Erinni Ludovisi*) is emphasised by its dark base.

In the *Sala della Duchessa*, decorated with mythological scenes in the 17C by Romanelli, is *Aphrodite bathing (Afrodite al Bagno)*, a work by the sculptor Doidalsas.

Museo Napoleonico★ (Napoleon Museum)

🕙*Open Tue–Sun 9am–7pm.* 🕙*Closed Mon, 1 Jan, 1 May and Christmas.* ✆€2.60. 📞*06 68 80 62 86; www2.comune.roma.it*

The museum was founded in 1927 by Giuseppe Primoli, a descendant of Lucien Bonaparte, and contains souvenirs of the Napoleonic presence here.

Two rooms are devoted to the emperor's son, declared king of Rome at his birth in 1811. Room VI, devoted to Pauline, Napoleon's sister, contains a couch similar to that in her portrait by Canova.

Casa di Mario Praz

Entrance in Via Zanardelli. 🕙*Open Tue-Sun 9am–1pm and 2:30–6:30pm; Mon, 2:30pm-6:30pm.* 👣*Guided tours only (45min).* 🕙*Closed 1 Jan and Christmas.* ✆€2. 📞*06 68 61 089; www.gnam.arti. beniculturali.it/prazco.htm*

This is the house of Mario Praz (d 1982), a renowned Anglicist and essayist, a renowned scholar of English 19C literature. A passionate collector, he accumulated a huge number of knick-knacks, pictures, sculpture, neo-classical furniture and *objets d'art*, crammed into every corner. Of particular note is the rare collection of 17C-19C wax models.

MONTE MARIO

MICHELIN MAP 38 C8-12, D7-12, E7-8, F7-10, G9-10.

The green slopes of Monte Mario form an attractive backdrop to this district, the city's sporting hub. National and international events are held here, either in the austere and impressive Stadio dei Marmi, so typical of the Fascist period, or in the more modern Palazzetto dello Sport. Football (soccer) fans should experience the excitement of a Roma–Lazio match at the Stadio Olimpico, wheresupporters exchange colourful insults in dialect.

▶ **Orient Yourself:** The district is bordered to the north by *Viale del Foro Italico*, to the west by the residential Balduina district, to the south by the Prati quarter, and to the east, by the Flaminio district.

Sights

Auditorium-Parco della Musica★

Viale Pietro de Coubertin 15/30. ○*Open Mon-Sat 11am-6pm and Sun 10am-6pm.* ☎*06 80 24 12 81.www.musicaperroma.it.* Opened in 2002, this large auditorium by Renzo Piano is the headquarters of the *Accademia di Santa Cecilia.* The complex comprises three halls, a *cavea* for exhibitions and the ruins of a Republican villa. The building has a hanging garden.

Foro Italico

The Fascist Government started construction of this huge sports centre on 5 February 1928. It is now occupied by the National Olympic Committee. The most important facilities are the **Olympic**, and **Marble Stadium**. The road – from the *Piazza L. de Bosis* to the *Piazzale del Foro Italico* – is paved with mosaics of *"Il Duce."*

Monte Mario

A strolling spot with a **view**★.

Monumento a Matteotti

This bronze gilt monument was erected by the Tiber in 1974. Its symbol – a shoot bursting from the earth – commemorates the Socialist MP Giacomo Matteotti, assassinated in June 1924 for denouncing the Fascists.

Palazzetto dello Sport

This concave concrete structure was designed by Annibale Vitel-lozzi and Pier Luigi Nervi for the 1960 Olympics.

Ponte Milvio (Milvian Bridge)

A bridge has spanned the Tiber here since the 2C BC: it has frequently been restored and rebuilt, particularly in the 15C, and 19C, when it was enlarged and a fortified gate added.

Nearby, the famous battle took place on 28 October 312 between **Constantine** and **Maxentius**, rival pretenders to the imperial throne. On the eve of the battle, Constantine had a vision: Christ told him to mark his soldiers' shields with a Christian symbol. The alternative legend – that a cross appeared in the sky with the words "You will conquer in this sign"– is less reliable. Some historians consider this the date of Constantine's conversion.

RAI (Palazzo della Radio e della Televisione)

The Radio and TV Centre is distinguished by a magnificent bronze statue of a rearing horse by Francesco Messina and is situated in the new district which has grown up around the **Piazza Mazzini.**

Villa Madama★

Walk up Via di Villa Madama. ⏱*Open Mon–Sat 9am–noon.* ⏱*Closed Sun and holidays.* ☎*06 36 91 42 84.*

This Renaissance villa, with an enchanting **position**★ on the slopes of Monte Mario, was built in 1515 by Cardinal Giulio de' Medici, the future Clement VII, to plans by **Raphael** and completed by Sangallo the Younger. it passed to Madam Margaret of Austria.

PANTHEON★★★

MICHELIN MAP 38 L 11-12

This square still retains its majesty despite the crowded tourists, Roma musicians, locals savouring aperitifs and McDonald's fast food wrappers. The Pantheon – remarkably intact and still stunning –dominates the Piazza della Rotonda. Classical and Baroque buildings form a court around this queen of antiquity.

▶ **Orient Yourself:** The Pantheon stands in the heart of the ancient *Campus Martius*. The Tiber runs to the west and the straight *Via del Corso* to the east.

⏱ **Organising Your Time:** Allow at least 1hr 30mins.

😊 **Don't Miss:** Return after dusk, when the square is lively with diners and drinkers. Sample coffees at San Eustachio and Tazzo d'Oro, rivals for "Rome's best". Masterworks in the Galleria Doria Pamphili. Pozzo's frescoes in San Ignazio.

🧒 **Especially for Kids:** The elephant obelisk in Piazza della Minerva. The mysterious giant foot the *Via Piè di Marmo*.

👣 **Also See:** *FONTANA DI TREVI-QUIRINALE; ISOLA TIBERINA-TORRE ARGENTINA; MONTECITORIO; PIAZZA NAVONA; PIAZZA VENEZIA.*

A Bit of History

The **Campus Martius** was a marshy plain for census-taking and soldier-drilling. However, in the 2C BC the Romans began to divide the area into lots. In the eastern half, between the Pantheon and the present Corso, Caesar erected the *Saepta*, an enclosure for the assemblies that elected the tribunes of the people (*comitia tributa*). In about 43 BC, two Egyptian temples – dedicated to Isis and Serapis –were built beside the *Saepta* (👣*see map of Rome during the empire*).

Each dynasty felt honour-bound to leave its mark here. Augustus' son-in-law, Agrippa, built the original Pantheon, which was rectangular, and, between 25 and 19 BC, the first public baths in Rome (*Terme di Agrippa*). The structure we see today was built by Hadrian between 118 and 125 BC on the old foundations. Domitian was responsible for a temple to Minerva and a portico to the deified Flavians. The Antonines added a temple to the deified Hadrian. Alexander Severus rebuilt Nero's Baths (*Terme di Nerone*).

In the 4C, the Christians held sway. They often cannibalized or adapted the ruins of pagan monuments. During the medieval struggle between the Ghibelline (empire) and the Guelf (papacy), Rome was peppered with towers. In the 16C and 17C, the higher clerics and citizens bought hovels and replaced them with unostentatious, but luxurious, palaces.

Piazza della Rotonda

This square, surrounding the Pantheon, is typically Roman. At the centre is a fountain designed in 1578 by Giacomo

MONTECITORIO

ISOLA TIBERINA- TORRE ARGENTINA   PIAZZA VENEZIA

Fontana del Facchino .... B   Piede gigantesco .... A

Address Book

🕭 See "Where to Eat" in the Your Stay in Rome section at the guide's end.

TAKING A BREAK

🕭 Locals consider these rival bars among the city's best.

Sant'Eustachio – *Piazza S. Eustachio 82.* ☎*06 6880 2048. www.santeustachioilcaffe.it. Open 8.30am-1am.* This café is famous for its delicious, creamy coffee known as a *gran caffè speciale*; the secret recipe is jealously guarded by its creator. Pay at the *cassa*, then request your espresso *amaro* (bitter) to avoid the signature sugar overdose.

Tazza d'Oro – *Via degli Orfani 84.* ☎*06 67 89 792. www.tazzadorocoffeeshop. com. Open Mon-Sat 7am-8pm.* This specialist coffee bar serves strong and aromatic coffee (counter service only). In the summer, don't miss the coffee granita with double helpings of cream.

BARS

Trinity College – *Via del Collegio Romano 6.* ☎*06 67 86 472. Open noon-3am.* On two floors of a splendid old palazzo, this Irish-style pub concentrates on good beer. Popular with Italian and foreign youngsters.

SHOPPING

Ditta G. Poggi – *Via del Gesù 74/75.* ☎*06 67 93 674. poggi@getnet.it. Open Mon-Wed, Fri and Sat 9am-1pm and 4-7:30pm; Thur 9am-7.30pm.* This shop, opened in 1825, provides students of the nearby Fine Arts School with materials from water-colours to drawing tables.

La Procure – *Piazza S. Luigi dei Francesi 23.* ☎*06 68 30 75 98. Open Tue-Sat 9:30am-7:30pm; Mon 3:30-7:30pm.* A wide range of books and guides, including texts on theology and law, for those who want to improve their knowledge of the French language and culture.

Libreria Antiquaria Rappaport – *Via Sistina 23.* ☎*06 48 38 26. Open Mon-Fri 9:30am-12:30pm and 3:15-7pm.* The perfect bookshop for collectors of old books, prints and old maps, some of which are particularly valuable and can fetch considerable prices.

Barbiconi – *Via di S. Caterina da Siena 59 (junction with Via dei Cestari).* ☎*06 67 94 985. Open Mon-Fri 9am-1pm and 3:30-7:30pm; Sat 9am-1pm.* This is the most famous of the shops along *Via dei Cestari*, selling religious garments, vestments and church ornaments.

Piazza della Rotonda, with the columns of the Pantheon in the foreground

Della Porta; in 1711 Clement XI stacked an obelisk on top. Like *Piazza della Minerva's*, it came from the Temple of Isis. The **Albergo del Sole** (Hotel of the Sun) at no. 63 dates from the 15C. One of the oldest inns in the city, its guests have included Ludovico Ariosto, the poet (1474-1533), and Pietro Mascagni, the musician (1863-1945).

Pantheon★★★

Note: The building is a church and should be treated as such. &. ⊙*Open Mon–Sat 8:30am–7:30pm; Sun 9am–6pm (1pm on weekday public holidays).* ⊙*Closed 1 Jan, 1 May and Christmas.*

Originally the Pantheon was a temple, built by Agrippa, the great town planner, in 27 BC; dedicated to all the gods, it faced south. In AD 80, it was damaged by fire and restored by Domitian. Then Hadrian (117-38) rebuilt it and gave it its present orientation to the north. The first Christian emperors closed the Pantheon, together with all other places of pagan worship. The ruins were sacked by the barbarians in 410, but saved from destruction by Pope Boniface IV, who received it as a gift in 608 from Phocas, the emperor in Byzantium (⌖ *see FORO ROMANO*).

Until 756, when the **Papal States** came into being, Rome was subject to Byzantium. The only eastern emperor to visit the Christian capital was **Constantinus II**

in 356, when the Pantheon was despoiled of its bronze tiles for the embellishment of Constantinople. It was restored early in the Renaissance. Then Urban VIII removed the nails and bronze plates that covered the beams of the porch roof and had them made into the magnificent baldaquin now in St Peter's. Pasquino, one of Rome's "talking statues," punned on the pope's family name: *Quod non fecerunt Barbari, fecerunt Barberini* (what the barbarians did not do, the Barberini have done).

Exterior

The Pantheon has a pillared porch, whose pediment bears two inscriptions: the most visible concerns Agrippa's original effort. A mighty bronze door leads into the circular interior, which could contain a 43m (142ft) globe.

Interior★★★

The entrance is under the porch, which is supported on 16 monolithic granite columns, all original except for three (replaced because of weakness under Urban VIII and Alexander VII).

The harmony and grandeur of the interior have an immediate impact. The proportions are striking; the diameter of the building is equal to its overall height. The **antique dome**★★★ is an incredibly bold feature; medieval architects lost this technology, which Renaissance artists –like Bramante and Michelangelo – recovered by studying the Pantheon. At the centre of the coffered ceiling is an enormous round opening (*oculus*), which lights the interior.

A series of superb monolithic columns punctuate round and rectangular recesses. The piers between have shrines with alternating triangular or rounded pediments. The upper stage – between the cornice and the base of the dome – was redesigned in the 18C with the present series of panels and blind windows. A section above the third chapel on the west side has been returned to the original decor.

The recesses have been converted into chapels: in the first to the west of the entrance is an attractive *Annunciation* attributed to Melozzo da Forlì. The next chapel contains the **tomb of Victor Emmanuel II** (1820-78), the first king of unified Italy.

Between the fifth and sixth chapels is the **tomb of Raphael**, composed of a fine antique sarcophagus. He died, aged 37, in 1520. On the upper edge is an inscription by Cardinal Pietro Bembo, poet and humanist (1470-1547), which Alexander Pope translated without acknowledgement for another epitaph:

> *"Living, great nature feared*
> *he might outvie*
> *Her works; and dying fears*
> *herself to die."*

Walking Tour

North of Piazza della Rotonda, Via del Pantheon leads to Piazza della Maddalena.

Santa Maria Maddalena

⏱*Open Mon-Fri 8am-noon and 5-8pm; Sat-Sun and public holidays, 9:30am-noon and 5-8pm.* ☎*06 67 97 796.*

The church, dedicated to Mary Magdalene, stands on the site of a 15C oratory and hospice. These were occupied in 1586 by St Camillus of Lellis, the founder of the Ministers of the Sick, a nursing order. The church was rebuilt in the 17C by Carlo Fontana, who was succeeded by followers of Bernini. The façade was erected in 1735; its contorted lines and abundant decoration are an exaggeration of Borromini's style.

The **interior**★ is a rare example of the Rococo in Rome. The elaborate plan, also suggesting Borromini's influence, gives the church a majestic appearance despite its small size. The rich decoration – in stucco, gold and marble – and the frescoes lend the church the charm of an old-fashioned drawing-room.

The relics of St Camillus are venerated at the altar in the south transept beneath the *Glory of St Camillus*, painted by Sebastian Conca. In the passage south of the chancel is a 15C wooden statue of Mary Magdalene. The sumptuous organ dates from the 18C, as do the attractive furnishings in the sacristy.

▷ *Return to Piazza della Rotonda.*

On the west side of the Pantheon (*Via Salita dei Crescenzi and Via di S. Eustachio*) is the site where the Crescenzi fortress stood in the Middle Ages. Nearby a tower was erected by the Sinibaldi family. Two ancient columns, once part of the baths of Alexander Severus, have been re-erected at the junction of the two streets. The famous Sant'Eustachio café is located in Piazza di S. Eustachio. Contrast this with Tazzo d'Oro, another famous nook on Via degli Orfani 8.

▷ *Go southeast along Via della Palombella to Piazza della Minerva.*

Piazza della Minerva

Kids Bernini suggested this obelisk be supported on an elephant's back. The Egyptian pillar dates from the 6C BC; it was once part of the nearby Temple of Isis. The fantastic marble elephant, affectionately called the "chick of Minerva," was sculpted by one of Bernini's pupils, Ercole Ferrata (1667).

Santa Maria sopra Minerva★★

⏱*Open daily 9am-7pm. Cloister open daily 8am-1pm and 3:30pm-7:30pm.*

Rome's only Gothic church – all elegant cobalt blue and gilt – contains a censored statue of Christ by **MIchelangelo**. Its name translates "Saint Mary over Minerva," a reference to the temple ruins nearby,

In 1280, it was rebuilt, then modified towards the middle of the 15C. The façade was constructed in the 17C; it is rectangular and very plain, with the original 15C doorways. Six plaques (*right*) mark the heights reached by Tiber flood waters. The church has long been the headquarters of the Dominicans, historical rivals of the Jesuits in the defence of Roman Catholic orthodoxy against the Reformation.

Interior

The **works of art**★ here rank this as one of Rome's first "museum churches".

South aisle – In the fifth chapel (**1**), the painting by Antoniazzo Romano recalls the beneficence of Cardinal Juan de Torquemada (uncle of the infamous inquisitor), who provided poor girls with dowries. This work, against a gold background, is typical of the style of this late-15C painter. The sixth chapel (**2**) was designed in the late-16C by Giacomo della Porta and Carlo Maderno. A la Counter-Reformation, the marble's extravagance is tempered with a certain severity. The next chapel (**3**) contains one of **Andrea Bregno**'s most famous works (*right*): the delicate decoration on the tomb of Cardinal Coca (d 1477).

South transept – The Carafa Chapel (**4**), which has a finely carved marble altar rail, was built and decorated between 1489 and 1493 with **frescoes**★ by Filippino

0   15 m   Piazza della Minerva

Lippi: above the altar, in a typical late-Renaissance frame, is an *Annunciation* in which Thomas Aquinas presents Cardinal Oliviero Carafa to the Virgin. The expressive faces, the slender figures and the deeply pleated garments are characteristic of Filippino Lippi's art. The rest of the wall is taken up with an *Assumption* in fine colours. The right-hand wall shows scenes from Thomas Aquinas' life. On the left of the Carafa Chapel is the 13C tomb of Guillaume Durand (**5**), Bishop of Mende in France (d 1296), by Giovanni Cosma.

Presbytery – Michelangelo's *Risen Christ*★ stands to the left of the high altar (**6**). The strong, confident pose expressed Christ's voluntary sacrifice. An assistant muddled some bits, yet the muscular, naked statue was much admired in the 16C. Baroque prudes added the bronze loincloth.

The tomb of **St Catherine of Siena**, patron saint of Italy, lies under the main altar.

The funeral monuments of the Medici Popes, **Clement VII** (**7**) and Leo V (**8**), modelled on commemorative arches, are the work of Antonio da Sangallo (1483-1546).

North transept – The first chapel (**9**) contains many fine **tombs**★; the one with the dead man resting on his elbow (*left*) is by Giacomo della Porta (late 16C). Set into the floor is the resting place of **Fra Angelico**: Giovanni da Fiesole, the Dominican painter who died in 1455. In the next chapel (**10**) is a 15C tomb composed of an antique sarcophagus (*Hercules and the lion*).

St Catherine of Siena's Chapel (11) – This chapel was built in the 17C using the walls of the room where the saint died (1380) in the neighbouring Dominican convent.

North aisle – Monument to Venerable Sister Maria Raggi (**12**): flowing garments, an ecstatic expression and lively cherubs exemplify the art of **Bernini** (1643). The Renaissance tomb of Francesco Tornabuoni (**13**) is one of Mino da Fiesole's most successful works because of its fine decorative carving.

▶ *Walk west along Via Piè di Marmo.*

Kids The street is named after the enormous stone **foot** that probably belonged to a Roman statue, although no one knows how it came to be in its present position. The **Roman College** (*Collegio Romano*), formerly the **Jesuit College**, was founded in 1583 by Gregory XIII, who strove to re-establish the primacy of Rome after the Council of Trent. At the corner of *Via della Gatta*, beneath a canopy, is a charming Madonna, so typical of Rome.

Palazzo Doria Pamphili★

This palace, one of the largest in Rome, was begun in the 15C and gradually enlarged by the succession of noble owners. Inside lies a gallery of the same name, which houses a fine collection of paintings and sculpture (*See full entry below*).

The façade facing the Corso is an imposing 18C construction in the Baroque style, whereas the front onto *Via del Plebiscito* dates from 1643. The *palazzo* extends the whole length of *Via della Gatta* behind a 19C façade and round two sides of *Piazza del Collegio Romano*.

Since 1966, it's housed the Anglican Centre in Rome, a tangible outcome of the formal visit paid by Archbishop Michael Ramsey to Pope Paul VI in that year. Students – particularly Roman Catholics curious about the Anglican Communion – can consult the library.

▶ *Take Via Lata between Santa Maria in Via Lata and Palazzo del Banco di Roma (Bank of Rome).*

Fontana del Facchino (Porter's Fountain)

Tucked against the wall (*right*) is an amusing little fountain composed of a porter (*facchino*) holding a barrel with water issuing from the bung hole. According to legend, the sculptor took as his model a drunken Renaissance water-carrier, who is thus obliged to stay sober for eternity.

▶ *Turn right into Via del Corso.*

Santa Maria in Via Lata (Church of St Mary in Via Lata)

The façade is of particular interest. Built between 1658 and 1662 by Pietro Cortona, it marks the transition in Baroque art to the period when detached col-

umns – no longer an integral part of the walls – took on an essential role. Set out along two storeys, the columns seem to support the whole building and create remarkable effects of light and shade.

Palazzo Salviati

It was built in the 17C by the Duke of Nevers, Cardinal Mazarin's nephew, to house the French Academy.

▶ *Retrace your steps along Via del Corso.*

San Marcello

🕐 *Open daily 7:45am–12pm and 4–7pm, Sun from 9:30am–12pm and 4–7pm.* The **church of St Marcellus** was founded in the 4C on the site of a *titulus*, a private house used as a place of Christian worship. It burned in 1519 and was completely rebuilt in the 16C and 17C. In 1683, Carlo Fontana designed the slightly concave Baroque façade. The palms linking the two storeys are typical of the Baroque style, which delighted in the unusual.

The single nave with side chapels, typical of the Renaissance, was designed by **Jacopo Sansovino** (1486-1570) in the 16C. The late-16C coffered ceiling is richly decorated in gold, blue and red.

To the left of the entrance is the tomb of Cardinal Giovanni Michiel, who was poisoned on Alexander VI's orders in 1503. Below it is the tomb of his nephew, Bishop Antonio Orso, who died in 1511. The work was begun in 1520 by **Andrea Sansovino** and finished in 1527 by his pupil **Jacopo Sansovino**.

In the fourth chapel on the right is a fine 15C wooden crucifix. The realistic figure of Christ gave rise to a lugubrious legend: the sculptor craved realism so much he killed a passer-by and studied the death throes. When the church burned down in 1519, it is said that the crucifix was recovered intact in the ruins. The frescoes in the vault are by Perin del Vaga, one of Raphael's pupils. In the altar's base is a 3C Roman stele, decorated with incrustations of marble in the 12C to serve as a reliquary.

The fourth chapel on the left contains busts of the noble family of the Frangipani; the three on the right were carved by Algardi in 1625.

Palazzo del Banco di Roma (Bank of Rome)

The palazzo was built between 1714 and 1722 for the Carolis, and converted early in the 20C. In the late-18C, it was the home of the French Ambassador, who held splendid receptions here; guests included the writer Chateaubriand.

▶ *Turn left and right into Via del Collegio Romano and left into Via del Caravita to reach Piazza Sant'Ignazio.*

Piazza Sant'Ignazio★

The square mimics a theatre set, in ochre and stone, and has an unusual charm, with curved façades on street corners.

Sant'Ignazio★★

○*Open daily 7:30am–12:30pm and 3pm–7:15pm.* The 1626 church is dedicated to the founder of the **Jesuit** Order and of the Roman College, the first free school. Jesuit Orazio Grassi designed the high façade; the two superimposed orders linked by scrolls produce a solemn and austere ensemble.

Central ceiling fresco★★ – For the best view of the stunning central vault fresco and the *trompe-l'œil* cupola, stand on the disc in the nave's centre. The fresco is the work of **Andrea Pozzo** (1684). A Jesuit, he chose a subject dear to the Counter-Reformation, which exalted the saints in the face of Protestantism. Here St Ignatius is bathed by a divine light, which is reflected on the four corners of the world, shown allegorically. Pozzo used his knowledge of perspective to create the *trompe-l'œil* effect.

The apsidal fresco, also by Pozzo, glorifies the miracles of St Ignatius. The altar at the end of the right transept is dedicated to St Luigi Gonzaga. Above the lapis lazuli urn containing the saint's relics – and between the beautiful green marble columns wreathed in fronds of bronze – is an admirable *Glory to St Luigi Gonzaga*, a carved "marble picture".

▶ *Take Via dei Burrò.*

Via dei Burrò owes its name to the administrative offices established by Napoleon Bonaparte ("*bureau*" is the French word for "office").

Piazza di Pietra

The south side of this colourful square is occupied by the Stock Exchange. In the 18C, it was the Customs House. Incorporated in the present building are 11 beautiful marble columns of the Corinthian order belonging to an ancient **temple**, that honoured **Hadrian**. The ancient columns lend much grandeur.

Galleria Doria Pamphili★★

In Palazzo Doria Pamphili, Piazza Collegio Romano 2. ♿○*Open Fri–Wed 10am–5pm (last admission 4:15pm).* ○*Closed Thurs, 1 Jan, Easter, 1 May, 15 Aug and Christmas. €8. Audioguides in various languages available.* ☎*06 67 97 323; www.doriapamphilj.it*

First are the **Sale di Rappresentanza** (Reception Rooms) including the **Sala dei Velluti** (Velvet Room), which retains its original 17C floor. The decorations include an eagle, symbol of the Doria family, of Ligurian origin, and a *fleur-de-lis*. Exhibited in the corner of the **Sala da Ballo** (Ballroom) – reserved for the musicians – is a 17C harp made from ivory and wood. The walls of the Rococo style **Saletta Gialla** (Yellow Drawing Room) to the right display tapestry panels depicting Allegories of the Twelve Months, made at the Gobelins factory in Paris during the reign of Louis XV.

The **gallery** itself is quadrilateral in shape. It was once the loggia over the internal 16C courtyard and was closed during the time of Camillo Pamphili (18C) to house the collection of paintings and sculpture. The discovery of a manuscript dating from 1767 has allowed the paintings to be displayed according to their original layout.

First gallery

This gallery houses paintings by **Annibale Carracci**, including the series of lunettes depicting the Stories of the Virgin Mary. In the *Flight into Egypt★★*, the religious scene seems to have a marginal role. The gentle, but realistic landscape, takes up almost all the picture, presaging a taste that developd throughout the 17C. In *Erminia Finding Tancred Wounded*, by

Guercino, the drama is intensified by the contrasts between light and dark. *The Usurers*★ by **Quentin Metsys** is an important painting. The characters depicted (especially the two userers on the left) have exaggerated features.

At the end of the gallery, a small studio houses the *Portrait of Innocent X*★★★, a masterpiece by **Velázquez**, painted in 1650 during his second visit to Rome. The painter produced an official portrait that is realistic and quite lacking in idealisation (note the stern expression). Here, also, is a bust of Innocent X by **Bernini**, an expressive interpretation of the pope's authoritative personality.

Galleria degli Specchi – This "Hall of Mirrors" makes up the gallery's second part. The decor is 18C and the **ceiling** is painted with frescoes by Aurelio Milani, depicting the Labours of Hercules.

Four **small rooms** lead off the gallery, dedicated to the 15C, 16C, 17C and 18C respectively. In the second, the visitor's attention is drawn to the magnificent *Rest after the Flight into Egypt*★★★ by **Caravaggio**. The scene is one of natural beauty: the tired Virgin sleeps with her head gently bent over her child; Joseph seems entranced by the music of the angel, a young man with large dark wings who stands in front of him (unusual). Just visible behind Joseph's shoulder is the donkey, who also seems enchanted by the music. Caravaggio has used the same model for his *Mary Magdalene*, cleverly positioned next to the painting of the Virgin. Even the pose is the same, though Mary Magdalene is depicted as a despairing woman with reference only to earthly pleasures; note the bottle of perfume and jewellery.

St Sebastian by Ludovico Carracci and *Endymion* by Guercino are exhibited in the same room. The main focus in the room dedicated to the 16C is the beautiful *Salome*★★ by **Titian**. Notice the play of expressions: the servant looks at Salome with a pious and reprimanding expression; Salome is only able to glance quickly, almost with horror, at the head of John the Baptist, as she flees; the hair of the Baptist almost seems to caress the hand of the man who killed him. In the same room the *Portrait of a Young Man* by Tintoretto, the *Portrait of Two People* by

Raphael and a delicate *Winter Landscape* by Peter Bruegel the Elder can also be admired. A masterpiece by Hans Memling, *Mourning the Death of Christ*★★, is exhibited in the 15C room. The dramatic composition is highlighted by the harsh traits and angular position of Christ.

Third Gallery

An unusual painting by Bruegel the Elder, *Battle in the Bay of Naples* (q21), can be seen in this gallery. The **Sala Aldobrandini**, a room to the left at the bottom of the gallery, houses statues from both the archaic and late imperial eras.

Fourth Gallery

At the entrance to this gallery is a **bust of Olimpia Maidalchini Pamphili**★★ by **Algardi**. She is said to have pestered and hounded her brother-in-law, Giovanni Battista Pamphili, until he attained the papal throne as Innocent X. Algardi, who was an accomplished portraitist, knew precisely how to express the energy and ambition of Donna Olimpia, as she was called by the Romans. She is shown in the distinctive headdress, which she alone wore. Paintings in this gallery include a 17C copy of *John the Baptist as a Child* (s57) by Caravaggio, which hangs in the Palazzo dei Conservatori, and the *Madonna and Child* (s71) by **Parmigiano**.

Appartamenti privati★ (Private Apartments)

These are the rooms inhabited from the 16C to 18C by the families who owned the palace. In the Wintergarden are an 18C sleigh and a fine sedan chair, painted and gilded. The Andrea Doria Room bears the name of the most famous member of the Genoese Doria family; a mercenary (*condottiere*), he commanded the French fleet for François I before being employed by Charles V.

The frieze in the dining room depicts the various properties belonging to the Doria Pamphili family (19C).

In the Green Drawing Room, one of the many paintings is a graceful *Annunciation* by the Florentine **Filippo Lippi** (1406-69), Botticelli's master. A large 15C Tournai tapestry illustrates the medieval legend of Alexander the Great.

PIAZZA NAVONA★★★

MICHELIN MAP 38 K 10, L 10-11

Domitian's old stadium now bears the gilding of Bernini's genius: the fountains of the Piazza Navona. Smack in the "centro storico" – Rome's heart – this square teems with tourists, vendors, mimes, musicians, portrait painters and seasonal festivals. Medieval streets emanate from this hub, lined with pizzerias, gelaterias, restaurants and shops: a reminder of when the district serviced pilgrims en route to St Peters.

▶ **Orient Yourself:** On a loop in the Tiber, this area is bordered by *Corso Vittorio Emanuele II, Corso del Rinascimento* and *Via Zanardelli* (opened in the late 19C and early 20C) and was once part of the *Campus Martius*. The piazza is few minutes' walk from the *Campo dei Fiori* and the Pantheon both.

🕐 **Organising Your Time:** Allow at least 2 hrs.

😊 **Don't Miss:** The delightful piazza of *Santa Maria della Pace* and its famous cafe, Pasquino "the talking statue", *San Ivo alla Sapienza*, and Caravaggio's masterwork in *San Luigi dei Francesi*.

🕯 **Also See:** *CAMPO DEI FIORI; CASTEL SANT'ANGELO; MONTECITORIO; PANTHEON.*

A Bit of History

Except for the outline of Domitian's Stadium, which is preserved in the shape of the Piazza Navona (🕯 *see below*), no traces of ancient Rome have survived here. The square is now adorned with fine Renaissance and Baroque buildings designed by the most famous architects of the 16C and 17C.

The popes attempted to smarten up the narrow, medieval streets around the piazza. Cardinals, ambassadors, papal officials, wealthy bankers and distinguished courtesans took up residence here. Around them intellectual life flourished: booksellers, engravers and miniaturists settled around Piazza Navona and Piazza Pasquino. To this day, numerous craftsmen still work here.

Piazza Navona★★★

This place perhaps characterises the true spirit of the Eternal City most effectively. Set apart from the thrum of traffic, Piazza Navona seems permanently on holiday: the balloon-seller has his pitch beside a caricaturist who sketches his customer with a few deft strokes of charcoal; an old woman lovingly feeds the pigeons next to a trade unionist exhorting his

comrades; tourists and locals come to savour a *tartufo* gelato at Tre Scalini. The long and narrow shape of the square is due to **Domitian**: in AD 86, he had a **stadium** built on this site (*Stadio di Domiziano*) and immediately instituted a series of games in the Greek style. Unlike the games in the amphitheatre, where the gladiators confronted one another with violence, these were contests of wit and physical fitness. The speaking, poetry and musical competitions were held in the Odeon, situated roughly where *Palazzo Massimo* and *Piazza S. Pantaleo* now stand, with running, wrestling, and discus and javelin in the stadium.

Stripped of its marble by Constantinus II, the staium was in ruins by the 5C. The Renaissance revived it, creating one of the most beautiful sights in Rome. In 1477, the Capitoline market was moved here and other attractions added, such as the *cuccagna*, a greased climbing pole, and puppet shows. In the mid-17C, the square was partially flooded to accommodate summer-weekend water games. Since 1869, market stalls only appear at Christmas and Epiphany.

Fontana dei Fiumi★★★

The **Fountain of the Rivers**, which occupies the centre, was created by **Bernini** for Innocent X. The pope wanted to provide worthy surroundings for his residence, the Palazzo Pamphili, which stood on the piazza. The brilliant Baroque architect contrived a pile of rockwork, hollowed into grottoes and crowned by an obelisk. The rigidity and symmetry of the latter contrasts strikingly with the fluid lines of the base. The wind seems to tear at the trees, as the marble statues gesticulate. They represent four rivers, symbolising the quarters of the world: the Danube for Europe, the Nile for Africa (the veiled head indicated that the source was unknown), the Ganges for Asia and the Plate for America.

The obelisk, a Roman work dating from Domitian's reign, was recovered by Innocent X from the Via Appia. The fountain was completed in 1651.

Fontana del Moro

The **Fountain of the Moor** was built at the end of the 16C. **Bernini** later designed the central figure of the Moor; one of his pupils was responsible for the vigorous interpretation. The statues on the tritons and the edge of the basin date from the 19C.

Fontana del Nettuno

The **Fountain of Neptune** was moved to Piazza Navona at the end of the 16C.

Artistic Rivalry

A number of stories illustrate the alleged rivalry between **Bernini** and **Borromini**, who designed the façade of St Agnes's Church. One Roman legend explains that the statues of the Nile and the Plate, their arms raised in a defensive gesture, are trying to protect themselves from the façade, which is about to collapse. In fact, the façade was built several years after the fountain.

The water god's central statue and those around it date from the 19C.

Sant'Agnese in Agone★★

🕐 *Open Tue, Wed and Fri, 2–6.30pm; Thu and Sat, 4–7pm; Sun and public holidays, 10am–1pm and 2–6.30pm.* 🕐 *Closed Mon.* ☎*06 68 19 21 34.*

According to tradition, a small oratory was built in the 8C on the site where St Agnes might have been martyred. In 1652, Pope Innocent X commissioned Girolamo Rainaldi and his son Carlo to rebuild the church as a family chapel attached to his palace. From 1653-57, **Borromini** took charge of the work. The church was completed at the end of the century by a group of architects. Bor-

Piazza Novona

B. Kaufmann/MICHELIN

Address Book

WHERE TO EAT

See "Where to Eat" in the Your Stay in Rome section at the end of the guide.

TAKING A BREAK

Tre Scalini – *Piazza Navona 28.* ☎*06 68 80 19 96. Open Thu-Tue, 9am-1am. Closed Wed, Jan.* This café is renowned for its excellent truffle ice cream. The sit-down prices are high), but it does boast ringside views of Bernini's fountain.

Cafè della Pace – *Via della Pace 3/7.* ☎*06 68 61 216. Open Tues-Sun 9am-2am, Mon 3pm-2am.* This chic, ivy-swathed bar attracts a number of personalities from the theatre, especially in the evening outdoors. The two rooms inside the café have a Central European feel, with padded sofas, soft lights and tinted mirrors.

Bar del Fico – *Piazza del Fico 26/27.* ☎*06 68 65 205. Open Wed-Mon 8am-2am.* This bar, one the of busiest in the district, has tables set out in the shade of the namesake fig. Exhibitions of paintings and photography can be admired inside the bar. It serves delicious canapés and snacks.

I Paladini – *Via del Governo Vecchio 29. Open usual pizzeria opening times, but closed 2.30-5pm –* 🍴*.* This joint serves excellent freshly-baked *pizza bianca* (pizza without a tomato base), topped with artichokes, cheese, different types of ham, or nutella.

Bar Piccolino – *Via del Teatro Valle 54/a.* ☎*06 68 80 17 46. Open 7am-11pm.* This tiny bar is known for its delicious hazelnut-flavoured coffee.

SHOPPING

Antonella Marani – *Via di Monte Giordano 27.* ☎*06 68 30 78 66. Open Mon-Fri 10:30am-6pm.* Miniature façades of Roman churches made from plaster casts are on sale here, as well as stuccoes, friezes, low reliefs and busts.

Galleria di Orditi e Trame – *Via del Teatro Valle 54/b.* ☎*06 68 93 372.* Two innovative artists create beautiful and original cotton hats for this boutique.

Jaracandà – *Via del Teatro Pace 2/a.* This workshop repairs and restores traditional Italian and foreign musical instruments.

Orsantico – *Via dell'Orso 60/61/63.* ☎*06 68 77 759. Open Tue-Sat, 10am-1pm and 4-7:30pm; Mon 4-7:30pm.* This shop specialises in furniture – and Italian and French antiques – and is housed in the *Palazzo della Scimmia* (Monkey's Palace). The name refers to a miracle said to have taken place here in the past).

Set – *Piazza del Fico 23.* This little shop, situated opposite the famous *Bar del Fico*, has a selection of splendid furniture and articles dating from 1900-50.

CHRISTMAS MARKET

Piazza Navona is particularly atmospheric around Christmas and the New Year, when the square is decorated with brightly coloured market stalls. Look for figurines of Befana, the witch that brings presents on Epiphany.

---

romini was responsible for part of the dome and for the façade, which demonstrates his taste for contrasting convex and concave lines.

The **interior**★ is captivating: the deep recesses in the pillars supporting the dome transform the Greek cross plan into an octagon.

The altars are adorned with beautiful "marble pictures" by Bernini's pupils. The decorations in stucco, gilt and painting are far from the spirit of Borromini's sober interiors and were added at the end of the 17C.

Palazzo Pamphili

The Pamphili residence was enlarged between 1644 and 1650 by Girolamo Rainaldi when Giovanni Battista Pamphili became Pope Innocent X.

Walking Tour

▶ At the north end of the Piazza, take *Via Agonale.*

The remains of **Domitian's Stadium** can be seen in *Via di Tor Sanguigna*, adjacent to the piazza.

Pasquino, the "talking statue"

The statue of **Pasquino**, probably part of a 3C BC group, was found in Piazza Navona in the 15C. No collector wanted this pitiable lump, and so it was marooned on a corner (which the Palazzo Braschi later graced) and there it stayed. People called it "Pasquino," after a local tailor with a very caustic tongue. Soon the sculpture became their mouthpiece. During the night, satirical or even libellous comments – sometimes in Roman dialect – were secretly hung here. The following day the "Pasquinades" spread through Rome, as far as the doors of the papal officials; some were even carried to the ears of foreign sovereigns and started more than one diplomatic incident. The draconian laws – sentencing the perpetrators of these libels to death – were rarely applied; or if they were, the prisoner was immediately pardoned. Pasquino was the most famous and most loquacious of the Roman "talking statues", which included Madama Lucrezia, Marforio and the Abate Luigi. He continues his ways in 2007 by decrying the Iraq war.

Santa Maria dell'Anima

▶ *As the main entrance is usually closed, enter by the Via della Pace.*

This is the church of German-speaking Roman Catholics. A pilgrim hostel stood here from 1386; the present building was begun in 1500.

Interior
Designed as a "hall church", where the nave and aisles are all of the same height, the plan is rather unusual for Rome, which has almost no Gothic architecture. The decoration dates from the 19C. Above the high altar is a *Holy Family with Saints* by Giulio Romano, one of Raphael's assistants.
The **façade** in Via dell'Anima was designed by Giuliano da Sangallo and built in 1511. Its flatness, which gives it the appearance of a screen, belongs to the Renaissance period. The pediment above the central door contains a sculpture of the Virgin between two figures, each representing a soul ("*anima*" in Italian), which is a copy of the painting that gave the church its name. The original is kept locked away (*apply to the sacristan*). To the right of the façade is a view of the bell-tower, capped by a slim cone faced with multicoloured ceramics.

Santa Maria della Pace★
🕐*Open Tues-Fri 10am-12:30pm.* 🕐*Closed Sat-Mon, public holidays. Donation welcome.* ☎*06 68 61 156.*

There was already a small church on this site in the 12C. Sixtus IV had it rebuilt in 1480. In the Baroque era, Alexander VII (1655-67) invited Pietro da Cortona to design a new **façade**. He created a pleasing combination: a semicircular porch flanked by two concave wings. The architect also sketched a charming square with elegant *palazzi*.

Interior
The 15C plan is very unusual; it comprises a short rectangular nave and an octagonal domed section. The first chapel's arch on the nave's right was decorated by **Raphael** in 1514. He painted the four **Sibyls**★ – inspired, no doubt after seeing Michelangelo's versions in the Sistine Chapel. His skill in turning an awkward surface to good account is to be admired. The first chapel on the left is decorated with frescoes by **Baldassarre Peruzzi** (1481-1536), who also worked on the Farnesina.
In the octagonal section over the high altar is an image of the Virgin, which is supposed to have bled when struck by a stone in 1480. Sixtus IV had the church rebuilt to house the miraculous image.

Cloisters
Entrance at Vicolo Arco della Pace 5.
Built in 1504, they were one of **Bramante**'s earliest Roman works. The handsome proportions give an air of great simplicity. The columns on the ground floor are complemented by those on the first, which alternate with smaller col-

CAMPO DEI FIORI

umns placed centrally over the lower arches. Today the cloister hosts a lovely cafe' and bookstore.

▶ *Between the chuches turn into Vicolo Arco della Pace which leads into Via della Pace. Follow this street to Via dei Coronari; turn left into Piazza Lancellotti to find Via della Maschera d'Oro.*

Via della Maschera d'Oro

No. 9, on the corner of Vicolo di San Simeone, is a small palace that shows how secular architecture developed in the 16C, as a result of Sixtus IV's essays in town planning.

At this period, the streets of Rome were lined by charming façades engraved and painted with monochrome frescoes. **Polidoro da Caravaggio** and **Maturino da Firenze** were the masters of this technique. The wall was first given a rough rendering blackened with smoke and then covered with a coat of plaster. The artist then engraved mythological scenes or motifs taken from antique art to reveal the dark undercoat. These

decorations were extremely fragile and almost all have disappeared.

▶ *Return to Via della Pace.*

The **Antico Caffè della Pace** has stood in the picturesque Via della Pace since the the early 19C (👁 *see Address Book*).

▶ *Continue south along Via di Parione; turn left into Via del Governo Vecchio to reach Piazza di Pasquino.*

Palazzo Braschi★

Pope Pius VI built this in the late 18C for his nephews; the last papal family palace erected in Rome. The neo-classical style produced the ponderous façades that dominate the surrounding streets.

Palazzo Massimo

The palace – which belongs to the Massimo, one of the oldest families in Rome – comprises three separate buildings. The one on the right of the **church of San Pantaleo** (designed by Valadier in 1806) is known as the Pyrrhus Palace, because of a statue which was kept there. The *Palazzo Massimo* (*facing on to Corso Vittorio Emanuele II*) is screened by a fine curved portico of Doric columns, designed (1532-36) by **Baldassarre Peruzzi**. The original windows of the upper storeys of the façade herald the Mannerist style. The oldest part of the palazzo is on the north side (*access from Corso Vittorio Emanuele II via a narrow lane into Piazza de' Massimi*) and is known as the "illustrated palace" because of the grisailles painted on the façade c 1523 by some of Daniele da Volterra's pupils.

The column standing in Piazza de' Massimi may have been part of the **Odeon** of Domitian. From the north end of the piazza there is a view of the Fountain of the Rivers in Piazza Navona.

▷ *Turn right and then left into Corso del Rinascimento.*

Palazzo della Sapienza

Until 1935, this palazzo was occupied by Rome University. Now it houses, among other things, the archives of the **Papal States** from the 9C to the 19C. The simple façade, begun in 1575 to a design by Giacomo della Porta and coloured burnt umber, gives no hint of the elegance of the inner courtyard.

Sant'Ivo alla Sapienza★★

🕐*Open Sun and public holidays, 9am-noon.* ☎*06 68 64 987.*

Equally unexpected is the audacity of Borromini's façade for St Ivo's Church, which closes the fourth side of the courtyard. Just as **Bernini** aimed at extensiveness, so Borromini tried to confine his ideas within a restricted space. His exaggeratedly curved lines were termed perverse and contrary. An amazing variety appear here: in the many-faceted drum, in the convex line of the dome and the concave buttresses, in the spiral surmounting the lantern.

The interior, very high and light, is a constant interplay of concave and convex surfaces, a foretaste of the Rococo style; it incorporates the bee from the Barberini coat of arms.

▷ *Exit by the side door (under the arcade on the right) into Via del Teatro Valle.*

In this street, where basket-makers still work, stands the 19C **Teatro Valle**.

▷ *Return up the street to Piazza San Eustachio.*

From the piazza, unfurls a splendid **view**★★ of the spiral dome of St Ivo's Church. On the south side stands the **Palazzo Maccarani** (1521), an austere building in the Renaissance style by Jules Romain; it incorporates one of the most popular cafés in Rome, the Caffè Sant'Eustachio.

The early-18C façade of the **church of Sant'Eustachio** is screened by a portico. The head of a deer bearing a cross between its antlers recalls the vision that St Eustace experienced in the hunting field while he was still a Roman general –that which led to his conversion.

▷ *Take Via della Dogana Vecchia to Piazza S. Luigi dei Francesi.*

San Luigi dei Francesi★★

🕐*Open 7am-12:30pm and 3:30-7pm.* 🕐*Closed Thu afternoons.* ☞*No charge.* ☎*06 68 82 71; Fax 06 68 82 72 28.*

The first stone of this building was laid in 1518 by Cardinal Giulio de' Medici, the future Pope **Clement VII**. The church was completed in 1589, partly with subsidies from Henri II, Henri III and Catherine de' Medici. It was consecrated as the national church of the French in Rome, dedicated to St Louis.

The façade was probably designed by Giacomo della Porta between 1580 and 1584. Its elegant lines accord well with Piazza di San Luigi dei Francesi. The prominent columns hint at the flamboyance of the Baroque style.

The interior, consisting of a nave, side aisles and lateral chapels, was embellished in the Baroque period and in the 18C with marble, paintings, gilding and stucco work. The church houses tombs of famous Frenchmen, the beautiful chapel of St Cecilia and the chapel of St Matthew with its magnificent frescoes by **Caravaggio**.

Frescoes by Domenichino★

In the chapel of St Cecilia (second chapel in the north aisle). The frescoes, which were executed in 1614, tell the story of St Cecilia. Domenichino, who had arrived in Rome in 1602, resisted the exuberance of the Baroque and strove after balance and clarity of texture.

Caravaggio's paintings★★★

In St Matthew's Chapel (*fifth on the south aisle*) are three works depicting the saint's life, painted between 1599 and 1600. The vault is by **Cavaliere d'Arpino**, in whose studio Caravaggio worked.

Above the altar the painting *St Matthew and the Angel* expresses the artist's delight in contradiction in the unusual posture of the old man, who has one knee balanced on a footstool and his face turned towards the angel, who is absorbed in the act of dictation.

On the left – *The Calling of St Matthew*: in a dark room five men, seated at a table, are distracted from their occupation by the entrance of Christ accompanied by St Peter. His pointing finger singles out Matthew, seated beside an old man counting out money. The light striking the wall and illuminating the faces is typical of Caravaggio and here symbolises the calling of the future disciple. The young man with a feather in his cap is a familiar figure.

On the right – The *Martyrdom of St Matthew*: in the middle lies the saint, wearing only a band of cloth around his hips, towered over by his persecutor, a soldier sent by the Ethiopian king. To the right, an altar boy runs away in terror. The most innovative element of the painting is the angel who emerges from a cloud to offer the saint the palm of martyrdom, thus immediately drawing the visitor into the action, which is both violent and dramatic in tone. To the left a face can be seen in the dark background: this is a self-portrait of the artist, who observes the scene with a contrite expression.

▶ *Take Via Salvatore; turn left into Corso del Rinascimento.*

Palazzo Madama

Open to public every first Sat of the month from 10am-6pm. It was built by the Medici in the 16C. In the days of Cardinal Giovanni de' Medici, the future Leo X, banquets and literary gatherings were held here. Later Pope **Clement VII** made it the residence of his great niece, Catherine de' Medici. When she became the queen of France, the palace passed to Alessandro de' Medici, whose wife, Madama Margherita d'Austria (1522-86), gave the palace its name. Since 1870, when Rome became the capital of Italy, the Senate has occupied the building. The Baroque façade in the Corso del Rinascimento was built c 1642.

At the southern end of the street rises the façade of *Sant'Andrea delle Valle* (&*see CAMPO DEI FIORI*).

Museum

Museo di Roma★

In Palazzo Braschi. & *Tues-Sun 9am-7pm.* *Closed Mon, 1 Jan, 1 May and Christmas.* *€6.20.* *06 67 10 83 46; www.museodiroma.comune.roma.it*

The paintings and frescoes exhibited in the Museum of Rome trace the history of the city from the Middle Ages to the present day. The colossal staircase leading to the first floor is by Cosimo Morelli, who designed the palace.

A number of anonymous paintings depict the jousts held in the 16C and 17C in the Belvedere courtyard in the Vatican, Piazza Navona and on the Testaccio. These are followed by **frescoes**★ taken from demolished buildings. The museum also houses various anonymous paintings, illustrating the bustle of the old Capitoline market in the 17C and the pageantry of the *Corpus Christi* processions in St Peter's Square, plus an attractive room with 18C Gobelins tapestries.

In the first room on the second floor hang three huge canvases on Greek mythological themes by **Gavin Hamilton**, a Scottish painter who settled in Rome in 1755 and spent most of his working life in Italy. Also on the second floor are the famous **watercolours**★ in the series "Lost Rome" (*Roma sparita*) and fragments of mosaic from the old St Peter's Basilica (late 12C-early 13C).

On the ground floor (*entrance in northeast corner of the courtyard*) is the papal train built for Pius IX in 1858. One of the coaches is fitted out as a small chapel.

PIAZZA DEL POPOLO★★

MICHELIN MAP 38 H 11-12, J 11-12
METRO LINE A: FLAMINIO OR SPAGNA

In the days of the Grand Tour, travellers approaching from the north would arrive through the Porta del Popolo. The surrounding piazza is one of the city's largest and most grandiose squares. A famous trio of streets run south from here; the quiet Via di Ripetta, popular for its boutiques; the bustling Via del Corso, the main commercial artery; and the elegant Via del Babuino, thick with antique shops.

▶ **Orient Yourself:** The area extends between the Tiber and the Pincian Hill, backed by the magnificent Villa Borghese gardens. Three main streets run south towards Augustus's Mausoleum and *Piazza di Spagna* from *Piazza del Popolo*, which is dominated by its twin churches and by the *Porta del Popolo*, a gate in the Aurelian walls.

😊 **Don't Miss:** Caravaggio's masterpiece in Santa Maria dep Popolo, a stroll through the Tridente, the view from the Pincian Hill.

Kids **Especially for Kids:** The water clock on the Pincio.

⌚ **Also See:** *PIAZZA DI SPAGNA; VILLA BORGHESE-VILLA GIULIA.*

Piazza del Popolo★★

The square was laid out by **Giuseppe Valadier** (1762-1839), the favourite architect and town planner of Pius VI and Pius VII. In an effort to open up Rome, he made *Piazza del Popolo* one of the largest squares in the city. He retained the *Porta del Popolo*, the central obelisk and the twin churches flanking *Via del Corso*, and opened out the space into two semicircles adorned with fountains and neo-classical statues. The east side of the square was linked to the Pincio Gardens by a series of monumental terraces with trees and shrubs. On 18 December 1813, the Government erected a guillotine to deter the local gangs.

Porta del Popolo★

This gateway in the 3C **Aurelian Wall** stands more or less on the site of the ancient *Porta Flaminia*. The exterior façade was built between 1562 and 1565 by Pius IV, who wanted to impress visitors arriving from the north with an entrance worthy of his splendid capital. The Medici arms are the dominant feature. On 24 May 1814, Pius VII – liberated by Napoleon – was given a delirious welcome here.

Obelisk

The pillar was brought from Heliopolis in Lower Egypt in the Augustan era and set up in the *Circus Maximus*. It was Sixtus V and his architect, **Domenico Fontana**, who raised it in the centre of *Piazza del Popolo* in 1589. The basins and marble lions at the base were added by Valadier at Leo XII's request in 1823.

Twin churches

From the obelisk, you can appreciate the impact of good town planning on the south side of the square. **Carlo Rainaldi** designed the two churches to provide a background to the obelisk and a theatrical entrance to *Via del Corso*. Their apparent similarity is false: only the drums facing the square have the same dimensions. In fact, the church on the left is eliptical beneath a 12-sided dome and the righthand one is circular with an octagonal dome and occupies a broader site. The domes were covered with slates by Leo XII in 1825. **Santa Maria di Montesanto** was the first of the twins: built from 1662-67 by Carlo Rainaldi and from 1671-75 by Bernini. **Santa Maria dei Miracoli** was begun by Rainaldi and completed (1677-79) by Carlo Fontana.

Santa Maria del Popolo★★

Despite its simple exterior, the church contains **art treasures**★ worthy of a

Address Book

WHERE TO EAT

♿ *See "Where to Eat" in the Your Stay in Rome section at the end of the guide.*

TAKING A BREAK

Rosati – *Piazza del Popolo 4. ☎06 32 25 859. Open 7:30am–midnight.* This traditional meeting place is an elegant café-restaurant right on the piazza.

SHOPPING

Piazza del Popolo is in the heart of one of Rome's busiest shopping districts.
Via del Corso is home to a huge variety of boutiques and shops; antiques enthusiasts should make for **Via del Babuino**, and art collectors for **Via Margutta**.
Fattoria la Parrina – *Largo Toniolo 3. ☎06 68 30 01 11. Open Tue-Sat 8:30am–1:30pm and 4:30-7:30pm; Mon 8:30am–1:30pm.* The Tuscan producer La Parrina has a couple of stores in Rome.

Bomba – *Via dell'Oca 39. ☎06 36 12 881. Open Tue-Sat 11am–7:30pm. Closed Mon morning.* This boutique specialises in women's clothes: simple, elegant and sought-after designs.
David Saddler – *Via del Corso 103. ☎06 80 01 59 54.* This shop has a number of outlets in the city for those who like classical styles and sells a range of English-style jackets, trousers, gloves and shirts at reasonable prices.
Il Discount dell'Alta Moda – *Via di Gesù e Maria 14/16. ☎06 36 13 796.* Menswear and women's outfits from the previous season can be purchased here at a 40% or 50% discount.

ART EXHIBITION

Via Margutta – This normally quiet street attracts crowds of visitors in June and October, when artists exhibit in the *Fiera di Via Margutta*.

---

museum. The building, which was commissioned by Sixtus IV in 1472 and finished in 1477, is one of the first examples of the Renaissance style in Rome. Its façade rises, almost devoid of ornament, to a triangular pediment. The plainness is relieved by shallow pilasters and simple scrolls linking the lower and upper stages of the façade (the elaborate curves are Baroque additions).

The **interior** abounds in Renaissance features. The Latin cross plan is used in preference to a basilical one. The nave, which has groined vaulting, is flanked by two aisles lined by side chapels. The usual columns and walls of a basilical church have been replaced by massive square pillars.

During the Baroque period, Bernini added stucco statues above the nave.

Chapels

The chapel rail in the **Cappella della Rovere** (1) shows the coat of arms of the Della Rovere family to which Pope Sixtus IV belonged. Above the altar is the **fresco**★ depicting the *Adoration of the Child* by the Umbrian painter **Pinturicchio** (1454-1513). The scene is animated with incidental detail: a grazing goat, a lamb suckling its mother and a watchful ox.

The Cappella Cybo (2) is a Baroque chapel designed by Carlo Fontana (1682-87) on a Greek cross plan beneath a dome.

On the right-hand wall of the **Cappella Basso della Rovere** (3) lies the tomb of Giovanni Basso della Rovere (15C) by a pupil of Andrea Bregno; the frescoes above the altar and on the left-hand wall are by the Pinturicchio School.

Transept

The chapels opening off the east side of the transept and the apses at either end are characteristic of the Renaissance. The Baroque style is represented by the cherubs supporting the picture frames above the transept altars.

The dome above the crossing was probably the first of its kind in Renaissance Rome: the technology had been lost since ancient times.

The chancel arch is decorated with gilded stucco low reliefs, one *(right)* showing Pope Paschal II (1099-1118) chopping down a walnut tree. According to legend, the church was built on the site of the tomb of the terrible Nero, which was marked by said tree. Demons lived within the trunk and took the form of black crows. The population, fearing Nero's ghost, appealed to Paschal II. He felled the tree,

Monumento ai fratelli Enrico e Giovanni Cairoli .... A   Orologio ad acqua ....B

threw the emperor's remains in the Tiber and erected a chapel, which under Sixtus IV became *Santa Maria del Popolo*.

Apse and Chancel

Go round behind the high altar. The apse was extended by **Bramante** for Julius II (1503-13). The ceiling fresco is by Pinturicchio. The stained glass – in predominantly neutral tones picked out with flashes of brilliant colour – is the work of Guillaume de Marcillat (16C). The two **tombs**★, carved around 1505 by **Andrea Sansovino**, are elegant.

Caravaggio's Paintings★★★

The **Cerasi Chapel (4)** houses two magnificent pictures painted in 1601, which illustrate scripture scenes. In the *Conversion of St Paul* (*right*), as in all **Caravaggio**'s works, light is the dominant feature. Here the divine rays fall first on the horse, which is out of proportion, before touching the foreshortened saint.

The *Crucifixion of St Peter* (*left*) illustrates Caravaggio's taste for creating a diago-

nal axis. The treatment avoids all reference to the sublime: three brawny men, whose faces are hidden, raise a cross bearing a man of rugged, but noble, mien. Above the altar is *The Assumption of the Virgin* by **Annibale Carracci**.

Cappella Chigi★ (5)

The design of this chapel was entrusted to **Raphael** in 1513 by his champion, Agostino Chigi, banker, patron and consort of princes and popes. The dome mosaic, from a drawing by Raphael, dates from the Renaissance, as do the figures of Jonah (after Raphael) and the Prophet Elijah, and the altarpiece, a muted Nativity by Sebastiano del Piombo.

In the Baroque period, **Bernini** faced the base of the pyramid-shaped tomb of Agostino and Sigismondo Chigi with green marble, carved the figures of Daniel, the lion, Habakkuk and the angel, and inserted in the floor a winged skeleton with the Chigi coat of arms.

Il Tridente
(The Trident)

To Romans this name indicated the three streets that diverge from *Piazza del Popolo* like three prongs: *Via di Ripetta, Via del Corso* and *Via del Babuino*.

Via di Ripetta

This street follows the course of an ancient Roman one beside the Tiber. Originally called *Via Leonina*, it was remodelled in 1515 by Leo X and perhaps financed by a brothel tax. *Via di Ripetta* contains a multitude of shops and boutiques.

Via del Corso

Following the route of the ancient *Via Flaminia*, the modern street runs in a straight line (1 500m/1 640yd) from *Piazza del Popolo* to *Piazza Venezia*. Its medieval name was *Via Lata,* but now it is called after the famous horse races organised by Pope Paul II in the 15C. Handsome Renaissance palaces line this frantic thoroughfare. Nowadays "the Corso" is Rome's main shopping street.

This area is where people from overseas traditionally gathered. Indeed, before the railways extended to Rome, most travellers arrived southwards down the *Via Cassia*, crossing the Tiber over the *Ponte Molle* (now called the *Ponte Milvio*) to enter through the *Porta del Popolo*.

Via del Babuino

The street was opened by Clement VII for Jubilee Year in 1525. Its present name came from popular usage; the statue of a silenus was discovered in such a hideous state that the Romans compared it to a baboon. The statue is now next to the fountain by St Athanasius' Church (*San Atanasio*) (*opposite no 65*). Today the street is known for its antique shops, often in the 17C and 18C *palazzi*.

Chiesa Anglicana (All Saints Anglican Church) – Now a protected building, it was designed by **GE Street** in the early 1880s, shortly before his death. He built in the English Gothic style of specially made bricks, with a distinctive white travertine spire erected in 1937. The spacious interior is enriched by a variety of coloured marble from different parts of Italy: white and green Carrara, red Perugia, black Verona, yellow Siena and white Como. The pulpit designed in 1891 by AE Street, the architect's son, is reminiscent of the early Christian basilicas. Above

At the Heart of the Festivities

Throughout the years, fashionable Romans have always made an appearance on the *Corso*. In the 18C, it was good form for a lady to be seen there with her *sigisbeo*, a faithful admirer. Even the Church tolerated this custom, and clauses permitting a wife to have one or more admirers were included in marriage contracts. During the **Carnival** in February, masquerades proceeded along the *Corso*. The horse race was the high point of the celebrations. Each evening in the week before Ash Wednesday, grooms led the horses round the course. On the last, the *moccoli* (wax tapers) appeared; everyone carried a lighted candle and tried to put out their neighbours' flames. Only in 1809 did the Romans boycott the Carnival to protest the French Government. Pasquino – the famous talking statue that presides over his own square (*see PIAZZA NAVONA*) – mocked: "The bear may dance under the rod, but not men".

the high altar hang seven lamps bought in Venice by a former Honourable Assistant Chaplain from money given him by the congregation "to be spent on himself". The stained glass, depicting various saints and commemorating people connected with the church, is English. So too is the organ, a large and complex instrument, originally made in Huddersfield and in demand by famous musicians for recitals and master classes.

Via Margutta

This street in the artistic heart of Rome is named after a famous little 15C theatre. Here parodies of chivalrous epic poems – such as Luigi Pulci's comedy *Morgante* with its two heroes, Morgante and Margutta – were performed.

The houses, often decorated with balconies and courtyard gardens, often contain groundfloor art galleries.

Via Margutta leads into **Vicolo d'Alibert**, which in the 18C contained the *Teatro delle Dame*, where women first sang on stage in the Papal States. Formerly *castrati* played female roles in opera.

Il Pincio (Pincian Hill)

Take the flight of steps leading to Piazzale Napoleone I, on the Pincian Hill.

The Pinci family, who had a garden here in the 4C, have left their name to this little hill, which is still covered by a garden, one of the pleasantest in Rome. The Pincio was laid out in its present style during the Napoleonic occupation (1809-14), according to designs by **Giuseppe Valadier**. Magnificent umbrella pines, palm trees and evergreen oaks shade the avenues. Giuseppe Mazzini (1805-72) added the statues of patriots.

From the terrace of Piazzale Napoleone I, there is a magnificent **view★★★**, particularly at dusk. Below the terrace is *Piazza del Popolo* with the domes of the twin churches marking the beginning of the *Corso*. Opposite are the buildings of the Vatican grouped round the dome of St Peter's next to the slopes of the Janiculum; in front stand Castel Sant'Angelo and the white bulk of the Law Courts. **Kids** The water clock in *Viale dell'Orologio* was built in 1867 by a Dominican monk,

Giovan Battista Embriago and presented to the Universal Exhibition in Paris (1889). Halfway along *Viale dell'Obelisco*, which leads to the gardens of the *Villa Borghese*, stands an obelisk. Pius VII set it here in 1822. Found near the *Porta Maggiore* in the 16C, it was originally erected by the Emperor Hadrian in memory of his young friend Antinoüs.

The **Cairoli Monument** commemorates two brothers, Enrico and Giovanni, Italian patriots who fought beside Garibaldi and died in 1867 in the bloody struggles for Italian unity. From here stretches an extensive view of the city of Rome.

Museum

Museo di Hendrik Christian Andersen★

Via Mancini 20. ♿ 🕐*Open daily (except Mon) 9am–8pm (last admission 7.20pm).* 🕐*Closed Mon, 1 Jan and Christmas.* ☎*06 32 19 089.*

Villa Helene was built by the Norwegian sculptor and painter Hendrik Christian Andersen at the beginning of the 20C as his residence and art studio. Now a museum, it houses around 700 works, including sculptures, paintings and graphic art. Most were produced for his World City futurist project, in which art, philosophy and science all played a major role. Note the finely decorated ceilings in the magnificent first-floor apartments, now used for temporary exhibitions.

The unusual water clock on the Pincian Hill

PIAZZA DI SPAGNA★★★

MICHELIN MAP 38 J 11-12, K 11-12
METRO LINE A: SPAGNA

This district was once popular with artists and writers such as Goethe, Keats, De Chirico and Stendhal, and later became a favourite meeting place for actors and film stars. Now it's one of the main tourist sights; crowds mill around Piazza di Spagna day and night, stopping to sit and chat on the famous Spanish Steps, or wandering the narrow streets off the square. Despite the invasion of fast-food outlets in the area, these elegant alleys are still home to some of the most prestigious names in the worlds of fashion, jewellery and design.

▶ **Orient Yourself:** The walk illustrated in this section covers the district south of the *Piazza del Popolo*, between *Villa Borghese* and the Tiber. The area falls within the *"Tridente"*, the three streets leading south from *Piazza del Popolo: Via del Babuino*, which emerges into *Piazza di Spagna; Via del Corso*, which cuts the district in two; and *Via di Ripetta*, near the River Tiber.

📷 **Don't Miss:** The stairs of *Trinità dei Monti* at night, a treat at *Caffè Greco*, the controversial shelter for the Ara Pacis, window shopping in *Via del Condotti*.

👣 **Also See:** *FONTANA DI TREVI-QUIRINALE; MONTECITORIO; PIAZZA DEL POPOLO; VILLA BORGHESE-VILLA GIULIA.*

Piazza Di Spagna★★★
(Spanish Square)

The square is famous throughout the world and the steps are a favourite meeting place, as well as a popular backdrop for fashion shoots and publicity events.

Shaped like a bow tie, the *piazza* got its name in the 17C when the Spanish ambassador to the Holy See took up residence in the **Palazzo di Spagna**. After that, the area bounded by *Via dei Condotti, Via del Corso* and *Via della Mercede* became Spanish territory and any non-national crossing the boundaries at night might be gang-pressed into the Spanish army. The French, however – who owned the land around the convent of the *Trinità dei Monti* – claimed the right to pass through. They named part of it "French Square" and set out to rival the Spanish by giving ever more sumptuous entertainments. In 1681, the Spanish celebrated the birthday of their queen, Marie-Louise, by transforming the square with a variety of paste-board decorations. In 1685, the French celebrated the Revocation of the Edict of Nantes; they covered the whole hillside with candelabra and decorated the church to look like a wayside altar; from here they set off fireworks that lit up the

whole town. In the 18C, it became very popular among the English on the Grand Tour. In 1820 Henry Matthews set down his first impressions in his diary:

"We were soon in the Piazza di Spagna, the focus of fashion and the general resort of the English... little more than an irregular open space, a little less nasty than the other piazzas in Rome because the habits of the people are in some measure restrained by the presence of the English..."

▶ *The Keats-Shelley Museum and the Casa-Museo di De Chirico are here/*

Fontana della Barcaccia★ (Boat Fountain)
At the foot of the steps. It was designed by Bernini's father, Pietro (1627-29) for Pope Urban VIII. The boat, which is decorated at either end with the suns and bees of the Barberini coat of arms, seems to be letting in water. The sculptor allegedly was inspired by a boat stranded in *Piazza di Spagna* by flood waters.

Scalinata della Trinità dei Monti★★★ (Spanish Steps)
Built between 1723 and 1726, the steps show the Baroque taste for perspective and *trompe-l'œil*. At certain times of the

Address Book

WHERE TO EAT

See "Where to Eat" in the Your Stay in Rome section at the end of the guide.

TAKING A BREAK

Caffè Greco – *Via dei Condotti 86* ☎*06 67 91 700. Open 9:30am–9pm.* One of the oldest literary cafés in Rome. Casanova once flirted here. Other famous patrons include Goethe, Wagner, Baudelaire, Shelley, Byron Buffalo Bill, Leopardi, D'Annunzio, Andersen (who lived in the same building) and Stendhal, whose last Roman residence was at no 48. Italians plotted to overthrow the French Occupation of 1849-70, in this building.

Ciampini – *Viale della Trinità dei Monti 1.* ☎*06 67 85 678. Open 8am–8pm.* Although this café is not as elegant as the one of the same name in *Piazza San Lorenzo* (Lucina 29), it has an unforgettable view of Rome. Outside tables only.

Babington's – *Piazza di Spagna 23.* ☎*06 67 86 027. http://babingtons.com. Open Wed-Mon 9am-8:15pm. Closed Tues.* Opened in 1893, these old tearooms are decorated in typically English style; the waitresses even wear a uniform. A good address for tea and cakes, scones, muffins and apple pie.

SHOPPING

De Clercq & De Clercq – *Via delle Carrozze 50.* ☎*06 67 90 988. Open Tue-Sat 10am–7pm; Mon 2–7pm.* All the exquisite jumpers (sweaters) and tops here are made from natural fibres, including cashmere and silk.

Fratelli Alinari – *Via Alibert 16/a.* ☎*06 67 92 923. www.alinari.com.* An excellent introduction to the work of these great photographers, depicting views and landscapes of ancient Rome.

Hausmann & C. – *Via del Corso 406.* ☎*06 68 71 501. www.hausmann-co.com. Open Tue-Fri 9:30am-1pm and 3:30-7:30pm; Mon 3:30-7:30pm; Sat 9:30am-1:30pm.* This shop was founded in 1794 and continues to mend and sell magnificent old clocks amid red velvet decor.

Myricae – *Via Frattina 36.* This shop specialises in hand-painted ceramics, especially from Puglia, Tuscany and Great Britain.

Sergio di Cori – *Piazza di Spagna 53.* ☎*06 67 84 439. www.dicorigloves.it.* This tiny, long-established shop has a wide selection of gloves.

Siragusa – *Via delle Carrozze 64.* ☎*06 67 97 085. Open Mon-Fri 10am-noon and 1:30-7:30pm.* Inspired by the jewels of antiquity, the works of art here are inspired by archaeological finds.

The Lion Bookshop – *Via dei Greci 33/36.* ☎*06 32 65 04 37. Open Tue-Sun 10am-7:30pm; Mon 3:30-7:30pm. www.thelionbookshop.com.* As well as a wide selection of books in English, this bookshop also has a small café.

year, they are smothered in flowers – azaleas in April – as well as idlers.

The idea of a stair linking *Piazza di Spagna* with the church of the *Trinità dei Monti* began in the 17C. Cardinal Mazarin proposed to make the steps a symbol of the greatness of the French monarchy in Rome. A grandiose design was prepared, dominated by an equestrian statue of Louis XIV. The idea of a king's statue in the papal city! Alexander VII objected. Neither the cardinal's death in 1661 nor the Pope's in 1669 ended the quarrel. It was not finally settled until Innocent XIII (1721-24) agreed to the French architect and the French abandoned the statue of Louis XIV. De Sanctis, in accordance with designs by De Specchi (a pupil of Carlo Fontana), built three successive flights of steps, some broader, some narrower, some divided, exaggerating the effect of height and creating a graceful and majestic effect. From the upper terrace is an excellent view of the city. In front of the church of the *Trinità dei Monti* stands an imitation Egyptian obelisk transported from the Gardens of Sallust (*Giardini di Sallusto*).

Trinità dei Monti★

The church of Holy Trinity on the Hill was founded in 1495 by Charles VIII. It was severely damaged by French revolutionaries and completely rebuilt in 1816. Now French property, the convent is occupied by the Ladies of the Sacred Heart.

Fontana della Barcaccia and the Spanish Steps

An elegant stairway, built in 1587 by Domenico Fontana, leads up to the **façade,** surmounted by two belfries, erected in 1588 and modelled on those designed by Giacomo della Porta for St Athanasius in *Via del Babuino*.

Interior

The single nave flanked by intercommunicating chapels is reminiscent of the Gothic churches in the south of France. The side chapels are decorated with Mannerist paintings. The third on the right contains a fresco of the *Assumption* by Daniele da Volterra. The figure in red on the right of the picture is a portrait of Michelangelo, which was much admired by the artist. The much-restored **Deposition from the Cross**★ (1541) in the second chapel on the left is a masterpiece by **Daniele da Volterra**. See how skilfully he has arranged his composition around the pale body of Jesus.

Walking Tour

▶ *From the Spanish Steps, turn left into Viale della Trinità dei Monti.*

On the right is a **bust of Chateaubriand**, better known as a writer: the French ambassador from 1828 to 1829.

Villa Medici

The Villa Medici now houses the French Academy (Accademia di Francia) and is *used for temporary exhibitions. At the moment, it's closed for restoration.* ☎06 67 611, *www.villamedici.it.* The villa was built c 1570 for Cardinal Ricci di Montepulciano and passed to Cardinal Ferdinando de' Medici in 1576. In the 1C BC, the site was covered by the Gardens of Lucullus (*Giardini di Lucullo*). There is a fine view of Rome from the terrace opposite the entrance.

The famous fountain, installed in 1587 by Cardinal Ferdinando de' Medici, is the subject of several 19C paintings and engravings, including *The Fountain at the Villa Medici* by Corot. Legend has it that the basin's cannonball was fired at the Villa from *Castel Sant'Angelo* by Queen Christina of Sweden, who adored practical jokes. She wanted to wake up the master of the house to join a hunting party. The main façade contrasts sharply with the richly decorated **inner façade**★; the latter faces the luxuriant gardens and was decorated by Bartolomeo Ammannati in the late-16C with statues, reliefs, and garlands from the Ara Pacis.

▶ *Return to Trinità dei Monti and continue along Via Gregoriana.*

In the 17C and 18C, **Via Gregoriana** provided lodgings for the wealthier visitors to Rome. N° 30, the **Casa dei Mostri**, built by Federico Zuccari, has a door and windows framed by carved monsters with gaping mouths.

▶ *Continue on Via Gregoriana; left at the end on Via Crispi. Take Via Capo le Case and cross Via Due Macelli.*

Palazzo di Propaganda Fide
This imposing building, the property of the Holy See, houses the Congregation for the Evangelisation of Peoples. **Urban VIII** (1623-44) began construction by inviting his protégé, **Bernini**, to design the façade overlooking *Piazza di Spagna*. The result is unexpectedly sober for this brilliant Baroque architect. On Innocent X's accession, Bernini fell into disgrace. The new pope wished to give his reign a new look and he turned to **Borromini** for the façade overlooking *Via di Propaganda*. A touch of fantasy was introduced, in the cornices and in the elaborate pediments over the windows.
Within the *palazzo* (on the left of the door in *Via di Propaganda* 1/c) is another building (1666) by Borromini, the tiny **Church of the Re Magi** (Three Wise Men). ◷*Open by appointment only. Contact the Congregazione di Propaganda Fide, Via Propaganda 1/C, 00187 ROMA or Fax 06 69 88 02 46, at least one week in advance.*

Sant'Andrea delle Fratte
St Andrew's Church, which originated in the 12C, stands in *Via di Capo Le Case* (end of the houses), which in the Middle Ages was the northeastern limit of the city. Its name recalls the thickets (*fratte*) that once abounded here. Early in the 17C, the rebuilding of the church was begun; the work was completed by **Borromini.** Higher up the street is a view of the **campanile**★ and the **dome**★, which he treated as precious objects. The dome, which would normally soar into the sky, is imprisoned in a space circumscribed by convex and concave surfaces.
Inside, at the entrance to the chancel, are two statues of **angels**★ presenting the Instruments of the Passion. When **Bernini** sculpted them in 1669, his art was very close to the extreme delicacy characteristic of the Rococo period.

▶ *Take Via della Mercede.*

Piazza San Silvestro is dominated by the façade of the Central Post Office, which was established in the 19C in the monastery of the church of *San Silvestro in Capite*. Every bus route and taxi fare seems to end in this square. Its church and post office, café and newspaper stall make this a good people-watching spot.

▶ *Turn right into Via del Gambero and left into Via Frattina to reach Piazza S. Lorenzo in Lucina.*

San Lorenzo in Lucina
The **church of St Lawrence** was built in the 12C on the site of a 4C *titulus*, the house of a woman called Lucina. The bell-tower, the porch and the two lions flanking the door date from the medieval period. The fourth chapel on the right contains a bust of Dr Gabriele Fonseca by **Bernini**, a late and rather theatrical work (1668).

▶ *Take Via del Leone, which leads into Largo Fontanella Borghese.*

From the piazza, there is an interesting view of the church of *Trinità dei Monti*.

Palazzo Borghese (Borghese Palace)
This late-16C palace overlooks the *Piazza Borghese* and demonstrates the dignity and austerity of the Counter-Reformation. The palace was acquired by Cardinal Camillo Borghese, who became Pope Paul V in 1605. The courtyard (*entrance in Largo della Fontanella di Borghese*) – with its loggias, statues, fountains and rockeries – is a beautiful evocation of the luxurious life of the noble families.

▶ *Take Via di Ripetta north as far as Piazza Augusto Imperatore.*

Botticella Fountain
It was built in 1774 at the expense of the Ripetta watermen's association. There is a fine view of the apse and dome of San Carlo al Corso.

Mausoleo di Augusto
The ruins of the **Mausoleum of Augustus** are now surrounded by the modern buildings of *Piazza Augusto Imperatore*, which was laid out in 1940.
This mausoleum was one of the most sacred monuments in antiquity. Built

between 28–23 BC, it has a cylindrical base surmounted by a conical hillock of earth (*tumulus*) planted with cypress trees. A bronze statue of the emperor stood in the middle of the monument, at its highest point. On the south side, flanking the entrance, stood two obelisks, Roman imitations of Egyptian models, which now stand in *Piazza dell' Esquilino* and *Piazza del Quirinale*.

In the Middle Ages, the mausoleum was converted into a fortress by the Colonna family; Gregory IX (1227-41) dismantled it and stripped it of its blocks of travertine. In 1936, its concert hall was closed and the remains were restored.

▶ *The Ara Pacis is housed in a modern building between the Mausoleum of Augustus and Lungotevere in Augusta. Follow Via dell'Ara Pacis and Via dei Pontefici; right on Via del Corso.*

San Carlo al Corso

In 1471, the Lombard community in Rome was given a small church in the *Corso* by Sixtus IV. They rebuilt it and dedicated it

to **St Ambrose**. In 1612, they enlarged the building in honour of Charles Borromeo, Archbishop of Milan, who had just been canonised. The full name of the church is therefore *Sant'Ambrogio e San Carlo al Corso*. The majestic interior is in the shape of a Latin cross with an ambulatory, a rarity in Rome, more usually found in northern churches. The heart of St Charles Borromeo now rests in the chapel behind the high altar. The **dome**★ is the work of **Pietro da Cortona** (1668). The *Apotheosis of St Ambrose and St Charles* on the high altar is one of the best works of Carlo Maratta (1685-90), restored in the 19C.

Palazzo Ruspoli

This 16C palace is now a bank. After the downfall of Napoleon in 1825, it became the refuge of Hortense de Beauharnais, ex-Queen of Holland, under the name of the Duchess of St Leu. Her salon became the centre of attraction for every pleasure-loving member of society. Her son, Prince Charles Louis Napoleon, the future Napoleon III, brought this sumptuous

Busto di Châteaubriand	A
Chiosco	B
Fontana della Botticella	C

life to an end. He was implicated in a scheme to declare a republic in Rome and, with his mother, was expelled. Throughout the year temporary exhibitions are held in the *palazzo* (*Via del Corso* 418/A).

▶ *Go back to Via dei Condotti.*

Via dei Condotti

The street is named after the conduits (*condotti*) that brought water to Agrippa's Baths (*Terme di Agrippa*) in 19 BC. *Via dei Condotti* is one of the most famous streets in Rome and is lined with smart boutiques and elegant *palazzi* housing some of the most prestigious names in fashion. The famous **Caffé Greco** can be seen at no 86 (👝 *see Address Book*).

Sights

Ara Pacis Augustae★★ (Altar of Augustus)

Lungotevere in Augusta. ◷*Tues-Sun 9am-7pm.* ◷*Closed Mon, 1 Jan, 1 May and 25 Dec.* ◲◲€6.50. ☎ 06 82 05 91 27. www.arapacis.it.
The monumental altar was inaugurated in 9 BC in honour of the peace that Augustus established throughout the Roman world and in the capital, where he ended 20 years of civil war. The *Ara Pacis* originally stood in the *Campus Martius*, beside the *Via Flaminia* (now *Via del Corso*), where the *Palazzo Fiano* stands today. The altar was the major work of the Augustan "golden age" and marks the apogee of Roman art.

Casa-Museo di Giorgio de Chirico★

Piazza di Spagna 31. ◷*Tues-Sat 10am-1pm. By appointment only.* ◷*Closed Sun-Mon.* ◲€5. ☎06 67 96 546; www.fondazionedechirico.it.
The house in which this artist lived from 1947 to 1978 (the year he died) occupies the top three floors of a 16C *palazzo*. The visit starts in a small entrance hall, which houses two oval works, inspired by the great masters, and the *Thinker*. A collection of self-portraits – depicting the artist in a range of costumes, but always

with the same expression – is exhibited in the drawing room, which overlooks *Piazza di Spagna*. This room also contains portaits of the artist's wife and a few pieces of sculpture. De Chirico's armchair can be seen in his favourite corner, where he used to watch the television with the sound turned down. The dining room is decorated with a number of still-life paintings. The second drawing room, added around 1970, is very different from the rest of the house, both in its furnishings and in the works on display here. These are known as the "neo-metaphysical works", produced towards the end of the artist's life, and include *Piazza d'Italia* and *Hector and Andromache★*.
De Chirico's tiny bedroom and his wife's room can be visited on the top floor. The artist's studio, lit by a skylight, houses the paintings he was working on at the time of his death.

Casina di Keats (Keats' House)

Piazza di Spagna 26. ◷*Open Mon-Fri 9am-1pm and 3-6pm; Sat 11am-1pm and 3-6pm.* ◷*Closed Sun, Christmas.* ◲€3.50. ☎06 67 84 235; www.keats-shelley-house. org
The "Young English Poet" passed away here of tuberculosis on 23 February 1821. The painter Joseph Severn nursed him to the end. The author of the romantic *Odes* and *Endymion* requested his tomb bear no name, only by the bitter epitaph: "here lies one whose name was writ on water." He died believing he'd failed his talent's early promise.
Shelley wrote *Adonais* about this tragic fate. On 8 July, 1822, he drowned off Livorno. His goldbricking friend Edward Trelawney snatched the author's heart from the beachside pyre. It's also buried in the Protestant Cemetery, not far from Keats (👝 *See Piramide Cestia-Testaccio*).
The poet's' rooms on the first floor contain a collection of manuscripts, letters, mementoes and documents on the lives not only of Keats but also of Shelley, **Byron** and Leigh Hunt, together with a library of 10 000 volumes. In the entrance hall on the ground floor hang portraits of Keats and his contemporaries by English artists of the period.

PIAZZA VENEZIA★

MICHELIN MAP 38 L11-12, M12

Piazza Venezia was transformed at the end of the 19C and is dominated by the overwhelming and controversial monument to Victor Emmanuel II, which obscures the view of Capitol Hill from Via del Corso. Not far from the piazza, close to one of the centres of political power in the city, stands the magnificent Baroque Chiesa del Gesù. Because of its position and its imposing 19C monuments to the glory of Victor Emmanuel, Piazza Venezia is a convenient meeting point for those new to the city. Today, Rome's principal thoroughfares all converge on the square, resulting in all-too-frequent gridlock.

Also See: *CAMPIDOGLIO-CAPITOLINO; FONTANA DI TREVI-QUIRINALE*

Walking Tour

Piazza Venezia★

Formerly the square was much more compact. The south side – going towards the Victor Emmanuel II monument (*Monumento a Vittorio Emanuele II*, below) – was closed by the smaller *Palazzetto Venezia*, a building in harmony with the tower of the more famous *Palazzo Venezia*. In 1911, however, the *palazzetto* was "moved" to its present position at the far end of *Piazza San Marco*. Although this change allows a better view of the monument, it has undoubtedly spoiled the balance of a Renaissance square.

Behind the *Palazzo Venezia* stands the beautiful *Gesù Church*, the main Jesuit church in Rome.

Monumento a Vittorio Emanuele II (Vittoriano)

⏱*Open 9:30am–6pm (winter 9:30am–4:30pm).* ⏱*Closed Christmas, I Jan.* ☎*06 69 91 718. www.ambienterm.arti.beniculturali.it/vittoriano/*

This huge monument by **Giuseppe Sacconi** was begun in 1885 and inaugurated in 1911. It honours **King Victor Emmanuel II**, who achieved the unification of Italy in 1870 with Rome as the capital city. The dazzling white marble clashes with the warm tones of the cityscape and the grandiloquent style strikes a jarring note. The monument has many insulting nicknames, including "wedding cake" and "typewriter".

A very broad flight of steps, flanked by two allegorical groups in bronze gilt representing *Thought* and *Action*, leads up to the *Altar to the Nation*. An eternal

Victor Emmanuel II monument

J. Malburet/MICHELIN

flame burns before the tomb of the unknown soldier, guarded by stone-faced *carabinieri*. Legend claims the vast equestrian status once hosted dinner parties in its belly. Local wags insist the top of the monument provides the finest **view**★★ of the city – namely the only one sans the *Vittoriano*...

Palazzo Venezia★

With this building, which extends from Piazza Venezia to Via del Plebiscito and Via degli Astalli, the Renaissance made a timid debut into civil architecture.

Construction of the palace was begun in 1455 by Pietro Barbo, who required a palace worthy of his rank as cardinal; when he became Pope in 1464 as **Paul II** he continued his project on a larger scale. In 1471, the Pope died before his house was finished, and the palace was completed by his nephew. It was later altered several times: under Sixtus IV (1471-84) a smaller palace (palazzetto) was added opening onto a garden surrounded by a portico.

It was Pius IV, in 1564, who gave the palace its present name, when he allowed the ambassadors of the Republic of Venice to lodge in part of the building. Following the Treaty of Campoformio between Austria and Napoleon in 1797, the Republic of Venice ceased to exist and almost all its property (including Palazzo Venezia) reverted to Austria.

By order of Napoleon in 1806 the palace became the seat of the French administration, and was again at the forefront of Roman history in 1910 when the Italian Government decided to lay out a huge square in front of the monument to King Victor Emmanuel II; the *palazzetto* which stood at the foot of the tower in the southeast angle was pulled down and put up again where it stands today on the corner of Piazza di San Marco and Via degli Astalli. At the same time the **Palazzo delle Assicurazioni Generali di Venezia** was built on the other side of the square, in imitation of Palazzo Venezia.

During the Fascist era, Mussolini set up the Grand Council of Fascism and his office in the palace; he used to address the crowds gathered in the piazza from the palace balcony. Now Palazzo Vene-

CAMPIDOGLIO-CAPITOLINO

Altare della Patria ....A	Statua equestre di Vittorio Emanuele II ....B	
Statua di Madama Lucrezia C		

zia is one of the most prestigious buildings in the capital, housing a museum and the library of the Institute of Art and Archaeology.

Exterior – The crenellations on the façade overlooking Piazza Venezia and the huge tower in the southeast corner show how the severe style of the fortified houses of the Middle Ages persisted. The mullion windows, the doors onto the square and in Via del Plebiscito and above all the attractive façade of St Mark's Basilica are pleasing manifestations of the Renaissance.

Statue of Madama Lucrezia – The statue stands in Piazza di San Marco in the angle where Palazzo Venezia and the *palazzetto* join and may have belonged to the Temple of Isis, which stood on the Campus Martius.

It was one of the four "talking statues" of Rome, the others being Pasquino, Marforio and the Abate Luigi – Madama Lucrezia's favourite.

Interior – *Access from Piazza di San Marco; entrance beside the statue of Madama Lucrezia.*

The unsophisticated outward appearance of Roman Renaissance palaces gives no hint of the elegant decor often to be found within.

The **courtyard** has a flourishing garden, partially flanked on two sides by an elegant but incomplete portico by Giuliano da Maiano (1432-90). The east side is formed by St Mark's Basilica, which stands within the palace, beneath its medieval belfry. The attractive fountain dates from the 18C: Venice, the lion of St Mark at its feet, is throwing a ring into the sea, a symbol of the marriage between the Serenissima and the sea.

The Museo di Palazzo Venezia is housed on the first floor of the palace (*see below*).

Basilica di San Marco
(St Mark's Basilica)

Founded in 336 and dedicated to St Mark the Evangelist, this basilica was rebuilt by Gregory IV in the 9C. Excavations beneath have uncovered traces of an earlier building and of the 9C crypt where Gregory IV had the relics of Abdon and Sennen, Persian martyrs, deposited. In the 12C, a belfry was added and in 1455 the church was rebuilt and incorporated into the *Palazzo Venezia* by Cardinal Pietro Barbo. In the 17C and 18C, further restoration and alterations took place. The **façade**★ overlooking *Piazza San Marco* is attributed to Giuliano da Maiano or Leon-Battista Alberti: the double row of arches, in which the upper ones are carried on slimmer supports, lends elegance to this charming Renaissance composition. The sumptuous **interior**★ is a typical Roman example of the overlapping of styles down the centuries. The medieval basilica plan of a nave and two aisles remains. In the 15C, the elegant coffered ceiling was added with the arms of Paul II, and clerestories were inserted in the nave above the alternate panels of stucco and 18C paintings.

▶ *Head to the beginning of Via del Corso.*

Palazzo Bonaparte

This 17C *palazzo* of modest appearance was once the property of Napoleon's mother, who lived here from the fall of the empire until her death in 1836. She supposedly spent much of her time sitting in the first-floor loggia, watching the busy street from behind shutters.

▶ *Via del Plebiscito to Piazza del Gesù.*

Chiesa Del Gesù★★★
(Gesù Church)

◷*Open 7am–12:30pm and 4-7pm. Donation welcome. ☎06 69 70 02 32.*

The *Chiesa del Gesù* is the main **Jesuit** church in Rome and stands in *Piazza del Gesù*, once home to the Christian Democrat Party and now the headquarters of the *Partito Popolare*. The Society of Jesus was founded in 1540 by Ignatius of Loyola (1491-1556), a Spaniard. After the Council of Trent, the society became the prime mover in the Counter-Reformation, which sought to rebut the ideas put forward by **Martin Luther** and Calvin. In 1568, the decision was taken to build a church in the centre of Rome. Cardinal Alexander Farnese undertook to provide the funds and insisted on his choice of architect: **Vignola**.

The design chosen for the façade in 1575 was by **Giacomo della Porta**. Very solemn and severe, it became a model for a transitional style, halfway between Renaissance and Baroque art, known as the "Jesuit style", often copied by Italian and foreign architects.

In the interior, a distinction must be made between the architecture, a fairly plain product of the Counter-Reformation, and the ornate decoration, added a century later in the Baroque period.

The majestic Latin cross **plan** was ideal for the Society's main purpose, preaching. In the single broad nave, unobstructed and well lit, the worshippers could concentrate on the celebrant and read the prayers with him. Special attention was paid to the acoustics to give resonance to the canticles.

The **decoration** was intended to celebrate the victory of the Roman Catholic Church and reinforce the conclusions of the Council of Trent. For example, the third chapel on the right shows angels and the Virgin interceding for the souls in Purgatory, illustrates ideas which were contested by the Reformers.

Baciccia Frescoes★★

In 1672, through the good offices of Bernini, Giovanni Battista Gaulli, called "Il Baciccia", was commissioned to fresco the Gesù Church. *The Triumph of the Name of Jesus*, which he painted on the nave ceiling, was certainly his masterpiece. The work, which was completed in 1679, combines the technique of composition with the exuberance of *trompe l'œil*; the eye moves without check from the painted surface to the sculptures by Antonio Raggi. He also painted the *Adoration of the Lamb* in the apse and the *Assumption* on the dome.

Chapel of Sant'Ignazio di Loyola★★★

This chapel (*left of the transept*), where the remains of St Ignatius rest in a beautiful urn, was built by **Andrea Pozzo**, a Jesuit, between 1696 and 1700. Behind a bronze rail embellished with cherubs stands the altar, bearing a statue of the saint in marble and silver. The original, the work of Pierre Legros, a Frenchman, was of solid silver, but was melted down

by Pius VI for taxes imposed by Napoleon under the Treaty of Tolentino.

On the sides of the altar, two groups of allegorical statues illustrate the work carried on by the Jesuits. On the left *Faith Triumphing over Idolatry* by Giovanni Théodon and on the right *Religion Vanquishing Heresy* by Pierre Legros, a pupil of Pozzo.

In the building to the right of the church are the rooms where St Ignatius lived and died (*access Piazza del Gesù 45*). The ceiling and walls of the flanking passage are decorated all over in Pozzo's *trompe l'œil* frescoes (17C). ⏰*Open Mon-Sat, 4-6pm; Sun and public holidays, 10am-noon.* 🚶*Guided tours available (30min).* ☎*06 69 20 58 00.*

Museo di Palazzo Venezia

(Palazzo Venezia Museum)

On the first floor of Palazzo Venezia. (♿) ⏰ *Open Tues–Sun 8:30am–7:30pm.* ⏰*Closed Mon, 1 Jan, 1 May and Christmas.* 💶*€4.* ☎*06 69 99 43 18; www.ticketeria. it/palazzovenezia-ita.asp.*

The first few rooms, devoted to medieval art, contain some particularly interesting antique ceramics, which include several 14C pieces from Orvieto. In the subsequent rooms, note the fine Byzantine enamel **Christ Pantocrator★★** from the second half of the 13C, a very finely carved ivory **Byzantine Triptych★★** from the 10C and a small bronze head sculpted by Nicola Pisano in 1248.

The museum also contains paintings on wood by primitive artists from Florence and Siena belonging to the **Sterbini Collection★★**, as well as the 14C "Orsini" cross, made of embossed silver. In the last room, note the painted ceiling taken from Palazzo Altoviti (1533) with its central figure, Ceres, framed by medallions of the agricultural labours of the year.

Paul II's suite of rooms (*overlooking Piazza Venezia and Via del Plebiscito*) comprises the Royal Room, where ambassadors waited to be received by the pope; the Battle Room (from the battles of the First World War); and the Map Room (thanks to a 15C map).

PIRAMIDE CESTIA-TESTACCIO★

MICHELIN MAP 38 R 11-12, S 11-12
METRO LINE B: PIRAMIDE
CENTRALE MONTEMARTINI – 800M/880YD FROM STATION

Ancient Rome's wharf zone contains a hill made of discarded amphorae: it was cheaper to smash the terracotta than ship back empties. Later a slaughterhouse zone, it's now the heartland of the blue-collar-heroes of AS Roma, the football (soccer) club. Clubs, bars and avant garde associations now dot this traditional neighbourhood. Centrale Montemartini, a rare example of industrial architecture, showcases collections from the Capitoline Museums. Perhaps the most moving sight is the Protestant Cemetery, where Keats and Shelley both rest, overlooked by the pyramid of Caius Cestius, a quirky 1C tomb. Celebrate the area's roots with meat dishes like "la coda alla vaccinara" at Checchino dal 1887.

▶ **Orient Yourself:** The Testaccio district lies between the Tiber and *Piazzale di Porta S. Paolo*, the latter a busy intersection of major roads such as *Viale della Piramide Cestia* from the Aventine Hill to the north and *Via Ostiense* to the south. The *Centrale Montemartini* stands on *Via Ostiense* opposite the General Market.

◉ **Don't Miss:** The Protestant Cemetery, resting place of Keats and Shelley; Centrale Montemartini, a power station turned museum of classical art; Mount Testaccio, the potshard hill; the famous Volpetti deli.

◷ **Organizing Your Time:** Allow 2 hrs.

◔ **Also See:** *AVENTINO; SAN PAOLO FUORI LE MURA*.

Walking Tour

Piramide di Caio Cestio★
(Mausoleum of Caius Cestius)

Caius Cestius, praetor and tribune of the people, (d 12 BC), devised Rome's most original mausoleum. The marble pyramid testifies to the grandeur of the Augustan era, when a citizen could erect a tomb worthy of a Pharaoh.

Porta San Paolo★
(St Paul's Gate)

Once part of the 3C **Aurelian Wall** (*Mura Aureliane*), this gate was originally called the *Porta Ostiensis*; it opened into *Via Ostiense*, which led to St Paul's Basilica – hence the medieval name, which stuck. In Aurelian's day, the gate consisted of two arches flanked by two semi-circular towers on the outside.

Via Ostiensis

The road dates from the 4C BC; it was one of the most important commercial arteries in antiquity. Use continued in the Christian era, since it led to the site of St Paul's martyrdom (*Tre Fontane*) and to his tomb in St Paul's Basilica.

▶ *Take Viale della Piramide Cestia, turn right up the steps in Via Baccio Pontelli and then left into Via Annia Faustina.*

The San Saba district occupies one of the peaks of the Aventine. Its elegant mansions – interspersed with open spaces, dating from early this century – have made it a model of town planning.

San Saba★

The church is dedicated to St Sabas, who founded a monastery called the Great Lavra in Palestine in the 5C. Two hundred years later, its monks were dispersed by the Persians and then by the Arabs. Many took refuge in Rome in a building inhabited a century earlier by St Sylvia, the mother of St Gregory the Great. Towards the end of the 10C, the eastern monks constructed the present church on top of their smaller 7C oratory. Over the centuries the building was subject to various alterations, but was restored from 1911.

Façade – The portico is contemporary with the church, but the columns have been replaced with thick pillars. In the 15C, a single storey surmounted by a

S. PAOLO FUORI LE MURA | **CENTRALE MONTEMARTINI** ★★

loggia was built on top of the portico by Cardinal Piccolomini, nephew of Pius II. The main door was attractively decorated in 1205 by one of the **Cosmati**.

Interior – The basilica plan, with a nave and two aisles each ending in an apse, has been conserved. The lack of uniformity between the pillars (bases, shafts and capitals) is typical of medieval buildings, which recycled chunks of ancient sculpture. An unusual feature is the additional aisle on the east side of the church; it probably linked the church to the monastery of the eastern monks. It was the Cluniac monks who rebuilt the convent in a new position in the 13C, thus exposing the additional aisle on the exterior of the church.

The paving was part of the refurbishment carried out by the **Cosmati**. In the frieze at the top of the right-hand central pillar is a small sculpted head with black stones for eyes; both it and its inscription are an enigma.

▶ *Via di S. Saba down to Piazza Albania.*

In *Piazza Albania*, at the beginning of *Via Sant'Anselmo*, are the remains of the 6C BC **Servian Wall** (*Mura Serviane*). This part was probably rebuilt in the 1C BC.

▶ *Take Via M. Gelsomini and Via Galvani as far as Piazza Giustiniani.*

Testaccio

This down-to-earth district was abandoned for 1 500 years. In the late-19C, it became a working-class neighbourhood, organised according to trendy town-planning principles of the era.

The main attraction is the **Monte Testaccio** (some 35m/115ft high). It takes its name from the ancient *amphorae* reduced to potsherds (*cocci* in Italian) and piled up here. It is, therefore, also called "*Monte dei Cocci*". Excavations have uncovered several "grottoes", some of which revealed what appeared to be ancient restaurants and night spots. Modern proprietors are following suit – with much success.

▶ *Back to previous crossroads; right on Via N. Zabaglia; left on Via Caio Cestio.*

Cimitero Protestante (Protestant Cemetery)

Via Caio Cestio 6. ◷*Open Mon–Sat 9am–5pm.* ◷*Closed Sun and holidays.* ◷◷ *Donations welcome.* ☎ *06 57 41 900. www.protestantcemetery.it.*

Also known as the **Testaccio Cemetery** and **Cimitero Acattolico**, a better name, since the criterion here was "not Catholic". In the shade of pines and cypresses, many famous people rest: at the eastern end of the gravel path – **John Keats** and his faithful friend Joseph Severn, Axel Munthe, the author of *San Michele*; at the foot of the last tower in the Aurelian Wall – Shelley's tombstone on which Byron had some verses of Shakespeare engraved; halfway down the slope in the main cemetery between two tall cypress trees – a tombstone bearing a bronze medallion marks the

Centrale Montemartini★★

G. BLUDZIN/MICHELIN

Industrial architecture and Classical sculpture in the Centrale Montemartini

Close to the General Market on Via Ostiense, not far from the Pyramid. ♿ ⏰Open Tues–Sun 9:30am–7pm. ⏰Closed Mon, 1 Jan, 1 May and Christmas. ✆€4.20, €8.30 ticket with the Capitoline Museums. ☎06 57 48 030; www.centralemontemartini.org.

This 1912 centre was Italy's first public thermoelectric power station. The steam turbines and diesel engines are still an impressive sight. The power station ran until the 1950s, when technology passed it by. Restoration began in the early-1990s, when the structure, complete with original machinery, became a multimedia centre. Since 1997, the museum has housed sculptures from the Capitoline Museums, which create an interesting contrast between ancient art and industrial archaeology.

The Capitoline Museum

The collection is housed in three rooms. The first is the Sala Colonne on the ground floor, displaying the oldest exhibits from the Archaic period to the late Republican era. Among the most interesting artefacts is the group of Heracles and Athena (6C BC), which once adorned the Temple of Fortune and Mater Matuta in the sacred precinct of *Sant'Omobono*. Also noteworthy are two funerary monuments (1C BC), one decorated with bronze leaf finely inlaid with

grave of **Goethe**'s son. One of the most poignant monuments is the *Angel of Grief* by American sculptor William Story. He concluded this memorial for his wife, then died and was laid beside her.
The cemetery is home to one of Rome's cat colonies. Strays run rampant here; widows leave pasta for the starving hordes under parked cars.

▶ *Continue along Via Caio Cestio; turn left into Via della Marmorata.*

On the left is the **Post Office** (Ufficio Postale) of the Aventine district, a good example of Italian rationalist architecture, designed by the architects A Libera and M de Renzi, who adhered to the rules of the Modern Movement which formed the debate on architecture between the two World Wars.

Address Book

WHERE TO EAT
👁️See "Where to Eat" in the Your Stay in Rome section at the end of the guide.

TAKING A BREAK
L'Oasi della Birra – *Piazza Testaccio 38/41. ☎06 57 46 122. Open 7:30pm-midnight (1.30am Fri and Sat).* More than 500 beers are served with cheeses, soups, bruschette and German salamis.

SHOPPING
Il Canestro – *Via Luca della Robbia 12. Open Mon-Sat 9am-8pm. Closed Sun. ☎06 574 6287.* 🍴 Health foods and natural cosmetics jostle together in this

mellow, earthy store, which has an informal deli attached.
Le Bambole – *Via Luca della Robbia 11. ☎06 57 56 895. Open Tue-Fri 9am-1pm and 4-7:30pm; Mon and Sat 9am-1pm.* Two artists skilfully repair antique dolls in this unusual shop.
Volpetti – *Via Marmorata 47. Open Mon-Sat 8am-2pm and 5-8:15pm. Closed Sun. ☎06-574-2352. www.volpetti.com.* Umbrian brothers supply Rome's gourmands with wild boar ham, Piedmontese cheese with white truffles (*crutin*), Italian caviar (*Calvisius*) and other deli offerings.

silver and copper, the other covered with bone. The decoration of both monuments was inspired by the cult of Dionysus. On the walls, a fragment of mosaic depicting fish, thought to be part of the atrium of a house, bears witness to the expressive delicacy and realism achieved in naturalistic reproductions. At the end of the gallery, housing portraits from the late Roman Republic, the **Togato Barberini** and statues of his ancestors are particularly striking (the head is a 17C restoration). The rich drapery of the toga and the transversal folds, showing how the toga would actually have been folded, are good examples of the desire for realism and fine sculpting. On the first floor, the *Sala Macchine* (Machinery Room) houses a sculpture gallery, with its two powerful diesel engines as a backdrop. Two images of Athena face each other at the ends of the room; one is a huge Roman copy of an original Greek statue dating from the 5C BC, the other was part of the **decoration** of the pediment of the

Temple of Apollo Sosianus. The sculptures are Greek originals, dating from the second half of the 5C BC. The *cella* of the temple has been partially reconstructed on the back of the pediment. Before entering the third room, note the beautiful basanite **statue of Agrippina praying**: the head is a copy of the original on display in Copenhagen. The *Sala Caldaie* (Steam Room) houses exhibits from the *horti*, villas and gardens on the outskirts, which were surrounded by greenery and richly decorated with statues, fountains, vases and mosaics. The splendid *Winged Victory*, an original Greek statue (5C BC), comes from the Gardens of Sallust (now in the Ludovisi district). The beautiful **Esquiline Venus**★★, a Roman copy from the Imperial period, was found in an underground room in the Gardens of Lamia (*Giardini di Lamia e Maia*). The gracious *Seated Girl*★★ and the two stern magistrates, captured in the act of opening the circus games, come from the Gardens of Licinius (*Giardini di Licinio*).

PORTA PIA-TERMINI★

MICHELIN MAP 38 H 15-16, J 14-15, K 14-15
METRO LINE A: TERMINI OR REPUBBLICA

Rome's main train station, Stazione Termini, is often the first introduction visitors have to Rome. Sadly, most flee the dirt and hustlers –and miss the gentrifying elegance and worthy sights, such as the Baths of Diocletian and the collections of the Museo Nazionale Romano. The area is typical of many station districts: large urban spaces, noisy traffic, fast-food outlets, small hotels and travel agents. It is also characterised by wide avenues and grand ministerial palazzi.

▶ **Orient Yourself:** Northwest of the station stands the *Porta Pia* in the old Aurelian walls, as well as the Nomentano district.

🅐 **Don't Miss:** The *Aula Ottagona* (aka Baths of Diocletian Planetarium) and the collection of the *Palazzo Massimo alle Terme*.

🕑 **Organizing Your Time:** Allow 1 hr, excluding museums

🅒 **Also See:** *SAN LORENZO FUORI LE MURA; SANTA MARIA MAGGIORE-ESQUILINO; VIA VENETO.*

Terme Di Diocleziano
(Baths Of Diocletian)

The few extant rooms and the bold vaulting are evidence of the original splendour of the building, part of which now houses the church of St Mary of the Angels (🅒 *see below*).

In the 4C, there were some 900 bathhouses in Rome, but the largest (13ha/32 acres) and most beautiful were the baths of the **Diocletian**. Construction took 10 years (295–305) under the direction of Maximian (the emperor lived in Nicomedia in Asia Minor until he moved to Split after his abdication in 305; he

Address Book

WHERE TO EAT

See "Where to Eat" in the Your Stay in Rome section at the end of the guide.

TAKING A BREAK

Quelli di Via Nizza – *Via Nizza 16.* This pizzeria stays open until 3-4am and serves croissants too. Specialities include original toppings such as turkey, porcini mushrooms and rocket salad, prawns or apple purée and nutella.

Pasticceria Antonio Lambiase – *Via Cernaia 49/a. ☎06 49 41 363. Open Mon-Fri midnight-2pm; Sat midnight-8am.* This pasticceria is particularly well known for its croissants with cream and nutella.

It's easily identifiable by the crowds waiting outside in the middle of the night. Hungarian and Austrian cakes are available by prior order.

SHOPPING

Latticini Micocci – *Via Collina 14. ☎06 47 41 784. Open Mon-Sat 8am-1:30pm and 5-7:30pm.* Known throughout the city as *"Micocci on Via Collina"*, this friendly shop is paradise for cheese lovers, with its excellent buffalo mozzarella and a wide selection of French and Piedmontese cheeses. Make sure you sample the sheep's ricotta and the creamy yoghurt.

---

never visited Rome). The bathhouse could accommodate up to 3 000. The complex also included libraries, concert halls, gardens, galleries, and gyms.

The baths were abandoned in 538, when the aqueducts were destroyed by the Ostrogoths under Witigis. Michelangelo was commissioned by Pius IV (1559-65) to convert the ruins into a church and Sixtus V (1585-90) removed a great deal of material for his many buildings.

Santa Maria degli Angeli★★

Entrance in Piazza della Repubblica. According to tradition, the Baths of Diocletian were built by 40 000 Christians condemned to forced labour; in 1561 Pius IV decided to convert the ruined baths into a church and a charterhouse. Michelangelo, by then 86 years old, was put in charge. His design, which closely followed the architecture of the original baths, was continually altered after he and the pope died within a year of one another (1564 and 1565 respectively). By 1749, the church was a jumble of dissociated features and **Vanvitelli**, the Neapolitan, was commissioned to reintroduce a degree of uniformity.

The outer façade which he designed was demolished in the early 20C, revealing the unusual unadorned curved wall of the *calidarium* of the original baths.

Interior

The interior, which is designed to the Greek cross plan, was extensively remodelled by Vanvitelli.

Vestibule

This was the *tepidarium* of the baths. On the left is the tomb (1) of the Neapolitan poet and painter **Salvatore Rosa**, who died in 1673. To the right, the tomb (2) of **Carlo Maratta** (1625-1713), who designed it himself. Between the vestibule and the transept stands the statue of **St Bruno** (3 –

TERME DI DIOCLEZIANO

— Extant parts   — Non-extant parts

■ Museo Nazionale Romano

□ Space reserved for temporary exhibitions

right), founder of the Carthusian order, by the French sculptor Houdon (1741-1827). On either side of the entrance to the transept are two **stoops**; the one on the right is 18C Baroque (**4**), the other modern (**5**).

Transept★

This part of the church gives the best idea of the solemn majesty of the ancient building. It occupies the central bath hall, with its eight monolithic granite columns. To create a uniform effect, Vanvitelli copied the columns in painted masonry, adding four more.

The transept is a virtual picture gallery, particularly of 18C works. The majority come from St Peter's, where they were replaced by mosaics. Here in St Mary's, Vanvitelli arranged them to cover the wall spaces between the pillars.

Of particular significance is the painting depicting *St Basil Celebrating Mass before Emperor Valens* (**6**) by the French painter Subleyras (1699-1749), who settled in Rome in 1728; the Emperor, overwhelmed by the dignity of the ceremony, has fainted; his uniform and background are treated in the classical manner. *The Fall of Simon Magus* (**7**) by **Pompeo Batoni** (1708-86) is typical of this artist's work, with its fine colours and effects of contrasting light and shade. *The Virgin with St Bruno and other saints* (**8**) is a gentle and luminous work by Giovanni Odazzi (1663-1731), a pupil of Baciccia; he worked in the Baroque Mannerist style.

The south transept contains the **tombs** of three First World War heroes: Marshal Armando Diaz (**9**), who won the Battle of Vittorio Veneto in 1918; Admiral Paolo Thaon di Revel (**10**), commander-in-chief of the Allied forces in the Adriatic 1917-18; Vittorio Emanuele Orlando (**11**), Minister of State.

Running across the floor from the south transept to the chancel is a meridian (**12**). Between 1702 and 1846, the clocks of Rome were regulated by it.

Presbytery – Like the transept, the presbytery is generously decorated with paintings, the most notable being *The Martyrdom of St Sebastian* (**13**) by **Domenichino** (1581-1641), and *The Baptism of Jesus* (**14**) by Carlo Maratta. Behind the high altar is a much-vener-

S. MARIA DEGLI ANGELI

ated picture (**15**) showing the Virgin surrounded by adoring angels. It was commissioned from a Venetian artist in 1543 by Antonio del Duca, a Sicilian priest, who had a vision in which he saw a cloud of angels rising from the Baths of Diocletian. From then on he never stopped demanding the construction of a church on the site of the baths; eventually Pius IV acceded to his request.

Aula Ottagona★★★ (or Baths of Diocletian Planetarium)

Entrance on Via Romita. ⏱*Open Mon-Sat 9:30am-1:30pm and 2:30-5pm.* *Guided tours with an archaeologist by appointment.* ⏱*Closed Sun, 1 Jan and Christmas.* ⊛€5, €20 for a "Roma archeologica" card valid for nine archaeological sites. ☎06 39 96 77 00; www.pierreci.it

Painted in the 1920s to resemble a planetarium, this wonderful domed octagonal room houses bronze and marble sculptures taken from Roman baths (2-4C BC). The **works of art**★★★ exhibited include:

● *Pugilist resting*: this superb figure cast in bronze is an original from the Hellenistic period. This fighter is no longer the ideally handsome hero represented by the classical artists, but a man overwhelmed with fatigue. The figure was found in 1884 at the same time as the *Youth leaning on his spear*. Not only are these statues rare examples of craftsmanship, they are also in the most remarkable condition.

- *Venus of Cyrene*: this fabulous statue is made from Parian marble, which has the consistency of ivory. It was discovered during the excavations of the baths at Cyrene in Libya. Venus is tying up her hair while still rising from the sea.
- *Venus Anadyomene*: Venus emerging from the waves, tying up her hair.
- *Hercules*: fine example of an athletic figure in motion.
- *Lycean Apollo* and head of *Aesculapius* (who was invoked against pestilence).

Set into the central part of the floor is a glass panel, revealing the foundations.

Epigraphical and Prehistoric Museum★

Entrances on Piazza della Repubblica, Viale Einaudi and Viale de Nicola. Audio guides recommended. ♿🕐*Open Tues-Sun 9am-7:45pm (last admission 7pm).* 🕐*Closed Mon, 1 Jan, 1 May and Christmas.* ✆€5. ☎06 48 80 530.

Garden – This 16C garden, which acts as an entrance to the museum in Diocletian's Baths, houses a collection of archaeological fragments. The huge central vase once adorned the villa of a wealthy Roman citizen.

Museum – This 1920s building has been completely rearranged to house the rich epigraphical collection of the *Museo Nazionale Romano*, displayed on three floors. The ground floor covers the archaic era to the late republican period (8C-1C BC). The two upper levels are dedicated to inscriptions (1C BC-4C AD), which inform about the emperor and his entourage, social structure, political and economic activity, and religion.

The raised floor around Michelangelo's cloisters (*access from the second floor of the Epigraphical Museum*) houses a section dedicated to the prehistory of the Latins between the 9C and 7C BC.

Chiostro Michelangiolesco – The Great Cloisters of *Santa Maria degli Angeli* are sometimes attributed to Michelangelo, although he died in 1564, aged 89, and the cloisters were probably completed in 1565.

Palazzo Massimo Alle Terme★★★

Entrance on Largo Villa Peretti, at the end of Viale Einaudi. ♿🕐*Open Tues-Sun 9am-§7:45pm (last admission 6.45pm).* 🕐*Closed Mon, 1 Jan and Christmas.* ✆€6, €20 for a "Roma archeologica" card valid for nine archaeological sites.* ☎06 39 96 77 00. www.pierreci.it. The largest part of the **National Roman Museum's** collection is now permanently housed in the former *Collegio Massimo*. The collections are displayed on four floors in a few rooms arranged around the inner courtyard and divided into bays, using glass. Greek and Roman statues are exhibited on the ground and first floors, frescoes and mosaics on the second, and gold and numismatics in the basement.

Ground floor

The entrance to the museum is dominated by a statue of **Minerva** (seated) (**1**), which dates from the 1C BC and is made of pink alabaster, basalt and Luni marble; the face is a plaster cast of another statue of the goddess.

Gallery I houses a series of portraits from the Republican era.

Room I: The two fragments on display in this room (**2**) represent a typical calendar and a list of consuls and censors who held office between 173 and 67 BC.

The **Tivoli General** (**3**) is an excellent example of the union of the ideal of Greek idealism and Italian portraiture. The classical beauty of the body contrasts with the realistic features of the face, which clearly shows signs of age.

A beautiful **floor mosaic** (**4**) (end 2C-beginning 1C BC) can be seen at the end of Gallery I; the emblem panel in the centre shows the abduction of Hylas (depicted with his cloak billowing in the wind) by water nymphs. In the middle of Room IV is a **young girl** (**5**), similar to Artemis, depicted wearing a richly draped chiton. Attention to detail is shown in the footwear, which has been carved with panthers' heads.

Room with three arches – Room V is the only one to give directly on to the inner courtyard and is therefore one of the best lit. It encloses the **statue of Augustus**★★★ (*Statua di Augusto*). The emperor is shown at about the age of 50, dressed in the High Priest's toga, with his head covered, as was the custom for priests about to offer a sacrifice. The face is treated with simple realism, and perhaps a little flattery.

On the back of the **Altar to Mars and Venus (6)** can be seen the *Lupercale*, which tells the legend of Romulus and Remus, suckled by a she-wolf. The personification of the Palatine can be seen at the top to the left, with, beneath it, the eagle, symbol of Jupiter, and to the side the two shepherds, Faustulus and Numitor, the former the adoptive father of the twins. The personification of the Tiber can be seen at the bottom.

The theme of Rome's founding is also taken up in the **frescoes from a Columbarium on the Esquiline (7)**. A colourful and realistic **mosaic (8) of a cat and ducks** can be admired in **Gallery III**.

Gli Horti Sallustiani (Gardens of Sallust) – The exhibits in Room VII include some original Greek statues from this residential district of the city, including the noteworthy **Wounded Niobe**★★★ (*Niobide ferita*), dating from 440 BC (*see also Palazzo Altemps and Centrale Montemartini*). The statue represents an episode in Greek mythology: **Niobe** was mother of 14 children, and was scornful of Leto, who had borne only two. The angry goddess asked her children, Artemis and Apollo, to avenge her by killing all of Niobe's offspring. This statue was one of the first representations of the naked female figure in Greek art after the Cycladic statues from the third millenium BC.

Neo-Attic period – *Room VIII*. Note the statue of the **Melpomene Muse (9)**, dating from the 1C BC, and the various ornamental garden pieces, including a base of dancing maenads (10).

First floor

These imperial works reveal the propagandist use of portraits.

Portraits – Among the portraits from the Flavian dynasty (*Room I*), that of **Vespasian (11)** is particularly worthy of note. This realistic work depicts an old man with a wide and solid face, small eyes and a furrowed brow. The portrait of **Sabina (12)** (*Room II*), Trajan's wife,

shows a woman of quite advanced years, but is fairly idealised in tone.

Villas and gymnasia – *Rooms V-VI*. This large double room, once the theatre of the college, houses works from three of the large imperial villas: Nero's at Subiaco and Anzio, and Hadrian's at Tivoli (🔎*see Tivoli*).

The **Ephebe of Subiaco (13)** is thought to represent one of Niobe's children, hit by Apollo's arrow (see Room VII). Admire the beautiful drapery of the chiton of the **Young girl from Anzio**★★ (*Fanciulla di Anzio*), shown with the upper half of her body twisting slightly. The statue of **Apollo (14)** is also from the villa at Anzio and is a Roman copy (1C AD); typical features from the Hellenistic period (4C BC) include the gentle, swaying pose, the shoulders at different heights and the slightly bowed head. These features contrast with those of the **Apollo of the Tiber (15)**, which is typical of the classical period in its statutary pose, level shoulders, strong body and idealised beauty – perhaps a replica of a Phidias masterpiece. The **Aphrodite crouching**★★★ (*Afrodite Accovacciata*) is one of the most beautiful copies of an original Greek work of the 3C BC; the goddess is shown bathing, a theme often reproduced by the Romans.

The **Lancellotti Discobolus**★★★ (*Discobolo Lancellotti*), named after its former owner, is considered to be an excellent copy. The athlete has already grasped the discus in his right hand and is flexing the muscles of his whole body prior to the throw. The impassive expression, devoid of any sign of physical effort, is characteristic of Greek works from the classical period. The hair and the veins in the arms are highly detailed.

The other replica is the **Castelporziano Discobolus**★ (*Discobolo "di Castelporziano"*), named after the estate where it was found in 1906.

Portraits of gods – *Room VII*. The **Sleeping Hermaphroditus**★★ (*Ermafrodito Addormentato*) is a beautiful copy of a Greek original thought to date from the 4C BC. The graceful, pure lines and the gently twisting body emphasise the ambiguity (the sexual organs are not visible from one side of the statue). Myths claim *Hermaphroditus* (son of

The Calendar

The first recorded Roman calendar is attributed to Romulus and consisted of 304 days divided into 10 months (March was the first). Numa Pompilius then added January and February, bringing the total number of days to 355. An extra day (23 February) was inserted every three years, so that the course of the sun and moon would coincide. Julius Caesar radically reformed the calendar: he increased the days to 365 and added an extra one in February every four years. The names of the months were taken either from gods and goddesses (March from Mars, May from Maia, June from Juno), from emperors (August from Augustus and July from Julius Caesar) or from their position in the calendar (September was the seventh month and October the eighth). The name February is an exception; it derived from the verb *februare*, meaning to purify, as this was the time of cleansing ceremonies.

Hermes and Aphrodite, hence the name) was sitting by a lake, when he was spotted by Salmacis, a water nymph. She fell in love with him. Rejected by the youth, the nymph requested to be joined to Hermaphroditus for ever. Her wish was granted and a new being of both genders emerged from the lake. The headless statue of **Apollo with his lyre** (16) is wearing a full chiton, which emphasises the movement of the body. Also exhibited in this room are two very different statues of Dionysus. The first, in bronze, shows **Young Dionysus** (17) with his traditional attributes: the thyrsus and the *taenia* (headband) with vine leaves in his hair; note the copper inserts (nipples and lips) and the glass paste eyes. The second – a marble copy of an original, probably by Praxiteles – portrays an older **Dionysus** (18), with a long beard and dressed in a long chiton covered with a himation thrown over the left shoulder. It presents a different representation of the god, and is known as **Sardanapalo**, from the name carved by one owner on the back of the statue.

Room X houses a collection of **bronzes** from the ships in Lake Nemi. Note the balustrade decorated with herms (19).

Historical events – *Room XII*. The large **Portonaccio Sarcophagus**★ (*Sarcofago del Portonaccio*) is decorated with a rich battle scene between the Romans and barbarians. The figures are crowded together and overlap to highlight the fighting. Two defeated figures to one side show their unbound hands to symbolise *Roman Pietàs*. The commander, seen in the middle, is faceless, probably because he would have been among the last figures completed.

Iconography and celebrations from Severus to Constantine – *Room XIV*. The 3C AD oval-shaped **Acilia Sarcophagus**★★ (*Sarcofago di Acilia*) is finely and elegantly decorated with high-relief carvings, illustrating a consular procession. The youngest figure wears the consular ring and is possibly the consul's son (on his shoulders to the right). The character wearing the toga and diadem is the personification of the Roman Senate. From a later period are the **Sarcophagus with Muses** (20), fitted with internal recesses, and the **Annona Sarcophagus** (21), with a wedding scene shown in the middle of the sarcophagus. The **Sarcophagus of Marcus Claudianus** (22) was made after the edict of Constantine and is carved with scenes from the Old and New Testaments. The commander in the centre is portrayed as Christ praying.

Second floor

This floor features mosaics and frescoes. Most of the floor is in Galleries I and III.

Triclinium della Villa di Livia★★★ – *Room II*. This is the reconstruction of a semi-underground room, probably a summer *triclinium* (dining room) from a villa where Livia, wife of Augustus, lived at *Prima Porta* (north of Rome). The fine decoration, dating from 20-10 BC, runs along the four walls and depicts a garden in full bloom. An incredible variety of plants (firs, cypresses, oaks, pines, pomegranates, oleanders and palm trees) and birds can be seen. Perspective is heightened by the skilful use of *chiaroscuro* and the varying heights of the plants. Muted fresco colours suggest depth and

PALAZZO MASSIMO ALLE TERME

SECOND FLOOR ▢ Villa della Farnesina rooms

XI, 30, X, 29, 28 IX, II, I — Triclinium della Villa di Livia

VIII, 25, 26, 27, VIII 24, VII, VI, 23, GALLERY III, GALLERY I

Colour frescoes

Winter triclinium

III, V — Cubicula

IV

GALLERY II

Criptoportico

FIRST FLOOR

Sarcofago di Acilia

Sarcofago del Portonaccio

IV, 22, 21, XIV, 20, XIII, XII, XI

GALLERY II

III, 12, 11, II, I, 18, 17, 16, 19, X

Ermafrodito addormentato

Discobolo Lancellotti

VII, IX

Conference room

13, V, 15, VI, VIII

14

Fanciulla di Anzio

Afrodite accovacciata

Discobolo "di Castelporziano"

GALLERY I

GROUND FLOOR

Niobide ferita

Peretti / Villa / Largo / di

10, 9, VIII, VII, VI

GALLERY III

8

Statua di Augusto

6, V, 5, IV

7, 4

1

2, I, 3, II, III

GALLERY I

GALLERY II

0   20 m

	Tourist information	⇕	Lift		Toilets
🎧	Audioguide	Ⓐ	Stairs		Bookshop
♿	Wheelchair access	△	Cloakroom		Telephone

relief, making this cycle of frescoes a masterpiece of Roman painting.

Villa della Farnesina★★★ – The stuccoes and paintings in this part of the museum come from a suburban villa dating from the Augustan era. Built on the banks of the Tiber, it had a large semicircular porch facing the river. The stuccoes, which decorated the ceilings, are marvellously delicate. The paintings are typical of the second and third styles (& see Introduction: Roman art: Painting) and were probably executed for the marriage of Giulia, the daughter of Augustus and Agrippa. The frescoes which decorated the cryptoporticus (*criptoportico*), an underground corridor lit by narrow slits, can be admired in Gallery II. The decoration shows a fine colonnade with panels of Bacchic and Dionysiac scenes painted on a white background between the columns. At the end of the corridor is a reconstruction of the **winter triclinium** (*triclinium invernale, Room III*). Slender columns hung with vegetal festoons are painted on a black background. The panels have an Egyptian theme and contain illustrations of sphinxes and trial scenes. Panels showing scenes from everyday life and tragic and comic masks can be admired on the other side of the corridor. The magnificent frescoes from the three *cubicola* (bedrooms) of the villa (Room V), two with a Pompeian red background (the colour of passion) and one with a light background, are very well preserved. The ceilings still retain some of the beautifully executed stuccoes.

Gallery III – The mosaic of a Nike (*centre*) surrounded by Dionysiac masks (23) dates from the end of the 1C BC. Small openings run off the gallery (*Room VIII*) which house the **Water Nymph from Anzio** (24) with, in the middle recess, a portrait of Hercules resting (the hero is easily recognisable by his club) and **frescoes** (25) of underwater fauna (2C AD) found near a river port on the Tiber. At the end of the gallery is a beautiful **mosaic with a Satyr's head and Pan** (26) and a large **mosaic of Nile landscape** (27) from the 2C AD, characterised by the presence of crocodiles and hippotami, similar to the fresco on display at the *Museo Archeologico Prenestino*.

Villa di Baccano – *Room IX*. This room houses floor mosaics from *Villa di Baccano* (on *Via Cassia*), which date from the 3C AD. The large **marine mosaic** (28) – centered around the personification of Neptune, god of the sea – would have decorated the bathing area. The four panels depicting the charioteers (29) (the colours of their tunics correspond with the four factions competing) would have decorated a bedroom.

Megalographs – *Room X*. Dedicated to a collection of *megalographs* (large paintings), this room contains a fresco (30) portraying a goddess understood in the 17C to be Roma (helmet), but since identified as Venus.

Basement

The basement houses a large display of coins and antique gold.

Numismatic Collection★★ – This large room displays coins from the 4C BC onwards, including models for the euro. Equipment, measures and weights used for minting coins are exhibited too.

Prices and wealth in Rome – In AD 301, Diocletian promulgated an edict to fix prices and measures. In the first display case is a collection of calculus equipment, including an abacus (n°14). The second contains an unusual statuette. The "convivial skeleton" was placed in the middle of the table during banquets as a *memento mori* (eat, but remember that you must die). The other cases exhibit collections of Roman goldwork. A reliquary in the centre of the room contains the perfectly preserved mummy of a child of about eight years old, thought to date from the 2C AD.

Fresco detail from Cubiculum C of the Villa Farnesina on display in the Palazzo Massimo

Walking Tour

Piazza dei Cinquecento

This vast, open space is the terminus for all public transport services in the city and home to the main **railway station**, **Stazione Termini**. The present building was begun before the Second World War to replace the old station(1846-78). Interrupted during the war, work began again in 1947 and was completed to mark the Holy Year in 1950. The roof, with its undulating lines, is considered one of the most significant examples of architecture of this period. In the station forecourt are imposing remains of a wall that girdled the city after the Gauls invaded in the 4C BC.

On the south side of Viale Luigi Einaudi stands a monument to 500 Italians (see the piazza's name) that died at Dogali in Eritrea in 1887. This was an incident in the wars of Italy's colonial expansion. The crowning obelisk comes from the Temple of Isis in *Campus Martius*.

In *Piazza Beniamino Gigli*, south of *Piazza della Repubblica*, is the **Teatro dell'Opera**, a theatre begun by A Sfondrini and completed in 1880. The façade is the work of M Piacentini, who restored and enlarged part of the building in 1926.

▶ *Follow Via Torino alongside the theatre, then turn right into Via Nazionale.*

Via Nazionale – This long, busy street links **Stazione Termini** with *Piazza Venezia*. It is one of the city's most important commercial centres, and is lined with a shops that attract both tourists and Romans. Halfway down is the **Palazzo delle Esposizioni**, which houses art exhibitions of international reputation. Near the south is the **Teatro Eliseo**.

Piazza della Repubblica (Piazza dell'Esedra)

Despite the heavy traffic, the roundabout (rotary) is one of the better post-1870 examples of town planning. Sometimes it's called *Piazza dell'Esedra*, because of the semicircle formed by the two palaces that flank the southwest side. They were designed in 1896 by Gaetano Koch to trace the line of the exedra in the southwest wall of the Baths of Diocletian. The porticoed buildings are reminiscent of the architecture of Turin. The attractive Naiad Fountain at the centre is adorned with bronze water nymphs and sea monsters, sculpted by the Sicilian artist Mario Rutelli (1901).

▶ *Via V.E. Orlando to Via XX Settembre.*

Via XX Settembre

The street is named after the date – 20 September 1870 – when Italian troops entered the papal capital. It replaced the old *Strada Pia* and was the first street developed in the post-1870 boom. Designed to link the ministries and reflect the grandeur of the city's new status, it was therefore lined with pompous buildings in imitation of the Renaissance and Baroque styles. The Ministery of Finance, to the right, is home to the *Museo della Zecca Italiana* (👤 *see below*). At the end of the street (right) is a very modern building by Sir Basil Spence, which houses the **British Embassy** (*Ambasciata del Regno Unito*).

Museo Nazionale Romano

Villa Paolina

🕐Open by appointment to groups only. Contact M. l'Ambassadeur, Via Piave 23, 00187 Roma. ☎06 42 03 09 00.

The villa is named after Napoleon's sister Pauline, who in 1803 married Prince Camillo Borghese, great-nephew of Pope Paul V. She took up residence here after the fall of the empire, since her husband, whom she had abandoned earlier, banished her from the family property. She spent long periods in the house until her death in 1825.

Porta Pia

The **inner façade**★ of the gate, facing down Via XX Settembre, is spectacular, the last architectural design by **Michelangelo**. It was erected between 1561 and 1564 at the request of Pope Pius IV. At the centre are six balls, the device of the Medici family. The curious white motif is said to be a barber's basin wrapped in a fringed towel, a reminder to Pius IV that one of his ancestors was a tradesman. The outside façade, facing down Via Nomentana, is the work of Benedetto Vespignani (1808-82), who was very active during the 19C.

▶ Continue along Via Nomentana and turn right into Via dei Villini.

Via dei Villini – This road is an excellent example of early-20C urban planning. Observe *palazzini*, four- or five-storey flat blocks for rentals, and the *villini*, smart little houses with gardens.

Museum

Museo Numismatico della Zecca Italiana (Currency Museum)

On the ground floor of the Treasury building. 🕐Open Tue–Sat 9am–12:30pm. 🕐Closed Mon, Aug and holidays. ☎06 47 61 33 17; www.museozecca.ipzs.it

The treasury building dates from 1877. The Numismatic Museum displays the currencies of every country in the world, including coins issued by the popes from the 15C. There is also a fine collection of wax impressions (about 400) by Benedetto Pistrucci (1784-1855), who was chief engraver to the Bank of England for 40 years: heads of George IV, Victoria, Duke of Wellington, Napoleon, Pauline Borghese.

S. MARIA MAGGIORE-ESQUILINO

SAN GIOVANNI IN LATERANO★★★

MICHELIN MAP 38 P 15-16 N 16-17, M 16
METRO LINE A: SAN GIOVANNI OR MANZONI

As in so many parts of the capital, pagan ruins sit beside important Christian churches: the basilica of St John Lateran – the pope's seat as Bishop of Rome – and Santa Croce in Gerusalemme, one of the seven pilgrimage churches. Today, the noisy junction *Piazza di Porta San Giovanni* contrasts with the calm solemnity of the east front of the basilica.

▶ **Orient Yourself:** This district stretches from the city's southeast to the Caelian Hill and is almost wedged inside the Aurelian walls. The *Tangenziale* provides a fast road link with the districts of San Lorenzo and Nomentano.

🕘 **Organising Your Time:** Allow 3hrs.

😎 **Don't Miss:** The small, busy clothing market that runs along Via Sannio, on the other side of Porta San Giovanni

🖐 **Also See:** Neighbouring sights are described in the following chapters: *COLOSSEO-CELIO; SAN LORENZO FUORI LE MURA; SANTA MARIA MAGGIORE-ESQUILINO.*

A Bit of History

The name is taken from the wealthy Laterani family who owned a property confiscated by Nero and restored by Septimius Severus. Excavations in Via dell'Amba Aradam (beneath the INPS building) have revealed traces of a house identified as belonging to the **Laterani**. It was combined with a neighbouring property in the 4C and may have been the residence of Fausta, who was Maxentius's sister and Constantine's wife. In 313, she lent her house to Pope Melchiades so that he could hold a council of bishops, one of the first official manifestations of Christianity.

Beneath the St John Lateran Hospital (Ospedale di San Giovanni in Laterano) are traces of a building which has been identified as the house of the Annii, Marcus Aurelius's family. The remains of the base of a statue were found in a peristyle; it may have carried the statue of the Emperor which now stands in the Capitoline Museum. **St John's Gate** (Porta San Giovanni) was erected in the 16C in the **Aurelian Wall** (Mura Aureliane), which was built around Rome in the 3C and is very well preserved.

The **monument to St Francis of Assisi** is a reminder that the saint and his companions came to the Lateran one day in 1210 to have their rule approved by Innocent III.

Basilica di San Giovanni in Laterano★★★

(St John Lateran)

🕘*Open 7am-6.30pm.* ☎*06 77 20 79 91.*
This basilica was the first church to the Holy Redeemer; it symbolised the triumph of Christianity over paganism and thus deserved its title of "Mother and Head of all the churches in the city and the world". It is the cathedral of Rome. The dedication to St John came later.

Constantine's Basilica – On 28 October 312, after defeating Maxentius in battle, Constantine made a triumphal entry into Rome and immediately forbade the persecution of the Christians. In 314, Pope Sylvester I took up residence in the Lateran (a group of buildings comprising a palace, a basilica and a baptistry). The *palazzo* became the official papal residence from the 5C until the papacy departed to Avignon.

Before starting St Peter's in the Vatican, Constantine built the Lateran basilica on the site of Maxentius's bodyguards' barracks. He thus asserted his victory by destroying one of the signs of his enemy's greatness and by stressing his intention of giving the Christians his approval. After being sacked by barbarians in the 5C, damaged by an earth tremor in 896 and destroyed by fire in 1308, the basilica was rebuilt in the Baroque era and in the 18C. Over 20 popes contributed to its structure, from Leo the Great (440-61) to Leo XIII (1878-1903).

Lateran Councils – Some of the most decisive meetings in church history took place in the Lateran. In **1123,** the Diet of Worms was confirmed, putting an end to the Investiture Controversy. The council of 1139 condemned **Arnold of Brescia**, a canon, who challenged episcopal authority and preached in favour of a return to the poverty of the early Church. He founded a free commune in Rome and drove out Eugenius III.

Pediment of St John Lateran

In **1179,** Alexander III called for a crusade against the Albigensian (Cathar) heresy. Following the Council in **1215** – attended by 400 bishops and 800 abbots and at which every court in Europe was represented – it laid down that the faithful must confess once a year and take Communion at Easter. Innocent III decided to put an end to the Albigensian heresy and launched a crusade in the Languedoc. In **1512,** Julius II opened the fifth Lateran Council by asserting the supremacy of the Church of Rome.

Exterior

The well-balanced 18C **façade** is the major work of Alessandro Galilei (1691-1736), a Baroque architect. He had a masterly touch in contrasting the clear lines of the columns with the dark cavities behind them. On the roof, the gigantic figures of the saints surrounding Christ, St John the Baptist and St John the Evangelist preach to the heavens. The **huge statue of Constantine**, the first Christian emperor **(1)**, in the porch comes from the imperial baths on the Quirinal. Since 1656, the **central entrance (2)** has been fitted with the doors from the Curia in the Forum.

Interior

It is hard to envisage the basilican plan of Constantine's building. Today's central nave and four aisles are those of a Baroque church, sometimes considered cold and severe because of its grandiose dimensions and pale stuccoes. In fact, it is a very old building dressed in 17C taste.
Nave and aisles – This part of the church was designed by the great Baroque architect **Borromini**; his plan included a dome. Just as Urban VIII had commissioned Bernini to complete St Peter's, so his successor **Innocent X**, desired to mark his reign in a prestigious manner. He invited Borromini in about 1650 to refurbish St John Lateran. Where Bernini knew how to adapt Baroque art to earlier constructions, Borromini was unable to give free rein to his genius, as Innocent III asked him to retain the existing ceiling. It seems to crush the pillars in the nave, which replace the ancient columns and were designed to support a dome. The prominent niches faced with dark mar-

A Strange Trial

The trial took place in 896 in the Lateran. The accused was the corpse of Pope Formosus, dressed in his papal vestments. His enemies had not forgiven him for bestowing the emperor's crown on the "barbarian" Arnoul, last of the Carolingians.

He was set opposite his judge, Pope Stephen VI, declared unworthy and a perjuror, and thrown into the Tiber.

Stephen VI was, in his turn, punished and strangled in prison.

ble spoil the effect of the low-relief sculptures and the oval medallions.
Ceiling★★ – Pius IV began this in 1562; his arms are in the centre. It was completed in 1567 by Pius V, whose arms are near the chancel. In the 18C, it was restored by Pius VI, who added his arms near the main door. The original design was by a group of Michelangelo's pupils.
Statues of the Apostles★ (3) – They are in the late Baroque style by some of Bernini's followers. Borromini created 12 huge recesses in the pillars of the nave to receive them. The columns of green flecked marble, which Borromini shortened and re-employed, originally separated the nave and aisles in the ancient

basilica. Above each recess, he placed the dove from the arms of Innocent X.

The low-relief sculptures (*above*), executed under the direction of Algardi, depict stories from the Old and New Testaments. The prophets in the oval medallions *(top)* were painted in the 18C. This decoration replaced the 15C frescoes painted by Pisanello and Gentile da Fabriano for **Martin V** and Eugenius IV.

Corsini Chapel★ (4) – Alessandro Galilei, who designed the east front, was also responsible for this chapel, which is built on the Greek cross plan beneath a dome. The red porphyry coffer (*left*) beneath Clement XII's tomb came from the Pantheon. The allegorical statues are fine 18C work. The fragment of heavily restored **fresco** (5), attributed to **Giotto**, shows Boniface VIII announcing the Jubilee Year in 1300.

Transept – The nave is as bare of ornament, as the transept is adorned with frescoes, marble and gilding. It was renovated in about 1595 by Clement VIII, with **Giacomo della Porta** as architect. Mannerist decoration includes the great wall frescoes that resemble theatrical decor. These were painted principally by Cesare Nebbia, Pomarancio and Cavaliere d'Arpino who, in the *Ascension* (*end of left transept*), imitated the *Transfiguration* by Raphael (Vatican Gallery).

The elaborate marble decoration includes high-relief angels, placed in small niches, which do not show the liberty of movement which characterises Baroque art. The ostentatious **ceiling,★★** bearing the arms of Clement VIII, is rich in colour and gilding and was designed by Taddeo Landini (late 16C).

The pediment in the **chapel of the Holy Sacrament** (6) is supported by four beautiful Antique **columns★** in gilded bronze, the only ones of this kind in Rome. Legend recounts that in the 1C BC they belonged to the Temple of Jupiter.

The 14C **baldaquin** (7) was repainted during the Renaissance. At the top, some relics of the heads of St Peter and St Paul – placed in silver reliquaries – are kept, partly paid for by Charles V of France (repaired in the 18C). In the 19C, Pius IX had the high altar faced in marble. During this work it became apparent that the wooden altar contained some much older planks, one of which very probably belonged to the altar at which Pope Sylvester I officiated (314-35).

The confessio (8), created in the 9C, contains the tomb of Martin V, the first pope to reign after the Great Schism. His tomb is the work of Donatello's brother.

Apse – The apse of Constantine's Basilica was rebuilt in the 5C and again in the 13C, but was not substantially altered until the 19C, when Leo XIII moved it back in order to extend the chancel. The ogival windows and particularly the **mosaic** in the top of the apse were retained. This mosaic had already been restored in the 13C by **Jacopo Torriti**, who took several features from the original model: the representation of the Cross, celestial Jerusalem with the palm and the phoenix, symbols of the Resurrection (*beneath the cross*) and the Jordan full of fishes, birds and boats, which forms the base of his composition. To these he added the Virgin and Nicholas IV kneeling, St Peter and St Paul (*left*), St Andrew and the two St Johns, the Baptist and the Evangelist (*right*). He also included two smaller figures: St Francis of Assisi (*left*) – Torriti was a Franciscan monk – and St Anthony of Padua (*right*).

The first representation of Christ in the apse dates from the 4C. Not long before, paganism was still the state religion, so when Pope Sylvester consecrated the basilica, the appearance of such an image was considered miraculous by the faithful. In his desire to perpetuate the "miracle", Jacopo Torriti managed to transfer the ancient figure to his own composition. During the 19C, alterations this original figure was broken and replaced by a copy.

Museo della Basilica – *Right of the chancel. For information on admission times and charges call ☎06 77 20 79 91.* The Basilica Museum displays the treasures of the basilica – gold chalices and reliquaries. The **station cross** (Cabinet V) is in silver gilt (12C).

Chiostro★ – ◐*Open 9am–6pm.* ◈€2. *☎06 77 20 79 91.* These charming 13C cloisters are one of the most remarkable by the Vassalletti (father and son). Their art, like that of the Cosmati, consisted of cutting and assembling fragments of antique marble. The twisted columns with varied capitals, the mosaic frieze and the delicate carving of the cornice make this a poetic place for linger. A fine 9C is in the garden's centre.

▶ *Leave the basilica by the right transept.*

In the **porch** is a bronze statue of Henri IV of France (**9**) by Nicolas Cordier (1567-1612) in recognition of the king's gift to the Lateran Chapter of the Abbey of Clairac in Agenais. The **façade of the north transept** is so majestic it could be the main front: by Domenico Fontana in 1586.

Battistero★ (Baptistery)

Like the basilica, this was built by Constantine. In the 4C, every Christian was baptised there; nowadays it is used for the ceremonies of Holy Saturday. It was rebuilt in the 5C by Sixtus III, who set up the eight porphyry columns in the centre. The upper colonnade and the lantern are 16C additions. Various popes sponsored the adjoining chapels and Urban VIII added the 17C frescoes.

Chapels

Ask the keeper to open the doors. The **chapels of St John the Baptist** (**10**) and **St John the Evangelist** (**11**) were built by Pope Hilary (461-68).

The chapel of St John the Baptist has kept its original door, which is made of an alloy of silver, bronze and gold and is very heavy. The Evangelist chapel was given a new bronze door in the 12C. The ceiling is covered with a beautiful 5C mosaic (delicate colours on a gold ground).

Chapel of St Rufina and St Secunda (12)

In the 12C, the original narthex, which was the entrance to the baptistry, was converted into a chapel. It is rectangular in shape with an apse at either end, one of which is decorated with a fine 5C mosaic.

Chapel of St Venantius (13)

Built in the 7C by John IV, it is decorated with mosaics in the Byzantine style (slim, slightly stiff figures) and has a fine cedar ceiling.

Piazza di San Giovanni in Laterano

In the piazza stands a fine **Egyptian obelisk** made of granite, the tallest in Rome. It dates from the 15C BC and was brought to Rome in the 4C by Constantinus II to adorn the Circus Maximus at the foot of the Palatine, where it was found in 1587. It was repaired and re-erected in its present position by Domenico Fontana, at Sixtus V's behest.

Palazzo Lateranense (Lateran Palace)

When Gregory XI returned to Rome in 1377 after the Avignon era, the palace had been gutted by fire. He installed his household in the Vatican.

The present building was constructed in 1586 by **Domenico Fontana**, during the reign of Sixtus V. The **Lateran Treaty** (*see VATICANO – SAN PIETRO*) was signed here. The palace is now the headquarters of the Diocese of Rome (*Vicariate*), with the pope at its head, in his capacity as Bishop of Rome, and of the Vatican Historical Museum.

Museo Storico Vaticano (Vatican Historical Museum)

Entrance by the main portico. ○*Open Mon–Sat at set hours: 9am, 10am, 11am and noon.* ○*Closed 1Jan, 19 Mar, 9 Apr, 1 & 17 May, 7 &29 June, Aug 15-16, Nov 1, Dec 8 & 26–6.* ⊛*€4.* ☎*06 69 88 16 62. http://mv.vatican.va.*

The museum comprises two parts – the **Papal Apartment** and the **Historical Museum**. The apartment contains 10 rooms, each decorated with frescoes by late-16C artists. In the last salon, called the Conciliation Room, the Lateran Treaty was signed in 1929 by Cardinal P Gaspari and Mussolini. The Historical Museum celebrates to the history of the papacy, its ceremonies and guards.

Traces of the medieval palace

In the Middle Ages, the papal palace extended from its present site as far as *Via Domenico Fontana*. Two features from this building, the banquet hall of Leo III and the Sacred Steps, have been reconstructed on the east side of the square.

Triclinium of Leo III

This pope (795-816) built two rooms in the palace. All that remains of the *triclinium* (dining room) is an apse decorated with a mosaic, repaired in the 18C. It celebrates the alliance of Leo III with Charlemagne: the emperor reinstated the pope on his throne and the pope crowned the emperor in St Peter's in the Vatican.

Scala Sancta

○*Open 6:15am–noon and 3:30-6:30pm; Sancta Sanctorum: open Apr-Sep Tue, Thu and Sat 10:30-11:30am and 3:30-5pm; Oct-Mar Tue, Thu and Sat, 10:30-11:30am and 3-4pm.* ⊛*€2.58.* ☎*06 77 26 641.*

Sixtus V (1585-90) demolished what remained of the medieval palace with two exceptions: the stairs, which according to tradition came from Pontius Pilate's palace and had been used by Christ, and the private chapel of the popes. This was relocated to a building specially designed by Domenico Fontana to incorporate the famous steps, climbed by the faithful on their knees. An alterante on the other side permits foot-traffic.

At the top is the popes' chapel, known as the **Holy of Holies**★★ (*Sancta Sanctorum*), by analogy with the temple in Jerusalem, because of its precious relics. The interior is decorated with fine Cosmati work. The paintings in the chapel, damaged by rainwater over the centuries, were carefully restored in 1995. Now it's possible to see the 11C frescoes, considered by medieval experts to be one of the most important discoveries of the century. Above the altar is the famous icon of Christ called the *Acheiropoeton*, which means it was not made by human hand. Begun by St Luke, it was completed by an angel, then arrived in Rome miraculously from Constantinople in the 8C. The ancient bronze door –which gives access to the popes' chapel – can be seen from St Lawrence's Chapel (*right*).

Porta Maggiore District Tour

▶ *Piazza S. Croce in Gerusalemme.*

In antiquity, the district to the east of the Esquiline was a suburb of Rome, well wooded and covered with tombs that stretched for miles along the Praenestina Way and the Labicana Way (now *Via Casilina*). From Augustus's reign (31 BC to AD 14) onwards, the cemeteries gradually gave way to huge gardens laid out by rich Romans. Under the empire, these sumptuous properties, designed by skilful landscape gardeners, with temples and avenues lined with works of art,

Porta Maggiore, an example of innovative architecture from the 1C AD

G. Bludzin/MICHELIN

were absorbed into the imperial estates either by confiscation or by legacy (members of the patrician class often willed their property to the emperor). This practice restricted development to the east and aggravated the problem of lack of space in the city centre, which was becoming overcrowded with huge, prestigious buildings. In the 3C, the district was enclosed by the **Aurelian Wall** (*Mura Aureliane*). Untouched by the popes, it was not developed until the 19C, when Rome had become the capital of Italy.

Santa Croce in Gerusalemme★

🕐*Open 7am–1pm and 2–6:30pm. The garden is open only by reservation. ☎06 70 14 769; www.basilicasantacroce.it*
In this church, originally known simply as "Jerusalem", the legend of the Holy Cross is closely linked with history. Here stood the **Sessorium** where Constantine's mother, Helen, lived; built in the 3C, it remained an imperial palace until the 6C. In the 4C, Helen went on a pilgrimage to Jerusalem, as was customary. She returned in 329 bearing a fragment of the True Cross, which she kept in the palace. She died later that year. A legend developed that she had found the True Cross. The cult of the Holy Cross was not introduced to Rome until the 7C.
History of the church – In memory of his mother, the Emperor Constantine (or perhaps his sons) converted part of the Sessorian Palace into a church to house the precious relic. It consisted of one

large chamber with an apse, where the services were held, and a smaller room (the present St Helen's Chapel), which housed the relic. In the 12C, Pope Lucius II (1144-45) divided the larger chamber into three and built a campanile without altering the outside walls. He raised the level of the church, but not the chapel, perhaps because its floor was composed of soil brought back from Calvary. The church acquired its present appearance in the 18C.

Visit

The 12C campanile is flanked by a lively façade and oval vestibule in the 18C style, consistent with the principles dear to Borromini.
The nave vault was refashioned in the 18C; the impressive baldaquin over the altar is of the same period. The apse has conserved the mark of the Renaissance; it is decorated with an attractive fresco by Antoniazzo Romano (late 15C), illustrating the legend of the *Discovery of the Cross by St Helen*.
Cappella di Sant'Elena (Chapel of St Helen) – Access by one of the sets of steps beside the chancel). The chapel is decorated with beautiful **mosaics**★, designed by Baldassarre Peruzzi and, perhaps, by Melozzo da Forlì. The statue above the altar is a Roman work originally representing Juno, but converted into St Helen.
Cappelle della Croce e delle Reliquie (Chapel of the Holy Cross and Relics Chapel) – *Access by steps to the right of the left aisle*).

The relics of the Passion kept in the chapel of the Holy Cross attract large numbers of pilgrims. In the first chapel, they venerate the arm of the cross of the robber crucified beside Christ (*at the beginning of the flight of steps opposite the entrance*). In the Relics Chapel, a glass case behind the altar displays fragments of the True Cross; the "heading" on the Cross (the inscription it bore); two thorns from the Crown; St Thomas's finger; some fragments from the Flagellation stake, from the grotto in Bethlehem and the Holy Sepulchre; a nail from the Cross.

▶ *On leaving the church, bear left through the opening in the Aurelian Wall.*

Anfiteatro Castrense

Its name comes from the Latin word "*castrum*", which in the 4C meant an imperial residence. This amphitheatre, like the Sessorian Palace (*see above*), was probably part of the imperial properties in this district. The Aurelian Wall detours to enclose it, suggesting great importance. Built entirely of red brick, this 3C structure originally had three storeys, of which only the first is well preserved.

▶ *Take Via Eleniana to Porta Maggiore.*

Porta Maggiore★

The gate was built in the 1C AD to carry the Claudian Aqueduct across the Praenestina Way and the Labicana Way where it entered the city. The use of huge, roughly hewn blocks of travertine (even for the supports) is an innovation typical of the Claudian era.

In the 3C the gate was incorporated into the Aurelian Wall. When Honorius (395-423) restored the fortifications, a bastion was added on the outside; its demolition in the 19C revealed the tomb of Marcus Vergilius Eurysaces.

Sepolcro di Eurisace★ (Tomb of Marcus Vergilius Eurysaces)

Eurysaces was a baker who lived in Rome at the end of the republic. As supplier to the army, he probably grew rich during the civil wars. His enormous travertine tomb (dating from c 30 BC), commemorates this trade.

The cylindrical motifs, some vertical and some horizontal, recall the receptacles that held flour. The low-relief frieze round the top illustrates the different steps in breadmaking.

▶ *Go west along Via Statilia.*

On the left among the trees are the elegant arches of the Claudian Aqueduct.

Aqua Claudia (Claudian Aqueduct)

Aqueducts are without doubt the most remarkable public works in Roman architecture. This one, begun by Caligula in AD 38 and completed by Claudius in AD 52, is the most impressive. Starting in the mountains near Subiaco, it reached Rome after 68km/42mi, of which 15km/9mi were above ground. From Porta Maggiore, Nero (AD 54-68) built a branch channel, traces of which remain in the gardens of Villa Wolkonsky, in Piazza della Navicella and in the Arch of Dolabella, at the eastern end of Via di San Paolo della Croce. This aqueduct was extended by Domitian as far as the Palatine, to supply his palace.

▶ *Turn left into Via G. Giolitti.*

Tempio di Minerva Medica

The beautiful circular temple (4C) was originally covered by a dome and was probably a nymphaeum.

Additional Sight

Museo degli Strumenti Musicali★

🕒 *Open Tues-Sun 8:30am-7:30pm.* 🕒*Closed Mon, 1 Jan, 1 May and Christmas.* ⊜€2. ☎06 70 14 796.

The charming **Museum of Musical Instruments** sweeps from antiquity to the 19C. Antique whistles, horns and handbells are succeeded by exotic instruments, such as beautiful inlaid mandolins, tambourines and ocarinas. The sumptuous exhibits include the 17C Barberini harp, decorated with magnificent gilt carvings, and a rare example of a vertical harpsichord (17C) with a pretty painted lid.

SAN LORENZO FUORI LE MURA ★

The major point of interest is the Basilica of San Lorenzo Fuori le Mura, situated in the heart of the university district. Don't expect ivory towers here, but the area remains lively with its crowds of students, the constant noise of mopeds and trams, and the many specialised bookshops and other small outlets. This vibrant atmosphere is intensified since some of the departments have moved off campus and are now dotted around the quarter.

▶ **Orient Yourself:** This district lies to the east of the city and is bordered by the inner by-pass (the *tangenziale*) that leads to San Giovanni. From here, the suburbs of Rome stretch as far as the eye can see.

🕐 **Organizing Your Time:** Allow 1 hr.

🔗 **Also See:** *CATACOMBE DI PRISCILLA; PORTA PIA-TERMINI; SAN GIOVANNI IN LATERANO.*

San Lorenzo Fuori le Mura ★★
(St Lawrence Without The Walls)

The church is also known as *San Lorenzo al Verano* since it is built on land that belonged to a certain Lucius Verus in antiquity. To the north ran the *Via Tiburtina*, lined with pagan tombs and then with Christian catacombs. One contains the grave of St Lawrence, who was martyred in 258 under the Emperor Valerian, soon after Pope Sixtus II was put to death. According to legend, Lawrence was roasted on a grill; he was highly venerated in the Middle Ages.

As pilgrims to the tomb of St Lawrence became more and more numerous, the Emperor Constantine had a sanctuary built (330). By the 6C, it was in such a poor state of repair that Pope **Pelagius II** (579-90) had it redone.

Enlarged in the 8C, it underwent major alterations in the 13C under Pope **Honorius III** (1216-27). The apse of Pelagius's church was demolished, the church was extended westwards and its orientation reversed. The original nave was raised and became the chancel.

Later Baroque additions were removed by Pius IX in 1855; he also revealed the original nave but retained Honorius's chancel. On 19 July 1943, a bomb fell on the church; the roof, the upper part of the walls and the porch were demolished. Repair work aimed for the church's 13C appearance.

Façade

The very elegant porch, which dates from the time of Honorius III, was reconstructed after the 1943 bomb damage. Above the architrave is a beautiful mosaic frieze in vivid colours. Higher still is a cornice delicately carved with flowers, fruit and acanthus leaves punctuated with lion-head gargoyles. This fine example of medieval decorative sculpture is attributed to the Vassalletti, a family who worked in marble with the Cosmati from the early-12C.

The **"harvest" sarcophagus** ★ (**3** – *left*) is quite remarkable. It was carved in the 5C or 6C; the clear-cut relief and the large smooth surfaces are characteristic of the Middle Ages. Two modern works honour Pope Pius XII (**4**) and Alcide de Gasperi (**5**), President of the Council from 1945-1953, in recognition of their assistance in the work of restoration following the bomb damage. The two lions (**6**) on either side of the main door are Romanesque.

Interior

The two distinct parts of the church are immediately apparent, divided by the triumphal arch and built on two different axes: one by Honorius III (13C) and the other by Pelagius II (6C).

Church built by Pope Pelagius II (6C)
Church built by Pope Honorius III (13C)

Piazzale San Lorenzo

Church built by Honorius III

The funerary monument (7 – *right of entrance*) of Guglielmo Fischi (1256),

nephew of Pope Innocent IV, was reconstructed in 1943. Beneath a small temple resembling a 13C baldaquin is a 3C sarcophagus decorated with a marriage scene.

Honorius's church comprises a nave and two aisles separated by beautiful Antique granite columns of varying diameters. The Ionic capitals, like those in the porch, date from the Middle Ages and are attributed to the Vassalletti. They show with what happy results the medieval marble workers adapted their technique to Ancient columns.

The lighting of the nave has hardly changed since the 13C. After 1943 the ceiling was rebuilt exactly as it had been in the 19C when Vespignani, who was working for Pius IX, had inserted a wooden coffered ceiling beneath the open roof frame.

The floor, damaged by the bomb, is bright with 3C **Cosmati** work.

The two **ambones**★ are not identical. They are Cosmati work: a combination of white marble, porphyry and serpen-

---

Address Book

WHERE TO EAT

👍 *See "Where to Eat" in the Your Stay in Rome section at the end of the guide.*

TAKING A BREAK

Antico Forno – *Via dei Rieti 61.* 🍴. This bakery attracts locals, with its well priced *pizza bianca* and biscuits.
Superpizza – *Largo Osci.* 🍴. In the heart of San Lorenzo, opposite the market stalls along *Largo degli Osci*, Superpizza bakes delicious pizzas for students from the nearby university.

BARS

Internet Café – *Via dei Marrucini 12.* ☎06 44 54 953. www.internetcafe.it. *Open Mon-Fri 9am-2am; Sat-Sun 5pm-2am.* There are 22 computer screens for Internet enthusiasts to surf the web, while they enjoy a drink and a snack.
Lancelot – *Via dei Volsci 77/a.* ☎06 44 54 675. *Open 8pm-2:30am.* This bar is particularly popular with students and has over 300 board games available to customers. It boasts a good beer and

cocktail list, in addition to a reasonable selection of rolls and salads.
Squinternet – *Via dei Luceri 13.* ☎06 44 70 28 34. *Open 4pm-2am.* Surf the Internet for little more than €4 an hour, using one of the nine screens of this small café. The tea is imported directly from Ceylon.

SHOPPING

Claudio Sanò – *Largo Osci 67/a.* ☎06 44 69 284. Original leather bags in the most unusual shapes – cubes, triangles, trapezia, and even some in the shape of buttons –are sold here.
Disfunzioni Musicali Usato e Rarità – *Via degli Etruschi 4.* ☎06 44 61 984. www.disfu.com ⏰*Open Tue-Sat, 10:30am-7:30pm; Mon 3:30-7:30pm.* The first shop sells mainly imported, avant-garde and rare records, as well as second-hand CDs. The second, *(Via dei Marrucini 1; closed Sat afternoons)* opened just a few years ago and specialises in avant-garde and rock singles and LPs.

tine, encrusted with multicoloured insets gleaming with touches of gold.

Church built by Pelagius II

The central section containing the high altar has been raised and is approached by two sets of steps. Its original orientation with the apse projecting west of the present chancel arch was reversed so that it could serve as the chancel of Honorius' church, as it does today. Pelagius's church comprised a nave and two aisles. From the raised nave only the tops of the Ancient fluted columns are visible, supporting a magnificent sculpted architrave composed of disparate fragments which once belonged to a frieze or a door lintel. Over the aisles are galleries (*matrones*) for the women; the arcades rest on fine slim columns, their capitals decorated with leaves (6C).

The bishop's **throne**★ at the east end of the chancel is by the Cosmati (1254). The whiteness of the marble contrasts with the vivid colours and the gold inlays to create a fine effect.

In the **crypt** are the remains of St Lawrence, St Stephen and St Justin.

Cloisters

Entrance through the sacristy in the south aisle or from the outside on the right of the bell-tower. The 12C cloisters with their archaic charm formed part of the fortified convent, which was like a cita-del in the Middle Ages. St Lawrence's Basilica, outside the walls of Rome, was easy prey for thieves and looters. The cloister walk contains inscriptions from the neighbouring catacombs.

Città Universitaria (University)

In 1935, the University of Rome, which had suffered cramped conditions in the *Palazzo della Sapienza* (Palace of Wisdom), was transferred to the new campus near the Municipal Clinic (*Policlinico Umberto I*) built in 1890. The overall design was awarded to **Marcello Piacentini**, who was the major exponent of large-scale building projects (Ⓖ*EUR*). He applied the rules so dear to the "Twenties", as can be seen in the Rectorate and the vast entrance area. The overall impression is, however, one of balance and shows no grandeur for its own sake. The final effect was the work of various architects. One of the most important of the Rationalists was Giuseppe Pagano, whose style can clearly be seen in the Institute of Physics. The architects who collaborated on the project were: Pietro Aschieri – **Institute of* Chemistry; Giò Ponti – *Mathematics; Giovanni Michelucci – *Mineralogy and *Physiology; Giuseppe Capponi – *Botany.

SAN PAOLO FUORI LE MURA★★

MICHELIN MAP 38 W 11, T 5.
METRO LINE B: BASILICA S. PAOLO (METRO STATION 300M/330YD FROM THE BASILICA) AND LAURENTINA (1.5KM/1MI FROM THE ABBAZIA DELLE TRE FONTANE)

This area contains two sites outside the Aurelian Wall, which are linked by the history of St Paul: the basilica of St Paul Without the Walls, built over the saint's tomb, and the demesne of Tre Fontane, a few kilometres away, the site of his martyrdom. The Abbazia delle Tre Fontane is situated on Via Laurentina farther to the south.

▶ **Orient Yourself:** This region lies to the south of the capital on *Via Ostiense*, which joins with the *Via del Mare* to link Rome to Ostia.

Ⓞ **Organising Your Time:** Allow 1hr for *San Paolo Fuori le Mura* and 45min for the *Abbazia delle Tre Fontane*, excluding travelling time.

Ⓖ **Also See:** PORTA PIA-TERMINI, S. GIOVANNI IN LATERANO, VIA S. LORENZO FUORI LE MURA

A Bit of History

Saint Paul – Paul was a Jew called Saul, born early in the 1C AD at Tarsus in Cilicia in Asia Minor (southeast Turkey). At first he persecuted Christ's disciples; then on his way from Jerusalem to Damascus, he was blinded by a light, fell from his horse and heard Jesus's voice saying: "Saul, Saul, why persecutest thou me?" This event precipitated his conversion: he changed his name from Saul to Paul and became the chief agent in preaching Christianity to the gentiles.

Accused by the Jewish community of Caesarea in Palestine, he demanded to be brought before the Emperor Nero (Paul was a Roman citizen). He set out in AD 60. Two years, the imperial court acquitted him.

The date of Paul's martyrdom is not known for certain. Like Peter, he may have been a victim of the persecution of the Christians organised by Nero after the terrible fire in AD 64, which destroyed the greater part of Rome. As a citizen, St Paul was sentenced to beheading.

Basilica di San Paolo Fuori le Mura★★

(Saint Paul Outside the Walls)

🕐 *Open 7am–6:30pm (6pm in winter).* ☎06 54 09 374.

St Paul Without the Walls is one of the major basilicas in Rome. Its historical significance attracts visitors and pilgrims from all over the world. The saint's body was buried beside the *Via Ostiensis*, which was lined with tombs, as were all the major roads leading out of Rome. A small shrine (*memoria*) was erected over his grave. In the 4C, the Emperor Constantine undertook to build a basilica over the tomb, as he had done for St Peter's.

This first basilica was consecrated by Pope Sylvester I in 324. It was smaller than St Peter's Basilica and faced the *Via Ostiensis*. By 386, it had become such a popular place of pilgrimage that three Emperors – Valentinian II, Theodosius I and his son Arcadius – decided to enlarge the building. It could not be

extended across the road (because of the rising ground), and since the Apostle's tomb could not be moved, the orientation was reversed, with the apse on the *Via Ostiensis* and the façade facing the Tiber.

The new structure was magnificent; it was larger than the contemporary basilica of St Peter in the Vatican. The huge project was not completed until 395, in the reign of the Emperor Honorius. For the next 14 centuries, it was maintained with great care and attention.

When the building was sacked by the Lombards in the 8C and by the Saracens in the 9C, the damage was immediately repaired. John VIII (872-82) walled around the basilica and the community around it; this came to be known as "Johannipolis", after the Pope.

The greatest artists were employed to embellish the basilica: from Pietro Cavallini and Arnolfo di Cambio to Carlo Maderno. rebuilt after a 19C fire, St Paul's Basilica is now adorned with gleaming marble and vivid colours.

Tour

▶ *Enter by the main door from Viale di S. Paolo.*

Interior★★★ – No visitor can fail to be impressed by the multitude of columns – 80 granite monoliths – that divide the nave and four aisles.

The gold and white coffered ceiling bears the arms of Pope Pius IX (1846-78), who consecrated the new basilica.

The Ciborium★★★ is a Gothic work by **Arnolfo di Cambio** (1285). Detail and proportion are delicately blended: the many decorative figures are executed with great skill, from the pairs of angels supporting the pierced rose-window on each of the four pediments to the animals on the vault.

To the left of the apse is the **chapel of the Holy Sacrament★**, the work of Carlo Maderno (1629), which contains a 14C wooden crucifix, a statue of St Bridget kneeling by Stefano Maderno (c 1576-1636) and a wooden statue of St Paul dating from the 14C.

The Paschal **candlestick★★** by Nicolà di Angelo and Pietro Vassalletto (12C) is

Pilgrims have been coming here since the Middle Ages. Many oratories were built; one of them, still decorated with traces of 9C painting, is now the entrance gateway. Surrounded by green hillsides and the scent of eucalyptus trees is a group of buildings: a Trappist monastery, a convent of the Little Sisters of Jesus and three churches.

Santa Maria Scala Coeli

Cistercian monks settled here in 1140. The history of the church is connected with one of St Bernard's ecstatic visions. During mass in the crypt, he had a vision of the souls in purgatory ascending into heaven, released by his intercession. The present church (restored 1925), was built in 1583 by **Giacomo della Porta** to an octagonal plan beneath a dome. Behind the altar in the crypt is a room supposed to be where St Paul waited before his execution.

a remarkable piece of Romanesque art. The base is decorated with monsters and on the shaft are decorative motifs, scenes from the life of Jesus (note the expressions of the squat figures), tendrils and more monsters supporting the candle socket.

Cloisters★ – These probably formed part of the work done by a member of the Vassalletto family (13C) who, like the Cosmati, was skilled in marble incrustation work. The north gallery (backing on to the church) is particularly fine. The great variety among the columns, their marble incrustation picked out in gold and the exquisite workmanship of the mosaic frieze above the arcades make the cloisters a charming composition.

Santi Vincenzo e Anastasio alle Tre Fontane

The church, which is dedicated to **St Vincent** and **St Anastasius**, is the abbey church of the Trappist monks who have occupied the neighbouring monastery since 1868. The origins of the church go back to the 7C, when Pope Honorius I (625-38) built a convent to house some Oriental monks (as at St Sabas).
The church, which was rebuilt in the 13C, is austere in appearance and still retains traces of paintings of the apostles by some of Raphael's pupils.

San Paolo alle Tre Fontane (Saint Paul of the Three Fountains)

The church of **St Paul at the Three Fountains** was designed in the 16C by Giacomo della Porta to replace two chapels. Here, according to legend, the fountains had spouted from the earth on the spots where the saint's severed head bounced. A small building commemorating his martyrdom stood here as early as the 7C.
The statues of St Peter and St Paul on the façade are by Nicolas Cordier. The ancient mosaics come from Ostia. The sites of the three fountains are marked by three shrines set at different levels.

Abbazia Delle Tre Fontane★
(Three Fountains Abbey)

▶ *From Via Laurentina a drive leads to Three Fountains Abbey.*

The place known in antiquity as *Ad Aquas Salvias* is where St Paul was beheaded. Legend has added an epilogue: the apostle's head bounced three times and three fountains sprouted from the ground.

SANTA MARIA MAGGIORE-ESQUILINO ★★★

MICHELIN MAP 38 L 14, M 14-16
METRO LINE A: VITTORIO EMANUELE

Augustus transformed this sprawling slum into a desirable district, where the mad emperor Nero later built his Golden House (Domus Aurea). Now this lively, bustling quarter – with its myriad shops, offices and crowded streets – has a distinct ethnic flavour. The plaza's busy market sells mainly clothes and shoes. Oriental shops and supermarkets line the streets surrounding the square. Anchored by the major basilica of Santa Maria Maggiore, this area warrants a deeper exploration than most tourists (fleeing the Termini train station chaos and squalor) manage.

▶ **Orient Yourself:** The neighbourhood is largely concentrated around *Piazza Vittorio*, which extends from the northern slopes of the Esquiline Hill (the *Domus Aurea* once stood on the southern side, overlooking the Colosseum) and Termini Railway Station. The *Via Cavour* separates it from the Viminal Hill.

😊 **Don't Miss:** The mosaics in Santa Maria Maggiore and the chapel of San Zenone in San Prassede.

Kids Especially for Kids: On 5 August, Santa Maria Maggiore rains rose petals from the dome, commemorating the summer snowstorm here predicted to Pope Liberius by the Virgin, which inspired the church.

👣 **Also See:** *COLOSSEO-CELIO; FORI IMPERIALI; PORTA PIA; SAN GIOVANNI IN LATERANO.*

A Bit of History

The **Esquiline**, one of the seven hills of Rome, has been inhabited since the 8C BC. The uneven plateau has three peaks, which the Romans named the **Oppius**, now covered by the *Parco Oppio*, the **Fagutalis**, which overlooks the Imperial Fora, and the **Cispius**, now crowned by *Santa Maria Maggiore*.

The imposing basilica of Santa Maria Maggiore

B. Kaufmann/MICHELIN

Address Book

WHERE TO EAT
See "Where to Eat" in the Your Stay in Rome section at the end of the guide.

SHOPPING
Il Discount dell'Alta Moda – *Via del Viminale 35*. Menswear and women's outfits from the previous season can be purchased here at a 40% or 50% discount.

Metropoli Rock – *Via Cavour 72*. ☎ *06 48 90 35 29. Open Mon-Fri, 9:30am-8pm; Sat 9:30am-1.30pm and 4-8pm*. Stock includes over 8 000 classical music CDs.

Mercato di Piazza Vittorio – See "Shopping" in the *Your Stay in Rome* section at the end of the guide.

Long a burial ground for poor people, the Esquiline was one of the most sinister parts of Rome. Augustus gave it a new face. He divided the city into 14 districts, one of which was the Esquiline; he arranged for part of it to be given to his friend Maecenas, who built a magnificent villa surrounded by gardens. In a classic example of gentrification, the district came to be coveted by the emperors, and it was confiscated into the imperial domain. After a fire in AD 64 cleared the ground, Nero built his Golden House on the Oppius (*see COLOSSEO-CELIO*).

Piazza di Santa Maria Maggiore

The fluted column at the centre is the sole survivor of the eight columns that graced the basilica of Maxentius in the Forum. Brought here in 1614 by Pope Paul V, it was erected by Carlo Maderno and crowned with the Virgin.

Basilica Di Santa Maria Maggiore★★★
(St Mary Major)

For information and reservations for the basilica and the loggia call ☎06 488 10 94; Fax 06 48 90 43 92.
This church is one of the four Roman basilicas which bear the title "major" (the others are St John Lateran, St Paul Without the Walls and St Peter's in the Vatican) and enjoys the privilege of extraterritoriality conferred by the Lateran Treaty in 1929.

The basilica was built by Sixtus III (432-40) in honour of Mary a year after the Council of Ephesus, at which Nestorius, the Patriarch of Constantinople, had claimed that Mary was not the Mother of God. Subsequent popes have left their mark; in their desire to contribute to the glory of the Virgin, they made numerous alterations. The campanile, the highest in Rome, was added in 1377 by Gregory XI. In the 17C and 18C, the apse was remodelled. The main façade was given its present appearance in the 18C under Benedict XIV by Ferdinando Fuga (1743-50).

Façade
The porch and loggia are sandwiched between two identical wings, although more than a century elapsed between the construction of the one on the right (1605) and the one on the left (1721-43). Like the majority of architects in the first half of the 18C, **Ferdinando Fuga** had a taste for classical forms, but also adopted certain elements from the Baroque art of Borromini. The façade is enlivened by sculptures, the broken lines of the pediments and the interplay of the openings in the porch and the arcade of the loggia. In the porch stands a statue of Philip IV of Spain (**1**), a benefactor of the basilica; it is by a pupil of Algardi (1692). The loggia from which the Pope used to give his blessing *Urbi et Orbi* was added to the original façade. It still retains its early-14C mosaic decoration, restored in the 19C.

Loggia Mosaic★
Access by the steps on the left of the porch.
The upper part – Christ, angels, the evangelistic symbols, the Virgin and the saints

– is the work of **Filippo Rusuti** (late 13C), who took over from Pietro Cavallini.

Below are four scenes illustrating the **legend of the basilica**★, which was built here late in the 4C by Pope Liberius. The Virgin appeared in a dream to a Giovanni Patrizio, a rich man, and to Pope Liberius, inviting them to build a church in her honour; the site for the sanctuary was to be marked by a fall of snow on the morrow. When the pope and Patrizio consulted one another, they were astonished to find that, in spite of the time of year (5 August 356), there had been a snowfall on the Esquiline. The pope drew up a plan of the church; Patrizio financed the construction. The graceful lines, richly apparelled figures and fine, deep perspectives link these scenes with the Florentine style of Cimabue and Giotto.

Kids The basilica rains rose petals onto the congregation each 5 August to celebrate the portentous snowstorm.

Interior★★★

The interior has also undergone many alterations: at the end of the 13C Nicholas IV (1288-92) extended the chancel and, in the middle of the 15C, Cardinal Guillaume d'Estouteville, archpriest of the basilica, covered the aisles with vaulting in keeping with Renaissance taste. Despite that, the interior, with its almost perfect proportions and two rows of Ionic columns, is a remarkable early Christian architecture;

brilliant with colour, it is most spectacular on Sundays and feast days.

Mosaics★★★

Those in the nave, on the chancel arch and in the apse are beyond compare.

Nave – Dating from the 5C, they consist of a series of panels above the entablature. They are some of the oldest Christian mosaics in Rome, together with those in Santa Pudenziana, Santa Costanza and the Lateran Baptistry. This art rediscovered vivid narrative, after accepting the rigidity of the late empire. The scenes are taken from the Old Testament with Abraham, Jacob, Moses and Joshua in the leading roles. On the left-hand side of the nave, beginning at the chancel end, are incidents from Genesis:

(2) Melchizedek comes to meet Abraham.

(3) Abraham's dream near the oak.

(4) The separation of Abraham and Lot.

Next comes the arch opened up in the 17C during the construction of the Pauline Chapel, which entailed the destruction of the mosaics at this point. Then:

(5) Isaac blesses Jacob. Esau returns from hunting.

The next panel is a painting.

(6) Rachel tells Laban of the arrival of Jacob, his nephew. Laban and Jacob embrace.

(7) Jacob agrees to serve Laban for seven years and to receive Rachel as his wife.

(8) Jacob reproaches Laban for giving him Leah, his elder daughter, in marriage. Jacob marries Rachel.

(9) Jacob asks Laban for the speckled and spotted sheep. The division of the flock.

(10) God tells Jacob to leave. Jacob announces his departure to the women.

Next between two painted panels:

(11) The meeting of the two brothers, Jacob and Esau.

(12) Hamor and his son Shechem ask Jacob for the hand of his daughter Dinah, whose brothers are angry.

(13) Dinah's brothers insist that the men among Hamor's people be circumcised. Hamor and Shechem explain to their tribes.

The last three panels on this side are painted.

On the right-hand side of the nave, starting at the chancel end, there is first a painted panel and then:

(14) Pharaoh's daughter receives Moses. He speaks with the Egyptian doctors.

(15) Moses marries Zipporah. God appears in the burning bush.

Then comes the arch opened up during the construction of Sixtus V's Chapel, which takes the place of the mosaics (1741-50).

(16) The passage of the Red Sea.

(17) Moses and the people of Israel. The miracle of quails.

(18) The salt sea of Mara. The people of Israel reproach Moses who, after praying to God, touches the water with a rod sent by God and makes it fresh. The meeting of Moses and Amalek.

(19) The battle against the people of Amalek, and Moses praying.

(20) The return of the chiefs of the tribes who had gone to explore the Promised Land. The stoning of Moses, Joshua and Caleb.

(21) The tablets of Law are handed down. The death of Moses. The transport of the Ark.

(22) The passage of the Jordan. Joshua sends spies to Jericho.

(23) The angel of God (the captain of the Lord's host) appears to Joshua. The harlot Rahab helps the spies to scale the walls of Jericho. The return of the spies.

(24) The besieging of Jericho. The procession of the Ark to the sound of trumpets.

(25) The taking of Ai. Joshua before God and among the soldiers.

(26) Joshua fights the Amorites. Hail of stones on Israel's enemies.

(27) The sun and moon stand still upon Gibeon.

(28) Joshua punishes the rebel kings.

The last three panels are paintings.

Chancel arch – The arch dates from the 5C and has the liveliness of the first Christian mosaics. It is divided into four horizontal bands. Probably later than the mosaics in the nave, it shows Byzantine influence:

● In the *Annunciation* scene (*top row left*), where Mary is dressed like an Oriental empress;

● In the Epiphany scene (*second row left*), presented as a sumptuous court reception, where the Child Jesus is sitting on a throne decorated with precious stones. The cities of Jerusalem and Bethlehem, with sheep representing the Apostles, can be seen in the two lower rows.

Apse – This dazzling composition comprises elements taken from a 5C mosaic, which was transformed at the end of the 13C by **Jacopo Torriti** when Nicolas IV rebuilt the apse. All the figures are the work of Torriti, since the earlier mosaic consisted only of birds, foliage and scrolls. The main subject of the composition is the *Crowning of the Virgin*, surrounded by groups of angels and a procession of saints. Kneeling before them are Nicolas IV and Cardinal Colonna.

Baldaquin (29)

Designed by Fuga, it's supported on porphyry columns wreathed in fronds of bronze. Unfortunately, it hides some of the mosaic. Beneath is the **Confessio**, where Pope Pius IX (1846-78) is resplendent in bronze gilt, marble and frescoes (19C). Fragments thought to belong to Jesus's crib rest in the silver urn.

Ceiling★

The coffers were decorated with the first gold to come from Peru, which was offered to Pope **Alexander VI**, a Spaniard (1492-1503), by Ferdinand and Isabella of Spain. The pope continued the work begun by Calixtus III (1455-58) in constructing this ceiling. The roses at the centre of the coffers are 1m/3.75ft in diameter. Vasari, a 16C art historian and author of *Lives of the Artists*, attributes this work to Giuliano da Sangallo (1445-1516).

Floor

The 12C Cosmati work was radically restored by Ferdinando Fuga in the 18C.

Right aisle

The tomb of Cardinal Consalvo Rodriguez (30) (late 13C) is typically Gothic (a recumbent figure, flanked by angels beneath the Virgin). In the floor is the tombstone (31) of the family of Bernini.

Cappella di Sisto Quinto (Sixtus V's Chapel)

The chapel is named after Sixtus V, who, during his five year reign (1585-90), turned Rome into a huge building site with his restorations, conversions and new constructions. His favourite architect was **Domenico Fontana**, to whom he entrusted the design of this chapel. It is almost a church in itself. Designed on the Greek cross plan beneath a dome painted with frescoes, it is resplendent with gilding, stucco and marble. In the right and left arms of the cross are the monumental tombs of Popes Sixtus V (32) and Pius V (33), decorated with low-relief sculptures.

Beneath the high altar (34) in 1590 Domenico Fontana set up the Oratory of the Crib, which had held the relics of the grotto in Bethlehem since the 7C.

Baptistry

The baptistry is the work of the Baroque architect Flaminio Ponzio. The beautiful porphyry font was decorated in the 19C by Giuseppe Valadier. The high relief of the *Assumption* on the altar is by Pietro Bernini, father of Gian Lorenzo.

Left aisle

It contains, in particular, two beautiful chapels.

Cappella Sforza (Sforza Chapel) – Its highly original architectural style is by Giacomo della Porta, probably from designs by Michelangelo.

Cappella Paolina (Pauline Chapel) – It is also called the **Borghese Chapel**, after the family name of Pope Paul V, who commissioned it in 1611 from Flaminio Ponzio. It is identical in plan to Sixtus V's Chapel but with even more sumptuous decoration. In 1612, Cigoli painted the dome without first subdividing it with ribs; he was the first to follow this course and the result was not perfect. When, some 10 years later, Lanfranco (who also worked on the Pauline Chapel), painted the dome of *Sant'Andrea della Valle* using the same process, he achieved a masterpiece. The main altar (35) is incomparably rich, like a jewel, set with jasper, lapis lazuli, agate and amethyst.

The 12C altarpiece is of a *Virgin and Child* in the Byzantine style. She is greatly venerated among the faithful and has even been attributed to St Luke. Above is a sculpted panel by Stefano Maderno illustrating the legend of the tracing of the basilica's plan (see above). As in Sixtus V's Chapel, the right and left arms of the cross contain Papal tombs: Clement VIII (36) and Paul V (37).

▷ *Leave the church by the door at the end of the aisle to the right of the choir.*

Walking Tour

Piazza dell' Esquilino

From here sprawls a fine **view**★★ of the apse of *Santa Maria Maggiore*. When the Pauline and Sistine Chapels were added beneath their domes, they looked like two separate buildings. Clement IX (1667-69) therefore commissioned Bernini to integrate them with the basilica by altering the apsidal end of the church. **Bernini** conceived a grandiose design, but the excessive cost prevented its execution. The following pope, Clement X, therefore gave the work to Carlo Rainaldi.

The **Egyptian obelisk** at the centre of the square comes from the Mausoleum of Augustus. Sixtus V ordered it to be moved and set up by Domenico Fontana, a specialist in such matters.

▷ *Turn left into Via Urbana.*

Santa Pudenziana

The church, dedicated to St Pudens or the Roman virgin St Potentiana, is one of the oldest in Rome and is now very popular with the local Filipino community, who have their own chaplain here. Legend tells how Senator Pudens, who lived in a house on this site, welcomed Peter under his roof.

In the 2C, a bathhouse stood on the site. Late in the 4C, a church (*ecclesia pudentiana*) was established in the baths. The word resembles the name of the senator's daughter. Pudentiana, like her sister Praxedes, are shown with the martyrs, whose bodies they prepared for burial. The façade was repaired in the 19C. The bell-tower dates from the 12C, as does the elegant doorway, with its fluted columns and its sculpted frieze inset with five medallions. The interior shows the signs of many changes: in 1589 the dome was built and the chancel altered so that several figures in the fine 4C **mosaic**★ were lost. It is one of the oldest examples of a Christian mosaic in Rome.

Excavations

For information on opening hours, call ☎06 48 14 622.

On display are the remains of Pudens' house, mosaics and the baths, as well as the Roman road built in the 3C.

▷ *Return to Piazza di Santa Maria Maggiore and, beyond the church, bear right into Via Santa Prassede.*

Santa Prassede★

Entrance in the right aisle. The brick façade with the main doors leading to a small courtyard can be seen through the entrance arch (*often closed*), which opens into Via di San Martino ai Monti beneath a loggia supported on two columns.

The church is an old *titulus* – a private house where Christian services were held in antiquity. The present building was put up by Paschal I in 822.

Chancel mosaics★

They date from the 9C and show the influence of both Byzantine traditionalism and Carolingian art. Colour is paramount and no longer used in half-tones. Against a background of sky quite lacking in depth, the figure of Christ is flanked by St Peter and St Paul presenting Praxedes and Pudentiana. The other two figures are St Zenon and Pope Paschal I offering his church (his square halo an indication that he was alive at the time). The two palms represent the Old and New Testaments and the phoenix on the one on the left symbolises the Resurrection.

Cappella di San Zenone★★

Right aisle. St Zenon's Chapel was built between 817 and 824 by Pope Paschal I. The doorway is made up of various elements taken from earlier buildings. Above this are several portrait medallions arranged in two arcs, one centred on Christ surrounded by the apostles and the other on the Virgin and Child surrounded by various saints.

The interior is covered in mosaics with a gold background: on the central vault Christ, in strict Byzantine style, is supported by four angels; above the opening to the left of the altar is the Virgin accompanied by two saints and the mother of Paschal I, Theodora Episcopa, with a blue halo; the mosaic above the opening to the right of the altar was spoiled in the 13C when an oratory was built to house a fragment of the scourging column. This relic is greatly venerated by pilgrims, especially during Holy Week.

▶ *Take Via S. Vito.*

Arco di Gallieno

The **Arch of Gallienus** was erected in 262 in honour of the Emperor Gallienus (253-68), who was assassinated by Illyrian officers. It stands on the site of the Esquiline Gate (*Porta Esquilina*) in the Servian Wall (*�85 see plan of Rome during the empire in Welcome to the City*). Traces of this wall, which was probably started in the 6C BC and several times repaired, can be seen in Via Carlo Alberto (*next to the church of St Vito e Modesto*).

Piazza Vittorio

The square once hosted a daily market, now moved to the nearby *Via Turati* . Today the piazza is a park. It was laid out in the late 19C by Gaetano Koch and other architects, with arcades at street level, as in Turin.

In the north corner of the square are the ruins of a huge 3C fountain, which was adorned with the "Trophies of Marius". The adjacent **Magic Gate** (*Porta Magica*) continues to excite speculation; the signs inscribed round the doorway (bricked up) have never been deciphered.

▶ *Take Via Principe Eugenio, then turn left into Via Cairoli.*

Santa Bibiana

The church was rebuilt in the 17C and was one of Bernini's first architectural projects. His **statue**★ of St Bibiana (or Viviana) (*inside above the altar*) is also one of his early works; note her left hand gathering up the folds of the garment.

Additional Sights

San Martino ai Monti

🕓*Open Mon–Sat 9am–noon and 3–5:30pm. Book at least 10 days in advance by writing to Ufficio parrocchiale di S. Martino ai Monti, Via Monte Oppio 28, 00184 Roma, or by calling ☎06 70 01 728.*

This venerable church, dedicated to St Martin, was founded in the 5C next to a titulus existing in the 3C in the house of Equitius (*the underground remains can be visited: ask in the sacristy*).

The church was completely transformed in the 17C. The interior was divided into a nave and two aisles by two rows of ancient marble columns with 5C capitals (the bases date from the 17C). The aisles are frescoed with Roman landscapes and the story of the Prophet Elijah.

▶ *Leave and walk around to the apse.*

The apse of the church of San Martino ai Monti dates from the 9C. In the square, the two **Cappocci towers**, despite restoration, still evoke the power of the nobles in the Middle Ages.

Museo Nazionale d'Arte Orientale

♿🕓*Open Tue, Thu, Sun and holidays, 8:30am–7:30pm; Mon, Wed, Fri and Sat, 8:30am–2pm.* 🕓*Closed first and third Mon in the month, 1 Jan, 1 May and Christmas.* ☛*Guided tours available (1hr 30min).* ☞€4. ☎06 48 74 415.

On the *piano nobile* of **Palazzo Brancaccio** is the National Collection of Oriental Art. On the right before going upstairs, is the nymphaeum designed by Francesco Gai. The museum starts with the Near and Middle East, particularly Iran. Two other sections are devoted to exhibits from the Far East, notably Tibet and Nepal, Gandhara and finally China.

Auditorium di Mecenate

🕓*Open Tues–Sat Apr–Sep 9am–7pm; Oct–Mar 9am–5pm; Sun 9am–1:30pm.* 🕓*Closed Mon and public holidays.* ☞€3. ☎06 48 73 262; www.comune.roma.it/monumentiantichi*

The **Auditorium of Maecenas**, part of the luxurious Villa of Maecenas (early 1C) – which was surrounded by large gardens – was discovered in 1874. The underground structure, with its drainage system and frescoes, was probably a nymphaeum originally, but Maecenas used it as an auditorium, where he entertained his learned friends.

TERME DI CARACALLA★★

MICHELIN MAP 38 R 13-14, S 14-15
METRO LINE B: CIRCO MASSIMO

This pleasant district of shady trees and abundant greenery is home to ancient ruins and small medieval churches. From the impressive FAO building, follow the original Appia Antica, now a busy thoroughfare leading south to the EUR district, and step back in history at the Baths of Caracalla. Once frequented by senators and guttersnipes alike – up to 1 600 people at a time – the complex included soaking tubs, gyms, lecture halls and gardens, where ancients could strive for "healthy mind in a healthy body".

▸ **Orient Yourself:** The area surrounding the Baths of Caracalla is inside the Aurelian Walls, to the south of the Colosseum and Circus Maximus. The district of San Giovanni lies to the northeast, beyond the Caelian Hill. Those visitors travelling here by Metro should refer to the Walking Tour.

🕐 **Organising Your Time:** Allow about 3hrs including the baths (1hr) for the Walking tour (Tour: 2.5km/1.5mi).

✦ **Also See:** *APPIA ANTICA; AVENTINO; COLOSSEO-CELIO.*

A Bit of History

Four sets of baths had already been built – by Agrippa, by Nero on the *Campus Martius*, by Titus near the Golden House and by Trajan on the Aventine – when the Emperor **Antoninus Caracalla** began the largest Rome had ever seen (11ha/25 acres); only Diocletian's Baths were to be more extensive. Work started on the baths in AD 212 and they were opened in AD 216. They were finished by **Elagabalus** (AD 218-22) and **Alexander Severus** (AD 222-35), the last two Emperors of the Severan dynasty.

The sober exterior concealed a contrastingly rich interior: floors paved with marble and mosaic, walls covered with mosaic and gilded stucco work; the white marble capitals and cornices contrasting with the multicoloured marble, porphyry and granite of the columns. The huge building, with its massive walls and bold vaulting (30m/98ft high), was much admired; it offered facilities for 1 600 bathers at one time and was able to cater for 6 000 people a day. The Romans used the baths daily, around noon at the end of a day's work. The poorest people were not excluded, although they had fewer slaves than the rich to assist. Baths were an important element in Roman life; they offered facilities for keeping fit through bathing and physical exercise,

as well as libraries for the cultivation of the mind. They were also, however, places of assignation, and by Caracalla's time the Romans were already denouncing notorious episodes.

The Baths of Caracalla were in use until 537, when the Goths under Witigis damaged the aqueducts that supplied Rome. **Shelley's** poem *Prometheus Un-bound* "was chiefly written upon the mountainous ruins of the Baths of Caracalla."

A typical day at the baths – The Romans followed the routine prescribed by their doctors. From the changing rooms (traces of fine floor mosaics) they went into the gymnasiums for various forms of exercise; it is such a setting that Petronius described in his *Satyricon*, when Encolpius and his friends meet the rich Trimalchio, a "bald old man... who played ball with his long-haired slaves ..."

Already sweating, the bather went on into an oval room heated to a very high temperature *(laconicum)*, which induced greater perspiration. The heating system was very efficient; hot air from huge stoves in the basement circulated beneath the floors, which were supported on sturdy brick pillars, and spread into ducts in the walls.

Next the bather passed into the *calidarium* for a good soak, after which he scraped his skin to remove all impurities. The *calidarium* was a huge circular room

(34m/112ft in diameter), covered by a dome; some of the supporting pillars can still be seen. From here, they went into the *tepidarium* for a cooler dip, before plunging into the bracing water of the cold bath (*frigidarium*). They could then take a swim in the open-air swimming pool (*natatio*). Some then caroused. Less wealthy or more serious Romans stayed to talk to their friends, to walk in the gardens or to read in the libraries.

Excavations were carried out in the 16C (by Cardinal Farnese for the construction of his magnificent *palazzo* in the square of the same name), and later in the 19C and 20C. These uncovered magnificent statues, vases and mosaics, in addition to a **mithraeum** (temple of Mithras), and a network of underground tunnels. Here horse-drawn carts transported wood to the 50 ovens that heated the baths.

Exploring the Baths

&♿⊙*Open daily 9am–1hr before dusk.* ⊙*Closed Mon afternoon, 1 Jan and Christmas.* ⊛ €*5,* €*20 for a "Roma archeologica" card, valid for nine sites* ☎*06 39 96 77 00; www.pierreci.it.*

After passing the chambers *(right)*, which were perhaps used for meetings, one enters *(left)* the central block. Immediately on the right is an oval room (*laconicum*), where the temperature was kept constantly high for a Turkish bath. This leads to the gymnasium (*palaestra*), where some coloured mosaic fragments can still be seen. In the changing room (*apodyterium*), a fair amount of the mosaic floor is still intact. Next comes the swimming pool (*natatio*); the fresco *(right)* has a religious theme and was probably added in the 17C, when the baths housed the oratory of St Philip Neri. The tour returns to the startingpoint symmetrically via the second changing

TERME DI CARACALLA

| 0 | 100 m |

Extant parts

Non-extant parts

G. Bludzin/MICHELIN

Baths of Carcalla

room and the second gymnasium, which has fine mosaics.

Walking Tour

Visitors can either begin this tour from the Circo Massimo metro station or directly from the Baths of Caracalla. In the case of the latter, see the church of Santi Nereo e Achilleo below.

The **Porta Capena** is a gate in the defensive wall built by **Servius Tullius** in the 6C BC. Here Livy recounts that in the reign of Tullus Hostilius (672-640 BC), the last of the **Horatii**, who had defeated the **Curiatii** of Alba, slew his sister with his sword because she had dared to weep for her fiancé, one of the Curiatii; "Let that be the fate of any Roman who mourns the enemy".

▸ *Take Viale delle Terme di Caracalla and bear right into Via Guido Baccelli.*

On the right stands the building of the **FAO** (Food and Agriculture Organisation), an agency of the United Nations, which employs over 3 000 people of all nationalities. It studies food production, plant and animal diseases, and new strains.

Santa Balbina
Entrance is usually permitted from the courtyard of Santa Margherita rest home (Casa di Riposo), to the right of the church. ○*Open 8:30-11:30am.* ☎*06 78 08 756.*

In 1927, the church underwent a thorough restoration, which returned it to its medieval simplicity. It was probably a 4C house converted into a place of worship. A pitched roof covers a single nave punctuated by recessed chapels and lit by high barred windows.

On the right of the entrance is Cardinal Surdi's **tomb**★, bearing a recumbent Gothic figure and decorated with multicoloured marble inlay (1295).

Behind the high altar is the **episcopal chair**★, a fine piece of Cosmati work (13C). The frescoes in the apse are 17C.

▸ *Beyond the church turn left into Via Antonina and then sharp right. Turn left in front of the Baths of Caracalla.*

Santi Nereo e Achilleo
○*Open after Easter to Oct, Wed-Mon 4:30–6:30pm.* ☎*06 57 57 996.*

A little church stood here in the 4C called *Titulus Fasciolae*. Its presence is explained by the legend of the bandage *(fasciola)* that bound St Peter's leg, covering sores from the Mamertine Prison chains. When Peter fled Rome, the dressing fell from his leg on this spot, which was venerated as a place of worship. Further along the Appian Way came St Peter's meeting with Christ and his question *"Domine, quo vadis?"* (&*See APPIA ANTICA).*

The church was completely rebuilt by Leo III (795-816) and later restored by Sixtus IV (1471-84). In 1596, the incumbent appointed to the church was Clement VIII's confessor, Cardinal Baronius, who had a great devotion to St Nereus and St Achilleus. He had their relics transferred here from Domitilla's Catacombs. He also borrowed the high altar from the crypt of St Paul Without the Walls, decorated it with Cosmati work.

▶ *From Piazzale Numa Pompilio take Via di Porta San Sebastiano.*

Via di Porta San Sebastiano is bordered by buildings of historical and architectural interest set in attractive rural surroundings.

San Cesareo
To visit, contact Via di Porta San Sebastiano 4. Donations welcome.
Little is known of the church's history before 1600, when Clement VIII entrusted its restoration to Cardinal Baronius. The latter followed contemporary taste in the coffered ceiling bearing the arms of Clement VIII and the paintings by **Cavaliere d'Arpino**. Elsewhere he tried to reproduce medieval decoration.
Some Renaissance work surives: the two angels drawing back the curtains before the *confessio (below the altar)* and the pretty little fresco of the Madonna and Child *(above the throne).*

▶ *Continue along Via S. Sebastiano to the Casa del Cardinale Bessarione and the Sepolcro degli Scipioni (see below). Turn left immediately after the Sepolcro degli Scipioni to reach the temple of San Giovanni in Oleo.*

San Giovanni in Oleo
Key available from the rector of S. Giovanni a Porta Latina. This small octagonal temple was built in the Renaissance style in 1509 by Benoit Adam, a Frenchman and member of the *Rota* (Roman Catholic ecclesiastical court). Over the door, he placed his arms and his motto *"Au plaisir de Dieu"* (at God's pleasure).

▶ *Turn left into Via di Porta Latina, then right to Via di San G. a Porta Latina.*

San Giovanni a Porta Latina
The church of **St John at the Latin Gate** occupies a charming **site★**; the peaceful forecourt, flanked by the campanile, is decorated by a medieval well and shaded by a cedar tree. The beautifully simple interior is decorated with 12C frescoes; although much damaged, they are a fine example of Romanesque painting.

▶ *Return to Via di Porta Latina.*

Porta Latina (Latin Gate)
This gate in the Aurelian Wall *(Mura Aureliane)* was restored by Honorius (5C) and again by Belisarius (6C). The keystone bears a Greek cross on the town side and the *chi-rho* on the outside.

▶ *Turn right outside the gate into Viale delle Mura Latine.*

Mura Aureliane★
Work on the wall was initiated under the Emperor Aurelian in the 3C, as the existing walls could no longer contain the expanding city. Punctuated by towers, this is a compelling piece of Roman civil engineering, notably between the *Porta Latina* and *Porta San Sebastiano.*
Access up onto the wall itself is from *Porta San Sebastiano* (See below).

Porta San Sebastiano★ (St Sebastian Gate)
The gate is without doubt the most spectacular in Rome, with its base of tall marble blocks supporting crenellated towers. Known as the *Porta Appia* in ancient times, it was constructed by Aurelian (AD 271-75) when he built his defensive wall. Now it houses the **Museo delle Mura** (See below).

Arco di Druso (Arch of Drusus)
The arch dates from the 2C AD and was not therefore raised in honour of Drusus (39-38 BC), the younger brother of the Emperor Tiberius. It was used by Caracalla (AD 211-17) to support the aqueduct that supplied water to his baths.

Additional Sights

Casa del Cardinale Bessarione★ (Cardinal Bessarion's House)
Open by appointment only. €2.07. 06 77 20 15 99.

This handsome house belonged to Cardinal John Bessarion, the Humanist scholar (c 1402-72).

Sepolcro degli Scipionia (Scipio Family Tomb)

Via di Porta S. Sebastiano 9. ⊶ *Closed for restoration at the time of going to press.* ☏*06 67 10 38 19.*

The Scipio family tomb was discovered in 1614 and restored in 1926. The funeral inscriptions constitute a remarkable document of the republican period and of the infancy of Latin literature. Their concentration on the dead man's public spiritedness and his moral rectitude reveal the mentality of those days, when Roman civilisation was being forged.

Columbarium of Pomponius Hylas

Next to the small temple of San Giovanni in Oleo. ◑ *Open by appointment only* ☏*06 67 10 20 70.*

Decorated with stucco work and fine paintings, this cremation urn repository probably dates from the Julio-Claudian period (AD 31-68).

Museo delle Mura (Wall Museum)

In Porta San Sebastiano. ◑*Open Tues-Sun Apr–Oct 9am-7pm; Nov-Mar 9am-5pm.* ◑*Closed Mon, 1 Jan, 1 May and Christmas.* ⊚*€2.58.* ☏*06 70 47 52 84.*

The museum, housed within the gate, chronicles the Aurelian walls' evolution. It is possible to walk along an expanse westwards as far as *Via Christoforo Colombo.*

SEPOLCRO DEGLI SCIPIONI

3C BC   c 150 BC

TRASTEVERE★★

MICHELIN MAP 38 M 10, N 10-11

Trastevere, on the right bank of the Tiber, was for centuries inhabited by artisans and small traders, known for their proud, independent nature. Today, that rogue energy continues – and is celebrated each July during the traditional "Festa de Noantri." However, the neighbourhood is now "multo chic", attracting wealthy Italians and expats, all drawn by the vibrant atmosphere with its picturesque, narrow streets and small piazzas, excellent bakeries and "tipico" trattorias. The pace here tends to drawl during the day, but the quarter stirs at dusk, especially in its northern section, where most of the nightclubs, bars and eateries lie.

▶ **Orient Yourself:** This district, divided into two by *Viale Trastevere*, sits across the Tiber from the historic centre of Rome, facing *Isola Tiberina*. The Janiculum Hill and the vast green area of *Villa Pamphili* lie to the west.

🕐 **Organising Your Time***:* Allow at least 2hrs.

🖈 **Don't Miss:** Porta Portese flea market every Sunday, the animation of Piazza Santa Maria della Trastevere, *Giudizio Universale* by Cavallini in S. Agnese.

🖈 **Also See:** *BOCCA DELLA VERITÀ; GIANICOLO; ISOLA TIBERINA-TORRE ARGENTINA.*

A Bit of History

Trastevere (from *trans-Tiberim* meaning "over the Tiber") was not originally part of Rome; it was the beginning of Etruscan territory.

From the republic, it was inhabited mainly by Jews and Syrians and was incorporated into Rome by Augustus as the 14th administrative district. Not far from the present *San Cosimato* Hospital, Augustus created a *naumachia*, a vast pool where naval warfare spectacles were mounted. Close to the Mediterranean harbour of Ostia and the river port of *Ripa Grande*, trade flourished, especially in food produce. This continues in the number of small groceries and trattorias here – contrasted with the artisanal trades on the opposite bank. Few public buildings lay here; rather utilitarian services, such as a 2C fire station near *Via dei Genovesi,* of which traces were discovered in the 19C. Among the religious buildings is a Syrian sanctuary, traces surfaced under the *Villa Sciarra* near *Via Emilio Dandolo*.

In the 3C, the whole of Trastevere was enclosed by the **Aurelian Wall** (*Mura Aureliane*) pierced by three gateways: the *Porta Settimiana* to the north, the *Porta Aurelia* (now *Porta S. Pancrazio*) (🖈*See GIANICOLO*) to the west and to the

south the *Porta Portuensis* (further south than the present *Porta Portese*).

Though some powerful Roman families had palaces in Trastevere, the area never lost its popular character. Throughout the centuries the inhabitants have kept their reputation of stout fellows ready to lend strength and courage to a revolutionary cause. Stendhal thought it superb and "full of energy."

Poets who celebrated Rome in the local dialect have always found a response there. The exploits of the Trasteverians, who defied the inhabitants of the *Santa Maria Maggiore* district with catapults, have been the subject of several sonnets in Roman folklore.

Walking Tour

Torre degli Anguillara (Anguillara Tower)

The 13C tower, attached to a small palace of the same name, recalls one of the most powerful Roman families. Whether as warriors, magistrates, outlaws, forgers or clerics, the Anguillara were at the forefront of events from the Middle Ages to the Renaissance.

The palace, built in the 15C, underwent major restoration in the 19C and now houses the Institute for Dante Studies.

Address Book

WHERE TO EAT

See "Where to Eat" in the Your Stay in Rome section at the end of the guide.

TAKING A BREAK

Bar Calisto – *Piazza San Calisto 3. Open Mon-Sat 6-1:30am. Closed Sun, end of Aug. ☎06 583 5869. ⌷.*
A hedge separates this local "dive bar" from the piazza, grid-locked with bodies each night. Nicknamed "Marcello's", it serves cheap coffee, beer and ice cream. It's glamorous in a gritty way, a true slice of old Trastevere. Try the vodka and lemon sorbet *affogato*.

Bibli – *Via dei Fienaroli 28. Open Tues-Sun 11am-midnight, Mon 5:30 pm-midnight. ☎06 581 4534. www.bibli.it.*
This tiny bookstore café is best known for its "minibrunch". Dinner buffet kicks off at 7pm, along with live music.

Café di Marzio – *Piazza Santa Maria in Trastevere 15. Open Tues-Sun 7am-2am. Closed Mon. ☎06 581 6095.*
The tables are costly (justifiably so, given the view), but counter service remains affordable: pay at the *cassa* first. Should you linger, sip slowly on a creamy hot chocolate, a speciality.

La Boccaccia: Pizza e Focaccia – *Via di S. Dorotea 2. Open 10am–12:30am. Closed early August. ☎06 581 0043. ⌷.*
This *al taglio* joint serves the best potato pizza in the world. Boccaccia's version is still anti-Atkins, but has soft potato chunks and lush mozzarella.

L'Insalata Ricca – *Via G.C. Santini 12/16, Trastevere. Open daily 12:30–11:45pm. ☎06 588 1301. www.insalataricca.it.*
Salads and *bruschette* (toast with toppings) star here, alongside omelettes. The bilingual staff understands the need for a light bite in the gut-busting, five-course wonderland of Roman restaurants.

Latteria Ugolini – *Via della Lungaretta 161. ☎06 58 16 440. Open Mon-Sat 8am–1:30pm and 5-8:15pm.* This old dairy is one of the few in Rome to have retained its old marble counter. Here customers can taste traditional Gentilini biscuits.

Pizza Pazza – *Piazza Trilussa 42. Open daily 8am–3am. ☎58 333 924.*
World-champion slices sell here – over 180 varieties. Chef Mauro de Maio's signature: aged crust made from special soy flour and extra virgin oil.

Sora Mirella – *Lungotevere degli Anguillara.* Enjoy traditional Roman *grattachecce* – shaved ice – with a wonderful view of the Isola Tiberina. The *"superfrutta"* with kiwi, strawberries and melon is available on request.

SHOPPING

Al Tempo Ritrovato – *Via dei Fienaroli 31d/32. Open Tue-Sat 10:30am-1.30pm and 4-8pm; Mon 4-8pm. ☎06 58 17 724.* This store celebrates women writers.

Lattonieri – *Piazza de Renzi 22.* The old trade of the tinsmith is still practised here today, producing coffee pots, lanterns and oil cruets.

Porta Portese Flea Market – See "Shopping" in the *Your Stay in Rome* section at the beginning of the guide.

TRASTEVERE IN FESTA

From 15-30 July, the district celebrates the *Festa de Noantri* ("Festival of We Others") with parades and pomp.

San Crisogono

The church of **St Chrysogonus,** which dates from the 5C, evolved over the centuries. The **belfry**, erected in the 12C when the church was almost entirely rebuilt, was altered in the 16C by the addition of a spire.

The **façade** is the work of **Giovanni Battista Soria**, who was put in charge of the refurbishment of the building in the 17C by Cardinal Scipione Borghese, a nephew of the Pope and incumbent of the church at the time.

Interior★ – Only the basilical plan of a nave and two aisles has survived from the 12C; the floor is 13C work by Roman marble masons. The overall effect – half-Mannerist, half-Baroque – was created in the 17C by GB Soria, who retained the ancient pillars, refashioned their capitals in stucco, opened up great windows in the nave to let in more light and installed

The faint outline of a fresco adds to the attraction of this picturesque, crumbling façade

Palaeo-Christian church – *Access from the sacristy by an awkward iron stair.* ⏱*Open Mon-Sat 7-11am and 4-7pm; Sun and public holidays, 8am-1pm and 4-7pm.* ⏱*Closed for visits during church services.* ⊕*€2.* ☎*06 58 18 225.*

At a depth of 6m/20ft below floor level archaeologists have discovered traces of the 5C building, which was altered in the 8C and abandoned in the 12C, when the present church was built.

Here is the lower part of the apse (probably partially 5C) below which Gregory III hollowed out a *confessio* in the 8C; it follows the curve of the apse before drawing in on each side into a horseshoe shape, thus creating a semicircular corridor. Also it's bifurcated at the end: (*towards the nave*) is a relic chamber. This passage and the apse still bear traces of 8C painting. There are 10C paintings on the walls of the semicircular corridor. The baptistry (*left*), now divided into two by a wall, was used for the baptism of early Christians.

▸ *From Piazza Sonnino take Via della Lunaaretta. Piazza in Piscinula. Via*

a fine coffered ceiling of complex design, showing the arms of Cardinal Borghese. Two monolithic porphyry columns support the chancel arch. The baldaquin is also the work of Soria. The fine wood carving in the chancel dates from 1863. The mosaic in the apse, showing the Virgin and Child with St James and St Chrysogonus, comes from the Cavallini School (late 13C).

dei Salumi and Via dei Vascellari to reach Piazza Santa Cecilia.

Santa Cecilia★

🕐*Open 9:30am-12:30pm and 4-6:30pm.* 🎫*Crypt: €2.50.* ☎*06 58 99 289.*

A sanctuary dedicated to St Cecilia existed in a private house on this site in the 5C. Pope Paschal I (817-24) replaced it with a church, which was much altered in the 16C, 18C and 19C.

The church is preceded by a courtyard planted with flower beds around a large antique vase. A fine 12C campanile was remodelled in the 18C, but its coeval porch, with its ancient columns and mosaic frieze, was preserved.

Interior – The medieval appearance is generally lost, although it still retains the **mosaic** from Paschal I in the 9C. The influence that Byzantine art exerted on Roman mosaic workers in earlier centuries is evident in the way the figures are presented: on Christ's right – St Paul, St Agatha and Pascal I, with a square halo since he was still alive; on the left – St Peter, St Valerian and St Cecilia; the lively postures and the beautiful colours are also typically Roman.

The **baldaquin** over the high altar is by **Arnolfo di Cambio** (1293); it is eight years later than a similar work by the same artist for St Paul Without the Walls and shows a growing heaviness of style and the influence of classical works; in the left back corner is an equestrian statue of a saint, reminiscent of the statue of Marcus Aurelius now in the Capitoline Museum.

The statue of **St Cecilia**★ *(below the altar)*, a fine sculpture by Stefano Maderno (1599), recalls her history and legend. Paschal I (817-24) who was desperately searching all the Christian cemeteries for the remains of St Cecilia, was guided by a dream. He found the saint's corpse lying beside her husband, St Valerian, in a catacomb on the Old Appian Way. He had them transferred immediately to a place beneath the altar. Seven centuries later, during the reign of Clement VIII, Cardinal Sfondrati undertook alterations to the chancel. During the work the sarcophagi came to light and St Cecilia's body was discovered in the posture in which Maderno has represented it.

The cardinal also wanted to restore the little room venerated as the site of St Cecilia's martyrdom. This work disclosed several pipes against the wall, thought to have raised the temperature in the room where Cecilia was condemned to suffocate. She was saved by a miraculous dew, only to be beheaded so inefficiently that she lingered in agony for three days. The cardinal commissioned Guido Reni to paint the *Decapitation of the Saint,* now above the altar.

The tomb of Rampolla is a dramatic exercise in perspective (1929) and commemorates the cardinal whose generosity made it possible to open the crypt. It was created from 1899-1901 in the Byzantine style.

Excavations uncovered the remains of several ancient houses, among which was the first sanctuary dedicated to St Cecilia. Also visible is a room containing seven grain silos and another in which are exhibited *sarcophagi* and inscriptions: a low relief representing Minerva (2C BC) in a little recess and a column also from the Republican period.

Behind the grating in the *confessio (beneath the apse)* are several *sarcophagi,* including those of St Cecilia and St Valerian.

The Last Judgement by Pietro Cavallini★★★ – *In the convent.* 🕐*Open Tue and Thu 10-11:30am; Sun, 11:15am-noon.* ☎*06 58 99 289.*

This masterpiece of Roman medieval painting by Pietro Cavallini (c 1293) was formerly on the inside wall of the façade of the church and is now kept in the monks' chancel. A magnificent work of art, the painting was badly damaged in the 16C. All that remains is the figure of *Christ in Judgement* surrounded by angels with magnificent outspread wings, flanked by Mary and John the Baptist, hands raised beseechingly; below are the apostles, and angels blowing trumpets.

Note the perfect distribution of light and shade, the individual expression on each face and the subtle harmony of the colours.

▶ *Take Via di San Michele.*

After turning into *Via Madonna dell'Orto*, note the impressive 19C tobacco factory behind the church.

▶ *Turn left into Via Anicia.*

San Francesco a Ripa

In 1682, St Francis replaced the earlier church of the Franciscan order. The fourth chapel in the left-hand aisle contains a **statue of Blessed Ludovica Albertoni**★★ by **Bernini**; she was a member of the Franciscan Tertiaries (1474-1533) and is buried beneath the altar. Bernini shows her suffering and in this, one of his later works (1674), the marble perfectly expresses the final agony of a saintly life.

▶ *Take Via di S. Francesco a Ripa to reach Piazza Santa Maria in Trastevere.*

Piazza Santa Maria in Trastevere★★, the heart of the district, is probably the most charming corner of Trastevere, full of local colour. The fountain at the centre was remodelled by **Bernini** in 1659. On the left is the fine 17C façade of the **Palazzo di San Callisto.**

Basilica di Santa Maria in Trastevere★★ (Basilica of St Mary in Trastevere)

On this spot in 38 BC, a fountain of oil *(fons olei)* flowed for a whole day. Christians interpreted this as a sign of the grace that would spread world-wide. Pope Calixtus (217-22) is said to have built the first sanctuary, but it was the energetic Pope Julius I (337-52), a keen builder, who constructed a proper basilica. The building was altered in the 9C by Gregory V, to provide a crypt in which he laid the saintly remains of Calixtus, Pope Cornelius and Calepodius.

The present basilica dates from the 12C; it was built about 1140 during a brief period of calm in the troubled reign of Innocent II, who was beset by the anti-Popes, Anacletus II and Victor IV. Despite St Bernard's assistance, when Innocent II died, Rome was in the hands of revolutionaries, who proclaimed a Republic. His successors restored and embellished the church on many occasions right up to the 19C.

Façade

The belfry is 12C; a small recess at the top is decorated with a mosaic of the Virgin and Child, to whom the basilica is dedicated. The *Virgin and Child* are also celebrated in the mosaic on the façade (12–13C), which shows a procession of women approaching from both sides.

The statues of the saints on the balustrade over the porch were erected from the 17C to the 18C. The porch, which was restored early in the 18C, shelters several fragments, some from the buildings which preceded the present one. Two 15C frescoes (1), (one rather damaged), depict the *Annunciation*. The door frames are made of friezes dating from the time of the empire.

Interior

The basilical plan of Pope Innocent II's 12C church is still visible. As in all medieval Roman buildings, the columns dividing the nave from the aisles were taken from ancient monuments; all are crowned with their classical capitals in either the Ionic or the Corinthian orders. The figures of some Egyptian divinities were removed in the 19C by Pope Pius IX.

The cornice is composed of an assortment of Ancient fragments.

Chancel mosaics★★★ – The mosaics on the chancel arch (the Prophets Isaiah and Jeremiah and the symbols of the Evangelists) date from the 12C; so do those in the half-dome of the apse. To the right of Christ and the Virgin are St Callixtus, St Lawrence and Pope Innocent II offering his church to Mary; on the left are St Peter, St Cornelius, St Julius and St Calepodius. During the Romanesque period, mosaic art was still influenced by the Byzantine style: the Virgin is adorned with gold like an empress, the group of figures betrays a certain oriental rigidity and loses some of its expressive force in the multitude of detail (the Virgin's dress). At the top is paradise, with the hand of God placing a crown on Christ's head; at the bottom are lambs, symbols of the apostles, coming from the cities of Jerusalem and Bethlehem and facing the Lamb of God.

The mosaics between the windows and at the base of the chancel arch are a masterpiece by **Pietro Cavallini** (late

13C), representing scenes from the life of the Virgin. The medallion above the throne shows the Virgin and Child between St Peter and St Paul, with Cardinal Stefaneschi, who commissioned the work, on a smaller scale.

The bishop's throne (2) standing in the apse is made of marble (12C).

An inscription (3) before the chancel marks the site of the oil fountain.

Altemps Chapel (4) – The stucco and frescoes of this chapel are in the style of the Counter-Reformation, which developed after the Council of Trent (late 16C).

Transept – The fine coffered ceiling is late-16C work. The central low relief in gilded and painted wood illustrates the Assumption.

The **Sacristy** lobby contains two very fine old mosaics (5).

The **Avila Chapel** (6) with its dome is the exuberant creation of Antonio Gherardi (late 17C); the *trompe l'œil* has been used to create a Baroque effect.

Among the treasures of this church is the charming tabernacle (7) by Mino da Fiesole (late 15C).

A warren of narrow, picturesque streets lead to the square, making this an ideal spot for a leisurely stroll.

▶ *Take Via della Paglia, then turn right into Piazza S. Egidio, home to the Museo di Roma in Trastevere.*
▶ *Take Via Pelliccia and Vicolo di Moro to reach Piazza Trilussa.*

The Piazza Trilussa commemorates Carlo Alberto Salustri, who wrote poetry in the Roman dialect under the pseudonym **Trilussa** (1871-1950). In his racy and mildly satirical style, he highlights the spirit of the Roman people, describing their lives in a long and colourful story. A monument was set up in his honour in 1954. Nearby is a colossal fountain installed by Paul V in 1612 at the beginning of *Via Giulia* and moved here in the 19C, when the Tiber embankments were built.

Opposite is the **Sistine Bridge** (*Ponte Sisto*), named after Sixtus IV (1471-84), who had it built (modernised in the 19C).

Basilica di Santa Maria in Trastevere

▶ *Take Via di Ponte Sisto and then Via Santa Dorotea.*

According to local tradition, the house before the corner (n° 20), with the charmingly decorated window on the second floor, was the home of **La Fornarina,** Raphael's mistress, whom he immortalised in his famous painting now in the National Museum of Antique Art in *Palazzo Barberini*.

Additional Sight

Museo di Roma in Trastevere

  Open Tues-Sun 10am-8pm (last admission 7:30pm); weekday holidays, 9am-1:30pm. Closed Mon, 1 Jan, 1 May and Christmas. € 2.58. ☎ 06 58 99 359.

The museum occupies what was once the Convent of St Egidius in Trastevere. There are many artefacts (watercolours, prints and ceramics) thaat tell the story of life and popular dress in 18C and 19C Rome. As well as the various display cases showing scenes from everyday life, there is a reconstruction of the room where the poet Trilussa worked.

VATICANO-SAN PIETRO★★★

MICHELIN MAP 38 J 7-8, K 7-9
METRO LINE A: OTTAVIANO-SAN PIETRO
(500M/550 YD FROM THE ENTRANCE TO THE VATICAN MUSEUMS
AND 800M/880YD FROM PIAZZA SAN PIETRO)
OR CIPRO-MUSEI VATICANI
(600M/660 YD FROM THE ENTRANCE TO THE VATICAN MUSEUMS)

The Vatican City is home to the largest basilica in the world and a museum containing some of its greatest art treasures. This tiny fortified territory lies inside Italy's capital; it is literally a state within a state. As the heart of the Roman Catholic Church, its influence extends to all four corners of the globe. Religion aside, the Vatican contains many of Rome's highlights: Bernini's colonnade surrounding St Peter's Square, Michelangelo's frescoes on the ceiling of the Sistine Chapel, and the splendid basilica dome, where breathtaking views unfurl.

▶ **Orient Yourself:** The Vatican City is on the right bank of the Tiber, north of the Janiculum Hill, level with Castel Sant'Angelo, to which it is linked by Via della Conciliazione. The Prati district lies to the north.

☺ **Don't Miss:** Michaelangelo's *Pietà*, St Peter's tomb and views from the basilica's dome, the Vatican Museums' Raphael Room and the Sistine Chapel.

🕓 **Organising Your Time:** Allow 1 full day. Visit the Vatican museums early in the morning, as lines can stretch miles (🖝 *See Making the Most of Your Visit in the Address Book*).

🖝 **Also See:** *CASTEL SANT'ANGELO; GIANICOLO.*

A Bit of History

The Vatican State

The wide **Via della Conciliazione** was opened in 1950, Jubilee Year. The façades of the buildings on the southern end bear the arms of Pius XII (*right*) and of Rome (*left*). Two rows of street lamps – in the shape of obelisks – line the broad road, which leads directly to St Peter's Basilica (*San Pietro*).

Once in St Peter's Square, you've left Italy and are in the Vatican State. The Vatican City, north of the Janiculum Hill, is bounded on three sides by the wall overlooking *Viale Vaticano* and on the east by the curved colonnade in St Peter's Square. It's dominated by the basilica, the Vatican Palaces and the beautiful gardens surrounding the administrative offices of the Papal State.

Although the **Ager Vaticanus** lay outside the boundary of ancient Rome, it was nonetheless well known. In the days of the empire, Caligula established a circus here, which was embellished by Nero and hosted the massacre of the first Roman martyrs; their number may have included St Peter. Hadrian built his mausoleum, the present *Castel Sant'Angelo*, in the gardens belonging to the Domitii. The Emperor **Constantine** built over St Peter's tomb, a structure now world famous as the *Basilica di San Pietro*.

Bishop of Rome – From the first days of Christianity, the bishop was Christ's representative on earth. Rome's maintained that his *See* had been founded by the apostles, Peter and Paul, and therefore claimed first place in the ecclesiastical hierarchy. The title "pope", derived from the Greek *pápas*, meaning "father". The term initially applied to all patriarchs and bishops, but eventually was reserved for the Bishop of Rome.

Gift of Quiersy-sur-Oise – In 752, the Lombards occupied Ravenna and the imperial territory between the River Po, the Apennines and the Adriatic. In Rome the king of the Lombards, Astolphe, demanded a tribute of one gold piece per head. When the intervention of the emperor in Byzantium, Constantine V (to whom Rome was, in principle, subject), proved useless, Pope Stephen II approached the Carolingian dynasty. In

756, Pepin the Short, king of the Franks, liberated the occupied territory. Power passed, however, to the pope in this "Republic of the Holy Church of God" – and thus the Papal States were born.

"Leonine City" – On 23 August 846, the Saracens invaded Rome, pillaging the basilicas of St Peter and St Paul. In the following year, therefore, Leo IV energetically set to work raising a defensive wall round the Vatican district, known as the *Borgo*. The wall was restored in the 15C by Nicholas V, reinforced with bastions by Sangallo the Younger under Paul III in the 16C, and extended by Pius IV in 1564 to *Porta Santo Spirito*.

Lateran Treaty – The unification of Italy (1820-70) would have been incomplete without the Papal States. On 20 September 1870, the troops of King **Victor Emmanuel II** entered Rome and proclaimed the city the capital of the kingdom. On 2 May 1871, the Italian Parliament passed the **Law of the Guarantees** to show that it did not wish to subjugate the papacy. The pope would retain the Vatican City and receive an annual allowance. Pius IX excommunicated the act's authors and shut himself inside the Vatican, declaring that he was a prisoner. His successors maintained this stance and the Roman Question was not resolved until 1929, when the **Lateran Treaty** was signed on 11 February by Cardinal Gaspari, representing the Holy See, and Mussolini, the head of the Italian government.

The terms recognised the pope as sovereign of the Vatican State: the City itself and a number of properties that enjoy the privilege of extraterritoriality. These include four major basilicas (St John Lateran, St Peter's in the Vatican, St Paul Without the Walls, *Santa Maria Maggiore*), the Roman Curia, colleges and seminaries and the villa at *Castel Gandolfo*; in all 44ha/109 acres and just under 1 000 inhabitants. The treaty also included a financial indemnity and a religious settlement granting the Church a privileged position in Italy in respect of schooling and marriage. The Republican constitution of 1947 established a new relationship between the Roman Church and the Italian State on the basis of the Lateran Treaty. Another agreement

modifying the 1929 Lateran Treaty was signed on 18 February 1984 by the President of the Council and the Vatican Secretary of State.

Although the smallest state in physical size, the Vatican spreads the spiritual influence of the Roman Church throughout the world.

Head of the Roman Church

The pope is also called the Roman Pontiff, the Sovereign Pontiff, the Vicar of Christ, Holy Father and His Holiness. Sometimes he calls himself *"Servus Servorum Dei,"* the Servant of the Servants of God. In his mission as Pastor to the Church founded by Jesus Christ, he is assisted by the Sacred College of Cardinals and by the Roman Curia.

College of Cardinals – A cardinal is a high ecclesiastical official. His dress consists of a scarlet cape (a short hooded cloak) worn over a linen *rochet* (a surplice with narrow sleeves). The cardinals are the pope's closest advisers; they also elect him, assembled in "conclave". In 1586, Sixtus V fixed their number at 70, yet it's risen. Today Benedict XVI has 183; only 120 have electoral power.

Conclave – The cardinals withdraw into a secret meeting to chose the next pope. This method of election was established by **Gregory X** (1271-76), whose own election lasted nearly three years. He imposed very strict regulations, involving confinement and secrecy. For incentive, stalling cardinals would be reduced to one meal after three days, then – if two more passed –bread and water. Now the cardinals meet in conclave in the Sistine Chapel. A vote is held twice a day and after each inconclusive ballot, the papers are burned so as to produce dark smoke. A majority of two-thirds plus one is required; then a plume of clear smoke appears above the Vatican. The senior cardinal appears at the window in the façade of St Peter's and announces the election in the Latin formula: *Annuntio vobis gaudium magnum: habemus papam* (I announce to you with great joy: we have a pope). The freshly annointed leader then gives his first blessing.

Roman Curia – The Curia consists of a group of bodies, the dicasteries, which administer the Holy See.

Address Book

SAN PIETRO

Basilica – *Open Mar – Thurs-Tues 7am-6pm; Wed 1pm-6pm. Closed during Pontifical services.* ☎06 69 88 16 62. *www.vatican.va*. Inappropriately dressed visitors may be refused access to the basilica: this restriction applies to shorts, mini-skirts, sleeveless shirts and bare shoulders.

Museo Storico e Tesoro – *Open Mar-Oct 7am-7pm; Nov-Feb 7am-6pm. Closed Easter and Christmas.* €4.13. ☎06 69 88 16 62.

Grotte Vaticane – *Open 7am–6pm (5pm in winter). Closed during Pontifical services.* ☎6 69 88 16 62.

Necropoli Vaticana – *Guided tours only (1hr), 9am-5pm. Closed Sun and Catholic holidays. Apply well in advance to the Delegato della Fabbrica di San Pietro, Ufficio Scavi, Città del Vaticano, 00120 (offices open to the public Mon-Sat, 9am–5pm).* €10. *Children aged 11+ allowed with parents.* ☎06 69 88 53 18

Ascent to the Dome – *Open Apr-Sep, 8am-6pm; rest of the year 8am-5pm.* €5 (lift), €4 (stairs). ☎06 69 88 16 62.

PAPAL AUDIENCES

When in residence at the Vatican, the Holy Father gives a **public audience** on Wednesdays (10am in summer and 10:30am in winter), usually in *Piazza San Pietro*. Here also he celebrates the **Angelus** on Sundays and public holidays at noon. Access to both is free, but tickets are required for the Wednesday audience. These may be obtained by writing one to two weeks beforehand to the *Prefettura della Casa Pontificata, Città del Vaticano, 00120.* ☎06 69 88 32 73; *www.santasusanna. org/popeVatican/tickets.html*. To arrange groups, numbers of attendees and place of residence should be provided. Collect tickets between 3–8pm on the afternoon before the audience, or on the morning itself, from the *Prefettura* in *Piazza San Pietro* (large bronze door). Places are sometimes available at short notice, even the same day.

VATICAN MUSEUMS

Admission times and charges – Two tours have been designed for

disabled visitors. Tour A is dedicated to classical antiquity and the Etruscans, Tour B concentrates on the Vatican Palaces and the Picture Gallery).
Entrance: Viale Vaticano.
Open Mar-Oct Mon-Fri 8:45am-4:45pm (last admission 3:20pm); Sat, last Sun of the month and Nov-Feb 8:45am-1:45pm (last admission 12:20pm). Closed Sun (except the last in the month), 1 and 6 Jan, 11 Feb, 19 Mar, Easter Sun and Easter Mon, 1 May, Ascension Day, Corpus Domini, 29 June and public holidays.
Audioguides available in English, Italian, French, German, Spanish and Japanese. €12; no charge 27 Sept and last Sun of the month. *Bar, café and self-service cafeteria.* ☎06 69 88 46 76; *www.vatican.va*

Loggia di Raffaello – *Open to specialists only by prior written request to the museum. Access is through the Hall of Constantine. The loggia occupies the second floor of the building. This monumental addition to the façade of Palazzo Apostolico, which looked out over Rome, was commissioned by Julius II.*

Museo delle Carrozze – *Available on request only.* ☎06 69 88 38 60

MAKING THE MOST OF YOUR VISIT

Allow at least one full day for an in-depth visit to all the galleries. However, the ★★★ highly recommended sections only take approximately 3hr.
A plan detailing a "short tour" and a "detailed tour" is available from the information desk.
Some galleries in the Vatican Museums are open in rotation, and not all have the same opening times. ☎06 69 88 33 33. Visitors must follow the official one-way tour, which has options at various points.

VATICAN CITY AND GARDENS

Tours by prior application to the Musei Vaticani. €9. ☎06 69 88 46 76, fax 06 69 88 51 00.

WHERE TO EAT

See "Where to Eat" in the *Your Stay in Rome* section at the end of the guide.

TAKING A BREAK

Ottaviani – *Via Paolo Emilio 9/11* – ☎06 32 43 302. *Closed Mon.* – . This small shop serves "*pizza pazza*" (crazy pizza), topped with as many ingredients as customers want.

Non solo Pizza – *Via degli Scipioni 95/97.* ☎*06 37 25 820. Closed Wed.* 🚭. A popular place for a bite to eat after a visit to St Peter's or the Vatican Museums. Specialities include pizza with cep mushrooms (*funghi porcini*), broccoli and sausage (*salsiccia*).

BARS

Morrison's – *Via Ennio Quirino Visconti 88.* ☎*06 32 22 2652. Open Tue-Sun noon-5pm and 7pm-2am. Closed Mon.* This elegant pub has a wide range of beers, including the Guinness group, as well as a selection of international whiskies.

Quelli della Notte – *Via Leone IV 48. Open Tue-Sun 6pm-5am.* This crowded bar is popular for its excellent *cornetti alla crema* (cream-filled croissant).

SHOPPING

Italia Garipoli – *Borgo Vittorio 91/a* – ☎*06 68 80 21 96. Open Mon-Fri 10am-1pm and 4-7pm; Sat 10am-1pm.* As well as producing and selling precious lace and embroidery, this shop also restores valuable clothes and fabrics.

SOUVENIRS FOR MODERN-DAY PILGRIMS

Shops selling religious articles are mostly located in *Via della Conciliazione,* along with general souvenir shops (👉 *See PANTHEON*).

Savelli – *Via Paolo VI 27-29 (on the corner of Piazza del Sant'Uffizio)* – ☎*06 68 30 70 17. Open Mon-Sat 9am-6:30pm.* This large shop is known for its religious mosaics.

Councils – Within the Roman Church there are two rites (Oriental and Latin); all the constituent churches belong to one or the other and are grouped into dioceses under the direction of **bishops**. The spiritual authority of a bishop is symbolised by a crozier, ring, mitre and his pectoral cross. His dress resembles a cardinal's, but purple. The Episcopal College, consisting of about 4 000 bishops spread throughout the world, is presided over by the pope, who calls them together in an **Ecumenical Council** to discuss the life of the Church.

Papal Audiences – The audiences are held in St Peter's Square in summer. Come winter, they move inside St Peter's Basilica and the huge modern hall designed by Pier Luigi Nervi under Paul VI. During the ceremony, the pope gives his blessing, and preaches on the great questions of the Church and humanity. His homily is delivered in Italian and then translated into English, French, German, Spanish and Polish. Official groups of pilgrims are greeted by name in the appropriate language.

Head of State

The pope is the Sovereign of the Vatican State and in this capacity wields the full range of legislative, executive and judicial power. He is assisted in the internal administration of the Vatican by a **Pontifical Commission**, composed of cardinals and a lay member. Beneath the commission is the **Administration** (*Governatorato*), which, since 1969, has been assisted by a **Council of State**.

The Vatican State has a yellow flag, bearing a tiara and crossed keys. Gounod composed its hymn, the *Pontifical March*. The armed regiments were disbanded by Paul VI in 1970; only the **Swiss Guards** have been retained, dressed in their picturesque yellow, red and blue uniforms, supposedly of Michelangelo's design.

The Vatican issues its own stamps, mints coins (valid in Italy), operates a post office and has a railway station.

Cultural, scientific and artistic activity – The **Apostolic Vatican Library** ranks very high; it was founded by Papal Bull in 1475 and contains over 60 000 volumes of manuscripts, 100 000 autographs, 800 000 prints, 100 000 engravings and maps and a collection of coins, including an important section consisting of Roman money from the Republican era.

The **Secret Archives**, composed of documents dating from the 13C, have been open to the public for consultation since 1881 and are of worldwide importance in historical research.

The **Pontifical Academy of Science** was founded in 1936 by Pius XI and con-

Pilgrim Routes

Via Francigena (or *Romea*) was one of the most famous pilgrim routes of the Middle Ages. It followed the ancient *Via Cassia* and linked Rome (or more precisely, St Peter's, with northern Europe.

sists of 70 Academicians chosen by the pope from scholars worldwide.

The **Fabric of St Peter** is the body of architects and specialists in charge of the conservation of St Peter's Basilica. The mosaic workshop is annexed to it.

The Vatican has a printing works that produces texts in almost all languages; there is also a daily newspaper, the *Osservatore Romano*, and a weekly paper, the *Osservatore della Domenica*, which is published in several languages. The Vatican Radio transmits programmes in 40 different languages.

Jubilee

Its origins are buried deep in the Jewish religion. When Moses received the Ten Commandments on Mount Sinai, he was also given a set of laws to guide the behaviour of the people of Israel. One insisted: "you shall send abroad the loud trumpet on the tenth day of the seventh month (of the forty-ninth year)... you shall hallow the fiftieth year, and proclaim liberty throughout the land to all its inhabitants; it shall be a jubilee for you." (This is known as the *Yôbél* in Hebrew, from the name given to the goat-horn instrument.) In the year of the Jubilee, "each man shall return to his property and his family... you shall neither sow, nor reap what grows of itself." The year represented an act of peace and reconciliation with God. This idea was later adopted by Christians, for whom the Jubilee signifies a remission of sins.

Their first Jubilee took place in 1300, during the rule of **Boniface VIII**. A huge number of pilgrims battled to Rome, believing that a full remission of sins would be granted in the centenary of the birth of Christ. This amazing influx led the pope to issue a Bull, sanctioning the "rules" for receiving indulgences. Each pilgrim was required to pay 15 visits to the two basilicas of St Peter's and St Paul Without the Walls, which housed the relics of the two saints (30 visits if they were from Rome). Hereafter, Jubilee years were celebrated regularly every 50 years, as decreed by Clement VI (1342-52), with just a few omissions, and subsequently every 25 years, as established by Paul II (1464-71). Exceptional Jubilee years were also occasionally declared, such as 1983.

In 1750, Benedict XIV established the conditions for full indulgence, which included visiting all four major basilicas, confession, communion and prayer.

Ceremonies and visits – The Jubilee year traditionally starts with the special Christmas Eve ceremony: the pope opens the Holy Door, which is closed at all other times. With a gold and silver mallet, he knocks three times on the wall behind which the door is hidden. Workers then knock it down. Until 1983, the doors of Santa Maria Maggiore, St Paul Without the Walls and St John Lateran

Pilgrims' Dress and the Rite of Departure

Pilgrims needed to be easily recognisable to obtain hospitality and assistance during their journey – and distinguish themselves from other travellers. Before leaving home, they made wills and gathered together for Mass and a blessing, where they received a cape, hat, purse and knapsack. Each of these articles had a special name. The cape was dark in colour, usually brown or grey, and was known as the *sanrocchino, schiavina* or *pellegrina*; the broad-brimmed hat was a *petaso*; the knapsack (or bag) was a *capsella* or *pera*; the stave, fitted with a hook and an iron tip, was known as a *bordone, burdo, baculus* or *fustis*. These articles also had symbolic significance: the knapsack represented charity (because it could hold only one day's provisions), the stave could chase off demons and overcome temptation, and the hat was covered with "souvenirs" from the journey – proof of pilgrimage. Objects that the *Romei* would hang from their hats (and sometimes their capes) included crosses, images of St Veronica, keys and portraits of saints and relics.

were opened by the three cardinals of these churches. However, this tradition was changed for the Jubilee of 2000, when the pope opened all four doors.

The door at St Peter's is closed again on 6 January of the following year (5 January for the other three basilicas). The pope blesses the materials used to rebuild the wall and lays the first three bricks.

Arco delle Campane...R   Camposanto teutonico...S

The pilgrims were known as "*Romei*". They came to the city not only to visit the major churches, but also the catacombs, each of which held saints' relics. Their graffiti is still visible: invocations to the saints, prayers, or sometimes simply names carved in the stone.

Accommodation – Suitable shelter had to be found for this huge influx of people, many of whom were destitute. The hospices provided for pilgrims were originally known as *xenodochi*; they often included a hospital, school , and other provisions for the poor. These establishments later came to be known as *scholae peregrinorum*. Many nations built and ran ones for their citizens.

Basilica Di San Pietro

A Bit of History
For admission times and charges, permissible attire, etc. see San Pietro in the Address Book

The basilica is the largest of all Christian places of worship. Its origin is linked to the martyrdom of **Peter** (c AD 64). When a huge fire destroyed much of Rome, Nero held the Christians responsible and ordered many executions. Simon, named "Peter" by Jesus, was probably among the victims.

According to the law, he was simply a Jewish fisherman, a native of Capernaum in Galilee, sentenced therefore to crucifixion in Nero's Circus at the foot of the Vatican Hill. So as to distinguish his own death from Jesus's, Peter humbly begged to be crucified upside down.

Constantine's basilica – Following his conversion to Christianity, Constantine built a sanctuary in 324 over the tomb of St Peter, Christ's chief apostle. In 326, Pope Sylvester I consecrated the building, which was completed some 25 years later. The basilica had a nave, four aisles and a narrow transept; the apsidal wall stood just behind the present papal altar. The entrance was through an *atrium* graced with a fountain decorated with the beautiful pine cone (*la Pigna*), which can now be seen in a courtyard of the Vatican Palace. The façade gleamed with mosaics. The *confessio* (a crypt containing the tomb of a martyr) was not completely underground; an opening at floor level gave access to the tomb. At the end of the 6C, Pope

St Peter's Square

Gregory the Great raised the chancel; beneath it the *confessio* took the form of a corridor following the apse's curve and had a chapel called *ad caput*.

Barbarians pillaged for more than a century: Alaric in 410 and Totila in 546. In 846, it was raided by the Saracens. Its prestige remained intact. Imperial coronations were held in solemn state. On Christmas Day AD 800, Leo III crowned Charlemagne king of the Romans; 75 years later it was the turn of his grandson, Charles the Bald, during the Pontificate of John VIII, the first soldier Pope and the also the first assassinated. Arnoul, the last of the Carolingians, became Pope Formosus in 891. John XII, who lived surrounded by slaves and eunuchs, crowned Otho I the first Emperor of Germany on 2 February 962 and then conspired against him. His intrigues brought the papacy under the Emperor's control for over a century. After 1 000 years, despite frequent restoration and embellishment, St Peter's Basilica needed help.

1452, Nicholas V intervenes – The pope appointed Bernardo Rossellino to restore the basilica. He retained the dimensions of Contantine's building, but proposed a cruciform plan with a dome and a new choir. The pope died in 1455 and the project was abandoned. For the next 50 years his successors were content to shore up the existing building.

1503, Julius II, an energetic Pope – His plan for renovation was radical. His architects were **Bramante**, who had arrived in Rome in 1499, and **Giuliano da Sangallo**. The chosen design was Bramante's: a Greek cruciform plan with jutting apses beneath cupolas and over the crossing a central dome similar to the Pantheon's. On 18 April 1506, the first stone was laid at the base of a pillar; a temporary chancel had been provided and a large part of the apse and transept demolished, causing Bramante to be nicknamed the "Destructive Maestro".

Sometimes Michelangelo cam to watch the work. Julius II had commissioned him to design his tomb, which was to be placed at the heart of the new basilica. The sculptor admired Bramante's plan, but disapproved of his administration. Seen as an intruder, Bramante came to hate him.

Believing himself in danger, Michelangelo retreated to Florence, but returned after violently denouncing the pope and Rome, where "they turn chalices into swords and helmets".

Julius II died in 1513 and Bramante the next year. For the next 30, the design of the building was the subject of interminable discussion. Raphael and Giuliano da Sangallo argued a return to the Latin cruciform plan. Baldassarre Peruzzi drew designs based on Bramante's. Antonio da Sangallo, Giuliano's nephew, promoted the Greek cross footprint, but suggested a bay in the form of a porch, with two towers flanking the façade, and alter the dome; he died in 1546.

From Michelangelo to Bernini – In 1547 **Paul III** appointed **Michelangelo**, then 72 and chief architect to the Vatican, to end the chaos. "To deviate from Bramante's design is to deviate from the truth", declared the master. He therefore returned to the Greek cruciform plan, simplified to accentuate its circular base – the circle, the sign of infinity, glorifying the Resurrection. The dome was no longer the shallow dome of the Pantheon, but reached high. Michelangelo worked on St Peter's, surrounded by intrigues, refusing any payment, doing all for the glory of God and the honour of St Peter. When he died in 1564, the apse and transepts were complete and the dome had risen as far as the top of the drum. It was completed in 1593 by **Giacomo della Porta**, assisted by Domenico Fontana, who may have been inspired to raise the dome even higher by one of the master's alternative designs.

In 1606, **Paul V** (1605-21) finally settled for the Latin cruciform plan; it was more suitable for high ceremony and preaching. The new basilica was to cover all the area occupied by the original church, whereas Michelangelo's plan had not extended so far east. The façade was entrusted to **Carlo Maderno**. The new basilica was consecrated by Urban VIII.

The final phase in St Peter's architectural history was directed by **Bernini**, who took over on Maderno's death in 1629. He turned what would have been a fine example of Renaissance architecture into a sumptuous Baroque monument. From Bramante to Bernini, the construction absorbed 120 years, the reigns of 20 popes and the work of 10 architects.

Piazza San Pietro★★★ (St Peter's Square)

The square, which was intended to isolate the basilica without creating a barrier in front of it, acts, in fact, as a sort of vestibule. The gentle curves of the colonnades, like two arcs of a circle framing the rectangular space, are a gesture of welcome extended to pilgrims.

The square was begun by **Bernini** in 1656 under Pope Alexander VII and completed in 1667. By flanking the façade with a broader and lower colonnade, the architect minimised the width and accentuate the height of the basilica. To create the effect of surprise so dear to Baroque artists, he enclosed the square and masked the façade. The basilica would be hidden from view until visitors entered the gap in the colonnade. Bernini's intention was not fully realised: the triumphal arch intended to link the two arms was not built and Via della Conciliazione gives a distant view of the basilica. Two belfries were planned, but the foundations proved too weak to carry the additional weight. At its widest point, the square measures 196m/643ft across. The **colonnade** is formed by rows of columns, four deep, surmounted by statues and the arms of Alexander VII: a remarkably solemn composition. At the centre of the square stands an **obelisk**, a granite monolith, carved in the 1C BC in Heliopolis for Caius Cornelius Gallus, the Roman Prefect in Egypt. It was brought to Rome in AD 37 by Caligula, who had it set up in his circus (left of the basilica). **Sixtus V** decided to erect it in St Peter's Square. His official architect was **Domenico Fontana**. The work took four months and gave birth to a legend. The obelisk was to be re-erected on 10 September 1585; 800 men and 75 horses were required to raise the 350t of granite to its full height (25.5m/84ft). After giving his blessing, the pope enjoined absolute silence on pain of death; he set up gallows to underscore the point. The work began, but the ropes chafed on the granite and threatened to give way. Then one of the workers cried out, *"acqua alle funi"* ("water for the ropes"). Even the pope congratulated him for disobeying the order. A relic of the True Cross is preserved at the top of the obelisk.

The two fountains are attributed to Carlo Maderno (*right*) and **Bernini** (*left*). Between them and the obelisk are two discs set into the paving to mark the focal points of the two ellipses enclosing the square; from these points the colonnades appear to consist of only one row of columns. This perspective is achieved by increasing the diameter of the columns from the inner to the outer row and placing them an equal distance from one another.

East front

A majestic flight of steps, designed by Bernini, leads to the east front. On either side stand statues of St Peter and St Paul (19C). The east front, begun by **Carlo Maderno** in 1607 and completed in 1614, was the object of spirited comment; owing to its dimensions (45m/147ft high and 115m/377ft wide), it masks the dome. From the balcony beneath the pediment, the pope gives his blessing *Urbi et Orbi* (to the city and to the world). The horizontal pediment above it is crowned by Christ, John the Baptist and 11 Apostles (sans Peter).

Porch

It was designed by **Carlo Maderno**. On the left behind a grill stands an equestrian statue of Charlemagne (1) (18C). The Door of Death (2), with sober sculptures on its bronze panels, is by **Giacomo Manzù** (1964); low down on the right in the left-hand section is a low-relief figure of John XXIII. The bronze door (3) was sculpted in 1445 by Antonio Averulino, known as **Il Filarete**. The true artistic spirit of the Renaissance is seen in the juxtaposition of religious scenes (*in the six panels*), episodes from the life of Eugenius IV (*in the spaces below the panels*) and mythological figures, animals and portraits of contemporary personalities (*in the frieze surrounding the panels*). To the right is the **Holy Door**: only the pope may open and close this to mark the Holy Year.

The "*Navicella*" mosaic (4) by **Giotto** dates from 1300. Originally from Constantine's Basilica, it was restored and shifted many times since.

Pietà

At the north end of the porch, in the vestibule of the *Scala Regia* (closed to the public), stands a statue of Constantine (5), the first Christian Emperor, by Bernini (1670).

Interior

Here everything is so well proportioned that the scale, though large, is not overwhelming. The seemingly life-size angels supporting the holy water stoups (6) are, in fact, enormous. St Peter's Basilica, with its 450 statues, 500 columns and 50 altars, and its reputed capacity to hold 60 000 people, is a record of the history of Christianity and art in Rome.

Nave – The overall length of the church, including the porch, is about 211m/692ft. Comparisons can be made with the length of other world-famous churches by means of marks set in the floor. When **Charlemagne** received the emperor's crown from the pope on Christmas Day AD 800, he knelt on the porphyry disc (7), now let into the pavement of the nave, although originally before the high altar.

Michelangelo's Pietà★★★ – This masterpiece, sculpted in 1499-1500 by Michelangelo at the age of 25, can be seen in the *Cappella della Pietà* (8). The execution of the profoundly human figures is perfect, revealing an amazing creative power. The group was commissioned by a French cardinal in 1498 and immediately hailed as genius. Even so, Michelangelo already had enemies, who muttered that the work was not his. He therefore added his signature across the Virgin's sash – his only opus thus marked.

BASILICA DI SAN PIETRO

0   40 m

Constantine's Basilica

Apse

Baldaquin

to the Grotte Vaticane

TRANSEPT   TRANSEPT

Museo storico e tesoro

Sacristia

NAVE

Michelangelo's plan

built   not built

Additions by Maderno and Bernini

CAPPELLA SISTINA

Scala R

Regia

PALAZZO E MUSEI DEL VATICANO

Porch   Porta Santa

Arco delle Campane

PIAZZA SAN PIETRO

Cappella del Crocifisso o delle reliquie (Crucifix Chapel or Chapel of Relics) **(9)** – **Bernini** designed the elliptical chapel, which contains a fine wooden crucifix attributed to Pietro Cavallini (early 14C).

Queen Christina of Sweden's Monument (10) – In 1654 **Queen Christina** abdicated her throne; she was converted to Roman Catholicism and came to live here the following year. She is buried in the "grottoes". Her monument was executed by Jean-Baptiste Theodon from designs by Carlo Fontana (18C).

Countess Mathilda of Tuscany's Monument (11) – She was the first woman to be buried in the basilica. Mathilda received the Emperor Henry IV, when he submitted to Gregory VII at Canossa (1077). This incident is represented in the low-relief carving on the sarcophagus. The monument was designed by

Bernini, assisted by pupils (1635).

Cappella del Santissimo Sacramento (Chapel of the Blessed Sacrament) **(12)** – The wrought-iron screen at the entrance is by Borromini. The high altarpiece representing the Trinity is one of the few paintings of St Peter by Pietro da Cortona (most are mosaics). On the altar, the tabernacle, which is similar to the *tempietto* of San Pietro in Montorio, and the kneeling angels are by Bernini (1675); the angel on the right is by a student.

Bernini brings unity to the Basilica – The passage **(A)** marks the line between Maderno's later and Michelangelo's earlier work. Bernini's task was to create a harmonised whole. The first problem was the junction of the nave with the eastern wall of Michelangelo's square plan. As this wall supports the oblique thrust of the weight of the dome, it could not be pierced to create a wide monumental doorway. Bernini erected two columns, like those flanking the doorways in the nave, and filled the space below the arch and the pediment with a shield supported by two angels. The second problem was the pier (**B**), which could not be pierced as it supports the dome. He erected two columns and an arch of identical size to those in the passage. The visitor approaching along the north aisle of the church receives an impression of depth, accentuated by the two narrow arches.

Gregory XIII's Monument★ (13) – The low-relief carving on the white marble sarcophagus (1723) illustrates the 1582 Gregorian reform of the calendar (now adopted worldwide).

Gregory XIV's Monument (14) – According to legend, the monument was despoiled to meet the expense of the pope's illness, which had to be treated with a mixture of gold and precious stones. The plaster sarcophagus was not faced with marble until 1842.

Clement XIII's Monument★★★ (15) – The fine neo-classical design by Canova dates from 1792. The lack of emotion for which Canova's art is often criticised here contributes to the purity of line. The balance of the whole is, however, upset by the statue on the left, which represents the Triumph of Religion.

Pictures in mosaic – Famous pictures began to be copied in mosaic in the 16C. The Church hoped to make its glories more intelligible to the faithful. This practice was further developed when Benedict XIII founded a mosaic school in 1727. These illustrate the power of St Peter; his walking on the water (**16**) and his raising of Tabitha (**17**); they celebrate the martyrs, popes, saints and angels challenged by the Reformation.

Cappella di San Michele o di Santa Petronilla (St Michael's or St Petronilla's Chapel) (**18**) – The mosaic illustrates St Petronilla's martyrdom after a painting by Guercino. St Petronilla, whose relics lie beneath the altar, was venerated in St Peter's from 8C. Pepin the Short built a chapel to her, in which Michelangelo's *Pietà* was to have stood.

Apse – The dominant feature is **"St Peter's Chair"**★★★ (**19**), an extraordinary work designed by **Bernini** to contain the remains of an ancient episcopal chair perhaps used by St Peter. These 4C remains are encased in a throne, decorated with ivory, which was given to John VIII by Charles the Bold at his coronation in 875. Bernini's throne is made of sculpted bronze, apparently supported by the four great Doctors of the Church (measuring between 4.50m/15ft and 5.50m/18ft). Above is a gilded stucco "gloria", veiled in clouds and a host of cherubs. Silhouetted against a sun-like central opening, which lets in the light, is the dove of the Holy Ghost (its wing span is 1.75m/just under 6ft). This work, completed in 1666 when Bernini was in his 70s, is a crowning example of his astounding art, full of movement and light. **Urban VIII's Monument★★★ (20)**, commissioned from **Bernini** in 1628 and finished in 1647, is considered to be the masterpiece of 17C funerary art.

For **Paul III's Monument★★★ (21)**, **Guglielmo della Porta** (?1500-77), a follower of Michelangelo, conceived a grandiose project: the monument was to be surrounded by eight allegorical statues and placed in the centre of the chancel. Michelangelo objected and asked for the number of statues to be reduced to four. Bernini cut the number to two; the others are in the Farnese Palace.

St Leo the Great's Altar (22) – The **altarpiece★** is a "picture in marble" by **Algardi** of the pope halting Attila at the gates of Rome. **Alexander VII's Monument★★ (23)** – **Bernini** completed this in 1678, two years before his death. He was anxious that he should sculpt the head of the pope, his protector.

The pope kneels among allegorical statues, the work of pupils who have somewhat exaggerated the movement. Even Bernini's own art gives way to excess here (death is represented by a skeleton draped in mottled marble, beckoning the pope).

Baldacchino★★★ – **Bernini**'s canopy, begun in 1624, was unveiled by Urban VIII in 1633. Despite the weight of the bronze and its great height (29m/95ft – the height of the Farnese Palace), it has captured the lightweight effect of a traditional baldaquin, usually of wood and cloth, carried in processions.

The work attracted much criticism, because the bronze had been taken from the Pantheon and because it was thought to be too theatrical and in bad taste.

The high altar below the baldaquin, where only the pope may celebrate Mass, stands over the *confessio* (24), designed by Maderno, which contains St Peter's tomb.

Piers of the Crossing – Begun by **Bramante** and completed by Michelangelo, they stand at the crossing of the transepts. Their austerity did not please Baroque taste; in 1629 Bernini faced them in marble and created recesses at the base, in which he placed four statues (5m/16ft high).

Each statue represents the relics deposited in the basilica: a fragment of the spear (St Longinus [25] by Bernini commemorates the soldier who pierced Jesus's side); the napkin bearing the Holy Image (St Veronica [26] wiped Jesus's face on the road to Calvary); a fragment of the True Cross (St Helena [27] brought the re-mains of the Cross to Rome); St Andrew's head (28). The last three are by Bernini's collaborators: Francesco Mochi, Andrea Bolgi and François Duquesnoy.

Dome★★★ – Bramante's design resembled the Pantheon's, but **Michelangelo** made the dome larger and higher. He carried out the work up to the lantern; it was finished in 1593 by **Giacomo della Porta** and **Domenico Fontana**. The whole building seems designed to support the city's largest dome, supposedly a symbol of God's perfection.

The pendentives carry four mosaic medallions (8m/26ft across) of the Evangelists. Above are Christ's words: "Thou art Peter and upon this rock I will build my church; and I will give unto thee the keys of the Kingdom of Heaven".

Statue of St Peter★★ (29) – This 13C bronze by **Arnolfo di Cambio** is greatly venerated. Countless pilgrims have kissed its foot. It is said to have been made out of the bronze statue of Jupiter on the Capitol.

Pius VII's Tomb (30) – Pius VII died in 1823, after bearing the brunt of the Napoleonic storm. His tomb was designed by **Thorwaldsen**, a Dane.

Leo XI's Monument (31) – **Algardi** was responsible for the white marble monument (1642-44). The low-relief sculpture on the sarcophagus illustrates Henri IV's conversion to Roman Catholicism; the king is being received by the future pope, who was then Clement VIII's legate.

Innocent VIII's Monument★★★ (32) – This is a Renaissance work by Antonio del Pollaiolo (1431-98), one of the few monuments preserved from the earlier church. The tomb is designed in typical 15C style against a wall.

When the monument was re-erected in 162, the two figures were reversed; originally the recumbent figure was above the pope, signifying the supreme power of death. An error has crept into the epitaph, which says that the pope "lived" (*vixit*) rather than "reigned" for eight years, 10 months and 25 days.

John XXIII's Monument (33) – The low-relief sculpture on the right of the chapel of the *Presentation* is by Emilio Greco.

Stuart Monument (34) – **Canova** designed this work (1817-19) to the glory of the last members of the Scottish Royal family: James Edward, Charles Edward and Henry Benedict, who are buried in the crypt (*See below*). The monument was commissioned by the Prince Regent and paid for by George III. The **angels★** in low relief were much admired by **Stendhal**, who also remarked that "George IV, in keeping with his reputation as the most accomplished gentleman in the three kingdoms, wished to honour the ashes of the unhappy princes, whom he would have sent to the scaffold had they fallen into his hands alive".

Museo Storico e Tesoro★

The Treasury has been pillaged on many occasions – by the Saracens in 846, during the sack of Rome in 1527, by Bonaparte under the Treaty of Tolentino in 1797 – but it has always been rebuilt.

In **Room I** (35) are two mementoes of the 4C basilica: the "Holy Column", which is identical to those reused by Bernini in the balcony chapels, and the gilded metal cockerel (9C), which Leo IV had placed on top of the basilica.

Room II (36) displays a dalmatic, said to have belonged to Charlemagne; it is, in fact, a Byzantine-style liturgical vestment dating from the 10C at the earliest. This room also contains a copy of the wooden and ivory chair contained in Bernini's throne, and a 6C papal cross.

The beautiful tabernacle in the **Benefactors' Chapel (37)** is attributed to **Donatello**, the Renaissance master artist from Florence. The plaster mould of the *Pietà* proved valuable when the original was damaged in 1972.

Room III (38) contains the **tomb of Sixtus IV**★★★ (1493) by Antonio del Pollaiolo. The accuracy of the portraiture and the delicacy of its execution make it a true masterpiece of bronze sculpture. Several rooms, glittering with gold and silverware and liturgical objects, lead into the **gallery (39)**. Here is the tiara with which St Peter's statue is crowned on ceremonial occasions. Junius **Bassus's sarcophagus**★★★ (4C) was found beneath the basilica and is a remarkable example of Christian funerary sculpture, richly decorated with biblical scenes; on the sides are children gathering the harvest, a symbol of the souls saved by the Eucharist.

Grotte Vaticane

Access in the northeast pier supporting the dome. The grottoes embrace the area beneath the basilica containing the papal tombs and parts of the earlier basilica. They consist of a semicircular section that follows the line of Constantine's apse, with the *Ad Caput* Chapel (*See below*) on the eastern side, and three aisles projecting eastwards. Among the tombs in the aisles are those of Pope John Paul II, Christina of Sweden, Benedict XV and Hadrian IV, born Nicholas Breakspear, the only English Pope.

Salita alla cupola★ (Ascent to the Dome)

Access from the exterior to the right of the basilica. From an internal gallery at the base of the dome, visitors can best appreciate the vast dimensions of the basilica. Two people, opposite one another and facing the wall, can hold a conversation in low voices. An interior stair climbs to a terrace surrounding the lantern at 120m/394ft above St Peter's Square. The **view**★★★ is magnificent.

Necropoli Vaticana★★ (Vatican Necropolis)

Constantine filled a pagan necropolis to form a foundation for the original ancient basilica. Two rows of tombs (1C to early 4C) run east to west. One bears an inscription recording the occupant's wish to be buried *"in Vaticano ad circum"*, alluding to Nero's circus, where St Peter may have perished. In another, that of the Julian family, are the oldest known Christian mosaics. These show "Christ as the Sun", on a horse-drawn chariot, and Jonah and the fisherman.

▷ *Return in the direction of the apse of the present basilica.*

Set in the east side of the so-called "Red Wall" (*Muro Rosso*) is the recess (2C) known as the "Trophy of Gaius" (*Trofeo di Gaio*); beneath is the **tomb of St Peter**. The emperor enclosed the tomb and trophy – which supposedly marked the grave of an apostle –in marble.

According to the historian Jerome Carcopino, the saint's relics have had a hazardous existence. In 258, fearing desecration during the Valerian persecution, the Christians may have moved them to St Sebastian's Catacombs, which did not then belong to the Church and were therefore unlikely to attract attention from the authorities. Not until 336, when Christians were again entitled to practise their religion, would the relics have been returned to their original resting place in the Vatican.

Cappella Clementina★ (Clementine Chapel) – This is the **Ad Caput Chapel** ("At the Head" Chapel). It stands behind the shrine very close to the apostle's tomb. Some bones, found nearby, could be St Peter's. Musei Vaticani Tour.

Musei Vaticani (Vatican Museums)

Entrance in Viale Vaticano; from Piazza Risorgimento take Via Bastioni di Michelangelo and turn left. (See the Address Book at the beginning of the chapter).
The official tour starts with the Egyptian and Chiaromonti Museums. The visit of the Pio-Clementino Museum begins from near Bramante's Staircase. The number of masterpieces in the Vatican is so great that a rigorous selection of the outstanding items has had to be made. For a more detailed

description of the exhibits consult the *"Guide to the Vatican City"* and the *"Guide to the Vatican Museums"* published by *Monumenti, Musei e Gallerie Pontificie.*

The museums are housed in part of the palaces built by the popes from the 13C onwards. The old entrance hall, opened in 1932, is now solely an exit. A new bronze door, to the left, leads visitors into a spacious, modern area capable of handling 2 000 people at once. From here, a spiral ramp and an escalator lead up to the *Cortile delle Corazze* (Cuirasses), the *Atrio dei Quatt ro Cancelli* (Atrium of the Four Gates) and Simonetti's 18C staircases (**A** on the plan).

Palaces

During the reign of Pope Symmachus (498-514), some buildings probably were erected to the north of St Peter's Basilica. Nicholas III (1277-80) hoped to replace them with a fortress and towers, but his project was only partially realised. When the popes returned from Avignon, they stopped living in the Lateran Palace, destroyed by fire, and settled here.

Nicholas V (1447-55) decided to enlarge the accommodation. Around the Parrot Court (*Cortile del Pappagallo*), he constructed a palace incorporating the 13C buildings. He kept the fortress-like exterior, but the interior was sumptuously decorated. The chapel by **Fra Angelico** can still be seen. Almost all the popes have altered or enlarged Nicholas V's palace.

Sixtus IV (1471-84) established a library on the ground floor of the north wing (now a conference room) and built the Sistine Chapel to the west. About 300m/984ft north of Nicholas V's palace, Innocent VIII(1484-92) built a summer residence, the Belvedere Palace. From 1493-94, Alexander VI added the Borgia Tower (*Torre Borgia*) and created his own apartments above Sixtus IV's library.

Pope **Julius II** (1503-13) commissioned **Bramante** to link Nicholas V's and Innocent VIII's palaces with two long narrow galleries, thus creating the Belvedere Court (*Cortile del Belvedere*). A huge rectangular courtyard, it provided a setting for grandiose spectacles and was later divided into the present Library and Pine Cone Courts (*Cortile della Biblioteca e Cortile della Pigna*). He lived above Alexander VI's apartments in the rooms painted by Piero **della Francesca**, Benedetto Bonfigli and Andrea del Castagno, and had them redecorated by **Raphael**. The façade was too austere for his taste, so he had another built, consisting of three loggias, one above another. The second floor loggia was decorated by Raphael.

Pius IV (1559-65) commissioned Pirro Ligorio to alter the Belvedere Court. To the north, the architect constructed a large semicircular niche, before which he planted the *pigna*, a huge pine cone (formerly it adorned the fountain in the *atrium* of Constantine's Basilica). The design is based on classical architecture, particularly Domitian's Stadium on the Palatine Hill. To the south, backing on to Nicholas V's palace, he created a semicircular façade one storey high with a central niche. Later the Belvedere Court was divided by two transverse galleries: between 1587 and 1588, during the reign of Sixtus V, Domenico Fontana built the Papal Library (Sistine Rooms); later, between 1806 and 1823, **Pius VII** built the New Wing (*Braccio Nuovo*).

The Belvedere Court was thus divided into three separate courts: the Belvedere Court (*Cortile del Belvedere*), the Library Court (*della Biblioteca*), the Pine Cone Court (*della Pigna*).

During the Baroque period, the only addition to the Vatican Palace was the *Scala Regia* (Royal Stairway – not open), a monumental stairway constructed by **Bernini** between 1633 and 1666. From the Great Bronze Door (*Portone di Bronzo*), which is the main entrance to the palace a long corridor along the north side of St Peter's Square leads to the *Scala Regia.*

Papal Court

Sixtus IV (1471-84) created a virtual court like that of a secular prince. He provided his nephews with ecclesiastical titles and benefices, and surrounded himself with rich cardinals, artists and men of letters.

Pope's Apartments

The 16C buildings around Sixtus V's Court (*Cortile di Sisto V*) contain the present papal apartments. Heads of State, diplomats and other important people enter the Vatican City by the Bell Arch (*Arco delle Campane*). Papal receptions are held in the pope's private library, a large room between Sixtus V's Court and Major-domo Court (*Cortile del Maggiordomo*). In the summer the Pope moves to Castel Gandolfo, 120km/75mi SE of Rome.

Museums

Their origins go back to 1503, when Julius II displayed a few classical works of art in the Belvedere Court. His successors continued to collect Greek and Roman, palaeo-Christian and Christian antiquities. Clement XIV created a new museum, which was enlarged by Pius VI and is called the Pio-Clementino after the pair. The rooms joining the Belvedere Palace to the West Gallery, now occupied by the Apostolic Library, were constructed by the architect Simonetti.

Following the Treaty of Tolentino in 1797, many artworks were sent to Paris. Those that were left were arranged by Canova in a museum called the Chiaramonti Museum (after the Pope's family name). Canova had been appointed Inspector General of Fine Arts and Antiquities belonging to the State and the Church by Pope Pius VII. When the lost works were returned in 1816, Pius VII built the New Wing to house them.

In 1837, Gregory XVI opened an Etruscan Museum to house excavated material; an Egyptian Museum opened 1839; the Art Gallery (*Pinacoteca*) opened 1932.

The year 1970 saw the inauguration of a very modern building to house the Antique and Christian Art collections formerly in the Lateran Palace. The Missionary collections were transferred from the Lateran in 1973, the same year as the creation of the History Museum and the Museum of Modern Religious Art. For the interest and diversity of their treasures, the Vatican Museums rank among the best in the world.

▶ **First Floor**

Museo Egizio
(Egyptian Museum)

Founded by Pope Gregory XVI, it was laid out in 1839 by Father Ungarelli, an Italian Egyptologist. The collection includes antiquities acquired by the popes in 18C

and statues found nearby. These were brought back from Egypt during the empire or are Roman copies of 1C-2C works.

Room I contains inscriptions from the Old Kingdom (c 2650 BC) to the 6C AD: throne of the statue of Pharaoh Ramses II (19th dynasty; c 1250 BC).

Room II is devoted to ancient Egyptian funerary art: the mummy of a woman (c 1000 BC) with henna-dyed hair; sarcophagi in painted wood and stone; canopic vases (organs were mummified separately) and various amulets.

Room III displays reproductions of the sculptures which decorate the Canopus in Hadrian's Villa at Tivoli. The main theme is the reawakening, represented by twin busts on a lotus flower, of Osiris-Apis, also known as Serapis, a deity introduced in the 4C by Ptolemy.

In the **hemicycle (V)** are Egyptian statues discovered in Rome and its environs: the fine Pharaoh's head of the 11th dynasty (c 2100 BC) exemplifies the art of the Middle Kingdom. The colossal statue of Queen Thuya, Ramses II's mother (c 1250 BC), is a New Kingdom effort.

Museo Chiaramonti e Galleria Lapidaria

The **Chiaramonti Museum** – set up by Pius VII, whose family name was Chiaramonti – has kept the appearance created by Canova in 1807. It has Roman copies of Greek works, portraits and funerary monuments: one low relief, bearing a millstone and donkey, commemorates a miller (*on the right, Row X*). The **Lapidary Gallery** houses over 3 000 pagan and Christian inscriptions (*specialists only*).

▶ *The tour proceeds to the New Wing.*

Braccio Nuovo
(New Wing)

The **"Doryphoros"** (*3rd recess on the left of the entrance*) depicts a spear-bearer. It is a copy of a bronze original by Polyclitus (440 BC). In all probability the original was the model (*the Kanon*), which demonstrated Polyclitus' theories about proportions in sculpture. The **statue of Augustus**★★ (*4th recess on the right*) – known as "from the *Prima Porta*" because

MUSEI VATICANI

Highly recommended sections · Other sections · Not open to the public

APPARTAMENTO DI S. PIO V

Ⓒ

GALLERIA DELLE CARTE GEOGRAFICHE · GALL.

Sala Sobieski

Sala dell' Immacolata Concezione

Ⓓ

Torre Borgia

STANZE DI RAFFAELLO

Cappella di Niccolò V

Sala dei Chiaroscuri

Loggia di Raffaello

0 — 75 m

BASILICA DI

SAN PIETRO

N

MUSEO MISSIONARIO-ETNOLOGICO

Ⓚ

to Ⓛ

Sala delle Nozze Aldobrandine · Stradone · ai

Ⓗ

Ⓒ Cappella di S. Pio V

CAPPELLA

BIBLIOTECA APOSTOLICA

Cortile della Sentinella

Galleria di Urbano VIII · Sale Sistine

SISTINA

Sala degli Indirizzi

Museo sacro

Ⓓ Torre Borgia

Salone

Sala Regia

Cortile Borgia

Ⓔ

CORTILE

APPARTAMENTO BORGIA E ARTE MODERNA RELIGIOSA

Sistino

Sala Ⓖ

Cortile dei Pappagalli

DEL BELVEDERE

Ducale

Ⓕ

PIAZZA S. PIETRO

GALLERIA LAPIDARIA

Cortile di S. Damaso

of where it was found – is a fine example of official Roman art. The decoration of the emperor's breastplate is an extraordinarily precise illustration of the King of the Parthians returning the standards lost by Crassus in 53 BC. *The Nile* (*il Nilo*) is a 1C Roman work inspired perhaps by a Greek original. The river god is surrounded by 16 children, a symbol of the 16 cubits the river must rise to flood and fertilise the plain. The gilded bronze peacocks may be from Hadrian's Mausoleum.

A, B   Stairs   Toilets   Letter box

↕   Lifts   Refreshments   Telephone

Sala della Biga

DEGLI   ARAZZI   GALL.   DEI   CANDELABRI

A

SECOND FLOOR

MUSEO
GREGORIANO ETRUSCO

PALAZZO DEL
BELVEDERE

B

Scala del Bramante

MUSEO MISSIONARIO-ETNOLOGICO
(lower level)

MUSEO
PIO CRISTIANO
(upper level)

Viale

I

MUSEO   Giardino

PINACOTECA

delle

MUSEO

GREGORIANO

PROFANO

MUSEO

DELLE

Quadrato

Zitelle

PIO

CRISTIANO

CARROZZE

J

Viale

K

L

J

Cortile
Pinacoteca

della

Giardini

Vaticano

BIBLIOTECA   APOSTOLICA

FIRST FLOOR

Sale Paoline   **Galleria Clementina**   A

**Sala
Alessandrina**   **Museo profano**

Cortile
della

NUOVO

CORTILE

MUSEO

Biblioteca

BRACCIO

DELLA   PIGNA

MUSEO
GREGORIANO
EGIZIO

PIO CLEMENTINO

PALAZZO DEL
BELVEDERE

MUSEO   CHIARAMONTI   B

Scala del Bramante

The **statue of Demosthenes** (*recess on the entrance's left*) is a Roman copy of a Greek bronze (3C BC).

▶ *Return to Chiaramonti entrance; enter Pio-Clementino Museum (stair B).*

Museo Pio-Clementino★★★

The museum is in the Belvedere Palace and Simonetti's 18C extension. **Vestibolo Quadrato** (Square Vestibule) is the atrium of the former Clementino Museum. The sobriety of early Roman art shows in the sarcophagus of **Scipio Barbatus**, carved in peperine (3C BC). Its shape is inspired by the Greek models that the Romans discovered after the capture of Rhegium in 270 BC.

Gabinetto dell'Apoxyomenos – The **Apoxyomenos**★★★ is the name given to the statue of an athlete scraping his skin with a strigil post-exercise. It is a 1C AD Roman copy of a Greek original by Lysippus (4C BC). In the weary body, the artist reveals the living human being rather than an idealistic image, as in the classical period.

Scala del Bramante – Bramante's noble spiral stairway, used by men on horseback, was designed in the ealy-16C, during the alterations ordered by Julius II.

Cortile ottagonale del Belvedere★ (Belvedere Octagonal Court) – The internal courtyard, originally on a square plan and planted with orange trees, acquired its octagonal outline when Simonetti added a portico in the 18C.

The extraordinary **Laocoön**★★★ (**2**) was unearthed in Nero's Golden House by a group of peasants. This sculpture was the work of a group of artists from Rhodes (1C BC), It represents the death of Laocoön, priest of Apollo, who had incurred the god's anger and, with his two sons, was crushed to death by serpents. Here Hellenistic art attains an intense realism, dubbed "Greek Baroque".

The statue of **Apollo**★★★ (**1**) was placed in the Belvedere Court by Julius II in 1503. It is probably copied from a 4C BC Greek original by a Roman sculptor. The figure may have held a bow in the left hand and an arrow in the right.

The three **neo-classical statues** by **Canova** (1757-1822) were bought by Pope Pius VII to make up for the loss of certain works removed under the terms of the Treaty of Tolentino: **Perseus**★★ (**4**), who conquered Medusa, and the boxers Kreugas (**5**) and Damozenos (**6**), who met in fierce combat at Nemea in Argolis. The **Hermes**★★★ (**3**) is a 2C AD Roman work, inspired by an original Greek bronze,

MUSEO GREGORIANO EGIZIO

MUSEO PIO CLEMENTINO

1st FLOOR

0   20 m

representing the trickster god. Under the north portico sits the **Ara Casali**, a 3C altar presented to Pope Pius VI. On the front is a scene with Venus and Mars; the back shows Romulus and Remus.

Sala degli Animali (Room of the Animals) – The statue of **Meleager★ (7)** is a 2C Roman copy of a bronze sculpture by Skopas, a Greek artist (4C BC). Beside Meleager is the head of the boar that caused his death, at Diana's behest.

The fine floor mosaics are Roman. A crab made of green porphyry, a rare stone, is displayed in a showcase **(8)**.

The **Sleeping Ariadne★ (9)** is a Roman copy of a Greek original, illustrating the characteristic taste for unusual poses and elaborate draperies of the Hellenistic period (2C BC). On waking, Ariadne will be married to Dionysius and carried away to Mount Olympus.

The candelabra **(10)** are fine examples of 2C Roman decorative work from Hadrian's Villa at Tivoli.

The statue of **Apollo Sauroktonos★ (11)**, showing the god about to kill a lizard, is a Roman copy of a work by Praxiteles, a Greek artist of the 4C BC. An expert in feminine models, he made the girlish young god very graceful.

In the three rooms of the **Sala dei Busti** (Room of the Busts), divided by fine marble columns, note the austere busts of **Cato and Portia (12)**, a husband and wife group intended for a tomb (1C BC). Imperial portraits include a particularly expressive bust of Julius Caesar **(13)**.

Gabinetto delle Maschere (Cabinet of the Masks) – This room owes its name to the mosaic of masks (2C) removed from Hadrian's Villa and let into the floor. The **Venus of Cnidos★★** is a Roman copy of Praxiteles's statue for the sanctuary at Cnidos in Asia Minor (4C BC), which was famous for its artistic merits and for being the first representation of a goddess in the nude. The Greeks – versed in the legend of Actaeon, who was killed for watching a goddess bathing – were shocked.

▷ *Return to the Room of the Animals.*

Sala delle Muse (Room of the Muses) – Like the statue of the Pugilist (*in the Museo Nazionale Romano*), the **Belvedere Torso★★★ (14)** is the masterly work of the Athenian Apollonius, Nestor's son, who lived in Rome in the 1C BC. The expressive torso, much admired by Michelangelo and originally thought to represent Hercules, has recently been identified as the Trojan War hero Ajax. According to mythology, he went mad and killed himself when his dead friend Achilles' armour was given to Ulysses. The statue (of which only the torso remains) shows him overcome with shame.

Sala rotonda★ (Round Room) – This fine room by Simonetti (1780) was inspired by the Pantheon. The monolithic porphyry **basin** may have come from Nero's Golden House. The **statue of Hercules (15)** in gilded bronze dates from the late 2C. **Antinoüs (16)**, the young favourite of the Emperor Hadrian, drowned in the Nile in 130. After his death, the emperor raised him under the name "Osirantinoos" to the ranks of the gods. He bears the attributes of Dionysius and the Egyptian god Osiris (on his head is the *uraeus*, a serpent – part of the headdress of the Pharaohs). The bust of **Jupiter★ (17)** is a 4C BC Roman copy.

Sala a Croce Greca (Greek Cross Room) – Two large porphyry **sarcophagi★** have pride of place. The one belonging to St Helena **(18)**, the Emperor Constantine's mother, dates from the early 4C and is heavily sculptured with conquering Roman cavalry and barbarian prisoners, an inappropriate theme for such a holy woman. This suggests that the sarcophagus was originally intended for her husband or her son. The other is the sarcophagus of Constantia **(19)**, Constantine's daughter, and dates from the middle of the 4C.

▷ *Simonetti Stairs (A) to second floor.*

▷ **Second Floor**

Museo Etrusco★

Founded in 1837 by Gregory XVI, this museum houses objects from southern Etruria. The oldest artefacts (9C-8C BC cinerary urns in the form of a house) are in **Room I**. Two-horse chariots used by high-born members of 8C BC society are in **Room II**. The exquisite Greek black-

and red-figure vases indicate the considerable wealth of the dead.

Items retrieved from the **Regolini-Galassi tomb,** south of Cerveteri, are particularly fine; these include a bronze throne and jewellery. The incomparable golden **clasp**★★, decorated with lions and ducks, shows the Etruscan's skill in such work. The **Bronze Room (III)** houses the **Mars**★★ found at Todi, a rare example of a large late 5C BC bronze statue. The style is akin to rigourous classical Greek works. The oval cist (*last case to the right of the Mars*), a toilette receptacle, is decorated with the Battle of the Amazons; fantastic figures adorn the handle.

In the hemicycle, note the striking large black-figure **amphora**★★★ (*second middle glass case to the left of the entrance*), painted by Exekias; this object is a rare example of his artistry. It illustrates Achilles playing draughts with Ajax.

Halls and Galleries

Sala Della Biga (Biga Room)
Don't miss the 1C Roman **two-horse chariot**★★ (*biga*). It was reconstituted in the 18C, when the body of the chariot was recovered from St Mark's Basilica; it had served as an episcopal throne.

Galleria degli Arazzi (Tapestry Gallery)
The tapestries were hung by Gregory XVI in 1838. Facing the windows: the New School series, commissioned by Leo X in the early 16C, was woven by Pieter van Aelst's workshops in Brussels from cartoons by Raphael's pupils.

Galleria delle Carte Geografiche★
The ceiling is decorated with stuccowork and paintings by a group of 18C Mannerists: 80 scenes from the lives of the saints closely associated with the maps below. The extraordinary maps on the walls were painted from 1580-83 from cartoons by Fr Ignazio Danzi. Below, the 16C cartography is embellished with inscriptions, ships and turbulent seas.

Sala Sobieski e Sala dell'Immacolata Concezione
In the former hangs a 19C painting by Jan Mateiko of John III Sobieski, king of Poland, repulsing the Turks at the Siege of Vienna (1683). The 19C frescoes in the latter illustrate the dogma of the Immaculate Conception.

Stanze di Raffaello★★★
(Raphael Rooms)

During part of the year to avoid overcrowding, there is one-way access from the Room of the Immaculate Conception via an external terrace. The visit to the Raphael Rooms then starts in the Hall of Constantine. The rest of the year the tour circles in the opposite direction.

These rooms were built during the reign of Nicholas V (1447-55) and decorated with frescoes by Piero **della Francesca** among others, except the Hall of Constantine, which was part of the 13C wing of the papal Palace. On becoming pope in 1503, Julius II arranged to have the rooms redecorated by Sodoma, Perugino and others. In 1508, on Bramante's recommendation, he sent for a young painter from Urbino. Charmed by Raphael's youthful grace, he entrusted the whole to him; the other painters were dismissed and their work effaced. The frescoes here are among the masterpieces of the Renaissance. They were damaged by the troops of Charles V, during the sack of Rome in 1527, but have been restored.

Sala dell'Incendio del Borgo (Room of the Borgo Fire) (1514-17)
This was the last room painted by Raphael. The immediate success of his work and the large number of commissions that followed led him to rush. From 1515, he worked with a group of assistants, including Giulio Romano. In this room he only designed the frescoes and some of the cartoons, completed by his team. The ceiling frescoes are by Perugino.

In the fresco of the *Coronation of Charlemagne* (1) the emperor is portrayed as François I of France and Leo II as Leo X. *The Borgo Fire* (2) shows Leo IV quenching an 847 conflagration with the sign of the cross. Inspired, like all Renaissance artists, by antiquity, Raphael painted the colonnade of the Temple of Mars Ultor on the left; the old man supported by a youth recalls Virgil (Aeneas fleeing Troy). In the *Battle of Ostia* (3), Leo X is again represented in the guise of Leo IV, who defeated the Saracens nearby in 849.

A medieval legend is depicted in the *Oath of Leo III* (**4**). According to this account, when Leo III sought to clear himself of a libel in St Peter's itself, a voice rang out, declaring "It is for God not men to judge bishops" (*Latin inscription to the right of the window*). Leo III is portrayed as Leo X.

Sala della Segnatura (Signature Room) (1508-11)

This room was used as a library, a study and for signing papal Bulls. It was the first room painted by Raphael. The decorative theme, probably proposed by a court scholar versed in neo-Platonic philosophy, illustrates the three great principles of the human spirit: Truth, Goodness and Beauty.

The medallions on the ceiling and wall paintings illustrate closely linked subjects. Above the Triumph of Religion (*Dispute over the Blessed Sacrament*) is shown the allegory of Theology and, above that, Philosophy (*School of Athens*). They represent the two aspects of Truth – the supernatural and the rational. Above the fresco representing canon and civil law and the cardinal virtues is the allegory of Justice. These represent Goodness. The allegory of Poetry, representing Beauty, crowns *Parnassus*. Smaller paintings in the corners underline the significance of the allegories: *Adam and Eve*, in which a woman imparts motion to the universe; the *Judgement of Solomon, Apollo and Marsyas*.

Part of the ceiling decoration is attributed to Sodoma and the octagonal area to Bramantino (c 1465-1530). The name *Dispute over the Blessed Sacrament* (**5**) is wrongly attributed to the fresco illustrating the Glorification of Religion: at the top, surrounding the Trinity, appears the Church victorious with Mary, St John the Baptist, the Apostles, Prophets and Patriarchs, martyrs and angels.

On earth, grouped round the altar, stand the Doctors of the Church, the popes and the faithful, including Dante (*right*), crowned with laurel, Savonarola, Sixtus IV, Fra Angelico and Gregory the Great, with the features of Julius II. The lines converge on the Host, the incarnation of Christ, linking the Church on earth and the Church in heaven.

The *School of Athens* (**6**) depicts a crowd of philosophers standing beneath the vaults of a classical building designed by Bramante. In the centre are Plato and Aristotle, representing the two main streams of classical thought. Plato's raised finger indicates the realm of ideas, Aristotle's open hand indicates that without the material world ideas would have no existence. Raphael has given Plato the face of Leonardo da Vinci. On the left, Socrates, in a tunic, is speaking to his pupil Alcibiades. Euclid, who resembles Bramante, is tracing geometric figures on a slate. In the right-hand corner, Raphael included himself in a black beret beside Sodoma, in a tunic and white beret. In the foreground is the solitary figure of Heraclitus, his head resting in his left hand; he has the features of Michelangelo, who was at that time decorating the Sistine Chapel. Raphael added this figure when the fresco was almost finished, honouring his rival.

The Cardinal and Theological Virtues (**7**) – Above the window are Strength (oak branch, emblem of the Della Rovere family to which Julius II belonged), Prudence and Temperance, Faith, Hope and Charity (as cupids). On the right Raimond de Pennafort hands Gregory IX (1234) the body of rules which make up canon law (Decretals); on the left Justinian approves the "Pandects", a collection of Roman jurisprudence, comprising civil law. Gregory IX is a portrait of Julius II. Beside him stand Cardinal Giovanni de' Medici (future Leo X) and Alessandro Farnese (future Paul III).

Coronation of Charlemagne (detail), Raphael Rooms

Note the *"Parnassus"* (8) on the opposite wall. Around Apollo and the nine Muses are grouped the great poets, starting with Homer, Virgil and Dante.

Sala di Eliodoro (Heliodorus Room) (1512-1514)

This was the suite's private antechamber and was decorated by Raphael after the Signature Room. The theme is the divine protection of the Church.

The biblical subject of the *Expulsion of Heliodorus from the Temple* (9), taken from the Book of Maccabees (Heliodorus, intent on stealing the temple treasure, is expelled by the angels), was probably chosen by Julius II himself, whose own policy was to expel usurpers from papal property. He appears on the left. This excellent portrait reveals the authority of the pope, who fought alongside his own soldiers and one day broke his cane across Michelangelo's back. This fresco is exceptional for Raphael in the vigour and movement of the figures (including a person flattening himself against a pillar).

The *Miracle of the Bolsena Mass* (10) commemorates the miracle today celebrated as the feast of Corpus Christi. In 1263, a priest, who doubted the doctrine of the real presence, saw blood on the host at the moment of consecration, while celebrating Mass in Bolsena. Julius II is kneeling before the priest. The pope, his suite and the Swiss guards are among Raphael's masterpieces.

An episode described in the Acts of the Apostles is depicted in *St Peter Delivered from Prison* (11). According to this account, Peter, chained in Rome, dreamt that an angel liberated him and on waking found, lo, that he was free. Note the various light sources: the moon, the guard's torch, the angel. This anticipates the genius of Caravaggio and Rembrandt by more than a century.

In *St Leo the Great Repulsing Attila* (12), Raphael shows Leo I meeting the Huns and repelling their advance, aided by the appearance of St Peter and St Paul armed with swords. The artist has moved the event to the gates of Rome, indicated by the Colosseum, a basilica and an aqueduct. The calm of the pope and his suite contrasts with the disorder of the barbarian hordes. The painting was not finished when Julius II died in 1513. Raphael therefore substituted a portrait of Leo X, although he already appeared in the picture as Cardinal Giovanni de Medici (*left*) wearing the *cappa magna* (a long hooded cloak).

A large part of the painting (*right*) was executed by Raphael's pupils.

Sala di Costantino (Hall of Constantine)

In 1520, Raphael died. This room was finished by his followers, led by Giulio Romano and Francesco Penni. Here begins Mannerism; overwhelmed by the legacy of Raphael and Michelangelo, artists began to abandon national idealism in favour of exaggerated form and contorted movement.

The Apparition of the Cross (13) and the *Battle of the Milvian Bridge* (14) are by Romano. Penni crafted *The Baptism of Constantine* (15). Pope Sylvester, who baptised Constantine, is shown in the basilica of St John Lateran.

The two artists collaborated on *Constantine's Donation* (16), which is set inside the old St Peter's and shows the Emperor Constantine (306-37) giving Rome to the pope, thus founding the temporal power of the papacy. In his *Divine Comedy*, Dante derided the gift: "Ah, Constantine, what evil was spawned not by your conversion, but by that gift which the first rich Ppope accepted from you."

Loggia di Raffaello★★ (Raphael's Loggia)

🕐*Open to specialists only. Access via the Hall of Constantine. On the second floor of the galleried building.*

At the beginning of the 16C – before the construction of St Damasus's Court (*Cortile di San Damaso*) and the buildings on its north, south and east sides – the façade of the 13C palace gazed over Rome. Julius II (1503-13) decided to give it a new look. He engaged Bramante to design three superimposed loggias. Work began in 1508; when Bramante died in 1514, only the first tier had been built. Julius II's successor, Leo X, appointed Raphael to take over.

The loggia takes the form of a vaulted corridor, richly decorated (probably

Cortile di S. Damaso

between 1517 and 1519). The walls and arches are adorned with stuccoes and "grotesques" inspired by classical models Raphael and his friends found in Nero's Golden House. Various artists collaborated with Raphael: Penni and Romano, Giovanni da Udine and Perin del Vaga. Their work abounds with fantastic invention: garlands of fruit and flowers, animals, famous statues, people, scenes from contemporary life.

The loggia is divided into 13 bays; the vault of each is decorated with four paintings, representing scenes from the Old Testament, except in the first bay (**17**), which has scenes from the New Testament. The loggia is sometimes called "Raphael's Bible". These charmingly fresh paintings include *Moses in the Bullrushes* (**18**); *Building Noah's Ark* (**19**); *Creation of the Animals* (**20**).

Sala dei Chiaroscuri e Cappella di Niccolò V (Chiaroscuro Rooms and Nicholas V's Chapel)

The rooms owe their name to the monochrome paintings of saints and apostles executed from Raphael's cartoons by his followers (1517). The paintings were restored in the late 16C.

Cappella di Niccolò V★★ (Nicholas V's Chapel)

The chapel is one of the oldest parts of the Vatican Palace. It probably formed part of a tower, which was absorbed into the first papal palace in the 13C. Nicholas V converted it to a chapel and had it decorated by **Fra Angelico** (1447-51), a Dominican monk and master of Florentine art. He was assisted by Benozzo Gozzoli, also from Florence.

In the angles are the Doctors of the Church; the Evangelists are on the ceiling. The two-tier wall paintings illustrate the lives of St Stephen and St Lawrence (*upper tier*) and were extensively restored in the 18C and 19C.

The **Life of St Stephen** is depicted in the upper level. On the right are two legendary episodes in the saint's life: being ordained deacon (*left*) by St Peter (whose figure shows great nobility); distributing alms (*right*). Above the entrance door: preaching in a square in Florence (*left*) and addressing the Council (*right*). On the left: the stoning of St Stephen.

The **Life of St Lawrence** is represented in the lower level. Sixtus II, resembling Nicholas V, ordains St Lawrence as deacon. Above the door: St Lawrence receiving the treasure of the Church from Sixtus II and distributing alms to the poor. The portrayal of a blind man (*right*) is exceptional in the idealised art of the Renaissance. Left: the Roman Emperor Decius pointing to the instruments of torture; the saint's martyrdom.

▶ *Leave Nicholas V's Chapel, return to the first Raphael Room (Borgo Fire). Pass through Urban VIII's Chapel and turn right to the Borgia Apartment.*

Appartamento Borgia★
(Borgia Apartment)

These rooms, which formed the suite of Alexander VI, the Borgia Pope from Spain, now house examples of modern art. They are decorated (end of 1492-94) with paintings by **Pinturicchio**, full of pleasant fantasy. The first, known as the **Sybilline Room** (I), has figures of sybils and prophets. In the **Creed Room** (III) the prophets and apostles carry scrolls bearing the articles of the Creed.

Next is the **Liberal Arts Room** (IV), probably Alexander VI's study. It is decorated with allegories of the seven subjects taught in medieval universities.

The **Saints' Room** (V) was probably painted by Pinturicchio; elsewhere pupils assisted. The legendary lives of the saints are combined with mythology, a common practice in the Renaissance period. Facing the window is one of Pinturicchio's best works, St Catherine of Alexandria arguing with the philosophers, against his usual landscape of delicate trees, rocks and hills. In the centre is the Arch of Constantine. Before the emperor, St Catherine expounds her arguments in defence of the Christian faith. The vault is painted with mythological scenes.

The **Mysteries of the Faith Room** (VI) depicts the principal mysteries in the lives of Jesus and his mother. On the wall framing the entrance: the Resurrection; on the left: a very fine portrait of Alexander VI, in rapt adoration.

The **Pontiffs' Room** (VII) was used for official meetings. The ceiling, which collapsed in 1500 – narrowly missing Alexander VI – was reconstructed in the reign of Leo X and has stucco ornaments

and "grotesques" by Perin del Vaga and Giovanni da Udine. At one time, the room was hung with portraits of the Popes, hence its name.

Collezione d'Arte Moderna Religiosa★★

Some of the world's greatest artists mingle here. On the upper floor, the **Chapel of Peace** by Giacomo Manzù (Room XIV) leads into a room devoted to Rouault (Room XV). Then follows a series of smaller rooms revealing traces of the 13C palace and containing works by **Chagall, Gauguin**, **Klee, Kandinsky**, Utrillo, Odilon Redon, Braque, Moore, Morandi, De Pisis, etc.

Downstairs in rooms partially beneath the Sistine Chapel gleams stained glass by Fernand Leger, Jacques Villon, George Meistermann. There are several canvases by Ben Shahn, Jack Levine, Bernard Buffet, Yugoslavian naive paintings, sculptures by Marini, Lipchitz and Mirko, **Picasso** ceramics and Bazaine tapestries.

At the inauguration on 23 June 1973 Paul VI declared: "Even in our arid secularised world, there is still a prodigious capacity for expressing beyond the truly human what is religious, divine, Christian."

▶ *Return to first floor for the Sistine Chapel (Staircase H).*

▶ First Floor

Cappella Sistina★★★
(Sistine Chapel) (Staircase H)

Named after Pope Sixtus IV, it was built from 1477-80. As well as being the papal palace chapel, it served a defensive role and boasts external crenellations.

The long chamber is lit by 12 windows. **Sixtus IV** sent for painters from Umbria and Florence to decorate the walls. His nephew **Julius II** (1503-13) commissioned Michelangelo to redecorate the ceiling (originally it depicted a starry sky). Twenty years later, the artist was again engaged by **Clement VII** and **Paul III** to paint the wall behind the altar. The chapel is not only the setting for the most solemn ceremonies of the Holy See, where the cardinals meet in conclave,

Sala delle Nozze Aldobrandine
Cappella di Pio V
Sala degli Indirizzi
Sala dei Papiri
Sala delle Sibille
Torre Borgia
Sala del Credo
CORTILE
Sala delle Arti Liberali
DEL
Sala dei Santi
BELVEDERE
Sala dei Misteri della Fede
CHANCEL
CAPPELLA
SISTINA
Cortile della Sentinella
Cortile Borgia
Sala Regia
Sala Regia
lower floor
upper floor
Scala Regia
Cortile dei Pappagalli
Cortile del Maresciallo
Cortile dei Pappagalli
Cortile Borgia
Cortile di S. Damaso
Sala Ducale
Sala Ducale
Sala dei Pontefici
GALLERIA LAPIDARIA

APPARTAMENTO BORGIA
ARTE MODERNA RELIGIOSA } 1st FLOOR
CAPPELLA SISTINA

0   20 m

but also a masterpiece of Renaissance art. Its dimensions – 40.23m/132ft long, 13.41m/44ft wide and 20.70m/68ft high – are exactly the same as those given in the Bible for Solomon's Temple.

Side walls

Sixtus IV wanted to perpetuate the decorative tradition of the early Christian basilicas. The lowest section represents the curtains that hung between the columns of the old basilicas. Between the windows are portraits of the early popes from St Peter to Marcellus I (308-09). The figures of Christ and the first three popes were obliterated when the Last Judgement bloomed above the altar. The paintings halfway up the walls depict parallel scenes in the lives of

Moses and Jesus, showing human condition before and after the Messiah.

Restoring the Chapel

This vast undertaking, carried out by Italian experts and financed by Japanese patrons, took 18 years to complete. Twelve (1980-92) were spent on Michelangelo's frescoes. Most of the restoration work consisted of cleaning the frescoes, darkened by dust and candle smoke, with a mixture of bicarbonate of soda and ammonium. After 500 years, Michelangelo's original colours – ranging from bright orange, clear pink, pale green to brilliant yellow and turquoise – sparkle gloriously.

Life of Moses – (*South wall from the Last Judgement*). *Moses in Egypt* (ɪ) by **Perugino** is followed by *Moses's Youth* (ɪɪ) by **Botticelli**; the two female figures of Jethro's daughters show the more lyrical side of the artist's style. These are followed by *Crossing the Red Sea* (ɪɪɪ) and *The Giving of the Tablets of the Law on Mount Sinai* (ɪⱽ)

Ceiling of the Sistine Chapel

by **Cosimo Rosselli**. In *The Punishment of Korah, Dathan and Abiram* (V), for denying Moses's and Aaron's authority over the Jewish people, Botticelli set the

scene against a background of Roman monuments: the Arch of Constantine and the Palatine Septizonium (♿ *See FORO ROMANO-PALATINO*). The *Testament and Death of Moses* (VI) is by **Luca Signorelli**.

Life of Christ – (*North wall from the Last Judgement*). The series begins with the *Baptism of Jesus* (VII) by **Perugino** and **Pinturicchio**, featuring many members of Sixtus IV's court. The next panel, *The Temptation of Christ* and *The Healing of the Leper* (VIII), directly faces the papal throne; here **Botticelli** has given greater weight to the healing scene in deference to Sixtus IV, who had written a theological treatise on the subject; he also painted the Temple in Jerusalem to look like the Santo Spirito Hospital, which the pope reconstructed. The small scenes at the foot of the painting represent the *Temptation of Christ* (*left to right*). The next is an illustration of *The calling of St Peter and St Andrew* (IX) by **Ghirlandaio**. In *The Sermon on the Mount* and *The Healing of the Leper* (X), **Cosimo Rosselli**, assisted by Piero di Cosimo, made one of the first attempts to paint a sunset. *The Delivery of the Keys to St Peter* (XI) is a masterpiece by **Perugino**; the Arch of Constantine appears twice flanking the Temple in Jerusalem, as imagined by the artist. The final panel is *The Last Supper* (XII) by Rosselli: Judas is face to face with Jesus, apart from the other apostles.

Ceiling

When Julius II abandoned his project for a funerary sculpture, **Michelangelo** returned unhappily to Florence. In 1508, he was recalled to Rome by the pope, who asked him to paint the Twelve Apostles on the ceiling of the Sistine Chapel. He had barely started, when he realised the work was going badly. The pope then gave him a free hand and instead of the blue star-spangled vault (some 520m2/660sq ft), he created a masterpiece filled with powerful movement. The animated figures compose an epic of the creation of the world and the history of the human race.

Julius II came regularly to ask Michelangelo when he would finish. From atop the scaffolding came the regular reply, "when I can."

Nippon Television

West wall { The Last Judgment
Altar ↓

South wall : Life of Moses

North wall : Life of Christ

CAPPELLA SISTINA

On 14 August 1511, bursting with impatience, the pope insisted on seeing the fresco; he was overwhelmed. About a year later, it was finished.

From the Creation to the Flood – *Starting from the altar.*

(1) *God divides the light from the darkness.*
(2) *Creation of the sun, the moon and plant life.*
(3) *God divides the waters from the earth and creates living creatures in the seas.*
(4) *Creation of Adam.*
(5) *Creation of Eve.*
(6) *Original sin and expulsion from the Garden of Eden.*
(7) *Noah's sacrifice*: contrary to biblical chronology, this scene precedes the flood. Michelangelo may have wanted to stress Noah's loyalty to God, thus justifying his ark salvation.
(8) *The Flood*: the first scene painted. Some figures are too small in proportion to their surroundings.
(9) *Noah's Drunkenness*: Noah is scorned by his son. Michelangelo pessimistically reminds us that life on earth began again under a bad omen.

The "Ignudi" (**10**) – Michelangelo frescoed these figures at each corner of the central panels. They glorify the human body. Modelled on classical sculptures, the *Ignudi* influenced many Renaissance and Mannerist artists.

Prophets and Sibyls – There is great variety in these 12 portraits: *Zacharias* (**11**), the old man with a beard; *Joel* (**12**), the critic; the *Erythraean sibyl* (**13**), not knowing where to begin her study; *Ezekiel* (**14**), in earnest debate; the *Persian sibyl* (**15**), short-sighted and bowed with old age; *Jeremiah* (**16**) in his melancholy; *Jonah* (**17**), symbol of Christ's Resurrection, ejected from the whale in a movement recalled by Baroque artists; the *Libyan sibyl* (**18**), her study completed, descending from her throne with gracefulness; *Daniel* (**19**), inspired by a new idea; the *Cumaean sibyl* (**20**), a muscle-bound giant apparently puzzled by what she is reading; *Isaiah* (**21**), troubled by an angel; the young *Delphic sibyl* (**22**).

Bible Stories – At the centre of these four scenes are the heroes of the Jewish people – David, Judith, Esther, Moses. Also *Judith and Holophernes* (**23**), *David and Goliath* (**24**), *the Punishment of Haman* (**25**), *the Brazen Serpent* (**26**).

Jesus's Forefathers (**27**) – Their names (*above the windows*) correspond to the scenes in the triangular sections. Jewish families wait for deliverance.

The Last Judgement

Twenty years after painting the ceiling, in 1534, **Michelangelo** was sent for by Clement VII to complete the decoration of the chapel. The Pope, who had seen Rome sacked by Charles V's troops in 1527, wanted *The Last Judgement* to deliver its message boldly from above the altar as a warning to the unfaithful. Paul III took up his predecessor's idea and work began in 1535. The 15C frescoes were obliterated, as well as two panels in the series depicting Jesus's ancestors. When the fresco was unveiled on 31 October 1541, people were amazed and dumbfounded. Stamped with the mark of violence and anger, this striking work, with its mass of naked bodies writhing in a baleful light, is an expression of misfortune: Rome had been sacked in 1527; Luther's doctrine was dividing the western Church. In the 16C and 18C, the fresco was touched up. The austerity of the Counter-Reformation moved Pius IV to have the naked figures clothed by Daniele da Volterra; in all about 30 figures were clothed.

This fresco introduced a new style in the history of art, which led to the Baroque. The composition follows a strict scheme: the elect are welcomed on high by the angels (*left*) as the damned tumble headlong into hell (*right*).

At the bottom (*left*) the dead slowly awake; in vain the devils try to restrain them. Above, the elect seem drawn by the movement of Christ's right hand. Beside the terrifying figure of Christ the Judge, the Virgin turns away from the horrific spectacle. Around them are the saints, bearing the instruments of their martyrdoms: St Andrew with his cross beside the Virgin, beneath them St Lawrence and his gridiron, St Bartholomew with his skin (in its folds appears the distorted face of Michelangelo).

In his boat, Charon waits for the damned, whom he throws into the river of hell. Minos, the master of hell, his body wreathed by a snake (*in the corner*), resembles Biagio da Cesena, the master of ceremonies at the papal court. The latter complained to the pope, Paul III, who retorted that he did not have the power to rescue someone from hell.

The fresco as a whole is dominated by angels bearing the Cross, the Crown of Thorns, the Column and the other instruments of the Passion.

Pavement and Choir Screen

The chapel has a 15C Cosmati pavement. The choir screen and the choristers' gallery are by **Mino da Fiesole** (15C).

Biblioteca Apostolica★
(Vatican Library)

Cappella di San Pio V (Pius V's Chapel) – On display are the varied treasures of the *Sancta Sanctorum*, the private chapel of the popes in the Lateran Palace.
Sala degli Indirizzi (Room of the Addresses) – Secular items from the Roman and early-Christian era are exhibited together with religious items from the Middle Ages to the present day.

Sala delle Nozze Aldobrandine (Aldobrandini Marriage Room) – A fresco from the Augustan period depicts wedding preparations (*centre wall*).
Museo Sacro (Sacred Museum) – Founded in 1756 by Benedict XIV, it contains early-Christian antiquities.
Sale Sistine (Sistine Rooms) – Beyond the Gallery of Urban VIII, with its instruments of astronomy and *mappa mundi*, are the Sistine Rooms, created by Sixtus V (1585-90) to hold archives.
Salone Sistino★ (Sistine Salon) – *Used for temporary exhibitions*. The salon was built in 1587 by Sixtus V and was the reading room of the Vatican Library. The Mannerist decoration by Cesare Nebbia shows episodes of Sixtus V's Papacy, the history of books, the Councils of the Church and the inventors of the alphabet (*on the pillars*). It contains 17C cupboards painted in the 19C.

The Vatican Library is followed by the Pauline Rooms, created by Paul V (1605-21). Next come the Alexandrine Room, created by Alexander VIII (1690), and the **Clementine Gallery**, commissioned by Clement XII. Next is the **Profane Museum**, which was founded in 1767 by Clement XIII (Etruscan, Roman and medieval artefacts).

Pinacoteca★★★
(Picture Gallery)

Italian Primitives – *Room I*. The 12C *Last Judgement* (**1**), painted on wood, exemplifies the Roman School and is very similar to Byzantine art.
Giotto and his School – *Room II*. The **Stefaneschi Triptych** (**2**) is named after the cardinal who commissioned it and was executed by **Giotto**, no doubt with the assistance of his pupils, in 1315. It was intended originally for the high altar of Constantine's Basilica.
Florentine School: Fra Angelico and his pupil Benozzo Gozzoli, Filippo Lippi – *Room III*. These artists are among the great 15C painters. Fra Angelico's (1400-55) slightly old-fashioned style, which links him to the Middle Ages, nonetheless expresses his deep religious feeling, as the small painting of the *Virgin and Child with saints and angels* (**3**) demonstrates; the two *scenes from the Life of St Nicholas of Bari* (**4**) come from an altar-

piece predella. The *Coronation of the Virgin* (**5**) is by **Filippo Lippi** (1406-69) and *St Thomas receiving the Virgin's girdle* (**6**) by Benozzo Gozzoli (1420-97).

Melozzo da Forlì (1438-94) – *Room IV*. The graceful **Musical Angels** (**7**), with their bright colours, elegant curls and delicate features, are remarkable. They are fragments of a fresco depicting the *Ascension of Christ* from the basilica of the Holy Apostles (*Santi Apostoli*). The fresco (transferred to canvas) of *Sixtus IV and Platina the Librarian* (**8**) adorned the pope's library.

Polyptychs – *Room VI. The Virgin and Child* (**9**) is by **Carlo Crivelli** (1430-93), a Venetian. While the Florentines were experimenting with line, the Venetians were taking an interest in colour. In addition, Crivelli had a marked taste for gold decoration (very beautiful painted fabrics).

15C Umbrian School – *Room VII. The Virgin and Child* (**10**) by **Perugino** and the Coronation of the Virgin (**11**) by Pin-

turicchio illustrate the clear and poetic style of the Umbrian artists.

Room VIII: Raphael★★★ (1483-1520) – The artistic development of the painter of the Stanze is illustrated by three works. The *Coronation of the Virgin* (**12**), painted in 1503 has a youthful freshness and shows the influence of Perugino. The *Madonna of Foligno* (**13**) was painted in 1511-12 while Raphael was in Rome at the height of his glory; the fine portrait of Sigismondo dei Conti, on his knees, which dominates the picture, the exquisite pose of the Virgin and the luminosity surrounding her are the work of a master. The beautiful *Transfiguration* (**14**), with its dramatic contrasts in chiaroscuro, was intended for Narbonne Cathedral in France and was completed by Raphael shortly before he died in 1520.

Room IX – With his *St Jerome★★* (**15**) **Leonardo da Vinci** (1452-1519) shows his mastery of anatomy, expression and light. The picture was reassembled from two pieces, one found in an antique shop and the other at a shoemaker's. The **Pietà** (**16**) by the Venetian **Giovanni Bellini** (1429-c 1516) combines accurate drawing with fine tonality.

Room X – In his *Madonna of San Nicola dei Frari* (**17**) Titian uses the marvellous Venetian palette. The *Coronation of the Virgin* (**18**), by Giulio Romano *(upper part)* and Francesco Penni *(lower part),* shows the Mannerist style.

In Veronese's *Sant'Elena* (**19**) the saint is depicted in an unusual position, her hand supporting her head.

Mannerists – *Room XI.* The works include *Rest on the Flight into Egypt* (**20**) by **Frederico Barocci** (1528-1612), as delicate and luminous as a pastel.

Caravaggio and his followers – *Room XII.* The *Descent from the Cross★★* (**21**) by **Caravaggio** (1573-1610) clearly expresses the painter's reaction to Mannerist sentimentality. His characters, even in the most religious scenes, are drawn from life. The firmness of his line and the way the light falls further emphasise his realism (note how Nicodemus and St John hold the body of the dead Christ). Mary Magdalen, her head bowed, is a truly remarkable figure. Caravaggio had a great influence on the French painter **Valentin** (1594-1632) – *Martyrdom of St Processus and St Martinian* (**22**). **Guido Reni** (1575-1642) was

PINACOTECA

0   20 m

Cortile della Pinacoteca

also inspired – *Crucifixion of St Peter* (23).
Rooms XIII-XIV – These rooms contain works from the 17C and 18C, particularly by **Pietro da Cortona**, the great Baroque artist. Note the portrait of Clement IX (24) by Carlo Maratta (1625-1713).

Musei Gregoriano Profano e Cristiano★

A fine modern building begun in 1963 houses the **Profane** and **Christian Museums**, opened to the public in 1970. It contains the Museum of Antique Art assembled by Gregory XVI (1831-46) and the Museum of Christian Art founded in 1854 by Pius IX.

Gregorian Profane Museum

It is divided into four sections: imperial copies, 1–2C Roman statues; sarcophagi and 2–3C Roman sculpture. The modern materials – metal, concrete and wood – provide an ideal setting for the exhibits, which can be viewed from all sides. Among the major pieces are the **Cancelleria Reliefs**★. One sculpture shows Vespasian's arrival in Rome after his election to the imperial throne. The other sculpture shows his son Domitian's departure on a campaign. When the Senate banned memorials of Domitian, his head was with that of his successor, Nerva.
Mosaics from the Baths of Caracalla★ – *Visible from the Christian Museum.* They date from the 3C and show the figures of athletes, gladiators and their trainers. This brutality is evidence of the Roman taste for violent spectacles.

Christian Museum *(up Staircase I)*
Statue of the Good Shepherd – It is heavily restored and probably dates from the 3C. The Christian artist adapted the pagan image of a shepherd offering his finest animal to the gods.
Sarcophagi – Christian artists decorated the sarcophagi with garlands, baskets and putti, using the pagan motifs to which they added the symbolic themes of sheep – Christ's flock, vine branches – symbol of union with God through the Eucharist, etc.

Museo Missionario-Etnologico (Missionary-Ethnological Museum)

▶ *Take staircase K.*

Founded in 1927 by Pius XI, it was first housed in the Lateran Palace, but moved into ultra-modern premises in the Vatican during Paul VI's reign.
Items include illustrations of the great world religions (Buddhism, Hinduism, Islam) and Christian artefacts designed in ethnic styles from every continent except Europe.

Museo delle Carrozze (Carriage Museum)

▶ *Take staircase L.*

The museum, opened in 1973 in an underground chamber, displays the first popemobile.

Vatican City and Gardens

The Bell Arch (*Arco delle Campane*) leads into *Piazza dei Protomartiri Romani*, which sits more or less in the centre of the Circus of Caligula and Nero, where many early Christians were martyred. A black stone with a white border marks the former site of the obelisk, now in St Peter's Square. On the left is the German and Dutch burial ground, which legend insists has earth brought from Jerusalem. Next, on the left, comes the church dedicated to St Stephen, where Charlemagne spent the night before being crowned in 800. After the **Mosaic School** (*Scuola del Mosaico*) are buildings where the Vatican State is administered.
The tour finishes with a view of the dome of St Peter's, designed by Michelangelo, rising majestically above the magnificent **gardens**★★★; the fountains and statues are gifts from various countries. Pius IV's "Casina" is a charming 16C building decorated with paintings and stucco work.

VIA VENETO ★

MICHELIN MAP 38 J 13, K 13
METRO LINE A: BARBERINI OR SPAGNA

This famous street once defined glamour, as film stars and the local glitterati mingled here. "Dolce Vita" – the sweet life – soured in the 70s–80s, the "years of lead," when terrorism scared wealthy Italians inside. Today the Via Veneto is the haunt of well-heeled tourists. Although it has now lost some of its former glamour, the Via Veneto is still lined with some of the smartest hotels and restaurants in the city. This wide avenue is lively at night, when crowds stroll past its famous cafés and magnificent palazzi.

▸ **Orient Yourself:** Near the Villa Borghese gardens, the *Via Veneto* winds downhill from *Porta Pinciana* in the Aurelian Walls (now the *Muro Torto*), through the Ludovisi quarter to *Piazza Barberini*. *Via Veneto* is easily reached from the Spagna Metro station, take the underpass connecting *Piazza di Spagna* with the Villa Borghese underground car park.

⊗ **Don't Miss:** *The Ecstasy of Saint Teresa* by Bernini in *Santa Maria della Vittoria*, the Triton Fountain in Piazza Barberini, the Palazzo Barberini masterpieces.

◷ **Organizing Your Time:** 1 hr and 30 min.

Kids Especially for Kids: The bone crypt in *Santa Maria della Concezione*

◔ **Also See:** *FONTANA DI TREVI- QUIRINALE; PIAZZA DI SPAGNA; PORTA PIA; VILLA BORGHESE-VILLA GIULIA.*

Walking Tour

Porta Pinciana

The gateway in the 3C Aurelian walls was fortified in the 6C by Belisarius, the Emperor Justinian's great general, who strove to regain the western territories. He captured Rome in 537 and expelled the Ostrogoths and Pope Silverius.

Via Vittorio Veneto

This street, created after 1879, bears the name of the commune of the Veneto, which, in 1866, adopted the name of King **Victor Emmanuel II** (Vittorio Ema-

nuele) and in 1918 was the scene of the battle in which the Austro-Hungarian army was beaten by Italian troops. The Via Veneto, as it is often called, runs through the heart of the beautiful **Ludovisi district**, which was divided into building lots in 1883 when Prince Ludovisi sold up his magnificent 17C property. Its luxury hotels, boutiques and elegant cafés have made it a meeting place for the smart set: rich tourists and those who like the sophisticated life.

Palazzo Margherita

It was designed by Gaetano Koch in 1886 and was the residence of Margaret of Savoy, King Humbert I's wife; it is now the United States Embassy.

Santa Maria della Concezione

Via Vittorio Veneto 27. ◷*Open 7am-12pm and 3:45pm-7:30pm, crypt open 9am-12pm and 3-6pm.* ◷*The crypt is closed Thurs.* ☎*06 48 71 185. www.cappuccini viaveneto.it.* The 1624 church has an austere Counter-Reformation style. At the chanel's entrance lies the tombstone of Cardinal Antonio Barberini, the church's founder, with the Latin inscription "Here lie dust, ashes and nothing".

WHERE TO EAT

◔ See "Where to Eat" in the *Your Stay in Rome* section at the end of the guide.

TAKING A BREAK

Café de Paris – *Via Vittorio Veneto 90.* ☎*06 48 85 284.* Open Wed-Mon 8am-1am. A favourite meeting place during the *Dolce Vita* years, this bar is now mainly frequented by tourists.
Doney – *Via Vittorio Veneto 145.* ☎*06 47 08 28 05.* This elegant café has a legendary piano bar and a rather old-fashioned atmosphere.

PIAZZA DI SPAGNA

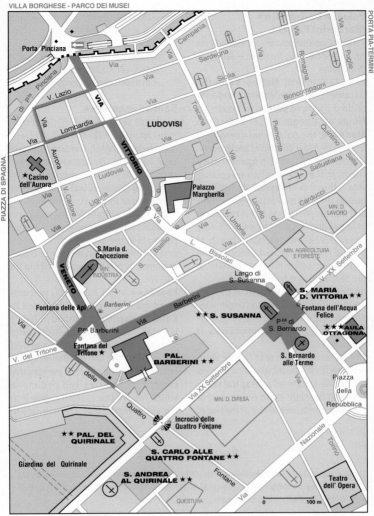

FONTANA DI TREVI-QUIRINALE

Kids Below the church (*access on the right of the front steps*) is the **Cappuccini crypt** ★★, where the friars prayed before bed. The bones and skulls of 4 000 decorate this galley, woven into Baroque artworks: a rosette of shoulder blades, a skull with shoulder-blade wings, and a baldacchino made of pelvises with a vertebrae. The *memento mori* message is simple: "death closes the gates of time, and opens those of eternity."

Fontana delle Api
The fountain, which incorporates the **bees** (*api*) from the Barberini coat of arms, is the work of **Bernini** (1644).

▶ Turn into Piazza Barberini.

Fontana del Tritone★
Bernini's **Triton Fountain** (c 1642) is a happy example of Roman Baroque. The composition – four dolphins supporting an open scallop shell, where a triton sits blowing into a conch – demonstrates the powerful and lively qualities of his art. The Barberini bees on the coat of arms recall that a Barberini, Urban VIII, was then pope.

307

Palazzo Barberini★★
(Barberini Palace)

Via delle Quattro Fontane 13 or Via Barberini 18. See Galleria Nazionale Antica in this chapter.

In 1623 Cardinal Maffeo Barberini became Pope Urban VIII and decided to build a Baroque palace to house his family. Work began in 1627 under Carlo **Maderno**; the palace was completed from 1629-33 by Borromini and Bernini. The main façade, which is framed by two wings, in the style of a Roman country villa, is the work of **Bernini**. By superimposing three tiers of attached columns and shallow pilasters to frame two floors of huge windows *(slightly splayed on the upper storey)* over an open porch at ground level, he created a sense of the dignity and solemnity appropriate to the Barberini family.

Borromini has left his mark in the two small curiously pedimented upper windows in the intermediate sections linking the wings to the central block of the palace.

The windows in the rear façade were decorated by Borromini, who also designed the couple-columned **oval spiral staircase★** at the right-hand *(south)* end of the front porch *(also visible at the end of*

the visit to the Galleria di Arte Antica, which is housed in the palazzo).

▶ Return to Piazza Barberini in order to turn down Via Barberini, which is lined with travel agencies and airline offices.

Santa Susanna★★

Via Venti Settembre 15 Open daily 9am–noon and 4-7pm. American church. Mass held in English, Sat 6pm, Sun 9am and 10:30am. Donations welcome. ☏06 42 01 45 54. www.santasusanna.org

A Christian sanctuary was probably established here in the 4C in the house of Pope Caius, where St Susanna was thought to have been martyred. Rebuilt by Leo III in the 9C and restored at the end of the 15C by Sixtus IV, the church assumed its present appearance in the late 16C.

Façade★★ – This beautifully proportioned masterpiece was designed by **Carlo Maderno** and finished in 1603. It is derived from the Counter-Reformation style typified by the façade of the Gesù Church, but the use of semi-engaged columns and the effect of perspective, created by recesses and pediments which relieve the austerity, give it an individual distinction. The two storeys

Restoration Work

The Palazzo Barberini collections are described here according to their current layout, which follows a roughly chronological order. Plans for the new floorplan –to debut in 2009, hopefully – are as follows:

Ground floor (Via Barberini side): Visitor reception area, including a cloakroom, bookshop, educational rooms, audio-visual rooms, etc.

Ground floor North Wing: 12C to 15C paintings.

First floor North Wing: 17C works, the largest part of the museum's collection.

First floor South Wing: This section of the palace has retained much of its original appearance. It will display what remains of the Barberini sculpture collection and the 17C collection of figurative arts.

Second floor: Paintings by non-Italian artists and 18C offerings. Some of the rooms will contain minor works or works, which have little relevance to the rest of the collection. The 18C apartment can be seen at the end of the rooms.

Third floor: The area originally occupied by Cardinal Francesco Barberini's library (17C) will house the cartoons by the School of Pietro da Cortona and tapestries made by the Barberini factory. The four cartoons depicting the life of Constantine by Pietro da Cortona and the cartoons showing scenes from the life of Christ by Ramonelli, his pupil, are worthy of note.

are harmoniously linked by the repetition of the two superimposed pediments and the elegant lateral scrolls.

Interior – The decoration is typical of the Roman Mannerist style (late 15C): the walls of the nave are covered with paintings made to look like tapestries, which illustrate the biblical story of Susanna. The scenes in the chancel also depict the history of this saint. The wreathed columns framing the paintings in the nave were probably added in the 17C, after Bernini had designed the baldaquin in St Peter's (1624).

Santa Maria della Vittoria★★

Open 7am–12:30pm and 3:30–7pm. **Carlo Maderno** was commissioned to design the church in 1608. Although the façade was built some 20 years after that of Santa Susanna (*see previous entry*), between 1624 and 1626, it is not so daring; with its flat pilasters in place of columns, it is closer to the Counter-Reformation style. It was designed by **Giovanni Battista Soria** for Cardinal Scipione Borghese.

Interior★★★ – Maderno's plan is based on the Gesù Church: a nave, a broad shallow transept and a dome over the crossing. The simple lines of the design enhance the elegant decoration of the cornice. During the 17C, a very rich Baroque decor was applied throughout. The vault, originally white and coffered, and the dome, were painted with *trompe-l'œil* frescoes of the Virgin triumphing against heresy and entering into Heaven. The walls were faced with multicoloured marble, their tones mingling with the gilded stucco and the white cherubs.

The Baroque decoration culminates in the **Cornaro Chapel** (*left transept*), which was designed by **Bernini** in 1652 to resemble a theatre: eight members of the Cornaro family, as if in boxes at the theatre, gaze at the *Ecstasy of St Theresa of Avila★★★*. Marble has never been made to look so supple nor to express so accurately the texture of rough cloth (the Carmelite habit), the angel's light veiling and the delicacy of the flesh. The paintings in the chapels include the Life of St Francis by Domenichino (*second chapel on the right*).

Fontana dell'Acqua Felice

This huge fountain was designed in 1587 by Domenico Fontana. It is supplied by an aqueduct built by Sixtus V, which bears his Christian name: Felice Peretti. A colossal statue of Moses reigns here, sculpted by Prospero Bresciano, who was, no doubt, inspired by Michelangelo's *Moses*. He died from disappointment when he saw the finished work.

San Bernardo alle Terme

St Bernard's Church was created late in the 16C in a rotunda, formerly the southwest corner of the Baths of Diocletian (*See PORTA PIA-TERMINI*). The handsome coffered dome, similar to the Pantheon's, lends dignity to the interior.

Galleria Nazionale d'Arte Antica★★

Palazzo Barberini. Via delle Quattro Fontane 13 or Via Barberini 18. *Open Tues-Sun 8:30am–7:30pm.* *Closed Mon, 1–2 Jan and Dec 25–27.* *€5.* *06 32810. www.galleriaborghese.it.*

First Floor

12C-16C Paintings – *The visit starts in the first room to the left of the entrance.* The *Virgin and Child* by the **master of the Palazzo Venezia** is an elegant drawing where the influence of Simone Martini can be seen. The *Virgin and Child* and the *Annunciation* are by **Filippo Lippi** (1406-1469). Note the attention paid to perspective via architectural elements (the windows and columns): a novelty in early Italian art. Such attention to detail was due to contact with Flemish artists. Also interesting are a fine *Mary Magdalene* by **Piero di Cosimo** and *San Nicolò da Tolentino* by **Perugino**. Three works by **Antoniazzo Romano**, chief exponent of the firm style being used in Latium at the end of the 15C, are also exhibited, among them the *Nativity with St Lawrence and St Andrew*.

Worthy 16C works include *The Holy Family* by **Andrea del Sarto** and a fine *Virgin and Child with St John* by Domenico Beccafumi, which plays with contrasting light and uses the *sfumato* technique perfected by Leonardo da Vinci. Works by **Sodoma** (1477-1549) – a great admirer of Raphael's flowing lines and his friend and collaborator in Rome – include *The Mystical Marriage of St Catherine* and *The Rape of the Sabine Women*. The collection also boasts a masterpiece by **Raphael**, *La Fornarina*★★★, painted by the artist during the year he died. The authorship of this work was the subject of much argument for many years and was attributed to a pupil of Raphael, then to Sebastiano del Piombo. The painting is a portrait of Raphael's beautiful mistress, Margherita, known as *La Fornarina* because she was the daughter of a baker ("*fornaio*" in Italian). *La Fornarina* often features in Raphael's work (👁*See also the Madonna della Seggiola and the Veiled Lady in the Palazzo Pitti in Florence and Santa Cecilia in the Pinacoteca in Bologna*) and is depicted here with an unusual sensuality and a hint of cunning in her expression.

The *Portrait of Stefano Colonna* (1546) is by **Bronzino** and is typical of this refined artist and portrait painter. He endeavoured to present subjects in a suitably noble pose, rather than bring out their more ordinary characteristics. The gallery also houses works by **Titian** and **Tintoretto**, as well as the beautiful *Holy Conversation* by Lorenzo Lotto, a magnificent painting notable for the detailed portrayal of clothes and jewels.

Central Salon★★★ – The ceiling is the best work ever produced by **Pietro da Cortona**, who showed the true measure of his talent here. It was painted between 1633 and 1639 to celebrate the glory of the Barberini family, whose coat of arms (bees in a crown of laurel) is carried by allegorical figures representing the Virtues. On the left, Divine Providence, holding a sceptre, reigns from the clouds. Note how skilfully the painter has used grisaille to separate the scenes.

Second floor

17C-18C Paintings – Works by **Guido Reni** (1575-1642) include the delicate *Portrait of Beatrice Cenci*★ and a beautiful foreshortened fresco, the *Sleeping Putto*★★. The *Portrait of Bernini*★ by **Baciccia** (1639-1709) is a rare portrait by this artist, who was famous mainly for

his decorative skill. Two other Baroque masters are **Pietro da Cortona** with his *Guardian Angel* and **Bernini** with his two paintings *David with the Head of Goliath* and the *Portrait of Urban VIII*.

Two famous paintings can be seen among the works by non-Italian artists. The *Portrait of Henry VIII*★★★ (1540) is by **Hans Holbein the Younger**, who became the official painter at the English court and produced portraits with impartiality and keen insight. The very expressive *Portrait of Erasmus*★★★ (1517), by **Quentin Metsys**, also shows deep analysis.

The *Narcissus*★★ illustrates the novel style of **Caravaggio** (1573-1610), who was a contemporary of Guido Reni and Guercino. Dispensing with background, he portrays Narcissus bending over the water, lost in admiration for his own reflection, his hands almost brushing against their reflected image. As always, light plays a primordial role, highlighting the rapt face, immaculate corset and knee and hiding Narcissus's expression with shadow. Contrasting sharply with this painting is *Judith and Holofernes*★. The cruelty and violence here is conveyed in dramatic detail – made even more striking by the troubled figure of the old woman. Only Judith, thrusting her sword into Holofernes's neck, appears in control, frowning with the effort of her physical exertions.

18C apartments – These elegant, Rococo-style rooms were decorated between 1750 and 1770 for Cornelia Costanza Barberini, who married Giulio Cesare Colonna in 1728. Note the furniture angled to hide the service passage in the dining room. The *Sala delle Sete Aipinte* (Painted Silk Room) has delightful tapestries illustrating the life of "savages" in the Americas.

Additional Sight

Casino dell'Aurora★

🕐*For information on admission times and charges, call ☎06 48 39 42.*

The Aurora Casino is the only extant building of this estate. Cardinal Ludovico Ludovisi, Gregory XV's nephew, invited Guercino, a Carracci pupil, to decorate.

VILLA BORGHESE – VILLA GIULIA★★

MICHELIN MAP 38 G-H 11-13
METRO LINE A: FLAMINIO.

Home to three of Rome's most important museums, this district is also graced by one of the largest areas of greenery (5.5k /3.5mi in circumference). The 17C pleasure garden is now a park, dotted with small lakes, temples and fragrant umbrella pines. Major international equestrian events are held here.

▶ **Orient Yourself:** This walk explores Rome's largest public park, which borders on the elegant Parioli district and contains two museums, an art gallery and various national academies of art in a setting of lakes, lawns and groves of trees.

🕒 **Organising Your Time:** Allow 1 day, including the museums.

🄺🄸🄳🄸 **Especially for Kids:** The bikes, rowboats and the static-line balloon in the leafy green Villa Borghese. The carousel is beside the *Teatro dei Piccoli*, which shows cartoons and movies for *bambini*. Pack a picnic to avoid overpriced snacks from vendors. The Bioparco (Rome's zoo) often disappoints.

ᘐ **Also See:** *PIAZZA DEL POPOLO; PIAZZA DI SPAGNA; VIA VENETO.*

A Bit of History

In the early 17C, Paul V became pope – and lavished gifts upon his family. His nephew even inherited his name: Scipione Borghese. When this newly made man became a cardinal, he built a little palace (*palazzina*) in his vineyards. The section of the **Aurelian Wall** from the *Porta del Popolo* to the *Porta Pinciana* follows such an irregular line that the Romans call it the crooked wall (**Muro Torto**) and tell many legends about it. When the Goths besieged the city in the 6C, they failed to take advantage of a fortifications breach here. Locals concluded that the area had St Peter's protection. In the Middle Ages, this was a cemetery for people denied Christian burial.

Borghese Gardens★★

This walk wanders through a romantic landscape of lakes, trees and flower gardens set with imitation antique sculpture.

▶ *Take Viale di Valle Giulia and then the first path on the right which leads to Viale Pietro Canonica; turn left.*

The little **castle** (*castello medievale*) was the house and studio of the sculptor Pietro Canonica (1869-1959). The **Temple of Antoninus and Faustina** was built in the late 18C.

▶ *Continue along the path as far as Viale dell'Uccelliera; turn right.*

The building topped by a wrought-iron cage is a 17C aviary. The *Viale dell'Uccelliera* (Aviary Avenue) leads to the Villa Borghese.

Villa Borghese★★★

This little palace (*palazzina*) was designed in 1613 by Flaminio Ponzio for Cardinal Scipione Borghese and is a delightful example of a rich prelate's house. Construction was continued after Ponzio's death by a Dutchman, Jan van Santen (called "Vasanzio" in Italian).

During a late-18C restoration, the southwest façade (the present front entrance) was considered too ornate; builders stripped some decoration and altered the steps. Early in the 20C, the balustrade bounding the forecourt (but not the statues, which were classed as works of art) was acquired by Lord Astor and removed to Cliveden.

Between 1801 and 1809, the Borghese horde was greatly depleted: Prince Camillo, Pauline Bonaparte's husband, sold over 200 sculptures to the Louvre. In 1891, the Borghese Palace paintings were moved to the *palazzina*. Its silvan setting, its elegant late-18C decor and its outstanding collections make this gallery one of Rome's best.

The massive square villa is embellished by two avant-corps topped with towers and framed by a portico. Statues peer from the facade.

▶ *Take Viale dei Pupazzi.*

The **Sea-horse Fountain** was commissioned in 1791 by Prince Marcantonio Borghese, who renovated the gardens. The **Piazza di Siena** further on is named after the native town of the Borghese. Set among umbrella pines, it sometimes hosts international equestrian events. On the northeast side stands the late-18C **Casina dell' Orologio**. *Viale dei Pupazzi* leads to the **Temple of Diana**, modelled on an ancient building. From there, an avenue runs north to the

Lake Garden (*Giardino del Lago*), one of the most popular corners of the park. The architect Asprucci created it; he helped enlarge the Borghese Gardens at the end of 18C. The lake reflects the columns of the little **Temple of Aesculapius**, another imitation.

▶ *Return to Viale di Villa Giulia and turn left into Viale delle Belle Arti.*

Various academies stand on both sides of this avenue, between the *Galleria Nazionale d'Arte Moderna* and the *Museo Nazionale di Villa Giulia*. One of these is the **British Academy** (*Scuola Britannica d'Arte*), which brings artists, architects and scholars to the Eternal City. (⏱*Lectures are regularly held on alternate Weds. Exhibition dates vary. Via Gramsci 61; ☎06 326 4939 ; www.bsr.ac.uk. ⌘See "French Academy" in PIAZZA DI SPAGNA).*

▶ *Follow Via delle Belle Arti to the intersection with Via Flaminia.*

Via Flaminia

This modern artery follows the line of the ancient Flaminian Way (220 BC). The road ran almost straight from the city centre to Rimini on the Adriatic (314km/195mi). The **Stadio Flaminio**, on the northern section of *Via Flaminia* (*off the map*), was designed by Pier Luigi Nervi for the 1960 Olympic Games.

Palazzina di Pio IV

The little palace was built by Pius IV (1559-65), who offered it to his nephew Cardinal Charles Borromeo. The slightly concave façade exhibits the mannered style typical of late-Renaissance works. Since 1929, the building has housed the Italian Embassy to the Holy See.

▶ *Turn right into Via Flaminia.*

Sant'Andrea

St Andrew's Church was built in the 16C by Vignola for Julius III. It is an unusual little building, with a clear-cut silhouette, stressed by heavy dentilated cornices, an elliptical dome resting on a solid base and plain brick walls.

Galleria Borghese★★★
(Borghese Gallery)

&⏱*Open Tues-Sun 9am-7pm.* ⏱*Closed Mon, Christmas, and 1 Jan. The visits are scheduled for 2hr for a maximum of 360 people. Entrance times are 9am, 11am, 1pm, 3pm and 5pm.* ✎€8.50. *Tickets must be reserved and collected at least 15 min before entry.* ☎ 06 32 810. www.galleriaborghese.it

The collection – Cardinal Scipione Borghese, nephew of Pope Paul V, was an avid collector of ancient, Renaissance and neo-classical art, although he showed little interest in the medieval period. He accumulated a substantial art collection and also commissioned some of the best-known sculptors of his time, such as Bernini and Cordier. Unfortunately, Camillo Borghese sold part of the collection to his brother-in-law Napoleon. These works are now exhibited in the Louvre. The cardinal also bought and commissioned paintings from Caravaggio, Rubens, Reni, Guercino and other great artists.

Ground Floor

Cross the portico to enter the **main hall**, which is decorated with antique statues (originals and copies), paintings and reliefs, and provides a good idea of **neo-classical** taste. The 4C mosaic fragments were discovered near Tusculum and depict hunting and wrestling. On the ceiling, a fresco by Mariano Rossi, illustrates the deification of Romulus, who is welcomed to Olympus by Jupiter (*centre*).

Also exhibited in the main hall is an unfinished sculpture by **Bernini**, *Truth Being Unveiled by Time* (the figure of Time is missing).

Canova – *Room I*. The **statue of Pauline Bonaparte**★★★ as Venus was immediately accepted as a masterpiece, despite its scandalous nature. The polished, translucent goddess lounges half naked, holding the "apple of discord". The model – Napoleon's sister – was the "idol of high society"; appearing without drapery was a risqué move. Yet her celebrity, combined with the wattage of Canova, proved irresistible.

The ceiling fresco by Domenico de Angelis repeats this theme. The small hooded marble statues in the corners are the Roman precursors of gnomes, said to bring fortune or disaster.

Opere del Bernini★★★ (Bernini Rooms) – The artist was 25 when he sculpted *David* (Room II). Michelangelo, working during the Renaissance, presented the hero calm and victorious. Bernini instead captured the moment of most intense effort, emphasised by the twisting body and the lips pursed in concentration, making this statue a masterpiece of Baroque sculpture.

WHERE TO EAT

See "Where to Eat" in the *Your Stay in Rome* section at the end of the guide.

TAKING A BREAK

The museum cafés are open to passersby, as well as ticket-holders. Enter the restaurant-bar at the *Villa Giuila* from inside or the gardens. The *Museo Nazionale d'Arte Moderna* café – renowned for tasty sandwiches and its fine terrace – is at *Via Gramsci 73*. The *Galleria Borghese* eatery is in the entrance hall.

SHOPPING

Boutique Jaguar Collection – *Via Francesco Siacci 36*. ☎*06 80 82 547* – Open Mon-Fri 9am-1pm and 3:30-7:30pm; Sat 10am-1pm and 4:30-7:30pm. Closed Sun. http://jaguar.evignastores.com. In the exclusive Parioli district, this shop sells luxury bags, suitcases and accessories produced by this famous brand.

In his *Apollo and Daphne* (Room III), Bernini shows the metamorphosis of Daphne from nymph to laurel bush. Note the movement of the hair, almost indistinguishable from the branches. Behind this sculpture, a painting by **Dosso Dossi** (c 1489-1542) treats the same theme quite differently. Apollo mourns his lost love, a tiny figure to the left. Metamorphosis is also the theme of a second masterpiece by this artist from Ferrara: *Circe the Sorceress*.

The *Rape of Proserpina* (Room IV) is one of **Bernini**'s early commissions of Scipione and was given as a gift to Cardinal Ludovisi. Although the statue of Pluto, god of the Underworld, shows traces of the academic style, the supple modelling of Proserpina foreshadows Bernini's works of genius. The subtle tears streaking her face and the fingermarks in her thigh show the artist's attention to detail and texture.

Aeneas carrying Anchises (Room VI) – rather stiff figures with set expressions – is now considered a collaboration between Bernini and his father.

Room V – The focus is the *Sleeping Hermaphroditus*★, a beautiful Roman copy of an original 2C BC Greek statue. Note the feminine shape of the back of the body and the way the head rests, turned to one side, on the arm.

Caravaggio room★★★ – (*Room VIII*). This room houses six masterpieces by **Caravaggio** (1573-1610). The artist led an adventurous and occasionally unlawful life. Yet he revolutionized painting, drawing his inspiration from nature. His figures sprang from the canvas with dazzling effects of light and were extremely realistic. Angry patrons often refused works they had commissioned.

This was the case with the altarpiece of the *Madonna dei Palafrenieri*, intended for an altar in St Peter's Basilica. It remained there only two days, before being banished to the *Chiesa di Santa Maria dei Palafrenieri*. The traditional iconography of the characters is distorted: St Anne –here an old woman – stands to one side, her hands clasped on her stomach. The Virgin supports Jesus, who helps crush the serpent's head. The scene may refer to a theological debate, in which the Protestants

FIRST FLOOR

denied the Immaculate Conception (and therefore the Virgin's power to overcome evil). The Rosario Bull of Pius V (1569) could well be reflected in the painting: the Virgin can triumph with her son's assistance.

The *Boy with a Basket of Fruit* is an admirable still life. For the *Ailing Bacchus*, Caravaggio gave the god his own features. He appears frail and wan (possibly following a leg injury that required hospitalisation). Death infuses this work, suggested not only by the colour palette, but also by the yellowed leaves and the bare grey slab that evokes a tombstone. These early works were most likely painted for the open market, without a specific patron in mind. The same sorrowful atmosphere can be sensed in *David Showing Goliath's Head*. The boy is hardly a triumphant victor. He wears an expression of sadness, compassion and horror; the expression of one who has carried out a just act, but is aware of the grave consequences.

An event in the artist's life may shed some light. Caravaggio was in exile in Naples when he painted this work, having killed a companion in a brawl. Anyone who came across his path had the right to behead him. It is not surprising that he has represented himself as Goliath, and perhaps also as David, who vaguely resembles the ailing Bacchus. He sent the painting to Cardinal Scipione, asking him to plead his cause.

St Jerome was painted by Caravaggio for the cardinal. The saint is portrayed as a thin and muscular figure, absorbed in his task of translating the holy texts. The last work by the artist is a sorrowful *St John the Baptist*.

First Floor

The **entrance hall** houses two superb mosaics by Marcello Provenzale (**1**) (1577-1639). These portray Orpheus, with references to Scipione Borghese (the eagle and the dragon on the left), and Paul V Borghese.

Room IX – The *Crucifixion with St Jerome and St Christopher* (**2**) by **Pinturicchio** (1454-1513) reflects the artist's liking for miniatures, which characterised the art of the 15C Primitives. In the *Virgin and Child with St John the Baptist* (**3**) by **Lorenzo di Credi** (1459-1537) and the *Adoration of the Child* (**4**) by **Fra Bartolomeo** (1475-1527), the influence of **Leonardo da Vinci** and the Renaissance is clearly evident. The room also houses three remarkable **works**★★★ by **Raphael** (1483-1520). The *Deposition* (**5**) was commissioned by Atalanta Baglioni. The patron had just lost his son (the character on the right) in the struggle for the Signoria of Perugia, hence the importance of the Virgin, grieving her child.

The portrait of a *Lady with a Unicorn* (**6**) – spoiled by being changed into a St Catherine but restored in 1935 – is a fine example of the nobility of Raphael's art. Note the delicacy of the necklace and pendant. The *Portrait of a Man* (**7**), a work of admirable vigour, still shows signs of

15C art with a full-face presentation and an indistinguishable background.

Room X – Arranged in their original positions are *Venus* (**8**) by **Lucas Cranach** (1472-1553), one of the rare works by a northern artist in Cardinal Borghese's collection, and the more sensual *Venus* (**9**) by **Brescianino**. In his painting of the *Virgin and Child with St John the Baptist* (**10**), **Andrea del Sarto** (1486-1531) was influenced by Michelangelo's drawing and by Leonardo da Vinci's *sfumato* technique. The outstanding painting in the back of the room is *Danaë*★★★ (**11**) by **Correggio** (c 1489-1534), which illustrates the myth of Zeus as a shower of gold. The use of oils has produced very subtle colour tones.

Room XII – This room is dedicated to works from the Lombardy-Veneto and Sienese regions (Sodoma). The *Portrait of a Man* (**12**) by the Venetian **Lorenzo Lotto** (c 1480-1556) is thought to represent the widower Mercurio Bua.

Room XIV – The three **Bernini** paintings depict a young man (**14**), possibly the artist's cousin, and two self-portraits, one as a youth (**16**) and another as an old man (**15**). Of the two fine busts of Cardinal Scipione Borghese, the second (**13**) was executed because there was a vein in the marble in the first one (**18**) on the cardinal's forehead. *Young Jupiter with the Goat Amalthea* (**19**) was probably the artist's first work (c 1615). A small bronze statue, *Sleep* (**17**) by Algardi, can be seen in the middle of the room.

Room XV – Works by Dosso Dossi and **Jacopo Bassano** (1516-1592) are exhibited in this room. Bassano was a Venetian who used exceptional colour effects. He enjoyed painting country scenes and interiors, which he used even in his religious works, as demonstrated in his *Last Supper* (**20**). This lively colourful scene represents a gathering of ordinary people, such as peasants and fishermen, crowded around a table. Some are deep in discussion, others gesture wildly, others still are lost in their thoughts and appear to be on the point of falling asleep. Only the figure of Christ in the centre of the picture remains calm and composed. *Tobias and the Angel* (**21**) by **Girolamo Savoldo** (1480-1548) presages Baroque painting in the powerful figures and the bold effects of light.

Room XVIII – The *Mourning the Death of Christ* (**22**) by **Rubens** was painted early in the 17C during the artist's visit to Rome. The *Portrait of Monsignor Merlini* (**23**) by **Andrea Sacchi** (1559-1661) shows a restraint unusual in the Baroque era.

Room XIX – After the insipid Mannerist style, two currents brought about the transition to Baroque painting. In Bologna, a style based on tradition developed around the Carracci, which **Domenichino** (1581-1641) helped to propagate; his painting of *Diana the huntress*★★★ (**24**) demonstrates the Bologna expertise very well (the detail of the trees and the bird hit by arrows). The beautifully coloured *Sibyl*★ (**25**) is by the same painter. Annibale Carracci succeeds in capturing expression in just a few strokes in his *Laughing Boy* (**26**).

Room XX – The *Portrait of a man*★★★ (**27**) by **Antonello de Messina** (1430-79), with its powerfully expressive look, its precision (garment folds) and the delicate modelling of the face, is a masterpiece. The *Holy Conversation* (**28**) by **Palma the Elder** (1480-1528) is remarkable for its colours and for the keenly observed portrait of the pious woman (*left side of the painting*). In the *Virgin and Child* (**29**) by the Venetian **Giovanni Bellini** (c 1429-1516) the firm line of the figures is bathed in a beautiful luminosity.

Sacred and Profane Love★★★ (**30**) by **Titian** (c 1490-1576) shows the young artist's search for an ideal of beauty. When he painted *Venus tending Love* (**31**) at 75, his art had been utterly renewed. As well as Titian in 16C Venice there was **Veronese**; *St John the Baptist preaching* (**32**) demonstrates Veronese's attraction to the narrative picture.

Museo Nazionale di Villa Giulia★★★

(Villa Giulia National Museum)

Piazzale di Villa Giulia 9. ♿ 🕐*Open Tues–Sun 8:30am–7:30pm* 🕐*Closed Mon, 1 Jan and Christmas.* ⬬€6. ☎06 32 26 571. *www.archeologia.beniculturali.it/pages/atlante/S75.html*

The Etruscans

This people's origin is lost in prehistory. Around the year 1000 BC, Indo-Europeans from the north settled in central Italy. These new arrivals were skilled in the use of iron and they also cremated their dead. This civilisation, which seems to have spread northwards from central Italy, is known as the **Villanovan** culture. The sophisticated Etruscans may have blossomed from these roots.

More advanced than their neighbours, the Etruscans governed Rome from the end of the 7C BC. Their domain stretched from Corsica to the shores of the Adriatic and from Capua to Bologna, but centred in modern Lazio, Umbria and Tuscany (which bears their name). Decline set in at the end of the 6C BC. Rome rebelled, expanded and attacked their cities; in the 1C BC the Etruscans became Roman citizens.

Traces of their civilisation have mostly disappeared. Their tombs still reveal much: richly decorated and full of funeral goods, these cluster together into *necropoli,* cities of the dead. Until the 18C, Etruscan art was thought to be a derivative of the Greek tradition, without any aesthetic value. Now its elegance and rogue spirit are very much in vogue – and scholars honour this people for style, as well as substance (their elegant engineering, urban planning and liberal social structure).

The exceptional interest of the collection is enhanced by its charming situation in Julius III's country villa.

The museum is devoted to **Etruscan civilisation**. In his classic 1932 book, *Etruscan Places*, DH Lawrence mourned the passing of this mysterious people "who occupied the middle of Italy in early Roman days and whom the Romans, in their usual neighborly fashion, wiped out entirely in order to make room for Rome with a very big R."

Etruscan Art

(&See also VATICANO-SAN PIETRO).

Pottery – The impasto technique used for rudimentary clay pots was succeeded in the 7C BC by **bucchero** (black terracotta). At first the vases were simply decorated with a stippled design, but the shapes grew ever more ornate up to the 5C, when they were fashioned in the form of humans or fantastic animals.

Ornamentation – The work is exquisitely rich: engraved on bronze, in gold filigree or granulation, in finely carved ivory.

Sculpture – The Etruscans never used marble; they worked in bronze and clay. Their statues are distinguished by an enigmatic smile and large staring eyes.

Frescoes – Art historians praise the painters' fluidity, but struggle to categorize the style, usually falling back on a lame "mixture of Greek, indigenous and eastern influences". Only a handful, 6-2C BC tomb decorations, survived. The Villa Giulia displays replicas; the originals are in Tarquinia, 90km /56mi northwest.

Architecture – An Etruscan temple was approached by a flight of steps that led up to a columned portico. The sanctuary itself was a rectangular building, standing on a high podium and containing three shrines (cellae) at the rear.

Villa Giulia★

Although Julius III's reign (1550-55) was contemporary with the Council of Trent, the pope did not lose his taste for the cultivated life of a Renaissance prince. In 1551, he invited Vignola to design a summer villa. The plain and sober façade is typical of this artist, who also studied and wrote about architectural theory. The first courtyard is framed by a semicircular portico with **frescoed vaulting**★, decorated with trellises of vines, climbing roses and jasmine.

In the main courtyard beyond is a charming Mannerist construction by Bartolomeo Ammanati, who collaborated on the Villa Giulia from 1552. The little loggia, perfectly proportioned, opens onto horseshoe steps descending to a *nymphaeum* adorned with caryatids, rockeries and false grottoes. Several pieces of Roman sculpture are on display. In the past, the public was permitted to enjoy the tranquillity of this villa and to gather the fruit and flowers. When the poet Joachim du Bellay visited, he disapproved severely of the pope for leading a life of pleasure to the detriment of affairs of State. When Julius III raised a young man of 17, who led a troop of performing monkeys, to be a cardinal, Du Bellay did not omit to poke fun at the new Jupiter and his Ganymede.

The courtyard is laid out in pleasant gardens bordered by the wings built at the beginning of the 20C to house the museum. To the right of the *nymphaeum* the Etruscan temple of Alatri has been reconstructed.

Ground Floor

Vulci – *Rooms 1-4*. This major centre of Etruscan civilisation occupied the area corresponding to the present-day Maremma and excelled in bronzework. Particularly worthy of note is the laminated bronze cinerary urn shaped like a hut (*Room 2*).

Maroie Tomb – *Beneath Room 5*. This is a reconstruction of a tomb dating from the 6C BC, with two funeral chambers, found in the Banditaccia necropolis at Cerveteri to the northwest of Rome.

Bisenzio Tombs – *Room 6*. Among the objects found in the tombs in this city are two remarkable **pieces of bronze**★, typical examples of early Etruscan art (late 8C to early 7C BC): a **miniature chariot** adorned with figures in the round depicting various aspects of everyday life (such as ploughing, hunting, and a duel), and a covered **vessel** decorated with warriors (also in the round), who are taking part in a ritual dance around an animal, on top of the vessel.

Veii (Veio) Sculptures★★★ – *Room 7*. The statue of **Apollo and Heracles** represents a dispute between the god and the hero over possession of the Ceryneian Hind, which lies at Heracles' feet; the sculpture dates from the end of the 6C BC, when Etruscan art was at its zenith. The display echoes the original configuration on the temple's roof ridge: the statues once were silhouetted against the sky. They are made of terracotta and are strikingly realistic and animated.

The other sculptures include a goddess with a child, which probably represents Apollo and his mother Leto, a fine head of Hermes and several *antefixae* in the shape of Gorgon, Maenad, Silenus and Achelous heads, which masked the ends of the roof beams and the painted pediments. These sculptures all come from the same temple and may be the work of **Vulca**, the only Etruscan sculptor known by name. The king of Rome sent for him in 509 BC to ornament the Temple of Jupiter on the Capitoline (👉 *See CAMPIDOGLIO – CAPITOLINO*).

Terracotta sarcophagus★★★ – *Room 9*. One of the masterpieces of Etruscan terracotta sculpture, it dates from the end of the 6C and comes from Cerveteri. The husband and wife, reclining as if at a banquet, seem to be pursuing their life in the beyond. In contrast to the stylised lower bodies, the torsos are realistic in tone, emphasising the couple's bond. Note the husband's loving stance, his head slightly turned towards his wife and his arm across her shoulders.

The Evolution of Ceramic Techniques

From the beginning of the 5C to about 480 BC, the red-figure technique made Athens the capital of Attic vase painting. Articles produced during this period show the heads in profile, but the eye is drawn full face. The quality is remarkable; the detail within the outline of the body and garments is done with a fine brush.

Artefacts from the 4C BC demonstrate a clear change in style. Hellenistic artists started to experiment with other techniques, not only in Athens, but in *Magna Graecia* (southern Italy) and Apulia. Flowers, fronds and elaborate decorations appeared in white, yellow and dark red against a background of black varnish. The ceramics from Egnatia in Apulia belong to this period.

The raised decoration on some pieces cheaply imitated metal vessels.

First floor

The **Antiquarium** (*Rooms 11-17*) of the museum is chiefly devoted to small **bronze objects**★, both useful and decorative. Bronze was one of the main Etruscan exports, which contributed largely to their wealth. They fashioned it with great creative skill: rudimentary **clasps** dating from the 8C to the 6C BC, **mirrors** finely etched with elegant scenes from family life or mythology, statuettes with astonishingly modern forms. The Etruscans' liking for bronze is explained by the rich copper deposits in Etruria and the island of Elba, which belonged to them. The tin may have been imported from Great Britain or the neighbouring islands.

One of the most famous exhibits in the collection is the **Chigi wine pitcher**★★, found at Veii (Veio); it is one of the most beautiful examples of Greek art from the middle of the 7C BC. This is the proto-Corinthian period when the ceramics produced in Corinth, an important port on the sea routes to the East, were decorated with subjects treated in miniature in bands of delicate silhouettes. On the upper part, two groups of warriors march into battle. The incision work shows each detail clearly. The lower part is covered with figures and hunting scenes.

The same display cabinet shows two *bucchero* **vases**★ dating from the 6C BC (*bucchero* is a sort of clay); the technique for producing this particular type of Etruscan ceramic, which is black, is not well understood.

One of the vases bears the Etruscan alphabet, the other a long inscription. Their alphabet has been deciphered, but the meaning is still unknown.

Biga di Castro – *Room 18*.
Of particular interest is the reconstruction of this chariot, with the skeletons of two horses sacrificed in the burial place.

Castellani Collection★ – *Semicircular corridor* (*Room 19*).
The collection traces the evolution of Greek and Etruscan ceramics from the 8C BC to the Roman era. The Etruscans imported a considerable amount of Greek pottery.

The following exhibits are particulary worthy of note:

- The elongated **vases**, which date from the 7C and 6C BC and come from eastern Greece. These are imitations of Egyptian alabaster vessels and were used by athletes for the perfumed oil with which they massaged their bodies; hence the flat lip. There are several *bucchero* vases dating from the 7C and 6C BC.

– The beautiful **wine bowl** made in Sparta in about 570 (*stile laconico*) and decorated with lotus flowers, an Eastern motif.

– The two **water pitchers**, dating from between 530 and 520. These Caere *hydriae* are a type of water pot found in a necropolis in Cerveteri (ancient *Caere*). The decoration of picturesque mythological scenes includes the abduction of Europa by Zeus on one and on the other Hercules in his lion skin leading Cerberus against Eurystheus, who is hiding in a large jar in terror.

– The **red-figure Attic vases**. From 540-530 BC, Attic ceramic art was transformed by the change from black- to red-figure technique. Henceforth artists signed their work, as can be seen on the two *amphorae* signed by Nicosthenes. Note the two vases by Cleophrades; one is decorated with a very realistic painting of Hercules and the Nemean lion.

Castellani Collection of Jewellery★
– *Room 20*. This stunning collection of over 2 500 pieces was assembled by the Castellani family of jewellers. The antique ornaments date from the 8C BC to the Roman and medieval periods. Also on display are 19C copies and arrangements of antique jewels. (*Reorganisation in progress*).

Pyrgi Antiquities – *Rooms 21-22*.
The old port of Cerveteri, where excavation work has uncovered the foundations of two temples, was mostly famous as a religious centre. The pediment of temple A (460 BC) can be admired in these rooms. The decoration on the back pediment (470-460 BC) recounts two of the most dramatic episodes of the legend of the Seven against Thebes. In the first, Zeus faces Capaneus, one of the seven rebels, and in the second, Tydeus lies mortally

wounded on the ground, about to devour Melanippus's brain.

▶ *Return to the semicircular corridor. Take the two flights of steps on the right at the far end of the corridor that lead down to the first floor of the south wing of the museum.*

Tombs from Capena and the Faliscan region – *Rooms 26-31*. The Capenans and Faliscans occupied neighbouring areas to the north of Rome, bordered to the east by the River Tiber. The two regions became known at the beginning of the 7C BC for their production of *impasto* ceramics. The black-varnished ceramic **plate** is a more recent (3C BC) example of their art. It was found at Capena and is decorated with an elephant accompanied by its calf and guided by an Indian; archers perch on the animal's back. The decoration is thought to refer to a parade that took place after the Roman victory over Pyrrhus (275 BC) in Benevento. There the enemy lost eight elephants, four of which were brought to Rome. The beautiful gold trousseau (necklace with granulated decoration) comes from the *Tomba degli Ori*, in Narce, a Faliscan centre in southern Italy.

Among the exhibits from Falerii Veteres, the capital of the Faliscans, now occupied by Città Castellana, note the beautiful **Aurora wine bowl**. This mid-4C BC piece shows Aurora and Cephalus in their chariot and Peleus abducting Thetis; round the neck a deer and a bull are being attacked by griffins.

Ground floor

Temples of Falerii Veteres★ – *Rooms 30-31*. The architecture of these buildings is known to us from plans left by Vitruvius, a Roman architect and theorist (1C BC). The room contains interesting partial reconstructions of pediments, examples of *antefixae* and *acroteria* (decorative elements, often in terracotta, which were placed on the peak and at either end of the pediments, from the 4C). The **bust of Apollo**★ (*Room 30*) shows late-Greek classical influence.

Praeneste: "Barberini" and "Bernardini" Tombs – *Room 34*. These rich tombs, situated near Palestrina (Ancient *Praeneste*. ⓒ *See Excursions Outside Rome*.) contained mid-7C BC articles, including carved **ivory pieces** – the result of trading relations between the Etruscans and Phoenicians.

The Etruscans were expert goldsmiths and worked in this metal from the 7C BC using the filigree technique. They also perfected granulation: splitting the gold into beads only a few tenths of a millimetre in diameter. The **jewellery**★ on display includes some beautiful brooches and **rectangular plates**★★, adorned with animal figures, such as chimera, lions, mermaids and horses, and embellished with granulations; these were used as ornaments worn over the chest.

Ficoroni Cists★★★ – The cists were marriage coffers; they were also sometimes used for toilet or religious articles. Some magnificent examples were produced by the Etruscans between the 4C and 2C BC. Their manufacture was a speciality of *Praeneste*, (ⓒ *See Palestrina in Excursions Outside Rome*.) where the largest known example – called the Ficoroni cist after its owner – was found in the 18C. Its feline feet are attached to the body by carved plaques; it is decorated with fine engravings of the Argonauts arriving among the Bebryces, with Pollux tying King Amycos to a tree. On the lid are hunting scenes and three statues in the round – the central figure is Dionysius.

Galleria Nazionale d'Arte Moderna★

(National Gallery of Modern Art)

Viale delle Belle Arti 131 ♿ⓒ*Open Tues–Sun 8:30am–7:30pm (last entrance 6:50pm).* ⓒ*Closed Mon, 1 Jan and Christmas.* ☛*Guided tours available (1hr) in various languages.*⊜€9.☎06 322 98 221. www.gnam.arti.beniculturali.it.

The museum has recently been reorganised; some of the works may no longer be exhibited in the order below.

The 1911 building houses the national collection of 19C–20C painting and sculpture; it also accommodates temporary exhibitions and a good library.

▶ *After passing through the barrier in the entrance hall, bear left.*

Entrance corridor and Spadini Room – These pieces by Galileo Chini, an exponent of the Italian Liberty style, explore the subject of spring.

In the **room** housing the **Giacomo Balla** (1871-1958) donation, three of the four panels that make up the *Polittico dei Viventi* (*Polyptych of the Living*) are particularly worthy of note: The *Beggar* and *The Sick* verge on the monochrome whereas *The Mad Woman* is a riot of colour.

Futurism – Light, colour, movement and speed were the principal concerns of Futurism. By 1910, a year after Filippo Marinetti (1876-1944) had published its manifesto, the group's cohesion was apparent in the works of such artists as Balla (*Dynamic demonstration + velocity*) and **Umberto Boccioni** (1882-1916) (*Horse + rider + building*).

Giorgio de Chirico Room – The gallery houses some of the artist's early works (*The Mother*), a number of paintings which demonstrate his return to classicism in the 1920s, as well as examples of his metaphysical phase (*Hector and Andromache*). Besides pieces by **Giorgio Morandi** (1890-1964), there is a Dada composition by Duchamp, which characteristically desecrates the concept of Art.

Glass Room – Sculptures from the 1920s and 1930s, including works by Arturo Martini and Marino Marini.

Central Room – In the 1920s–30s, Italian painting returned to the classical tradition set by the early primitives and developed by masters before the Renaissance in the 15C. The principal protagonists are **Carrà** (*Horses*), **De Chirico, Mario Sironi** (*Solitude*) – an artist associated with Fascism – **Guidi** (*Street Car*), **Trombadori** (*Female Nude*), **Felice Casorati** whose paintings (*Apples*) tend towards a palette of icy-cold colours, **Rosai** and **Morandi**, represented here by a selection of landscapes.

Filippo de Pisis Room – This artist used Impressionist techniques to infuse his perception of reality with magic and mystery. In his *Quai de Tournelles*, figures

are reduced to patches of colour, which on occasion merge with their inanimate surroundings of houses, trees and street.

Abstract Art – Paintings displayed in this room include **Kandinsky**'s *Angular Line* and works by the **Turin Six**. They aspired to a more European vision, looking to new movements emerging in France, notably at the hands of the Impressionists, Cézanne and Matisse.

▶ *Up the stairs.*

Upper Room – This is dominated by the **Guttuso** gift (*Crucifixion*) and post-1945 Italian works, which seek to interpret new figurative experiences in reaction to international avant-garde ideas. By 1960, the break with tradition was complete. The artist **Fontana** was free to pierce, tear or split the canvas and use whatever materials he wished.

▶ *The section to the left of the main entrance is dedicated to painting from the 19C and early 20C.*

After neo-classical works by Canova (*Hercules and Lica*) come pieces from the Romantic Age and the likes of **Francesco Hayez** (*Sicilian Vespers*). Paintings of the **Neapolitan School** by Toma (*Luisa Sanfelice in Prison*), Mancini and Morelli show an uncanny sympathy with the French landscape painters of the Barbizon School.

On the floor above are displayed efforts from the late 19C and early 20C. Alongside works of Italian origin are works by overseas artists, which exemplify new international trends: The *Three Ages* by **Klimt**, the *Portrait* by **Boldini**, which bears a striking resemblance to Manet and Cézanne, **Monet's Waterlilies**, Van Gogh's Portrait of the *Gardener* and *l'Arlésienne*, or Rodin's *Age of Bronze*.

The Pointillists and later the Divisionists practised a special technique juxtaposing primary colours with their complementary colour to obtain a heightened, intense luminosity. The leading Italian exponent of this technique was **Giovanni Segantini** (*Mountain Huts in the Snow, Alla Stanga*).

Rocca di Papa

LAGO DI BRACCIANO★★
39KM/24MI NW OF ROME
MICHELIN MAP 563, P 18

North of Rome, Lake Bracciano occupies a series of craters in the Sabatini Mountains (Monti Sabatini), not far from Viterbo. The peaceful scenery make this a popular getaway for Romans. A boat service plies the lake, allowing visitors to explore the villages with their charming old houses and narrow alleyways. At nightfall, rustling reeds and lapping water provide a welcome contrast to the noise and traffic of the capital. **Lago di Bracciano** is of volcanic origin, like the lakes at Castelli Romani, and is the eighth largest lake in Italy. It produces a fairly rich variety of fish including pike, eel, carp and *latterino,* a local fish. In AD 109, Trajan built an aqueduct (30km/19mi long) to carry water to Trastevere in Rome.

▶ **Orient Yourself:** By bus (COTRAL): departure from Via Lepanto. By train (FS): departure from Ostiense, Termini or Tiburtina Stations. By car: take S 2 (Via Cassia), direction Viterbo; after crossing the *Grande Raccordo Anulare* (Rome ring road) and passing through Giustiniana, bear left towards Bracciano-Anguillare; after about 7.5km/5mi bear right in Osteria Nuova into *Via Anguillarese* to Anguillara-Sabazia.

Kids Especially for Kids: The military aerospace museum at Vigna di Valle

Lake Tour

36km/22mi

Anguillara-Sabazia★
The village is set on a rocky promontory (185m/607ft above sea level). Access to this medieval town is through an impressive 16C gate decorated with a clock. Opposite is *Via Umberto I*, which climbs to the top of the village. Immediately after the gate is a small belvedere (*left*) that has a fountain containing eels. A

flight of steps (*left*) leads to the 18C Collegiate Church of the Assumption (*Collegiata dell'Assunta*): from the small square stretches a magnificent **view** across the lake. Narrow, but enchanting streets, lead down to the lake.

▶ *On leaving the town, turn left after the garden into Via Trevignanese.*

Trevignano Romano
This characteristic village has developed round an outcrop of basalt beside the

Castello Orsini-Odescalchi – the Arms' Room

lake. The medieval town extends along the lake shore like a fish bone and climbs the hill, crowned by the ruins of the Orsini Rock (*Rocca degli Orsini*). From *Via Umberto I* (right), the road climbs to the church of the Assumption and its frescoes inspired by the School of Raphael. Beyond the clock tower in *Piazza Vittorio Emanuele III* is the town hall (right) with its 16C door.

▷ Take Via IV Novembre to Bracciano.

Bracciano★

All the main streets converge on *Piazza 1 Maggio*. On the right is the town hall in *Piazzetta IV Novembre*. To the left *Via Umberto I* leads to *Piazza Mazzini*, where there is a splendid view of the cylindrical towers of the impressive **Orsini-Odescalchi Castle** (*Castello Orsini-Odescalchi*).

Castello Orsini-Odescalchi★★★

🕐*Open Apr-Sep, Tue-Sat 10am–noon and 3-6pm, Sun and holidays 9am-12:30pm; Oct-Mar, Tues-Sun 10-noon and 3-5pm, Sun and holidays 9am-12:30pm.* 🎧*1hr guided tours are given every hour on the hour Tue–Sat and every 20/30min on Sunday and holidays.* 🕐*Closed Mon, 1 Jan and 25 Dec.* 💶*€7, ages 6-10 €5.* ☎*06 99 80 43 48. www.odescalchi.it*

The castle was originally built around the medieval Rock of the Prefects of Vico, who governed till the 13C. It passed to the Orsini family in 1419.

Six impressive cylindrical – but somewhat irregular towers – mark the outer limits of the castle, which was built almost entirely of lava rock atop volcanic tufa. Two walls surround the monument and the medieval township.

Interior★ – A spiral staircase leads up to the first rooms on the main floor. **Room I** (library): Pope Sixtus V stayed there in 1481, fleeing the plague in Rome. The ceiling fresco is by Taddeo Zuccari. **Room III**: interesting original coffered ceiling. **Room VII**: a bust of *Paolo Giordano II Orsini* by **Bernini** and a bust of *Isabella de' Medici* by one of Bernini's pupils. **Room XVII**: room leading to a loggia with a magnificent view of the old rock.

The **Sentry Walk** (*cammino di ronda*) connects the towers (another glorious panorama here). Steps then lead down to the charming **Central Courtyard★** (*cortile centrale*) with its double doors and external staircase made of lava.

▷ Return to Piazza Mazzini and turn left into Via della Collegiata.

In the square beyond the archway is **St Stephen's Church**, once inside the Rock of the Prefects. Walk through the old town's narrow, picturesque streets.

▷ From Bracciano go to Anguillara-Sabazia. After about 5km, turn to Vigna di Valle.

Museo Storico dell'Aeronautica

Aeroporto Vigna di Valle. 🕐*June-Oct Tues-Sun 9:30am-5:30pm (4:30pm in win-*

---

ter). Closed Mon, 1 Jan, Easter, 1 May, 25 Dec. ☎06 99 88 75 08. www.aeronautica. difesa.it/museostorico

Kids The **Aerospace Museum** explores the history of flight via photographs, weapons, uniforms, and, of course, shining ranks of restored planes.

▷ *Take Via Agostino Fausti and then Via Braccianese to return to Rome.*

CASTELLI ROMANI★★

MICHELIN MAP 563, Q 19-20

This attractive region of gently rolling hills, old villages and volcanic lakes, is a popular weekend destination. The landscape is dotted with fine 17C mansions and graced with magnificent gardens, ponds and fountains, and a Greek-Orthodox abbey.

The "Castelli" are in the Alban Hills (Colli Albani), volcanic in origin. They form a circle, whose circumference is the edge of an immense burnt-out crater. Meadows and sweet chestnut trees spread up the hillsides; the lower slopes are covered with olive groves and vineyards that produce the area's famous wines.

▷ **Orient Yourself:** A car is most comfortable, but most villages mentioned are also accessible by train from Termini Station, or by bus (COTRAL) from Anagnina, the last station on Metro line A.

☺ **Don't Miss:** The enchanting position and strawberries of Nemi, Rocca di Papa, the Palazzo Chigi and roast pork of Aricca, the papal palace at Castel Gandolfo.

◷ **Organizing Your Time:** Allow one day.

A Bit of History

The history of the Alban Hills is linked to that of Rome. Cicero, the Emperors Tiberius, Nero and Galba had country houses here. Cato the Censor was born near Tuscolo in 234 BC.

During the Middle Ages, the region southeast of Rome became known as the *Castelli Romani*, or "Roman fortresses". While anarchy reigned in Rome, the noble families sought refuge. Thirteen outlying villages were fortified: Frascati, Grottaferrata, Marino, Castel Gandolfo, Albano, Aricccia, Genzano, Nemi, Rocca di Papa, Rocca Priora, Monte Compatri, Monte Porzio Catone and Colonna.

Castelli Romani★★ Driving Tour

▷ *122km/76mi – 1day. From Rome take Via Tuscolana S 215 (exit 21 on Michelin map 563). After crossing the GRA (ring road) continue to Frascati.*

On the outskirts of Rome, the route passes **Cinecittà**, the Italian equivalent of Hollywood. ☛ *The studios at Cinecittà, which are open to the public at certain times of year, are closed for restoration at the time of going to press.*

Frascati★

Antiquity's affluent and insouciant youth loafed here. From the main square, *Piazza G. Marconi*, sprawls an extensive view downhill as far as Rome.

Frascati has gained a reputation for its white wine and for its 16C and 17C villas, particularly the **Villa Aldobrandini★**, set high above its terraces, clipped avenues, fountains and rockeries. *Gardens open in summer Mon-Fri 9am-1pm and 3-6pm (5pm winter). Closed Sat-Sun, holidays. By appointment only. Contact the Ufficio del Turismo, Piazza Marconi 1, ☎06 94 20 331. www.aldobrandini.it*

▶ *From Piazza G. Marconi, drive to Ville Tuscolane and Monte Porzio Catone.*

The road offers a good view of **Monte Compatri** and **Monte Porzio Catone** as it climbs up to **Rocca Priora,** which clings to the north rim of the crater.

▶ *Continue downhill; turn right into Via Latina; after 4km/2.5mi turn right to Tuscolo (no sign) into a winding road leading to the ruins.*

Tuscolo

It was in his villa in Ancient Tusculum that Cicero set his series of philosophical treatises known as the *Tusculanes*.

The city was once the fief of the counts of Tusculum; from the 10C to the 12C this powerful family owned most of the Castelli and extended its power as far as Rome, also providing several of the Popes. Tusculum was completely destroyed in 1191 in an engagement with the Romans and never rebuilt. A few traces survive: up the slope to the left near the large cross, which is now half hidden in the trees on what was once the citadel, are the ruins of a small theatre, with the remains of a water cistern at the back.

▶ *Return downhill; turn right into Via Latina. In Grottaferrata take Corso del Popolo (main street).*

Grottaferrata

In 1004, Greek monks settled in the ruins of a Roman villa, once perhaps owned by Marcus Tullius Cicero.

Abbazia★ – The fortress-like **abbey** is at the end of the main street. In the

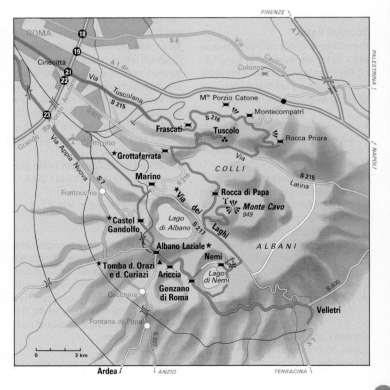

courtyard of the castle, there is a bronze statue of St Nilus.

Museo – ⚷ *Closed for restoration.* ☎*06 94 59 309.*

The large doorway opens onto a beautiful courtyard flanked by the church of St Mary of Grottaferrata (🕯 *see below*) and the Sangallo Doorway. The **museum** is housed in the rooms previously occupied by the commendatory cardinals. On display are Roman and Greek finds and paintings from the Old Testament that had been in the church's central nave. One of the rooms is decorated with frescoes by Francesco da Siena in 1547.

Santa Maria di Grottaferrata★ – *2nd castle terrace*. In the narthex (*on the left*) is an attractive marble font (10C). The Byzantine-style doorway is carved with animals and leaves. St Nilus's Chapel (*right*) has a 17C coffered ceiling and is adorned with frescoes (1608-10) by Domenichino. In the right aisle is the *cripta ferrata*, the villa room converted for Christian worship (5C).

▶ *On leaving the church, turn left into Viale San Nilo; after the lights, turn right into Via Roma to Rocca di Papa.*

Rocca di Papa

The village fans out on a picturesque **site**★ on the slopes of Monte Cavo, facing the Alban lakes and hills. It lies at the heart of hunting country and known for rabbit dishes (*coniglio alla cacciatora*).

▶ *Before Via dei Laghi, turn left to Monte Cavo, surmounted by TV masts.*

Monte Cavo

Alt 949m/3 114ft. Road toll €1 per person. Huge paving stones remain from the ancient Sacred Way leading to the Temple of Jupiter atop Monte Cavo. Here the Latin League met. In the 4C BC, however, Rome defeated the other cities and set her cap on the peninsula. From the square is a fine **view**★.

▶ *Return downhill; turn left and left again into S 217, Via dei Laghi.*

Via dei Laghi★

This is a beautiful road winding between oak and sweet chestnut woods.

▶ *After 3.5km/5.5mi turn right to Nemi.*

Nemi

The village occupies a charming **site**★★ in a natural amphitheatre on the steep slopes of a crater now filled by Lake Nemi. One tower of the Ruspoli Castle still stands, the only trace of the medieval *castello*. In June, delicious wild strawberries are served in Nemi.

▶ *Drive towards the lake.*

Lago di Nemi (Lake Nemi) – The road down passes through fields of daisies, poppies and strawberries. The lake is called "Diana's Mirror", because it reflects the sacred wood next to the Temple of Diana. In 1929, the water level was lowered to recover two ancient boats (AD 37–41). They were burned during the war; a few charred remains are in the **museum**. ♿🕐*Open Mon-Sat 9am-6pm; Sun and holidays 9am-1pm.* 🕐*Closed 1 Jan, 1 May and 25 Dec.* ✎€2. ☎*06 32 14 300.*

▶ *Continue on Via dei Laghi to Velletri.*

Velletri

The town has been prominently involved in Italian history: it resisted Joachim Murat, was captured by Fra Diavolo, the Calabrian brigand chief, was fought over by the troops of Garibaldi and Naples and damaged by bombardments during the Second World War. It is now a prosperous modern town on the south-facing slope of a crater in the Alban Hills, at the centre of a wine-producing region.

The imposing 14C **Torre del Trivio** rises from the main square, Piazza Cairoli.

▶ *From Velletri drive to Ariccia.*

Ariccia

The main square, with its two fountains, bears the styling of **Bernini**. The **church of the Assumption** on the left (*south side*) is elegantly flanked by two porticoes (the circular interior, capped by a dome, is worth a visit). However, this town is most famous for its roasted suckling pig (*porchetta*).

▶ *Stop on the outskirts of Ariccia.*

G. Biudzin/MICHELIN

Nemi

Tomba degli Orazi e dei Curiazi★ (Tomb of the Horatii and the Curiatii)

At the entrance to the Albano, on the left, over a wall and below the level of the road. The late-Republic tomb is made of huge blocks of peperine.

Albano Laziale

The town probably derives its name from Domitian's Villa Albana. Monuments worthy of note include the brick church of **Santa Maria della Rotonda**★ (*take Via Cavour, turn right into Via A. Saffi, then left into Via della Rotonda*), a converted *nymphaeum*, with a bold Romanesque bell-tower (13C). The town has also preserved part of an old Roman gate, the **Porta Pretoria** (*return to Via Cavour, then turn into Via A. de Gasperi*). The **Villa Communale**★ (*Piazza Mazzini*) is a huge public garden with vestiges of Pompey the Great's villa.

▶ *Continue to Castel Gandolfo.*

Castel Gandolfo★

On the edge of a crater, now Lake Albano, stands Castel Gandolfo, famous as the pope's summer residence .
Alba Longa – The oldest town in Latium was founded, according to legend, c 1150 BC. Its rivalry with Rome led to the famous battle between the Horatii and the Curiatii. (*See Appia Antica*)
Papal Villa – ⚓ *Not open to the public.* In 1628, **Urban VIII** commissioned **Mad-**

erno to build on the site of Domitian's earlier villa (81-96 AD), which had extended as far as *Albano Laziale*. The Vatican Observatory (*Specola Vaticana*) was established here in Pius XI's reign.

Lake Albano★

A **view**★ unfurls from a terrace at the entrance to the village.

▶ *Continue north; turn right into S 7, Via Appia Nuova. In Frattochie, detour south (30km/ 19mi) to Ardea.*

Ardea

According to legend, Aeneas defeated Turnus, king of the Rutuli, here. The town stands on tufa rock. Some remains of the city walls, in the form of square blocks of tufa, can still be seen.

▶ *The museum is 100m/110yd after the junction with Via Laurentina.*

Museo della Raccolta Manzù★★ (Manzù Collection) – ♿ ◷*Open Mon 2–7pm Tues–Sun 9am–7pm.* ◷*Closed 1 Jan and Christmas.* ☎*06 91 35 022; www.gnam. arti.beniculturali.it*
Most of the work belongs to the artist's mature period (1950-1970), when he reworked some of themes of his earlier years. The 462 items include sculpture, drawings, engravings and jewellery.

▶ *Take Via Laurentina, S 148, to return to Rome.*

OSTIA ANTICA★★
24KM/15MI SW OF ROME
MICHELIN MAP 563 Q 18

The best-preserved Roman ruins outside Pompeii, this archaeological site lies near the coast, amid umbrella pines and cypress trees. Wander the ruined streets of Rome's old port, admiring temples, pubs, baths, blocks of flats and the vast main square. The long grey sandy beach at **Ostia Lido**, the nearest to Rome, stretches to the south of the river mouth.

▸ **Orient Yourself:** Access by car: along Via del Mare; by underground: (Metro Line B), direction Laurentina to Magliana and then by train to Ostia Antica.

A Bit of History

Ostia, where the Tiber once met the sea, takes its name from the Latin *"ostium"* – mouth. According to Virgil, Aeneas disembarked here. Livy says the fourth king of Rome "extended his dominion to the sea, founded Ostia at the mouth of the Tiber and established salt pans all around". Archaeologists however, place its origins in the 4C BC, but also admit that an earlier village of salt extractors may have existed. Ostia was a military port when Rome embarked on her conquest of the Mediterranean and a commercial port when the victorious city established an organised trade.

Nothing medieval remains except the 15C **castle** built by Cardinal Giuliano della Rovere (Julius II).

Evolution of a port

Roman control of the mouth of the Tiber – set at c 335 BC – corresponds with her expansion in the Mediterranean. Several years earlier, the Romans had won their first naval victory at Antium. During the war against Pyrrhus (278 BC), the fleet sent by Carthage to assist the Romans docked in Ostia. During the Punic Wars (264-41 BC and 218-01 BC), Ostia served as an arsenal; Scipio's army embarked

here for Spain (217 BC) to prevent reinforcements reaching Hannibal, who had already crossed the Alps and defeated Flaminius at Lake Trasimeno. Two years later, about 30 ships set sail from Ostia for Tarentum, which was planning an alliance with Hannibal. In 211 BC, Publius Cornelius Scipio (known as Scipio Africanus Major) took ship for Spain to avenge the defeat of his ancestors. Barely 25 years old and exceptionally invested with proconsular power, he covered himself with glory.

The commercial port – At first there was simply a castle (*castrum*) to protect the port from pirates, but by the 1C BC Ostia had become a real town. In 79 BC, Sulla built a rampart round three sides, using the Tiber to protect the fourth. The last bend in the river was then further east, so the river flowed in a straight course along the town's north flank. Rome imported food from her numerous overseas provinces. A cargo of wheat from Sardinia was unloaded in Ostia as early as 212 BC. Protection was essential. The efforts of Pompey in 67 BC and of Agrippa from 63-12 BC had rid the sea of pirates. Only the problem of entering port remained: frequent strong winds restricted access to the summer months and the adjacent coastline consisted of dunes, lagoons and shallows. As a result, the merchant ships usually docked in the Neapolitan ports and the goods had to be carried overland to the capital.

Claudian Harbour – In antiquity, the shoreline ran parallel to the west side of the excavated site. Claudius's engineers avoided the mouth of the Tiber because of a sandbar created by the currents.

Instead they sited the harbour on the right bank of the river (roughly the site of Leonardo da Vinci Airport). It covered about 70ha/173 acres and was protected by two incurving breakwaters with an artificial island between.

Trajan's Harbour – When the Claudian Harbour became too small, Trajan (98-117) built a second one inland. It was hexagonal in shape, covered 30ha/74 acres and was lined with docks and warehouses. It was joined to the Claudian Harbour by a broad channel and to the Tiber by a canal (*Fossa Trajana*).

Decline and excavation

Like Rome, Ostia began to decline in the 4C. The harbours silted up and malaria depopulated the town. Ostia suffered the fate of all Roman ruins and was pillaged for materials. Regular excavations have been undertaken since 1909; the western sectors of the town were excavated from 1938-42.

Between the town and the harbour the **necropolis of Trajan's Harbour** was discovered on the Sacred Island (*Isola Sacra*), which had been created by digging the Fiumicino channel. Since antiquity, the land has advanced several miles towards the sea.

Life in Ostia

Ostia was a very busy commercial town and under the empire its population rose to 100 000. Its main streets were lined with shops; administrative buildings clustered round the forum; warehouses and industrial premises were concentrated near the Tiber; the residential districts extended towards the seashore.

The cosmopolitan citizens welcomed a variety of overseas religions. Several places of worship have been discovered: the oriental cults of the Great Mother (Cybele), of Isis and Serapis, of Jupiter Dolichenus and particularly of Mithras. Christianity, too, had its adherents; writer Minucius Felix chose the sea baths at Ostia for his conversation with Octavius Januarius, another Christian, and Caecilius, a pagan they tried to convert.

In 387, St Augustine's mother, Monica, died in Ostia on her way home to Africa.

Ostia houses – The most common dwelling in this densely populated town was the **insula**, a block of flats to let, several storeys high. Wealthier citizens lived in a **domus**, a detached house with a courtyard and garden.

All the buildings were of brick and probably unrendered. Some have elegant entrances framed by a triangular pediment resting on two pillars. Here and there, a porch or a balcony adds interest to the street front. Sometimes the brickwork is finished with a decorative effect. **Opus reticulatum** is the technique most frequently used: small squares of dark tufa and lighter limestone are laid on edge to form a net pattern. This technique was practised from the 1C BC to the 2C AD. Later the corners were sometimes reinforced with courses of brick. Another technique used in Ostia, particularly in the 2C AD, is **opus testaceum**: pyramid-shaped bricks laid very regularly on their sides – point inwards, flat bottom outwards.

Excavations (Scavi)

Viale dei Romagnoli 717 ♿ (with assistance, and only for the museum). ⊙*Museum and excavations: open Apr-Oct Tues-Sun 8:30am-7:30pm; Nov-Mar Tues-Sun 8:30am-5:30pm.* ⊙*Closed Mon, 1 Jan, 1 May and 25 Dec.* ✆€4. ☎06 56 35 809.

On the left, inside the entrance, but outside the town limits is **Via delle Tombe**, reserved for burials of various types: sarcophagus, *columbarium* or chapel.

Porta Romana (Rome Gate) – This was the main entrance to the town and led into the **Decumanus Maximus**, the east-west axis of all Roman towns. In Ostia, it was paved with large slabs and lined with porticoed buildings and warehouses (*horrea*). From the outer side of the gate the broad and busy *Via Ostiense* carried traffic to Rome.

Piazzale della Vittoria – The square took its name from a **statue of Minerva Victoria** (1C) **(1)**, a copy of a Greek work, which probably adorned the town gate.

Terme di Nettuno (Baths of Neptune) – This 2C building has a terrace (*steps up from main street*) with a view of the fine **mosaics**★★, which depict the marriage of Neptune and Amphitrite **(3)**.

Via dei Vigili – The construction of this

OSTIA

Non-extant parts

🍴 Refreshments

🚻 Toilets

Previous course of the Tiber (Tevere)

TEVERE

Previous course of the Tiber (Tevere)

Firemen's barracks

Fullonica

V. Fullonica

V. dei Vigili

6

★★★ p.ZALE DELLE

CORPORAZIONI

8

V. della Fontana

2

5 **Terme di Nettuno** 3

4

V. dei Balconi

Casa di Apuleio

7

Mitreo

Theatre ★

Museo★

11

Grandi Horrea

★ **Horrea di Hortensius**

Insula dei Dipinti

Cardo Maximus

V. dei Molini

9

Casa di Diana

DECUMANUS

★ **Horrea Epagathiana**

10

Early fortress

★★ **DOMUS DI AMORE E PSICHE**

THERMOPOLIUM ★★

Terme di Mitra

CAPITOLIUM ★★

Curia

15

Domus della Fortuna Annonaria

★ **Casa del Larario**

FORO ★ ★★

★ **Terme del Foro**

★ **Insula del Serapide**

Area Sacra Repubblicana

Basilica

Circular Temple

14

Mill

Domus del Protiro

★ **Terme dei Sette Sapienti**

Tempio di Roma e Augusto

Cardo Maximus

Insula degli Aurighi

Christian basilica

Market

Porta Laurentina

Insula delle Muse

SCHOLA DEL TRAIANO ★★

Ara della Magna Mater

17

DECUMANUS MAXIMUS

16

Garden suburb

Insula delle Volte Dipinte

Insula delle Pareti Gialle

Casa dei Dioscuri

Domus del Ninfeo

12

SILLANA

Porta Marina

13

CINTA

NECROPOLI DEL PORTO DI TRAIANO

Terme della Marciana

Previous

Coastline

S 296

Synagogue

S 8

LIDO DI OSTIA

street in the 2C meant the demolition of earlier buildings which contained a **mosaic**★ **(2)** showing the heads of figures symbolising the Winds and four Provinces (Sicily, Egypt, Africa, Spain). At the end of the street stand the **firemen's barracks** (*caserna dei vigili*) built in the 2C; on the far side of the courtyard is the *Augusteum* (for the cult of the emperor) **(6)**; the mosaic shows a bull sacrifice.

▶ *Turn left into Via della Palestra which leads into Via della Fontana.*

Via della Fontana – This well-preserved street still contains its fountain **(5)**. On the corner with the Decumanus Maximus stood a tavern; the mosaic orders: *"Dicit Fortunatus: Vinum cratera quot sitis bibe"* (Fortunatus says: Drink wine from the bowl to quench your thirst) **(4)**.
Horrea di Hortensius★ (Hortensius's Warehouses) – These grand 1C warehouses (*horrea*), built round a pillared courtyard and lined with shops, are a striking example of *opus reticulatum*. On the right of the entrance is a small shrine

The **temple (8)** in the centre of the square (only the podium and two columns remain) is sometimes attributed to Ceres and sometimes to the *Annona Augusta*, the imperial corn supply that was worshipped like a god.

Casa di Apuleio (Apuleius's House) – This house has a pillared atrium and mosaic floors.

Mitreo delle Sette Sfere (Seven Spheres Mithraeum) – This is one of the best preserved of the many temples dedicated to Mithras in Ostia. One can still see the two benches for the initiates and a relief showing the sacrifice of the bull.

▶ *Return to the Decumanus Maximus; turn right into Via dei Molini.*

Via dei Molini – The street is named after some millstones found in one of the buildings **(9)**. Opposite are the ruins of several warehouses.

▶ *Return to the beginning of the street and turn right into Via di Diana.*

Piazza dei Lari (10) – In the square (*left*) is an altar dedicated to the Lares. Here also are traces of a primitive fortress (*castrum*) made of huge blocks of tufa.

Casa di Diana★ (Diana's House) – Facing onto the square is a striking example of an *insula* (block of flats), with rooms and passages arranged round an internal courtyard; note the fine corbel in the side street (*Via dei Balconi*).

Thermopolium★★ – This bar's name means "sale of hot drinks". The building had a marble counter, shelving and paintings of the produce on sale.

▶ *Turn right into Via dei Dipinti.*

Insula dei Dipinti – Block containing several dwellings grouped round a garden; fine mosaics on the wall. At the end of the *Via dei Dipinti* on the right an oil store **(11)** was found with huge jars half buried in the ground.

Museo★ – **Rooms I** to **IV** are devoted to crafts, illustrated by low reliefs and to the Oriental religious cults, which flourished in Ostia. The Mithras group about to sacrifice the bull (**Room III**) is a clear indication of the strength of this

TIBER DELTA IN 2C AD
AND TODAY

– – – – The coastline early in 2C AD

Leonardo da Vinci
Museo delle Navi
Porto di Claudio
Via Portuense
TEVERE
Fiumicino
Fiumicino (Fossa Traiana)
Porto di Traiano
ISOLA
SACRA
★ Necropoli
Ostia Antica
Via Ostiense
SCAVI DI OSTIA ★★
Lido di Ostia
0   2 km

dedicated to Hortensius (floor mosaic).

Teatro★ (Theatre) – Ostia was probably provided with a theatre under Augustus. It has been much restored. The three fine masks **(7)** come from the stage.

Piazzale delle Corporazioni★★★ – Under the portico in the square were the offices of the 70 trading corporations. Mosaic emblems show what commodity they traded and their country of origin: grain assessors, caulkers, rope-makers, shipbuilders and fitters, from Alexandria, Arles, Narbonne, Carthage etc.

cult, which had some 15 shrines here. **Room VIII** contains a fine 1C BC statue of a Hercules by Cartilius Poplicola as well as a series of **portraits**★, especially of the Antonines; the quality of expression and the fine detail indicate the high standard of 2C Roman portraiture.

Room XI and **XII** contain examples of the rich interior decoration found in Ostia: walls covered with mosaics, paintings and frescoes from the 1C to 4C.

▶ *Take the Via del Capitolium which opens into Cardo Maximus.*

Cardo Maximus – This important street, at right angles to the Decumanus, kinks left to skirt the temple **Capitolium**.

▶ *Enter the Forum.*

Capitolium and Forum★★ – The **Capitolium** was the largest temple in Ostia, built in the 2C and dedicated to the Capitoline trio – Jupiter, Juno and Minerva. Although the marble facing is missing from the walls, the brick remains are impressive, as are the steps leading up to the *pronaos*; in front of the steps is a partial reconstruction of the altar.

The **forum** was enlarged in the 2C; the few pillars still standing belonged to the surrounding portico. At the far end stands the **Temple of Rome and Augustus** (1C), a grandiose building once faced with marble, which indicates the loyalty of Ostia, the first Roman colony.

As in all Roman towns, the forum had a **basilica**, a covered building where citizens mingled, and a senate house (**Curia**), where the council met.

▶ *Return to Decumanus Maximus.*

Tempio Rotondo (Circular Temple) – It was probably dedicated to the cult of the emperors in the 3C.

Casa del Larario★ (House with Lararium) – The building consists of shops ranged around an internal court. The recess, decorated in attractive red and ochre bricks, housed the statues of the Lares.

▶ *Continue along the Decumanus Maximus; turn right into Via Epagathiana.*

Horrea Epagathiana★ **(Epagathus's Warehouses)** – This 2C complex has a fine doorway with columns and a pediment. It belonged to two rich freedmen: Epagathus and Epaphroditus.

Casa di Amore e Psiche★★ (House of Cupid and Psyche) – Like most of the buildings facing the shore, this was a private house (4C). It had mosaic and marble floors, and *nymphaeum* decorated with niches, arcades and columns.

▶ *Turn left into Via del Tempio di Ercole, right into Via della Foce and right again into Via delle Terme di Mitra.*

Terme di Mitra (Baths of Mithras) – An arcade leads into the 2C building. Inside is a flight of steps descending to the underground *hypocaust* (heating system) and traces of a *frigidarium* (pool and columns with Corinthian capitals).

Ruins of the once impressive Forum and Capitolium at Ostia Antica

B. Kaufmann/MICHELIN

▶ *Return to Via della Foce and walk through the Insula del Serapide.*

Insula del Serapide★ (Serapis Flats) – The 2C blocks had porticoes round a courtyard and a bathhouse
Terme dei Sette Sapienti★ (Baths of the Seven Sages) – There is a mosaic floor in the large circular room and one room is roofed with a dome decorated with mosaics on a white ground.
Insula degli Aurighi (Charioteers' Flats) – Includes a court and portico.

▶ *Turn left into Cardo degli Aurighi and right into Via delle Volte Dipinti.*

Insula delle Volte Dipinte; Insula delle Muse; Insula delle Pareti Gialle – 🕐*Specialists only; apply to the Soprintendenza di Ostia.* Houses from the 2C with mosaics and paintings.
Città-Giardino (Garden Suburb) – *Right.* Example of a 2C residential complex with blocks of dwellings surrounded by gardens and fountains (remains of several fountains, one containing mosaic).
Casa dei Dioscuri (Dioscuri House) – It was built in the 4C in one of the garden suburb blocks. The rooms are paved with beautiful multicoloured mosaics, one of which shows the Dioscuri.
Domus del Ninfeo (House with Nymphaeum) – Incorporated in the 4C into a 2C building; one room is screened by three arches supported on slim columns.

▶ *Return to Decumanus Maximus; right.*

Porta Marina (Marine Gate) – This gate in Sulla's walls gave access to the seashore. A few huge blocks of tufa remain. Inside the gate (*left*) was the tavern of Alexander Helix **(12)** and outside (*right*) a tomb **(13)**.
The Decumanus came to an end outside the gate in a large colonnaded square.

▶ *Left on Cartilio Poplicola; walk to end.*

Terme della Marciana (Marciana Baths) – Behind the massive pilasters of the *frigidarium* apse, a beautiful **mosaic**★ shows athletes in the pose characteristic of the various sports, with trophies and equipment on a table in the centre.

▶ *Return to the Porta Marina and walk back along the Decumanus Maximus.*

Schola del Traiano★★ – *Right.* This impressive 2–3C building was the headquarters of a guild of merchants. On the left of the entrance is a plaster copy of a statue of Trajan found here, hence the name. Next comes a court with a rectangular central basin surrounded by brick columns. The central room, preceded by two columns, contains a fine mosaic floor. During excavations, a 2C house was discovered on the court's east side, furnished with a *nymphaeum* (paintings and mosaics) and a peristyle.
Basilica Cristiana (Christian Basilica) – *Left.* 4C; a row of columns separates the aisles, which end in apses.
Mercato (Market) – There were two fishmongers' shops **(14)** on either side of an alley, which led to a pillared podium on the west side of the market square. On the third pillar on the left, it says in Latin: "read and know that there is a lot of gossiping in the market."

▶ *Right into Via del Pomerio; left into Via del Tempio Rotondo and continue past the Tempio di Roma e Augusto (left) and Cardo Maximus (right).*

Terme del Foro★ (Forum Baths) – The largest baths in Ostia had heating ducts in the walls and a public lavatory **(15)**.

▶ *Turn left into Cardo Maximus.*

Mulino (Mill) – On the left of the Cardo Maximus are several millstones.
Ara della Magna Mater (Altar of the Great Earth Mother) – This sacred enclosure contains the remains of a temple dedicated to Cybele (the Great Mother – *Magna Mater*) **(16)**. The Sanctuary of Attis **(17)** has a statue of the goddess in the apse and two faun sculptures.
The Cardo Maximus ends at the Laurentina Gate (**Porta Laurentina**) in Sulla's Wall (**Cinta Sillana**).

▶ *Turn left into Via Semita dei Cippi.*

The **Domus del Protiro** (*right; closed for restoration*) is an exception in Ostia for its marble pediment above the door.

Domus della Fortuna Annonaria – 🔓
Closed for restoration. A 3–4C house with a well in the garden and mosaic floors.

▷ *Take Via del Mitreo dei Serpenti to return to the Decumanus Maximus.*

Outskirts

Necropoli del Porto di Traiano★ (Trajan's Port Necropolis)
5km/3mi from the excavations. Access by car: by S 296 (direction Leonardo da Vinci Airport at Fiumicino); right turn into Via Cima Cristallo; entrance to the necropolis on the left of the access road. ⏱*Open Tues–Sun Nov–Feb 9am–4pm; Mar 9am–5pm; Apr–Oct 9am–6pm.* ⏱*Closed Mon, 1 Jan, 1 May and 25 Dec.* ☎*06 65 83 888; www.itnw.roma.it/ostia/scavi*

Isolated and silent, the necropolis is an impressive place, studded with umbrella pines, cypresses and laurels. The inhabitants of Trajan's Harbour buried their dead here from the 2C-4C.
The simplest tombs are marked by an amphora or a ridge of tiles. Others of brick had one or more chambers for sarcophagi. Sometimes there is a fore-ourt columbarium (with recesses for the cinerary urns), which the owner made available to his household.
The majority of the tombs have a low door beneath a lintel resting directly on the uprights. The inscription gave the name of the dead person, with sometimes a low-relief sculpture depicting their occupation.

Museo delle Navi Romane (Ship Museum) In Fiumicino
Access: Roma Ostiense Station to Leonardo da Vinci Airport and then by train. ☎*06 65 01 00 89.*

The maritime museum is on the site of the Claudian Harbour. It houses the hulls of five Roman **vessels** and smaller articles: pottery, fishing floats, rope, nails, wooden pegs, needles, money. A low relief sculpture (*copy*) shows the boat that transported Caligula's Obelisk, now in St Peter's Square. The boat was sunk as a foundation for the lighthouse at the harbour mouth. It stood 50m/164ft high and shone 30km/18mi out to sea.

PALESTRINA ★
42 KM/26 MI SE OF ROME

MICHELIN MAP 563 Q 20

According to legend, Ancient Praeneste was founded at the dawn of Roman history by Telegonus, the son of Ulysses and the enchantress Circe. Palestrina, now an attractive small medieval town, still occupies the same position, perched on the slopes of the Prenestini Hills, offering stunning views of the surrounding countryside. Highlights include the ruined temple of the goddess Fortune and the famous Hellenistic Nile mosaic, further examples of the splendour of ancient Rome.

🛈 **Information:** Palazzo Colonna-Barberini, Via della Cortina. Open Mon-Fri 9am-12:30pm and 3–7pm, Sat 9am-1pm ☎06 957 3176.
▷ **Orient Yourself:** Palestrina was built on the southern slopes of Monte Ginestro, an outcrop in the chain of Prenestini Hills overlooking the valley. From Rome, drive along *Via Prenestina;* by bus from Roma Ponte Mammolo (Metro line B).

A Bit of History

Praeneste rose to its full glory during the early days of its existence, in the 8C and 7C BC; it was besieged subsequently through the centuries because of its strategic position. Under the rule of Rome from the 4C BC, the town became a favourite country retreat in Imperial times for dignitaries and nobles. The cult of Fortune lasted well into the 4C AD, when the temple was abandoned and its site became encroached upon by the medieval city.

The superb 8C necropolis, together with the Barberini and Bernardini tombs, in which fabulous funerary ornaments were found (now displayed at the Museo Nazionale di Villa Giulia in Rome), are a lasting testament to Palestrina's illustrious past.

Sights

Tempio della Fortuna Primigenia★

This temple was once a grandiose sanctuary dedicated to the goddess Fortune. Built during the 2C-1C BC, it stands as one of the most important examples of Roman architecture based upon Hellenistic archetypes in Italy.

The complex would have occupied most of the area now covered by the town; it comprised a series of terraces linked by a system of ramps and stairways aligned one above the other. A large basilica-shaped room, two lateral buildings, a natural cave and an apse paved with the famous *Nile Mosaic* (◉ *See Museo Archeologico Prenestino*) survive from the lower sanctuary that was accommodated on the site of the old forum, on the second level of the temple. The upper was located on the fourth terrace of the temple complex, where *Piazza della Cortina* now preens. On this platform, once graced with steps arranged in semicircles, was built the *Palazzo Colonna* (11C) – later known as the *Palazzo Barberini* (1640). Here, behind the elegant façade, is the museum.

Museo Archeologico Prenestino

The entrance to the museum is at the top of the stairs up to the Terrazza degli Emicicli. ♿ ⊙*Open 9am-7.30pm.* ▦€3. ☎06 95 38 100; www.archeologia.beniculturali.it/pages/atlante/S66.html

The palace curves dramatically, embracing the ancient Temple of Fortune. The Palazzo Colonna-Barberini contains one of the largest and finest Hellenic mosaics. The late-2C BC **Nile Mosaic**★★ depicts the river in flood: stranded animals, hunters, boaters and partiers, all among islands

and elaborate architecture. Alexandrian artists pieced together this tableau, heavily restored in the 17C (sliced up and sent to Rome, then reassembled incorrectly). It was evacuated in WWII to prevent bomb damage. Conservators used Grand Tour sketches to reassemble it.

The museum also showcases the recently discovered sculpture, **Il Triade Capitolina**★★. The only known depiction of Rome's three tutelary gods, the Capitoline Triad shows Minerva, Jupiter and Juno squashed onto one throne. Police recovered this staute – stolen in 1992 – from the underworld. On leaving the museum, cross the street and descend the terraces.

▸ *Follow the one-way road system into town by means of the Via Anicia.*

Town centre

The main square, Piazza Regina Margherita, replaces the old forum. The 11C duomo, flanked by a Romanesque bell-tower, was constructed among the ruins of a Roman temple. It is dedicated to St Agapito, the town's patron.

At the centre of the piazza is a statue of **Giovanni Pierluigi da Palestrina** (1524-94), the renowned composer of polyphonic religious music. His house is now a music research center with a 6,000-volume library (*Centro di Studi Palestriniani, Vicolo Pierluigi 3 Palestrina. Open Tues-Sun 9:30am-12:30pm.* ☎06 953 8083. www.fondpalestrina.org).

TIVOLI★★★
31 KM/19 MI E OF ROME
MICHELIN MAP 563 Q 20

One of the most impressive sites of antiquity lies just outside the town of Tivoli to the east of Rome. The evocative setting and magnificent architecture of Hadrian's Villa has long fascinated visitors, despite its extensive plundering over the centuries. This picturesque little town sits on the lower slopes of the chalky Apennines (Monti Simbruini), where the River Aniene cascades into the Roman plain before joining the Tiber. Famous for its sunset vistas, Tivoli also has two famous and contrasting gardens: the manicured fantasia of Villa d'Este and the shaggy exuberance of Villa Gregoriana.

- **Information:** Piazza Garibaldi. Open Mon-Fri 9am-1pm and 3-5pm, Sat 9am-1pm. ☎0774 31 12 49
- **Orient Yourself:** Drivers should take the *Via Tiburtina* or turn off the autostrada 28km from Rome at the Tivoli Exit A24. Access by coach from Rebibbia (last stop on Metro line B).
- **Don't Miss:** Hadrian's Villa, the Villa d'Este, sunset views of Rome.
- **Organizing Your Time:** Visit Hadrian's Villa in the morning: 2hr 30min. Save the cooler Villa d'Este and Villa Gregoriana –each 1hr 30min – for later in the day.

A Bit of History

A Greek seer and a Roman sibyl – Tivoli, Tibur in Antiquity, is said to have been founded earlier than Rome by Tiburtus, grandson of the Greek seer Amphiaraos, whom Zeus caused to be swallowed up in the earth outside Thebes. Tibur came under Roman control in the 4C BC and became a holiday resort under the Empire.

Several centuries later, according to a medieval legend, two great prophecies were made by a sibyl. When Augustus asked her whether there would be anyone greater than he, she sent him a vision of the Virgin and Child on the Capitol in Rome and added that on the Child's birthday a spring of oil would bubble up from the ground; this is supposed to have taken place in Trastevere. In 1001 Tivoli rebelled against the German Emperor Otho III, who was in Italy with Pope Sylvester II. The Romans, who had no love for their neighbours in Tivoli, made common cause with the Emperor. The Pope intervened and the Emperor spared the town and the rebels but, when the Pope and the Emperor returned to Rome, the Romans reproached them for their leniency; both had to flee the mob. The following year Otho died and Sylvester the year after. Tivoli retained its independence until 1816, when it joined the Papal States.

Villa Adriana★★★
(Hadrian's Villa)

Hadrian's Villa is 6km below the main town: about 1.5km off the highway, turn right onto Via Rosolino. Tivoli–Rome buses stop on request, just a 15-minute walk from the site, or take the local CAT #4 from Largo Garibaldi. The car park, which wraps around the ticket booth, costs €2.
Open May–Sep 8:30am–8pm; Oct–Apr 8:30am–5pm. Closed 1 Jan, 1 May and Christmas. €8.50. ☎0774 53 02 03. www.villa-adriana.net

WHERE TO EAT
Hotel Adriano Ristorante – *Via Villa Adriana 194, Tivoli.* ☎*0774 535 028.* *www.hoteladriano.it.* Savour contemporary Italian fare across from Hadrian's Villa: herb risotto in a Parmesan *tuille* basket and *panna cotta al mandarino* (clotted cream with mandarin orange slices). Dining in the shady garden park is delightful in summer.

VILLA ADRIANA

0   100 m

CANOPO ★★★

Praetorium

Museum

Grandi
Terme

5

★★ Piazza
d'Oro

Sala dei
pilastri dorici ★★

★★ TERME   Vestibule

Piccole
Terme

6

4

7

PALAZZO
IMPERIALE

8

Nymphaeum

3

Cortile delle
Biblioteche

9

★★★
TEATRO
MARITTIMO

PECILE ★★

11   10

12

Terrazza
di Tempe

P

Museo
Didattico

13

Theatre

N

TIVOLI / ROMA

The perimeter (5km/3mi) enclosed an estate: vast gardens adorned with works of art, an imperial palace, baths, libraries and theatres. Probably the richest building project in antiquity, it was designed largely by the emperor Hadrian. The complex was a mix of pleasure and politics, private and public spaces, akin to Versailles. Historians suggest it was also a diorama of the world, a sort of ancient Epcot Center, inspired by Hadrian's extensive travels. Grief-stricken at the death of his young favourite Antinoüs, he died in Baiae in 138. His remains were buried in his huge mausoleum in Rome. The emperors who succeeded him probably continued to come to Tivoli. It was here that Zenobia, Queen of Palmyra, ended her days as Aurelian's prisoner. Then the villa fell into ruin. From the 15C to the 19C, the site was explored; over 300 works were recovered, which now enrich museums and private collections in Rome, London, Berlin, Dresden, Stockholm and St Petersburg.

Since 1870, the site has belonged to the Italian Government, which has organised its excavation. The vegetation has been cleared from the ruins, revealing magnificent vaults, columns, stucco work and mosaics.

The present entrance is probably not the one used in Hadrian's day. The design of the villa is so unusual that archaeologists have not been able to identify the buildings or their uses with any certainty. Before exploring the site it is advisable to study a model of the villa that is displayed in a room next to the bar. The toilets are 300m from the entrance.

Pecile★★

The **Poikile** was the name of a portico in Athens which Hadrian wished to reproduce. Only the north wall remains, through which the visitor enters the excavation site. Notice the lattice-work effect created by small blocks of tufa – *opus reticulatum* – Hadrian's Villa is one of the last examples of this technique, which fell into disuse in the 2C. The horizontal grooves in the wall were filled with bricks, which disappeared when the villa was plundered for its materials, in particular for the *Villa d'Este*.

The *Poikile* was built in the shape of a large rectangle with slightly curved ends and lined with a portico; it was sited so that one side was always in the shade. The apsidal chamber was the **philosophers' room (1)**, possibly for reading.

Teatro Marittimo★★★

This circular construction consists of a portico and a central building. It is surrounded by a canal, spanned by small swing bridges. The theatre was an ideal retreat for the misanthropic Hadrian.

▸ *Walk south towards the Ninfeo and climb the steps.*

The ruins look down on a *nymphaeum*, which can be reached by part of the **cryptoporticus**, a network of passages. These made it possible to traverse the site underground

▸ *Cross the Cryptoporticus (right).*

Ninfeo

The *nymphaeum*, the flat area enclosed between sections of high wall, was originally thought to be a stadium. The building (*west*) was composed of three semicircular rooms on a courtyard **(3)**.

Terme★★

The **baths** consist of the Small Baths (*Piccole Terme*) and the Great Baths (*Grandi Terme*). They both show the high architectural standards attained in the villa: rectangular rooms with concave walls, octagonal rooms with alternate concave and convex walls, circular rooms with recesses alternating with doors. The most impressive room is in the Great Baths; it has an apse and the remains of some superb vaulting.

The tall building, called the **Praetorium** (*Pretorio*), was probably a storehouse.

Museo (Museum)

The **museum** contains the results of the most recent excavations: Roman copies of the Amazon by Phidias and Polyclitus; copies of the Caryatids from the Erechtheion on the Acropolis in Athens. These statues adorned the sides of the Canopus. There are more ruins belonging to the villa to the west of the museum in a large olive grove, but it is private property.

Canopo★★★ (Canopus)

The route to Canope from Alexandria was a canal lined with temples and gardens. Hadrian had part of his estate landscaped to look like the Egyptian site. He completed the effect with a canal down the centre and a copy of the Temple of Serapis (*Tempio di Serapis*) at the southern end. He combined the cult of Serapis with the cult of Antinoüs, his young favourite who had been drowned in the Nile.

▸ *On leaving the Canopus, bear right between the Grandi Terme and the Pretorio, climb to the upper level and continue towards the Ninfeo before bearing right.*

The path goes round a large **fish pond** surrounded by a portico (*Quadriportico con peschiera*) **(4)**.

▶ *Return to the Pretorio and the Grandi Terme and walk as far as the ruins overlooking the Ninfeo and bear right.*

Palazzo Imperiale

The **Imperial Palace** complex extended from the *Piazza d'Oro* to the libraries.

Piazza d'Oro★★ – The rectangular area was surrounded by a double portico; the piazza was an aesthetic caprice. On the far side are traces of an octagonal chamber **(5)**: each of the eight sides, which are alternately concave and convex, was preceded by a small portico (one of these has been reconstructed). On the opposite side is a chamber **(6)** covered by a dome and flanked by two smaller chambers: the lefthand one contains traces of a black-and-white mosaic.

Sala dei pilastri dorici★★ – The **Doric Pillared Hall** takes its name from the surrounding portico, which was composed of pilasters with Doric bases and capitals supporting a Doric architrave (partial reconstruction in one corner). Opposite stood the **firemen's barracks** (*caserma dei vigili*) **(7)**.

Adjoining the **Pillared Hall** (*north side*) is a huge section of curved wall which may have been part of a summer **dining room** (triclinio estivo) **(8)**; the oval basins further east mark the site of a **nymphaeum** (ninfeo di palazzo). These buildings overlook a courtyard which is separated by a *cryptoporticus* from the **library court**; the east side of the latter court is composed of a complex of 10 rooms ranged down both sides of a corridor; this was an infirmary **(9)**; each of the rooms held three beds; the **floor**★ is paved with fine mosaics. The library courtyard offers a pleasant **view**★ over the countryside.

Biblioteche – The ruins of the **library buildings** are on the north side of the courtyard (*Cortile delle Biblioteche*); according to custom, there was a Greek library **(10)** and a Latin library **(11)**.

Next to the libraries (*east side*) is a group of rooms paved with mosaic, which belonged to a dining room (*triclinio imperiale*) **(12)**.

Terrazza di Tempe

A grove of trees hangs on the slope above a valley, which Hadrian called his **Vale of Tempe**, after the Greek beauty spot in Thessaly. The path runs through the trees past a **circular temple (13)** (reconstructed). It contained a statue of the goddess Venus and was thus attributed to her. Further along (*left*) is the site of a **theatre**.

▶ *Proceed to Tivoli (town plan in the Michelin Guide Italia).*

The **Rocca Pia**, a fortress built by Pius II (1458-64), dominates *Piazza Garibaldi*.

Villa d'Este★★★

The center of Tivoli, down the street from Largo Garibaldi. Entrance from the old convent cloisters. ◷*Open Tues–Sun 8:30am-1hr before sunset.* ◷*Closed Mon, 1 Jan, 1 May and 25 Dec.* ▧€6.50. ☏0424 60 04 60. www.villadestetivoli.info

The fountains are the real draw in this Renaissance pleasure garden. Over 1,200 liters of water per second flowed through its pipes and pumps, during its prime. Today the spectacle varies – depending on the season, time of day and nearly completed restoration – but the UNESCO world heritage site is always worth a look.

The Cardinal Ippolito II d'Este, squeezed out of Rome after an unsuccessful papal bid, sponsored this extravaganza in 1550. Under his guidance, Neapolitan architect Pirro Ligorio transformed a convent into the ultimate villa, after a careful study of Hadrian's ruins, which he then quarried.

The simple architecture contrasts with the elaborate gardens (3ha/7.5 acres), which descend in a series of terraces on the western slope of the hill. The statues, pools and fountains enhance the natural beauty with all the grace of the Mannerist style. Many distinguished guests visited the villa, including Pius IV and Gregory XII, and after the cardinal's death, Paul IV, Paul V, Pius IX and writers and artists: Benvenuto Cellini, Titian, Tasso, and Liszt.

In 1759, when the avenues were overgrown with brambles and the fountains silent, Fragonard and Hubert Robert, who were staying at the French Academy in Rome, came to spend the summer in Tivoli with their patron the Abbé de Saint Non. There is scarcely a corner of the gardens where they did not set up their easels, nor a perspective that escaped their brushes.

Villa and Gardens★★★

The Old Apartment (*Vecchio Apparta-mento*) on the first floor of the villa now holds temporary exhibitions.

▷ *Descend to the floor below.*

Sala grande – The **central Salon** is deco-rated in the Mannerist style by pupils of Girolamo Muziano and Federico Zuccari. The fountain, a riot of mosaics, faces a wall panel showing the gardens in the 16C. On the ceiling is a fresco of the *Ban-quet of the Gods*. From the Salon loggia is a lovely **view**★.

Next is a series of four rooms in the west wing. The mythological paintings in the first room are attributed to Muziano and Luigi Karcher: the *Labours of Hercules* surround a fresco of the *Synod of the Gods* (*ceiling*). Federico Zuccari and his school painted the allegorical frescoes in the next room, known as the Philoso-phers' Hall, and the *Glory of Este* in the third room. In the Hall of the Hunt, Tem-pesta's efforts show hunting trophies and countryside scenes.

From the balcony is a pleasant view of the gardens and Tivoli itself.

▷ *Double flights of steps lead down to the upper garden walk.*

Fontana del Bicchierone – The foun-tain, often attributed to Bernini, consists of a huge moss-covered **beaker**. Water overflows into a shell-shaped basin.

La "Rometta" – This fountain, known as **"mini Rome"** was an attempt by the cardinal to reproduce some of the most famous monuments of classical Rome: a pool bearing a boat (representing Tiber Island) surmounted by an obelisk; higher up near some artificial ruins an allego-rical statue of Rome and the she-wolf.

Viale delle Cento Fontane★★★ – The **Avenue of a Hundred Fountains** is one of the most charming spots here. One side of the straight walk is lined by fountains of water spouting from small boats, obelisks, animal heads, eagles and lilies, which recall the Este coat of arms.

Fontana dell'Ovato★★★ – The **Oval Fountain** is dominated by the statue of the sibyl, flanked by allegorical figures of rivers. Round the edge of the basin, half covered in moss, are statues of naiads pouring the water of the River Aniene from their water pots. An attractive ceramic decoration adorns the front rim of the oval basin.

Fontana dell'Organo★★★ – The **Organ Fountain** once played music on a hidden water-powered organ. This ingenious mechanism was invented by a Frenchman, Claude Venard, in the 16C. After seeing and hearing the fountain, Montaigne, the French writer and philosopher, wrote in his journal that "the organ music is made by water falling into a cave with such power that the air is forced out through the organ pipes while another stream of water turns a toothed wheel, which operates the keyboard; one can also hear the distorted sound of trumpets".

Spianata delle Peschiere – The three basins were **fishponds** that supplied the cardinal's table on fast days. There is a fine **view★★** of the water spouts and the Organ Fountain.

Fontana della Madre Natura – The **Fountain of Mother Nature** is decorated with a statue of Diana of Ephesus, goddess of fertility.

Fontana dei Draghi – The **Dragon Fountain** was created in honour of Pope Gregory XIII, who visited the villa in September 1572, shortly before the cardinal's death; the dragons recall the arms of the pope's Buoncompagni family.

Fontana della Civetta – The **Owl Fountain** is more commonly known as the "Bird Fountain" because of the hydraulic mechanism, originally concealed in a recess, which twittered. Periodically an owl appeared and uttered a mournful screech. Several times restored, the fountain is now silent.

Fontana di Proserpina – (*left*). The **Fountain of Proserpina** (*restored*) recalls the mythological girl abducted by Pluto.

▶ *It is possible to walk down to the Villa Gregoriana through the streets of the old town (città vecchia).*

The town is agreeably lively and some traces of the past still remain.

The **cathedral**, rebuilt in the 17C and flanked by a 12C Romanesque campanile, contains a fine group of carved wooden figures depicting the **Deposition★** (13C).

Santa Maria Maggiore.

This old abbey church of St Mary Major belongs to the Benedictine convent. It has an attractive Gothic façade and a 17C bell-tower. The interior contains two 15C triptychs (*in the chancel*). Above the one on the left is a painting of the Virgin by Jacopo Torriti, who also worked in mosaic at the end of the 13C.

Villa Gregoriana★

Largo Sant'Angelo. ◑*Open Tues–Sun Apr–mid-Oct 10am–6:30pm; late-Oct–Noc and March 10am–2:30pm.* ◑*Closed Mon and Dec–Feb.* ◎*€4.* ☎*0246 761 583. www.villagregoriana.it*

A tangle of paths winds down wooded slopes to where the Aniene plunges through the craggy ravine. Pope Gregory XVI diverted the river to ease flooding in 1831, veiling the cliff in diaphanous spray.

Take the path down from the entrance and bear right to the **Great Waterfall★★**(*Grande Cascata*).

A smaller waterfall, engineered by **Bernini**, flows at the canyon's neck. The path winds past two grottoes, where the torrent spits at visitors in the gloom. The walk's strenuous, but a dramatic payoff awaits: a late-Republic **Temple of Vesta**. The hearth goddess's circular shrine later served as a medieval church (*Santa Maria della Rotunda*). Eighteen Corinthian columns still adorn the hillside, now in the garden of the Ristorante Sibilla restaurant, which welcomes curious travelers (*Via della Sibilla 50;* ☎*0774 335 281*).

☻ Solid, nonskid shoes are advisable.

Piazza Navona
B. Kaufmann/ MICHELIN

WHERE TO STAY

From modest *pensioni* to luxury hotels, Rome has a wide range of accommodation, although finding value for money can sometimes prove difficult. Visitors should book well in advance as the capital is popular throughout the year.

Generally speaking, the low season includes January, the first half of February, the last two weeks of July, the months of August and November and the first two weeks of December. During these periods many hotels offer reasonable rates and special weekend deals or short breaks.

Choose a hotel with air-conditioning during the summer, as it is particularly hot during this period (*See list below*). Breakfast may be an additional charge - and even towels in more modest establishments.

Address Book

SELECTING A DISTRICT

A good selection of *pensioni* and hotels can be found in the **historic centre,** where the atmosphere and high concentration of tourist sights and shops make it particularly popular. However, many of these establishments have limited capacity and often full. The attractive quarter of **Trastevere,** with its lively nightlife, is also pleasant, although accommodation options here are somewhat limited.

Quieter and cheaper, the **Vatican and Prati** districts are also close to the centre. The choice around **Via Cavour** (near *Monti*), between Termini Station and the *Fori Imperiali*, is also good, especially for mid-range hotels.

Many of the cheaper pensioni and smaller hotels are concentrated in the area around **Termini Station**, slightly away from the centre and somewhat lacking in character, but well served by public buses and the metro system. Most of Rome's luxury hotels are on the **Via Veneto** and around **Villa Borghese**.

Driving in Rome is not advisable as parking can be a major problem (most central hotels do not have private garages or parking). The few private car parks that do exist are extremely expensive and access to the city centre requires a special permit.

TYPES OF ACCOMMODATION

HOTELS AND PENSIONI

Generally, the word *pensione* describes a small family-run hotel, sometimes within a residential building. It offers simple, basic rooms, often without a private bathroom. The hotels can of course be more lavish, but there are plenty of attractive and convenient pensioni on offer. Wherever you choose to stay, it is worth doing some inital research to get the right place for you. Rates vary depending on the time of year and availability of rooms. Given the shortage of rooms in Rome, hoteliers usually request confirmation of booking by fax, as well as a credit card number. Breakfast is usually included in the price of the room, although this may not be the case in smaller hotels.

HOSTELS AND BUDGET ACCOMMODATION

There is no age limit for Youth Hostel Association membership, which must be renewed annually. The **Associazione Italiana Alberghi per la Gioventù** (AIG) is situated at Via Cavour 44, ☎06 48 71 152. The main office of the Comitato Regionale Lazio, is at Viale delle Olimpiadi 61. Those wishing to arrange hostel accommodation in advance from the UK can contact the **Youth Hostels Association,** Trevelyan House, Dimple Road, Matlock, Derbyshire DE4 3YH,

☎(0870) 870 8808; Fax 01629 592 702; www.yha.org.uk or **Hostelling International-American Youth Hostels,** 733 15th Street, NW, Ste. 840, Washington DC 20005, ☎(202) 783 6161; www.hiayh.org More general information on hostels in the US can be obtained by visiting www.hostels.com

Other organisations and properties offer dormitory accomodation or shared rooms at reasonable rates.

BED AND BREAKFAST

The B&B formula has gained in popularity in Italy in recent years, offering visitors the chance to stay in private homes. The house or apartment is also often lived in by the hosts, who let out a few of their rooms (usually between one and three) to guests cheaply. However, guests are usually required to stay for a minimum period and credit cards are rarely accepted. For a list of over 200 bed and breakfast addresses, contact the B&B reservation offices from 8am-9pm on ☎06 67 89 222. There is no charge for reservations.

Information is also available on the Italian Bed and Breakfast Web site at www.bbitalia.it

SHORT-TERM RENTAL

An apartment (*appartamento*) is often the most atmospheric option. For privacy and authenticity, a short-term rental can't be beat. Generally cheaper than hotels, apartments also have basic cooking implements and facilities. Good companies include www.realrome.com, www.cross-pollinate.com; www.romesweethome.it and www.flatinrome.com.

HOME SWAP

Increasingly popular, these services allow homeowners to trade places. Find a reputable service, like Home Exchange (Post Office Box 787, Hermosa Beach, CA, 90254, USA; ☎310 798 3864; www.homeexchange.com) or HomeLink International (Viale Frassinetti 84, 31046 Oderzo (Treviso), Italy; ☎422 815 575; www.homelink.org). Check references carefully.

CONVENTS AND MONASTERIES

As well as providing accommodation for pilgrims, convents and monasteries are also a good option for those on a limited budget. Rooms are reasonably priced, although visitors are usually expected to be in by a specified hour (usually 10:30pm). Occasionally men and women are required to sleep in separate rooms.

For further information, contact the **Peregrinatio ad Petri Sedem,** *Piazza Pio XII 4 (Vaticano-San Pietro district),* ☎*06 69 88 48 96; Fax 06 69 88 56 17.*

CAMP SITES

Although Rome's campsites are a fair distance from the centre, they are cheap and in attractive green surroundings. Shade is particularly welcome in the hot summer months, when the downtown humidity becomes almost unbearable. Campsite addresses are given below.

HOTEL RESERVATIONS

Visitors can book hotel rooms through the **Hotel Reservation Service,** ☎06 69 91 000, open 7am–10pm. This service is free of charge and offers a choice of 350 hotels in the capital. Visitors booking any of these hotels may also take advantage of a shuttle service from Fiumicino Airport, at a cost of €11 per person. Reservations can be made by phone or from the airport desk (in the International, European and National arrival halls), from Termini Railway Station (opposite platform 20), at Ciampino Airport and at the Tevere-Ovest service station on the A1 Milan-Rome motorway. The same service is also available on the Internet at www.hotelreservation.it

FOR ALL BUDGETS

The hotels in this guide are grouped according to district and subdivided into three categories, each based on the price of a double room. Hotels included in the **Budget** section are usually small and basic, but are fairly comfortable and in a particular good location; expect to pay less than €60. This category includes youth hostels and modest *pensioni,* some of which offer rooms without private facilities.

Those with a larger budget will find hotels offering greater comfort and charm in our **Moderate** category, where prices range from €60–130. A selection of luxury and atmospheric hotels guaranteeing a memorable stay is given in the **Expensive** section.

Prices are given for breakfast, if not included in the rate. The hotels listed have been chosen for their value for money, level of comfort and character. Although every hotel has been carefully inspected, it is possible that things have changed since our last visit. We would be grateful for any comments or suggestions from readers. *For coin ranges, see the Legend on the cover flap.*

DON'T FORGET THE MICHELIN RED GUIDE

The Michelin Guide Italia
For a more exhaustive list of hotels consult *the Michelin Guide Italia,* which provides a whole host of details on Rome's hotels and restaurants.

ACCOMMODATION BY AREA

For coin ranges, see the Legend on the cover flap.

AVENTINO/PIRAMIDE CESTIA – TESTACCIO

Hotel Santa Prisca – *Largo M. Gelsomini 25, Aventine.* ☎06 57 41 917. Fax 06 57 46 658. *50 rooms.* ☐☐☐ – *Restaurant* ☐☐. Palms, pines and flowers wreathe this pleasant hotel on the flanks of the Aventine hill. The rooms – formerly nuns' cells – are like cameos: small but finely wrought.

Sant'Anselmo – *Piazza Sant'Anselmo 2, Aventine.* ☎06 574 5231. www.aventinohotels.com. *44 rooms.* ☐. Swags of marble, faded gilt mirrors and citrus trees lend a Belle Epoque air to this retreat, nestled high on the green-swathed hill. A lovely property.

CATACOMBE DI PRISCILLA (VIA NOMENTANA, VIA SALARIA)

Hotel Santa Costanza – *Viale 21 Aprile 4, Via Nomentana.* ☎06 86 00 602. Fax 06 86 02 786 ☐☐ ☐*68 rooms.* ☐. Comfortable, colourful armchairs furnish the lobby of this hotel, which has good transport connections to the city centre. The breakfast room, with its attractive floral designs, has large windows looking on an internal garden. Comfortable, well-appointed rooms.

COLOSSEO – CELIO/FORI IMPERIALI/ PIAZZA VENEZIA/RIONE MONTI

Hotel Sandy – *Via Cavour 136, (5th floor, no lift), Fori Imperiali.* ☎06 48 84 585. www.sandyhostel.com. *24 beds.*

This hostel is very popular with international visitors and young people. Spacious, colourful rooms are shared by three to five people, with a communal bathroom. Breakfast not available.

Hotel San Paolo – *Via Panisperna 95, (1st floor, no lift), Rione Monti.* ☎06 47 45 213. Fax 06 46 45 218 . hsanpaolo@tin. it. *24 rooms.* ☐*€5.16.* This simple hotel is in Monti, which still retains a flavour of old Rome. The rooms are small, but colourfully decorated.

Hotel Perugia – *Via del Colosseo 7, Colosseo.* ☎06 67 97 200. Fax 06 67 84 63. htlperugia@isl.it. *13 rooms.* ☐. Given its excellent location close to the Colosseum, this small hotel is very reasonably priced. One fourth-floor room has a small balcony with views of the amphitheatre, but no bathroom.

Hotel Solis Invictus – *Via Cavour 311, Fori Imperiali.* ☎06 69 92 05 87. Fax 06 69 92 33 95. *16 rooms.* ☐☐. This small, comfortable hotel is family run and is on the first floor of a building a few steps away from the Colosseum. The large rooms are the most modern.

Hotel Celio – *Via dei Santi Quattro 35/c, Colosseo.* ☎06 70 49 53 33. *18 rooms.* ☐☐. Splendid fragments of frescoes add a touch of originality to the rooms in this elegant family hotel. The hotel also has a suite with a view of the Colosseum. Breakfast is served in the rooms.

FONTANA DI TREVI – QUIRINALE

Hotel Fontana – *Piazza di Trevi 96, Fontana di Trevi .* ☎06 67 86 113. Fax 06 67 90 024. www.hotelfontana-trevi. com. *25 rooms.* ☐. Admire the Trevi Fountain without having to fight through the crowds. Charming rooms in an old convent will satisfy the most romantic of travellers.

ISOLA TIBERINA – TORRE ARGENTINA

Pensione Barrett – *Largo Torre Argentina 47, Torre Argentina district –* ☎06 68 68 481. www.pensionebarrett. com *20 rooms.* ☐ *€8.* ☐ *€5.16.* Simple, but well looked after and in an excellent location. The rooms have thoughtful and unusual touches, such as a small footbath and tea- and coffee-making facilities. Visitors in search of peace and quiet should avoid the rooms overlooking the busy square.

*Campo dei Fiori market, with a statue
of Giordano Bruno in the background*

◉◉ **Hotel Arenula** – *Via Santa Maria
de' Calderari 47, (1st floor, no lift), Torre
Argentina.* ☎*06 68 79 454. www.
hotelarenula.com. 50 rooms.* ☲. This
charming hotel is in a 20C palazzo in
the Jewish quarter. The light rooms,
brightened by colourful curtains, are
decorated in grey and white.

MONTE MARIO

◉ **Ostello Foro Italico A. F. Pessina** –
*Viale delle Olimpiadi 61, Monte Mario district
– From Termini Station, Metro A to Ottaviano,
then bus 32 (7 stops).* ☎*06 32 36 267.
www.ostellionline.org. 400 beds.* ☵ ☲
Restaurant. ◉ This modern building
surrounded by gardens is Rome's only
official hostel and has a self-service
restaurant and a bar. Dorm accommodation only, with 6-bedded rooms for
men and 10-bedded rooms for women.
Closed between midnight and 7am.

PANTHEON/MONTECITORIO

◉ **Hotel Mimosa** – *Via Santa Chiara 61,
(2nd floor, no lift), Pantheon.* ☎*06 68 80
17 53. www.hotelmimosa.net. 11 rooms.*
☵ ☷ ☲. The main attraction is its
excellent location in an old building
behind the Pantheon, close to Santa
Maria sopra Minerva. The rooms are
basic, but clean and quiet.

◉◉ **Hotel Coronet** – *Piazza Grazioli 5,
Pantheon.* ☎*06 67 92 341. www.
hotelcoronet.com. 13 rooms.* ☲. In the
17C Palazzo Doria Pamphili, this small
hotel is well maintained and offers
spacious, com-fortable rooms. A
romantic atmosphere and good service.

◉◉ **Hotel Portoghesi** – *Via dei
Portoghesi 1, Montecitorio.* ☎*06 68 64
231. www.hotelportoghesiroma.
com. 27 rooms.* ☷ ☲. Opposite the
legendary "*Torre della Scimmia*"
(Monkey Tower), this hotel has pleasant
rooms decorated with antique furniture.
The glass conservatory, used as the
breakfast room, and the terrace, with
its views of the rooftops of Rome,
are particularly delightful. Wi-fi.

◉◉◉ **Albergo del Sole al Pantheon**
Piazza della Rotunda 63, Pantheon. ☎*06
678 0689. www.hotelsolealpantheon.
com.* ☲. One of the world's oldest
hotels, this establishment traces its
roots to 1467. Elegant and aristocratic, it
overlooks the ancient Roman temple
and the lively square it anchors. Jean-
Paul Sartre and Simone de Beavoir
favored this hotel.

**PIAZZA NAVONA/CAMPO DEI FIORI/
CASTEL SANT'ANGELO**

◉◉ **Hotel Navona** – *Via dei Sediari 8,
(1st floor, no lift), Piazza Navona district –*
☎*06 68 21 13 92 – Fax 06 68 80 38 02 –
info@hotelnavona.com –* ☵ ☷ –
30 rooms. ☲. This delightful hotel has
cool, attractive rooms decorated in
English style, as a result of the owner's
long period of residence in Australia.
The hotel is located in a 16C palazzo
which was built on top of much older
foundations. Breakfast is served at a
long table.

◉◉ **Hotel Due Torri** – *Vicolo del
Leonetto 23, Piazza Navona.* ☎*06 688
069. www.hotelduetorriroma.com* ☲.
Once the home of cardinals and
bishops, this brick-colored residence
stands slightly north of the Piazza

Navona. Each room has its own unique decor and is furnished with a parquet floor and high quality furniture, including some genuine antiques. One of our favourite addresses in Rome.

⊜⊜▤ **Hotel Teatro di Pompeo** – *Largo del Pallaro 8, Campo dei Fiori.* ☎*06 68 30 01 70. www.hotelteatrodipompeo. it. 13 rooms.* ▤ ▭. A boutique hotel now nestles in a medieval palazzo, once the Theatre of Pompey – the site of Caesar's assassination in 44BC. The charming hotel rooms are spacious and simply furnished, with coffered ceilings and tiled floors.

PIAZZA DEL POPOLO/ PIAZZA DI SPAGNA

⊜⊜ **Pensione Panda** – *Via della Croce 35, Piazza di Spagna.* ☎*06 67 80 179. www.pensionepanda.com. 20 rooms.* This well-kept pensione in a 19C palazzo not far from the Spanish Steps has quiet, simply furnished rooms, some with shared bathroom. Although lacking in overall charm, the hotel is recommended for its excellent location and reasonable rates.

⊜⊜ **Hotel Margutta** – *Via Laurina 34, Piazza di Spagna district.* ☎*06 32 23 674. www.hotelmargutta.it . 24 rooms.* ▭. This simple hotel is in a side street off the busy Via del Corso – an ideal location for shoppers! Only double rooms: very clean and quiet.

⊜⊜ **Hotel Parlamento** – *Via delle Convertite 5, Piazza di Spagna.* ☎*/Fax 06 69 92 10 00. 23 rooms.* ▭. High ceilings and rooms decorated with plants provide this hotel with a pleasant, relaxing atmosphere. In summer, breakfast is served on an attractive terrace facing Piazza San Silvestro.

⊜⊜▤ **Hotel d'Inghilterra** – *Via Bocca di Leone 14, Piazza di Spagna.* ☎*06 69 98 11. http://hoteldinghilterra.warwickhotels. com. 88 rooms.* ▤▭€22.72. Restaurant ⊜⊜▤. In the old guest-quarters of Palazzo Torlonia, this hotel has retained the elegance and charm of a 15C residence. Furnishings of the period, valuable paintings and precious carpets recall its prestigious past.

PORTA PIA – TERMINI

⊜ **The Beehive** – *Via Marghera 8, Termini.* ☎*06 44 704 553. www.the-beehive.com.* This "hotel and art space" is an aesthetic, yet affordable, haven. Ikea-influenced, contemporary minimalism replaces yard-sale-rejects. The Beehive prides itself on ecologically friendly products, including handmade soaps. Three independent apartments are available off-site as well.

⊜ **Hotel Pensione Tizi** – *Via Collina 48, (1st floor, lift), Porta Pia.* ☎*06 48 20 128. 25 rooms.* ▭ ▭ €5.16. The hotel is named after the owner's daughter, Tiziana, who is usually at reception to welcome guests. Quiet, attractive rooms, both with and without bathrooms. Good value for money.

⊜⊜ **Hotel Venezia** – *Via Varese 18, Stazione Termini district.* ☎*06 44 57 101. 61 rooms.* ▤ ▭. A comfortable, well-kept hotel, with good facilities. The public rooms of the hotel are particularly attractive, with wrought-iron candelabras, rustic furniture and delicate fabrics. Recommended.

SANTA MARIA MAGGIORE/ SAN GIOVANNI IN LATERANO

⊜ **YWCA** – *Via Cesare Balbo 4, Santa Maria Maggiore.* ☎*06 48 80 460. www. ywca-ucdg.it. 70 beds.* ▭ ✕ ▭ *Restaurant* ⊜. Accommodation available to women, couples and groups (not single men) in simple, clean rooms. Many of the rooms, both with and without private bathrooms, are rented out by the year to students. Closed from midnight to 7am.

⊜⊜ **Hotel Piccadilly** – *Via Magna Grecia 122, San Giovanni in Laterano.* ☎*06 70 47 48 58. www.bestwestern.it/ BW/EN/98025_hotel_Rome. 55 rooms.* ▤ ✕ ▭. This modern hotel extends over eight floors, with the upper one used as a panoramic breakfast room. The hotel is near the basilica of St John Lateran and the market at Via Sannio.

TRASTEVERE

⊜ **Casa del Bradipo** – *Via Portuense 495, Trastevere.* ☎*328 679 2067. www. casabradipo.com. 3 rooms.* ▭ Vast paintings and bold-hued walls distinguish this Trastevere pensione. Furnishings are equally funky, though the marble floor creates unfortunate echoes. Three rooms share a kitchen, living room and terrace. Towels available on request, as well as Internet access and laundry facilities. Minimum four-night stay.

Antico Borgo di Trastevere – *Vicolo del Buco 7, Trastevere.* ☎06 588 3924. *www.trasteverehouse.it.* 🖥🛏.
This modest 18C palace has exposed beams, French windows, wooden shutters and balcony flower pots. All rooms have a private bath, color television and ait conditioning. Expect some late-night noise in this trendy area.

🍽🛏 **Ripa Hotel** – *Via degli Orti di Trastevere 1, Trastevere.* ☎06 58 611. *www.ripahotel.com. 170 rooms. Restaurant.* 🍽🍽
Self-conscious minimalism rules here. The lobby resembles a contemporary art exhibit: scarlet and purple pouffes sprout like toadstools. DJs spin tunes in the downstairs club, dubbed Suite.

VATICANO – SAN PIETRO

🍽 **Colors** – *Via Boezio 31, Vatican.* ☎06 687 4030. *www.colorshotel.com.* 🖥
Polished floors reflect great swathes of bright paint and Italian contemporary flair. A terrace surveys the skyline in this quiet quarter just north of the Vatican. Linen, hot water and a self-catering kitchen number among the amentities. Colors is 10–15-minutes' from the Metro Line A stop Ottaviano-San Pietro.

🍽🍽 **Hotel Alimandi** – *Via Tunisi 8, Vatican.* ☎06 39 72 39 48. *www. alimandi.it. Closed for 10 days in Jan. 35 rooms.* 🅿🛏. The rooms near the Vatican Museums are well appointed and comfortable (safety deposit boxes available). The hotel has a terrace on the first floor and a roof garden for summer barbecues. Medieval decor in the hotel bar. Free shuttle service to the airport.

🍽🍽🛏 **Hotel Atlante Star** – *Via Vitelleschi 34, Vatican.* ☎06 68 73 233. *www.atlantehotels.com. 70 rooms.* 🖥 – 🛏. This elegant hotel close to St Peter's has a lovely roof garden with a magnificent view of the basilica. The hotel restaurant, Les Étoiles, makes the most of this splendid location in summer.

VIA VENETO

🍽🍽 **Hotel Pensione Merano** – *Via Vittorio Veneto 155, (4th floor, lift), Via Veneto.* ☎06 48 21 796. *Fax 06 48 21 810. hotel.merano@tiscalinet.it. 30 rooms.* 🛏. This quiet, charming pensione is situated in one of the smartest streets in the capital. The

wooden chairs and floral designs in the attractive breakfast room give the hotel a typically English ambiance.

🍽🍽 **Hotel Invictus** – *Via Quintino Sella 15, Via Veneto district.* ☎06 42 01 14 33. *www.solisinvictus.com. 13 rooms.* 🖥 🛏. The rooms in this well-maintained hotel are pleasant and comfortable with good quality furnishings. A good location for those wishing to experience the "*Dolce Vita*" ambiance.

VILLA BORGHESE – VILLA GIULIA

🍽🍽🛏 **Hotel Lord Byron** – *Via de Notaris 5, Villa Giulia.* ☎06 32 20 404. *www.lordbyronhotel.com. 32 rooms.* 🖥 🛏. *Restaurant* 🍽🍽. This small, elegant hotel overlooks the Villa Borghese gardens and has an attractive 1920s atmosphere.

🍽🍽🛏 **Aldrovandi Palace Hotel** – *Via Aldrovandi 15, Villa Borghese.* ☎06 32 23 993. *www.aldrovandi.com. 125 rooms.* 🖥 ⌦ 🛏 €22. *Restaurant* 🍽🍽🛏.
This prestigious hotel just a few steps from the Villa Borghese has fine lounges furnished with antique items and magnificent chandeliers, and elegant bedrooms, tastefully decorated in pink and green tones.

CAMPSITES

🍽 **Happy Camping** – *Via Prato della Corte 1915, 10km/6mi from the centre. From Termini Station, take Metro line A to Piazzale Flaminio, then the train to Prima Porta and a shuttle bus that operates between 8:30am–noon and 5–10:30pm.* ☎06 33 62 64 01. *www.happycamping. net . Open Mar–mid-Sep. 150 pitches* 🏊. This pleasant campsite in the northwest of the city has a restaurant, bar, super-market, children's playground and a swimming pool.

🍽 **Village Flaminio Camping** – *Via Flaminia Nuova 821, 8km/5mi from the centre. From Termini Station, take bus n° 910 to Piazza Mancini and then bus n° 200.* ☎06 33 32 604. *www.village-flaminio.com Closed mid-Nov to mid-Dec and Feb to mid-Mar. 300 pitches.* 🏊. Shaded by acacia trees, this campsite has a restaurant, grocery store, an open-air swimming pool, and a residential area for chalets. In high season, staff organise games and dance lessons.

WHERE TO EAT

The Eternal City ranks among the world's culinary capitals. Long a proponent of Slow Food – local recipes and fresh, indigenous ingredients – its eateries shine, from the humblest pizzeria or trattoria to temples of haute cuisine.

Address Book

DINING ETIQUETTE

In Rome, lunch (*pranzo*) runs from 12:30-3pm and dinner (*cena*) from 8-11pm; restaurants generally close around midnight. Most places shut one day a week – and for two to three weeks in August.

Here the table is sold for the evening. Customers are expected to linger through at least two or three of the following courses: *antipasto* (hors-d'oeuvre), *primo* (pasta or soup), *secondo* (meat or fish), then perhaps an *insalata* (salad) or *contorni* (vegetable), followed by *formaggio* (cheese) or *dolce* (dessert) and, finally, *caffè* (espresso) or liqueur, such as amaro or grappa.

Avoid tourist menus (*menu turistico*): choice is limited and, too often, the food inferior. Likewise, steer clear of touts: what decent eatery needs one, when locals queue hours for prime tables? Some ritzy establishments, however, offer a *menu degustazione* (tasting menu), spotlighting kitchen pyrotechnics.

BEVERAGES

Italians wash down meals with *acqua minerale* (**bottled water**), either flat (*naturale*) or carbonated (*gassata, frizzante, con gas*). Ordering tap water – *l'acqua rubinetta* – is poor form. However, Rome's municipal water is fine to drink, though locals prefer to fill bottles from the *nasone*, the street spigots that free-flow from aqueducts. Carafes of h**ouse wine** (*vino della casa*) come in litres (*litro*), half-litres (*un mezzo litro*) and sometimes quarters (*un quattro*), akin to two glasses. Standard wine bottles hold 750ml; it's easy to underestimate the 25% extra wallop of a litre. Though Italians savour *un po di vino* – a little wine – they frown on public drunkeness.

WHAT'S IN A NAME?

In general, a **ristorante** offers elegant cuisine and service, whereas a **trattoria or osteria** is more likely to be family-run and serve homemade dishes in a more informal atmosphere. Prices are usually lower in the latter and house wine (of varying quality) is available by the carafe. In typical trattorias, the waiter recounts the day's specials – determine a price before ordering.

WINE BARS

Wine bars (*enoteche*) have become increasingly popular in Italy. Some offer tapas-style snacks.

PIZZERIAS

A pizzeria is a sit-down restaurant, which may serve pasta for lunch and only fire the wood oven at night (See "pizza al taglio" under snacks below). Fluffy Neapolitan-style pizza is becoming more and more popular. However, the traditional Roman ones are thin, crispy and drenched in olive oil. Locals rarely share: one pizza apiece is the drill. They generally start with **bruschetta** (toast rubbed with raw garlic, sprinkled with salt, drizzled with olive oil and topped with fresh tomatoes and basil) or **fritto misto alla romana.** *Fritto misto* comprises different seasonal delicacies, such as zucchini flowers stuffed with mozzarella and anchovies, fillets of salted cod, stuffed giant green Ascoli olives, and potato croquettes dipped in batter and deep fried. Those not wishing to order pizza may like to try a **crostino** instead: this toasted bread is similar to *bruschetta*, but is covered with melted cheese and Parma ham, or perhaps with *porcini* (cep) mushrooms.

INTERNATIONAL RESTAURANTS

As Italians tend to be very attached to their culinary traditions, ethnic restaurants are rather thin on the ground. Rome has a handful of Asian and Indian eateries, as well as Spanish, Mexican and American ones. Still novelties, these may not satisfy a sophisticated palette.

SNACKS AND CAFFÈ

A *pizza al taglio* shop turns out takeaway slices. Long slabs of **pizza** line the counter. Request the type and amount: the server then bisects the strip, presses the topping-faces together, and wraps the impromptu sandwich in wax paper (about €2.50). Many cafés serve **grilled sandwiches** and pastries, alongside the ubiquitous espresso. Enjoying coffee *al banco* (at the counter) is often much cheaper than *al tavolo* (at the table), especially in tourist hotspots. More informal establishments have customers pay at the *cassa* (register), then present the *scontrino* (receipt) to the server. Purists drink *caffè* (**espresso**). *Lungo* dilutes the mix with water and *Americano* roughly equates to the standard cup of joe. *Caffè latte* means espresso with hot milk, while *cappuccino* adds froth to the cup – expect a sneer if you order either after 4pm, however. Many Italians believe that milk prompts nightmares.

PASTICCERIAS AND GELATERIAS

Pastry shops, (*pasticcerie*) offer mouth-watering delicacies. Typical Roman ones include *panpepato*, made from flour mixed with almonds, crystallised fruit, honey, orange rind and spices; *pangiallo*, prepared with maize flour, almonds, walnuts, pine nuts and raisins, *torta di ricotta e visciole* (ricotta and sour cherry tart) of Jewish origin, *zuppa inglese* and *bignè di San Giuseppe*, puff pastry filled with cream.
Retreat to a *gelateria* to sample Rome's other confectionery triumphs. Ice creams and sorbets – often made in-house – are served in cones and cups (order at least two flavours). *Grattachecca* is the local version of *granita*, the crushed ice drink. The pieces of ice, scraped off large blocks with a spatula, are covered with sweet, colourful syrups and topped with fresh fruit. Vendors also sell these and water-cooled coconut slices in summer;

roasted chestnuts and pumpkin seeds in cooler months.
Addresses for snacks, such as pizza slices, ice-cream and patries are given in the central section of the guide (*⌖ See Discovering Rome section*).

FOR ALL BUDGETS

The eateries in this guide have been selected to suit all tastes and budgets, divided by district. Once again, recommendations run least to most expensive. The price brackets are based on the average cost of a meal per person, excluding drinks.
The Budget category includes typical trattorias, pizzerias or wine bars where the cost of a meal is under €16.
Restaurants with a more refined atmosphere serving fine cuisine for €17–50 are considered Moderate.
The Expensive category includes some of the best and most elegant restaurants in the city – with prices to match.

BILLS, TIPS, FINE PRINT

Il conto (**the bill**) may include a small charge for *coperto* (cover) or *pane* (bread). These shouldn't impact the modest *resto* (**tip**), usually €2–3. Italians tip about 5% in a pizzeria or trattoria. The rate rises in posher places, but rarely tops 10%.
Some restaurants only note the service charge – *servizio incluso* – in Italian. Stay alert and tip accordingly.
Visitors should be aware that credit cards are rarely accepted in small restaurants or family-run trattorias. Large bills (€20s, 50s, 100s) often cause consternation, especially in cafes. Save coins for small transactions like this.

BOOKING

Book in advance on Fridays and Saturdays, although some small trattorias and pizzerias do not accept reservations. Go ahead and queue – the lively street scene is part of the Roman experience. In the *centro storico*, any establishment worth its salt has patrons waiting; the alternatives probably aren't busy for good reasons. Touts, in particular, are a sign of culinary catastrophe... Run, don't walk, away.

DON'T FORGET
THE MICHELIN RED GUIDE

TYPICAL ROMAN CUISINE

Roman cuisine is often referred to as *"cucina povera"* – peasant cooking – because of its simplicity and reliance on fresh produce. A *trattoria* meal may start with an *antipasto* (hors d'oeuvre) of vegetables or mixed cold meats. The *primo (first)* course could be any one of a number of pasta dishes – the famous **fettuccine** egg pasta, **bucatini all'amatriciana** (a sauce made with olive oil, pecorino cheese, tomatoes, onions and streaky bacon), **spaghetti alla gricia** (a type of amatriciana, but without tomato), **tonnarelli con cacio e pepe** (a cheese and pepper sauce), **gnocchi alla romana** (dumplings made from bran dough) or potato *gnocchi* (traditionally prepared on Thursdays), as well as the well-known **carbonara** dish. The most typical *secondi* – main courses – include **saltimbocca** (veal escalope rolled around a slice of ham and sage), **abbacchio** – suckling lamb cooked in a chasseur sauce *(alla cacciatora)* or grilled on a spit (*alla scottadito* in the Roman dialect), **trippa** (tripe cooked with tomatoes and herbs), **coda alla vaccinara** (oxtail cooked with bacon fat, garlic, green vegetables, salt, pepper, herbs, spices and white wine), **pajata** (lamb offal) and **baccalà** (dried cod), usually fried. Typical *contorni* (side dishes) include **puntarelle** (greens flavoured with garlic and anchovies), **agretti** (another kind of very delicate salad vegetable served with vinegar), **carciofi alla giudìa** (whole fried artichokes), and **rughetta** (rocket, known as *rucola* in northern Italy). Cheese, especially pecorino, is often accompanied by broad beans. In the more simple *trattorias* the choice of desserts is usually limited to tiramisù, *panna cotta,* crème caramel or ice cream. Elsewhere, visitors may be able to sample a home-made **torta di ricotta** or **zuppa inglese,** which, despite its name, has Roman origins.

House wines are usually Montepulciano d'Abruzzo (red – *rosso*) and some Castelli Romani blend (white –*bianco*). Orvieto is a reliable and affordable option, as is Montefiascone's Est! Est!! Est!!!. Lazio's most famous vintages are the dry whites — *Vini dei Castelli* (Frascati, Grottaferrata, Genzano, Marino and Velletri).

RESTAURANTS BY AREA

For coin ranges, see the Legend on the cover flap.

AVENTINO/PIRAMIDE CESTIA – TESTACCIO

Pizzeria Addò Masto 2 – *Via G. Bove 43, Piramide Cestia-Testaccio.* ☎*06 57 46 372. Closed Mon, mid-to-late Aug, end of Dec.* Deep, soft pizzas for those who enjoy the Neapolitan style. Despite the spacious dining room and outdoor sprawl in summer, there is never an empty table.

Tuttifrutti – *Via Luca della Robbia 5, Testaccio.* ☎*06 57 57 902. Open Tues–Sat 8–11pm. Closed Aug, Mon and school holidays. Booking recommended.* This restaurant is run by a cultural association that employs young artists. The cuisine is simple, yet original, and includes appetizing *antipasti.* The white wine and chocolate are produced by Trappist monks.

Checchino dal 1887 – *Via Monte Testaccio 30, Testaccio.* ☎*06 57 46 318. www.checchino-dal-1887.com. Closed Sun–Mon, 24 Dec-2 Jan, Aug. Booking recommended.* This restaurant specializes in butchers' off-cuts – oxtail, offal and tripe – as befits it location across from the old slaughterhouse. Specialities include *rigatoni alla pajata,* sweetbreads in a white wine sauce and oxtail. Cheaper meals of cheese and vegetables are available at lunchtime.

Da Oio a Casa Mia *Via Galvani 43–5, Testaccio.* ☎*06 578 2682. Open Mon–Sat 12– 3 and 7:30– 11pm. Closed Sun, Aug.* Brick arches soar over red-check tables in this neighborhood trattoria. The menu concentrates on Roman organ meats like tripe and a scramble of heart, liver, spleen and lung with artichokes or onions. Vegetarians prefer the chickpea soup or *tagliolini cacio e pepe* (broad noodles with sheep cheese and pepper).

Estro Bar – *Abitart Hotel, Via Pellegrino Matteucci 20, Ostiense. Open daily 6.30pm–1.30am.* ☎*06 454 3191. www.estrobar.com.* This trendy eatery does triple duty: as a pizzeria, gallery and wine-bar in the hipster outpost of the Abitart Hotel, which almost single-handedly is gentrifying Ostiense (www.abitarthotel.com). The minimalist menu includes nibbles like salami selections and *involtini di melanzana* (eggplant-wrapped cheese).

CATACOMBE DI PRISCILLA (VIA NOMENTANA, VIA SALARIA)

La Mora – *Piazza Crati 13, Catacombe di Priscilla.* ☎*06 86 20 66 13. Closed Mon and Aug.* This friendly, informal restaurant serves Tuscan cuisine and wood-fired pizzas. Other dishes include focaccia with provola cheese and pork sausage, and, for steak-lovers, a delicious *bistecca alla fiorentina* from cattle raised in the Chiana Valley.

Dai Toscani – *Via Forlì 41, Via Nomentana.* ☎*06 44 23 13 02. Closed Aug and Sun.* 📋 *10% service.* As the name suggests, Tuscan cuisine rules here: crostini, ribollita stew and *bistecca alla fiorentina*. Finish with traditional *cantucci* biscuits served with Vin Santo.

COLOSSEO – CELIO/FORI IMPERIALI/PIAZZA VENEZIA/RIONE MONTI

Taverna Romana – *Via Madonna dei Monti 79, Monti.* ☎*06 47 45 325. Closed on Sun and in Aug – Booking recommended.* Seasonal Roman cuisine includes pasta matriciana, *cacio e pepe*, grilled lamb and typical vegetable dishes. The service is not the friendliest, but the food is worth it.

Enoteca Al Vino al Vino – *Via dei Serpenti 19, Monti.* ☎*06 48 58 03. Closed the last three weeks in Aug – Booking recommended.* This charming wine bar has an excellent selection of wine, colourful ceramic tables and a lively atmosphere. Try the selection of cooked meats and cheeses (the saltiest of which are served with honey) and delicious Sicilian specialities. Friendly service.

Hasekura – *Via dei Serpenti 27, Monti.* ☎*06 48 36 48. Closed Sun, Aug, four days at Christmas.* This simply furnished Japanese restaurant is noted for its fresh ingredients and excellent sushi. This trendy address offers better value for money at lunchtime.

Relaxing in Piazza Navona

B. Pérousse/MICHELIN

EUR

Shangri Là-Corsetti – *Viale Algeria 141, EUR.* ☎*06 59 18 861. Closed 10-26 Aug* 📋. This restaurant – in the hotel of the same name – is surrounded by greenery and has spacious contemporary dining rooms. In summer, tables also surround the pool. House specialities include an *antipasti* buffet and fish dishes. Attentive service.

FONTANA DI TREVI – QUIRINALE

Pizzeria Est Est Est – *Via Genova 32, Quirinale.* ☎*06 48 81 107. Closed Mon and Aug* 🖉. One of the oldest pizzerias in Rome, its decor dates from the early 20C. (Look for the small cherub pouring the so-called "mayor's water".) The white wine that gives its name to the restaurant is highly recommended.

Il Giardino di Albino – *Via Zucchelli 29, Trevi.* ☎*06 48 85 202.* 📋. This warm, friendly family offers typical Sardinian cuisine. Both the fish and meat are excellent.

ISOLA TIBERINA – TORRE ARGENTINA

Enoteca La Bottega del Vino da Anacleto Bleve – *Via S. Maria del Pianto 9/a, Largo Argentina.* ☎*06 68 65 970. Closed evenings and public holidays – Booking recommended.* This wine bar is in the heart of the Jewish quarter. Before sitting down, choose from the delicate soufflés, roulades, salads and cheeses displayed at the bar. Delicious lemon or coffee ice cream.

Quelli della Taverna – *Via dei Barbieri 25, Torre Argentina.* ☎*06 68 69 660. www.renatoeluisa.it . Open Tues–Sun*

8:30pm–12:30am. Closed Mon, Aug, 24-26 Dec. Booking recommended. Run by two friends, this friendly taverna serves drinks and pasta in terracotta crockery, as in days gone by. Try the focaccia.

Al Pompiere – *Via S. Maria de' Calderari 38, Torre Argentina.* ☎06 68 68 377. Closed Sun and 15 Jul-30 Aug. A range of Roman-Jewish traditional dishes served in the spacious rooms of an old palazzo. The *crostata di ricotta e visciole* (ricotta and sour cherry tart) is highly recommended.

Piperno – *Via Monte de' Cenci 9, Ghetto.* ☎06 6880 6629. *www. ristorantepiperno.com. Open Tues–Sat 12:45–2;30pm and 8–10:30pm. Closed Sun–Mon and Aug.*
This ghetto favorite serves Jewish-Roman fare, including *carciofi alla giudia* (deep-fried artichokes) and *zuppa di ceci* (garbanzo-bean soup). The elegant cuisine is matched by the setting, a secluded piazza engulfed by the 15C Palazzo Cenci, where a noble family self-destructed.

Sora Lella – *Via di Ponte Quattro Capi 16, Isola Tiberina.* ☎06 68 61 601. Closed Sun, 1 Jan, Easter, Aug and 24-26 Dec. 🖂. This famous restaurant was once run by Lella Fabrizi, the sister of the actor Aldo. It is now managed by her son, who has extended the traditional range of family recipes to include new specialities. Don't miss the *formaggi alle marmellate* (cheese with sweet fruit jelly) and the desserts.

MONTE MARIO

Osteria dell'Angelo – *Via G. Bettolo 24, Monte Mario.* ☎06 37 29 470. Closed Sun and public holidays, lunch-time (except Tue and Fri) and for 10 days in Aug. 🖂. This lively trattoria, decorated with rugby shirts, serves a selection of traditional Roman dishes, including *tonnarelli cacio e pepe, rigatoni con pajata, coda alla vaccinara* and *trippa alla romana* (See Typical Roman Cuisine). The fixed-price dinner menu is good value for money.

La Pergola – *Via Cadolo 101, Hotel Cavalieri Hilton, Monte Mario.* ☎06 35 0912 152. Open Tues–Sat 7:30pm–12am. Closed Sun–Mon. Free shuttle bus from the city center. Atop Monte Mario preens this famous restaurant, reputed to be Rome's best. German Chef Heinz Beck intuits Italian fare, turning out dishes like lobster with orange sauce and fennel ravioli with anchovies.

PANTHEON/MONTECITORIO

Eau Vive – *Via Monterone 85, Pantheon.* ☎06 68 80 10 95. Closed Sun and Aug. 🍽 Booking recommended. This restaurant is run by missionary nuns of different nationalities and is inside the 16C Palazzo Lante. French specialities can be sampled in the large, frescoed dining room on the first floor.

Vecchia Locanda – *Vicolo Simibaldi 2, Pantheon.* ☎06 68 80 28 31. Closed Sun and 22 Dec-22 Jan. Booking recommended. In a typical narrow street between Largo Argentina and the Pantheon, this small, elegant restaurant is known for its beef and fresh home-made pasta. The atmosphere resembles a Roman inn's, with tables outside in summer.

Da Settimio – *Via delle Colonnelle 14, Pantheon.* ☎06 678 9651. Open Tues–Sat noon–3pm and 7:30–11:30pm. Closed Sun and Mon, Aug. Reservations recommended. Wrought iron and abundant piles of fruit greet diners. Recommended plates include *tagliolini al tartufo bianco* (white truffle) and *gorgonzola polenta* (corn-meal cake). This intimate spot was once an alley: look for the old fountain and roof-tiles.

Osteria dell'Ingegno – *Piazza di Pietra 45, Montecitorio.* ☎06 67 80 662. www.osteriadellingegno.it. Closed Sun and Aug. Booking recommended. This charming bistro is always crowded at lunchtime. The menu includes elaborate dishes flavoured with herbs and a wide selection of charcuterie and cheeses.

La Rosetta – *Via della Rosetta 9, Pantheon.* ☎06 68 61 002. Closed Sat lunchtime, Sun and 8-22 Aug. 🍽 Booking recommended . This restaurant is well known because of its excellent seafood, including *sashimi* (raw fish).

PIAZZA NAVONA/CAMPO DEI FIORI/CASTEL SAN ANGELO

Pizzeria Da Baffetto – *Via del Governo Vecchio 114, Piazza Navona.* ☎06 68 61 617. Open 6:30pm–1 am. Closed Sun, except in summer, and Aug. 🖂 Summer of Love radicals made this trendy – now everyone jostles for a seat at this straightforward establishment. The pizzas are crisp and the service brusque in classic Roman style.

◉ **Osteria Ar Galletto** – *Piazza Farnese 102, Vicolo del Gallo 1, Campo dei Fiori.* ☎*06 68 61 714. Closed Sun, 14-21 Aug and 23 Dec-mid-Jan.* This Piazza Farnese restaurant was founded in 1484 and was once known as the *Osteria dei Borgia*. Ham is still cut by hand in front of customers and there is a wide choice of sauces for pasta.

◉ **Tonino** – *Via del Governo Vecchio 18, Piazza Navona. Only open in the evening.* 🍴 This trattoria, too small even for a sign, often asks customers to share tables in the congenial atmosphere. Mop up delicious pasta and meat sauces with home-made bread.

◉ **Enoteca L'Angolo Divino** – *Via dei Balestrari 12, Campo dei Fiori.* ☎*06 68 64 413. Closed Sun lunchtime and Mon evening.* This old wine and oil store has been converted into a rustic, simply furnished wine bar, lined with bottle-filled shelves. The snacks on offer include tarts and roulades.

◉ **Da Francesco** – *Piazza del Fico 29, Piazza Navona.* ☎*06 68 64 009. Closed Tue lunchtime.* 🍴 The attractive *Piazza del Fico* is home to this lively trattoria that serves typical Roman dishes, including pizzas, an excellent focaccia with dry-cured ham and various types of pasta. A cheerful atmosphere.

◉◉ **Enoteca Al Bric** – *Via del Pellegrino 51, Campo dei Fiori.* ☎*06 68 79 533. Closed Mon and for two weeks in Aug. Booking recommended.* This popular bistro offers a wide choice of wines, cheeses and charcuterie from several countries, with an emphasis on France.

◉◉ **Grotte del Teatro di Pompeo** *Via del Biscione, Campo dei Fiori.* ☎*06 683 03686. OpenTues–Sun noon–3:30pm and 7:30–11pm. Closed Mon.* Dine near the site of Julius Cesar's assassination. A *palazzo* gradually barnacled the ruins of the Theater of Pompey. The chef does impressive things with *radicchio*, the maroon chicory-like plant beloved by Italians, and also with fish.

◉◉ **Il Drappo** – *Vicolo del Malpasso 9, Piazza Navona.* ☎*06 68 77 365. Closed Sun, lunch and Aug* 🍽 *Booking recommended.* Traditional Sardinian specialities are the order of the day in this quiet, friendly restaurant, which is

decorated with draped curtains, mirrors, candles and tables set close together.

◉◉◉◉ **Pierluigi**– *Piazza dé Ricci 144, Campo dei Fiori.* ☎*06 68 61 302. Closed Mon, 13-22 Aug* 🍽 *Booking recommended .* The menu focuses on fish. Pasta dishes are delicious and service is impeccable. The lovely piazza adds to the overall experience.

PIAZZA DEL POPOLO/ PIAZZA DI SPAGNA

◉◉ **Gina** – *Via San Sebastianello , 7/A, Piazza di Spagna.* ☎*06 67 80 251. www. ginaroma.com. Open Mon–Thurs 11am–9pm and Fri–Sun 11am–midnight.* 🍽. This tasteful white-on-white restaurant is perfect for a quick bite or a relaxed meal. Gina also provides hampers for picnickers in the nearby Villa Borghese.

◉◉◉ **La Penna d'Oca** – *Via della Penna 53, Piazza del Popolo.* ☎*06 32 02 898. Closed Sun, Sat lunch, for 10 days in Jan and 20 days in Aug. Booking recommended.* This charming restaurant serves traditional cuisine, innovative fish and seafood dishes (try the conch pie served with red onion) and home-made bread. Summertime veranda.

◉◉◉ **La Terrazza** – *Via Ludovisi 49, Piazza di Spagna.* ☎*06 47 81 21. www. starwoodhotels.com. Open 7–10:30am, 12:30–2:30pm, 7:30–10:30pm.* 🍽 *Booking recommended.* The roof garden of the Hotel Eden is home to this elegant restaurant, which offers stunning views of the city and is popular with famous personalities. The creative cuisine served here is mainly based on fish and seafood recipes. Prices for Sunday brunch are more affordable.

PORTA PIA – TERMINI

◉ **Africa** – *Via Gaeta 26–8, Termini.* ☎*06 494 1077. Open Tues–Sun noon–4pm and 7–11.30pm. Closed Mon, Aug.* 🍴 Scoop meat and vegetables inside spongy whole-wheat bread (*inghera*). A favorite breakfast dish is the *ful* (mashed broad beans and yoghurt). The menu ranges from falafel to the mixed vegetarian platter with stewed lentils.

◉◉ **Pizzeria Al Forno della Soffitta** – *Via dei Villini 1e/1f, Porta Pia.* ☎*06 44 04 642.* 🍴 Genuine Neapolitan pizza is the speciality: all the ingredients come from the Campania region. The pies are erved on a round, wooden board.

🍴 **Er Buchetto** – *Via del Viminale 2F, Termini.* ☎*06 488 3031. Open Mon–Fri 9am–9pm, Sat 9am–1pm. Closed Sat pm. Closed Sun.* 🍴 A stuffed boar guards the exterior of this carvery, which has specialized in *porchetta* since 1890. This rosticceria is an old-school experience with just three tables. Wash down cold buffet selections with Castelli wines.

🍴 **Trimani il Wine Bar** – *Via Cernaia 37/b, Porta Pia.* ☎*06 44 69 630. Closed Sun. holidays and mid-to-late-Aug.* This bar, run by one of the oldest families in the Roman wine business, offers an impressive selection and fine cuisine. Summer brings outdoor seating.

SAN LORENZO FUORI LE MURA

🍴 **Pizzeria Il Ministero della Pizza** – *Via die Campani 65, San Lorenzo Fuori le Mura.* 🍴. In the student district, this pizzeria offers a number of first courses and specialities from Calabria, plus wood-fired pies. The owner is welcoming.

🍴 **Il Pulcino Ballerino** – *Via degli Equi 66/68, San Lorenzo Fuori le Mura.* ☎*06 49 41 255. www.pulcinoballerino.com. Open Mon–Fri 12:45–3:45pm and Mon–Sat 8pm–midnight. Closed Sat lunch, Sun and holidays.* 🍴 This pleasant and informal eatery has hit on an original formula for Rome: customers cook their own vegetables, meat or cheese on a stone placed in the middle of their table.

🍴🍴 **Il Dito e la Luna** – *Via dei Sabelli 51, San Lorenzo Fuori le Mura.* ☎*06 49 40 726. Closed lunch.* 🍴 Booking recommended. This restaurant has a pleasant bistro atmosphere. Theme evenings are occasionally held here, when Sicilian recipes, such as fish cuscus and caponata (Mediterranean vegetables served cold in a sweet-sour sauce), and fine wines are served.

SANTA MARIA MAGGIORE/ SAN GIOVANNI IN LATERANO

🍴 **Pizzeria La Gallina Bianca** – *Via A. Rosmini 9, Santa Maria Maggiore.* ☎*06 47 43 777.* 🍴. This popular, rustic-style pizzeria also serves excellent *fritti* (deep-fried specialities). Indulge in home-made desserts, including a tiramisù with strawberries.

🍴🍴 **Charly's Saucière** – *Via di San Giovanni in Laterano 270, San Giovanni in Laterano.* ☎*06 70 49 56 66. Closed Sat and Mon lunchtimes, Sun and 5-20 Aug –* 🍴 *– Booking recommended.* Renowned as one of Rome's genuinely French outlets, it has an old-fashioned, welcoming ambiance. Traditional meat and fish dishes predominate, in addition to Swiss specialities, in honour of the chef's country of origin.

🍴🍴🍴 **Agata e Romeo** – *Via Carlo Alberto 45, Santa Maria Maggiore.* ☎*06 44 66 115. Open Mon–Fri 1–2:30pm and 7:30–10:30pm. Closed Sat–Sun. Closed mid-Jan and Aug.* 🍴 *Booking recommended.* Sophisticated versions of Rome's *cucina povera* star in this elegant establishment. The menu shifts with the seasons, but might include saffron risotto, ox-tail stew, duck cannelloni and breaded lamb chops. The *baccalà* (salted cod) is especially popular, as is Romeo's astute wine list. Chef Agata is also a cooking instructor and cookbook author (and expert on local oils and vinegars). Don't miss the excellent desserts, including the *millefeuille*.

TRASTEVERE/GIANICOLO

🍴 **Pizzeria Panattoni** – *Viale Trastevere 53, Trastevere* – ☎*06 58 00 919. Open Thurs–Tues 6:30pm–2:30am. Closed Wed, Aug.* 🍴. Huge slab tables earn this classic pizzeria two nicknames: *I Marmi* (the Marbles) and the less-appetizing **l'Obitorio** (the Morgue). That – and the cranky service – still don't scare off customers. Waiters slam vast, crispy pizzas, chilled Peroni beer and serviceable house red, scowling at celebrities and common people alike.

🍴 **Pizzeria Dar Poeta** – *Vicolo del Bologna 45, Trastevere.* ☎*06 58 80 516. www.darpoeta.it . Open Tues–Sun 7:30pm–1am. Closed Mon* 🍴. The queue is worth the wait here. Expect quirky combinations (like apples and Gran Marnier) and soft, dripping pizzas on slow-risen bases. The bill is scrawled on the tablecloth, but the atmosphere is jovial and the food extraordinary.

🍴🍴 **Jaipur** – *Via San Francisco Ripa 56, Trastevere.* ☎*06 580 3992. www. ristorantejaipur.it. Open Tues-Sun noon–3pm and 7–11:30pm. Closed Mon lunch.* Rome's best Indian restaurant serves North Indian specialties from a clay tandoori oven. Dine outside on this pleasant side-street. Spice-fans should exaggerate their normal preferences:

Italians prefer ethnic food far more mild than most foreigners.

Enoteca Ferrara – *Via del Moro 1a, Piazza Trilussa 41A, Trastevere. ☎06 58 333 20. www. enotecaferrara.it. Open 11am–12.30am. Meals served 6pm–12am.* Nibble at the bar – or book a table to seriously imbibe. The international wine list, 850-bottles strong, is the main draw, however the kitchen turns out thoughtful dishes like perch with red cabbage and *involtini di pesce spada* (swordfish fillets rolled around cinnamon-flecked filling).

La Paella 2 – *Vicolo della Luce 3-4, near the Ponte Cestio, Trastevere. ☎06 58 331 179. Open Thurs–Tues noon–3pm and 7:30–11pm. Wed noon–3pm. Closed Wed lunch.* Savour sangria and paella near the Tiber. Options include fish, meat, vegetarian, lobster and squid ink. Kitsch, murals red-check tablecloths and exposed brick arches complete the rustic look of this endearing eatery.

Thai Inn – *Via Federico Ozanam 94, Gianicolo. ☎06 582 03145. Open Tues–Sun 12–2:30pm, 7–11:30pm. Closed Mon, Aug.* These Thai chefs would standout in any city –and are worth the bus trip. Christmas lights, blue lanterns, aquariums, bamboo matting, fake flowers and butterflies create a tranquil atmosphere. *From Piazza Venezia, take bus 44, which stops across from the Inn, just before Via Nadina Helbig.*

Antico Arco – *Via San Pancrazio 1, Piazzale Aurelio, Gianicolo. ☎06 581 5274. Open Mon–Sat 7:30–11:30pm. Closed Sun, Aug.* Internationally acclaimed nouvelle cuisine stars here such as onion flan, pheasant breast with truffles on a potato tart; *risotto al castemagno* (Piedmontese cheese) in wine sauce and home-made Sicilian cassata made from ricotta. The cellar contains over 400 blends. The vine-swathed restaurant is inside an 18C palazzo.

VATICANO – SAN PIETRO

Al Limone – *Viale Angelico 64/66, Vaticano. ☎06 37 22 003. Closed Sat lunchtime and Sun.* Lemon is the focal point for this restaurant, including the decor and the cuisine. Innovative

An old façade in Trastevere

regional cuisine, barbecued dishes and home-made bread.

Hostaria dei Bastioni – *Via Leone IV 29, Vatican. ☎06 39 723 034. Open Mon–Sat noon–3pm and 7–11:30pm. Closed Sun, mid-July–mid-Aug.* Celebrated for its mussels and pasta, this restaurant is convenient to the Vatican Museums. Though the terrace is noisy, the price is right here.

VIA VENETO

Sans Souci – *Via Sicilia 20/24, Via Veneto. ☎06 42 01 45 10. Closed lunch and 10-20 Aug* 🗐 *Booking recommended.* A well-established restaurant offering traditional and regional cuisine with an innovative flavour. The decor recalls the golden age of the *Dolce Vita* period.

VILLA BORGHESE – VILLA GIULIA

Al Ceppo – *Via Panama 2, Villa Borghese. ☎06 85 51 379. Closed Mon and 8-24 Aug. Booking recommended.* In the smart Parioli district, this restaurant has a rustic, yet elegant, feel. Innovative cuisine uses seasonal produce and is based on traditional recipes. Desserts include chestnut ice cream with hot chocolate.

Papa Giulio –*Via Giulia 14, Campo de' Fiori. ☎06 6813 5920. Open Wed–Mon 11:30am–3pm, 7:30pm–12:30am. Closed Tues, maybe Aug.* Dusky mirrors and leather banquettes grace this local favorite. The decor inside – crisp linen, candles and crystal – has a mellow elegance. Menu highlights include seafood and innovative dishes, such as smoke and champagne risotto. Garden seating sprawls in summer.

ENTERTAINMENT

👃See Discovering Rome for additional bars, pubs or other night spots.

Performing Arts

SHOWS

👃*See also Address Book.* Venues range from traditional theatres, usually in the old centre, to modern venues staging more contemporary and experimental shows, often near the university.
Tickets for plays, concerts and sporting events can be purchased from a number of agencies in Rome. The most central include **Orbis** (*Piazza Esquilino 37, Santa Maria Maggiore district,* ☎*06 47 44 776, www.cdflash.com),* **Gesman 92 Primafila** (*Via A. Emo 65,* ☎*06 39 74 07 89)* and **Interclub Service** (*Piazza I. Nievo 3/5,* ☎*06 58 94 54 31, www.interclubservice. com).* The **Box Office di Ricordi** (*Via del Corso 506, Piazza del Popolo district,* ☎*06 36 12 68; Viale Giulio Cesare 88, Vaticano district,* ☎*06 37 20 216; and Via Cesare Battisti 120, Fontana di Trevi district,* ☎*06 67 98 022)* offers a comprehensive ticketing service.
AMIT (☎*06 80 88 352, www.chartnet.it)* takes telephone and Internet bookings (by credit card) for concerts in the Santa Cecilia auditorium and performances in Rome's major theatres. A whole range of musical events can be also booked through **Il Sogno – Gente e Paesi** (*Via Adda 111,* ☎*06 85 30 17 55).*

PUBLICATIONS

Information on films, plays, concerts and exhibitions is listed in the **Roma C'è** magazine, every Friday (www.romace.it), and in **Trovaroma,** a supplement of the *La Repubblica* daily newspaper (Thurs). Cultural events are detailed in **Time Out Rome** (www. timeout.com) and **Wanted in Rome** (www.wantedinrome.com).
Theatre by bus – Bus no 116 serves the various theatres within the city centre, departing from Via Veneto and Via Giulia. Buses run Mon–Fri, 8pm–1.30am, every 15min.

Nightlife

NIGHTCLUBS

👃*See also Address Book.* Rome, after-hours, mainly concentrates in three areas, each attracting a different patrons. The district between **Piazza Campo dei Fiori** and **Piazza Navona** has a wide choice of pubs and bars, drawing a mix of young students, tourists and the theatre crowd (especially in the elegant bars around Piazza Navona). On the streets of **Trastevere,** the bars and restaurants are typically Roman in character and host live music. The majority of the city's most popular night-clubs are concentrated in the **Testaccio** district, particularly in *Via di Monte Testaccio,* and more recently, in the nearby *Via di Libetta.*
👃*A list of suggestions for bars, pubs and nightclubs is given below.*

THE ESTATE ROMANA FESTIVAL

During the summer, most nightclubs move out to their cooler premises along the exclusive Fregene Beach. A number of open-air concerts are held in the various "villages" within the capital, where books, records, home-made products and clothes – as well as sandwiches and drinks –can be bought, before dancing the night away or sitting at a table to enjoy the music. The most famous of these include **Testaccio Village,** which welcomes a number of international artists every year; the **Foro Italico,** where annual cabaret shows are held; **Parco di Villa Celimontana,** for jazz concerts; **Parco di Villa Ada Savoia,** for new sounds and for Latin-American music, the **Fiesta** (www.estateromana.it).

A NIGHT-TIME SNACK

Some city bakeries open their doors to night owls. Some of the best known

are in **Trastevere** and **Testaccio**
(*See TRASTEVERE and PIRAMIDE-TESTACCIO in Discovering Rome*).

Cinemas

See also Address Book. The number of screens more than doubled in the 1990s. In addition to the arthouses and multiplexes, the Eternal City has small clubs, like **Filmstudio**, which may require a membership card (*Via degli Orti d'Alibert 1/c, Trastevere; 06 68 192 987*). Don't be alarmed: these are free or very cheap, much like social clubs' (*centri sociale*). Cinemas typically screen at 4:30, 6:30, 8:30 and 10:30pm. Credit card payments are still rare. Smaller venues shut for summer but outdoor screens take up the slack.

Open-Air Cinemas

During July and August, the open-air "villages" set up during the *Estate Romana* festival offer cinema-lovers the chance to see a number of films. Among the long-standing venues taking part in this festival, **Cineporto** screens the most successful films of the previous season every year under the pine trees near the *Ministero degli Affari Esteri* (*www.cineporto.com; 06 323 0930 Monte Mario*), **Sotto le Stelle di San Lorenzo** provides visitors with the opportunity to watch films in their original language in the beautiful *Villa Mercede* gardens, and the most recent **Notti di Cinema a Piazza Vittorio** has both successful and lesser-known films

on its programme, as does the **Isola del Cinema** (*L'Isola Tibertina between the Ponte Cestio and Ponte Fabricio; 06 58 333 113; www.isoladelcinema. com; open from 8pm July–Sept*). At the **Nuovo Sacher**, owned by Italian film legend Nanni Moretti, a projector outside in summer. English offerings are typically Mon–Tues (**Largo Ascianghi 1, Trastevere; 06 581 8116**).

The **Massenzio Film Festival** migrates, but always celebrates cinema under the stars. Given its scale, it tends to linger on the outskirts like EUR and the Via Appia area (06 700 1719; www.massenzio.it).

Film center and festival

The *Casa dei Cinema* celebrates western filmmaking. The elegant building – formerly "home of the roses" – stands in a pastoral stretch of the Village Borghese, just 50m from the Via Veneto. Visitors can attend screenings, view archival DVDs, browse the bookshop or loiter in the café (*Largo Marcello Mastroianni, enter from the Piazzale del Brasile, Parcheggio di Villa Borghese; 06 423 601; www. casadelcinema.it; evening programs daily; the library is open 10am–2pm and 3–7pm café 10am–7pm*).

The **Roma Independent Film Festival** takes place in early April each year (*Via Po 134; 06 45 425 050; www.riff.it*). In autumn, the city hosts the progressive **Cinecittà Internet Film Festival** (www. cinecitta.com).

Address Book

NIGHTCLUBS

Akab-Cave – *Via di Monte Testaccio 69, Piramide Cestia-Testaccio. 06 57 82 390. Open Mon-Sat, 10pm-4am.* A large number of new venues have opened in this district in the last few years. Akab has a cellar and an upper floor, which is used for concerts and theme evenings.
Alexanderplatz – *Via Ostia 9, Vaticano-San Pietro. 06 39 74 21 71. www. alexanderplatz.it . Open Mon–Sat 9pm–2am.* Some of the greatest jazz musicians in the world have played here

in the past 12 years. Concerts start at 10.30pm.
Alpheus – *Via del Commercio 36, Piramide Cestia-Testaccio. 06 57 47 826. Open 9pm–3.30am. Closed in Aug.* One of the district's many nightclubs, located in one of the market's old warehouses. The club has three dance floors and hosts concerts and cabaret shows.
Big Mama – *Vicolo S. Francesco a Ripa 18, Trastevere. 06 58 12 551. www. bigmama.it. Open Tue–Sun 9pm–1.30am.* Bricks walls and huge names: this club has international jazz chops.

Centro Sociale Brancaleone – *Via Levanna 11, NE of the Catacombe di Priscillia.* ☎*06 82 00 09 59. www. brancaleone.it. Open 8pm–2am (dawn on Fri–Sat).* Housed in a renovated social centre, this trendy venue is known for bringing in famous DJs from Italy and abroad, who spin mainly in electronica.
Il Locale – *Vicolo del Fico 3, Piazza Navona.* ☎*06 68 79 075. Open Tue–Sun 10pm–3am.* This old garage is divided into a number of simply furnished rooms. New Italian rock groups have gigs here.
Jonathan's Angels – *Via della Fossa 16, Piazza Navona. 06 68 93 426. Open 5pm–4am.* It's often difficult to find a seat in this popular piano bar, deliberately kitsch and decorated with paintings by the owner, an enigmatic figure who dominates the till. Rome's most famous toilet preens here.
Piper – *Via Tagliamento 9, Catacombe di Priscilla.* ☎*06 85 55 398. www. piperclub.it. Open 10:30pm–4am; Sat, 4–8pm.* ⏰*Closed Mon–Wed.* Opened in 1965, this famous nightclub now organises theme evenings, including rock, underground, and 1970s music.

THEATRES AND CLASSICAL MUSIC CONCERTS

Teatro dell'Opera – *Piazza Beniamino Gigli 1, Santa Maria Maggiore.* ☎*06 48 16 02 55. www.opera.roma.it. Ticket office open Tue and Sat 9am–5pm; Sun 9am–1.30pm.* Tickets can also be purchased 1hr prior to shows. Recommended for fans of classical music, opera and ballet, this large theatre provides subtitles for shows in foreign languages. In summer, open-air perform-ances are organised in the romantic setting of Caracalla's Baths.
Teatro Olimpico – *Piazza Gentile da Fabriano 17, Monte Mario.* ☎*06 32 65 991. www.teatroolimpico.it. Ticket office open 11am–1pm and 3–7pm, and 8–9pm on the day of performance.* This theatre on the banks of the Tiber is the headquar-ters of the Accademia Filarmonica Romana. Musical shows, ballet and some comic opera are staged here.
Teatro Sistina – *Via Sistina 129, Piazza di Spagna.* ☎*06 42 00 711. www.ilsistina. com. Ticket office open 10am–1pm and 3:30–7pm.* Renowned for its excellent acoustics, this theatre hosts famous

musicals, as well as concerts by acclaimed international performers.
Auditorium dell'Accademia Nazionale di Santa Cecilia – *Via della Conciliazione 4, Vaticano.* ☎*06 68 80 10 44. www. santacecilia.it.* This prestigious concert hall is the setting for concerts by some of the best-known orchestras and conductors from across the globe.
Teatro Argentina – *Largo Argentina 52.* ☎*06 68 80 46 01 /2. Ticket office open Tue–Sat, 10am-2pm, 3-7pm and 8-10pm.* Built at the beginning of the 18C, this large theatre staged the first performance of the Barber of Seville in 1816. The theatre enjoys an excellent location opposite the Roman ruins of Largo Argentina, and offers a programme of mainly drama.
Teatro Quirino – *Via Marco Minghetti 1, Fontana di Treve.* ☎*06 67 94 585. www. teatroquirino.it . Ticket office open Tue–Sun 10am–2pm, 3–7pm and 8–10pm.* The theatre is known for its emphasis on traditional drama, although experimental plays are also performed here.
Teatro Valle – *Via del Teatro Valle 21, Piazza Navona.* ☎*06 68 80 37 94. www. teatrovalle.it. Ticket office open Tue-Sun, 10am-7pm.* This magnificent 18C building, situated near Piazza S. Eustachio, hosts performances of many of the Italian classics.
Teatro Eliseo – *Via Nazionale 183, Quirinale.* ☎*06 48 82 114. www.teatroeli seo.it. Ticket office open Tue, Thu, Fri and Sat 8:30am–2:30pm, 3:30-7pm and 8-8:40pm; Wed and Sun 9:30am-7pm.* In addition to well-known drama, this theatre hosts works by the greatest 20C Italian writers, such as Aldo Palazzeschi and Eduardo de Filippo. Dance perform-ances are also occasionally held here.
Teatro Parioli – *Via Giosue' Borsi 20, Parioli.* ☎*06 80 83 523. www.teatroparioli. it. Ticket office open Tue–Sat 10am–1:30pm and 2:30-7pm; Sun 10–1:30pm and 3-5pm.* Theatre tickets (usually for comedies) also include entrance to the live recording of the popular Italian television programme, the Maurizio Costanzo Show. Binoculars provided.
Alfellini – *Via Francesco Carletti 5, Piramide Cestia district* – ☎*06 57 57 570.* The Alfellini is a popular comedy venue that hosts a range of cabaret and variety shows.

SHOPPING

Unlike other capital cities in Europe, Rome does not have many large department stores, preferring a wide range of small shops and boutiques to suit all tastes and budgets. Visitors will have no difficult in buying antiques, craft products and high-quality food produce throughout the city, especially in the historic centre, as well as an excellent selection of the latest fashions. The following section gives information on where to shop in Rome, with descriptions of the different areas of the city that specialise in certain products. Each category lists shops, detailed in the *Discovering Rome* section.

In general, clothes stores are closed on Monday morning; food shops close on Thursday afternoon. With the exception of the historic centre, where shops tend to stay open all day, shops are open from 10am–1pm and from 4–7:30pm (winter) or 5–8pm (summer). Credit cards are accepted in most stores, with the exception of small food shops.

Address Book

FASHION

Many luxury stores are located in **Via Veneto,** and some of the best-known names in the Italian fashion world can be found in the area between **Via del Corso** and **Piazza di Spagna,** especially in *Via Frattina, Via Borgognona* (Laura Biagiotti, Versace, Fendi etc) and *Via Bocca di Leone* (Versace). Particularly worthy of mention in this district is **Bulgari,** one of the original goldsmiths in Rome, which is situated at the beginning of **Via dei Condotti.** In the same street, **Raggi** is very popular with young people for its reasonably priced and striking jewellery. Other famous names in this district include Armani, Gucci, Prada and Valentino.

Via del Corso, packed with youngsters on a Saturday afternoon, is home to a variety of shops selling all kinds of goods, as are **Via Nazionale, Via del Tritone** and **Via Cola di Rienzo.**

These shops have been selected for their prices and original goods:

- Bomba –
  see PIAZZA DEL POPOLO
- Claudio Sanò –
  see SAN LORENZO FUORI LE MURA
- David Saddler –
  see PIAZZA DEL POPOLO
- De Clercq & De Clercq –
  see PIAZZA DI SPAGNA
- Il Discount dell'Alta Moda –
  see PIAZZA DEL POPOLO and SANTA MARIA MAGGIORE – ESQUILINO
- Franco Borini –
  see CAMPO DEI FIORI
- Fratelli Viganò –
  see FONTANA DI TREVI-QUIRINALE
- Galleria di Orditi e Trame –
  see PIAZZA NAVONA
- Sergio di Cori Gloves –
  see PIAZZA DI SPAGNA

ANTIQUES

Stroll in the Piazza di Spagna district along **Via del Babuino,** home to the city's most prestigious antique dealers, and **Via Margutta,** with its many art galleries and craft shops, which still specialise in the restoration of marble and silver objects. The most lively area, especially during fairs, is **Via dei Coronari,** not far from Piazza Navona. Wandering through the narrow alleyways around **Piazza Campo dei Fiori** and **Piazza Farnese,** don't be surprised to see second-hand dealers and craftsmen busy at work in the sunshine.

Particularly worthy of note are some of the long-established shops and those with a real flavour of the past, though far from the city's famous streets.

- Antica Erboristeria Romana –
  see ISOLA TIBERINA-TORRE ARGENTINA

*For an unusual souvenir, why not have
your portrait painted in Piazza Navona?*

- Antonella Marani –
  see PIAZZA NAVONA
- Le Bambole –
  see PIRAMIDE CESTIA-TESTACCIO
- Comics Bazar –
  see CAMPO DEI FIORI
- Ditta G Poggi –
  see PANTHEON
- Farmacia Pesci –
  see FONTANA DI TREVI-QUIRINALE
- Fratelli Alinari –
  see PIAZZA DI SPAGNA
- Hausmann & C –
  see PIAZZA DI SPAGNA
- Italia Garipoli –
  see VATICANO-SAN PIETRO
- Lattonieri –
  see TRASTEVERE
- Libreria Antiquaria Rappaport –
  see PANTHEON
- Maria Favilli – *see MONTECITORIO*
- Orsantico – *see PIAZZA NAVONA*
- Set – *see PIAZZA NAVONA*
- Siragusa – *see PIAZZA DI SPAGNA*

FOOD AND DRINK

- Biscottificio Artigiano Innocenti –
  see TRASTEVERE
- La Bottega del Cioccolato –
  see FORI IMPERIALI
- Cooperativa Agricola Stella –
  see CATACOMBE DI PRISCILLA
- Fattoria la Parrina –
  see PIAZZA DEL POPOLO
- Gatti e Antonelli –
  see CATACOMBE DI PRISCILLA
- Latteria Ugolini – *see TRASTEVERE*
- Latticini Micocci – *see PORTA PIA*

BOOKSHOPS

The most famous bookshops tend to
sprawl in spacious premises in the
centre of Rome, often on a number of
floors. They offer a wide selection of
books of all kinds, and also sell videos,
CD-ROMs and stationery. **Feltrinelli**
(www.lafeltrinelli.it) has opened three
bookshops at stategic locations
throughout the city, such as *Via del
Babuino 39, ☎06 36 00 18 42, Via
Orlando 78/81 (near Piazza della
Repubblica)*, where the whole shop is
dedicated to foreign books, and *Largo
Argentina 5A/6 (b06 68 80 32 48)*. Rizzoli
has stores at *Via Tomacelli 156 (in
Montecitorio)* and in *Largo Chigi (near
Galleria Colonna* in the *Fontana di Trevi*
district); **Mondadori** (www.mondadori.it)
has branches at *Via Cola di Rienzo 51
(Vaticano)* and *Via Appia Nuova 51 (San
Giovanni in Laterano)*. Other bookshops
include Mel Book Store (*Via Nazionale
254/255*) and Rinascita (*Via delle
Botteghe Oscure 1*).

The smaller bookshops mentioned
below either contain interesting and
original features or offer visitors a
chance to purchase rare literary works.

- Al Tempo Ritrovato –
  see TRASTEVERE
- All American Comics –
  see SAN GIOVANNI IN LATERANO
- Bibli – *see TRASTEVERE*
- Farenheit 451 –
  see CAMPO DEI FIORI
- Invito alla Lettura –
  see CASTEL SAN ANGELO

B. Kaufmann/MICHELIN

Off shopping in Rome

- Libreria del Viaggiatore –
  🛇*see CAMPO DEI FIORI*
- Mel Bookstore –
  🛇*see FONTANA DI TREVI-QUIRINALE*
- La Procure – 🛇*see PANTHEON*
- The Lion Bookshop –
  🛇*see PIAZZA DI SPAGNA*

MUSIC SHOPPING

- Archivio Fonografico –
  🛇*see AVENTINO*
- Art & Music –
  🛇*see PIRAMIDE CESTIA-TESTACCIO*
- Città 2000 –
  🛇*see CATACOMBE DI PRISCILLA*
- Disfunzioni Musicali –
  Disfunzioni Musicali Usato e Rarità –
  🛇*see SAN LORENZO FUORI LE MURA*
- Metropoli Rock – 🛇*see SANTA MARIA MAGGIORE-ESQUILINO*
- Tendenza –
  🛇*see PIRAMIDE CESTIA-TESTACCIO*

OTHER SHOPS

- Arredamento Liturgico – 🛇*see ISOLA TIBERINA-TORRE ARGENTINA*
- Barbiconi – 🛇*see PANTHEON*
- Becker & Musicò –
  🛇*see FONTANA DI TREVI-QUIRINALE*
- Boutique Jaguar Collection –
  🛇*see VILLA BORGHESE-VILLA GIULIA*
- Jaracandà – 🛇*see PIAZZA NAVONA*
- Myricae – 🛇*see PIAZZA DI SPAGNA*
- Savelli – 🛇 *see VATICANO-SAN PIETRO*

DEPARTMENT STORES

The most exclusive department stores include **La Rinascente** *(Via del Corso 189, on the corner of Largo Chigi, ☏06 67 97 691,*

Montecitorio district, and Via Aniene 1, on the corner of Piazza Fiume, Porta Pia district; open Sun 10:30am–8pm), and **Coin** *(Piazzale Appio 7, ☏06 70 80 020, San Giovanni in Laterano district, and Via Cola di Rienzo 177, Vaticano district; open 9:30am–8pm)*, whose larger outlets also have a household articles and furnishings department.

MAS – *Via dello Statuto 11, Santa Maria Maggiore. ☏06 44 68 078. Open Mon–Sat 9am–1pm and 4–7:30pm (open Sun from 10am).* This store, located a stone's throw from Piazza Vittorio, allows customers to rummage through the shelves looking for the perfect dress, jumper, trousers, shoes or even a leather jacket, all of which are sold at reasonable prices.

Ricordi Mediastore – *Via del Corso 506, Piazza del Popolo. ☏06 36 12 370. www. ricordimediastores.it. Open Mon–Sat 9:30am–8pm; Sun 10am–1pm and 3–8pm.* With five shops in the most central districts of Rome, Ricordi is one of the largest music stores in the city. Other branches are at: *Via Orlando 73 (Piazza Repubblica district), Via C. Battisti 120/c (Piazza Venezia district), Viale G.Cesare 88 (east of the Vaticano – San Pietro district) and Galleria Stazione Termini.*

LATE-NIGHT SHOPPING

🕙Shops in Rome close at around 7:30pm in winter and 8pm in summer, although some may stay open later. The Galleria Colonna shopping center *(Via del Corso)* and the Rinascente

"Er Cicala"

recently extended their hours until 10pm.

Newspapers can now be bought late at night or early in the morning almost as soon as they are printed from a number of **newsstands.** Some of the most centrally located can be found at *Via Veneto, Viale Trastevere* and *Piazza Sonnino, Piazza dei Cinquecento, Piazza Colonna, Piazza Cola di Rienzo, Viale Manzoni* and *Via Magna Greci*a.

For those visitors who require more than just an early morning croissant after a long night in the capital, the **Museum Drugstore** (*Via Portuense 313*) offers a wide range of groceries and other items, and is open 24hr a day; the store also has a bar and an archaeological area with graves dating from the 2C AD.

Other 24hr outlets include **Rosati Due** (*Piazzale Clodio, 06 03 97 41 138, Monte Mario district*), which has a supermarket and a fast-food counter, and **Tiburtina Station** with a pizzeria, pastry shop and gift store.

Inveterate smokers have been able to buy cigarettes from automatic machines for some years now and will also find a few **tabacchi** (tobacconists) that stay open late. These include those at *Piazza d'Ara Coeli, Piazza Venezia* (Open all night), *Via del Tritone 144, Piazza del Popolo 16, Viale Trastevere 354, Tiburtina Station* and *Via Cesare Battisti 135*.

To buy **fresh flowers** at any time of the day or night, head for the flower stalls at *Lungotevere Milvio, Piazzale degli Eroi* and *Via Latina* on the corner of *Piazza Galeria, Piazzale del Parco della Rimembranz*a and *Via Portuense* on the corner of *Via Rolli*.

MARKETS

Fruit and vegetable markets are held in the different districts of the city. These offer a panoply of bright colours and fresh smells, where the lively conversation of the locals, punctuated by the cries of the stallholders, provide a genuine flavour of everyday Rome. It is also pleasant to wander through the many antique and flea markets, where you might just pick up an unusual souvenir or original item of clothing.

Borgo Parioli – *Via Tirso 14, Catacombe di Priscilla. Open Sat–Sun 9am–8pm.* This antique market is held in a large garage and has a selection of paintings, prints, frames, clocks, embroidery, lace, books and magazines. Unusual culinary specialities may also be sampled here.

Garage Sale. Rigattieri per Hobby – *Piazza della Marina, Borghetto Flaminio 32, Villa Giulia.* ☎*06 47 82 42 71. Open Sun, 10am–7pm.* Stalls vend clothes and other items at this market, which specialises in chic second-hand goods, antiques and general bric-a-brac.

La Soffitta sotto i Portici – *Piazza Augusto Imperatore, Piazza di Spagna. Open 3rd Sun in the month, 10am–dusk.* Frequented by collectors of paintings, prints, frames, small items of furniture, ceramics and lace.

Mercatino Biologico – *Via Cardinale Merry del Val, Trastevere. Open 2nd Sun in the month, 9am–7pm.* This market sells environmentally friendly produce, including organic food, recycled paper, plant-based soaps and wooden toys.

Mercatino di Ponte Milvio – *Lungotevere Caporati, Monte Mario. Open 1st weekend in the month, Sat 3–7pm; Sun 8am–7pm.* This market is held under Milvio Bridge and sells furniture, craftwork, art and other articles.

Mercato dell'Antiquariato di Fontanella Borghese – *Piazza Borghese, Piazza di Spagna. Open Mon–Sat 7am–1pm.* An excellent market for those interested in old books and prints.

Mercato dell'Antiquariato di Piazza Verdi – *Piazza Verdi, Villa Borghese. Open 4th Sun in the month, 9am–8pm.* As well as antiques and arts and crafts, this market also sells amphorae, old friezes and coats of arms. Entertainment and a wide selection of books for children.

Mercato di Campo dei Fiori – *Campo dei Fiori. Open mornings, daily.* Once the largest in Rome, this now sells vegetables, fish, kitchen gadgets and gorgeous cheap floral bouquets.

Mercato di Piazza Alessandria – *Piazza Alessandria, Porta Pia. Open mornings, Mon–Sat.* A food market inside a Liberty-style building.

Mercato di Piazza S. Cosimato – *Piazza San Cosimato, Trastevere. Open mornings Mon–Sat.* This market is one of the busiest in central Rome, and is divided into two sections: the *fruttaroli*, who buy their produce every morning from the wholesale market, and the *vignaroli*, who sell produce grown in their own garden.

Mercato di Piazza Vittorio Emanuele – *Piazza Vittorio Emanuele, Santa Maria Maggiore. Open mornings, all week.* This is one of the cheapest markets in Rome. Renowned for its fresh fish at reasonable prices, its excellent selection of cheeses and horse meat, and its choice of Oriental spices.

Mercato di Testaccio – *Piazza di Testaccio. Opem Mon–Sat, all morning.* Nicknamed *"er core de Roma"*, the heart of Rome, this market has a wide selection of goods. A large number of stalls vend shoes at factory prices.

Mercato di Via Sannio – *Via Sannio, San Giovanni in Laterano. Open Mon–Sat 10am–1pm.* A wide choice of reasonably priced new and second-hand clothes, as well as shoes sold at factory prices.

Mercato di Viale Parioli – *Viale Parioli, Catacombe di Priscilla. Open Sat–Sun 10am–7pm.* This market starts in *Viale Parioli* with stalls selling costume jewellery, household goods and clothing, and continues into *Via Locchi*, where the main food stalls are located.

Porta Portese – *Via Portuense, Trastevere. Open Sun from dawn–2pm.* This market sells a bit of everything and is often referred to as the flea market. It opened officially during the Second World War. Articles on sale include general bric-a-brac, new and second-hand clothes, photographic equipment, books and records.

Suk – *Via Portuense 851. Open Sun–Fri – 7pm; Sat 11am–7pm.* This ethnic market is held in a supermarket car park. Ethnic goods, antiques and unusual items.

Underground – *Via Crispi, Parcheggio Ludovisi 96, Piazza di Spagna.* ☎ *06 99 40 40. Open 1st weekend of the month, Sat 3–8pm; Sun 10:30am–7:30pm.* This 5 000m^2/54 000sq ft exhibition area, in the old centre, has a wide variety of antiques, collectors' items, modern articles, jewels and costume jewellery.

INDEX

INDEX

WHERE TO EAT

WHERE TO STAY

MAPS AND PLANS

LIST OF MAPS

COMPANION PUBLICATIONS

MICHELIN PLAN OF ROME 38:

- a complete 1:10 000 scale plan of Rome, including major thoroughfares, one-way streets, main car parks, post offices and the most important public buildings in the city
- an alphabetical street index
- practical information

MAPS OF ITALY

Map of central Italy 563

- a 1:400 000 scale map of central Italy with an index of place names

Italy Road Atlas

- a useful spiral-bound atlas with a full index of towns and cities

LEGEND

	Sight	Seaside resort	Winter sports resort	Spa
Highly recommended	★★★	☆☆☆	✲✲✲	♇♇♇
Recommended	★★	☆☆	✲✲	♇♇
Interesting	★	☆	✲	♇

Selected monuments and sights

◉ ⇥	Tour - Departure point
🏛 ⴕ	Catholic church
🏛 ⴕ	Protestant church, other temple
✡ ⊡ ☾	Synagogue - Mosque
▰	Building
■	Statue, small building
ⴕ	Calvary, wayside cross
◎	Fountain
▬●▬■	Rampart - Tower - Gate
✕	Château, castle, historic house
∴	Ruins
◡	Dam
✿	Factory, power plant
✩	Fort
∩	Cave
▱	Troglodyte dwelling
⚲	Prehistoric site
▼	Viewing table
ⱴ	Viewpoint
▲	Other place of interest

Special symbols

Ⓐ	Underground line A (Battistini-Anagnina)
Ⓑ	Underground line B (Rebibbia-Laurentina)

Additional symbols

🇮		Tourist information
═══ ═══		Motorway or other primary route
❶ ❶		Junction: complete, limited
⬌ ═══		Pedestrian street
⊥≡≡≡⊥		Unsuitable for traffic, street subject to restrictions
⌐⌐⌐	----	Steps – Footpath
🚃	🚉	Train station – Auto-train station
🚌	SNCF	Coach (bus) station
─┴─┴─		Tram
⊙		Metro, underground
🅿		Park-and-Ride
♿		Access for the disabled

Sports and recreation

🏇	Racecourse
⛸	Skating rink
≈ ≋	Outdoor, indoor swimming pool
🎬	Multiplex Cinema
⚲	Marina, sailing centre
⛺	Trail refuge hut
▫▪▪▪▫	Cable cars, gondolas
▫+++++▫	Funicular, rack railway
🚂	Tourist train
◆	Recreation area, park
🎢	Theme, amusement park
ⵌ	Wildlife park, zoo
⊛	Gardens, park, arboretum
◔	Bird sanctuary, aviary
🚶	Walking tour, footpath
😊	Of special interest to children

Abbreviations

H	Town hall (Municipio)
J	Law courts (Palazzo di Giustizia)
M	Museum (Museo)
P	Local authority offices (Prefettura)
POL.	Police station (Polizia) (in large towns: Questura)
T	Theatre (Teatro)
U	University (Università)

✉	Post office
📞	Telephone
⊠	Covered market
⚔	Barracks
△	Drawbridge
∪	Quarry
✕	Mine
🅱 🅵	Car ferry (river or lake)
🚢	Ferry service: cars and passengers
⛴	Foot passengers only
③	Access route number common to Michelin maps and town plans
Bert (R.)...	Main shopping street
AZ B	Map co-ordinates

381

Michelin Apa Publications Ltd

A joint venture between Michelin and Langenscheidt

Suite 6, Tulip House, 70 Borough High Street, London SE1 1XF, United Kingdom

© 2007 Michelin Apa Publications Ltd
ISBN 978-1-906261-15-3
Printed: September 2007
Printed and bound in Germany

ROME

25

Chief Editor   Cynthia Clayton Ochterbeck

THE GREEN GUIDE ROME

Editor   Jonathan P. Gilbert
Principal Writers   Amanda Castleman
Production Coordinator   Natasha G. George
Cartography   Alain Baldet, Michèle Cana, Peter Wrenn
Photo Editor   Lydia Strong
Layout & Design   Nicole Jordan and John Higginbottom
Cover Design   Laurent Muller and Ute Weber

Contact Us: The Green Guide
                                  Michelin Maps and Guides
                                  One Parkway South
                                  Greenville, SC 29615
                                  USA
                                  www.michelintravel.com
                                  michelin.guides@us.michelin.com

                                  Michelin Maps and Guides
                                  Hannay House
                                  39 Clarendon Road
                                  Watford, Herts WD17 1JA
                                  UK
                                  ☎ (01923) 205 240
                                  www.ViaMichelin.com
                                  travelpubsales@uk.michelin.com

Special Sales: For information regarding bulk sales,
                                  customized editions and premium sales,
                                  please contact our Customer Service
                                  Departments:
                                  USA   1-800-432-6277
                                  UK   (01923) 205 240
                                  Canada 1-800-361-8236

Note to the Reader
While every effort is made to ensure that all information printed in this guide is correct and up-to-date, Michelin Apa Publications Ltd. accepts no liability for any direct, indirect or consequential losses howsoever caused so far as such can be excluded by law.